Healthcare Delivery in the Information Age

For further volumes:
http://www.springer.com/series/8783

Nilmini Wickramasinghe with
Latif Al-Hakim • Chris Gonzalez • Joseph Tan
Editors

Lean Thinking for Healthcare

Springer

Editors
Nilmini Wickramasinghe
Epworth HealthCare & RMIT University
School of Business Information Technology
Melbourne, VIC, Australia

Chris Gonzalez
Department of Urology
Northwestern University
Chicago, IL, USA

Latif Al-Hakim
University of Southern Queensland
Toowoomba, QLD, Australia

Joseph Tan
DeGroote School Business
McMaster University
Hamilton, ON, Canada

ISBN 978-1-4614-8035-8 ISBN 978-1-4614-8036-5 (eBook)
DOI 10.1007/978-1-4614-8036-5
Springer New York Heidelberg Dordrecht London

Library of Congress Control Number: 2013947473

Printed on acid-free paper

Springer is part of Springer Science+Business Media (www.springer.com)

For our Families

Series Dedication

This series is dedicated to Leo Cussen: Learned scholar, colleague extraordinaire, and good friend.

Foreword

Healthcare, by all accounts, is fraught with problems and lack of sustainability under the current circumstances. Service quality is perennially challenged. Embracing IS/IT is a temptation (and deservedly so) as new application possibilities are introduced at ever-increasing rates. However, simply dropping technology into complex environments generally does not succeed. Numerous examples of unused or under-used technology exist in the annals of healthcare. There is a wide range of stakeholder considerations and sensitivities including an informed public with the ability for comparison and contrast that warrants consideration.

This book artfully brings together a wide range of issues around a common theme that is important to all of us—efficient yet quality healthcare—through application of lean thinking. Recognizing that the "majority of medical errors are caused by faulty systems, processes, and conditions that lead people to make mistakes or prevent them" sets the stage for innovative interventions. Bringing quality concepts having originated in manufacturing (e.g. six-sigma) is novel. However, even though the principles may be OK, people are different and transformation requires a fair amount of interpretation, at least in practice. Machines don't complain and, for better or worse, tend to consistently produce the same output. Such is not the case in healthcare where circumstances resist being mechanized.

However, embracing a "sociotechnical" approach presents a solution strategy and operational way forward that bridges technological capabilities with sensitivity to human practice. The sociotechnical approach has a long history of application in complex circumstances. Fundamentally, the approach centres around people and embraces their knowledge and wisdom as well as their desires to make effective use of technology, often in ways unimagined by its creators. Aspects of process and social value are integral to productive application. The issues are many and varied. Under these circumstances, lean thinking need not be devoid of human sensitivity and quality can emerge in an efficient and caring fashion.

The parts and chapters in this book navigate and map this space in a comprehensive fashion that provides much for many. The first part on key concepts, tools, and techniques provides a solid background for the second part emphasizing applications of lean thinking around the healthcare world. This is followed by the third part which deals with macro issues and the fourth part dealing with micro issues. Culminating with case studies in Part V effectively brings things to a close. Overall, this is a book of interest to a broad readership crossing multiple disciplines and areas of practice. I expect it to be well read.

City University, Hong Kong Douglas R. Vogel

Preface

At a very fundamental level quality of care is about meeting the physical, psychological, and social expectations of patients who search for care. The American Institute of Medicine (IOM) refers to quality of care as "the degree to which health services for individuals and populations increase the likelihood of desired health outcome consistent with current professional knowledge" (Kumpersmith 2003). The term "health service for the individuals" in the definition is a reference to service quality as well as the link between service quality and patients, i.e. customers. This link is further strengthened in this definition with the application of professional knowledge. In fact the link between quality and customers has been established in the healthcare industry as early as 1910. In 1910, the American surgeon, Ernest Codman, developed the concept of "end result idea" in hospitals. The concept requires the following: "Every hospital should follow every patient it treats long enough to determine whether the treatment has been successful, and then to inquire 'if not, why not' with a view to preventing similar failure in the future" (NCBI 2005). While initially this may not have been embraced readily (Who_Named_It 2005), today, Dr. Codman is remembered as a guru for quality of care and The Ernest A. Codman Award was created in 1996 to showcase the effective use of performance measures and to encourage the quality of care. Ironically, in this same year, the Advisory Commission on Consumer Protection and Quality in the Heath Care Industry was established. The Commissions notes the following quality problems in hospitals (Advisory_Commission 1998):

1. *Avoidable error*: the report points out that too many Americans are injured and died prematurely as a result of avoidable errors. The report claims that "from 1983 to 1993 alone, deaths due to medical errors rose more than twofold, with 7,391 deaths attributed to medication errors in 1993 alone".
2. *Underutilization of services*: the report claims that millions of people do not receive necessary care. It estimated that about 18,000 people die each year from heart attacks because they did not receive effective interventions.

3. *Overuse of services*: the claim was that millions of Americans receive healthcare services that are unnecessary.
4. *Variation in services*: there is a continuing pattern of variation in healthcare services, including regional variations and small-area variations.

More recently, in 2000, IOM released its landmark report, entitled "To Err is Human: Building a Safer Health System" (Kohn et al. 2000). This report concentrates on errors within the American healthcare systems and concludes that majority of medical errors are caused by faulty systems, processes, and conditions that lead people to make mistakes or fail to prevent them. Moreover, the report stresses that "when an error occurs, blaming an individual does little to make the system safer and prevent someone else from committing the same error (ibid)".

About 15 months after releasing its landmark report on medical errors, the IOM released its second report, titled "Crossing the Quality Chasm: A New Health System for the 21st Century" (IOM 2001). This second report emphasizes a gap or "chasm" between the quality of care for the existing health system and the expected quality of health that should be delivered and set forth a vision for transforming quality of the health system. In consistency with the findings of the Advisory Commission (Advisory_Commission 1998), the IOM report calls for improvements in six dimensions of healthcare performance: safety, effectiveness, patient-centeredness, timeliness, efficiency, and equity (Table 1). It asserts that "those improvements cannot be achieved within the constraints of the existing system of care" (Berwick 2002). In response to this challenge, the Institute of Medicine (IOM) and the National Academy of Engineering (NAE), released a third report, titled "Building a Better Delivery System: A New Engineering/Health Care Partnership" (Reid et al. 2005). In an attempt "to bridge the knowledge/awareness divide separating healthcare professionals from their potential partners in systems engineering and related disciplines", the NAE/IOM study identifies system engineering applications that could contribute significantly to improvements in healthcare delivery and emphasizes that tools transforming the quality and productivity performance of other large-scale complex systems could also be used to improve healthcare delivery. The report highlights the role of information and recognizes the importance of human factors techniques and the significance of adapting Toyota Production System (TPS) concepts to healthcare performance. The TPS is a collection of ideas, techniques, and procedures developed by Toyota mainly afterWorld War II. The focus of TPS is to produce cars that satisfy customers and fits their requirements. The principles are producing cars with best quality at the lowest costs and with shortest lead time through systematic elimination of waste and improving performance.

Given this growing importance placed on quality and value creation for healthcare delivery, coupled with the plethora of technology solutions now being developed that facilitate (or at least claim to facilitate) better healthcare delivery, we believed it was timely to examine the issue of lean thinking for healthcare together

Table 1 Six quality aims for the twenty-first-century healthcare system proposed by IOM (2001)

• *Safe*—avoiding injuries to patients from the care that is intended to help them
• *Effective*—providing services based on scientific knowledge to all who could benefit and refraining from providing services to those not likely to benefit (avoiding underuse and overuse, respectively)
• *Patient-centred*—providing care that is respectful of and responsive to individual patient preferences, needs, and values and ensuring that patient values guide all clinical decisions
• *Timely*—reducing waits and sometimes harmful delays for both those who receive and those who give care
• *Efficient*—avoiding waste, including waste of equipment, supplies, ideas, and energy
• *Equitable*—providing care that does not vary in quality because of personal characteristics such as gender, ethnicity, geographic location, and socioeconomic status

Source: IOM (2001), pp. 5–6

with related and complementary concepts such as six sigma, kaizen, and constraint management. Hence, together with our colleagues around the world, we set about creating this magnum opus that serves to explore and present in one volume critical issues relating to lean thinking and its application in a variety of healthcare contexts in order to facilitate and enable superior healthcare delivery to ensue.

Introduction to Lean Thinking

During 1980s, Professors Womack and Jones of Massachusetts Institute of Technology (MIT) conducted a 5-year project for studying TPS and publish their book, entitled "The Machines that Changed the World" in 1990 and they coined the term "lean production" as synonymous to the TPS (Womack et al. 1990). The term "lean" is used because the lean production uses less of everything compared to other production systems. Since its introduction, the concept of lean production has changed considerably (Joosten et al. 2009). It is diffused from car industry to other manufacturing industry and then to service industry (Hines et al. 2004). Originally, the application of lean at Toyota was a process-oriented concept. Currently, lean extends beyond the original Toyota operational shop floor concept to include "respect-for-human system" aspects besides the technical aspects of the system under study (Joosten et al. 2009; Sugimori et al. 1977). In other words, application of lean requires looking to the system as "sociotechnical" system in which human factor engineering and technology plays the central role. Womack and Jones (1996b, 2003) enhance further the "sociotechnical" aspect of lean production through introducing five principles within which the customer value and waste reduction are the cores of the lean system (Joosten et al. 2009; Womack and Jones 2003). Womack and Jones coin their principles with the term "lean thinking" with emphasize to applicability of lean thinking to service industry including healthcare services. Table 2 describes the five principles of lean thinking.

By definition, customer value is a reference to activities which from the viewpoint of the customer add value and the customer is ready to pay for (Womack and Jones 1996a). Accordingly, activities of a process or system can be divided into two

Table 2 The five principles of lean thinking (adapted from Inozu et al. 2012; Black 1984)

No.	Principle	Meaning
1	Value	Value is any activity, step, or event that improves the customer experience (Powell et al. 2009). This principle requires specifying the values the customer actually wants in order to provide them
2	Value stream	Value stream—steaming a process means mapping (dividing) activities within the process. It may require dividing each activity to its sub-activities or steps and so on. Value stream means that the activities of a process should provide value. This requires streaming the process into activities and then sub-activities/steps and identifying those steps that add no value from the customer perspective (i.e. waste) with the aim to eliminate them
3	Flow	The principle requires smoothing the flow of work, material, and information. It may require redesigning the process to create continual flow and eliminate bottlenecks
4	Pull	Align the supply of services or product with customer demand. Services or goods are only provided upstream when the customer downstream requests for them (Powell et al. 2009). It also means that all work, material, and information should be pulled to perform tasks when needed (Jones and Mitchell 2006)
5	Perfection	This principle requires continual improvement such that each improvement in the process creates a platform for the next one (Jones and Mitchell 2006)

main types of activities; value adding activities and non-value adding activities. Value adding activities contribute directly to the production of products or services while non-value adding activities do not make such contribution and, accordingly, can be considered as waste that should be considered for possible reduction or elimination. Waste is anything other than the minimum amount of equipment, effort, material, parts, space, and time, which are absolutely essential to add value to the product [or service] (Cho and Makise 1980; Russell and Taylor 1999). There are two kinds of non-value adding activities; activities add no value but are necessary such as transportation and those activities that can be avoided and can be considered as complete waste (Monden 1993). Lean thinking attempts to eliminate or reduce waste by eliminating unnecessary non-value adding activities and reducing as much as possible the necessary non-value adding activities. Literature specifies seven elements of waste (Ohno 1988). Table 3 provides description of the seven types of waste with examples from healthcare services (Table 3).

The aim of lean thinking is to provide what the customer wants, quickly, efficiently, and with little waste (Jones and Mitchell 2006; Young et al. 2004). It aims to substantially smooth the flow and drastically reduce waste and process variations (Womack et al. 1990; Taj and Berro 2006; Reichhart 2007). From the customer's value perspective, waste is defined as the activity or activities that a customer would not want to pay for, and that do not add value to the product or service from the customer's perspective (Shinohara 2006). Once waste has been identified in the current or existing state, a plan is formulated to eliminate this to attain a desired future

Table 3 The seven elements of waste (adapted from Inozu et al. 2012; Black 1984)

	Waste element	Lean principle	Quality aim	Comments/examples from healthcare services
1	Defect	Value stream	Safe, patient-centred	A defect occurs when the output was not as intended or does not fit with the requirements and specifications. It may require corrective action, or repeating the activity. Examples include medical assessment errors, adverse drug reaction, providing wrong drug, performing surgery on the wrong side, and readmission patient because of wrong discharge
2	Transportation	Flow/value stream	Timely, efficiency	This is a reference to the movement of material and equipment. It includes also the transportation of a patient from one place to another. Transportation may be necessary and cannot be avoided but can be considerably reduced using process re-engineering. For instance, having preoperative area adjacent to operating room reduces considerably the patient movement
3	Motion	Flow/value stream	Timely, efficiency	It refers to the movement of medical staff to obtain material or information. Electronic transferring the medical test results or x-ray images eliminate the staff movement to obtain the results or images. Motion includes extra effort and movement in performing action such as using arm and shoulder rather arranging work place for less effort movement (human factor engineering)
4	Waiting	Pull/value stream	Patient-centred, timely, efficiency	This includes any delay in performing an activity or waiting for an action to occur. Examples include waiting for general practitioner, for medical results, for trolley to move a patient, or for medical information
5	Inventory	Value, value stream, perfection	Efficiency	It refers to excess material stocks in a storage. For healthcare, it refers to long waiting lists for surgery, medical assessments, or special treatments
6	Over-processing	Value, value stream, perfection	Effectiveness	Unnecessary repetition of an action. Examples include unnecessary recounting instruments, requesting same information from a patient several times, and receiving additional information which is not required
7	Overproduction	Value, value stream, perfection	Effectiveness	Unnecessary reproduction of the same product/service: example, repeating unnecessary x-ray or medical test, have unnecessary extra beds in discharge room, and leaving lights and air conditioning switch on after leaving offices

state in as effective and efficient a manner as possible. Lean Thinking provides the following benefits (Jones and Mitchell 2006): improved quality and safety, improved delivery, improved throughput—the same resources with higher efficiency, and accelerating momentum—A stable working environment with clear, standardized procedures creates the foundations for constant improvement.

Lean thinking comprises a set of approaches and techniques utilized to efficiently reduce waste in a way that achieves the five principles of lean thinking. Some of these approaches are old and developed during the second and third decades of twenty-first century such as method study and work measurement (Barnes 1980) while other approaches are recently developed such as Just-in-time (Womack et al. 1990) and process reengineering (Hammer 1990). The list of approaches and techniques is growing with the time. The main question that first needs to be answered is which technique(s) is (are) most suitable to achieve the aim of lean thinking for specific situation under study. However, lean thinking differs from other traditional approaches in that:

1. It looks to the entire process rather than specific activity of it. Improving an activity without addressing the whole process may not improve efficiency at all (Jones and Mitchell 2006).
2. It aims to achieve the five principles of lean thinking.

In order to achieve lean principles, the commitment to create lean thinking culture should start at the very top management of the organization (Miller 2005), keeping in mind that Lean "has to be locally led and be part of the organisational strategy" (Jones and Mitchell 2006). From operational side, there is a need to integrate more than one approach to achieve the requirements for lean thinking. The set of approaches may differ from one process to another. In addition, many approaches may require adaptation in order to be integrated with other approaches.

Lean Thinking for Healthcare Services

The literature emphasizes the applicability of lean thinking to healthcare services (Balle and Regnier 2007; Jones and Mitchell 2006; Young et al. 2004). Although some healthcare professionals may argue that lean thinking is more suitable to manufacturing and does not translate well to healthcare services; Bowen and Youngdahl (1998) show how it does apply to healthcare by providing theory, case studies, and context for lean applications. Flinders Medical Centre, a medium-sized public sector teaching hospital in Adelaide, South Australia, has, for some time, been implementing lean strategies (King et al. 2006) and has been able to operate below its budgeted costs (Jones and Mitchell 2006). Lean thinking has also been advocated in the healthcare setting of the USA through the use of the Six Sigma methodology, which in many ways resembles lean production techniques (Dahlgaard and Dahlgaard 2006; Tolga Taner et al. 2007; Young et al. 2004). Other related literature also reveals that the implementation of lean thinking brings benefit to healthcare

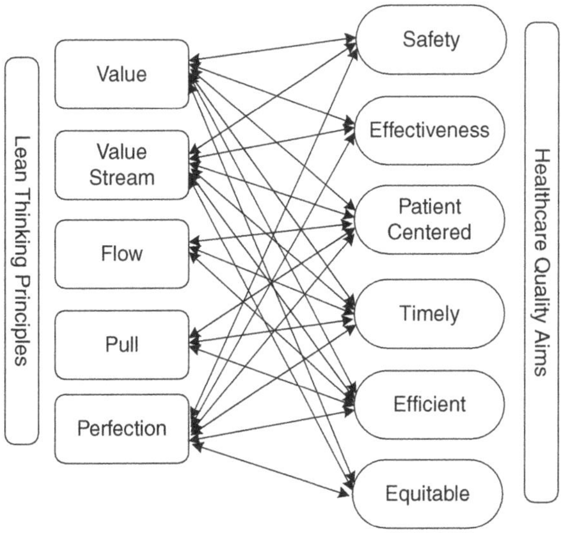

Fig. 1 Lean principles and aims of healthcare quality (adapted from Inozu et al. 2012; Black 1984)

(DeKoning et al. 2006; Jimmerson et al. 2005; Young and McClean 2008; Ahluwalia and Offredy 2005). It has been emphasized that lean thinking provides the following benefits (Jones and Mitchell 2006):

1. *Improved quality and safety*—fewer mistakes, accidents and errors, will result and better quality goods and services will be produced.
2. *Improved delivery*—the work gets done faster.
3. *Improved throughput*—the same people, using the same equipment, find they are capable of achieving much more results.
4. *Accelerating momentum*—a stable working environment with clear, standardized procedures creates the foundations for constant improvement.

The customers for healthcare services are mainly patients but also include society, government, or even the legislations. The quality aims proposed by IOM (2001) comprises the main values required by the customers. Any activity or step that contradicts, prevents, or shifts attention from any of these aims is considered as non-value adding activity and should be targeted for elimination as required by value stream principle. Perfection should be targeted to achieve all the quality aims. Lean principles "flow" and "pull" deal with the healthcare quality aims "timely" and "efficient". All lean principles are patient-centred (Fig. 1).

Challenges Faced by Lean Thinking

Like any other improvement philosophies or approaches, lean thinking faces a range of criticisms both from philosophical and practical perspectives (Hines et al. 2004; Powell et al. 2009). Powell et al. (2009) list 13 particular challenges in applying lean thinking in healthcare settings as identified by various authors. Most of these challenges are similar to these challenges that have been facing manufacturing organizations before or during the application of lean thinking. Having complex patient pathways in healthcare services is a factor that may contribute to the importance of applying lean thinking rather than the opposite. Powell et al. (2009) state in their list that Just-in-time requires demand prediction. This is not a true statement. The pull strategy of Just-in-time is particularly designed to deal with real demand rather than predictions or forecasts (Simchi-Levi et al. 2008). Nevertheless, the study of the NHS Institute for Innovation and Improvement stresses demand on healthcare is mostly predictable with a range (Westwood et al. 2007). The study emphasizes that it is the way the process is designed and operated that causes any instability that is important to note.

Falling to understand the real challenges is one of the main reasons that limit the application of lean thinking in healthcare services and in particular in areas such as operating rooms or in dealing with the actual work of medical professionals. Understanding these challenges allows us to adapt lean thinking to suit the healthcare settings. We should first look to the main differences between healthcare and manufacturing settings. These differences are summarized below.

Differences Between Healthcare and Manufacturing Settings

Hospital and manufacturing production systems vary in a number of dimensions. There are several reasons for the notion that the concept of lean thinking should be adapted to fit the hospital system (Woodward-Hagg et al. 2007). Gong (2009) considers the work of Al-Hakim (2006) and lists major areas of differences between manufacturing and healthcare settings. The differences include human involvement, level of product uniformity, cycle time, waiting time, object behaviour, ease of performance measurement, and process effectiveness.

Advanced machinery could be designed and then skilled labour involvement could be minimized in a manufacturing setting; whereas, in healthcare, involvement of skilled professionals is necessary. In manufacturing, performance of workers in the production process is easier to measure. In contrast, performance of professionals in the process is not easily measurable. Again, this is because healthcare professionals differ in skills and expertise, and it is hard to measure their effectiveness in dealing with various complexities during operation processes. Also, products have defined characteristics in manufacturing; however, in healthcare, since the level of complexity and variability of activities is high, it is not always possible to predict the degree of the success of surgery.

In addition, while products are uniform in manufacturing, every patient may require a different service in healthcare. Even health problems that appear to be similar could require a unique treatment. As a result, the designed process needs to be modified to fit the circumstances of each particular patient. Also, unlike manufacturing products which have defined characteristics, patients' behaviour is not predictable and could vary substantially.

Table 4 Summary of differences between the manufacturing and healthcare services settings (Gong 2009)

Organization type Differences	Lean thinking in manufacturing	Lean thinking in healthcare
Human involvement	Automation is a major role to reduce human involvement; it reduces the need for high skill and knowledge	Skill, knowledge, and experience of professionals play major role
Ease of performance measurement	Performance of workers in the production process is easy to measure	Performance of professionals in the process is not easily measurable
Process effectiveness	Process outcome is predictable	It is hard to predict the degree of the success of healthcare service
Product uniformity	Machine produces identical products	It is difficult to perform a medical operation (say surgery) that will have exactly same output. In addition, every patient requires different service
Object behaviour	Products have defined characteristics	Patients' behaviour is not predictable and could vary
Cycle time	Cycle time of the production could be precise and determined in advance	Healthcare service cycle time could vary and is difficult to determine prior to the service
Non-added value activity time	All types of inspection are waste and should be reduced or eliminated	In healthcare environment, monitoring and testing are essential
Information flow	Mainly depends on process flow	Healthcare activities are information-based activities

Further, production cycle time could be precise in a production setting, but it is not possible to fix an operation time in healthcare as each service might be unique. Also, zero waiting time could be targeted in a manufacturing environment; whereas waiting time is not always a waste in healthcare. Sometimes it can even be considered as a value-added activity. If an operating theatre of the hospital is taken as an example, an anaesthetist does the job mainly at the beginning of the operation, while the other surgical team is involved in monitoring activities. In contrast, in a production line of manufacturing, if a worker is waiting or monitoring a process, it is considered as a waste that should be eliminated to improve efficiency (see Table 4 for summary of differences).

Considering that modern lean thinking deals with human factor aspects, most of the main listed differences can be managed including human involvement, performance measurement, and object behaviour. Similar to any service process, information flow plays major role besides human (employees) involvement (Evans and Lindsay 2008). Several important differences missed from the list of Gong (2009), among them are that the patient (customer) is directly involved in the healthcare services and the healthcare services are consumed and produced simultaneously (Evans and Lindsay 2008). Another important difference missed from Gong's list is that the defect as a waste could result adverse event that is very costly and cannot be rectified. Performing surgery in the wrong side (removing the wrong breast or cutting wrong leg) cannot be rectified by performing corrective action or repeating the wrong activity. Defect even can be vital and may lead to death. This is not the case in manufacturing or other service settings. It is the value principle, particularly safety factor, forms the main difference between healthcare and other settings. From lean thinking perspective, value should be specified by customers. Value stream should stream activities of the process throughout the patient journey within the processes in order to identify non-value adding activities and eliminate or reduce them. The quality aims provided by IOM (2001) specifies these values as shown in Table 2. The first aim, i.e. safe, is specifically critical value from customer perspective. The safe principle may require changes in the definition of waste, in some circumstances may be different from waste as defined for the purpose of applying lean thinking settings other than healthcare service. For instance, monitoring may be considered as waste from manufacturing perspective while it could be extremely important in certain healthcare services such as monitoring patients inside intensive care units. The position of the scrub table inside operating room is another example. From manufacturing perspective, having scrub table near the door of the operating room may have logistical advantage as there is wide range of circumstances in which there are needs to bring sterilized materials or instruments from outside operating rooms to the table during surgery. Opening or closing OF doors may generate airborne contamination. In addition, having scrub table near the door increases the movements around the table and subsequently increases airborne contamination. What could be considered as logistical waste from manufacturing perspective may create value from healthcare perspective. This fundamental difference requires us to look to value stream from customer value as specified by IOM (2001) and not by the traditional perspective adopted for other settings. According to the NHS study (Westwood et al. 2007), identifying the value stream means identifying the components of the patient journey which add value to their care. This can be done through process mapping. Most current process mapping methodologies deal with work flow and from which the information flow can be identified. These methodologies are suitable for manufacturing as well as the majority of service settings. Healthcare service is an information-based service (McLaughlin 1996). Accordingly, information flow plays a major role in healthcare services. This fact creates another major difference with other setting where the work flow plays a major role. This fundamental difference leads us to search for methodology that first maps information flow in order to identify the components of the process rather than the opposite. Lillrank (2003) suggests that the primary problem in healthcare services is not the quality of the actual implementation of the process, such as surgery, but the quality of information that controls the process. The recognition of data and information quality becomes a key area of both strategic and operations management in the healthcare industry (Lorence and Jameson 2002). This adds another difference in that the information quality and the quality of information flow play more superior role than in manufacturing settings where machines, automation, and quality of work flow are more important. Table 5 shows the main additional difference between

Table 5 Additional difference between manufacturing and healthcare settings that requires adaptation or more attention

Lean thinking principle	Issue	Manufacturing settings	Healthcare settings
Customer value	Customer involvement	Customers are not involved in manufacturing the product	Customers are directly involved in producing the services
	Waste: defect	Defect in manufacturing is rectifiable. It may require repletion of the process	Defects could result adverse event that is very costly and cannot be rectified
	Waste: definition	Waste is any activity or activities that a customer would not want to pay for, and that do not add value to the product or service from the customer's perspective	Similar definition. However, the activities which may be considered waste in manufacturing setting may not be considered waste from healthcare perspective
Value stream	Consumption	Products are produced and consumed at a later stage	Products are produced and consumed simultaneously
	Basis of the processes	Work-based process	Information-based process
	Quality	The primary quality problem in manufacturing settings is the quality of the final product	The primary problem in healthcare services is not the quality of the actual implementation of the process but the quality of information that controls the process (Lillrank 2003)
	Process mapping	Requiring methodology that first maps the components of work flow	Requiring methodology that first maps the information flow in order to identify the components that add value
Flow	Priority	Priority is given to work flow	Priority is given to information flow

healthcare and manufacturing settings that needs further attention and more adaptation from lean thinking perspective.

Applications of Lean Thinking in Healthcare Services

As the proceeding has hopefully highlighted the area of lean for healthcare is both broad and rich. Given the importance for healthcare delivery today to grapple with challenges such as escalating costs, demands for high-quality care, ageing populations, increase in chronic diseases such as diabetes as well as the increase in technology, it becomes more essential than ever before for healthcare organizations to embrace the principles of lean and adopt many of the related tools, techniques, and practices to effect superior healthcare delivery. The following pages serve to guide the reader through the complex and rich world of lean thinking for healthcare. We do this by first introducing key principles, concepts, techniques, and technologies in Part I. Then in Part II we present the reader with a miscellany of applications taken from various healthcare contexts throughout the world which serve to highlight either the benefits of applying lean thinking and/or how lean thinking principles may have facilitated a better and more successful result. Parts III and IV, respectively, serve to illustrate macro-level and micro-level considerations with regard to the application of lean thinking in healthcare contexts and finally Part V provides case studies that demonstrate the benefits of simulation in various emergency departments in order to illustrate how lean thinking can actually facilitate current state operations, streamline workflow, and enable heightened healthcare value to be realized.

The world of lean thinking for healthcare is still at its infancy. It is a very broad and rich world and thus it is not possible to fill the pages of one book with all possible scenarios and contexts. However, we hope this book will provide our readers be they academics or practitioners, graduate students or members of the general public all with one common desire to understand how to create and support superior healthcare delivery by applying lean thinking for healthcare, a road map to illumination and thereby the getting of better healthcare delivery for us all.

Melbourne, VIC, Australia — Nilmini Wickramasinghe
Toowoomba, QLD, Australia — Latif Al-Hakim
Chicago, IL, USA — Chris Gonzalez
Hamilton, ON, Canada — Joseph Tan

References

Advisory_Commission. (1998). Advisory Commission's final report.

Ahluwalia, S., & Offredy, M. (2005). A qualitative study of the impact of the implementation of advanced access in primary healthcare on the working lives of general practice staff. *BMC Family Practice, 6*, 39.

Al-Hakim, L. (2006). Web-based hospital information system for managing operating theatre waiting list. *International Journal of Healthcare Technology and Management, 7*, 266–682.

Balle, M. & Regnier, A. (2007). Lean as a learning system in a hospital ward. *Leadership in Health Service 20*(1), 33–41.

Barnes, R. M. (1980). *Motion and time study design and measurement of work*. New York: Wiley.

Berwick, D. M. (2002). A user's manual for the IOM's 'Quality Chasm' report. *Health Affairs, 21*, 80.

Black, J. (1984). *The Toyota Way to Healthcare excellence*. AHE Managmeent Series. Chicago: Health administration Press.

Bowen, D. E. & Youngdahl, W. E. 1998. Lean service: In defense of a production-line approach. *International Journal of Service Industry Management, 9*, 207–225.

Cho, F., & Makise, K. (1980). Toyota kanban, the ultimate in efficiency and effectiveness. New York: American Production and Inventory Control Society.

Dahlgaard, J. J., & Dahlgaard, S. M. (2006). Lean production, six sigma quality, TQM and company culture—A critical review. *The TQM Magazine, 18*, 263–281.

DeKoning, H., Verver, J., Heuvel, J., Bisgaard, S., & Does, R. (2006). Lean six sigma in healthcare. *Journal for Healthcare Quality, 28*, 4–11.

Evans, J. R. & Lindsay, W. M. 2008. *Managing for Quality and Performance Excellence,* Cincinati, Ohio, South-Western, Thomson Learning.

Gong, X. Y. (2009). *Identifying and minimising preventable dealy within the operating theatre management process.* MBA, The University of Southern Queensland.

Hammer, M. (1990). Reengineering work: Don't automate, obliterate. *Harvard Business Review, 68*, 104–112.

Hines, P., Holweg, M., & Rich, N. (2004). Learning to evolve: A review of contemporary lean thinking. *International Journal of Operations & Production Management, 24*, 994–1011.

IOM. (2001). *Crossing the quality chasm: A new health system for the 21st century*. Washington, DC: Institute of Medicine, National Academy Press.

Inozu, B., Chauncey, D., Kamataris, V., & Mount, C. (2012). *Performance improvement for healthcare*. Chicago: McGrawHill.

Jimmerson, C., Weber, D., & Sobek, D. K. (2005). Reducing waste and errors: Piloting lean principles at IHC. *Joint Commission Journal on Quality and Safety, 31*, 249–257.

Jones, D., & Mitchell, A. (2006). Lean thinking for the NHS. London: National Health Service (NHS) Confederation Report, UK.

Joosten, T., Bongers, I., & Janssen, R. (2009). Application of lean thinking to health care: Issues and observations. *International Journal for Quality in health care, 21*, 1–7.

King, D. L., Ben-Tovim, D. I., & Bassham, J. (2006). Redesigning emergency department patient flows: Application of lean thinking to health care. *Emergency Medicine Australasia, 18*, 391–397.

Kohn, L. T., Corrigan, J. M., & Donaldson, M. S. (2000). *To err is human: Building a safer health system*. A report of the Committee on Quality of Health Care in America, Institute of Medicine. Washington, DC: National Academy Press.

Kumpersmith, J. (2003). *Quality of care in teaching hospitals: Executive summary*. Association of American Medical Colleges. Retrieved December 2011, from http://www.aamc.org/quality/surveys/start.htm

Lillrank, P. (2003). The quality of information. *International Journal of Quality and Reliability Management, 20*, 691–703.

Lorence, D. P., & Jameson, R. (2002). Adoption of information quality management practices in US healthcare organisations: A national assessment. *International Journal of Quality & Reliability Management, 19*, 737–756.

McLaughlin, C. P. (1996). Why variation reduction is not everything: A new paradigm for service operations. *International Journal of Service Industry Management, 7*, 17–30.

Miller, D. (2005). *Going lean in health care*. Cambridge, MA: Institute for Healthcare Improvement.

Monden, Y. (1993). *Toyota production system: An introduction to just-in-time*. Norcross, GA: Industrial Engineering and Management Press.

National Centre for Biotechnology Information (2005). Ernest Codman's contribution to quality assessment and beyond. Accessed December 2012, from http://www.ncbi.nlm.nih.gov

Ohno, T. (1988). *Toyota production system: Beyond large-scale production*. New York: Productivity Press.

Powell, A., Rushmer, R., & Davies, H. (2009). Effective quality improvement: Lean. *British Journal of Healthcare Management, 15*, 270–275.

Reichhart, A. (2007). Lean distribution: Concepts, contributions, conflicts. *International Journal of Production Research, 45*, 3699–3722.

Reid, P. P., Compton, W. D., Grossman, J. H., & Fanjiang, G. (2005). *Building a better delivery system: A new engineering/health care partnership*. Washington, DC: National Academy Press.

Russell, R. S., & Taylor, B. W. (1999). *Operations management*. Upper Saddle, NJ: Prentice-Hall.

Shinohara, M. (2006). *European and Japanese logistics paradigms: An explorative and comparative study of the dynamics of logistics management.* Thesis, Erasmus University, Rotterdam.
Simchi-Levi, D., Kaminisky, P. & Simchi-Levi, E. 2008. *Designing and Managing the Supply Chain: Concepts, Strategies and Case Studies,* Buston McGraw-Hill.
Sugimori, Y., Kusunoki, K., & Cho, F. (1977). Toyota production system and kanban system materialization of just-in-time and respect-f-human system. *International Journal of Production Research, 15*, 553–564.
Taj, S., & Berro, L. (2006). Application of constrained management and lean manufacturing in developing best practices for productivity improvement in an auto-assembly plant. *International Journal of Productivity and Performance Management, 55*, 332.
Tolga Taner, M., Sezen, B., & Antony, J. (2007). An overview of Six Sigma applications in healthcare industry. *International Journal of Health Care Quality Assurance, 20*, 329–340.
Westwood, N., James-Moor, M., & Cooke, M. (2007). Going lean in the NHS. Warwick, UK: Institute for Innovation and Improvement, NHS.
Who_Named_It. (2005). *Ernest Armory Codman.* Retrieved November, 15 2005, from http://www.whonamedit.com/doctor.cfm/2558.html
Womack, J. P., & Jones, D. T. (1996a). Beyond Toyota: How to root out waste and pursue perfection. *Harvard Business Review, 74*, 140–172.
Womack, J. P., & Jones, D. T. (1996b). *Lean thinking.* New York: Simon & Schuster.
Womack, J. P., & Jones, D. T. (2003). *Lean thinking: Banish waste and create wealth in your corporation.* New York: Free Press.
Womack, J. P., Jones, D. T., & Roos, D. (1990). *The machine that changed the world.* New York: Rawson Associates.
Woodward-Hagg, H., Suskovich, D., Workman-Germann, J., Scachitti, S., Hudson, B., Swartz, J., & Vanni, C. (2007). *Aaptation of lean methodologies for healthcare applications.* Retrieved from http://docs.lib.purdue.edu/cgi/viewcontent.cgi?article=1035&context=rche_rp
Young, T., Brailsford, S., Connell, C., Davies, R., Harper, P., & Klein, J. H. (2004). *Using industrial processes to improve patient care* [Online]. Retrieved from http://www.bmj.com/cgi/content/extract/328/7437/463
Young, T. P., & Mcclean, S. I. (2008). A critical look at Lean Thinking in healthcare. *British Medical Journal, 17*, 382.

Acknowledgements

This book would not have been possible without the cooperation and assistance of numerous people: the contributors, reviewers, our respective institutions, our colleagues, students, families, friends and the staff at Springer. In today's networked environment when we are not co-located but distributed across various continents and continually meeting the challenges of the respective local demands on our time, we are especially appreciative to all the contributors and reviewers for not only your timely responses but also the high quality of your submissions and feedback. Finally, we would especially like to thank the production staff at Springer, in particular Khristine Queja, for all their efforts in helping us to make this book possible.

Contents

Contributors

Mohamed Abouzahra Degroote School of Business, McMaster University, Hamilton, ON, Canada

Seyed Mohammad Seyedi Alavi School of Information Systems and Technology, University of Wollongong, Wollongong, NSW, Australia

Latif Al-Hakim School of Management and Marketing, Faculty of Business, University of Southern Queensland, Toowoomba, QLD, Australia

Ray Arias Arias Information Solutions LLC, Chicago, IL, USA

Melanie Bathelt University of Hohenheim, Stuttgart, Germany

Mirjam Bathelt University of Hohenheim, Stuttgart, Germany

Mari Botti Epworth Research Institute, Richmond, VIC, Australia

Ayse Cakmak University of Hohenheim, Stuttgart, Germany

Suresh Chalasani MIS Department, School of Business and Technology, University of Wisconsin-Parkside, Kenosha, WI, USA

Daniel Denkert University of Hohenheim, Stuttgart, Germany

Raphael Di Francesco Epworth HealthCare & Department of BITL & HIRi, RMIT University, Melbourne, VIC, Australia

Michael S. Dohan DeGroote School of Business, McMaster University, Hamilton, ON, Canada

Faculty of Business Administration, Lakehead University, Thunder Bay, ON, Canada

Carolin Durst Institute of Information Systems, University Erlangen-Nürnberg, Nürnberg, Germany

Steffen Ebach University of Hohenheim, Stuttgart, Germany

Katharinen hospital, Stuttgart, Germany

Steve Goldberg INET International Canada, Thornhill, ON, Canada

Chris Gonzalez North Western Memorial Hospital, Chicago, IL, USA

Emanuel Grabler University of Hohenheim, Stuttgart, Germany

Mark Gregory School of Electrical and Computer Engineering, RMIT University, Melbourne, VIC, Australia

Stefanie Guder University of Hohenheim, Stuttgart, Germany

Peter Haddad School of Business IT and Logistics, RMIT University, Melbourne, VIC, Australia

Sabrina Hamm University of Hohenheim, Stuttgart, Germany

Andreas Hamper Institute of Information Systems, University Erlangen-Nürnberg, Nürnberg, Germany

Lara Henzler University of Hohenheim, Stuttgart, Germany

Sally Rao Hill University of Adelaide Business School, Adelaide, SA, Australia

Nathan Houchens Department of Internal Medicine, University of Michigan, Ann Arbor, MI, USA

Bridie Kent Epworth Research Institute, Richmond, VIC, Australia

Nils Kern University of Hohenheim, Stuttgart, Germany

Christopher S. Kim Department of Internal Medicine, University of Michigan, Ann Arbor, MI, USA

Corinna Klink University of Hohenheim, Stuttgart, Germany

Sridevi Koritala Lakeshore Medical Clinic, Saint Francis, WI, USA

Kwok Hung Lau School of Business IT and Logistics, RMIT University, Melbourne, VIC, Australia

Jan Lipka University of Hohenheim, Stuttgart, Germany

Tobias Lörch University of Hohenheim, Stuttgart, Germany

Daniel Mengele University of Hohenheim, Stuttgart, Germany

Fatemeh Hoda Moghimi School of Business IT and Logistics, RMIT University, Research Institute, Epworth HealthCare, Melbourne, VIC, Australia

Tino Müller Institute of Information Systems, University Erlangen-Nürnberg, Nürnberg, Germany

Imran Muhammed School of Business IT & Logistics, RMIT University, Melbourne, VIC, Australia

Lemai Nguyen Epworth Research Institute, Richmond, VIC, Australia

Mohammad Rezazadeh Niavarani School of Business IT and Logistics, RMIT University, Melbourne, VIC, Australia

Tahnee Platz University of Hohenheim, Stuttgart, Germany

Bernice Redley Epworth Research Institute, Richmond, VIC, Australia

Tobias Reutemann University of Hohenheim, Stuttgart, Germany

Kristina Riemann University of Hohenheim, Stuttgart, Germany

Juergen Seitz Department of Business Information Systems, DHBW Heidenheim, Heidenheim, Germany

Ningqiao Shen Information Engineering Department, Jiangsu Province Hospital of TCM, Nanjing, China

Anke Simon Baden-Wuerttemberg Cooperative State University, Stuttgart, Germany

Jeffrey Soar School of Information Systems, Faculty of Business & Law, University of Southern Queensland, Toowoomba, QLD, Australia

Janine Steffen University of Hohenheim, Stuttgart, Germany

Malte Stien SmartWard Pty Ltd, Canberra, Australia

Ying Su Institute of Scientific and Technical Information of China, Beijing, China

Joseph Tan Degroote School of Business, McMaster University, Hamilton, ON, Canada

Nyree Taylor Epworth Research Institute, Richmond, VIC, Australia

Say Yen Teoh HIRi and BITL, RMIT University, Melbourne, VIC, Australia

Indrit Troshani University of Adelaide Business School, Adelaide, SA, Australia

Mario Vargheamidis University of Hohenheim, Stuttgart, Germany

Janine Viol Institute of Information Systems, University Erlangen-Nürnberg, Nürnberg, Germany

Nilmini Wickramasinghe Epworth HealthCare & Department of BITL & HIRi, RMIT University, Melbourne, VIC, Australia

Khin Than Win School of Information Systems and Technology, University of Wollongong, Wollongong, NSW, Australia

Sou Wei Wong School of Business IT and Logistics, RMIT University, Melbourne, VIC, Australia

Ted Xenodemetropoulos Division of Gastroenterology, Department of Medicine, McMaster University, Hamilton, ON, Canada

Trudy Yuginovich School of Information Systems, Faculty of Business & Law, University of Southern Queensland, Toowoomba, QLD, Australia

Manuel Zwicker Department of Business IT and Logistics, RMIT University, Melbourne, VIC, Australia

Part I
Key Concepts, Tools and Techniques

1.1 Introduction

The seven chapters in this section all serve to highlight key concepts, tools and techniques that are relevant and necessary to effect lean thinking for healthcare.

Chapter 1 "Lean Principles for Healthcare" by Wickramasinghe serves to introduce the key principles of lean thinking and related concepts and techniques that are relevant and thus should be incorporated into healthcare design and reform.

Chapter 2 "Artificial Neural Network Excellence to Facilitate Lean Thinking Adoption in Healthcare Contexts" by Moghimi and Wickramasinghe explores the benefits of applying Artificial Neural Network (ANN) techniques to help to identify lost values and facilitate lean thinking adoption in healthcare contexts.

Chapter 3 "The Suitability of Artificial Neural Networks in Service Quality Control and Forecasting" by Nirvani and Wickramasinghe further explores aspects of ANN from the perspective of service quality in healthcare contexts.

Chapter 4 "The Application of Lean in the Healthcare Sector: Theory and Practical Examples" by Houchens and Kim.

Chapter 5 "Business Value of IT in Health Care" by Haddad et al. examines the important aspect of business value and how lean thinking principles can enhance value creation for healthcare.

Chapter 6 "Initiatives in Service Orientated Architecture towards Performance Improvement in Healthcare" by Moghimi and Wickramasinghe looks at key IT technical considerations that can support the application of lean principles for healthcare contexts.

Finally, Chap. 7 by Al-Harkim "Adapted Lean Thinking for Emergency Departments: Information Quality Perspective" examines the benefits of lean in effecting information quality perspectives.

Taken together these chapters help to set the stage for the need for the application of lean principles in healthcare as well as to identify the key tools, techniques and technologies that can facilitate healthcare organisations to embrace and develop appropriate lean strategies and thereby effect superior healthcare operations.

Chapter 1
Lean Principles for Healthcare

Nilmini Wickramasinghe

Abstract Lean thinking, which developed from lean manufacturing or the Toyota Production System, is centred around elimination of waste and preserving value. Lean became especially important, some may go so far to say a fad, in manufacturing in the 1990s. So why in the twenty-first century might the principles of lean be relevant to healthcare? In order to understand this, we need to recognise that healthcare delivery today is facing many pressures much like much of the manufacturing industries in the 1990s. The following serves to introduce key concepts that fall within taking a lean philosophy and explore how/why they might be relevant to healthcare.

Keywords Lean thinking • Kaizen • Total quality management • Six sigma

1.1 Introduction

Healthcare delivery today throughout the world is in a conundrum. Escalating costs, ageing populations, increase in chronic diseases and growth in medical technology solutions are some of the major challenges with which all healthcare systems must contend. Governments, policy makers and clinicians are all in agreement that healthcare reform is necessary and new strategies, protocols and procedures are required if healthcare delivery is to in fact provide appropriate access, quality and value to patients and the community at large. Most are turning to ICT (information communications technologies) as the silver bullet. However, this is only part of the

N. Wickramasinghe, Ph.D., M.B.A. (✉)
Epworth HealthCare & School of BITL & HIRi, RMIT University,
GPO Box 2476, Melbourne, VIC 3001, Australia
e-mail: nilmini.wickramasinghe@rmit.edu.au; nilmini.work@gmail.com

N. Wickramasinghe et al. (eds.), *Lean Thinking for Healthcare*, Healthcare Delivery in the Information Age, DOI 10.1007/978-1-4614-8036-5_1,

solution. The other part of the solution lies in the embracement of leading management principles and techniques which support and enable lean thinking and value creation and generation. The following serves to introduce the key concepts in lean thinking as relevant for healthcare.

1.2 TQM and Kaizen

Integral to lean manufacturing are the concepts of total quality management (TQM) and Kaizen. Both concepts focus on continuous improvements, the importance of process and performance to achieve positive outcomes and the key role of people. TQM is a philosophy (Deming 1986) while Kaizen is a technique. The later tends to focus on quality and customer satisfaction, while the latter takes a top-down approach and focuses on small incremental stages.

1.2.1 TQM

While there are many definitions of TQM, simply stated TQM is a continuous quality improvement approach (Nawar 2008). It has also been described as a total organisation approach (Oakland 1993), an effort to improve the whole organisation's competitiveness, effectiveness and structure (Dale 1999) and requires the mutual co-operation of management, employees, suppliers and customers (Dale 1999). Many scholars and proponents (Deming 1986; Juran 1993; Scholtes 1992) have noted that TQM and more especially a quality focus are important for long-term success.

TQM can be thought of as having a soft side and a hard side or the tools of TQM. Table 1.1 depicts the soft aspects of TQM while Table 1.2 summarises the key tools which make up the hard side.

1.2.2 Kaizen

In contrast to TQM Kaizen is a technique (Imai 1986, 1997). Kaizen means continuous improvement and assumes managers and employees work together to achieve this and such efforts do not require tremendous resources.

The key elements of Kaizen include:

1. Team work
2. Personal discipline
3. Improved morale
4. Quality circles
5. Suggestions for improvement
6. Elimination of wastes and inefficiency

Table 1.1 Soft aspects of TQM

Soft aspects of TQM	Description
Employees	TQM involves all employees at all levels of an organisation
Process	It is a continuous improvement philosophy. Continuous process improvement is a natural evaluation of TQM
Training	Continuous training of employee is necessary for the successful implementation of TQM in an organisation
Top management	Top-management commitment and support is an essential element of successful implementation of all the principles of TQM
Customers	TQM is a customer-focused management approach
Culture	Cultural change is necessary for the successful implementation of TQM in an organisation
Systems	TQM is a system approach through a process management. Processes must be improved to improve the results of an organisation
Decisions	TQM based on actual data is a factual approach to decision-making
Suppliers	TQM develops a mutually beneficial supplier relationship

7. The 5S framework (Saleem et al. 2012): (1) Seiri (sorting out), (2) Seiton (systematic arrangement), (3) Seiso (spic and span), Seiketsu (standardising) and Shitsuke (self-discipline)

These aspects are all captured in Fig. 1.1.

In addition to the elements of Kaizen, Kaizen techniques can be applied at three different levels:

1. Individual vs. team
2. Day to day vs. special events
3. Process level vs. subprocess level

Finally, there exist several tools that can be employed in order to ensure the Kaizen technique ensues. Table 1.3 provides a comprehensive list of these tools.

1.3 Six Sigma and Constraints Management

In addition to the philosophy of lean and the techniques of Kaizen, other complementary management methodologies and theories include six sigma and constraints management. The following briefly looks at each in turn.

1.3.1 Six Sigma

Six sigma has emerged as a primary vehicle for improving both manufacturing and service processes (Inozu et al. 2012). Specifically, "six sigma is a rigorous and

Table 1.2 Hard aspects of TQM (adapted from Saleem et al. 2012)

Name of tools	Description
7 Basic QC tools	These are basic tools used for data collection, data presentation and data analyses, for the improvement of quality of the products and processes. They include check sheets, Pareto diagram, histogram, control charts, cause and effect diagram, scatter diagram, and graphs (Ishikawa 1985)
Fishbone or Ishikawa diagram	This is a brainstorming method to guess different causes of problems related to each, man, machine, material and method, without using statistical methods
The matrix diagram	This tool is used to grade the relationship among different variables. It encourages them to think in terms of relationships, their strengths and patterns (Besterfield et al. 1999)
Tree diagram	According to Dale (1999), it is a tool which arranges targets, problems or customer's needs in a specific order
Critical path analysis (CPA)	CPA seeks to establish a sequential order of activities including time and their priority for the completion of a project, through the use of a network of arrows or nodes
Statistical process control	This tool is used to reduce both assignable and unassignable variation in the process, e.g., control charts. It helps the managers to control the production process
Pareto analysis	Pareto analysis helps the management teams to identify major 20 % causes which are giving 80 % variation in the production or service processes. Management team should concentrate on these 20 % causes first to improve the quality and performance of the system
ISO 9000 series	ISO series is an international standard written by a worldwide organisation known as the ISO/Technical Committee 176 (Lamprect 1992). This set of standards requirement ensures that a company has a specific quality improvement policy, which makes it more competitive in the market
Benchmarking	It involves selecting a demonstrated standard of product or process, costs or practices that represent the very best performance for processes or activities very similar to the company's own
Just in time (JIT)	It is one of the cost, time and inventory reduction techniques. It is designed to produce products or deliver services just as and when they are needed
Quality lost function (QLF)	It identifies all costs associated with poor quality and shows how these costs increase as the products/services move away from being exactly what the customer wants
Quality function deployment (QFD)	QFD is the process of determining customer's desires/requirements and translating those desires into the target product design. A graphic yet systematic technique for defining the relationship between customer desires and the developed product or service is known as House of Quality

systematic methodology that utilises information (management by facts) and statistical analysis to measure and improve a company's operational performance, practices and systems by identifying and preventing 'defects' in manufacturing and service-related processes in order to anticipate and exceed expectations of all

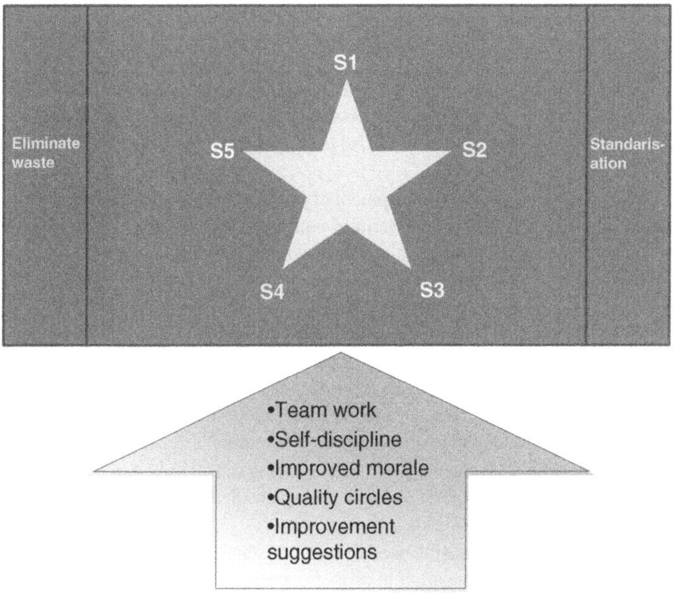

Fig. 1.1 Elements of Kaizen

stakeholders to accomplish effectiveness" (Inozu et al. 2012, p. 20). A five-step define-measure-analyse-improve-control (DMAIC) methodology is used where each step outlines distinct and key activities that must be performed as follows:

1. Define the business issue.
2. Measure the process.
3. Analyse the data and verify root causes of variation.
4. Improve the process.
5. Control the process and sustain improvements.

Six sigma has the power to save healthcare millions of dollars. Usually this is achieved by combining the key components of six sigma with one of the major principles of lean, namely, the seven deadly wastes. Table 1.4 outlines the deadly wastes and how they relate to healthcare.

1.3.2 Constraints Management

The last complementary methodology that will be presented in this chapter is that of constraints management. Constraints management is made up of a suite of techniques used in operations and supply chain management. The key being to enable a systematic approach to manage complex organisations by identifying and

Table 1.3 Kaizen tools and techniques

Name of tools	Description
Single-Minute Exchange of Die (SMED)	Technique which refers to significant reductions in set-up times. In this technique main emphasis is given on reduction in set-up time, like "changeover of die, clamping and unclamping of work piece/die on the machine"
Total productive maintenance (TPM)	TPM enhances equipment efficiency through establishment of a preventive maintenance system of equipment throughout its working life. It involves and empowers every employee, from shop floor worker to top management to initiate preventive and corrective maintenance activities
Kanban	Kanban is a specially designed box/container having a kanban card in it, which moves from workstation to store on requirement bases. This Kanban card is a green signal for store to forward material to workstation for processing. Toyota motor used Kanban system to reduce the work in process inventory
5 S practice	The 5S framework (1) Seiri (sorting out), (2) Seiton (systematic arrangement), (3) Seiso (spic and span), Seiketsu (standardising) and Shitsuke (self-discipline)
Poka-Yoke/Jidoka	It is mechanisms used to make mistake-proof an entire process; Poka-Yokes ensure that proper conditions exist before actually executing a process step. This prevents defects from occurring in the first place. Where this is not possible, Poka-Yokes detect and eliminate defects in the process. Stop the machine whenever problem occurred. This ensures the reliability of the process
Standardised work	A work in which the successive activities have been properly structured so that it can be done efficiently is called standardised work. The aim of standardised work is to bring the process under control by reducing variation. This in turn eradicates wastages and increases the productivity
Value stream mapping	A value stream mapping is a flow diagram of all the activities required to bring a product from raw materials to delivery to the customer. The objective is to identify and get rid of the waste in the process
Takt time	Takt time is time taken from the receipt of order from customer till the product is handed over to him or her. It should be minimised through reduction of waste in the processes
Standard operating procedure	Means standardise all operating procedures for comparison and further improvement purpose
Kaizen blitz/Kaizen event	Kaizen event or kaizen blitz is a focused small incremental improvement project completed by cross-functional team in a limited time frame (Doolean et al. 2008)
7 W (waste)	Seven Ws are 7 commonly accepted wastes out of the manufacturing operations. They include waste from overproduction, waste of waiting time, transportation waste, inventory waste, overprocessing waste, waste of motion and waste from production defects

Source: Singh and Singh (2009)

controlling key leverage points within the system. Some of the basic constraint types include:

1. Market
2. Resources

Table 1.4 The seven deadly wastes of lean

Wastes	Examples
Transport	1. Moving patients from room to room 2. Charts not centrally located 3. Poor layouts, lab located a long distance from the ED
Inventory	1. Overstocked medications on units/floors 2. Multiple locations for consumable goods 3. Multiple suppliers of surgical supplies 4. Any work in progress
Motion	1. Heavy items on top shelf, light items on bottom 2. Excessive bending, reaching, walking to complete a progress step
Waiting	1. Specimens waiting analysis 2. Patients waiting to make appointments 3. Patients waiting to be seen for an appointment 4. Time lag with physician's orders 5. Patients on hold for admission
Overproduction	1. Duplicate charting 2. Copies of reports sent automatically 3. Multiple forms with same information
Overprocessing	1. Clarifying orders 2. Increased size of patient records 3. Multiple blood specimen collections
Defects requiring rework or scrap	1. Label on the wrong tube 2. Over-/under-coding 3. Decrease in revenue based on insurance claims 4. Decree in patient satisfaction scores

3. Materials
4. Supplier/vendor
5. Financial
6. Knowledge/competence
7. Policy

For healthcare this involves looking at the five focussing steps. These steps are presented in Table 1.5.

1.4 Discussion and Conclusions

Healthcare delivery today is under pressure to deliver high-quality outcomes, contain costs as well as contend with other challenges such as increase in chronic diseases and the impact of technology advances on healthcare delivery. All are agreed that healthcare reform is necessary, and we are witnessing in all OECD

Table 1.5 Focusing steps of constraints management (adapted from Inozu et al. 2012)

Five focusing steps	Translation for healthcare
1. Identify the system's constraint(s)	Identify the constraint at the system level: what most impedes the delivery of care? • Resource: lack of nurses • Policy: payer-network participation • Artificial: nurses transporting patients • Market: lack of patients • Supplier: flu vaccine unavailability
2. Decide how to exploit the system constraint(s)	Determine how to get the most out of the constraint: • Decrease the time it takes to prepare patients • Shift portions of treatment to other resources with available capacity or where capacity could be added easily • Modify treatment procedures to reveal hidden capacity • Reduce the idle time of the constrained resource • Operating rooms and other similar nonhuman resources do not need to take lunch breaks and can be scheduled to remain in use during such times • A transporter does not abandon his or her post before a porter replacement arrives
3. Subordinate/synchronise everything else to the above decision	All elements of the system support the constraint via coordination and synchronisation so that the bottleneck is never starved (assuming that the system constraint is a resource): • Purchase drugs and supplies based on demand and consumption • Schedule patients based on doctors' capacity • Stagger lunch breaks so that the phones of the call centre are always answered
4. Elevate the system's constraint(s)	Having completed exploit and subordinate, if the revealed/exposed capacity is insufficient, then additional capacity may be added, usually at some expense: • Buy an additional MRI scanner • Hire more nurses • Increase hours of operation • Hire temporary workers for morning registration
5. Warning! If in the previous steps a constraint has been broken, go back to step 1 and do not allow inertia to become the system constraint!	Be alert to adapt to change in the operational, regulatory and competitive environments, as well as changes to patient population, because constraints can shift: • Healthcare reform • Accountable care organisation • Group purchasing organisations • If the system constraint changed, go back to step 1

countries a focus on healthcare reform with a key enabler being e-health. The preceding has introduced the principle of lean thinking and other complementary concepts all aimed at effecting more efficient and effective operations to ensue. These tools and techniques have proved their value in the manufacturing sector. It is the thesis of this book that they are as important for and can facilitate the attainment of superior healthcare delivery. It is therefore essential that practitioners and researchers alike try to embrace lean principle and related concepts as they set about designing and developing new healthcare initiatives.

References

Besterfield, H., Besterfield-Michna, C., Besterfield, H., & Betserfield-Sacre, M. (1999). *Total quality management* (2nd ed.). London: Prentice-Hall.

Dale, B. (1999). TQM: An overview. In B. Dale (Ed.), *Managing quality* (3rd ed., p. 296). Oxford: Blackwell.

Deming, E. (1986). *Out of the crisis*. Cambridge: Cambridge University Press.

Doolean, T., Van Aken, E., Farris, J., Worley, J., & Huwe, J. (2008). A field study of Kaizen events and organizational performance. *International Journal of Productivity and Performance Management, 57*(8), 637–658.

Imai, M. (1986). *Kaizen: The key to Japanese competitive Success*. New York: McGraw-Hill.

Imai, M. (1997). *Gemba Kaizen: A common sense, low cost approach to management*. New York: McGraw-Hill.

Inozu, B., Chauncey, D., Kamataris, V., & Mount, C. (2012). *Performance improvement for healthcare: Leading change with lean, six sigma, and constraints management*. Chicago: Novaces, LLC.

Ishikawa, K. (1985). *What is TQC? The Japanese way*. Englewood Cliffs: Prentice-Hall.

Juran, J. (1993). Made in USA: A renaissance in quality. *Harvard Business Review, 71*(4), 42–50.

Lamprect, L. (1992). *ISO 9000 preparing for registration*. New York: Marcel Dekker.

Nawar, K. (2008). *Total quality management*. Rawalpindi: NUST Publishing.

Oakland, J. (1993). *Total quality management: The route to improving performance*. London: Butterworth Heinemann.

Saleem, M., Khan, S., Hameed, S., & Abbas, M. (2012). An analysis of relationship between total quality management and kaizen. *Life Science Journal, 9*(3). Accessed August 2012, from http://www.lifesciencesite.com

Scholtes, R. (1992). *The team handbook*. Madison: Joinder Associates.

Singh, J., & Singh, H. (2009). *Kaizen philosophy a review of literature*. Working Paper, The Icfai University.

Chapter 2
Artificial Neural Network Excellence to Facilitate Lean Thinking Adoption in Healthcare Contexts

Fatemeh Hoda Moghimi and Nilmini Wickramasinghe

Abstract Over the years, healthcare organisations have improved their processes, services, and outcomes significantly. However, with the increasing importance placed on value making, healthcare organisations too often are struggling to demonstrate best performance and/or appropriate and sustained quality of care. Hence, in this chapter we explore the benefits of using artificial neural network (ANN) techniques to identify lost value for the healthcare organisations and to facilitate Lean thinking adoption.

Keywords Lean thinking • Artificial neural networks • Quality of care • Performance

2.1 Background

The key concept in Lean thinking is "value" (Joosten et al. 2009). Value has different connotations in each organisational context. However, Womack and Jones (2003) provide a comprehensive and general definition of value which is defined as "the capability to deliver exactly the (customised) product or service a customer wants with minimal time between the moment the customer asks for that product or service and the actual delivery at an appropriate price" (Womack and Jones 2003, p. 23).

F.H. Moghimi
School of Business IT and Logistics, RMIT University, Research Institute, Epworth HealthCare, GPO Box 2476, Melbourne, VIC 3001, Australia
e-mail: fatemeh.moghimi@rmit.edu.au

N. Wickramasinghe, Ph.D., M.B.A. (✉)
Epworth HealthCare & Department of BITL & HIRi,
RMIT University, GPO Box 2476, Melbourne, VIC 3001, Australia
e-mail: Nilmini.wickramasinghe@rmit.edu.au

N. Wickramasinghe et al. (eds.), *Lean Thinking for Healthcare*, Healthcare Delivery in the Information Age, DOI 10.1007/978-1-4614-8036-5_2,

Although quality and safety are significant values of healthcare delivery, there are lots of hidden layers across them which should be discovered and developed to improve efficiency of care.

On the other hand, widespread use of medical information systems and the explosive growth of medical databases require traditional manual data analysis to be coupled with methods for efficient computer-assisted analysis (Lavrač 1999).

Therefore, taking these two issues into consideration, artificial intelligence techniques and intelligent systems have found many valuable applications to assist in this regard (Teodorrescu et al. 1998). Specifically, neural networks have been found to be very useful in many biomedical areas, to help with the diagnosis of diseases and studying the pathological conditions, and also for monitoring the progress of various treatment outcomes. Also, Shi et al. (2004) state that artificial neural networks (ANNs) are powerful tools to model the non-linear cause-and-effect relationships inherent in complex processes, usually for quality control (Shi et al. 2004).

ANNs are computational paradigms based on mathematical models that unlike traditional computing have a structure and operation that resembles that of the mammal brain (Margarita 2002). An artificial network performs in two different modes, learning (or training) and testing. During learning, a set of examples is presented to the network. At the beginning of the training process, the network "guesses" the output for each example. However, as training goes on, the network modifies internally until it reaches a stable stage at which time the provided outputs are satisfactory. Learning is simply an adaptive process during which the weights associated to all the interconnected neurons change in order to provide the best possible response to all the observed stimuli. Neural networks can learn in two ways, supervised or unsupervised (Beg et al. 2006):

- Supervised learning: The network is trained using a set of input–output pairs. The goal is to "teach" the network to identify the given input with the desired output. For each example in the training set, the network receives an input and produces an actual output. After each trial, the network compares the actual with the desired output and corrects any difference by slightly adjusting all the weights in the network until the output produced is similar enough to the desired output, or the network cannot improve its performance any further (Margarita 2002).
- Unsupervised learning: The network is trained using input signals only. In response, the network organises internally to produce outputs that are consistent with a particular stimulus or group of similar stimuli. Inputs form clusters in the input space, where each cluster represents a set of elements of the real world with some common features (Margarita 2002).

In both cases, once the network has reached the desired performance, the learning stage is over and the associated weights are frozen. The final state of the network is preserved and it can be used to classify new, previously unseen inputs. At the testing stage, the network receives an input signal and processes it to produce an output. If the network has correctly learnt, it should be able to generalise, and the actual output produced by the network should be almost as good as the ones produced in the learning stage for similar inputs.

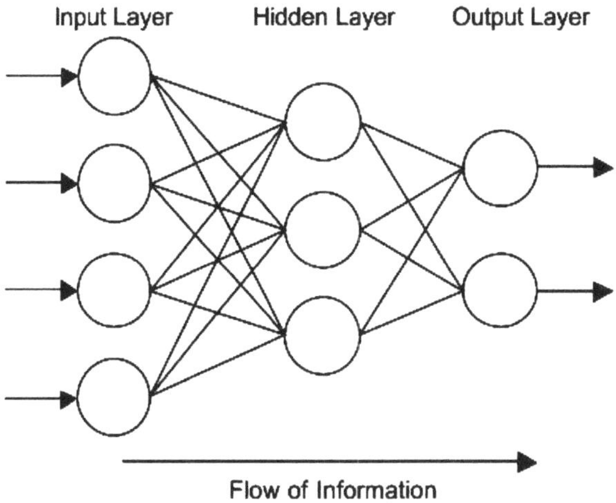

Fig. 2.1 A multilayered feedforward network. Adapted from (Margarita 2002)

Neural networks are typically arranged in layers. Each layer in a layered network is an array of processing elements or neurons. A common example of such a network is the multilayer perceptron (MLP) (Fig. 2.1). MLP networks normally have three layers of processing elements with only one hidden layer, but there is no restriction on the number of hidden layers (Margarita 2002).

2.2 Neural Networks in Healthcare Contexts

Neural networks have been applied within the medical domain for clinical diagnosis (Baxt 1995), image analysis and interpretation (Miller et al. 1992; Miller, 1993), signal analysis and interpretation, and drug development (Weinstein et al. 1992a, b). The classification of the applications is presented below (Table 2.1).

2.3 The Case Study Analysis

This recent case presents an example of how ANNs can be applied in healthcare contexts. This case is presented from the research study conducted by Takehira et al. (2011). The aim of this study was to investigate the difference between the professional perspectives of pharmacists and nurses in Japan with regard to evaluation of the quality of life (QOL) of cancer patients. It is therefore a suitable case from which to develop an initial assessment of key concepts of ANNs and map them in order to present how ANNs can facilitate applying a Lean thinking approach to increase quality of care. Thus, the assessment criteria are set up based on Lean thinking key components.

Table 2.1 Some of ANN applications in healthcare contexts

Clinical issue	ANN application
Clinical diagnosis	Papnet (Beg et al. 2006) is a commercial neural network-based computer programme for assisted screening of Pap (cervical) smears. A Pap smear test examines cells taken from the uterine cervix for signs of precancerous and cancerous changes. A properly taken and analysed Pap smear can detect very early precancerous changes. These precancerous cells can then be eliminated, usually in a relatively simple office or outpatient procedure. Detected early, cervical cancer has an almost 100 % chance of cure. Traditionally, Pap smear testing relies on the human eye to look for abnormal cells under a microscope. It is the only large-scale laboratory test that is not automated. Since a patient with a serious abnormality can have fewer than a dozen abnormal cells among the 30,000–50,000 normal cells on her Pap smear, it is very difficult to detect all cases of early cancer by this "needle-in-a-haystack" search. Imagine proofreading 80 books a day, each containing over 300,000 words, to look for a few books each with a dozen spelling errors! Relying on manual inspection alone makes it inevitable that some abnormal Pap smears will be missed, no matter how careful the laboratory is
	In fact, even the best laboratories can miss from 10 to 30 % abnormal cases "Papnet-assisted reviews of [cervical] smears result in a more accurate screening process than the current practice leading to an earlier and more effective detection of pre-cancerous and cancerous cells in the cervix"
	The electrocardiography (ECG) signal is a representation of the bioelectrical activity of the heart's pumping action. This signal is recorded via electrodes placed on the patient's chest. The physician routinely uses ECG time-history plots and the associated characteristic features of P, QRS, and T waveforms to study and diagnose the heart's overall function. Deviations in these waveforms have been linked to many forms of heart diseases, and neural network has played a significant role in helping the ECG diagnosis process. For example, neural networks have been used to detect signs of acute myocardial infarction (AMI), cardiac arrhythmias, and other forms of cardiac abnormalities (Baxt 1991; Nazeran and Behbehani 2001). Neural networks have performed exceptionally well when applied to differentiate patients with and without a particular abnormality, for example, in the diagnosis of patients with AMI (97.2 % sensitivity and 96.2 % specificity; Baxt 1991)
	Electromyography (EMG) is the electrical activity of the contracting muscles. EMG signals can be used to monitor the activity of the muscles during a task or movement and can potentially lead to the diagnosis of muscular disorders. Both amplitude and timing of the EMG data are used to investigate muscle function. Neural networks have been shown to help in the modelling between mechanical muscle force generation and the corresponding recorded EMG signals (Wang and Buchanan 2002). Neuromuscular diseases can affect the activity of the muscles (e.g. motor neuron disease), and neural networks have been proven useful in identifying individuals with neuromuscular diseases from features extracted from the motor unit action potentials of their muscles (Pattichis et al. 1995)
	The EEG signal represents electrical activity of the neurons of the brain and is recorded using electrodes placed on the human scalp. The EEG signals and their characteristic plots are often used as a guide to diagnose neurological disorders, such as epilepsy, dementia, stroke, and brain injury or damage. The presence of these neurological disorders is reflected in the EEG waveforms. Like many other pattern recognition techniques, neural networks have been used to detect changes in the EEG waveforms as a result of various neurological and other forms of abnormalities that can affect the neuronal activity of the brain. A well-known application of neural networks in EEG signal analysis is the detection of epileptic seizures, which often result in a sudden and transient disturbance of the body movement due to excessive discharge of the brain cells. This seizure event results in spikes in the EEG waveforms, and neural networks and other artificial intelligence tools, such as fuzzy logic and support vector machines, have been employed for automated detection of these spikes in the EEG waveform. Neural networks-aided EEG analysis has also been undertaken for the diagnosis of much other related pathology, including Huntington's and Alzheimer's diseases (Jervis et al. 1992; Yagneswaran et al. 2002)

	Another important emerging application of neural networks is in the area of brain computer interface (BCI), in which neural networks use EEG activity to extract embedded features linked to mental status or cognitive tasks to interact with the external environment (Culpepper and Keller 2003)
	An Entropy Maximization Network (EMN) has been applied to prediction of metastases in breast cancer patients (Choong and deSilva 1994). They used EMN to construct discrete models that predict the occurrence of axillary lymph node metastases in breast cancer patients, based on characteristics of the primary tumour alone. The clinical and physiological features used in the analysis are the age of the patient at the time of diagnosis of the primary tumour, mitotic count (the number of relative hyperchromatic nuclei per 10 hpf) in the primary invasive tumour, tubule formation of the primary tumour, assessment of the size of the tumour nuclei, assessment of the variability of the shape and size of the tumour nuclei, tumour grading, gross size of the primary tumour, and the presence/absence of carcinoma in peritumoural vessel. Results indicated that EMN is an effective way of constructing discrete models from small data sets
	Serum electrophoresis is used as standard laboratory medical test for diagnosis of several pathological conditions such as liver cirrhosis or nephrotic syndrome. A multilayer perceptron trained using the backpropagation learning algorithm and a radial-based function network were used to implement an effective diagnostic aid system. Preliminary results confirm the suitability of such neural network architectures as aids for medical diagnosis (Costa et al. 1998)
Image analysis and interpretation	Aizenberg et al. (2001) present examples of filtering, segmentation, and edge detection techniques using cellular neural networks to improve resolution in brain tomographies and improve global frequency correction for the detection of microcalcifications in mammograms
	Miller et al. 1992 trained different neural networks (NNs) to recognise regions of interest (ROIs) corresponding to specific organs within electrical impedance tomography images (EIT) of the thorax. The network allows automatic selection of optimal pixels based on the number of images, over a sample period, in which each pixel is classified as belonging to a particular organ. Initial results using simulated EIT data indicate the possible use of neural networks for characterisation of such images
	Hall et al. (1992) compared neural networks (cascade correlation) and fuzzy clustering techniques for segmentation of magnetic resonance imaging (MRI) of the brain. Both approaches were applied to intelligent diagnosis. Results, validated by experienced radiologists, provided good insights as to the suitability of the applied techniques for automatic image segmentation in the context of intelligent medical diagnosis
	Rajapakse and Acharya (1990) implemented a self-organising network multilayer adaptive resonance architecture (MARA) for the segmentation of CT images of the heart. Similarly, Däschlein et al. (1994) implemented a two-layer neural network for segmentation of CT images of the abdomen. The method required the discrimination of various tissues like kidney, liver, and bone and pathologic tissue like renal calculus and kidney tumour
	An ANN was successfully applied to enhance low-level segmentation of eye images for diagnosis of Grave's ophthalmopathy (Ossen et al. 1994). The neural network segmentation system was integrated into an existing medical imaging system. The system provides a user interface to allow interactive selection of images, neural network architectures, training algorithms, and data

(continued)

Table 2.1 (continued)

Clinical issue	ANN application
	In another study, Özkan et al. (1990) used neural networks trained with the backpropagation learning algorithm for segmentation and classification multispectral MRI images of normal and pathological human brain. Results indicate that sharp and compact segmentation of MRI images can be obtained with neural networks with a small architecture. Anthony et al. (1990) evaluated the performance of neural networks (NNs) in image compression of lung scintigrams. They discussed the suitability of NNs and presented limitations and recommendations with special reference to medical imaging
	A multi-module system was used to focus, segment, and classify lung-parenchyma lesions in standard chest radiographies. A Laplacian-of-Gaussian kernel filter is applied to the X-ray images to remove low-frequency components, while preserving detail contrast. An input mask of 19×19 units serves as input to the classification module, which consists of a feedforward network. The output of the network identifies ROIs in the image, which later are analysed by other modules in the system (DeDominicis 1994)
	Houston et al. (1994) compared an expert system rule induction and a neural network to determine the optimal diagnostic strategy for colorectal cancer using MRI and tumour markers. Data from 39 patients was used to assess the suitability of such methodologies. Inconclusive results indicated that both methods strongly rely on large number of samples
	ANNs have been used for automatic screening of blood cell classification from microscope images
	82 objects extracted from 133 digitised images were isolated using classical image enhancement algorithms. A single-layer perceptron was trained with the backpropagation learning algorithm. The output produced a binary output, indicating whether the input corresponded to a normal or a pathologic cell network correctly classified 65 out of 82 objects (Karakas et al. 1994)
	Xing and Feltham (1994) and Zheng et al. (1994) are two of multiple examples of neural networks applied to pattern recognition in mammograms. Xing and Feltham used 14 image features extracted from mammograms by experienced radiologists. A pyramidal neural network detects malignant tumours or clustered calcifications in preprocessed mammograms. Results indicate that abnormal patterns observed in mammograms can be mapped into a unique data set. Similarly, Zheng et al. used a multistage neural network (MNN) for locating and classification of microcalcifications in digital mammograms. The network is trained using backpropagation with Kalman filtering. Experimental results show 100 % detection with a false positive detection rate of less than 1 micro calcification cluster per image

Signal analysis and interpretation	Sordo (1999) implemented a knowledge-based neural network (KBANN) for classification of phosphorus (31P) magnetic resonance spectra (MRS) from normal and cancerous breast tissues. Data from 26 cases was used as input to the network. A priori knowledge of metabolic features of normal and cancerous breast tissues was incorporated into the structure of the neural network to overcome the scarcity of available data. Classification rates of 62.4 % for "knowledge-free" neural networks and 87.36 % for KBANNs showed how KBANNs outperformed conventional neural networks in the classification of 31P MRS. This indicates that the combination of symbolic and connectionist techniques is more robust than a connectionist technique alone
	Waltrus et al. (1993) reported results from the application of tools for synthesising, optimising, and analysing neural networks to an Electrocardiogram (ECG) Patient Monitoring task. A neural network was synthesised from a rule-based classifier and optimised over a set of normal and abnormal heartbeats. The classification error rate on a separate and larger test set was reduced by a factor of 2. Sensitivity analysis of the synthesised and optimised networks revealed informative differences. Analysis of the weights and unit activations of the optimised network enabled a reduction in size of the network by a factor of 40 % without loss of accuracy

Project Title: Artificial Neural Network Modelling of Quality of Life of Cancer Patients, Relationships Between Quality of Life Assessments, as Evaluated by Patients, Pharmacists, and Nurses (Takehira et al. 2011)[1]

Methods: A group of cancer hospital inpatients ($n=15$) were asked to rate the condition of their health and their QOL by filling in a questionnaire. On the same day, a group of pharmacists ($n=8$) and nurses ($n=18$) also evaluated patient QOL. Three-layered ANN architecture was used to model the relationship between the different QOL evaluations made by patients, pharmacists, and nurses.

Results: Although there was no statistical difference between the QOL scores obtained from pharmacists and nurses, the correlation between these scores was weak (0.1188). These results suggest that pharmacists and nurses evaluate the QOL of their patients from different perspectives, based on their respective profession. QOL parameters were modelled with an ANN using the scores, given by patients in answer to questions regarding health-related QOL as input variables. Both the predictive performance of the ANN and the robustness of the optimised model were acceptable. The response surfaces calculated by ANN modelling showed that pharmacists and nurses evaluate patient's QOL using different information and reasoning, which is likely related to the nature of their contact with the patients.

Project Design and Outcomes

Patients: A group of cancer patients ($n=18$) hospitalised in Nippon Medical University Hospital (Sendagi, Tokyo, Japan) were initially included in this study. All patients took opioid analgesics for pain control, and a pain control team, organised by physicians, pharmacists, and nurses, provided appropriate inhospital care. Patients were excluded if they began chemotherapy during the study period or if they did not complete the questionnaire, owing to the severity of their illness. Thus, 15 patients (eight females and seven males, age 64.7 ± 7.2 years, mean$\pm$SD) were enrolled in the study and gave written consent to answer the study questions. A questionnaire was designed to assess the HRQOL of patients referring SF36, Functional Living Index Cancer (FLIC), and Functional Assessment of Cancer Therapy, General (FACT-G); it consisted of four important domains, EWB, FWB, SWB, and PWB. The number of questions included was limited to 18 in order to avoid unnecessary burden on the patients, in accordance with the suggestion of a local research committee. Patient health-related status and subjective QOL were collected by pharmacists in the form of a bedside interview and data collection was conducted four times every week, using a questionnaire. Time required to fill the questionnaire by interviewing was about 5–10 min.

[1]This case study & its results is extracted exactly from (Takehira et al. 2011) research study to present how exactly Artificial Neural Network can be apply in healthcare contexts.

(continued)

(continued)

Pharmacists and nurses: Pharmacists (n=8) and nurses (n=18) providing patient care in a pain control team were involved in this study. Details regarding the amount of professional experience are possessed by the participating pharmacists and nurses. Pharmacists evaluated patient QOL when interviewing patients using the questionnaire. Nurses evaluated patient QOL on the same day as the patient answered the questionnaire. Patient QOL was evaluated on a simple scale ranging from 1 (very bad) to 5 (very good), rather than in a structured manner. The intended number of the answers in the research was 60 (each of 15 patients would answer 4 times). However, some patients, pharmacists, and nurses did not complete the questionnaires, so a number of paired (patient, pharmacist, and nurse) forms (n=40) were used in the analysis. Table 2.2 shows the items of the questionnaires which were selected to be used for the SEM and mean values of their score, as well as the mean QOL scores given by patients, pharmacists, and nurses. The study design and questionnaires were reviewed by a local research committee. The background of the patients and details of the questionnaires they were given are described in our previous study.

ANN

A three-layered ANN architecture was used and optimisation of the weights between neurons to match the evaluated QOLs with those that were predicted was carried out using a second-order, conjugate, gradient descent algorithm. In this algorithm, a search is performed along conjugated directions, which generally produce faster convergence compared with a backpropagation of the error algorithm. Scores obtained from patients are shown in Table 2.2 and were used for input data (independent parameters). These eight questions were from the initial 18 questions and sufficed to perform exploratory factor analysis. The subjective patient QOL scores and QOL evaluations made by pharmacists and nurses were used for output data (dependent parameters). The determination of the number of neurons in the hidden layer will be described subsequently. The optimised ANN model had initial value dependence, so at least ten runs were performed using reinitialised weights between neurons, after which the model with the best fit between observations and predictions from the training data was adopted as the optimised ANN model.

Statistica 06J, featuring a neural networks module, was used for ANN calculation. A sigmoid function was adopted for activation function of the hidden layer. Robustness of optimised ANN was investigated with leave-one-out cross-validation. The procedure is as follows: The data obtained from one patient was removed from the data set and the data from the remaining patient were used as the training data set. The ANN was optimised using the training data set, and then the outcome of the excluded patient was predicted by the optimised ANN model.

(continued)

Table 2.2 Prediction performance of QOL by ANN modelling

	QOL evaluated by patients		QOL by evaluated pharmacists		QOL evaluated by nurses	
QOL score	Answered	Predicted[1)]	Answered	Predicted[1)]	Answered	Predicted[a]
5	0	0	1	1	2	1
4	5	5	15	15	11	11
3	13	13	9	9	20	19
2	19	19	15	15	4	4
1	3	3	0	0	3	3
Performance[b]	100.0		100.0		95.0	

[a]Number of correct scores predicted
[b]Performance is the rate of correct scores predicted (%)

Table 2.3 Robustness of optimised ANN evaluated by leave-one-out cross-validation

	QOL evaluated by patients		QOL evaluated by pharmacists		QOL evaluated by nurses	
	Answered	Predicted[1)]	Answered	Predicted[1)]	Answered	Predicted[a]
5	0	0	1	0	2	0
4	5	4	15	8	11	8
3	13	8	9	3	20	12
2	19	13	15	13	4	1
1	3	1	0	0	3	1
Performance[b]	65.0		60.0		55.0	

[a]Number of correct scores predicted
[b]Performance is the rate of correct scores predicted (%)

Results

QOL was evaluated by patients, pharmacists, and nurses. As shown in Table 2.2, the subjective QOL scores given by patients were significantly lower than those given by both pharmacists and nurses, and the latter did not show statistical difference ($p=0.7649$ by Wilcoxon signed-rank test). At least to compare among QOL scores given by patients, pharmacists, and nurses, pharmacists and nurses may have a tendency to underestimate the condition of the patients. Table 2.3 shows the Spearman's correlation coefficient between the QOL scores given by patients, pharmacists, and nurses. The correlation between patient and pharmacist scores was moderate ($r=0.4481$), and the correlation between the scores of patients and nurses was very weak to negligible($r=0.1187$). The correlation between those QOL scores given by pharmacists and those given by nurses was also very weak to negligible ($r=0.1188$). It has been suggested that doctors would underestimate the number of symptoms experienced by cancer patients. However, Sneeuw et al.

(continued)

(continued)

reported that healthcare providers tend to assess patients as having more symptoms than did the patients themselves. Some other studies have reported that healthcare providers are likely to underestimate the physical symptoms of patients. Their results show that pharmacists and nurses seem to have the same tendency as doctors to underestimate the condition of health of patients. Furthermore, although there were no statistically differences in QOL as evaluated by pharmacists and nurses ($p=0.7649$), the correlation between them was very weak to negligible ($r=0.1188$). These results suggest that pharmacists and nurses evaluate the QOL of their patients from different perspectives, based on their respective profession.

ANN model for QOL of patients. They had previously reported that the QOL of cancer patients was modelled well with a score of eight answers (Table 2.2) in the questionnaire, using SEM. As described, pharmacists and nurses evaluate the QOL of their patients from different professional perspectives. We used an ANN to investigate the difference in perspectives between pharmacists and nurses with regard to evaluation of QOL using. As ANN architecture, we used a three-layer perceptron, an input layer comprises eight processing elements (the scores obtained from the answers to the questions), a hidden layer comprises processing elements with a sigmoid function as an activation function, and an output layer comprises the QOL scores obtained from patients, pharmacists, and nurses. The network diagram that was used in the present investigation is shown in Fig. 2.1. The neurons in the hidden and output layers work to calculate the sum of products of values of previous layers and the weight between connections. The neurons then transfer a value to neurons in the next layer according to an activation function. All weights among neurons were optimised to minimise differences between observed and modelled QOLs.

Figure 2.1 shows the effect on prediction performance of QOL of the number of neurons in the hidden layer, using the ANN model. The best fit was obtained when more than 11 neurons were arranged in the hidden layer. In order to avoid "over-fitting" a smaller number of neurons are preferable, so a three-layered architecture with 11 neurons in the hidden layer was used for modelling in this study.

Table 2.2 shows the prediction performance of QOL as evaluated by patients, pharmacists, and nurses using the ANN model. In the final model, subjective QOL, as assessed by patients, and the QOL scores given by pharmacists were all successfully predicted, and only a few of the data obtained from nurses were not predicted by the ANN model that was established. These results suggest that the necessary information to predict how pharmacists would evaluate QOL is contained in the input data.

(continued)

(continued)

The robustness of the ANN model was evaluated with the leave-one-out cross-validation. Table 2.3 shows the prediction performance of QOL with leave-one-out cross-validation. The rate of correct prediction was approximately 60 % for the QOL scores obtained from patients, pharmacists, and nurses, which seems to indicate that the use of the ANN model to predict QOL is not robust. However, only 2/40 patients, 5/40 pharmacists, and 6/40 nurses had differences between evaluated and predicted QOL that were greater than 1 (results not shown). These results indicate that approximately 90 % of QOL data (from 107/120 individuals) could only be roughly, rather than precisely, predicted by the ANN model. QOL is a broad concept, including not only the condition of physical health, but also mental health, education, and social belonging. The patients evaluated their QOL subjectively, based not only on the condition of their own health, but also on their concept of values. We argue that pharmacists and nurses scored patients QOL primarily based on the condition of health of each patient, as assessed from their professional perspective. Therefore, it would be very difficult to make a precise prediction of patient QOL score using data from health professionals. Furthermore, each respective patient was not evaluated by a particular pharmacist and nurse every time. This may have lead to individual differences in the evaluation of QOL. If these were considered, a roughly predictive performance of approximately 90 % by ANN would be acceptable.

The QOL of cancer patients was evaluated by the patients themselves and by pharmacists and nurses on the same day. When QOL was self-evaluated by the patients, the scores were different from the QOL scores obtained from pharmacists and nurses. The correlation between QOL scores given by patients and those given by pharmacists and nurses was low. Although the QOL scores given by pharmacists and nurses were not different statistically, the correlation coefficient between them was weak to negligible ($r=0.1188$). These results suggest that pharmacists and nurses evaluate the QOL of their patients from different perspectives, based on their respective profession. The QOL scores were modelled using the scores regarding the HRQOL of patients as input variables using an ANN with three-layer architecture. The predictive performance given by ANN and the robustness of the model were acceptable. Health professionals affect QOL scores as a result of the difference of the profession-based perspectives they hold.

2.4 Discussion and Conclusions

Due to the complexity of processes and the importance of quality improvement in the healthcare contexts, ANN techniques can play a significant role to discover hidden knowledge and values through huge data sets. Indeed Lean thinking key concepts and models can facilitate value making in the healthcare contexts; however, ANN techniques can also be beneficial to facilitate value discovery. Therefore, taking this into consideration, we propose that ANN techniques should be incorporated to facilitate Lean thinking adoption especially for critical areas within the healthcare domain.

For example, the optimised ANN model in the case study above showed the "information flow" in the case of cancer patients by presenting the difference in perspectives between the pharmacists and nurses in their evaluations of QOL. "Flow" is a key concept in a Lean System (Black and Miller 2008) and "information flow" is one of the seven essential improvement targets to the healthy operation of a healthcare using Lean approach (Black and Miller 2008). Therefore, the presented case study could clearly demonstrate how the ANNs can facilitate Lean thinking adoption in healthcare contexts.

In conclusion, the power of ANNs is considerable in care performance improvement as well as Lean action plans. It is left to further studies to examine or even start to prototype the other numerous benefits of ANNs, and thereby provide a more in-depth analysis that will in turn serve to facilitate Lean thinking adoption in healthcare contexts.

References

Aizenberg, I., Aizenberga, N., Hiltnerb, J., et al. (2001). Cellular neural networks and computational intelligence in medical image processing. *Image and Vision Computing, 19*(4), 177–183.

Anthony, D., Hines, E., Barham, J., & Taylor, D. (1990). A comparison of image compression by neural networks and principal component analysis. *International Joint Conference on Neural Networks* (Vol. 1, pp. 339–344). San Diego, CA, USA: IEEE

Baxt, W. G. (1991). Use of an artificial neural network for the diagnosis of myocardial infarction. *Annals of Internal Medicine, 115*, 843–848.

Baxt, W. G. (1995). Application of artificial neural networks to clinical medicine. *Lancet, 346*, 1135–1138.

Beg, R., Kamruzzaman, J., & Sarker, R. (2006). *Neural networks in healthcare: Potential and challenges* (pp. 16–20). Hershey, PA: Idea Group Publishing.

Black, J., & Miller, D. (2008). *The Toyota way to healthcare excellence, American College of Healthcare Executives Management Series* (p. 106).

Choong, P. L., & deSilva, C. J. S. (1994). Breast cancer prognosis using EMN architecture. *Proceedings of IEEE International Conference on Neural Networks*. Orlando, FL, USA: IEEE.

Costa, A., Cabestany, J., Moreno, J., & Calvet, M. (1998). Neuroserum: An artificial neural NetBased diagnostic aid tool for serum electrophoresis. *Third International Conference on Neural Networks and Expert Systems in Medicine and Healthcare* (pp. 34–43). World Scientific.

Culpepper, B. J., & Keller, R. M. (2003). Enabling computer decisions based on EEG input. *IEEE Transactions on Neural Systems and Rehabilitation Engineering, 11*(4), 354–360.

Däschlein, R., Waschulzik, T., Brauer, W., et al. (1994). Segmentation of computertomographies with neural networks based on local features. In E. Ifeachor & K. Rosen (Eds.), *Proceedings of the International Conference on Neural Networks and Expert Systems in Medicine and Healthcare: Moat House Hotel, Plymouth, UK.*, August 23–26, (pp. 240–247). University Medical Centre.

De Dominicis, R., Bocchi, L., Coppini, G., & Valli, G. (1994). Computer Aided Analysis of LungParenchyma Lesions in Standard Chest Radiography. In Ifeachor, E., & Rosen, K. (Eds.), International Conference on Neural Networks and Expert Systems in Medicine and Healthcare, pp. 174–180.

Hall, L., Bensaid, A., Clarke, L., Velthuizen, R., Silbiger, M., & Bezdek, J. (1992). A comparison of neural network and fuzzy clustering techniques in segmenting magnetic resonance images of the brain. *IEEE Transactions on Neural Networks, 3*(5), 672–682.

Houston, A., Kemp, P., Macleod, M., Norsworthy, J., et al. (1994). Analysis of a nuclear medicine database for colorectal cancer using expert system rule induction and neural networks. In E. Ifeachor & K. Rosen (Eds.), *Proceedings of the International Conference on Neural Networks and Expert Systems in Medicine and Healthcare: Moat House Hotel, Plymouth, UK.*, August 23–26, (pp. 303–309). University Medical Centre.

Jervis, B. W., Saatchi, M. R., Lacey, A., Papadourakis, G. M., Vourkas, M., Roberts, T., et al. (1992). The application of unsupervised artificial neural networks to the sub-classification of subjects at-risk of Huntington's Disease. *IEEE Colloquium on Intelligent Decision Support Systems and Medicine* (Vol. 5, pp. 1–9). London: IEEE.

Joosten, T., Bongers, I., & Janssen, R. (2009). Application of Lean thinking to health care: Issues and observations. *International Journal for Quality in Health Care, 21*(5), 341–347.

Karakas, M., Duru, H., Tipi, V., et al. (1994). A system for an automated classification of blood cells from microscope images, CELL v. 1.0. In E. Ifeachor & K. Rosen (Eds.), *Proceedings of the International Conference on Neural Networks and Expert Systems in Medicine and Healthcare: Moat House Hotel, Plymouth, UK.*, August 23-26, (pp. 248–256). University Medical Centre.

Lavrač, N. (1999). Selected techniques for data mining in medicine. *Journal of Artificial Intelligence in Medicine, 16*(1), 3–23.

Margarita, S. (2002). *Introduction to neural networks in healthcare, knowledge management for medical care, for open clinical* (pp. 12–15). Harvard University.

Miller, A. (1993). *The application of neural networks to imaging and signal processing in astronomy and medicine*. Ph.D. thesis, Faculty of Science, Department of Physics, University of Southampton.

Miller, A., Blott, B., & Hames, T. (1992). Review of neural network applications in medical imaging and signal processing. *Medical and Biological Engineering and Computing, 30*(5), 449–464.

Nazeran, H., & Behbehani, K. (2001). Neural networks in processing and analysis of biomedical signals. In M. Akay (Ed.), *Nonlinear biomedical signal processing: Fuzzy logic, neural networks and new algorithms* (pp. 69–97). IEEE Press. Published in Wiley Online Library.

Ossen, A., Zamzow, T., Oswald, H., & Fleck, E. (1994). Segmentation of medical images using NeuralNetwork classifiers. In E. Ifeachor & K. Rosen (Eds.), *Proceedings of the International Conference on Neural Networks and Expert Systems in Medicine and Healthcare: Moat House Hotel, Plymouth, UK., August 23–26,* (pp. 427–432). University Medical Centre.

Özkan, M., Sprenkels, H., & Dawant, B. (1990). MultiSpectral magnetic resonance image segmentation using neural networks. *IJCNN-90-Wash DC: International Joint Conference on Neural Networks,* January 15–19, Omni Shoreham Hotel, Washington, (Vol. 2, pp. 429–434). Erlbaum.

Pattichis, C. S., Schizas, C. N., & Middleton, L. T. (1995). Neural network models in EMG diagnosis. *IEEE Transactions on Biomedical Engineering, 42*(5), 486–496.

Rajapakse, J., & Acharya, R. (1990). Medical image segmentation with MARA. *International Joint Conference on Neural Networks* (Vol. 2, pp. 965–972).

Shi, X., Schillings, P., & Boyd, D. (2004). Applying artificial neural networks and virtual experimental design to quality improvement of two industrial processes. *International Journal of Production Research, 42*(1), 101–118.

Sordo, M. (1999). *Neural networks for detection of Down's syndrome*. Master's thesis, Department of Artificial Intelligence, University of Edinburgh.

Takehira, R., Murakami, K., Katayama, S., Nishizawa, K., & Yamamura, S. (2011). Artificial neural network modeling of quality of life of cancer patients, relationships between quality of life assessments, as evaluated by patients, pharmacists, and nurses. *International Journal of Biomedical Science, 7*(4), 255–262.

Teodorrescu, T., Kandel, A., & Jain, L. C. (1998). *Fuzzy and neuro-fuzzy systems in medicine*. Boca Raton, FL: CRC Press.

Watrous, R., Towell, G., Glassman, M., Shahraray, M., & Theivanayagam, D. (1993). Synthesize, optimize, analyze, repeat (SOAR): Application of neural network tools to ECG patient monitoring. In Proceedings of the Symposium on Nonlinear Theory and its Applications (p. 565).

Wang, L., & Buchanan, T. S. (2002). Prediction of joint moments using a neural network model of muscle activation from EMG signals. *IEEE Transactions on Neural Systems and Rehabilitation Engineering, 10*, 30–37.

Weinstein, J., Kohn, K., Grever, M., et al. (1992a). Neural computing in cancer drug development, predicting mechanism of action. *Science, 258*, 447–451.

Weinstein, J. N., Kohn, K. W., et al. (1992b). Neural computing in cancer drug development, predicting mechanisms of action. *Science, 258*, 447–451.

Womack, J., & Jones, D. (2003). *Lean thinking* (pp. 23–35). New York, NY: Simon & Schuster.

Xing, G., & Feltham, R. (1994). Pyramidal neural networking for mammogram tumour pattern recognition. *IEEE International Conference on Neural Networks* (Vol. VI, pp. 3546–3551). IEEE.

Yagneswaran, S., Baker, M., & Petrosian, A. (2002). Power frequency and wavelet characteristics in differentiating between normal and Alzheimer EEG. *Proceedings of the Second Joint 24th Annual Conference and the Annual Fall Meeting of the Biomedical Engineering Society (EMBS/ BMES)* IEEE. (Vol. 1, pp. 46–47).

Zheng, B., Qian, W., & Clarke, L. P. (1994). Multistage neural network for pattern recognition in mammogram screening. *IEEE International Conference on Neural Networks* IEEE. (Vol. VI, pp. 3537–3441).

Chapter 3
The Suitability of Artificial Neural Networks in Service Quality Control and Forecasting

Mohammad Rezazadeh Niavarani and Nilmini Wickramasinghe

Abstract There has been considerable research into service quality over the last couple of decades. Services, however, as intangible, perishable, and heterogenic transactions are very difficult to quantify and measure, and little success has been reported on a systematic approach in modeling of quality of service transactions (with SERVQUAL and its derivatives as the notable exception). In this chapter, we propose artificial neural networks (ANNs) to monitor quality of service transaction as a dynamic and real-time control and forecasting system. ANNs are widely used in many engineering fields to model and simulate complex systems. The resulting near-perfect models are particularly suited for applications where real-world complexities make it difficult or even impossible to mathematically model and control the system. The proposed approach alleviates restrictions and limitations of applying questionnaire-based static methods, even in cases where there are large number of correlated attributes as well as obscure and unobservable quality characteristics. We illustrate with a case vignette in a healthcare context, thereby demonstrating the suitability of such techniques for healthcare delivery a vital, at times lifesaving service.

Keywords Service • Service systems • Service science • Service quality • Service quality forecasting • Artificial neural network (ANN) • Healthcare delivery

M. Rezazadeh Niavarani (✉)
School of Business IT and Logistics, RMIT University,
GPO Box 2476, Melbourne, VIC 3001, Australia
e-mail: arash.r.n@gmail.com

N. Wickramasinghe, Ph.D., M.B.A.
Epworth HealthCare & Department of BITL & HIRi, RMIT University,
GPO Box 2476, Melbourne, VIC 3001, Australia
e-mail: Nilmini.wickramasinghe@rmit.edu.au; nilmini.work@gmail.com

N. Wickramasinghe et al. (eds.), *Lean Thinking for Healthcare*, Healthcare Delivery in the Information Age, DOI 10.1007/978-1-4614-8036-5_3,

3.1 Introduction

The service sector in developed countries such as the United States and Australia currently accounts for some 80 % of all economic activity (DFAT 2008; Spohrer et al. 2007). The service economy encompasses not only private enterprise but also the diverse services provided by government, such as education and health care. Service systems can be described as dynamic configurations of resources (people, technologies, organizations, and shared information) that can create and deliver value to customers, providers, and other stakeholders (IfM and IBM 2008, p. 18).

Despite the sheer size of economic activities that are classified as services, service quality remains an abstract and elusive construct mainly because of its three unique features: intangibility, heterogeneity, and inseparability of production and consumption of services (Parasuraman et al. 1985). There is not even a global consensus on what constitutes quality in service transactions. One of the most comprehensive definitions of quality is the "degree to which a set of inherent characteristics fulfils requirements" (ISO 2005). In this definition, requirements are defined as the "need or expectation that is stated, generally implied or obligatory" (ISO 2005). This definition of quality is different from that usually employed in manufacturing, for example, where definition of the requirements and hence the quality are set and measured objectively by such indicators as durability and number of defects (Crosby 1979; Garvin 1983). In the absence of objective measures, subjective methods such as SERVQUAL (Parasuraman et al. 1988), SERFPERF (Cronin and Taylor 1992), and Qualitometro (Franceschini et al. 1988) have been developed and used extensively in service sector.

Computational techniques and simulation methodologies have played a significant role in modeling and optimization of production and process management over the past few decades. The lack of objective measures in services, however, has hindered adoption of simulation, control, and computational techniques in this section of the economy. There is now a clear and growing understanding amongst service scientists that there is a need for a modeling or simulation tool for services.

Artificial neural networks (ANNs) are computational networks that attempt to crudely mimic the networks of neurons of biological system such as that of humans or animals (Graupe 2007). ANNs belong to a category of meta-heuristic modeling, control, and optimization algorithms, called evolutionary algorithms (EAs). EAs are inspired by nature through exhibiting complex collective behavior from a collection of seemingly simple agents. These include ANNs, genetic algorithm, tabu search, ant colony optimization, and simulated annealing. Most of these techniques have long been used in engineering and in industry; there are reports of the application of ANNs, for example, in quality control (Abbasi 2007). Their application in quality control, however, has been mostly limited to manufacturing industry. We propose there is merit in considering EAs in service quality control and service quality forecasting.

In the following section we cover service quality as it has been studied in academia, followed by an introduction to ANNs. We conclude this paper by summarizing advantage and disadvantage of using ANNs in service quality control and service quality forecasting.

3.2 Service Quality

In today's world and in this competitive market, service enterprises attempt to achieve competitive advantage by fulfilling customers' needs and expectations, resulting in higher customer satisfaction. Furthermore, customers' ease of access to services and ease of supplier change have resulted in reduced customer loyalty, with the implication that service quality is more important than ever before in retaining and attracting new customers (Mahdavinia 2007).

The concept of service quality as a whole construct is large and varied. The conceptual foundation for service quality was emerged from the works of a handful of researchers who examined the meaning of service quality (Sasser et al. 1978; Gronroos 1982).

Service quality is usually expressed from a customer point of view as a function of customer's expectations of the service compared to the perception of the actual service experience (Gronroos 1984; Parasuraman et al. 1985; Johnston and Heineke 1998). Imrie et al. (2002) showed that using service quality as a key point of market differentiation positively influenced customer retention and market growth. Interestingly, Parasuraman et al. (1988) stated that in measuring perceived service quality, the level of comparison is what a customer *should* expect, whereas Mahdavinia (2007) prefers that in measuring customer satisfaction, the appropriate comparison is what a customer *would* expect.

Some other researchers have focused on the role of employee in service quality and consequently customer satisfaction. Hartline et al. (2002) highlighted the fact that in many cases, employees are most often the first and the only representatives of a service firm to customers. Therefore, customer often base their impressions of the firm on the service received from customer-facing employees (Mahdavinia 2007).

Due to the illusive nature of service quality and its dependence on the type of services being provided, it has been suggested that managers need to understand the types of service quality factors relevant to their own services and understand various relationships between perception and performance in order to design, measure, and control the services. Service levels need to be set and strategies devised that first recognize the relative impact of individual factors on overall perceptions and secondly, link them to organization's quality strategy (Johnston and Heineke 1998).

Overall there have been five predominant service quality measurement tools reported in literature since 1991. These tools can be summarized in chronological order as follows:

- SERVQUAL is used to measure consumer's and service providers' expectations and perceptions. This approach enables the exceptions and perceptions gaps to be assessed, while providing a measure of service quality gap and service delivery gap. According to Parasuraman et al. (1988) model, the gap between consumer's expectations and perceptions is a function of several other gaps in the service delivery process (Mangold and Emin 1991). Some other models were proposed after the first introduction of SERVQUAL.
- Qualitometro (Franceschini et al. 1988) is founded on the determinants of service quality. Customer expectations and perceptions are evaluated in two distinct moments. Quality evaluation is carried out by means of a comparison between quality and expectations and perception profile. Qualitometro employs the same semantic scale and dimensions as SERVQUAL (Mahdavinia 2007).
- Two-way model used latent evaluation factors based on the theory that service quality is evaluated by answers given by customers about "objective" (quality attribute) and "subjective" (satisfaction level) (Schvaneveldt and Enkawa 1991; Mahdavinia 2007).
- Cronin and Taylor (1992) proposed SERVPERF based on their survey on theory that service quality is evaluated by perception only. The key difference with SERVQUAL is that only perceptions are evaluated (Mahdavinia 2007).
- Normed quality model (Teas 1994) uses the distinction between ideal expectation and feasible expectation to calculate service quality. It also employs the same semantic scale and dimensions as SERVQUAL. Normed is the second well-known model (after SERVPERF) that is derived from SERVQUAL (Ghoseiri and Pishdad 2006).

In addition to the well-known service quality models described above, there are other less-known models (technical and functional quality model (Gronroos 1984); GAP model (Parasuraman et al. 1985); attribute service quality model (Haywood-Farmer 1988); synthesized model of service quality (Brogowicz et al. 1990); performance-only model (Cronin and Taylor 1992); ideal value model of service quality (Mattsson 1992); evaluated performance and normed quality model (Teas 1993); IT alignment model (Berkley and Gupta 1994); attribute and overall affect model (Dabholkar 1996); model of perceived service quality and satisfaction (Spreng and Mackoy 1996); PCP attribute model (Philip and Hazlett 1997); retail service quality and perceived value model (Sweeney et al. 1997); service quality, customer value, and customer satisfaction model (Oh 1999); antecedents and mediator model (Dabholkar et al. 2000); internal service quality model (Frost and Kumar 2000); internal service quality DEA model (Soteriou and Stavrinides 2000); Internet banking model (Broderick and Vachirapornpuk 2002); IT-based model (Zhu et al. 2002); model of e-service quality (Santos 2003)).

All the above service quality models share a common feature; they evaluate quality of services through the same approach; they apply questionnaire or other data gathering tools and evaluate the quality based on their respective subjective concepts.

Many quality characteristics can be measured and stated as a numerical value. For instance, service delivery may be timed and reported in seconds or minutes or hours. These types of quality characteristics are called "variable characteristics." Advantage of questionnaire-based approaches is in their ease of collecting and the use of variable characteristics. There are, however, other types of measurements that can only assume nominal (reject, accept), ordinal (bad, good, excellent), or categorical (married, single, divorced) values. These are called "attribute characteristics." Collecting and processing of attribute characteristics are a much harder proposition as they inherit subjective principal and values. We propose the use of ANNs in order to overcome the complexity in processing these tacitly implied and subjective measurements. ANNs have been used in engineering and manufacturing, and to the best of the author's knowledge they have not been applied in service quality control and forecasting.

3.3 Artificial Neural Network

ANNs mimic biological neural networks to model and solve a variety of problems arising in forecasting, function approximation, pattern classification, clustering, and categorization (Pao 1989).

It is estimated that there are approximately ten billion neurons in the human cortex and 60 billion synapses or connections. Synapses are elementary structural and functional units that mediate the interaction between neurons. Axons and dendrites play their role as the transmission lines and the receptive zones, respectively. Figure 3.1 illustrates the shape of a pyramidal cell, which is one of the most common types of cortical neurons. Like many other types of neurons, it receives most of its inputs through dendritic spines (Haykin 1999).

From technical point of view, the block diagram of Fig. 3.2 shows the model of neuron, which forms the basis for designing ANNs. Three basic elements of the neural model are:

1. A set of *synapses* or *connecting links*, each of which is characterized by a weight or strength of its own. Specially, a signal x_j at the input of synapse j connected to neuron k is multiplied by a synaptic weight w_{kj}.
2. An *adder* for summing the input signals, weighted by respective of the neuron; the operation described here constitutes a *linear combiner.*
3. An *activation function* for limiting the amplitude of the output of a neuron (Haykin 1999).

The neuronal model of Fig. 3.2 also indicates an externally applied *bias*, denoted by b_k. The bias has the effect of increasing or lowering the net input of the activation function, depending on whether it is positive or negative, respectively.

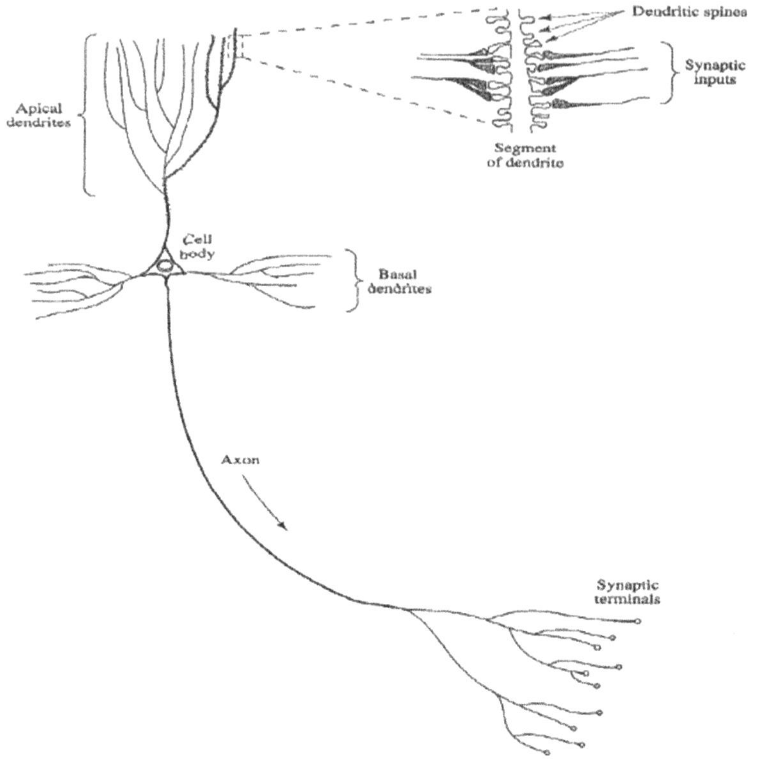

Fig. 3.1 The pyramidal cell

Fig. 3.2 Nonlinear model of neuron

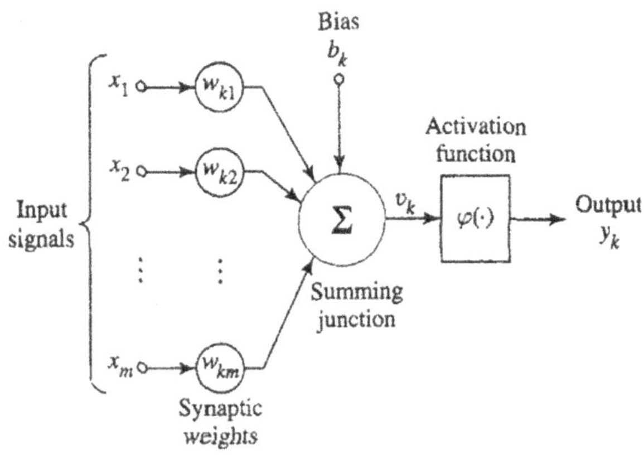

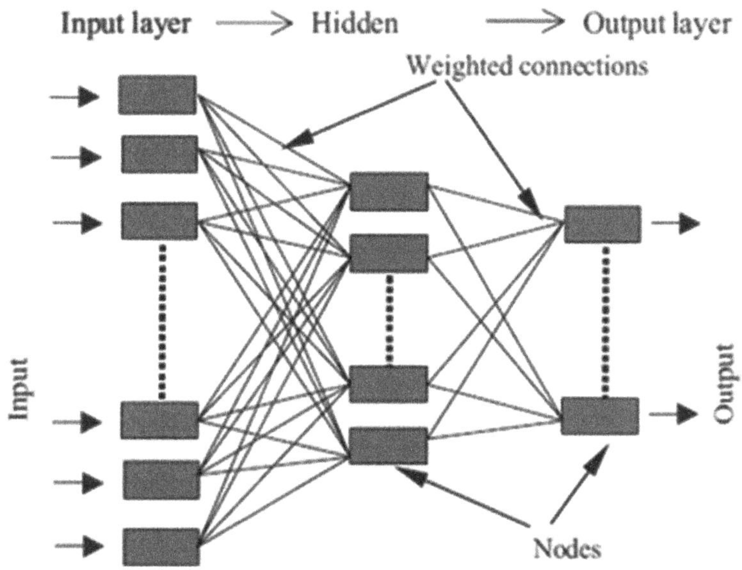

Fig. 3.3 The structure of a multilayer feed-forward network

In mathematical terms, we may describe a neuron *k* by writing (3.1) and (3.2):

$$u_k = \sum_{j=1}^{m} w_{jk} x_j \tag{3.1}$$

$$y_k = \Phi(u_k + b_k) \tag{3.2}$$

where $x_1, x_2, \ldots, x_m$ are the input signals; $w_{k1}, w_{k2}, \ldots, w_{km}$ are the synaptic weights of neuron k; u_k is the *linear combiner output* due to the input signals; b_k is the bias; Φ is the *activation function*; and y_k is the output signal of the neuron.

The activation function defines the output of a neuron in terms of the induced load field Φ. There are different activation function such as *threshold* function, *piecewise-linear* function, and *sigmoid* function which are applied for different types of outputs (Haykin 1999).

In terms of structuring of a network, there are different classes of network architectures including *single-layer feed-forward networks*, *multilayer feed-forward networks*, and *recurrent networks* (Haykin 1999). As an example, a multilayer feed-forward model is shown in Fig. 3.3.

After constructing a neural network, it needs to be trained based on some available data (different inputs and their corresponding outputs) to be able to forecast the output for future inputs with an acceptable error level through an ongoing modification process. The property that is of primary significance for a neural network is the ability of the network to learn from its environment and to improve its performance through learning. Learning is a process by which the free parameters of a neural network are adapted through a process of stimulation by the environment in which the network is embedded. The type of learning is determined by manner in which the parameter changes take place. There are different types of learning including *unsupervised learning* and *supervised learning*. In the supervised training process, the user plays an important role as the network learns. However, in an unsupervised process the user lets the network train itself (Haykin 1999).

3.3.1 Merits and Demerits

Generally, the use of neural networks offers useful properties and capabilities including but not limited to (Haykin 1999):

- *Nonlinearity*. An artificial neuron can be linear or nonlinear.
- *Input–output mapping*. The network is presented with an example picked at random from the set, and the synaptic weights (free parameters) of the network modified to minimize the difference between the desired response and the actual response of the network produced by the input signal in accordance with an appropriate statistical criterion.
- *Adaptivity*. Neural networks have a built-in capability to adapt their synaptic weight to changes in the surrounding environment.
- *Uniformity of analysis and design*. Basically, neural network enjoy universality as information processors. We say this in the sense that the same notation is used in all domains involving the application of neural network.
- *Neurobiological analogy*. The design of a neural network is motivated by analogy with the brain, which is a living proof that fault-tolerant parallel processing is not only physically possible but also fast and powerful.

Regardless of all aforementioned merits, neural network has the following drawbacks (Friedman et al. 2001):

- Trial and error element to building good models (in training phase).
- It is hard to interpret what is happening in the model (Black Box), and people only see the inputs and outputs.
- Model performance relates to starting input values and parameters.

3.4 Application of Artificial Neural Network to Service Quality

In spite of considerable number of available service quality methods, there are some shortcomings shared between them:

1. Firstly, all proposed methods for quality control in service industry are somehow subjective and they are mostly designed based on SERVQUAL. These models employ static methods for data analysis. A periodical analysis can be performed

Table 3.1 A model for applying ANN in service quality

Phase	Description
Problem definition	Case description, problem assumptions (service quality model, etc.)
Designing	Type of model, type of connections, number of layers, number of neurons, activation function, cutting value
	Estimating parameters (based on historical data)
	Generating training data based on estimated parameters
Training	Training of neural network
Verification	Testing trained network based on random generated or historical data
Programming	Coding and running the network based on related assumption (cutting value, etc.)
Validation	Validation of network in real case study

in a regular base (e.g., monthly, every 6 months, and yearly) if trends are to be determined. These methods are retrospect and are not able to monitor service quality in real time. Whereas, in dynamic methods, one can monitor quality of delivered service in real time (as the service is being delivered). Based on the past history (training data set), and real-time data gathering, ANNs have the ability to forecast the outcome (service quality). Exactly as humans deal with imprecise data, service quality forecasting can be performed even in the case of imprecise or imperfect real-time data.

2. Secondly, in subjective methods, the correlation between different factors is not reckoned, and each characteristic (e.g., reliability and responsiveness) is monitored through one or more questions in the questionnaire. However, in reality characteristics and attributes of service transactions do correlate and can affect service quality indirectly. Considering these characteristics in isolation ignores such indirect consequences.
3. Thirdly, in applying subjective model based on questionnaire or other means of data gathering, some variable data are missed or converted to numeric attribute. For instance, qualitative values are usually given numeric rankings. ANNs can deal with qualitative values as they are, alleviating this limitation.

Based on the above, it seems the use of ANNs for service quality control and service quality forecasting is well justified. A model for applying ANNs in service quality control is proposed in Table 3.1.

As a very general example, we assume that for controlling quality of a banking service, there are "responsiveness," "reliability," and "information technology" as three attribute characteristics and "time" and "cost" as two variable characteristics. Designing an ANN for such a scenario would require five input neurons and six output neurons, the first one for overall quality and the rest for showing the effect of each characteristic on the overall quality status. In this example, the output [0, 1, 1, 0, 1, and 0] means that the customer is not satisfied with the quality due to information technology and cost ("0" values).

3.5 Application to Healthcare Context

There are some different services that can be nominated in application case study, e.g., education, public transportation, banking, and health care. In comparison with other types of servicing, healthcare providers face many challenges, while they are concurrently under public scrutiny as consumer demands escalate. Medical care quality control and improvement as confidence in the medical community providing safe and effective patient care. Note that poor quality in patient care processes can run the spectrum from minor dietary issues to patient morbidity and fatality. It seems that applying a biological-origin concept in healthcare industry would be interesting (Frings and Laura Grant 2005). Health care is the most crucial service industry because of its nature of zero tolerance for mistakes and potential for reducing medical (Kwak and Anbari 2006). Health care is the largest service industry accounting for 17 % of the US GDP ahead of education at ten percent (Larson 2009). There are about 7,500 hospitals in the United States but about 4,000 institutions of higher education (Larson 2010).

The Commonwealth Fund, in its annual survey, "Mirror, Mirror on the Wall," compares the performance of the healthcare systems in Australia, New Zealand, the United Kingdom, Germany, Canada, and the United States. The Organization for Economic Co-operation and Development (OECD) also collects comparative statistics and has published brief country profiles as in Table 3.2 (The Commonwealth Fund 2007; Organization for Economic Co-operation and Development 2008; Wikipedia 2010).

The Institute of Medicine's definition of quality has proved of enduring usefulness: "Quality is the extent to which health services for individuals and populations increase the likelihood of desired health outcomes and are consistent with current professional knowledge" (Chassin 1998).

Table 3.2 Brief country healthcare profiles

Country	Per capita expenditure on health (USD)	Healthcare costs as a percent of GDP	% of government revenue spent on health	% of health costs paid by government
Australia	3,137	8.7	17.7	67.7
Canada	3,895	10.1	16.7	69.8
France	3,601	11.0	14.2	79.0
Germany	3,588	10.4	17.6	76.9
Japan	2,581	8.1	16.8	81.3
Norway	5,910	9.0	17.9	83.6
Sweden	3,323	9.2	13.6	81.7
United Kingdom	2,992	8.4	15.8	81.7
United States	7,290	16.0	18.5	45.4

Some operational inefficiencies are associated with the direct medical service delivery process. Others are associated with the administrative, logistical, and operational side of the healthcare delivery system. Both areas can benefit from systematic process innovation activities (Henk de Koning et al. 2006).

A lot of different attributes and variable quality characteristics can be considered in health care to monitor, predict, and improve (Loey Sehwail and Camille De Yong 2003; Richard Stahl et al. 2003) the posit that the quality characteristics in health care can be classified into four categories:

- Service level (e.g., access to care, wait time, service time)
- Service cost (e.g., cost per unit of service, labor productivity)
- Customer satisfaction (e.g., patient or family, referring physician, employee)
- Clinical excellence (e.g., guidelines for medication or treatment, standard procedures for patient monitoring)

From different angle, McGlynn et al. (2003) proposed different quality indicator in three types of care including preventive, acute, and chronic and in four different functions including screening, diagnosis, treatment, and follow-up. In an analytical paper published by the Quality in Australian Health Care Study (QAHCS), Ross McL Wilson et al. analyzed the cause of adverse events resulting from health care in Australia from different categories like human error categories, delay categories, treatment categories, and investigation categories (Ross McL Wilson, Harrison et al. 1999).

3.6 Concluding Remarks

Service quality and methodologies of measuring it were discussed and then from the case vignette contextualized for a healthcare context. In this way we demonstrated the potential benefits of applying ANN into health care to facilitate the achievement of superior healthcare delivery. The gaps in the currently available methodologies were highlighted. Based on the lessons learnt in manufacturing in dealing with analogous problems, the use of evolutionary algorithms (EAs) in service quality control and forecasting is proposed, and a simple model for applying ANNs (a subclass of EA) is presented.

For completeness, it is noted that the application of ANNs in service quality control and forecasting has the following characteristics:

1. No restriction on the type of inputs and outputs (qualitative values, quantitative attributes, or any combination thereof).
2. No assumption is made on the statistical distribution of variables and their interdependence.
3. No limitation on the number of inputs and outputs (although it is noted that as the number of inputs and outputs increase, the network might become prohibitively complex).

4. No requirements on access to large data sets. EV can be trained and used with much smaller data sets than statistical methods afford.
5. Computationally very efficient, which can translate into much faster data analysis; affording near real-time data analysis in the case of ANNs.

We believe ANNs are a prime candidate in service quality control and service quality forecasting. Research is already underway in designing and applying an ANN as a dynamic model for monitoring and forecasting of service quality in a nominal service industry. Further, ANNs have the potential to bring numerous benefits to healthcare contexts and we close by recommending their incorporation into healthcare contexts.

References

Abbasi, B. (2007). *Developing multi-attribute control charts*. PhD, Industrial Engineering, Sharif University of Technology, Tehran.

Berkley, B. J., & Gupta, A. (1994). Improving service quality with information technology. *International Journal of Information Management, 14*, 109–121.

Broderick, A. J., & Vachirapornpuk, S. (2002). Service quality in internet banking: The importance of customer role. *Marketing Intelligence & Planning, 20*(6), 327–335.

Brogowicz, A. A., Delene, L. M., et al. (1990). A synthesised service quality model with managerial implications. *International Journal of Service Industry Management, 1*(1), 27–44.

Cronin, J. J., & Taylor, S. A. (1992). Measuring service quality: A reexamination and extension. *Journal of Marketing, 56*(3), 55.

Crosby, P. B. (1979). *Quality is free: The art of making quality certain*. New York: New American Library.

Dabholkar, P. A. (1996). Consumer evaluations of new technology-based self-service operations: An investigation of alternative models. *International Journal of Research in Marketing, 13*(1), 29–51.

Dabholkar, P. A., Shepherd, C. D., et al. (2000). A comprehensive framework for service quality: An investigation of critical conceptual and measurement issues through a longitudinal study. *Journal of Retailing, 76*, 2131–2139.

DFAT (Department of Foreign Affairs and Trade, Australia). (2008). *About Australia service sector world class tertiary industries*. March 2008 version. Retrieved November 7, 2008, from http://www.dfat.gov.au/facts/service_sector.pdf

Elizabeth A. McGlynn, Steven M. Asch, et al. (2003). "The Quality of Health Care Delivered to Adults in the United States." *The new england journal of medicine 348*, 2635–45.

Franceschini, F., Cignetti, M., et al. (1988). Comparing tools for service quality evaluation. *International Journal of Quality Science, 3*(4), 356–367.

Friedman, J., Hastie, T., et al. (2001). *The element of statistical learning-data mining, inference and prediction*. New York: Springer.

Frost, F. A., & Kumar, M. (2000). INTSERVQUAL: An internal adaptation of the GAP model in a large service organization. *Journal of Services Marketing, 14*(5), 358–377.

Garvin, D. A. (1983). Quality on the line. *Harvard Business Review, 61*, 65–73.

Ghoseiri, K., & Pishdad, S. (2006). Service quality measurement in information technology departments. *Journal of Management Knowledge, 19*, 74.

Ginny W. Frings and Laura Grant (2005). "Who Moved My Sigma . . . Effective Implementation of the Six Sigma Methodology to Hospitals." QUALITY AND RELIABILITY ENGINEERING INTERNATIONAL 21, 311–328.

Graupe, D. (2007). *Principles of artificial neural networks*. River Edge, NJ: World Scientific Publishing.

Gronroos, C. (1982). *Strategic management and marketing in the service sector*. Helsinki: Swedish School of Economics and Business Administration.
Gronroos, C. (1984). A service quality model and its marketing implications. *European Journal of Marketing, 18*(4), 9.
Hartline, M., III, Maxham, J., et al. (2002). Corridors of influence in the dimension of customer-oriented strategy to customer contact service employee. *Journal of Marketing, 64*(2), 35–51.
Haykin, S. (1999). *Neural network. A comprehensive foundation*. New Delhi: Pearson Education.
Haywood-Farmer, J. (1988). A conceptual model of service quality. *International Journal of Operations & Production Management, 8*(6), 19–29.
Henk de Koning, John P. S. Verver, et al. (2006). "Lean Six Sigma in Healthcare." *Journal for Healthcare Quality 28*(2), 4–11.
IfM & IBM. (2008). *Succeeding through service innovation: A service perspective for education, research, business and government*. Cambridge: University of Cambridge Institute for Manufacturing, ISBN: 978-1-902546-65-0. http://www.ifm.eng.cam.ac.uk/ssme/
Imrie, B. C., Cadogan, J. W., et al. (2002). The service quality construct on a global stage. *Managing Service Quality, 12*(1), 10–18.
ISO 9000:2005. (2005). *Quality management systems—Fundamentals and vocabulary*. Switzerland: International Organization for Standardization (ISO).
Johnston, R., & Heineke, J. (1998). Exploring the relationship between perception and performance: Priorities for action. *Service Industries Journal, 18*, 1101–1112.
Kwak Y. H. and Anbari F. T. (2006). "Benefits, obstacles, and future of six sigma approach." Technovation 26, 708–715.
Loey Sehwail and Camille De Yong (2003). "Six Sigma in Helath Care." *International Journal of Health care Quality Assurance incorporating leadership with health services 16*(4).
Mahdavinia, H. (2007). *Customer satisfaction in four star Isfahan hotels: An application of SERVQUAL model*. Master, Department of Business Administration and Social Science, Porson-Sweden, Lulea University of Technology.
Mangold, G., & Emin, B. (1991). Service quality: The front-stage vs. the back-stage perspective. *Journal of Services Marketing, 5*(4), 59–70.
Mark R. Chassin (1998). "Is Health Care Ready for Six Sigma Quality?" *The Milbank Quarterly 76*(4), 565–591.
Mattsson, J. (1992). A service quality model based on ideal value standard. *International Journal of Service Industry Management, 3*(3), 18–33.
Oh, H. (1999). Service quality, customer satisfaction and customer value: A holistic perspective. *International Journal of Hospitality Management, 18*, 67–82.
Pao, Y. H. (1989). *Adaptive pattern recognition and neural network*. Reading, MA: Addison-Wesley.
Parasuraman, A., Zeithaml, V. A., et al. (1985). A conceptual model of service quality and its implication in future research. *Journal of Marketing, Fall*, 41–50.
Parasuraman, A., Zeithaml, V. A., et al. (1988). SERVQUAL: A multiple-item scale for measuring consumer perception of service quality. *Journal of Retailing, 64*(1), 12–40.
Philip, G., & Hazlett, S. A. (1997). The measurement of service quality: A new P-C-P attributes model. *International Journal of Quality & Reliability Management, 14*(3), 260–286.
Richard Stahl R, Schultz B, et al. (2003). "Revamping healthcare using DMAIC and DFSS." *iSix-Sigma Healthcare Newsletter v3.01b, 0.0-b.*, 246.
Richard C. Larson (2009). "Education: Our Most Important Service Sector." *Service Science 1*(4), 1–3.
Richard C. Larson (2010). Shared Services: Libraries, Universities and More, Massachusetts *Institute of Technology*, Cambridge.
Ross McL Wilson, Bernadette T Harrison, et al. (1999). "An analysis of the causes of adverse events from the Quality in Australian Health Care Study". *The Medical Journal of Australia 170*, 411–415.
Santos, J. (2003). E-service quality: A model of virtual service quality dimensions. *Managing Service Quality, 13*(3), 233–246.

Sasser, W. W., Olsen, R. P., et al. (1978). *Management of service operations*. Boston, MA: Allyn and Boston.

Schvaneveldt, S., & Enkawa, T. (1991). Consumer evaluation perspectives of service quality: Evaluation factors and two-way model of quality. *Total Quality Management, 2*(2), 13.

Soteriou, A. C., & Stavrinides, Y. (2000). An internal customer service quality data envelope analysis model for bank branches. *International Journal of Bank Marketing, 18*(5), 246–252.

Spohrer, J., Maglio, P. P., Bailey, J., & Gruhl, D. (2007). Steps toward a science of service systems, *IEEE Xplore*. Retrieved October 29, 2008.

Spreng, R. A., & Mackoy, R. D. (1996). An empirical examination of a model of perceived service quality and satisfaction. *Journal of Retailing, 722*, 201–214.

Sweeney, J. C., Soutar, G. N., et al. (1997). Retail service quality and perceived value. *Journal of Consumer Services, 4*(1), 39–48.

Teas, R. K. (1993). Expectations, performance evaluation, and consumer's perceptions of quality. *Journal of Marketing, 57*(4), 18–34.

Teas, R. K. (1994). Expectations as a comparison standard in measuring service quality: An assessment of a reassessment. *Journal of Marketing, 58*(1), 132–139.

The Commonwealth Fund (2007). "Mirror, Mirror on the Wall: An International Update on the Comparative Performance of American Health Care".

The Organization for Economic Co-operation and Development (OECD) (2008).

Wikipedia (2010). Health care system. Health care system. t. f. e. From Wikipedia.

Zhu, F. X., Wymer, W. J., et al. (2002). IT-based services and service quality in consumer banking. *International Journal of Service Industry Management, 13*(1), 69–90.

Chapter 4
The Application of Lean in the Healthcare Sector: Theory and Practical Examples

Nathan Houchens and Christopher S. Kim

Abstract Many companies in the manufacturing sector, such as Toyota, have enjoyed immense financial and commercial success by utilizing lean principles to identify value for the customer, eliminate waste in the production process, and deliver high-quality products. Lean encourages participation by the "frontline" workers to generate ideas, enact changes in workflow, and constantly pursue perfection in learning systems. Modern healthcare organizations comprise complex processes and are in significant need of improvement in the domains of safe, efficient, timely, and appropriate delivery of care to patients. It is these complex processes that are targets for improvement using the systematic and scientific lean approach. Lean has been implemented in numerous healthcare organizations within the United States and other nations. From decreased patient wait times to improved patient throughput in emergency departments to more efficient bedside rounding practices, lean has improved the quality of healthcare delivery in institutions that teach its ideals and goals. By going and observing where the work is performed, asking why to determine the root cause of problems, and respecting and supporting involved parties, organizations may have a positive transformative effect on the way healthcare is delivered.

Keywords Lean approach • Healthcare systems • Patient safety • Efficiency • Problem solving

Key Questions

1. What is the lean approach?
2. How can lean principles be applied in healthcare?
3. Who are the customers in the healthcare system and what are the values specific to each?

N. Houchens, M.D. (✉) • C.S. Kim, M.D., M.B.A.
Department of Internal Medicine, University of Michigan, Ann Arbor, MI, USA
e-mail: an9188@gmail.com

N. Wickramasinghe et al. (eds.), *Lean Thinking for Healthcare*, Healthcare Delivery in the Information Age, DOI 10.1007/978-1-4614-8036-5_4,

4. How are value and waste defined in the healthcare arena?
5. What is the lean practitioner's approach to solving healthcare process problems?
   What are the steps involved and how is quality improvement executed?
6. What are examples of effects of the lean approach in healthcare?

4.1 The History of Lean: A Quality Revolution from Manufacturing to Healthcare

Provision of a high-quality product with maximal value to the customer and minimal waste to the organization is the critical endeavor of any industry. Toyota Motor Corporation epitomizes this statement by maintaining its unremitting devotion to continuous quality improvement and safety for both its employees and its customers. In doing so, it has achieved remarkable success. Toyota is widely recognized as a world-class automotive manufacturer and consistently garners top rankings and awards for quality and customer satisfaction by reporting agencies (Liker 2004). Much can be learned from the ways in which this industry giant conducts its business.

The management philosophy of the Toyota Production System, known generically as lean production, is a set of principles and practices that assist in delivering the ultimate goal of improving quality by the constant transformation of waste into value from the customer's perspective. Waste can be defined as anything that does not add value to the final product or service; conversely, value is the capability to provide the right product or service, at the right time, and at an appropriate price (Womack and Jones 2003). Lean production refined twentieth-century scientific management concepts pioneered by Frederick Winslow Taylor and Henry Ford. Taiichi Ohno, an engineer at Toyota during the 1940s, identified deficiencies in Western automotive production systems. He believed that excess inventory led to costly capital, increased need for storage space, and product defects. He also noted the inability of inflexible systems to honor dynamic customer preferences due to line-based production systems (Holweg 2007).

With these insights, he developed the principles of *jidoka* and "just-in-time." *Jidoka* can be loosely translated as "automation with a human touch" and refers to automated and standardized processes that are able to detect problems requiring human attention in real time, thereby preventing defects in the final product. The "just-in-time" philosophy leads to production of only that which is needed by the next process in order to achieve a smooth and continuous workflow. These process-oriented concepts, combined with methods suggested by American statistician and quality expert W. Edwards Deming, serve as the foundation for the Toyota Production System and lean thinking. Over generations, Toyota as an evolving organization, has undergone continuous iterative learning cycles with a goal of eliminating waste and creating value (Womack et al. 1990).

A derivation of this strategy is known as lean thinking or the lean approach. A descendent of the quality improvement method known as the Plan-Do-Study-Act (PDSA) cycle, lean has been incorporated into numerous other industries such as construction, aerospace, and insurance in an effort to improve performance and productivity. This philosophy has also extended to healthcare. Indeed, many hospitals, clinics, and medical groups are rapidly adopting its tenets across the world and establishing it as the systematic approach to enhancing quality, efficiency, and patient safety (Blackmore et al. 2011; Kim et al. 2009; Waldhausen et al. 2010). In this chapter, we will investigate the numerous challenges the healthcare industry faces, the key steps and tools of lean as it relates to the care of patients, and examples of successful execution of lean principles by forward-thinking healthcare institutions.

4.2 Healthcare Challenges in the Twenty-First Century

Healthcare systems are intricate organizations that comprise not only the physical locations of care delivery but also a myriad of medical provider disciplines, varying acuity of patient disease processes, and an ever-expanding database of literature describing disease pathophysiology, diagnostic approaches, and therapies. Achievements in technology and innovation have equipped providers to deliver higher levels of care than ever before. However, as a natural by-product of this evolution, care of patients has become more subspecialized, and the processes that must coordinate to produce quality medical care are increasing in number and complexity.

More than a decade ago, the United States Institute of Medicine published two reports entitled *To Err Is Human* and *Crossing the Quality Chasm* that investigated the ways in which healthcare is delivered and placed focus on quality improvement and patient safety issues (Kohn et al. 2000; Committee on Quality Health Care in America, Institute of Medicine 2001). The recommendations put forth in these reports highlight patient care that should be safe, effective, efficient, patient-centered, timely, and equitable. Despite the time that has since passed and the substantial amount of resources that have been allocated toward achieving these goals, many challenges in the United States and other nations remain.

It is clear that healthcare delivery and financial systems require significant intervention in order to create the ideal care experience that patients require and deserve. While this represents a global view of the challenges facing healthcare, the processes and tools of change will likely need to be engaged at the local or individual organization level. The lean philosophy has been utilized in multiple industries such as automotive manufacturing, finance, and metalworking to improve processes with massive improvements in quality, efficiency, and profit margins. The time has come to harness the power of lean in order to improve the state of healthcare. Indeed, the Institute for Healthcare Improvement has advocated for healthcare leaders to take up the lean approach for this purpose (Institute for Healthcare Improvement 2005).

Those who state that patients are not composed of parts needing to be assembled correctly to function are correct. However, the healthcare system is a complex organization that comprises multiple processes similar to other industries, and it is these processes that are targets for improvement using lean techniques. In order to gain a better understanding of lean thinking, it is imperative to first consider the fundamental concepts of lean.

4.3 The Principles of Lean (in Healthcare)

In their book entitled *Lean Thinking: Banish Waste and Create Wealth in Your Corporation* (Womack and Jones 1996), James Womack and Daniel Jones specify the lean thinking approach as consisting of five steps:

1. Specify value from the customer's perspective.
2. Identify the value stream (from order to delivery) for each product or service and remove the waste.
3. Make value flow without interruption from the beginning to the end of the process.
4. Let the customers pull what they value from processes when they need it.
5. Pursue perfection through continuous improvement.

In healthcare, one can also view the approach to lean thinking following these five steps. The goal of lean thinking in healthcare is to focus continuously on how appropriate healthcare can be delivered most efficiently, safely, and with the highest quality by transforming waste into value from the perspective of the customer.

1. Value from the customer's perspective

Customers in healthcare do not solely refer to patients, but also include other internal and external partners of the healthcare system. In addition to patients, external customers could also include regulatory agencies such as the Joint Commission and the Centers for Medicare and Medicaid Services, as well as third-party payers such as private and public insurers. Internal customers could include providers referring to one another and other ancillary support staff collaborating to provide clinical and nonclinical healthcare service to patients. Organizations striving to provide the best care possible need to understand the value as determined by both its internal and external customers to the healthcare delivery process.

2. Identify the value stream and remove waste

The healthcare organization operates in a series of processes, where each successive step in a process should deliver a value-added piece of work in the overall goal of taking care of the needs of its patients. Many of these processes are far less than optimally efficient. Consider, for example, the number of steps and waiting time required for an outpatient office visit. The total time that elapses from when the patient picks up the phone to make an appointment until the time when she is seen and evaluated at the clinic can be quite long and variable. The patient could spend minutes on hold waiting to speak to a scheduler and then wait up to several days to weeks before the actual appointment date. Upon arrival at the clinic, the patient again waits in a reception area prior to moving through other clinic areas at which point there is typically additional wait time (i.e., moving from the waiting room to the area where vital signs are taken, moving into the exam room, being evaluated by a medical assistant or nurse) before finally being seen by the medical provider. The patient may experience further wait time at checkout. If she needs a prescription, further diagnostic tests, or is referred to a specialist, she may need to repeat many aspects within this series of inefficient steps. This process, taken as a whole, often frustrates patients regarding the length of time required to schedule and be seen by their physicians. Yet, for all those involved in coordinating and providing the medical care for the patient, the overall primary goal *is* to help the patient with her medical problem as best they can. There appears to be a gap between what the patient desires from the healthcare delivery system and what the organization is actually delivering as its product.

A lean approach to investigating this problem example would (a) sort through which of these facets of the work would be considered of value to the patient, (b) try to ensure those parts are as closely linked to each other as possible, and (c) minimize (or eliminate) any other aspects the patient would not want as part of her healthcare utilization process. These steps comprise the process of creating a value stream map (VSM). Dohan et al. (2012) in this same volume discuss the use of VSM in lean healthcare with illustrative diagramming techniques. Delving deeper, the lean approach to identifying and eliminating waste would entail specifying the types of waste. In this example, waste would be defined to the customer as all aspects of the process that contribute to wait times either before or after being seen by the medical provider. The Toyota Production System categorized waste into seven areas of *muda*, a Japanese word describing waste or uselessness within a system (Womack and Jones 2003). Classifying waste into more specific areas may allow for organizations to better identify the underlying root causes of waste production that might serve as targets for improvement. Table 4.1 describes these categories of wastes and provides examples from the healthcare sector.

3. Make value flow without interruption
4. Pull what is valued from the process just in time

In analyzing the situation, the observer(s) and operator(s) of the process ask themselves if each of the steps is creating value for the customer and if the steps of this process can be accomplished with less waste. So often in healthcare, in their devotion to patient care, workers are focused only on their particular segment of the patient's journey and they often fail to see how their work affects other individuals who are also part of the process both upstream and downstream. Continuing on the previous example of the patient seeking an outpatient appointment, the overall goal of the lean thinking healthcare organization is to be able to make each of the steps involved in obtaining an appointment and evaluating the patient at the clinic visit flow as smoothly as possible with minimal interruptions. In fact, examples of these organizations exist.

Table 4.1 The seven types of waste (*muda*) in manufacturing and examples of their correlates in healthcare

Type of *muda*	Manufacturing example	Healthcare example
Correction: Rework to correct defects in work previously done	A car reaches the end of the assembly line and is found to have a part misplaced that needs to be corrected	Calling the lab for missing test results that were misdirected to the wrong clinician
Overproduction: Excess and unnecessary work	Production by a factory stamping group of several hundred more parts than are needed by the welding group (the next step in the process)	Ordering a computed tomography scan when clinical suspicion for a disease process is low and does not justify ordering the study
Motion of people: Unnecessary movement of people	An assembly line worker, who has 15 s to attach a part to each car moving down the assembly line, having to walk 5 steps every time to get the part	Nursing staff having to walk down the hall each time they need the key to the cabinet for narcotic pain medications
Material movement: Unnecessary transporting, rearranging, storing/moving materials great distances while waiting to be used	Storing parts for a production process in a warehouse on the other side of town, rather than at or near the production facility	Movement of laboratory specimens to a central receiving station for logging and sorting prior to being delivered to the final destination of various laboratories
Waiting: Waiting for equipment to finish running before the next phase can be initiated; or waiting for people, information, or materials before meetings	Waiting for equipment to finish running, before it can be changed to a different function, is idle time for the operator	Clinicians in the clinic waiting for patients to be put into exam rooms
Inventory: Excess supply that has no intended use in immediate future	A manufacturer has several months of completed products on hand, for which customers have not yet placed orders	Patients waiting in a long telephone queue to speak to a health provider
Processing: Doing something that the customer does not perceive as adding value	There are an excessive number of steps involved in ordering a part for the assembly line	Lengthy review and evaluation of patient records by the specialist before a patient can be scheduled in the specialty clinic

Source: Adapted from Womack and Jones (2003)

The mnemonic "COMMWIP" can be used to remember the seven types of *muda*, as originally described by Taiichi Ohno of Toyota: *C* correction, *O* overproduction, *M* motion of people, *M* material movement, *W* waiting, *I* inventory, *P* processing

Depending on the needs of the particular patient, there have been clinics established to allow for patients to make an appointment, show up to the clinic that same day, be seen by a provider, have their prescriptions sent to the pharmacy electronically via "e-prescribing," and have the medication ready for patient pick up, all without significant delays.

5. Pursue perfection through continuous improvement

An ultimate intention of a lean organization and management is to have the individual workers in the front line continuously work to improve processes of their everyday activity. When this happens, as Toyota has been able to achieve, a lean organization can start to become a learning organization. This type of organization addresses problems immediately through onsite, timely experimentation that identifies further problems and waste in the process steps. As individuals work and identify these problems, rapid deployment of improvement ideas can lead to dissemination to other individuals doing the same type of work. Once the improvement ideas are depicted and implemented as a new way of performing the work, further refinements can be made to stabilize and optimize the process, thereby becoming the "future state." Further experimentation leads to new process methods, further refinements and implementation ultimately determine the new current state, and the process repeats indefinitely in a continuous improvement cycle.

4.4 Lean Healthcare Organizations

The goal of lean thinking in healthcare is to focus continuously on the large and small changes that must be made in the processes of how clinical care is delivered, so that healthcare can be delivered in a way that simultaneously optimizes quality, safety, efficiency, and appropriateness. Some healthcare systems and organizations that were early adopters of lean production management have been able to demonstrate meaningful results.

- Virginia Mason Medical Center in Seattle, Washington, has been able to reduce the incidence of ventilator-associated pneumonias from 34 to 4 cases utilizing lean thinking methods (Institute for Healthcare Improvement 2005; Spear 2005). Their ongoing commitment to improve patient care and safety utilizing the approaches of lean healthcare has propelled them to become recognized as one of the safest hospitals in the country.
- ThedaCare Inc. is a health delivery system located in northeast Wisconsin that utilizes the ideals and tools of ThedaCare Improvement System. This organization has been able to achieve a $3.3 million cost savings in 2004; reduce the number of days outstanding in accounts receivable by 21 %, equating to about $12 million in cash flow; and redeploy staff in several areas by improving the efficiency of their operations, which have led to a savings of 33 full-time equivalent employees (Institute for Healthcare Improvement 2005).

- At the University of Pittsburgh Medical Center, nursing administration utilized the Toyota Production System model of Lean production to improve the quality and first-time accuracy of medication delivery which has led to cost savings of more than \$200,000; increased the percent of patients who received their medications on time as scheduled; virtually eliminated a non-value-added work of searching for a special narcotics key, leading to 2,900 nursing hours saved annually and patients obtaining pain relief on demand; and reduced the preparation time for antibiotic administration by 4 min per dose, thus leading to an estimated savings of nearly 5,000 nursing hours per year (Thompson et al. 2003).
- At Flinders Medical Center in South Australia, Emergency Department (ED) overcrowding was such a significant issue that providers were forced to see patients outside of the usual ED space. Through a series of value stream mapping exercises and process improvement work groups, this group was able to visualize their workflow and separate patient cases out into distinct "streams" based on their triage categories. Flinders was able to reduce the total amount of time spent in the ED by all types of patients, and the average number of patients being seen in the ED at any given time was also reduced, both of which led to the goal of decreasing ED overcrowding (King et al. 2006).

Case Example

Hospital-based rounding physicians have traditionally utilized batched processing in their approach to evaluation of patients. This process usually prioritizes the examination of patients who are reported to be the most ill, followed by those with urgent questions or issues, followed by routine patients who are likely to need ongoing hospital care services, and finally those patients who will be discharged that day. It is not clear as to the reason for this rounding order, but the behavior has been passed on from one generation of physicians to the next. However, it is not necessarily the order of patients that matters to workflow, but rather the order of provider actions.

To illustrate this concept, a process flow map of a typical rounding order and the subsequent batched work steps of calling specialty consultants and entering orders (daily orders, discharge orders, etc.) is shown in the figure below. Even this simplified depiction of a hospital-based provider's morning workflow demonstrates that batching activities together, while possibly convenient for the provider, can lead to the untoward by-products of wait times for other healthcare workers—such as providers receiving consult calls or allied health professionals having to carry out physician orders—as well as "bursts" of activity among these groups (e.g., specialty consultants, nurses, phlebotomists, pharmacists). This alternation between idling and overload leads to a lack of efficient and effective workflow that can produce delays in providing timely care to patients.

(continued)

(continued)

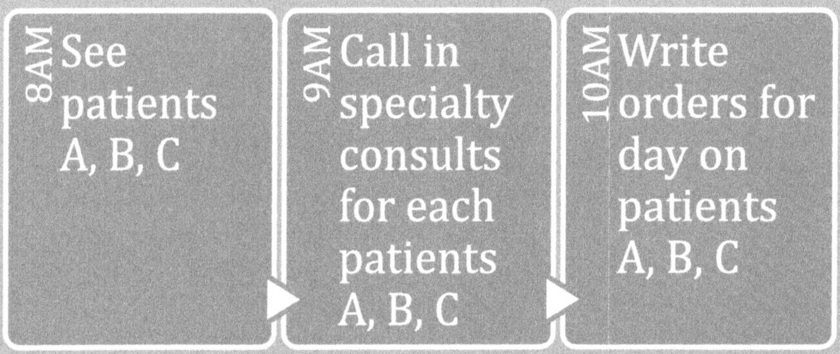

Source: Author

A practitioner utilizing lean principles, however, may envision an alternative approach for the same set of work steps. By redesigning the workflow to allow patient-related tasks to be started and completed for one patient at a time (also known as one-piece work), the patients as customers reap the benefits that are less directly apparent. Care delivered is safer and more efficacious because it is more efficient. Downstream healthcare workers are no longer sitting idle but are instead examining patients and executing orders in sync with the provider as he or she sets the cadence for the healthcare delivery process.

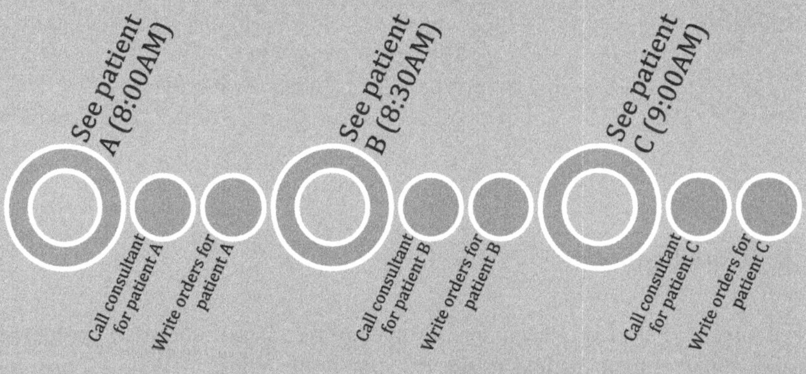

Source: Author

(continued)

(continued)

A keen observer will also note that by working in a one-piece workflow process, the opportunities to catch and correct defects or errors are much more rapid and close to the source of the error than in the traditional batching workflow process. One can see that in the batching process, entering orders for all the patients together creates an opportunity for error if the hospital-based provider is trying to toggle among multiple patients to enter orders. Further, if an error in order entry is going to be caught by an allied health professional—a clinical pharmacist, for example—he or she will not have all the information on patient A until well after 10:00 AM, the point at which the provider has completed writing all orders for all patients in a batched fashion. Alternatively, a pharmacist could catch and prevent an order error for patient A immediately after the provider enters orders on that patient if the provider utilizes one-piece workflow. The opportunity to fix the error becomes easier also as all involved parties are still proximal to the work and the needs of the patient as customer.

As hospitals have sought to improve the efficiency of care delivered in the hospital, they should consider incorporating a one-piece workflow from the patient's perspective to allow for quicker processing of each patient and to allow for opportunities to catch errors as proximal to the situation as possible. It is obvious to see the benefits of improving hospital and patient flow if one simply substitutes "writing a discharge order for patient A" to replace "writing a prescription order for patient A." In a busy health system, increasing efficiency of bed turnover even hours earlier can have a significant impact on the overall operation of all care settings including the hospital, the emergency department, and the clinic from which the patient was admitted.

4.5 Conclusions

Lean thinking has clearly been demonstrated to be a highly successful process and quality improvement method in the manufacturing industry (Womack and Jones 2003; Womack et al. 1990). Healthcare abounds with opportunities for improvement in quality, safety, efficiency, and appropriateness of care delivery. Organizations that oversee various perspectives of healthcare delivery, from quality and safety to economics and efficiency, recognize that delivery of healthcare can and should operate at a much higher level of performance. The practice of lean thinking has the potential for great application in the healthcare arena, where it may have a transformative effect on how care is delivered to our patients. Those able to adapt to the ways of lean healthcare methods can anticipate that they will benefit as an institution, but more importantly the "customers" will receive greater value in the form of higher quality, safer, more efficient, and more appropriate care, as those organizations focus on the "customers'" journey through the complex maze of the healthcare system.

As healthcare providers, we are rooted in the belief of scientific experimentation and evidence-based practice. Lean is designed to make work a series of experiments that immediately reveal problems. These problems can be acted upon rapidly to develop, implement, and disseminate a successful solution across the health system to work toward continuous improvement. This type of systemic learning based on sound theoretical and quantitatively driven change has been dubbed as "pragmatic science" (Berwick 2005) which we hope the scientific community will embrace for its capability to improve the delivery and practice of healthcare.

References

Berwick, D. M. (2005). Broadening the view of evidence-based medicine. *Quality & Safety in Health Care, 14*, 315–316.

Blackmore, C. C., Mecklenburg, R. S., & Kaplan, G. S. (2011). At Virginia Mason, collaboration among providers, employers, and health plans to transform care cut costs and improved quality. *Health Affairs (Millwood), 30*(9), 1680–1687.

Committee on Quality Health Care in America, Institute of Medicine. (2001). *Crossing the quality chasm: A new health system for the 21st century*. Washington, DC: National Academy Press.

Dohan, M., Xenodemetropoulos, T., & Tan, J. (2012). *Value stream mapping in lean healthcare: A brief introduction and application*. New York: Springer.

Holweg, M. (2007). The genealogy of lean production. *Journal of Operations Management, 25*(2), 420–437.

Institute for Healthcare Improvement. (2005). *Going lean in health care*. White Paper. Boston, MA: Institute for Healthcare Improvement, January and February 2005.

Kim, C. S., Spahlinger, D. A., Kin, J. M., et al. (2009). Implementation of lean thinking: One health system's journey. *Joint Commission Journal on Quality and Patient Safety, 35*(8), 406–413.

King, D. L., Ben-Tovim, D. I., & Bassham, J. (2006). Redesigning emergency department patient flows: Application of lean thinking to health care. *Emergency Medicine Australasia, 18*(4), 391–397.

Kohn, L. T., Corrigan, J., & Donaldson, M. S. (Eds.). (2000). *To err is human: Building a safer health system*. Washington, DC: National Academy Press.

Liker, J. K. (2004). *The Toyota way*. Madison, WI: McGraw-Hill.

Spear, S. J. (2005). Fixing health care from the inside, today. *Harvard Business Review, 83*(9), 78–91.

Thompson, D. N., Wolf, G. A., & Spear, S. J. (2003). Driving improvement in patient care: Lessons from Toyota. *Journal of Nursing Administration, 33*(11), 585–595.

Waldhausen, J. H., Avansino, J. R., Libby, A., et al. (2010). Application of lean methods improves surgical clinic experience. *Journal of Pediatric Surgery, 45*(7), 1420–1425.

Womack, J., & Jones, D. (1996). *Lean thinking. Banish waste and create wealth in your corporation*. New York: Simon and Schuster.

Womack, J. P., & Jones, D. T. (2003). *Lean thinking* (p. 396). New York: Free Press.

Womack, J. P., Jones, D. T., & Roos, D. (1990). *The machine that changed the world*. New York: Rawson Associates.

Chapter 5
Business Value of IT in Healthcare

Peter Haddad, Mark Gregory, and Nilmini Wickramasinghe

Abstract With the rapid increase of healthcare expenditures and the parallel increase of doubts about the efficiency of current healthcare systems, due to increasing number of medical incidents and problems, decision- and policy-makers in healthcare industry have started looking for adopting new management practices and strategies to reduce costs and increase healthcare quality, in other words, maximizing the value and minimizing waste. Investing more on information technology has been one of these new strategies. At the same time, lean thinking and Lean Six Sigma promises have been appealing for healthcare, after achieving good results in different industries. However, due to its uniqueness, healthcare industry should have its own definition of "value" as it extends this concept beyond the operational level to cover sociotechnical aspects. Thus, the role that information technology can play to facilitate business value, and later value, in healthcare is discussed in this chapter. Also, lean and Lean Six Sigma in healthcare and their link to business value of IT are to be discussed, on a quest to draw a road map to better IT investments in healthcare to improve value generating in this industry.

Keywords Information technology • Value • Business value of IT • Healthcare quality • Lean thinking • Lean Six Sigma

---

P. Haddad
School of Business IT and Logistics, RMIT University,
GPO Box 2476, Melbourne, VIC 3001, Australia
e-mail: peter.haddad@rmit.edu.au

M. Gregory
School of Electrical and Computer Engineering, RMIT University,
GPO Box 2476, Melbourne, VIC 3001, Australia
e-mail: mark.gregory@rmit.edu.au

N. Wickramasinghe, Ph.D., M.B.A. (✉)
Epworth HealthCare & Department of BITL & HIRi, RMIT University,
GPO Box 2476, Melbourne, VIC 3001, Australia
e-mail: nilmini.wickramasinghe@rmit.edu.au; nilmini.work@gmail.com

N. Wickramasinghe et al. (eds.), *Lean Thinking for Healthcare*, Healthcare Delivery in the Information Age, DOI 10.1007/978-1-4614-8036-5_5,

5.1 Introduction

Healthcare costs are skyrocketing around the world, which has made decision- and policy-makers in this massive industry look desperately for solutions to control these costs and enhance the medical procedures as much as possible. Investing in information technology has been shown as a key strategy to achieve this complex balancing. Thus, healthcare organizations have started investing, relatively heavily, in implementing information technology-based healthcare systems. This tremendous international trend to make the movement from the traditional healthcare to what has been known as "e-health" has motivated lots of researches to focus on the role that information technology can play to enhance the productivity in healthcare. However this interest came a bit late as too many healthcare organizations had started spending more and more on information technology with little to show for it in the output statistics.

Although there has been much work done in this area, measuring "the business value of IT" in healthcare is yet to be investigated. The concept of "business value of IT" has been a major point of interest and research in the last few decades, and it links the impact of IT and the organizational performance. This chapter introduces the implementing of this concept in healthcare and proposes a model to conceptualize the business value of IT in healthcare. That will be after briefing the economy of healthcare, healthcare delivery, the current state of information technology in health delivery, and summarizing the main features and elements of the concept of "business value of IT" in the light of prior research in this area. Finally, value and the lean thinking principles will be introduced, and how, and why, business value of IT in healthcare is so essential in such a paradigm will be discussed.

5.2 The Economy of Healthcare

The rising of health spending is much faster than incomes in most developed countries, which makes the question about how these countries will pay their health needs in the future a key to more studies and researches. The issue is particularly penetrating in the USA, where more per capita on healthcare is being spent and also one of the highest spending growth rates can be found. Although both public and private health expenditures are growing at rates which outpace comparable countries, according to the figures coming from the Organization for Economic Co-operation and Development (OECD), the USA does not achieve better outcomes on many important health measures, like the dangerous combination of high costs, irregular quality of care, frequent errors as well as limited access to care (Porter and Teisberg 2006).

In this section we use information from (OECD) to compare the level and growth rate of healthcare spending in the USA to those of other OECD countries.

Figure 5.1 and Table 5.1 show, respectively, (1) Total health expenditure per capita, in selected countries (2) Total Expenditure on Health as a share of GDP.

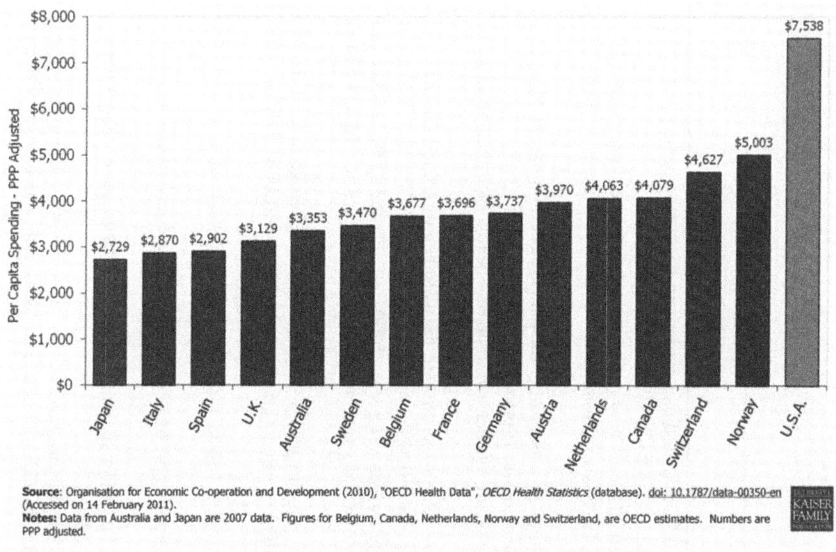

Fig. 5.1 Total health expenditure per capita, the USA and selected countries, 2008

Table 5.1 Total expenditure on health as a share of GDP

Country	1970 (%)	1980 (%)	1990 (%)	2000 (%)	2008 (%)
Australia	4.1	6.1	6.7	8.0	8.5
Austria	5.2	7.4	8.3	9.9	10.5
Belgium	3.9	6.3	7.2	9.0	11.1
Canada	6.9	7.0	8.9	8.8	10.4
France	5.4	7.0	8.4	10.1	11.2
Germany	N/A	N/A	N/A	10.3	10.5
Italy	N/A	N/A	7.7	8.1	9.1
Japan	4.6	6.5	6.0	7.7	8.1
The Netherlands	N/A	7.4	8.0	8.0	9.9
Norway	4.4	7.0	7.6	8.4	8.5
Spain	3.5	5.3	6.5	7.2	9.0
Sweden	6.8	8.9	8.2	8.2	9.4
Switzerland	5.4	7.3	8.2	10.2	10.7
UK	4.5	5.6	5.9	7.0	8.7
USA	7.1	9.0	12.2	13.4	16.0
Average	*5.2*	*7.0*	*7.8*	*9.0*	*10.1*

5.2.1 Different Healthcare Systems

This section will summarize in Table 5.2 three different healthcare systems: private healthcare (the USA as an example), public healthcare system (UK), and the 2-tier healthcare system which is a system, where, besides a guaranteed public health

Table 5.2 Different healthcare systems

HC system	Country	Description
Private	USA	In 2008, the USA had a total expenditure on healthcare (% GDP) of 16.0 %, and total expenditure on healthcare per capita (US$) was $7,538. Both figures are the highest value within the OECD countries (OECD 2010b)
		Healthcare coverage in the USA is partitioned between several payers. In 2008, 60 % of residents were covered through private insurers, while 24 % received their coverage from federal programs. Forty-six million residents had no insurance, which represented 15 % of the population
		The problem with the US healthcare system is not only the problem of high costs but rather the dangerous combination of high costs, irregular quality of care, frequent errors as well as limited access to care (Porter and Teisberg 2006)
Public	UK	The National Health Service (NHS) is the fundamental part of UK's healthcare system, while private health insurance plays a significantly smaller role
		In 2008, the UK had a total expenditure on healthcare (% GDP) of 8.7 %, which was close to the average ratio of the OECD countries. Furthermore, the UK's total expenditure on healthcare per capita (US$) was $3,129 (OECD 2010b)
		NHS provides a big variety of free healthcare services to UK's ordinarily residents (Greener 2009), reliable for 87 % of UK's total healthcare spending, while private health insurance accounted for 1 % of UK's total spending on healthcare according to 2006 figures
2-tier	Germany	In 2008, Germany had a total expenditure on health (% GDP) of 10.5 %, which was 1.5 % higher than the average ratio of the OECD countries. Concurrently, Germany's total expenditure on health per capita (US$) was $3,737, whereas the OECD countries spent on average $3,060 per capita (OECD 2010c)
		The healthcare actors in Germany are divided into enrollees, service providers (medical doctors, pharmacists, hospitals), and cost units (health insurance companies)
		Germany has around 82.14 million inhabitants, where around 70.23 million people have public health insurance and around 8.62 million people use a private health insurance
		In Germany, health insurance is compulsory for all citizens. Depending on factors like income and job status, the enrollees have either public or private health insurance (The Commonwealth Fund 2010)
		As of July 2009, the employee contributed 7.9 % of their gross wage, while the employer added 7.0 % on top of The gross wage, which is in total a premium of 14.9 % of each individual's gross wage. In addition, dependents like kids and spouses without income were also included (The Commonwealth Fund 2010)

Australia	In 2009, Australia had a total expenditure on health (% GDP) of 8.5 %, and in 2010 Australia's total expenditure on health per capita (US$) was $3,353 (OECD 2010b) The healthcare system in Australia consists of both a public and private component. The key feature is public health insurance under Medicare, which is funded by taxation. Here enrollees have the possibility to use subsidized medical services and pharmaceuticals as well as free of charge hospital treatment according to their status as a public health enrollee. Besides Medicare, Australian patients have the possibility to use, in addition, a private health insurance, which gives, for example, patients access to dental services and hospital treatment as a private patient (The Commonwealth Fund 2010) In 2007 till 2008, the governments funded 69 % of all health expenditures, while 43 % came from the Australian government and 26 % from State or Territory governments Since 1999, the Australian government has supported private health insurance by giving enrollees a rebate of 30 % of private health insurance premiums In mid of 2009, 44.6 % of Australia's population had a private hospital insurance; private health insurance is in Australia community rated, which means that "everyone pays the same premium for their health insurance" (Australian Government 2010) In 2007 till 2008, 16.8 % of Australia's health expenditures were out-of-pocket spending; examples are dental services and copayments on medical fees

insurance, a private healthcare system exists, which can have a substitutive or complementary function, and different factors like income and job status influence the classification of an enrollee (ArticlesBase.com 2009) (Germany and Australia).

5.3 Healthcare Delivery

Breakthroughs in medical science and innovations in clinical practices offer enormous opportunities and impressive improvements in the health and well-being of society. Returns on investments in these endeavors can be impressive. However, we will not realize the greatest returns unless we also better engineer the system of healthcare delivery (Rouse 2009).

5.3.1 The Enterprise of Healthcare

Consider the architecture of the enterprise of healthcare delivery shown below (Rouse and Cortese 2010). The efficiencies that can be gained at the lowest level (clinical practices) are limited by nature of the next level (delivery operations). For example, functionally organized practices are much less efficient than delivery organized around processes. Similarly, the efficiencies that can be gained in operations are limited by the level above (system structure). Functional operations are driven by organizations structured around specialties, e.g., anesthesiology and radiology. And, of course, efficiencies in system structure are limited by the healthcare ecosystem in which organizations operate. Differing experiences of other countries provide ample evidence of this (Fig. 5.2).

The fee-for-service model central to healthcare in the USA assures that provider income is linked to activities rather than outcomes. The focus on disease and restoration of health rather than wellness and productivity assures that healthcare expenditures will be viewed as costs rather than investments. Recasting of "the problem" in terms of outcomes characterized by wellness and productivity may enable identification and pursuit of efficiencies that could not be imagined within our current frame of reference (Rouse and Cortese 2010).

5.3.1.1 Defining Value

There is currently much commentary on two things in healthcare—universal availability and cost control. However, we do not think that people want the lowest cost, universally available healthcare system. We think the central issue should really be the creation of a healthcare system that provides the highest value (Rouse and Cortese 2010).

Value is often defined in terms of the benefits of the outcomes of expenditure, divided by the costs of the expenditure. The benefits of healthcare—from a

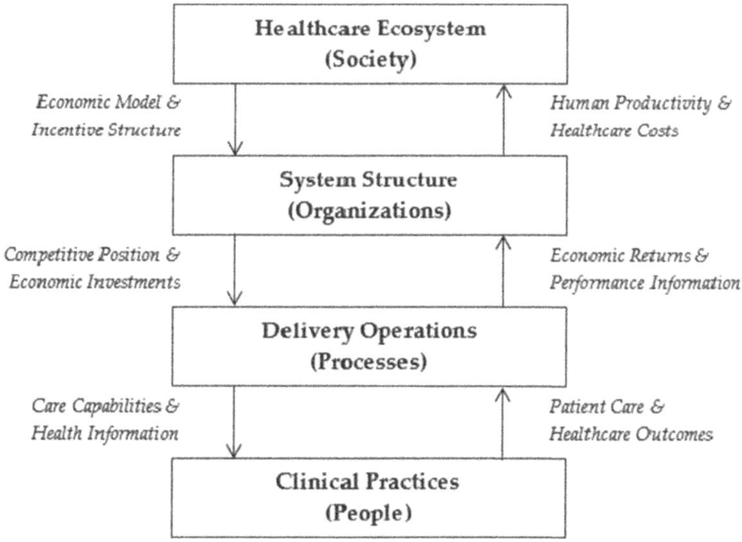

Fig. 5.2 The enterprise of healthcare delivery (Rouse and Cortese 2010)

patient's perspective—include the quality of health outcomes, the safety of the process of delivery, and the services associated with the delivery process (Porter and Teisberg 2006).

The benefits from the perspective of society also include the availability of healthy, productive people who contribute to society in a wealth of ways. When people are not healthy, these contributions are diminished. A recent study found that the cost of the lost productivity far exceeds the cost of the healthcare (DeVol et al. 2007).

For many reasons it is likely people will remain in the workforce longer than in the past (Rouse and Cortese 2010). In 1960s, before Medicare got started in the USA, the average age of death was 67; the average age at retirement was 65–66. By 2005, the average age of death had reached 75, and the average age of retirement was 62. We are now seeing some people planning on working longer, perhaps up to 70. Even Social Security has delayed the eligibility age for benefits, with the retirement age for people born after 1937 increasing to 66 if born before 1955 and up to 67 if born later.

If people in the USA who do not retire at the usual Social Security retirement age stay on employers' insurance, then employers will even have an increased interest in keeping people healthy for as long as possible and doing productive work for as long as possible until the worker retires and goes onto Medicare. Employer insurance companies are glad to see the older employees roll into Medicare for the same reasons; when the greater costs are incurred, it is the government's problem (Rouse and Cortese 2010).

Indeed, this is the exact reason some have proposed that people enrol in and own an insurance product and keep it even after they retire. That way the insurance company will now have an interest in keeping you as well as possible even after you retire, in other words, sun setting Medicare. A Federal Employees Health Care Plan model would facilitate this option (Rouse and Cortese 2010).

Thus, there will be an increasing need to keep people healthy because they will need to remain productive longer. More pervasive will be the need to keep everyone healthy and productive. Part of the value equation, therefore, should include the productivity in the future of all the workers that do not get diabetes or have heart attacks or cancer. For this to work, our value equation will have to account for future returns from today's investments.

5.3.2 Healthcare Delivery Systems: Current Challenges

According to (Reid and Compton 2010), large numbers of entities that operate collectively to meet a set of objectives are commonly referred to as "systems". Examples are telecommunications systems, trucking systems, and manufacturing systems. A well-designed, efficient operating system requires that the overall objectives be clearly understood by all elements of the system, that feedback loops be supported by good communications and control, and that some entity be in charge of the system and responsible for ensuring that its performance meets its stated goals. The main reason of this problem as (Reid and Compton 2010) believe is that healthcare delivery was never designed as a system and does not operate as one.

Statistics clearly indicate the magnitude of the task of improving the quality of healthcare delivery in the USA, for example. Every year, more than 98,000 Americans die, and more than one million patients are injured as a result of broken healthcare processes and system failures (Institute of Medicine 2005). The gulf between rapidly advancing medical knowledge base and its application to patient care is growing. According to one survey, 75 % of patients consider the healthcare system fragmented and fractured, a "nightmare" to navigate, and plagued by duplication of effort, lack of communication, conflicting advice regarding treatment, and tenuous links to the evolving medical evidence base (Picker Institute 2000).

Poor quality is costly (Reid and Compton 2010). David Lawrence estimates that \$.30 to \$.40 of every dollar spent on healthcare, more than a half trillion dollars per year, is spent on costs associated with "overuse, underuse, misuse, duplication, system failures, poor communication, and inefficiency" (Lawrence 2005). Meanwhile, healthcare costs have been rising by almost double digits (Table 5.1).

According to a study published back in 2001 by the American Institute of Medicine (IOM) *Crossing the Chasm: A New Health System for the 21st Century*, a committee of experts identified six interrelated characteristics of a healthcare delivery system that should guide efforts to improve the quality of care. The twenty-first century healthcare must be:

- Safe—avoiding injuries to patients from the care that is intended to help them
- Effective—providing services based on scientific knowledge to all who could benefit and refraining from providing service to those not likely to benefit (avoiding underuse and overuse, respectively)
- Patient-centered—providing care that is respectful of and responsive to individual patient preferences, needs, and values and ensuring that patient value guides all clinical decisions
- Timely—reducing waiting times and sometimes harmful delays for those who receive and those who give care
- Efficient—avoiding waste, including waste of equipment, supplies, ideas, and energy
- Equitable—providing care that does not vary in quality because of personal characteristics, such as gender, ethnicity, geographic location, and socioeconomic status

To meet these six objectives, the committee emphasized the role that engineering community can play to facilitate the complex process of transforming the healthcare delivery systems, each of which includes many aspects that are relevant to engineering, in terms of implementing ICT and other assets. For example, the meaning of efficiency can be broadened to include the optimization of operations, the reduction of costs, and the avoidance of errors; and "timely" healthcare delivery might include better scheduling of facilities and personnel (Reid and Compton 2010).

5.3.3 Information Technology for Healthcare Delivery

In a speech delivered in December 2008, then President-elected Obama pledged to "use information technology to lower the cost of healthcare; and invest $10 billion a year over the next 5 years to move the US healthcare system to broad adoption of standards-based electronic health information systems, including health records". The US Congress acted on this pledge by designating 519 billion for healthcare IT spending in the recently signed stimulus bill (Das et al. 2010).

Today, healthcare service providers benefit from different technologies so as to reduce cost and improve quality of the medical procedures (Gagnona et al. 2003). In particular, telemedicine resides on the center of these technologies. The American Telemedicine Association defines telemedicine as "the use of medical information exchanged from one site to another via electronic communications to improve patients' health status" (ATA 2009).

Telemedicine applications were used in a broad range including consultation (Berghout et al. 2007), education and training (Chen et al. 2008), and home care (Biermann et al. 2002).

Selecting the best telemedicine service among given ones is a complex task. The process needs considerations of trade-offs between cost and benefits of the service. Analytic Hierarchy Process (AHP) (Saaty 1996, 1997) is an outstanding method that can be used in multifactor decision-making environments. It presents a structured approach to determine individual weights of multiple attributes of a product or service so that they can be compared in a simple way. Then, it simplifies decision-making in the selection process. Recent technological developments enable advancements in delivery of medical services, appropriate healthcare at a reasonable cost, and access to quality healthcare in underserved areas in the medical sector. Telemedicine is one of these developments that "enable remote medical procedures and examinations between patients and medical providers via telecommunication technologies like the Internet, or telephone" (Al-Qirim 2007). Moreover, many previous researches show that compared to traditional medical care, telemedicine services present many benefits to the patients and physicians (van den Brink et al. 2005; Chae et al. 2001).

5.4 Business Value of Information Technology

This section will demonstrate in three interrelated subsections some of most important principles and concepts in delineating the idea of investigating the business value of IT in healthcare firms. First, a defining the concept of "Business Value of IT" through distillation will be given (Sect. 5.3.1), and then a brief summary of the IT portfolio and the proposed conceptual model will be introduced in (Sect. 5.3.2), and implementing the concept of business value of IT in healthcare firms will be explained in (Sect. 5.3.3).

5.4.1 Definition Through Distillation

When, several years ago, economists pointed out an apparent "productivity paradox" with respect to investments in information technology (IT), information systems (IS) professionals and academics had a rude awakening. The "fact" that organizations were spending more and more on information technology with little to show for it in the output statistics forced practitioners to redouble their efforts to justify investments in technology (Soh and Markus 1995).

The term IT business value is commonly used to refer to the organizational performance impacts of IT, including cost reduction, profitability improvement, productivity enhancement, competitive advantage, inventory reduction, and other measures of performance (Melville et al. 2004; Devaraj and Kohli 2003; Hitt and Brynjolfsson 1997; Kriebel and Kauffman 1988). For example, Mukhopadhyay et al. (1995, p. 138) refer to the "business value of IT" as the "impact of IT on firm performance" while Melville et al. (2004) define IT business value as "the organizational performance impacts of information technology at both the intermediate process level and the organization-wide level, and comprising both efficiency impacts and competitive impacts."

Information systems scholars have adopted diverse conceptualizations of information technology, extending beyond hardware and software to include a range of contextual factors associated with its application within organizations (Melville et al. 2004; Kling 1980; Markus and Robey 1987).

As always, seeking better theory is the first endeavor after reaching to mixed empirical results. Researchers believe that a productive approach is to move from the question of whether IT creates value to how, when, and why benefits occur or fail to do so (Melville et al. 2004). One of the first researchers to fill this theory gap was Weill (1992), who introduced the concept of "IT conversion effectiveness" to account for the failure of some of IT investments to reach the firm's bottom line. Since then, many researchers have proposed theoretical models that trace the path investment inputs take on the way to becoming the outputs of "productivity increases," "realized business value," "organizational performance improvements," and the like. The most recent evidence is that IT is associated with increased output (thus refuting the productivity paradox), but not with business value as measured by return on asset and return on equity (Brynjolfsson and Hitt 1996).

As a precise specification of what we mean by IT business value is dependent upon what we mean by IT, we briefly summarize the information technology portfolio that would be our base in developing, analyzing, and testing the proposed conceptual model.

5.4.2 Information Technology Portfolio

Like any investment portfolio, investing in information technology is made up of investments with different objectives—each with different risk-return profiles to be balanced to meet the goals of the firm (Weill and Broadbent 1998). The information technology portfolio of an organization is its entire investment in information technology, including all people dedicated to providing information technology services, whether centralized, decentralized, distributed, or outsources. The investments include all computers, telecommunication networks, data, software, training, programmers, support personnel, point-of-sale systems, database, and fax machines, whether integrated or standalone (Weill and Broadbent 1998) (Fig. 5.3).

Managers make decisions about information technology investments based on a cluster of factors, including capacities required now and in the future, the role of technology in the industry, the level of investments are viewed, and the role and history of information technology in the firm.

Principally, firms invest in information technology to achieve four fundamentally different management objectives: transactional, infrastructure, informational, and strategic (Weill and Broadbent 1998). Theses management objectives then lead to

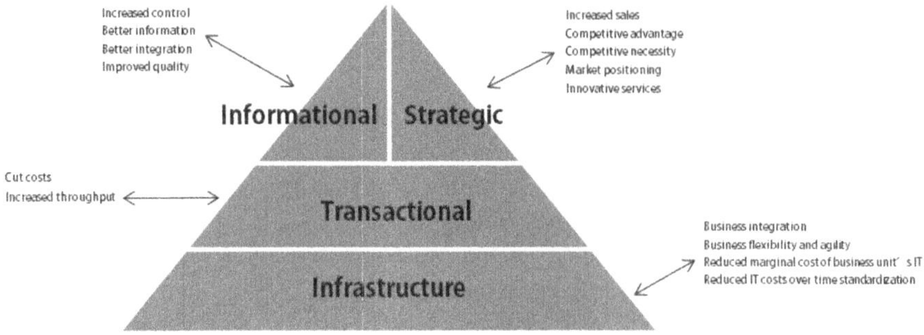

Fig. 5.3 Management objectives for the information technology portfolio (Weill and Broadbent 1998)

information, transactional, infrastructure, and strategic systems, which make up the information technology investment portfolio. Figure 5.4 depicts these different management objectives and their relationship as they form the information technology portfolio. Table 5.3 describes the objectives of this portfolio briefly.

5.4.3 Implementing of Business Value of IT in Healthcare Firms

Organizations, convinced that information technology (IT) provides business value, have been acquiring increasing amounts of IT capital over the past 2 decades. The average amount of IT investment varies considerably by industry. The healthcare industry, for example, has implemented IT relatively slowly (Memon et al. 2000). Only in the last few years have hospitals invested heavily in IT (Kettelhut 1992). Tremendous international interest in healthcare costs (Fuchs 1996) and conflicting results from IT productivity studies in other industries (e.g., Brynjolfsson and Yang 1996) motivate any sort of study on the value created by IT in the healthcare industry.

The healthcare informatics literature is relatively new. In the past decade, the healthcare industry has started to invest heavily in various healthcare information technologies to boost "quality of patient care," which has therefore been a major criterion variable for related studies on hospitals (Burke and Menachemi 2004). For example, Menachemi et al. studied the relationship between adoption of IT in healthcare and quality of care, and Solovy presented an evidence of lower mortality rates in hospitals having higher rates of technology adoption. Some studies have focused on the effects of adoption of a specific type of healthcare IT, such as electronic medical records (EMRs). Others are limited in their sample size; therefore, their results are not easily generalizable to the overall healthcare industry, e.g., studies on the effect of EMRs on performance at a psychiatric hospital, and on the effect of EMRs and computerized physician order entry on efficiency measures in an academic medical center. However, there is a dearth of studies on the business value of

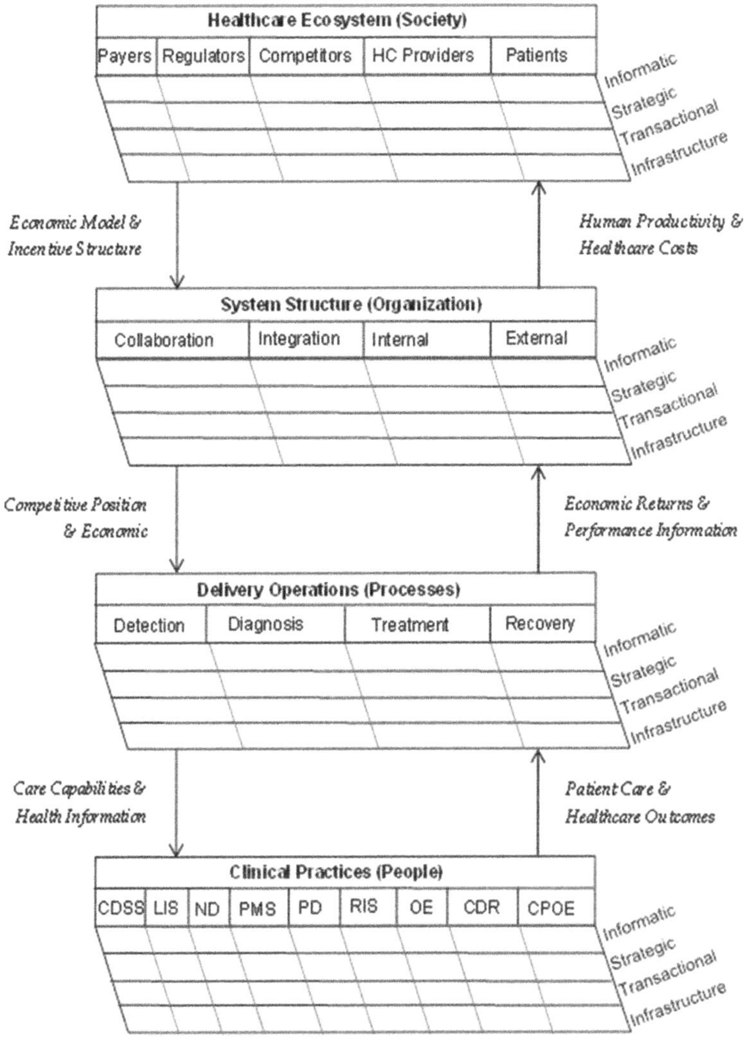

Key:

CDR: Clinical Data Repository
CDSS: Clinical Decision Support Systems
CPOE: Computerized Practitioner Order Entry
LIS: Laboratory Information Systems
ND: Nursing Documentation
OE: Order Entry
PMS: Pharmacy Management System
PD: Physician Documentation
RIS: Radiology Information Systems

Fig. 5.4 The proposed conceptual model

Table 5.3 The objectives of IT portfolio

Objectives	Description
Infrastructure	The foundation of information technology capacity which is delivered as reliable services shared throughout the firm and coordinated centrally, usually by the information technology group
	Include both the technical and the managerial expertise required to provide reliable services
	Having the required infrastructure services in place significantly increases the speed with which new applications can be implemented to meet new strategies, thus increasing the firm's strategic agility and flexibility
Transactional	Process and automate the basic, repetitive transactions of the firm. These include systems that support order processing, inventory control, bank cash withdrawal, statement production, account receivable, accounts payable, and other transactional processing
	Transactional systems aim to cut costs by substituting capital for labor or to handle higher volumes of transactions with greater speed and less unit cost. These systems build on and depend on a reliable infrastructure capacity
Informational	Provide information for managing and controlling the firm
	Systems in this category typically support management control, decision-making, communication, and accounting. These systems can summarize and report this firm's product and process performance across a wide range of areas
	Two examples of these systems come from Ford Australia (Electronic Corporate Memory) and from the consulting firm Bain & Company which developed Bain Resources Access for Value Addition (BRAVA)
Strategic	The objective of strategic technology investment is quite different from those of the other parts of the portfolio
	Strategic investments are made to gain competitive advantage or to position the firm in the marketplace, most often by increasing market share or sales
	Firms with successful strategic information technology initiatives have usually found a new use of information technology for an industry at a particular point at time
	Two good examples of these strategic initiatives are inventing automatic teller machines (ATMs) and designing a system that provides immediate 24-h, 7-day-a-week loan approvals in car dealerships using expert systems technology. Both of these innovative systems have changed their industries forever

investments in healthcare information technologies at the organizational level (Das et al. 2010).

One paper classifies hospital capital into three components: IT capital, medical capital, and medical information technology capital. IT capital includes data processing and communication capital (mainly for administrative purposes). Medical information technology capital includes equipment used for diagnosis and therapeutic purposes, i.e., to collect data from patients or report information to medical personnel (e.g., X-ray machines, magnetic resonance imaging). Medical capital consists of equipment used solely for therapeutic purposes (e.g., improvements in acute care wards or lasers). Labor is classified into two components; medical and IT labor. Productive capital is calculated as capital stock aggregated over the past several years using annual capital expenses. The validity of the capital stock measure requires a time window over the life expectancy of capital input at a minimum. Accordingly, researchers use an 18-year window (relatively long compared to prior research).

The methodology adopted for the study is the stochastic frontier approach. Since this approach assumes all production processes are inherently inefficient, the model parameters capture inefficiencies of the production process at the firm level (Devaraj and Kohli 2003). In addition to these research refinements, this paper adds to the existing literature in several ways.

Results obtained with these methodological refinements show that both IT and medical IT capital exhibit a positive influence on output. A positive mean marginal revenue contribution is also obtained for IT and medical IT capital investments. In addition, results indicate that IT labor and medical labor exhibit a positive influence on output as well as a positive impact on mean marginal revenue. However, the study finds that medical capital appears to be negatively associated with output during this time period. This finding may reflect hospitals' attempts to contain costs by substituting outpatient services for inpatient services, resulting in a decrease in length of stay for acute care wards (where medical capital is invested) and increasing outpatient visits for diagnostic tests and procedures (where medical IT capital is invested). Marginal revenue contribution of the inputs (in increasing order) is medical capital, IT capital, medical IT capital, medical labor, and IT labor. Medical IT capital contributed nearly 100 % more than IT capital, while labor components contributed over 200 % more than IT capital.

Similar to prior research that aggregates across various types of capital, this study is subject to problems that occur when the productivity impacts of different information technologies are averaged (Bryujolfsson 1993). When information technology is aggregated over mainframes, personal computers, and networks, the productivity impact of IT may be understated, since mainframes are frequently used past their accounting depreciation life and since the prices of PCs dropped over the period in question. Hospitals were slow in adopting new IT and most IT managers kept tight control over the mainframe installations, so IT capital was probably not replaced in a timely manner. While the lower prices of a unit of new IT and extended use of old IT may have somewhat balanced each other, the exact effects of these influences are difficult to gauge at this level of analysis.

Another paper (Das et al. 2010) develops a framework that disaggregates investments in IT in the healthcare industry into four distinct categories: investments in patient management IT (PMIT), transactional support IT (TSIT), communications IT (CIT), and administrative IT (AIT). It investigates two problems related to the effect of IT investments on productivity in a healthcare setting (as a branch from the tree of Service Industry)—the lag (i.e., when the effect is observed, which can be immediate, i.e., near term, or late) and the durability (i.e., duration of the effect, which can be short or long term).

Researchers tried to study the relationship between IT investments in healthcare and the overall performance, depending on two prior studies. First is a pioneering study by Weill which examined the lagged effect of different types of IT investments on four measures of performance. Using a sample of 33 small to medium-sized valve manufacturing firms, this study has found that only transactional IT had a positive association with some of the firm performance measures. On the other hand, Brynjolfsson and Hitt (1996) have studied the duration of the effect of IT investment. In their study of several hundred large firms, they have shown that investment in IT hardware has an effect on productivity and output growth that continues from the first year up to the sixth year, and that this effect is much greater over long periods. Focusing on the healthcare industry, there is sparse research on the lagged effect of IT. Devaraj and Kohli have shown the presence of lag in the effect of IT usage in the healthcare sector. In a field study using panel data from eight hospitals, they found that the improvement in hospital revenues after a decision-support application is implemented could be observed after a lag of 3 months for investments in IT labor and a lag of 4 months for investments in IT capital.

The authors of this paper conclude that:

1. Investing in IT in a healthcare setting is associated with improvements in several performance measures.
2. The suggested model reveals the types of healthcare IT investments that have an immediate effect and those that affect later.
3. Investing PMIT "may" increase operating cost intensity in hospitals, while having no effect on productivity.

5.5 Strategy and IT in Healthcare Firms

Strategy, as an art, science, and practice, has been a centerpiece of management and information technology (IT) literature and discussion for many years and will remain a major management concern for the foreseeable future (Glaser and Salzberg 2011). Effective strategies are key determinants of organizational performance, but developing effective strategies is difficult. A plethora of issues and approaches to assist in strategy formation have been developed over the years (Collis and Rukstad 2008).

5.5.1 Definition of Strategy

Strategy is the determination of the basic long-term goals and objectives of an organization, the adoption of the course of action, and the allocation of resources necessary to carry out those actions (Chandler 1962). Strategy seeks to answer questions such as, "Where does this organization need to go and how will it get there?" and "Where should it focus management attention and expenditures?" (Glaser and Salzberg 2011). The development of an organization's strategy has two major components: formulation and implementation (Henderson and Venkatraman 1993). Formulation involves making decisions about the mission and goals of the organization and the activities and initiatives it will undertake to achieve them.

In healthcare IT, there is a need for formulation, in keeping with an IT mission to use the technology to support improvement of the quality of care, maybe by having a goal to integrate clinical application systems.

Implementation involves making decisions about how to structure organizations, acquire skills, establish organizational capabilities, and alter organizational processes to achieve the goals and carry out the activities that have been defined during formulation of a strategy. For example, if reducing of care costs has been decided by reducing inappropriate procedure use, there will be a need to implement one or more of the following changes to the organization:

- An organizational unit of providers with health services research training to analyze care practices and identify deficiencies
- A steering committee of clinical leadership to guide these efforts and provide political support
- A provider order entry system to provide real-time feedback on order appropriateness
- Data warehouse technologies to support analyses of healthcare utilization

5.5.2 The Need for IT Strategy in Healthcare Firms

"If you don't know your target, you will not hit it." It looks 100 % true statement in linking IT investments and future vision. According to the previous definitions of business value of IT, there must be links between IT investments and organizational performance, and the main factor in determining how these investments are easy to justify would be how do they reflect positively on the overall performance. Thus, strategic planning in healthcare industry is needed to make such a bridge between the input (IT investments) and the outcomes (better medical care, higher standards of performance, safety, cost reduction, etc.). For example, an organization's decision to implement a computerized provider order entry system should reflect the organization's strategy of improving patient care. Developing sound strategy in these areas can be very important for one simple reason: if you define what you have to do incorrectly or partially correctly, you run the risk that significant organizational resources will be misdirected. This risk has nothing to do with how well you execute the direction you choose. Being on time, on budget, and on spec is of diminished usefulness if you are doing the wrong thing (Glaser and Salzberg 2011).

In addition, organizations can find it has failed to anticipate the future and its response to that future. When the future arrives (as it always does), the organization finds it is playing catch up with others who are capitalizing on the future. Catching up is a dangerous game; the organization may not catch up and lose, or the organization, in a fog of panic, may rush to catch up, waste money, and damage the organization in its haste. There are many times in IT activities in which the goal (or our approach to achieving the goal) is not particularly strategic; strategy formulation and implementation are not needed. Replacing an inpatient pharmacy system, enhancing help desk support, and upgrading an operating system, although requiring well-executed projects, do not always require that we engage in conversations of organizational goals or that we take a strategic look at organizational capabilities and skills. Often there is little likelihood that the way we achieve the goal will create a distinct competitive advantage. For example, an organization may decide it needs a common data network for its hospitals, clinics, and physicians' offices, but it does not expect that the delivered network, or its implementation, would be so superior to a competitor's network that it would confer an advantage on the organization (Glaser and Salzberg 2011).

Much of what IT does is not strategic, nor does it require strategic thinking. However, the fact that not all activities are strategic should not reduce the need for the IT organization to find the best technology and continuously improve its own performance (Glaser and Salzberg 2011).

5.6 The Proposed Conceptual Model

Based on the analysis of how IT business value researchers have treated the IT artifact, the predominant approach has been either (1) to use aggregate variables such as IT capital or counts of systems in quantitative empirical studies or (2) to take a holistic approach in exploring the interdependencies between IT and human resources in the creation of business value within case and field studies (Melville et al. 2004). Other researchers have attempted to develop a more generalized view of IT. For example, in their review and synthesis of quantitative empirical IT business value research, Dehning and Richardson (2002) identify three different formulations of IT: IT spending, IT strategy (type of IT), and IT management/capability. Likewise, Bharadwaj (2000) derives IT infrastructure, human IT resources, and IT-enabled intangibles such as customer orientation and knowledge as principal IT-based resources. Based on a survey of top IT executives at 50 firms, Ross et al. (1996) identify three IT assets underlying a firm's IT capability: human, technology, and relationship.

To operationalize the IT resource, from a technical perspective, we align with Weill and Broadbent's (1998) classification of IT portfolio into infrastructure IT, transactional IT, informational IT, and strategic IT (see Fig. 5.1). From an organizational perspective, this study will depend on The Enterprise of Healthcare Delivery Model (see Fig. 5.3) and adapt it to find the business value of information technology from a sociotechnical aspect in four interrelated levels: (1) clinical practices (people), (2) delivery operations (processes), (3) system structure (organizations), and (4) healthcare ecosystem (society). Figure 5.4 shows the proposed conceptual model for this research with a key that shows the definitions of clinical IT applications.

Although this conceptual model looks complicated and multilayered, it is expected to put the road map to study business value of the different layers of information technology in Weill's well-known model and in the four levels of the model of the enterprise of healthcare delivery. This study would benefit from the existence of these two models, and it will develop the use of them to start a new approach in evaluating how much healthcare firms get value from implementing information technology systems, solution, and resources. In this study we will examine the following:

- Layer 4: Healthcare Ecosystem (Society):
  - What is the impact of competition on business value of infrastructure IT
  - What is the impact of competition on business value of transactional IT
  - What is the impact of competition on business value of strategic IT
  - What is the impact of competition on business value of informational IT
- Layer 3: System Structure (Organization):
  - What is the impact of infrastructure IT on business value in terms of improving the system structure (internal and external)
  - What is the impact of transactional IT on business value in terms of improving the system structure (internal and external)
  - What is the impact of strategic IT on business value in terms of improving the system structure (internal and external)
  - What is the impact of informational IT on business value in terms of improving the system structure (internal and external)
- Layer 2: Delivery Operations (Processes):
  - What is the impact of infrastructure IT on business value in enhancing recovery processes
  - What is the impact of informational IT on business value in enhancing detection processes
  - What is the impact of transactional IT on business value in enhancing the diagnosis capabilities
  - What is the impact of strategic IT on business value in enhancing the treatment

- Layer 1: Clinical Practices (People):
  - What is the impact of transactional IT on business value in enhancing clinical practices, especially CPOE, LIS, and OE
  - What is the impact of informational IT on business value in enhancing clinical practices, especially CDR, CDSS, ND, and PD
  - The business value of infrastructure IT in enhancing laboratory and radiology practices (LIS and RIS)

5.7 Lean Thinking and Business Value of IT in Healthcare

In their book "Redefining Health Care: Creating Value-Based Competition on Results" (2006), Porter and Teisberg introduced a definition of "value" in healthcare industry in terms of the benefits of the outcomes of expenditure divided by the costs of expenditure. Furthermore, they stated that the benefits of healthcare—from a patient's perspective—include the quality of healthcare outcomes, the safety of the process of delivery, and the services associated with the delivery process (Porter and Teisberg 2006). Another perspective of "value" comes from the society, and it is based on the availability of healthy and productive people who will be able to contribute to society in a wealth of ways.

Thus, solving the conundrum of creating value in healthcare depends on maximizing these healthcare outcomes within the available resources which are limited, and scares in many cases. In other words, meeting the customer needs without waste through reconfiguring organizational processes (Womack and Jones 2003), which represents the heart of lean thinking, is a real challenge. Under these circumstances, the quest to explore the promises of lean thinking is compelling (Young and McClean 2008).

5.7.1 Lean Thinking and Value Creation

Value creation is seen as equal to cost reduction in lean thinking (Hines et al. 2004). As such, understanding of this concept will reinforce the understanding of lean thinking itself. According to this paper, after Womack and Jones (1996) had crystallized value as the first principle of lean thinking, lean moved away from a merely "shop-floor-focus" on waste and cost reduction, to an approach that contingently sought to enhance value (or perceived value) to customers by adding product or service features and/or removing wasteful activities. In other words, value was linked to customer requirements and no longer was simply defined through its opposite: waste. Figure 5.5 shows the interrelationship between value and cost, which states that the value is created in avenues: reducing waste (and activities produce waste) and increasing features and/or services being offered.

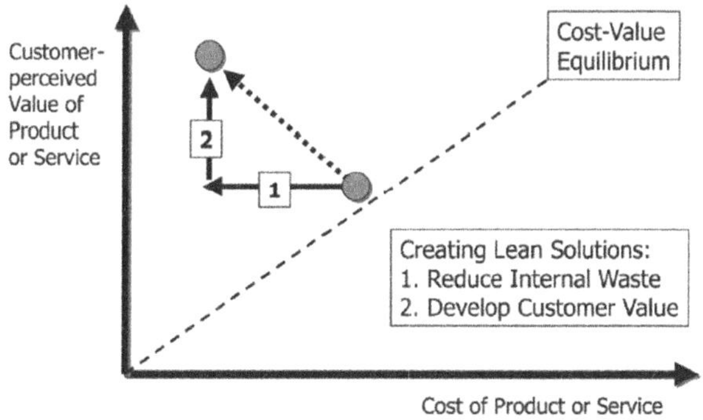

Fig. 5.5 Relation of value, cost, and waste (Hines et al. 2004)

5.7.2 Information Technology and Lean Thinking

Optimizing the organizational performance is claimed to be the target of implementing lean thinking from one side and pro-information technology on the other hand. However, a close look at the main principles of these two distinct solutions shows that they both depend on totally different principles. For pro-Lean, less is best. According to Piszczalski (2000) that means:

- Fewer inventories
- Less material movement
- Less floor space
- Less variability
- Fewer steps, options, and choices

On the other hand, information systems camp adopts more is best and goes for:

- More information
- More flexibility
- More functions
- More comprehensive business processes
- Faster and more frequent decision-making made by more people

Despite these massive differences between lean and Information Technology, the author encourages manufacturers to not adopt one of these strategies totally to the exclusion; rather, predicting that tomorrow's most successful manufacturers will learn how to artfully blend the best of both worlds to maximize productivity and quality and to minimize required resources, and that is exactly what happened, when lean extended from being an approach to optimize production to become lean enterprise where other business activities (e.g., product design, payments processing, order taking) are included (Bruun and Mefford 2003) and started using information technology to perform these crucial steps in the overall business activities.

Another paper (Bruun and Mefford 2004) demonstrates success stories from three different firms after using Internet and information systems to implement lean thinking; among these examples, Dell Computer Corporation looks unique in terms of the increases of sales, profit, and share prices, which all increased at astounding rates in the last few years after using IT to implement lean strategy. As a result of these observations, Internet and other information systems support the lean manufacturing principles, which results in a self-reinforcing development of broader business processes, like procurement, after-sales services, invoicing and payments, and even the adoption of virtual enterprises, cited to what Micheal Hammer (2001) urged that this success in cutting waste in internal operations should encourage looking beyond the wall of these organizations to streamline the process shared with other firms to form what he named it a "superefficient company."

5.7.3 Lean Thinking in Healthcare

Healthcare organizations have been investing considerable effort in the development and implementation of a variety of quality improvement initiatives, which include, for example, implementation of incident-reporting systems, risk management systems, quality assurance methods, and quality-oriented human resource management (Katz-Navon et al. 2007). At the same time, lean thinking has been appealing to be applied on healthcare to improve the outcomes. However, duplicating any management practice from first movers (first organizations to adopt it) is condemned to failure unless modified according to the unique conditions of the new adopting organizations (the organizations that adopt these practices later) (Kostova and Roth 2002; Tolbert and Zucker 1983). Applying this on lean thinking, as a management practice, classifies healthcare industry as a "second mover."

First movers, driven by a desire to improve performance, are mainly interested in technical efficiency, which results from the operating benefits of the practice and its effects on eliminating problems (Tolbert and Zucker 1983; Katz-Navon et al. 2007). On the other hand, second movers typically conform to institutional pressure, such as the demands of customers and the desire to appear as if they are keeping up with competitors. According to the institutional theory, the ultimate performance improvement belongs to the first movers because they implement a practice that fits their needs (Katz-Navon et al. 2007).

5.7.3.1 Lean Thinking in Healthcare: Sociotechnical Perspective

Although lean started originally on an operational aspect, lean theory nowadays extends to include human behavioral aspects and the interface between these two. It is argued now that for any lean effort to succeed, both a quality system (operational) and a quality culture (sociotechnical) are needed (Joosten et al. 2009; Hines et al.

2004; Osono et al. 2008; De Treville and Antonakis 2006; Savary and Crawford-Mason 2006). While much studies and researches have been done on the operational level of lean, research on sociotechnical dynamics in lean organizations, especially in healthcare, is virtually absent (Joosten et al. 2009).

Reports on lean-related improvements in healthcare have led some to conclude that "the lean message is 100 % positive (Joosten et al. 2009). Lean can improve safety and quality, improve staff morale, and reduce costs—all at the same time" (Jones and Mitchell 2006). However, the standards of this message are limited on operational level, with noticeable neglecting of sociotechnical aspects, which are crucial in healthcare. Joosten et al. (2009) suggest redefining lean thinking to include both operational and sociotechnical aspects urging the importance of such a trend to better understand the whole photo of lean.

5.7.4 Lean Six Sigma in Healthcare

During the past century, industry deployed a large arsenal of tools and innovation approaches to achieve high levels of operational efficiency (Koning et al. 2006). lean thinking and Six Sigma are two of these approaches that are being used widely in industry on a quest to improve customer satisfaction and quality, increase process speed, and reduce cost (Cheng and Chang 2012). These two management practices have been used in software development, administration and different contexts in service industry (Education, healthcare, etc.) although they were originally developed according to manufacturing settings.

In healthcare, Lean Six Sigma has received relatively good attention to discover its capabilities to improve healthcare outcomes. For example, (Koning et al. 2006) observed the implementation of Lean Six Sigma at The Red Cross Hospital in the Netherlands. In this case, the hospital started applying Six Sigma in 2002, and then deploying quality improvement QI on project to project basis, and third, the Lean Six Sigma approach was based on developing organizational competency for innovation by training a dedicated force for Lean Six Sigma project leaders. According to the authors, the application at the Red Cross Hospital provides an illustration of the significant benefits of the Lean Six Sigma approach in three dimensions: reducing complexity in hiring personnel, reducing operating theatres (OTs) starting times, and reducing maintenance costs by €200,000.

Another example on implementing Lean Six Sigma comes from Stanford Hospital and Clinics (George 2003), which started applying LLS mid-1980s, and had to increase profitability to sustain clinics' operations. Although no entire service vision was clear, this hospital could, after 10 years implementing quality system, develop flexible methods to improve outcomes through using flexible methods according to teams' needs and styles.

5.7.5 Discussion

Comparing the end goals of IT business value, lean and lean thinking shows that they are all "value-centric" and their ultimate aim is to maximize the value by reducing cost, improving profitability, productivity and enhancing competitive advantage. Thus, identifying the business value of IT in healthcare, and any other industry, will help better implementing of lean, by giving new indicators on IT whether it participates in generating value or it does not. It is really important to emphasize that business value of IT is not a value by itself; rather, it is a model that suggests the value that might be generated by implementing this sort of solutions or that. We think identifying the most value-generating areas in IT investments, which represents the heart of the proposed conceptual model, and later, will help lean implementers to better identify adding-value investments to be kept, and non-adding-values to be avoided after being tagged as Waste.

References

Al-Qirim, N. (2007). Championing telemedicine adoption and utilization healthcare organizations in New Zealand. *International Journal of Medical Informatics, 76*, 42–54.

ArticlesBase.com—McMillan. (2009). *Two-tier health care*. Retrieved November 20, 2011, from http://www.articlesbase.com/health-articles/twotier-health-care-1020480.html

American Telemedicine Association. (2009). What is telemedicine? Available online on: http://www.americantelemed.org/learn/what-is-telemedicine. Cited 23 June 2012.

Australian Government– Department of Health and Ageing. (2010). Private health insurance. http://www.health.gov.au/internet/main/publishing.nsf/Content/health-privatehealthconsumers-glossary.htm. Cited 15 November 2011.

Berghout, B. M., Eminovic, N., de Keizer, N. F., & Birnie, E. (2007). Evaluation of general practitioner's time investment during a store-and-forward teledermatology consultation. *International Journal of Medical Informatics, 76*, 384–391.

Bharadwaj, A. S. (2000). A resource-based perspective on information technology capability and firm performance: An empirical investigation? *MIS Quarterly, 24*(1), 169–196.

Biermann, E., Dietrich, W., Rihl, J., & Standl, E. (2002). Are there time and cost savings by using telemanagement for patients on intensified insulin therapy: A randomised, controlled trial. *Computer Methods and Programs in Biomedicine, 69*, 137–146.

Bruun, P., & Mefford, R. (2003). Lean production and the Internet. *International Journal of Production Economics, 89*, 247–260.

Bruun, P., & Mefford, R. (2004). Lean production and the Internet. *International Journal of Production Economics, 89*, 247–260. ISSN: 0925-5273.

Bryujolfsson, E. (1993). The productivity paradox of information technology. *Communications of the ACM, 36*(12), 66–77.

Brynjolfsson, E., & Hitt, L. (1996). Paradox lost? Firm-level evidence on the returns to information systems spending. *Management Science, 42*(4), 541–558.

Brynjolfsson, E., & Yang, S. (1996). Information technology and productivity: A review of literature. *Advances in Computers, 43*, 179–214.

Burke, D., & Menachemi, N. (2004). Opening the black box: Measuring hospital information technology capacity. *Healthcare Management Review, 29*(3), 207–217.

Chae, W., et al. (2001). Patient satisfaction with telemedicine in home health services for the elderly. *International Journal of Medical Informatics, 61*(2–3), 167–173. ISSN: 1386-5056.

Chandler, A., Jr. (1962). Strategy and structure: Chapters in the history of the American Industrial Enterprise. MIT.
Chen, I. J., Yang, K. F., & Tang, F. I. (2008). Applying the technology acceptance model to explore public health nurses' intentions towards web-based learning: A cross-sectional questionnaire survey. *International Journal of Nursing Studies, 45*, 869–878.
Cheng, C. Y., & Chang, P. Y. (2012). Implantation of the Lean Six Sigma framework in non-profit organisations: A case study. *Total Quality Management and Business Excellence, 23*(3–4), 431–447.
Collis, D. J., & Rukstad, M. G. (2008). Can you say what your strategy is? *Harvard Business Review, 86*(4), 82–90.
Das, S., Yaylacicegi, U., & Menon, N. M. (2010). The effect of information technology investments in healthcare: A longitudinal study of its lag, duration, and economic value. *IEEE Transactions on Engineering Management, 58*(1), 124–140.
De Treville, S., & Antonakis, J. (2006). Could lean production job design be intrinsically motivating? Contextual, configurational and levels-of-analysis issues. *Journal of Operations Management, 24*, 99–123.
Dehning, B., & Richardson, V. J. (2002). Returns on investments in information technology: A research synthesis? *Journal of Information Systems Management, 16*(1), 7–30.
Devaraj, S., & Kohli, R. (2003). Performance impacts of information technology: Is actual usage the missing link. *Management Science, 49*(3), 273–289.
Devaraj, S., & Kohli, R. (2003). Information technology payoff in the healthcare industry: A longitudinal study. *Journal of Management Information Systems, 16*(4), 41–67.
DeVol, R., Bedroussian, A., Charuworn, A., Chatterjee, A., Kim, I., Kim, S., et al. (2007). *An unhealthy America: The economic burden of chronic disease*. Santa Monica, CA: Milken Institute.
Fuchs, V. R. (1996). Economics, values, and health care reform. *American Economic Review, 86*(1), 1–24.
Gagnona, M. P., Godinb, G., Gagnéb, C., Fortina, J. P., Lamothec, L., Reinharza, D., et al. (2003). An adaptation of the theory of interpersonal behaviour to the study of telemedicine adoption by physicians. *International Journal of Medical Informatics, 71*, 103–115.
George, M. L. (2003). *Lean Six Sigma for services*. New York: McGraw-Hill.
Glaser, J. P., & Salzberg, C. (2011). *The strategic application of information technology in healthcare organizations*. San Francisco: Jossey-Bass.
Greener, I. (2009). *Healthcare in the UK: Understanding continuity and change*. Bristol: The Policy Press.
Hammer, M. (2001). The superefficient company. *Harvard Business Review, 79*(8), 82–91.
Henderson J., & Venkatraman N. (1993). Strategic alignment: leveraging information technology for transforming organizations. *IBM Systems Journal, 32*(1).
Hines, P., Holweg, M., & Rich, N. (2004). Learning to evolve: A review of contemporary lean thinking. *International Journal of Operations & Production Management, 24*(10), 994–1011.
Hitt, L., & Brynjolfsson, E. (1997). Information technology and internal firm organization: An exploratory analysis. *Journal of Management Information Systems, 14*(2), 81–101.
Institute of Medicine. (2005). *Building a better delivery system: A new engineering/health care partnership*. Washington, DC: National Academy Press.
Institute of Medicine—Committee on Quality of Healthcare in America. (2001). *Crossing the quality chasm: A new health system for the 21st century*. Washington, DC: National Academy Press.
Jones, D., & Mitchell, A. (2006). *Lean thinking for the NHS*. London: NHS Confederation.
Joosten, T., Bongers, I., & Janssen, R. (2009). Application of lean thinking to healthcare: Issues and observations. *International Journal for Quality in Healthcare, 21*(5), 341–347.
Katz-Navon, T., Naveh, E., & Stern, Z. (2007). The moderate success of quality of care improvement efforts: Three observations on the situation. *International Journal for Quality in Healthcare, 19*, 4–7.

Kettelhut, M. C. (1992). Strategic requirements for IS in the turbulent healthcare environment. *Journal of Systems Management, 43*(6), 6–9.

Kling, R. (1980). Social analysis of computing: Theoretical perspectives in recent empirical research. *Computing Surveys, 12*(1), 61–110.

Koning, H. D., Verver, J. P. S., van den Heuvel, J., Bisgaard, S., & Does, R. J. M. M. (2006). Lean Six Sigma in healthcare. *Journal for Healthcare Quality, 28*(2), 4–11.

Kostova, A., & Roth, K. (2002). Adoption of organizational practice by subsidiaries of multinational corporations: Institutional and relational effects. *Academy of Management Journal, 45*, 215–233.

Kriebel, C., & Kauffman, R. (1988). *Measuring and modeling the business value of information technologies*. Washington, DC: ICIT Press.

Lawrence (2005). National Academy of Engineering (US) and Institute of Medicine (US) Committee on Engineering and the Health Care System; Reid PP, Compton WD, Grossman JH, et al., editors. Building a Better Delivery System: A New Engineering/Health Care Partnership. Washington (DC): National Academies Press (US); 2005. Bridging the Quality Chasm. Available from: http://www.ncbi.nlm.nih.gov/books/NBK22849/.

Markus, M. L., & Robey, D. (1987). Information technology and organizational change: Causal structure in theory and research. *Management Science, 34*(5), 583–598.

Melville, N., Kraemer, K., & Gurmaxani, V. (2004). Review: Information technology and organizational performance: An integrative model of IT business value. *MIS Quarterly, 28*(2), 283–322.

Memon, N. M., Lee, B., & Eldenburg, L. (2000). Productivity of information technology in the healthcare delivery. *Information Systems Research, 11*(1), 83–92.

Mukhopadhyay, T., Kekre, S., & Kalathur, S. (1995). Business value of information technology: A study of electronic data interchange. *MIS Quarterly, 19*(2), 137–156.

OECD. (2010b). OECD health data 2010. http://stats.oecd.org/Index.aspx?DatasetCode=HEALTH. Cited 27 September 2011.

OECD. (2010c). OECD-Gesundheitsdaten 2010: Deutschland im Vergleich. http://www.oecd.org/dataoecd/15/1/39001235.pdf. Cited and translated into English 3 October 2011.

Osono, E., Shimizu, N., Takeuchi, H., et al. (2008). *Extreme Toyota: Radical contradictions that drive success at the world's best manufacturer*. Hoboken, NJ: Wiley.

Picker Institute. (2000). *Eye on patients: A report by the Picker Institute for the American Hospital Association*. Boston, MA: Picker Institute.

Piszczalski, M. (2000). Lean vs. information systems. *Automotive Manufacturing & Production, 112*(8), 26–28.

Porter, M., & Teisberg, E. (2006). *Redefining health care: Creating value-based competition on results*. Boston: Harvard Business School Press.

Reid, P. P., & Compton, W. D. (2010). *Handbook of healthcare delivery system, Chapter 2*. Boca Raton, FL: CRC Press.

Ross, J. W., Beath, C. M., and Goodhue, D. L. (1996). Develop long-term competitiveness through IT assets? *Sloan Management Review, 38*(1), 31–42.

Rouse, W. B. (2009). Engineering perspectives on healthcare delivery: Can we afford technological innovation in healthcare? *Journal of Systems Research and Behavioural Science, 26*(2009), 1–10.

Rouse, W. B., & Cortese, D. A. (2010). *Engineering the system on healthcare delivery*. Amsterdam: IOS Press.

Saaty, T. L. (1996). *The analytic hierarchy process*. Pittsburgh: RWS Publications.

Saaty, T. L. (1997). A scaling method for priorities in hierarchical structures. *Journal of Mathematical Psychology, 15*, 234–281.

Savary, L., & Crawford-Mason, C. (2006). *The Nun and the Bureaucrat: How they found an unlikely cure for America's Sick Hospitals*. Washington, DC: CC-M Productions.

Soh, C., and Markus, M.L. (1995). How IT creates business value: A process theory synthesis. *Proceedings of the Sixteenth International Conference on Information Systems* (pp. 29–41). Amsterdam, The Netherlands.

The Commonwealth Fund. (2010). *International profiles of health care systems*. http://www.commonwealthfund.org/~/media/Files/Publications/Fund%20Report/2010/Jun/1417_Squires_Intl_Profiles_622.pdf. Cited 3 April 2012.

Tolbert, P. S., & Zucker, L. G. (1983). Institutional sources of change in the formal structure of organizations: The diffusion of civil service reform, 1880–1935. *Administrative Science Quarterly, 28*(1), 22–39.

van den Brink, J. L., Moorman, P. W., de Boer, M. F., Pruyn, J. F. A., Verwoerd, C. D. A., & van Bemmel, J. H. (2005). Involving the patient: A prospective study on use, appreciation and effectiveness of an information system in head and neck cancer care. *International Journal of Medical Informatics, 74*, 839–849.

Weill, P. (1992). The relationship between investment in information technology and firm performance: A study of valve manufacturing sector. *Information Systems Research, 3*(4), 307–333.

Weill, P., & Broadbent, M. (1998). *Levering the new infrastructure: How market leaders capitalize on information technology*. Cambridge, MA: Harvard Business School Press.

Womack, J., & Jones, D. T. (1996). *Lean thinking: Banish waste and create wealth for your corporation*. New York, NY: Simon and Schuster.

Womack, J. P., & Jones, D. T. (2003). *Lean thinking* (2nd ed.). New York: Free Press.

Young, T., & McClean, S. (2008). A critical look at lean thinking in healthcare. *Quality & Safety in Health Care, 17*, 382–386.

Chapter 6
Initiatives of Service-Oriented Architecture Towards Performance Improvement in Healthcare

Fatemeh Hoda Moghimi and Nilmini Wickramasinghe

Abstract In healthcare contexts, performance improvement is always one of the top priorities for stakeholders. The performance improvement history demonstrates outcomes of applying lots of techniques and approaches to enhance performance in different healthcare dimensions. However, due to the increasing use of computer-based solutions in healthcare, performance of technology solutions has been also a critical dimension which should be improved. Therefore, considering the importance of healthcare technology solutions performance, this chapter outlines how service-oriented architecture can facilitate performance improvement using well-known methods of Lean Thinking. In addition, this study tries to identify key architectural requirements in order to propose a conceptual model based on key concepts of these methods.

Keywords Performance improvement • SOA (service-oriented architecture) • Lean thinking • Service-oriented enterprise (SOE)

F.H. Moghimi
School of Business IT and Logistics, RMIT University, Research Institute, Epworth HealthCare, GPO Box 2476, Melbourne, VIC 3001, Australia
e-mail: fatemeh.moghimi@rmit.edu.au

N. Wickramasinghe (✉)
Epworth HealthCare & Department of BITL & HIRi, RMIT University, GPO Box 2476, Melbourne, VIC 3001, Australia
e-mail: nilmini.wickramasinghe@rmit.edu.au

N. Wickramasinghe et al. (eds.), *Lean Thinking for Healthcare*, Healthcare Delivery in the Information Age, DOI 10.1007/978-1-4614-8036-5_6,

6.1 Introduction

Over the last few years, web services and the service-oriented architecture (SOA) have become main themes in IT across many industries (Rajini et al. 2012). SOA can be defined as a framework to integrate business processes and supporting IT infrastructures into secure, standardized components services that can be reused and combined to address changing business activities and priorities (Bieberstein et al. 2006). Gens believes the goal of investing in SOA is to be a fully deployed service-oriented enterprise (SOE) in integrating internal and external processes and services—processes of the firms as services (Gens 2009). The SOA is considered as highly suitable for a new software design model for the healthcare industry (Chu 2005).

SOA for healthcare integration helps healthcare organizations lower operating costs and speeds time-to-market by delivering a consistent user interface, management console, and monitoring environment, as well as healthcare libraries and templates for healthcare customer projects (Rajini et al. 2012).

Smith's study in 2009 presents that more than half of business sectors investing in SOA have had anticipated or more than expected benefits and less than half have had less than expected benefits or have not deployed it on operational systems, as demonstrated in Fig. 6.1.

A literature analysis conducted by Lawler and Joseph (2011) examines Levels of Maturity of SOA in 15 business firms of the 2010 and 2007 case studies and literature studies (Fig. 6.2).

As presented in Fig. 6.2, more SOA studies in 2007 and 2010 are related to deployment and exploitation of services based on SOE while in the other firms the most conducted studies in the same years are regarding the process integration, service architecture, restructuring of organization, and expansion of web services.

In analyzing and continually enhancing fundamental activities of the operation of business firms, the program management methodology is defined by Lawler and Howell-Barber (2008). It is a disciplined Methodology for Enabling Service-Oriented Architecture (Fig. 6.3), described in frameworks of best practices of governance, communication, product realization, project management, architecture, data management, service management, human resource management, and post-implementation on initiatives or projects of SOA (Lawler and Joseph 2011).

Table 6.1 describes the significant role of these frameworks to explore the SOA strategies or techniques in different firms.

SOA infrastructures have clearly matured and are at different stages of delivering on the promise of cost savings, efficiency, and business results (Ellis 2010). However, healthcare organizations are still in various stages of evolution of emerging SOAs without any deployed outcomes in this context. Therefore, in an attempt to overcome this issue we propose to identify key service-oriented architectural requirements in healthcare context in order to enhance care performance.

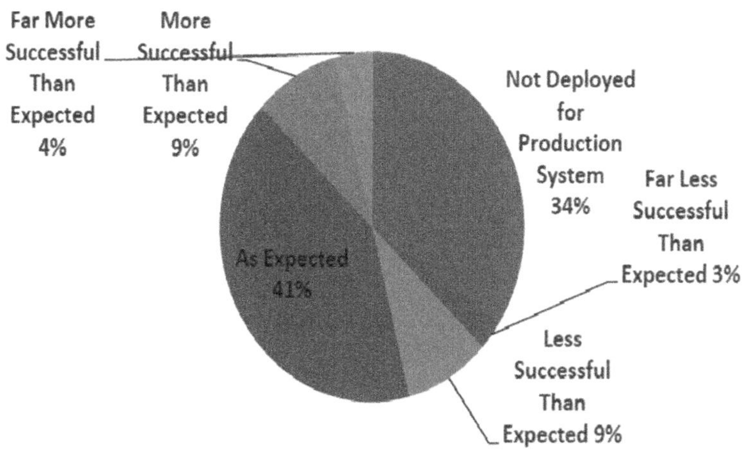

Fig. 6.1 Impact of SOA deployment in different business sectors (adapted from Smith 2009)

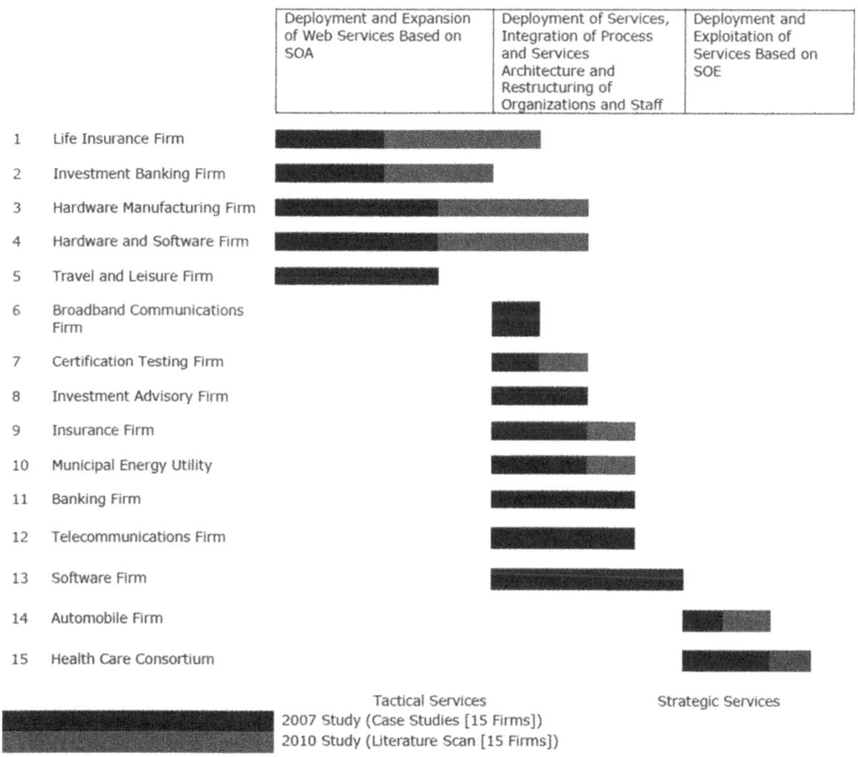

Fig. 6.2 Levels of maturity of SOA (adapted from Lawler and Joseph 2011)

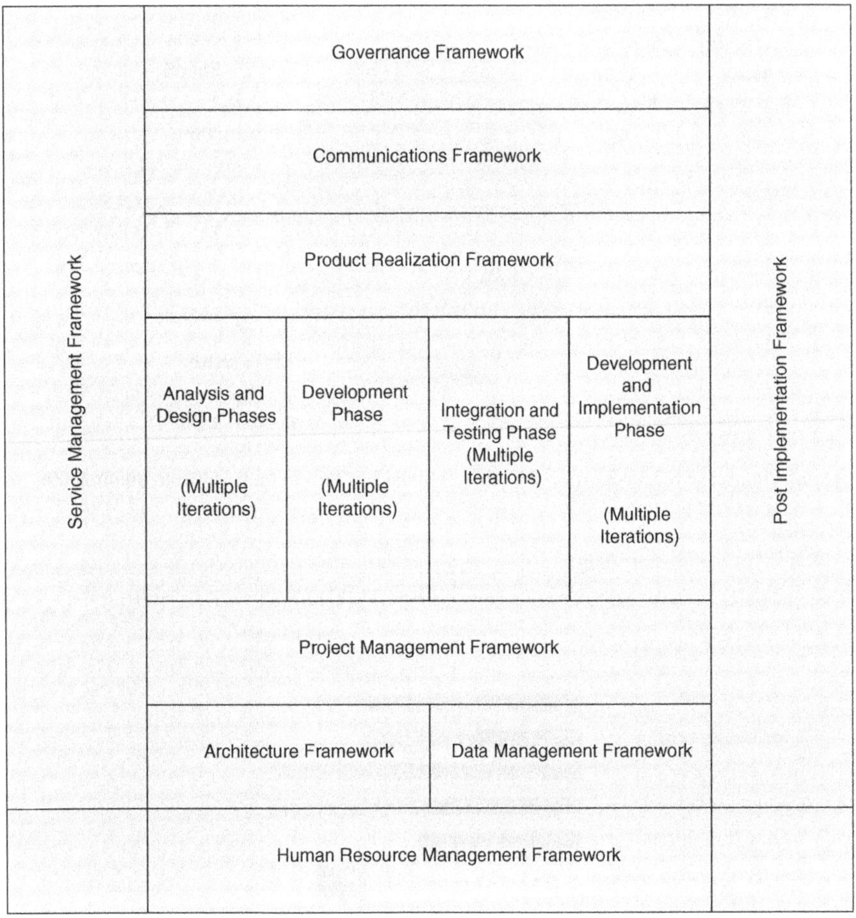

Fig. 6.3 Frameworks of the program management methodology (adapted from Lawler and Joseph 2011)

6.2 The Need for SOA in Healthcare Context

The aim of health information systems is primarily to contribute to a high-quality and efficient patient care system (Haux et al 2004). This aim is centered towards the patient, so it is first and foremost a patient-centered approach and then focuses on medical and nursing care, while the administrative and management tasks must support and facilitate such care (Haux 2006). However, besides increasing the number of information systems, some issues are also developing such as:

- Lack of interaction between these systems
- Duplications

Table 6.1 Frameworks of program management methodology towards SOA deployment (adapted from Lawler and Howell-Barber 2008)

Frameworks	Impacts to SOA deployment
Governance	Enables alignment of processes and services with business strategy and results in evolution towards SOE
	Ensures services conform to consistent corporate SOA strategy supporting business strategy of firm
	Facilitates learning of program management methodology
Communications	Enables emphasis on business criticality of SOA of business firm, articulated by Chief Information Officer (CIO), if not Chief Executive Officer (CEO)
	Ensures collaboration of business and technical staff in continued plan on endeavor, coupled
	Enables emphasis on business criticality of SOA of business firm, articulated by Chief Information Officer (CIO), if not Chief Executive Officer (CEO)
Product/service realization	Enables analysis and design, development, integration and testing, and deployment and implementation of SOA and is core of established project management methodology
	Is coupled with other frameworks and ensures focus of projects is on business processes to be evolved into SOA and not on technology
	Program to be realized may be implemented in interlinked iterations of internal department application projects to external firm process integration projects
Project management	Enables delivery of projects of SOA
	Ensures changes in business strategy are applied as appropriate on projects of SOA
	Ensures processes and services are functioning and implemented as planned in strategy
Architecture	Enables compliance of business processes with SOA model
	Ensures evolution from conversion of functions into services, creation of component services and integration into composite services, integration of internal applications, internal services and external services, to on-demand services in a gradual SOE
	Ensures seamless integration of hardware and software conforming to service standards and technology
Data management	Enables behaved SOA data services not disruptive of applications of firm
	Enables implementation of services, based on access, availability, breath and accuracy of data already in databases of applications
	Ensures consistency of data

(continued)

Table 6.1 (continued)

Frameworks	Impacts to SOA deployment
Service management	Enables continued conformity and coordination of processes and services to business strategy
	Is coupled with product realization on new projects of SOA and ensures requirements for new processes and new services, or revisions to them, are not redundant with existing processes or services
	Ensures reusability of services
Human resource management	Enables identification of new and revised responsibilities and roles of business and technical staff on SOA
	Ensures education of business and technical staff on change in culture of service orientation, and technical staff on technology of SOA, is furnished throughout projects of SOA
Post implementation	Enables service and process life cycle tasks following product realization
	Ensures availability of applications and services and of technologies, tools and utilities of SOA
	Is formulated in Service Level Agreements (SLA) between technology department, internal business departments and business units

- Lack of integrated systems
- Lack of a clinical information flow between the system users
- Lack of aggregations

Therefore to address these issues, SOA towards SOE appears to be a prudent technological solution to make a robust architecture obtaining the best care outcomes. To design the healthcare SOA, a managerial approach should be used as a lens to find the value stream of IT solutions in healthcare and make sure what the main components of this architecture are. As the critical starting of "Lean Thinking" is value and value stream with the aim of increasing performance and efficiency (Womak and Jones 1996), it is interesting to investigate how a lean approach can be used to capture the main requirements of healthcare SOA.

6.3 Lean Approach

Womak and Jones (1996) describe lean using five principles: precisely specify value by specific product/service, identify the value stream for each product/service, make value flow without interruption, let the customer pull value from the producer, and pursue perfection (Womak and Jones 1996).

Hines redefined those original principles into a new holistic framework known as the 8Ps of the Lean Business System. This framework helps companies in any industry and at any stage of Lean maturity to reflect on how they are deploying Lean in their business (Hines 2010) (Fig. 6.4).

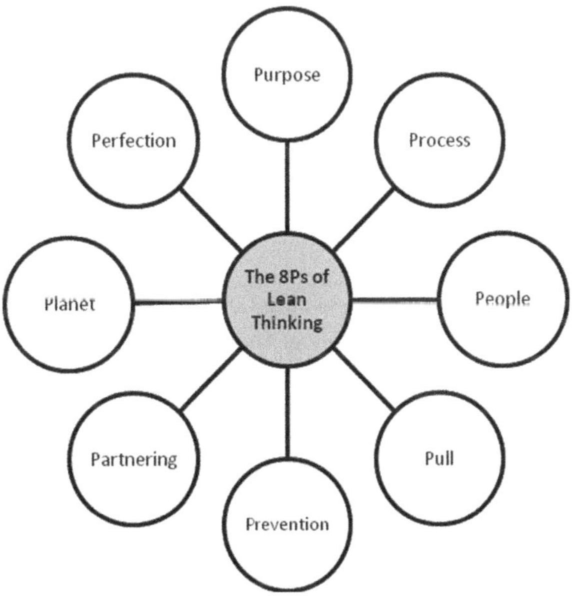

Fig. 6.4 The 8Ps of the lean business system (adapted from Hines 2010)

This new 8Ps approach is focused on purpose, process, people, pull, prevention, partnering, planet, and finally perfection, as described below:

- *Purpose*: Achieving an effective and sustainable purpose, before starting any activity by focusing on the voice of the owner, voice of the customer, voice of the employer, and voice of the society (Hines 2010).
- *Process*: Lean, as an approach to deliver improved customer service and waste reduction, should deliver an optimal balance between these two areas by improving a range of processes such as order creation and innovation as well as improving customer values (Hines 2010).
- *People*: Developing a culture of continuous improvement with respect for people (Liker 2004) to the success and sustainability of any lean transformation (Hines 2010).
- *Pull*: There are three main areas of pull that are necessary to consider within a lean business system as pull-based delivery, pull-based improvement, and pull-based training.
- *Prevention*: Focusing on preventing variation, problems, and subsequent rework of quality failures for the customer within the tool house of lean as presented in Fig. 6.5.
- *Partnering*: The leading practitioners of lean worldwide such as Toyota and Tesco have also heavily focused on creating a high-performing supply chain as a key competitive advantage.
- *Planet*: Womak and Jones (1996) stated "lean thinking must be green because it reduces the amount of energy and wasted by products required to produce a given product… ." Therefore respect to environment is also the other important approach in lean thinking.
- *Perfection*: Organizations, to improve their performance level should create ideal state through envisioning their most advanced position. This process calls moving forward towards perfection as presented in Fig. 6.5.

Considering the role of the 8Ps in the lean approach in order to reduce wastes and value creation, it is also crucial to understand the seven wastes in healthcare contexts (Black and Miller 2008) which include:

1. Overproduction (e.g., ordering of duplicate tests)
2. Wasting time (e.g., patients waiting for treatments)
3. Waste of stock on hand (e.g., medications and other items that are stored but not used and then must be disposed of)
4. Waste of movement (e.g., time spent walking from one location to another)
5. Waste of defective products (e.g., misinformation or recording of wrong information on patient record)
6. Waste in transportation (e.g., moving patient unnecessarily)
7. Waste in processing (e.g., duplication of forms and redundant capture of information)

As described above, these seven wastes already are captured in healthcare contexts and can be addressed through adopting a lean approach.

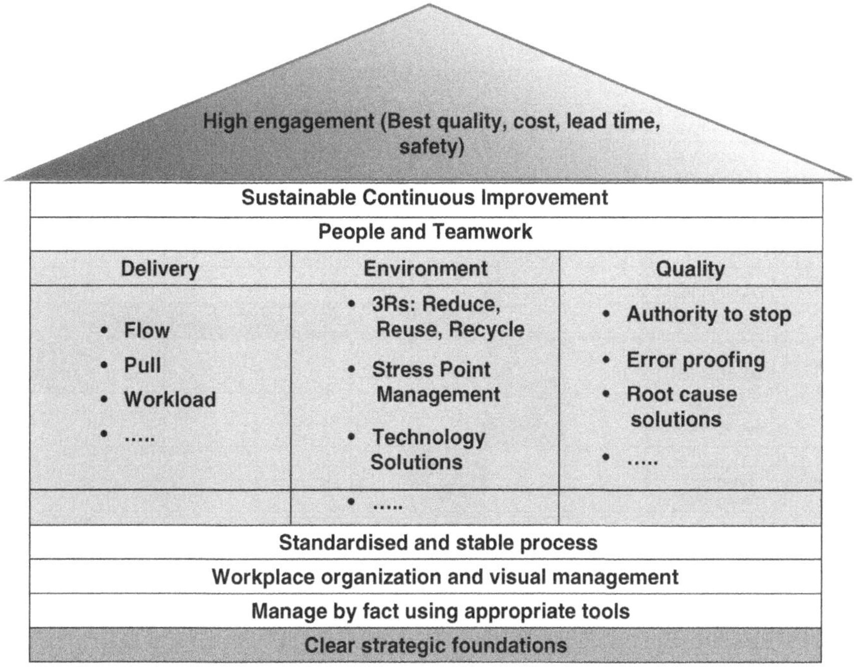

Fig. 6.5 Key tools of lean (adapted from Hines 2010)

6.4 Conceptualization

Regarding the aim of this study, the focus is on investigating how a lean approach can facilitate SOA architecture in healthcare contexts to improve mentioned issues. The objectives of the healthcare SOA architecture in our study are:

- To improve the interaction between current and future systems developing in the healthcare contexts
- To remove duplications in different clinical systems in various care environment
- To build a robust platform of integrated healthcare systems
- To improve the clinical information flow between the system users
- To make aggregations in the best way to make a well-designed e-health

Moreover, we also would like to understand how our healthcare SOA architecture may reduce seven wastes implicitly to improve care performance as followed:

- To reduce wastes through overproduction
- To reduce wasting time
- To reduce waste of stock on hand
- To reduce waste of movement

Table 6.2 A matrix to present how lean 8Ps can be applied to the healthcare SOA using frameworks of program management methodology

	8Ps	1P	2P	3P	4P	5P	6P	7P	8P
	Frameworks	purpose	process	people	pull	prevention	partnering	planet	perfection
1F	Governance	■						■	
2F	Communications			■	■		■		
3F	Product/service Realization		■						
4F	Project Management		■						■
5F	Architecture		■	■		■	■	■	■
6F	Data Management		■						■
7F	Service Management		■						
8F	Human Resource Management			■					
9F	Post Implementation								■

- To reduce waste of defective products
- To reduce waste in transportation
- To reduce waste in processing

Through the matrix below, the relation between 8Ps (Fig. 6.4) and frameworks of Program Management Methodology towards SOA deployment (Table 6.2) are presented to capture the main components and frameworks of healthcare SOA towards care performance.

6.5 Discussion and Conclusion

Although designing and developing new technology solutions for healthcare context has been encouraged significantly, increasing the number of systems is highly likely to create some new challenges in this context. Duplications, lack of systematic interactions, and lack of information flow are some potential issues that would be raised up by increasing the computer-based care solutions. Hence, developing a healthcare SOA would be a solution to make a robust platform to develop future solution compatible with this platform. To develop the healthcare SOA, using lean approach is proposed to improve the care performance through creating values as well as reducing wastes. Hence, in this study it is tried to understand how healthcare SOA can be developed using adopting the lean approach.

Considering the developed matrix (Table 6.2), it is anticipated that lean 8Ps can be applied to design the healthcare SOA to address defined explicit and implicit objectives of the healthcare SOA, as followed examples:

- 1P/1F: It means "purpose" through the lean approach by using "Governance" framework:
  - Enables alignment of processes and services with business strategy and results in evolution towards SOE
  - Ensures services conform to consistent corporate SOA strategy supporting business strategy of firm

  By:

  - Developing a set of KPIs
  - Aligning the organization

  In order to address below objectives:

  - To improve the interaction between current and future systems developing in the healthcare contexts
  - To improve the clinical information flow between the system users
- 1P, 2P, 3P, 5P, 6P, 7P, 8P/5F: It means "purpose" through the lean approach by using "Architecture" framework:
  - Ensures evolution from conversion of functions into services, creation of component services and integration into composite services, integration of internal applications, internal services and external services, to on-demand services in a gradual SOE
  - Ensures seamless integration of hardware and software conforming to service standards and technology

  By:

  - Developing a set of KPIs
  - Aligning the organization
  - Directional processes
  - Enabling processes
  - Respect to people
  - Continues improvement
  - Preventing variation, problems, and subsequent reworks
  - Performing a high performance supply chain in care contexts
  - Respect to clinical environment
  - Conducting the performance levels step by step as presented in Fig. 6.6.

  In order to address below objectives:

  - To improve the interaction between current and future systems developing in the healthcare contexts

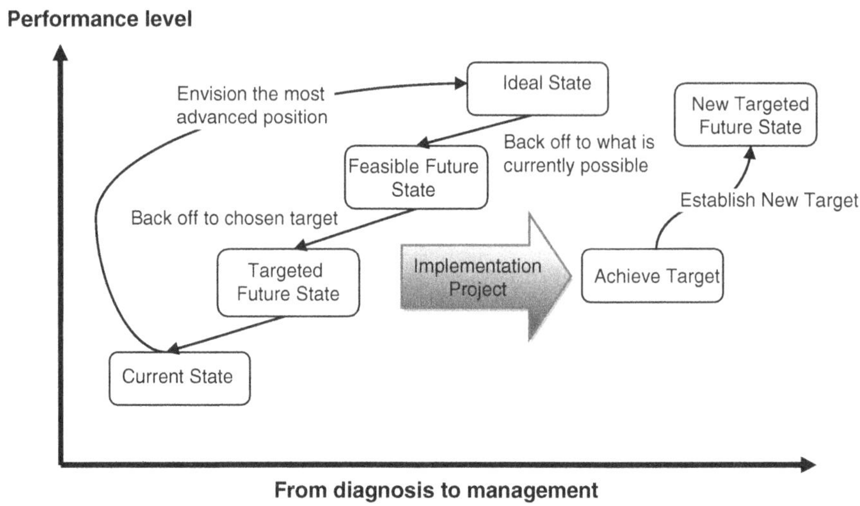

Fig. 6.6 Moving forwards perfection (adapted from Hines 2010)

- To remove duplications in different clinical systems in various care environment
- To build a robust platform of integrated healthcare systems
- To improve the clinical information flow between the system users
- To make aggregations in the best way to make a well-designed e-health
- To reduce waste in processing
- To reduce wastes through overproduction
- To reduce wasting time
- To reduce waste of stock on hand
- To reduce waste of movement
- To reduce waste of defective products
- To reduce waste in transportation

• 2P/3F: It means "process" through the lean approach by using "service Realization" framework:

- Enables analysis and design, development, integration and testing, and deployment and implementation of SOA and is core of established project management methodology
- Is coupled with other frameworks and ensures focus of projects is on business processes to be evolved into SOA and not on technology
- Program to be realized may be implemented in interlinked iterations of internal department application projects to external firm process integration projects

By:

- Capturing all clinical, managerial, and administration process

In order to address the below objectives:

- To improve the clinical information flow between the system users
- To reduce waste in processing

The proposed SOA designed and deployed through a lean approach would be able to address most of the developed SOA objectives in the healthcare contexts. The next steps include validating this through a qualitative research study. To do this, it is first necessary to develop both conceptual and technical frameworks, respectively, to design the healthcare SOA layers and components in details for specific healthcare contexts.

This chapter then served to introduce the benefits of incorporating SOA design in conjunction with lean thinking approaches into healthcare contexts. We close by calling for more research into this area.

References

Bieberstein, N., Bose, S., Fiammante, M., Jones, K., & Shah, R. (2006). *Service oriented architecture compass: Business value, planning and enterprise roadmap*. Upper Saddle River, NJ: Pearson Education.

Black, J., Miller D., (2008). *The Toyota Way to HealthCare Excellence, American College of Healthcare Executives Management Series*, p. 106.

Chu S. (2006). From component-based to service oriented software architecture for healthcare. *JITH, 4*(1), 5–14.

Ellis, P. (2010). *The key to SOA success: Application performance management*. Retrieved October 22, 2012, from http://esj.com/Articles/2010/03/02/Application-Performance-Mgt.aspx?Page=1

Gens, F. (2009). Here comes the cloud: New information technology (it) models for growth and innovation. *IDC Cloud Computing Forum: Getting Down to Business with the Cloud*, November 4, New York City.

Haux, R. (2006). Health information systems: Past, present, future. *International Journal of Medical Informatics, 75*, 268–281.

Haux, R., Winter, A., Ammenwerth, E., & Brigl, B. (2004). *Strategic information management in hospitals. An introduction to hospital information systems* (p. 30). New York: Springer.

Hines, P. (2010). *The principles of the lean business system*. Accessed October 23, 2012, from http://www.atem.org.au/uploads/publications/-The_Principles_of_The_Lean_Business_System.pdf

Lawler, J. P., & Howell-Barber, H. (2008). *Service-oriented architecture: SOA strategy, methodology, and technology* (pp. 27–59, 61–170, 171–180). Boca Raton, FL: Taylor and Francis.

Lawler, J. P., & Joseph, A. (2011). The potential reality of service-oriented architecture (SOA) in a cloud computing strategy. *Journal of Information Systems Applied Research, 4*(1), 57–72.

Liker, J. (2004). *The Toyota way* (p. 55). New York: McGraw-Hill.

Rajini, S. N. S., Bhuvaneswari, T., & Rajagopalan, S. P. (2012). Service based architecture in healthcare domain using fingerprint image identification. *European Journal of Scientific Research, 85*(1), 105–109.

Smith, R. (2009). Trouble ahead, trouble behind: Is soa on track for recovery, or has this technology been permanently derailed by the economic downturn? *Information Week, February*, 28–29.

Womak, J., & Jones, D. (1996). *Lean thinking*. New York: Simon and Shuster.

Chapter 7
Adapted Lean Thinking for Emergency Departments: Information Quality Perspective

Latif Al-Hakim

Abstract The criticality of information for reducing disruption in emergency departments has been emphasised in the literature, but there is no empirical study explicitly investigating the relationships between information quality and disruption. This study is an attempt to fill this gap. The research adapts lean thinking approach to suit emergency services taking into consideration the quality of information flow. The paper employs observational methodology and presents results of observations conducted in emergency services at two Chinese hospitals. The activities of 19 emergency doctors and 28 nurses were observed during the first 4 months in 2010.

Results indicate that approximately 16 % of emergency doctors' time and more than 29 % for the emergency nurses' time were wasted as a result of poor quality of information flow. About 42 % of the waste was the result of unavailability of information and failure to update information. Incomplete information causes 15.5 % of the waste while relevancy causes approximately 16 % of the total waste. Lack of accuracy in information prolongs emergency services by almost 11 %. The study shows that up to 24 % of the emergency time can be saved via improving the quality of information flow.

Keywords Disruption • Emergency departments • Information flow • Information quality • Observations • Waste

---

L. Al-Hakim (✉)
School of Management and Marketing, Faculty of Business, University of Southern Queensland, Toowoomba, QLD 4350, Australia
e-mail: hakim@usq.edu.au

N. Wickramasinghe et al. (eds.), *Lean Thinking for Healthcare*, Healthcare Delivery in the Information Age, DOI 10.1007/978-1-4614-8036-5_7,

7.1 Introduction

Lean thinking strategy is considered to have the capacity to enable delivery of better health care at the lowest overall cost (Jones and Mitchell 2006). Lean thinking originated in the Toyota Production system in the 1950s and has been further developed by Womack and Jones (1996a, b). The aim of lean thinking is to provide what the customer wants, quickly, efficiently and with little waste (Jones and Mitchell 2006; Womack and Jones 1996a, b; Young et al. 2004). It provides the following benefits (Jones and Mitchell 2006)—enhances quality and safety, improves delivery, increases throughput, produces stable working environment and creates the foundations for continuous improvement.

From a manufacturing perspective, lean thinking is a strategy to achieve competitiveness through driving organisations to continually add value to the products or services they deliver (Dickson et al. 2009; Womack and Jones 1996a, b). The key principle of lean thinking lies in the perception of value from the customer perspective. Activities that do not add value to the product or service from the customer's perspective are considered as non-value-added activities or waste (Shinohara 2006). However, it is recognised that some non-value-added activities, such as transportation, are necessary to perform the value-added activities (Moden 1993). Lean thinking uses a set of principles and techniques that aim to eliminate unnecessary non-value-added activities and significantly reduce the necessary non-value-added activities (Dickson et al. 2009; Reichhart 2007; Shinohara 2006; Taj and Berro 2006; Womack and Jones 1996a, b).

In a healthcare setting, it is argued that the patient should define what creates value rather than the healthcare providers (Young et al. 2004). Based on this perspective, the literature provides evidence that lean thinking offers significant improvement opportunities hospital-wide, including emergency departments (EDs) (Dickson et al. 2009; Ng et al. 2010; Parks et al. 2008). On the other hand, Winch and Henderson argue that lean manufacturing does not translate well to healthcare systems (Winch and Henderson 2009). To a certain extent, most healthcare systems, including EDs, have been tailored to serve the needs of providers, institutions and stakeholders rather than the patients (Dart 2011; Millard 2011). Most are organised around functional departments in which 'patients travel from one site to queue up at another and then, after "processing", are sent to yet another' (Aherne 2007). Holden (2011) critically reviews and analyses the limited applications of lean thinking in ED and concludes that 'more work remains in understanding Lean in the ED' and that 'we don't thoroughly understand the use of Lean in the ED, nor do we know how to apply Lean methods in the ED' (Dart 2011). Holden (2011) raises the question of how lean thinking can best be adapted to health care. This chapter attempts to partially answer the concern of Winch and Henderson and the question posed by Holden.

There are a number of differences between manufacturing and healthcare environments. These differences require adaptation of lean thinking to suit the healthcare environment. Neglecting to take into consideration these differences plays a major role in limiting the application of lean thinking in specific areas such as EDs.

The major difference is that lean thinking is designed to produce products with defined characteristics and quality. The progress of the work generates information. In healthcare environments and in particular in EDs, the system deals with human being and not machines. The available information relating to a patient's health status generates the ED work and, accordingly, workflow follows the information flow rather than the opposite. Waste in terms of errors and disruptions in ED may occur where the quality of information is poor. The criticality of information for the emergency process has been emphasised in the literature (Carey et al. 2011; Holden 2011), but there is no empirical study explicitly investigating the relationships between information quality and waste in EDs. This study is an attempt to fill this gap.

The paper is structured as follows. Firstly, the paper criticises the concept of treating patients in EDs like cars. This criticism is followed by a section emphasising the necessity for adapting lean thinking to suit the ED environment taking into consideration the quality of information flow. The paper then describes the dimensions of information quality which are most related to the ED environment. The paper frameworks the research methodology and presents the results of an empirical observational study conducted in EDs in two Chinese hospitals.

7.2 Should We Treat Patients Like Cars?

Assembly of cars is a highly automated system with limited, well-defined workflow paths. The car manufacturers use lean thinking methodology to achieve satisfaction of their customers who are, in the first instance, not part of the manufacturing system nor are they known to the workers directly involved in the manufacturing process. The system is divided into stations such that a product moves from one station to another without delay. Where a quality problem is detected (usually by using a mistake-proofing approach), the product is treated or removed from the main assembly system with no or minimal delay to the next product. Similar quality symptoms or problems are treated similarly. Under such settings, the workflow is very smooth and the system capacity can be predicted with very high precision. Inspired by such systems, Millard in his article entitled 'If Toyota run ED' emphasises that in 'certain clinical situations, perhaps even a majority of them, the secret to patient care may be to treat the patients like cars' (Millard 2011).

What Millard dreams to achieve is to design an ED system with a number of stations such that the patient is moved from one station to another with no delay or wait between stations. Such system assumes that medical diagnosis, analysis, tests, treatment, monitoring and other medical operations are automated with predicted durations. It is not clear how such a system can be achieved given that each patient has different health status and requires different diagnosis and medical treatment. Indeed, Millard does not consider in his perception the differences between manufacturing and health settings which has been emphasised repeatedly in the literature (e.g. Winch and Henderson 2009). More importantly, this hypothetical system is not a patient-centred system and its value would be defined by the management of the healthcare system rather than by patients who are considered as cars. It is possible to increase number of diagnosis's steps and move the patient from one 'station' to any other available one regardless of the benefits gained from such movement. The suggested system may drastically reduce wait and smooth the patient flow but will also drastically increase cycle time and the expenses which should be paid by the patients. In addition, such suggested system significantly increases medical errors resulting from automating medical operations.

7.3 Criticality of Information Flow

There are several reasons for the notion that the concept of lean thinking should be adapted to fit the hospital system (Woodward-Hagg et al. 2007). Hospital and manufacturing production systems vary in a number of dimensions (see Table 7.1). Major areas of difference include degree of human involvement, level of product uniformity, cycle time, waiting time, object behaviour, ease of performance measurement and process effectiveness (Al-Hakim 2006). The emergency process is a 'sociotechnical' process in which each action or activity is governed by information that

Table 7.1 Summary of the differences between the manufacturing and healthcare services settings

Organisation type		
Differences	Lean thinking in manufacturing	Lean thinking in health care
Necessity of human involvement	Automation is a major role to reduce human involvement; it reduces the need for high skill and knowledge	Skill, knowledge and experience of professionals play a major role
Ease of performance measurement	Performance of workers in the production process is easy to measure	Performance of professionals in the process is not easily measurable
Process effectiveness	Process outcome is predictable	It is hard to predict the degree of the success of healthcare service
Product uniformity	Machine produces identical products	Every patient requires different service
Object behaviour	Products have defined characteristics	Patients behaviour are not predictable and could vary
Cycle time	Cycle time of the production could be precise and determined in advance	Healthcare service cycle time could vary and be difficult to determine prior to the service
Non-added-value activity time	All types of inspection are a waste and should be reduced or eliminated	In healthcare environment, monitoring and testing are essential
Information flow	Mainly depends on process flow	Healthcare activities are information-based activities

enables coordination of ED professionals with various resources and technologies. The main differences between the emergency process and processes in other settings are summarised as follows:

1. There is no definite series of activities that construct emergency services. Every patient has a specific emergency status and should be treated differently based on information stemming from his/her health status.
2. There is a higher degree of fluctuation and unpredictability in the patient health status over the process time. Such fluctuations may require changes in the emergency workflow.
3. Tests and activities required to obtain information may differ from one patient to another. There is a high degree of complexity encountered in decision-making relating to selecting the correct workflow path.
4. Each activity within emergency services requires high information quality in terms of availability, accuracy, believability, completeness and up-to-dateness (timelessness). The quality of information at each stage of the ED process plays a major role in the success of the whole emergency process.
5. The quality of information is the main factor contributing to the amount of non-value-added activities or waste within the emergency process. The same test may need to be repeated either to ensure accuracy, complete missing information or to update information.

The above differences explicitly emphasise the criticality of information flow to the performance of EDs. It is the information flows from an activity that determine the subsequent workflow rather than the opposite. The work of an ED professional with a very high level of medical skill may lead to a medical error or an adverse event if the action of the professional is based on poor information quality (IQ). The literature emphasises the importance of information flows and communications in reducing disruptions within EDs (Carey et al. 2011; Gillespie et al. 2012; Holden 2011). Virtually, all disruption within EDs can be contributed to the lack of information quality. Examples include making a wrong decision, performing incorrect/inappropriate action, unnecessarily repeating an operation, confusing tests results, delaying implementation of an action, wasting time in communications and movements, excessive movement, searching for information or physical materials, supplying wrong instruments and providing inappropriate drug(s). The link between information quality and disruption events is not a new assertion. The contribution of this chapter lies in testing empirically the effect of information quality dimensions on disruption events in EDs.

7.4 Dimensions of Information Quality

Individuals have different ways of considering the quality of information as they have different wants and needs and, hence, different quality standards which lead to a user-based quality perspective (Evans and Lindsey 2008). This perspective is

Table 7.2 Dimensions of information quality applicable to emergency process

No.	Dimension	Definition
1	Accessibility/availability	The degree to which information related to the patient health status is available, easily obtainable or quickly retrievable when needed. Accessibility depends on the customer's circumstances
2	Accuracy	The degree to which information represents real status of the patient's health
3	Believability	This dimension measures the assessment of the emergency medical professional assessment of credibility of information
4	Coherency	This measures how information 'hangs together' and provides one meaning to different emergency professionals
5	Completeness	The degree to which information is sufficient enough to depict every state of the emergency task at hand or the represented system, that is, assesses the degree of missing information
6	Ease of understanding	The degree of comprehension of information by the emergency professional to perform the emergency task
7	Relevancy	Relevancy indicates weather information addresses the emergency professional's needs. It reflects the level of appropriateness of information to the emergency task under consideration
8	Timeliness	This dimension measures how up-to-date information is with respect to emergency professional's needs or the task at hand. It reflects also how fast the patient information is updated by the emergency system

based on the Juran definition of quality which defines quality as 'fitness for intended use' (Juran and Godfrey 1999). Thus, information and data can be regarded as being of high quality if they are fit for their intended use in operations, decision-making and planning (Redman 2004). Other related IQ perspectives are 'conformance to specifications' and 'meeting and exceeding consumer expectations' (Evans and Lindsay 2008).

While these perspectives capture the essence of IQ, they are very broad definitions and are difficult to use in the measurement of IQ. There is a need to identify the dimensions that can be used to measure IQ.

IQ is a multidimensional. This means that organisations must use multiple measures to evaluate the quality of their information or data. Several researchers have attempted to identify the IQ dimension (Wand and Wang 1996; Wang et al. 1995; Wang and Wang 2009). More than 20 dimensions have been identified in the literature. IQ dimensions more related to EDs are accessibility, accuracy, believability, coherency, completeness, ease of understanding, relevancy and timeliness. Table 7.2 provides definitions of the IQ dimensions used in the literature which are related to the information flow within emergency services.

7.5 Research Methodology

This research uses observation methodology to collect data. Observational studies of healthcare services usually report workflow activities and time spent on implementing the activities (Rosenbaum 2002). The emergency departments of two Chinese hospitals were selected as the setting in which to conduct the study. One of these hospitals is an academic hospital while the other hospital is a large public hospital.

The observation sheet comprises fields to record activities and time durations. The sheet uses symbols representing performed activities. Twenty-one types of activities were initially recognised in this study. These activities are grouped into two main categories: value-added activities and non-value-added activities. The latter are further divided into two subcategories: non-value-added but necessary activities and non-value-added activities or total waste. Table 7.3 illustrates symbols used to represent activities and provides a brief description of each type of activity. The study considers nine dimensions of information quality. These are availability, accuracy, believability, completeness, coherence, ease of understanding, relevancy and timeliness (Table 7.2). The observation sheet is divided into fields showing the start and end of each activity, observed disruption events, any notable features of the observed activity or event and quality features of associated information.

The research methodology comprised three stages: the introduction stage, the mapping and training stage and the observation stage. The introduction stage involved meeting with the ED senior officers at the hospital to introduce the project and obtain their consent to start the study. At this stage, the hospital assigned a liaison team of one professional ED doctor and two senior ED nurses to accompany the researcher and facilitate the observations.

The second stage was the mapping and training stage. This stage involved a series of four to six meetings with the liaison team. The first meeting was conducted to obtain initial information necessary to understand the ED process in the hospital. The subsequent meetings followed an iterative pattern. The first part of the meeting was used to review and revise the process and information flows completed as a result of information collected from the previous meeting. Then, certain activities and actions were highlighted for further analysis and examination. In this stage, the researcher presented and discussed the observation sheet with the liaison team. For training purposes, the researcher and the two nurses conducted 32-h trial sessions.

During the trial, the nurses handled small digital recorders to record events. In addition, the nurses recorded events on the observation sheet. Wherever possible, the observation sheets were provided to observed nurses and professionals to enter data at a time convenient to them relating to their opinion of the quality of information provided to them. After each trial a meeting was held with the liaison team. During the meeting, the recorded events and the data in the observation sheets prepared by the nurses were analysed and compared with the data in the observation sheet prepared by the researcher. Other ED professionals and nurses who

Table 7.3 Activity description

Category	Activity	Description
Value-added activities	Assessment	A mental action in the presence of a patient involving the assessment of the health status of the patient
	Diagnosis	A clinical, mental or emotional action in the presence of a patient exercised during the judgement of the patient's health status
	Acquisition	Acquisition of information, acquirement of medical test or deciding a clinical action
	Preparation	A clinical action preparing the patient for actual emergency process. Examples include cleaning injury, positioning patient for suturing injury or emergency surgery
	Operation	Any other value-added action in the presence or absence of the patient. Examples include performing CPR or processing medical test. This category of activities includes also supervision of emergency action or helping in performance of emergency action
Non-value-added but necessary activities	Movement	A movement of the observed ED professional with or without a patient, material or equipment
	Monitoring	Observe and supervise patient or monitoring devices connected to a patient
	Checking	Verifying forms, retrieve information, ensure suitability of a procedure or check connection of a patient to devices
	Setup	Preparing material, devices or space necessary for emergency process
	Stocking	Shelving material or records, procurement of material and devices
	Support	
	Paperwork	Writing information or preparing by handwriting a form
	Computer/electronic work	This activity includes any action using a computer or related devices. Copying and scanning is part of this activity
	Discussion	Face-to-face communication with other professionals, patient or patient's family
	Telephone	Communication via telephone, pagers or other communication system
Non-value-added activities	Redundant	Doing unnecessary action or performing an action that should be performed before and the current performance unnecessary obstructs the emergency service
	Rework	Repeating an action that was done before
	Defect	Correcting a defective action
	Delay/waiting	The observed professional is idle or waiting for another action or information
	Searching	Searching for information, material and devices
	Exterior obstructions	Noises and other exterior interruptions
Others	Others	Any other action not listed above

volunteered to record data were usually invited to attend the trial meetings. Emphasis was placed on the quality of information provided to the ED professionals. The trial meetings and discussions were very helpful in training both the nurses and the researcher in differentiating value-added activities from other types of activities, in detecting waste and errors during observation and in configuring the dimensions of quality of information before the professional at the time of performing the observed activity. The trial was also very useful in reformulating the observation sheet. There was some overlapping between assessment, acquisition and diagnosis actions. As these actions are considered as value-added activities, it was decided to record times for these activities under the 'diagnosis'. It was also decided to consider preparation as part of 'operation' activities.

The observation date was usually assigned after telephone communications between a liaison officer and the researcher indicating the availability of a nurse to accompany the researcher. Before the day of the observation, the liaison officer obtained the consent of the nurses and ED professionals to be observed and provided them with the observation sheets and written instructions including example of observations. Observed doctors, nurses and other emergency staff were told to conduct their normal duties and their filling of the sheet was voluntary and should not obstruct their normal duties.

At the end of observation, the data collected by the researcher, the liaison nurse and the volunteers were compared and analysed. Data were entered into a spreadsheet file. Data in the spreadsheet were discussed with the liaison team and ED professionals involved in the observation. Discussion with professionals emphasised observed obstruction events and the role of information quality. The willingness of ED professionals to participate in the observation was noticeable during this stage. The data provided by them and their strong willingness to participate in discussion provided valuable insights into waste and information quality problems they had faced. It is important to note that ED professionals strongly believed in the existence of a high percentage of waste in their work and in the role of information quality in creating waste.

7.5.1 Credibility and Limitations

The credibility of an observational study depends on the experience and expertise of the observer (Gillespie et al. 2012). The first observer has an industrial engineering and management background with experience spanning over 40 years in industry, research and development and academic institutions. He has published intensively in the area of information quality and conducted several ergonomic and observational studies, including studies dealing with lean thinking and disruptions inside operating rooms (Al-Hakim 2011; Al-Hakim and Gong 2012). The other observers were members of the liaison team and were senior ED nurses with high experience in ED processes. Further, this type of study is a revelatory study. The observations were conducted under difficult circumstances not normally welcomed or open for in-depth study and the opportunity to observe and analyse a phenomenon is usually not available due to access constraints (Yin 2009). The involvement of observed objects (ED professionals) in recording data and participating in meetings and discussions was essential to the success of the study. It also provides a platform for sharing information, validation and interpreting results. However, the results of the methodology should also be seen in light of several limitations. The observation was conducted by only two observers at a time. This may limit obtaining more comprehensive data comprising the whole ED system. The heavy duties of the liaison nurses limited the number of observational sessions. It follows that the sample size of the observed objects is relatively small and may not represent the whole ED system.

7.6 Data Analysis

The observations were conducted at the emergency departments of two large Chinese hospitals, each with an average of 400 patients per day. A total of 51 observation sessions were conducted over the first 4 months of 2010. The total observation time was 6,432 min (approximately 107 h). During the study the activities of 19 emergency doctors and 28 nurses were observed. Break, coffee time and other personal activities were disregarded. All observed doctors and nurses (ED professionals) volunteered to contribute to the study, filling in the observation sheets and participating in related meetings and discussions. They tried, whatever the time applicable, to record disruption events and their perception of the quality of information before them. The observation time for emergency doctors was 2,541 min while the observation time for nurses was 3,891 min. Session times ranged from approximately one and a half hours to about 3 h. It should be noticed that in many occasions observation sheets were submitted from volunteered ED professionals who were not under observation at that session. Their data provided insights relating to the quality of information and type of disruption. They were useful for validation of results and for discussions, but their data were not considered as part of the recorded data.

At the end of the observation day, the recorded data were scripted, discussed with the liaison team and entered into a draft spreadsheet. The draft spreadsheet was distributed by the liaison team among the observed ED professionals for their comments. Usually observed professionals discussed data and provided opinions via telephone or face-to-face meetings with the researcher and liaison team. Final results were also discussed during a meeting comprising senior management and senior ED professionals. Table 7.4 provides descriptive statistics of observed waste activities made by nurses and emergency doctors in the ED of the two Chinese hospitals. Table 7.5 illustrates reasons for waste in terms of information quality dimensions.

Table 7.4 Descriptive data of the ED professionals' activities (minutes) and percent of wasted time (minutes) in their activities

Activity	ED doctors				ED nurses				Doctors + nurses			
	Time (minute)	% activity	Waste (minute)	% waste	Time (minute)	% activity	Waste (minute)	% waste	Time (minute)	% activity	Waste (minute)	% waste
Value added	1,463	57.58	0	0	1,811	**46.54**	0	0	3,274	50.90	0	0
Supportive	771	30.34	101	3.97	1,390	**35.72**	441	11.33	2,161	33.60	542	8.43
Non-value added	307	12.08	307	12.08	690	**17.73**	690	17.73	997	15.50	997	15.50
Total	2,541	100	408	16.06	3,891	100	1,131	29.07	6,432	100	1,539	23.93

Table 7.5 Reasons for waste in terms of IQ dimensions

Activity	Waste (min)	Information quality dimensions															
		Availability		Accuracy		Believability		Coherence		Completeness		Understanding		Relevancy		Timeliness	
		Min.	%	Min.	%	Min.	%	Min.	%	Min.	%	Min.	%	Min.	%	Min.	%
Supportive	542	177	11.50	98	6.37	35	2.27	41	2.66	99	6.43	33	2.14	119	7.73	152	9.88
Non-added value	997	146	9.49	71	4.61	38	2.47	38	2.47	137	8.90	41	2.66	131	8.51	179	11.63
Total	1,539	323	20.99	169	10.98	73	4.74	79	5.13	236	15.33	74	4.81	250	16.24	331	21.51

Results indicate that ED doctors spent more than half of their working time (about 57 %) performing value-added activities, 30 % of their time doing supportive activities and about 12 % of their time representing preventable waste. ED nurses spent almost 47 % of their working time performing value-added activities with preventable waste representing approximately 18 % of their working time.

For the combined group of ED professionals, value-added activities contributed approximately 51 % of the total combined work of both doctors and nurses. The preventable waste in the combined work was 15.5 %.

Analysis of the results in terms of IQ dimensions (Table 7.5) shows that failure to update information (timeliness) and lack of information availability (availability) were the main dimensions contributing to waste in the work of ED professionals. Each of these dimensions contributed more than 20 % of the waste. The third dimension is 'relevancy' which contributed approximately 16 % of the waste. Incomplete information contributed more than 15 % of the wasted time. Results show that the IQ dimensions 'ease of understanding' and 'believability' have the lowest effect on waste (less than 5 %) indicating there was no lack in understanding or believing the information received by ED professionals.

7.7 Conclusion

This research deals with preventable waste within emergency departments. The aim of this chapter is to study the role of information quality in disturbing emergency services. The study observed the activities of emergency doctors and nurses in emergency departments at the two Chinese hospitals' emergency departments and presents results of 4 months of observations.

Results indicate that approximately 16 % of emergency doctors' time was wasted. The percentage of wasted time reaches more than 29 % for the emergency nurses. About 42 % of the waste was the result of unavailability of information and failure to update information. Incomplete information causes more than 15 % of the waste while relevancy causes approximately 16 % of the total waste. Lack of accuracy in information prolongs emergency services by 11 %. The IQ dimensions 'ease of understanding' and believability have the lowest effect on waste (less than % each) indicating there was no lack in understanding or believing the information received by ED professionals. The study shows that up to 24 % of the emergency time can be saved via improving the quality of information flow.

References

Aherne, J. (2007). Think lean. *Nursing Management, 13*(10), 13–15.

Al-Hakim, L. (2006). Web-based hospital information system for managing operating theatre waiting list. *International Journal of Healthcare Technology and Management, 7*(3), 266–682.

Al-Hakim, L. (2011). The impact of preventable disruption on the operative time for minimally invasive surgery. *Surgical Endoscopy, 25*(10), 3385–3392.

Al-Hakim, L., & Gong, X. Y. (2012). On the day of surgery: How long does preventable disruption prolong the patient journey? *International Journal of Health Care Quality Assurance, 25*, 322–342.

Carey, D., Chisholm, M., Christopher, S., Weaver, M., Laura Whenmouth, B., & Beverly Giles, R. (2011). A task analysis of emergency physician activities in academic and community settings. *Annals of Emergency Medicine, 58*(2), 117–122.

Dart, R. C. (2011). Can lean thinking transform American health care. *Annals of Emergency Medicine, 57*(3), 279–281.

Dickson, E. W., Singh, S., Cheung, D. S., Wyatt, C. C., & Nugent, A. S. (2009). Application of lean manufacturing techniques in the emergency department. *The Journal of Emergency Medicine, 37*(2), 177–182.

Evans, J. R., & Lindsay, W. M. (2008). *Managing for quality and performance excellence* (7th ed.). Cincinati, OH: South-Western, Thomson Learning.

Gillespie, B., Chaboyer, W., & Fairweather, N. (2012). Factors that influence the expected length of operation: Results of a prospective study. *Quality & Safety in Health Care, 21*, 3–12. doi:10.1136/bmjqs-2011-000169.

Holden, R. (2011). Lean thinking in emergency departments: A critical review. *Applied Ergonomics, 57*(3), 265–278.

Jones, D., & Mitchell, A. (2006). Lean thinking for the NHS. *National Health Service (NHS) Confederation Report, UK.*

Juran, J. M., & Godfrey, A. B. (1999). *Juran's quality handbook* (5th ed.). New York: McGraw-Hill.

Millard, W. B. (2011). If Toyota ran the ED. *Annals of Emergency Medicine, 57*(6), 13A–17A.

Moden, Y. (1993). *Toyota production system: An introduction to just-in-time* (2nd ed.). Norcross, GA: Industrial Engineering and Management Press.

Ng, D., Vail, G., Thomas, S., & Schmidt, N. (2010). Applying the lean principles of the Toyota Production System to reduce wait times in the emergency department. *Canadian Journal of Emergency Medicine, 12*(1), 50–57.

Parks, J. K., Klein, J., Frankel, H. L., Friese, R. S., & Shafi, S. (2008). Dissecting delays in trauma care using corporate lean six sigma methodology. *The Journal of Trauma, 65*(5), 1098–1105.

Redman, T. (2004). Data: An unfolding quality disaster. *Dm Review, 14*, 21–23.

Reichhart, A. (2007). Lean distribution: Concepts, contributions, conflicts. *International Journal of Production Research, 45*(16), 3699–3722.

Rosenbaum, P. (2002). *Observational studies* (2nd ed.). New York: Springer.

Shinohara, M. (2006). *European and Japanese Logistics Paradigms: An Explorative and comparative study of the dynamics of logistics management*. Thesis Erasmus University Rotterdam.

Taj, S., & Berro, L. (2006). Application of constrained management and lean manufacturing in developing best practices for productivity improvement in an auto-assembly plant. *International Journal of Productivity and Performance Management, 55*(3/4), 332–345.

Wand, Y., & Wang, R. Y. (1996). Anchoring data quality dimensions in ontological foundations. *Communications of the ACM, 39*(11), 86–95.

Wang, R. Y., Storey, V. C., & Firth, C. P. (1995). A framework for analysis of data quality research. *IEEE Transactions on Knowledge and Data Engineering, 7*(4), 623–640.

Wang, Y. M., & Wang, Y. S. (2009). Examining the dimensionality and measurement of user-perceived knowledge and information quality in the KMS context. *Journal of Information Science, 35*(1), 94–109. doi:10.1177/0165551508092260.

Winch, S., & Henderson, A. J. (2009). Making care and making healthcare: A critical review. *Medical Journal Australia, 191*(1), 28–29.

Womack, J. P., & Jones, D. T. (1996a). Beyond Toyota: How to root out waste and pursue perfection. *Harvard Business Review, 74*, 140–172.

Womack, J. P., & Jones, D. T. (1996b). *Lean thinking*. New York: Simon & Schuster.

Woodward-Hagg., et al. (2007, February 2007). Adaptation of lean methodologies for healthcare applications. *Proceedings of the 2007 Society for Health Systems Conference*. LA: New Orleans. Retrieved on October 20, 2012 from http://docs.lib.purdue.edu/rche_rp/24/.

Yin, R. K. (2009). *Case study research: Design and methodology*. Thousand Oaks, CA: Sage.

Young, T., Brailsford, S., Connell, C., Davies, R., Harper, P., & Klein, J. H. (2004). *Using industrial processes to improve patient care*. Retrieved on October 20, 2012 from http://www.bmj.com/cgi/content/extract/328/7437/463.

Part II
Applications of Lean Thinking Around the Healthcare World

1.1 Introduction

The chapters that make up this section focus on various lean thinking applications in healthcare around the world. It should be noted that healthcare is a global industry. Today all countries' healthcare systems are being challenged to deliver effective efficient quality care. Indeed, while each health are system is moulded to some extent by the unique cultural and structural contexts of that particular country there are many more similar issues across countries regarding how to deliver superior healthcare. By closer examination of many of these situations it is possible to develop a more holistic picture of healthcare delivery as well as identify some key nuggets and critical success factors.

Chapters 8 and 9 are both by Soar and his colleagues Adapted Lean Thinking for Hospitals in China and Lean Thinking in Smart Homes respectively.

Chapter 10 A Delphi Study on Developing a Conceptual Framework to Understand the Perception of Iranian Physicians Towards Electronic Health Records by Alavi and Win looks at key issues and challenges in Iran.

Chapter 11 Trying to Streamline Healthcare Delivery in Australia via the Personally Controlled Electronic Health Record(PCEHR) by Muhammad et al. examines the Australian healthcare scene in some detail.

Chapter 12 Identifying Critical Issues for Developing Successful E-health Solutions by Zwicker et al. provides an analysis of the German healthcare system.

Chapter 13 Applying the Principles of KM to Effect Streamlined Healthcare Operations: A Malaysian Case Study by Wong and Wickramasinghe provides an example from Asia, specifically Malaysia.

Chapter 14 Re-making Rosa Medical Center: A 5-Step Approach to Transitioning with Lean by Abouzahra and Tan looks at a North American case study and finally Chap. 15 Lean Thinking and Customer Focus by Simon and Wickramasinghe also examines issues in the German healthcare context.

Taken together these chapters present examples from across the different types of healthcare systems essentially private to various examples of two tiered systems to essentially public. What is interesting that all systems are facing similar challenges and lean principles are as relevant in all contexts.

Chapter 8
Adapted Lean Thinking for Healthcare Services: An Empirical Study in the Traditional Chinese Hospital

Ying Su, Jeffrey Soar, Ningqiao Shen, and Latif Al-Hakim

Abstract This chapter looks at how Lean Thinking can be adapted using a model derived from a case study of a large Traditional Chinese Hospital. After a restructuring in divisions and the implementation of the care programmers and clinical pathways, hospital management found that they had no tools to evaluate if these changes were resulting in a Lean Thinking approach on the work-floor. In agreement with hospital management, an existing tool of Business Process Re-engineering measurement was adopted and adapted to the specific context of health care. This chapter reports on how the quantitative model was changed and validated in order to come up with a useful instrument to measure the Lean Thinking of the employees in the hospital. The Hospital Lean Thinking (HLT) tool can be useful to measure the effects of changes that are assumed to lead to more Lean Thinking or even patient focus. In this way the pay-off of these investments can be made more tangible. The HLT tool offers hospitals a way to evaluate how they are evolving towards more Lean Thinking.

Y. Su (✉)
Institute of Scientific and Technical Information of China,
No. 15 Fu Xing Road, Beijing, China
e-mail: suy4@sem.tsinghua.edu.cn

J. Soar
School of Information Systems, Faculty of Business & Law,
University of Southern Queensland, Toowoomba, QLD, Australia
e-mail: Jeffrey.Soar@usq.edu.au

N. Shen
Information Engineering Department, Jiangsu Province Hospital
of TCM, Nanjing, China
e-mail: ningqiao@foxmail.com

L. Al-Hakim
School of Management and Marketing, Faculty of Business, University of Southern
Queensland, Toowoomba, QLD 4350, Australia
e-mail: hakim@usq.edu.au

N. Wickramasinghe et al. (eds.), *Lean Thinking for Healthcare*, Healthcare Delivery in the Information Age, DOI 10.1007/978-1-4614-8036-5_8,

Keywords Service innovation • Indigenous management • Performance measurement system • Hospital services industry • Quality of service • Quantitative model • Case study • Business process • Object-oriented • Analytic hierarchy process • System dynamics

8.1 Introduction

Issues of health care in Chinese hospitals include crowding and long waiting times; a visit to a hospital in China is rarely a smooth and satisfying experience. Nearly 400 outpatient departments (ODs) operate in Beijing and provide care for patients around the clock. There are annually 24 million OD visits, which result in 4 million hospitalisations (accounting for 60 % of hospital admissions overall). Patients in Beijing rely more heavily (40 %) on OD services than other big cities (22 % other cities).

Causes for OD overcrowding are well known (Jones and Mitchell 2006) and include hospital bed shortage, high medical acuity of patients, increasing patient volume, shortage of examination space and shortage of RN (Registered Nurse) staff. Even though these issues are well recognised, alleviation of these problems in OD is not trivial and requires addressing complex systems issues. This is not the focus of the paper which instead concentrates on exploration of improving effectiveness of OD operations.

It has been shown that despite various management, methods and techniques have been developed over the last years to approach the need for constant change and improvement in OD management. There are still many difficulties and obstacles between doctors and patients in the aspects of expression, transmission, understanding and communication of information. These obstacles affect the improvement of perioperative efficiency, such as reducing waste time or overtime of cases, adding more cases during regular diagnosing hours and increasing profitability of the hospitals. Thus, these impediments need to be reduced to shorten the overall outpatient time. The Lean Thinking approach potentially can play a vital role in improving outpatient performance and raising the level of hospital services (Womack and Jones 1996).

The Lean Thinking strategy is considered to have the capacity to enable delivery of better health care at the lower overall cost (Jones and Mitchell 2006). Lean thinking originated in the Toyota Production System in the 1950s and has been further developed by Womack and Jones (1996). The aim of Lean Thinking is to provide what the customer wants, quickly, efficiently and with little waste (Jones and Mitchell 2006; Womack and Jones 1996; Young et al. 2004). It can provide the following benefits (Jones and Mitchell 2006): improved quality and safety, improved delivery and improved throughput, that is, using the same resources with higher efficiency and accelerating momentum. A stable working environment with clear, standardised procedures can create the foundations for constant improvement.

From a perspective of manufacturing, Lean Thinking is a strategy to achieve competitiveness through identification and elimination of wasteful steps in products, services or processes (Womack and Jones 1996; Shinohara 2006). It aims to substantially smooth the flow and drastically reduce waste and process variations (Womack and Jones 1996; Shinohara 2006; Taj and Berro 2006; Reichhart 2007). Waste is defined as the activity or activities that a customer would not want to pay for and that do not add value to the product or service from the customer's perspective (Shinohara 2006). Once waste has been identified in the current or existing state, a plan is formulated to eliminate this to attain a desired future state in as effective and efficient a manner as possible. These activities belong to one of three sets of operations (Moden 1993):

- Non-value-added activities
- Necessary, but non-value-added activities
- Value-added activities

Similarly, in a healthcare service organisation, wasted time leads to high cost and affects the quality of patient care, and thus it should be reduced. To achieve the leanness target, the activities that add little or no value, or that adversely affect the smooth flow of the process, are considered for elimination. Because the main mission of health care is to treat and cure patients who are the end consumers in the care process, it is argued that the patient should have an input into defining what creates value in health care (Young et al. 2004).

Some management professionals argue that lean manufacturing does not translate well to service industries. Bowen and Youngdahl (1998) show how it can apply to health care by providing theory, case studies and context for lean applications. Flinders Medical Centre, a medium-sized public sector teaching hospital in Adelaide, South Australia, has for some time been implementing lean strategies (King et al. 2006) and has been able to operate below its budgeted costs (Jones and Mitchell 2006). Lean thinking has also been advocated in the healthcare setting of the USA through the use of the Six Sigma methodology, which in many ways resembles lean production techniques (Young et al. 2004; Tolga Taner et al. 2007; Dahlgaard and Dahlgaard 2006). Other related literature also reveals that the implementation of Lean Thinking brings benefit to health care (Jones and Mitchell 2006; King et al. 2006; De Koning et al. 2006; Jimmerson et al. 2005; Ahluwalia and Offredy 2005).

8.2 Literature Review

8.2.1 Lean Thinking in Health Care

The strategies of Lean Thinking are applicable to health care (Reichhart 2007; Moden 1993; Bowen and Youngdahl 1998). An application of Lean Thinking to health care lies in minimising or eliminating delay, repeated encounters, errors and inappropriate procedures (Moden 1993 p, 162). Hospitals may apply Lean Thinking to provide better services to their patients, especially in the use of operating theatres. One of the key principles of Lean Thinking is respect for the customer. In a healthcare setting, the patient is the primary customer to the healthcare services since the patient justifies the existence of such services. Applications of the Lean Thinking approach in health care need to consider how to engage patients who are the end consumers in the care process (Moden 1993; King et al. 2006). Literature indicates that the implementation of Lean Thinking has the potential to benefit health care (Tolga Taner et al. 2007). Some healthcare services around the world are considering applying the Lean Thinking approach. Applications of lean in health care have been published in academic journals and other media (see Table 8.1).

8.2.2 Performance Measurement Systems

Traditional performance measurement systems (PMSs) have often failed to measure and integrate all the factors critical to success of a business (Yurdakul and Ic 2005; Wegelius-Lehtonen 2001). To deal with the new environment, new PMSs have been proposed, such as the Activity-Based Costing System (Koota and Takala 1998), the Balanced Scorecard (Kaplan and Norton 2005), the SMART System (Hudson et al. 2001) and the Performance Measurement Questionnaire (Park et al. 1998). There are also approaches for proposing criteria for the design of PMSs (Neely et al. 2005).

Despite the availability of the various approaches to develop PMSs, there are a few performance systems that are exclusively designed and applied to service businesses (Bititci 1995). Atkinson et al. describe a stakeholder-based PMS and while they do not draw attention to the service measurement aspect, nevertheless they do apply their system to measure a bank's various outputs, one of which is service innovation (Atkinson et al. 1997).

The literature on Lean Thinking and *performance measurement* reveals that there is a lack of quantified and unique indigenous management models (Yu et al. 2000). Existing management models can be separated into three distinct types: the static, (Harding and Popplewell 2000; Candido and Morris 2000), the dynamic (Dobni and Luffman 2003; Dye 2004) and the mixed models (Zhang and Prybutok 2004; Candido 2005; De Toni and Tonchia 2005). Existing static models offer a representation of an organisation, dynamic models offer a generic process of strategy formulation and implementation and mixed models show what dimensions can be changed at each stage. The mixed model can be further developed in the form of quantification.

8.2.3 AHP Approach for Performance Assessment

The analytic hierarchy process (AHP) developed by Saaty (1980) provides a suitable and appropriate way of analysing a performance measurement model because

Table 8.1 Summary of Lean Thinking literature for healthcare services

Author	Title	Domain	Key area of study	Findings/conclusion
Ben-Tovim et al. (2008) Australia	Redesigning care at the Flinders Medical Centre: clinical process redesign using 'Lean Thinking'	Clinical process throughout the hospital	Lean Thinking Patient flow Process redesign	The Redesigning Care programme has enabled the hospital to provide safer and more accessible care during a period of growth in demand
Dickson et al. (2008) USA	Application of Lean Manufacturing Techniques in the Emergency Department	Emergency department	Lean Thinking Patient flow Process redesign	Lean improved the value of the care
Maier-Speredelozzi et al. (2005) USA	Applying Lean Principles to a Continuing Care Patient Discharge Process	Discharge process	Lean Thinking Time-motion study	The greatest benefits are derived through identifying and eliminating wastes in the process
Jimmerson et al. (2005) USA	Reducing waste and errors: Piloting Lean Principles at IHC	Intensive care unit Medical ICU Medical/surgical unit Emergency department	Lean Thinking Time-motion study	Discovered ample opportunity to improve efficiency and quality in health care by eliminating waste
USA	Going Lean in Health Care	Throughout the entire process	Lean Thinking	Demonstrated that lean management can reduce waste in health care with results comparable to other industries

(continued)

Table 8.1 (continued)

Author	Title	Domain	Key area of study	Findings/conclusion
Johnson et al. (2004) USA	Attacking waste and variation hospital-wide: a comprehensive lean sigma deployment	Surgery	Six sigma Lean Thinking	The hospital has realised both a financial and cultural return on investment
UK	NHS Modernisation Agency's way to improve health care	Across entire organisations	Six sigma Lean Thinking Theory of constraints	The idea of Lean Thinking can suit healthcare organisations
Womack and Jones (2003) USA	Lean Thinking: Banish Waste and Create Wealth in Your Corporation	Medical system	Lean Thinking	Having multi-skilled teams taking care of the patient and an active involvement of the patient in the process is emphasised
Young et al. (2004) UK	Using industrial processes to improve patient care	Diabetic retinopathy	Six sigma	Patients focused
			Lean Thinking	Coordinate and balance activities
			Theory of constraints	Identify those that constitute weak links or bottlenecks and take appropriate remedial action
Young et al. (2004) UK	A critical look at Lean Thinking in health care	Medical system	Lean Thinking	There is scope for methodological development, perhaps by defining three themes associated with value—the operational, the clinical and the experiential
Den Boer et al. (1999) Netherlands	Preoperative time-motion analysis of diagnostic laparoscopy with laparoscopic ultrasonography	Preoperative Surgical process	Time-motion study Lean Thinking	This time-motion study provided detailed insight into the preoperative process of operation, leading to improvements in the surgical process and instruments used

AHP is a multiple criteria decision-making technique that allows subjective as well as objective factors to be considered in a decision-making process (Rangone 1996; Dey et al. 2006). Performance measurement is usually a team effort and AHP is one available method for forming a systematic framework for group interaction and group decision-making (Saaty and Vargas 2001).

Although AHP has been used before to measure performance in service industries, Dey et al. (2006) applied AHP to performance measurement of intensive care units in hospitals, and Chow et al. (2005) adapted the AHP methodology to the service innovation of restaurant industry; it appears not to have been applied as a performance measurement model specifically for service innovation strategy. The objective of this study is to develop a quantitative performance measurement model that can be used for service process performance and strategy selection.

8.3 Research Objectives and Methodology

The objective of the research adopted under the heading of Quantitative Models for Service innovation Strategy (QMSQS) was to identify tools and techniques that would facilitate:

- Identification of factors affecting service innovation
- Identification of the relationship between factors affecting service innovation
- Quantification of the different factors affecting service innovation and on the overall performance of the service processes
- 'What if?' analysis on process performance and strategy selection

The six steps of the approach were developed as a result of the QMSQS methodology implementation as depicted in Fig. 8.1. The details of this approach have been explained and discussed through a case study in Sect. 8.5.

Stage 1: Establishing Strategic Perspectives
At the start of a QMSQS approach, the strategic perspectives should be established within the strategic plan. These perspectives should be used for all the service processes of a business. Perspectives are connected together with the help of the coupling operation. It is not necessary to establish a methodical sequence. However, if the perspectives structure (i.e. the sequence of individual perspectives) is logically established, the automatic generation of a model is considerably simplified and the logical structure of the cause-and-effect chain is made clear.

Stage 2: Defining Strategic Performance Measures
With the QMSQS method, strategic objectives and critical factors taken from different points of view are allocated to the company (the so-called perspectives). These include internal perspectives (e.g. learning and development perspective, process perspective) and external performance perspectives (e.g. patient perspective, hospital and economic perspective). This arrangement of the key performance indicators achieves a certain balance between short-term and long-term goals, hospital and

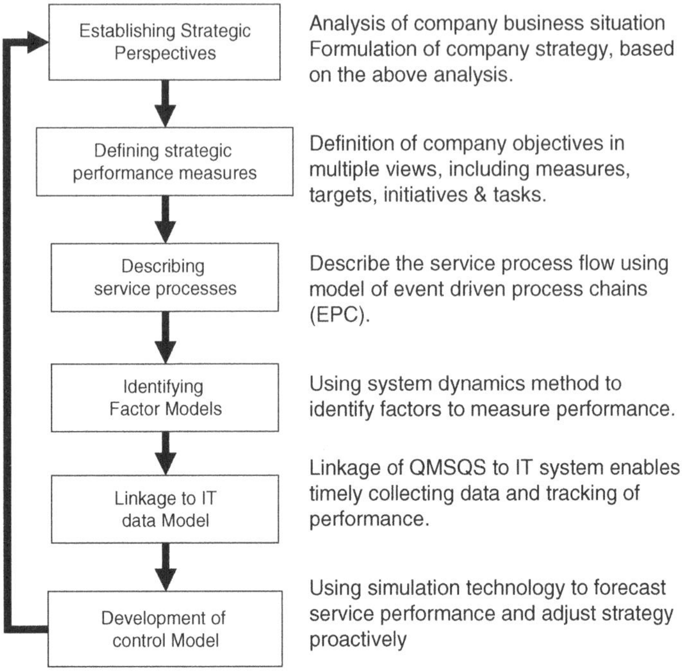

Fig. 8.1 A methodology for service innovation strategy

non-hospital key performance indicators, leading and lagging indicators and internal and external points of view. The introduction of specific key performance indicators for different sectors adds a further benchmarking component to the concept.

In general, the QMSQS approach classifies the relationships between critical factors which affect service innovation as follows:

- Direct (vertical) effect
- Indirect (horizontal) effect
- Self-interaction effect

Stage 3: Describing Service Processes

The quantitative model for service innovation strategy (QMSQS) developed in Sect. 8.4 uses system dynamics models (SDMs) to describe service processes.

The components necessary to provide a full description of a service process are thus procedures, events, products/statuses, processors, organisational units and information technology resources.

Considering all the effects on all the elements of the procedure for every event would severely complicate the model and lead to redundancies in the description. In order to reduce this complexity, the general context is divided into individual models that represent separate modelling and design aspects. These can be processed largely independently of each other. The models are divided in such a way that relationships between the components within a model are very high while those between the models are only relatively loosely linked.

The AHP approaches to the measurement of service innovation are presented in the *Evaluation Models*.

Stage 4: *Identifying Factors to Measure Performance*
The identification of the factors follows on from the service process model. Having created a service process model for the performance measure in question, in this step the activities within each process were analysed in order to establish factors which may contribute towards the particular performance measure. This was achieved through the use of cause-and-effect analysis. The cause-and-effect analysis shows how each service process (shown as a major cause) may have an impact on the performance measure.

These factors provide the structure view for that particular *result model*. In addition, they also lead to the identification of performance measures for use at the tactical and operational levels. The measures identified against each process are considered to be tactical performance measures corresponding to each process. The causes listed under each service process provide the basis for operational measures for that process.

The use of the cause-and-effect analysis technique as described above provides a useful approach to analysis and provides some form of guidance for modelling of the structure of performance measures. It is possible to transpose the information contained in the cause-and-effect model into a more visualised data structure commonly used in information systems analysis.

Stage 5: *Linkage of Resource Class to Data Model*
The project team should consider linking the PMSs to competency development. This enables employees to focus not only on their strategic goals but also on competencies that may be critical for strategy execution, such as teamwork and communication. A company's core competencies (including management competencies) should be selected based on the company's business strategy, core values and culture.

The PMSs should be linked to variable pay to motivate all employees to work together to achieve the company's strategic goals. When designing the variable pay component, it is important to consider the relative importance and priority of objectives in each perspective and at each level of the organisational structure. The decisions made about relative importance and priorities communicate clear messages to all managers and employees.

Stage 6: *Development of Control Models*
The *control model* is a model of the interactions between states and events of a real-time system. The system responds to outside events and passes through a series of modes or states. As events occur, they initiate changes in the system's state.

A possibility for creating the *control model*, which is a means to display how the measures are influencing each other, is the use of a system dynamics (SD)-oriented approach, using a matrix. In the vertical column the influencing measures are written and perpendicular to them the influenced measures. The levels are chosen according to the levels in the structure view.

In the matrix the level of relationship between individual measures is illustrated in the normal SD fashion. That is:

- ++ Strong positive impact
- + Positive impact
- Blank no impact
- – Negative impact
- –– Strong negative impact

This SD-oriented matrix approach provides a valuable technique to describe the dynamic view of a PMS, because it is simple and straightforward to understand.

The use of the SD approach also promotes deployment of priorities between various levels of the PMS. Once the business objectives and strategy are established this will allow prioritisation of the strategic performance measures according to the objectives and the strategy. Once the top-level priorities are in place these could be deployed to lower levels through the relationship matrix using the relationship level as a deployment aid. This type of deployment approach is well described in the widely available SD material. However, in using this approach one must practice particular attention to ensure that priority deployment is carried out between two distinct levels.

8.4 Quantitative Model for Service Innovation Strategy (QMSQS)

This chapter introduces four types of quantitative models, shown in Fig. 8.2, which can support the aforementioned methodology to service innovation indigenous management. Each model is a collection of operation formulae, which can capture the information necessary to describe a service process's state and behaviour. These models are considered essential: a business model, control model, result model and an evaluation model.

The business model also includes four classes of objects: an organisation object, an information object, a function object and an operator object as shown in Fig. 8.2. These classes are proposed based on the object-oriented approach (OOA).

The OOA makes the basic assumption that the world is made of an organised collection of objects. According to this hypothesis, anything within a service firm is also considered an object characterised by its unique and invariant identifier, its object class and its state, defined by the values of its attributes. A business object might be a concrete thing (e.g. a piece of equipment, an employee or a product), an abstract thing (e.g. an enterprise goal, a business process, an enterprise activity, a performance measure or a service) or a relationship between things (e.g. a logical link between two objects).

Individual models are not described in detail in this chapter, since the purpose of each model has been identified and a detailed explanation of its information content

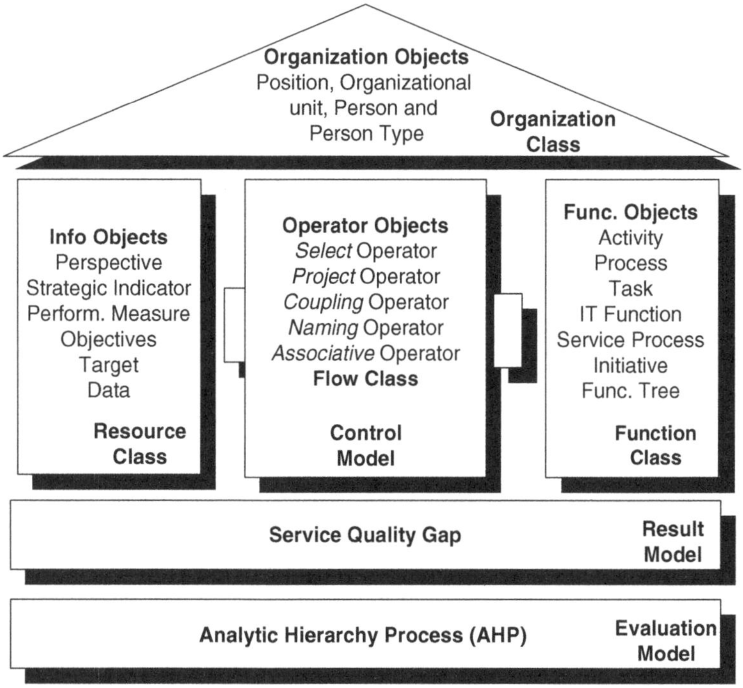

Fig. 8.2 Descriptive views of QMSQS

and functionality is given in Sect. 8.3 and an explanation of their application is given in the case study (see Sect. 8.5). The purpose of this section is to identify and describe the content and functionality of the QMSQS, since these quantitative models must satisfy the methodology requirements of all the steps.

8.4.1 Business Model

Business models are the most important building blocks of our quantitative models. From the OOA point of view, they are a description of a set of abstract business objects that share the same attributes. Our business models are divided from four classes:

8.4.1.1 Organisational Class

The organisational class is a typical form of representing organisational structures. This kind of class reflects the organisational units (as task performers) and their interrelationships, depending on the selected structuring criteria. In order to show the individual positions in the company that have, for example, job descriptions, the separate *position object type* is available. *Organisational units* and *persons* can also be assigned a type.

8.4.1.2 Function Class

The functions to be performed (processes) and their interrelationships with each other form a second view, the function class. It contains the description of the function, the enumeration of the individual sub-functions that belong to the overall relationship and the positional relationships that exist between the functions.

Modelling methods often display functions in connection with objects from the other descriptive views of QMSQS. The relationship between data and functions is displayed, for example, to specify the transformation process of a function via the input/output data of that function.

In the QMSQS architecture, however, the various areas of analysis are kept strictly separate. Within the function only those representational forms are used which illustrate the connections between the functions. One example is the relationship between functions and data displayed in the control model of QMSQS.

8.4.1.3 Information Class

Events such as ‘patient order received’ or ‘invoice produced’ define the point at which a change in the state of information objects (data) occurs. They are described in the *information class* of the QMSQS architecture.

An information class includes a description of the semantic data model of the field which is to be examined. According to the QMSQS division principle, this description contains both the objects which specify the start and end events of a process chain and the status descriptions of a service process chain’s relevant environment.

An entity-relationship model (ERM) is the most widely used designing method for semantic data models. This modelling method uses a number of specialised terms such as entity type, relationship type and attribute. The relationships which exist between these objects and information technology (IT) are linked via coupling operators which will be introduced in the next section.

8.4.1.4 Flow Class

The *flow class* is structured as an integrated view in which the relationships between the other object classes are described by the *operator object*.

The operator object consists of a set of operations that take one or two objects as the input and produce a new object as their result. The fundamental operations in the flow class are *select*, *project*, *Cartesian product* and *associative*.

The *select* operation selects tuples that satisfy a given predicate. We use the lowercase Greek letter sigma (σ) to denote selection. The predicate appears as a subscript to σ. The argument relation is in parentheses after the σ.

The *project* operation allows us to produce this relation. The project operation is a unary operation that returns its argument relation, with certain attributes left out. Since a relation is a set, any duplicate rows are eliminated. Projection is denoted by the uppercase Greek letter pi (Π). We list those attributes that we wish to appear in the result as a subscript to Π.

The *Cartesian-product* operation, denoted by a cross (×), allows us to combine information from any two objects.

The *associative* operation is a binary operation that allows us to combine certain selections and a Cartesian product into one operation. It is denoted by the ‘join’ symbol ‘)‘’. The associative operation forms a Cartesian product of its two arguments, performs a selection forcing equality on those attributes that appear in both relation objects and finally removes the duplicate attributes.

8.4.2 Control Model

Indigenous management is mainly concerned with detailed action planning and the preparations to take these action steps. Thus, all general decisions have already been made and—sometimes—a model might already exist. The purpose of system dynamics modelling in service innovation indigenous management is to communicate the decisions that have been made, involve stakeholders in the implementation and provide means for ‘optimisation’ within the given decision frame. The usage of system dynamics in indigenous management differs from system dynamics modelling in strategy formulation insofar that:

- The scope of changes that can be made to the actual strategy is very limited.
- Frequently, a high number of people from all organisational hierarchical levels are involved either in the modelling itself or in connected activities.
- The main purpose of modelling is for understanding and refining a decision that has already been made.

This section is a detailed discussion of the system dynamics modelling, which allows for simple representation of complex cause-and-effect relationships. For the discussion that follows, it is important to understand that it is the levels (or state variables) that define the dynamics of a system. For the mathematically inclined, we can introduce this in a more formal way. The following equations show the basic mathematical form of the QMSQS:

$$\begin{aligned} measures[i]_t &= \int_0^T levels[j]_t \, dt; \\ \frac{d}{dt} measures[i]_t &= levels[j]_t \end{aligned} \tag{8.1}$$

or

$$\begin{aligned} rates_t &= levels_t \, dt = \int_0^T rates_t \, dt \frac{d}{dt} levels_t \\ rates_t &= \mathbf{g}(levels_t, aux_t, data_t, const) \end{aligned} \tag{8.2}$$

$$aux_t = \mathbf{f}(levels_t, aux_t, data_t, const) \tag{8.3}$$

$$levels_o = \mathbf{h}(levels_o, aux_o, data_o, const) \tag{8.4}$$

In these equations **g**, **h** and **f** are arbitrary, nonlinear, potentially time varying, vector-valued functions. Equation (8.1) represents the evolution of the system over time, (8.2) the computation of the rates determining that evolution, (8.3) the intermediate results necessary to compute the rates and (8.4) the initialisation of the system.

The symbols *aux*, *const*, *data*, *levels* and *rates* represent different types of variables:

- aux_t Auxiliary. These are computed (see (8.3)) from Levels, Constants, Data and other Auxiliaries. Auxiliary variables have no memory and their current values are independent of the values of variables at previous times.
- *const* Constants. These do not change with time.
- $data_t$ Data (also called exogenous). These have values that change over time but are independent of anything that happens to other variables.
- $levels_t$ Levels (also called accumulations, stocks and states). These change only over time and the values they take on at any time depend on the value they (and other variables) took on at previous times. Equation (8.1) shows how the Levels integrate or 'accumulate' based on the values themselves and other variables in the system. The Level variables ultimately determine the dynamic behaviour of a system.
- $rates_t$ Rates (also called flows). These are the variables that directly change the Levels. Rates are essentially the same as Auxiliaries and differ only in the way they are used in a model.

Rates are implicitly determined based on Auxiliaries and other variables and are not broken out as a separate variable type. Put another way, an Auxiliary that is used to change a Level can also be thought of as a Rate.

In the following section, we underline our thesis by a case study from a traditional Chinese hospital trying to implement a strategy. After that, we discuss some general issues of system dynamics modelling for indigenous management of service innovation.

8.4.3 Result Model

The result model proposed here is capable of constructing a PMS, using a set of metrics generated by a control model.

Static models of service innovation gaps (SQGs) are, thus, representations of the organisation, at a given moment, which identify, define and interrelate the fundamental organisational dimensions for successful indigenous management.

By listing 20 essential dimensions—represented as ellipses—and by overlapping each ellipse with every other, Candido and Morris (2001) introduced a static model which emphasised the diversity of dimensions that can be involved in indigenous management and the intricacy of their relationships.

Essentially, the model aims to provide a list of all basic dimensions that can constitute important areas for management intervention during strategy formulation and implementation. The model, however, does not imply that managers must intervene on all 20 variables. The specific group of dimensions that a manager will choose to manipulate depends on his/her personal experience and knowledge. But, more importantly, the choice should depend on the current internal and external situation of an organisation, particularly on the SQGs that have been identified before and during implementation (Candido and Morris 2001).

8.4.4 Evaluation Model

Evaluation model uses simulation technology which enables experiments of 'what if?' scenarios to be carried out, giving the designer a better insight into how the proposed enterprise will work. This chapter focuses on the use of simulation for dynamic evaluation. Following the simulation experiments, the design can be refined further, possibly by revisiting the control model. Case studies in the next section will demonstrate the creation and population of evaluation models.

8.5 Illustrative Case

In order to test the concept of the QMSQS model described above, two alternative strategies have been carried out and detailed steps have been given in Sect. 8.3. In this section an application of the QMSQS to model the strategy to 'improve quality of service via e-business' at 'TCM' is presented. The case will show how the QMSQS was used to identify factors affecting performance and their relationships and quantify the effects of the factors on this indigenous management.

'TCM' is a leader in the non-prime automobile financing industry. For 10 years 'TCM' has fulfilled the auto financing needs of consumers across China. Today the company serves patients who may not qualify for loans for their new or used vehicle based on conventional criteria. With a reputation for quality control, an efficient processing system and sturdy capital to fund loans, 'TCM', delivers responsive service to its national network of dealers.

8.5.1 Establishing Strategic Perspectives

The QMSQS methodology's use of different perspectives for organising company objectives enables a significant improvement in the development of the company's strategic management infrastructure. We discuss five perspectives in this company: hospital, patient, process, employee and partner and innovation.

Customers' concerns tend to fall into four categories: time, quality, performance and service and cost. Lead time measures the time required for the company to meet its patients' needs. For existing products, lead time can be measured from the time the company receives an order to the time it actually delivers the product or service to the patient. For new products, lead time represents the time to market, or how long it takes to bring a new product from the product definition stage to the start of shipments. Quality measures the defect level of incoming products as perceived and measured by the patient. Quality could also measure on-time delivery or the accuracy of the company's delivery forecasts. The combination of performance and service measures how the company's products or services contribute to creating value for its patients. Senior managers at 'TCM' established general goals for patient performance: to get standard processes to make credit decisions quicker and to improve patients' time to wait. The managers translated these general goals into four specific goals and identified an appropriate measure for each, as shown in Fig. 8.3.

Using business objects in Information Class (see Sect. 8.4.1.3), the patients' perspective can be described as follows:

8.5.2 Creating Service Processes

The modelling of the company's service process is the starting point for indigenous management. The organisational units, positions, person and locations are shown in Fig. 8.4.

From organisation class (Sect. 8.4.1.1) the *person-type* and *organisation-type* objects can be instantiated as follows:

The organisational object is built by the operator object via links between the person type and organisational units. In this context, a link can have one of the three meanings: 'is technically superior to', 'is disciplinarily superior to' or 'is a component of'.

In this case the process model represents the underlying process which leads to achievement of the strategic objective. It was decided to use business models technique (see Sect. 8.4.1) to model the underlying process. Although it was possible to create a single-process model to encapsulate all activities which affect all the strategic performance measures, it was simpler to create a model of the process focusing on one measure at a time. This resulted in considerable duplication between the models, but it also simplified the model, making the process model more visible. Therefore, in this case study it has been necessary to create a process model for each one of the strategic performance measures identified. These duplication models can be eliminated via flow class objects. In this chapter, for illustration purposes, the strategic measure 'patient satisfaction' has been selected for illustration purposes. Figure 8.5 shows the process model developed for this particular strategic performance measure.

PT = {(1, *Head of SO*, *Listener*),
(2, *Employee of SO*, *Processor*)...
(4, *Assistant of SO*, *Dispatcher*)}

PT = {(1, *Board of management*, *Management*,2,3),
(2, *Internal transaction*, *Business*,4,7)...
(8, *Accounting*, *Technology*,8,2)}

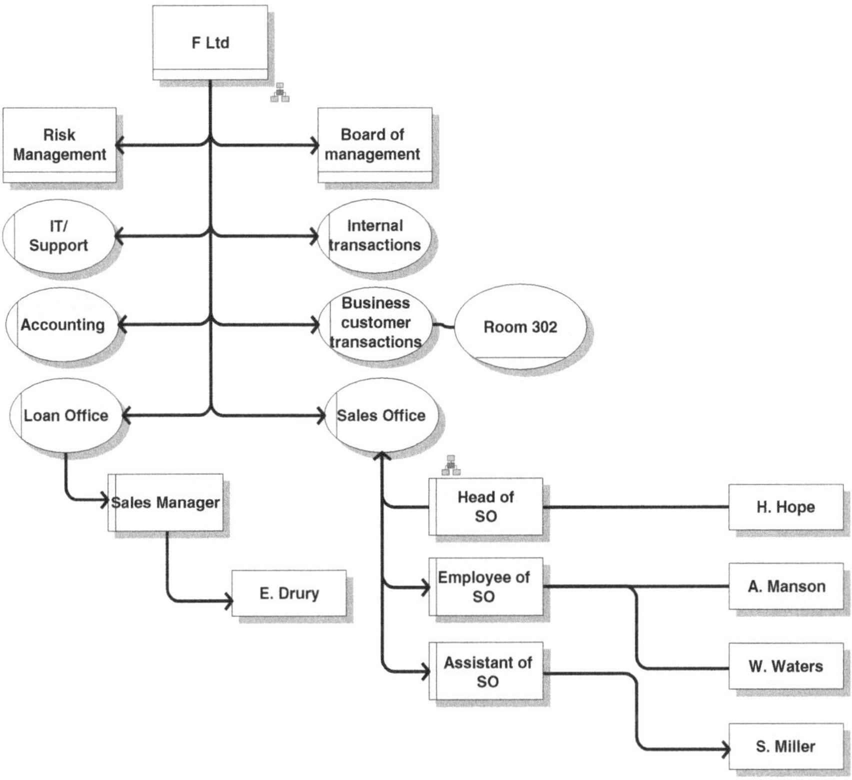

Fig. 8.3 Organisation structure graph of TCM

8.5.3 Establishing Cause-and-Effect Relationships

Having created a process model for the performance measure in question, in this step the activities within each process were analysed in order to establish factors which may contribute towards the particular performance measure. This was achieved through the use of cause-and-effect analysis as shown in Fig. 8.6.

Using organisation class, information class, function class and flow class, the cause-and-effect relationships views for TCM can be analysed to show how each process (shown as a major cause) may have an impact on the performance measure. For example, the Online Private Customer Transactions process can affect the performance of the organisation with respect to 'optimal e-processes'. In turn the

IR = {(1, time, 2007-5-12,2day, efferent),
(2, quality, 2007-3-12,10day, inner),
...(5, cost, 2007-12-12,35day, environmental)}

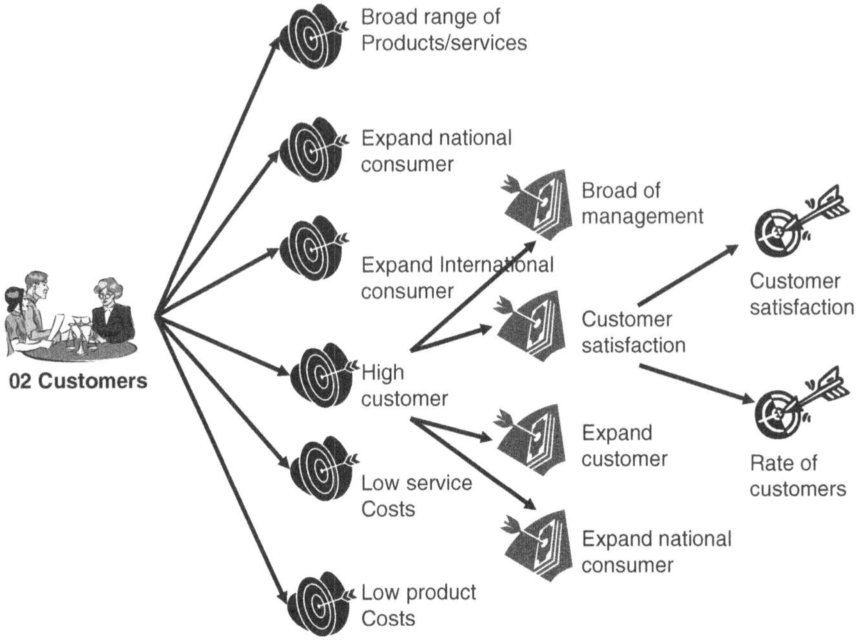

Fig. 8.4 Establish patients' perspective

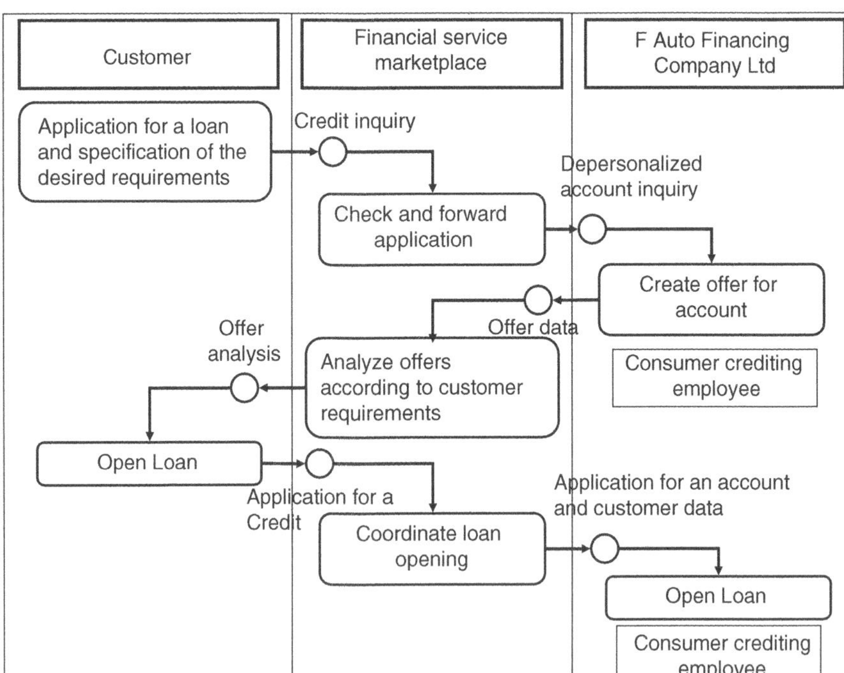

Fig. 8.5 Online services process of TCM

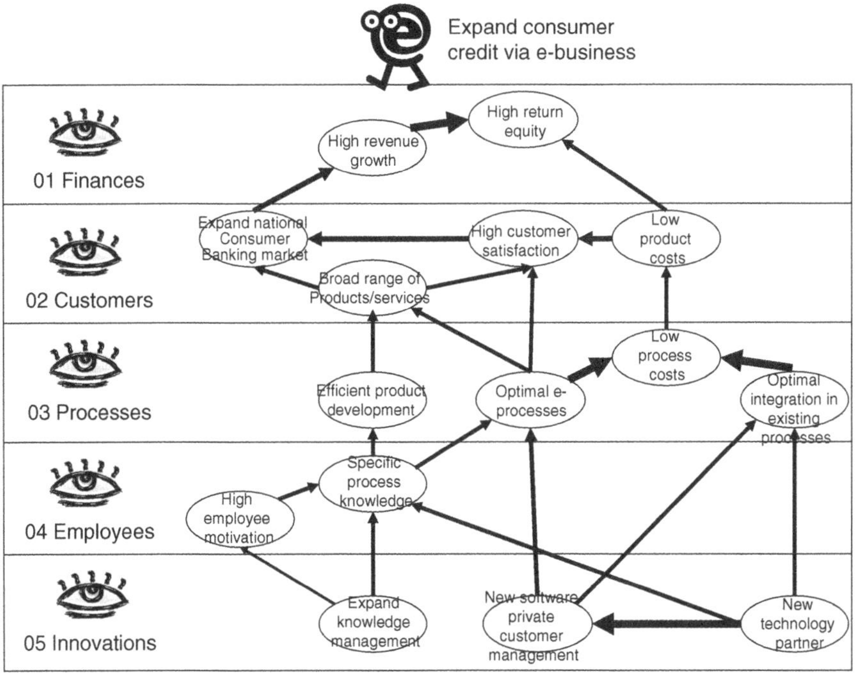

Fig. 8.6 Cause-and-effect views for 'TCM'

factors listed on the upward arrow, such as broad range of products/services, high patient satisfaction, low process costs and low product costs, can constrain the process's ability to fulfil the plan.

8.5.4 Linkage of IT Systems to Monitor Objectives

IT systems play an invaluable role in helping managers disaggregate the summary measures. When an unexpected signal appears on the performance measures, executives can query their information system to find the source of the trouble. If the aggregate measure for on-time delivery is poor, for example, executives with a good information system can quickly look behind the aggregate measure until they can identify late deliveries, day by day, by a particular plant, to an individual patient.

If the information system is unresponsive, however, it can be the Achilles' heel of performance measurement. Managers at 'TCM' are currently limited by the absence of such an operational information system. Their greatest concern is that the service innovation information is not timely; reports are generally a week behind the company's routine management meetings and the measures have yet to be linked to measures for managers and employees at lower levels of the organisation. The company is in the process of developing a more responsive information system to eliminate these constraints which are shown in Fig. 8.7.

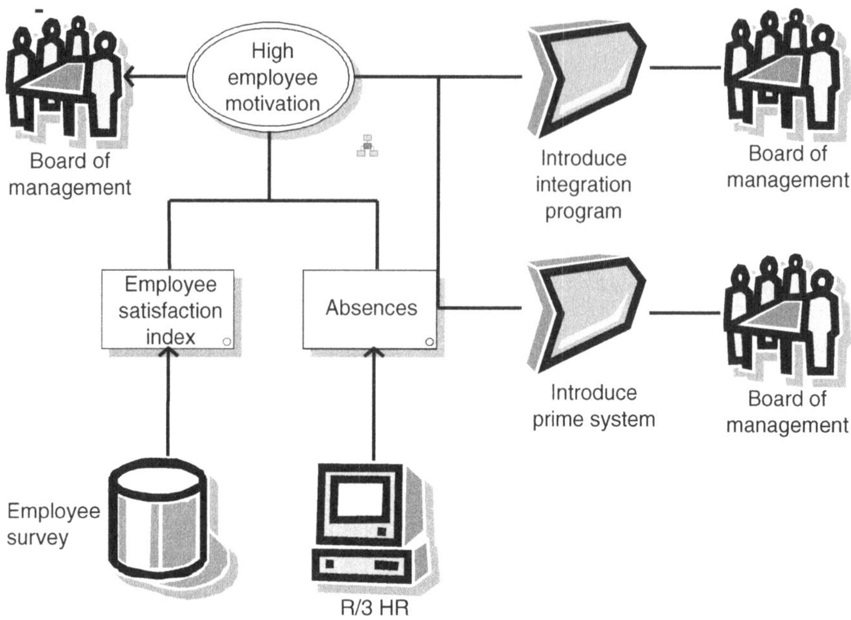

Fig. 8.7 Key performance indicator allocation model

8.5.5 Evaluating the Performance of Alternative Strategies

In the following, we discuss two alternative strategies that can be adopted by 'TCM' depending on the line of loan. If the line is high, the company should adopt the 'customised service' strategy. If line is low, the company should adopt the 'indirect face to patient' strategy. These two strategies require different competitive characteristics as illustrated in Table 8.2.

The differences between the two groups lie in the elements of the characteristics and their relative positions in the group (ranking). The customised strategy primarily stresses service innovation and the ability to perform the service dependably and

Table 8.2 Competitive characteristics of two alternative service innovation strategies

Customised service	Indirect face to patient
Perform the service dependably and accurately	Quick credit decisions
Caring and individual attention	Consistent personal skills
Reliability	Tangibles
Responsiveness	Assurance
Empathy	Responsiveness

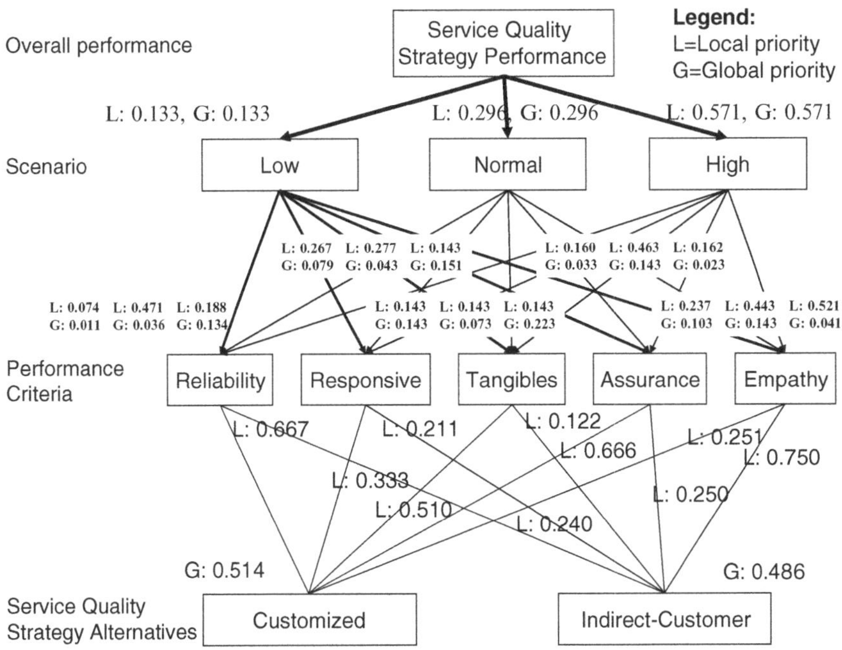

Fig. 8.8 Key performance indicator model

accurately. To have the ability to be reliable, the employees must be able to convey trust and confidence. In other words, they should have personal skills and knowledge. Referring to the banking performance of service innovation, the customised service must be excellent in reliability, responsiveness and empathy. Although it is necessary for TCM to control cost, it is not the principal characteristic for competitiveness.

The indirect-patient strategy prioritises quick credit decisions and dependable loans. To have the ability to make credit decisions rapidly, the service system must be able to shift from one type of loan to another very quickly. In other words, the service system should be flexible and automatic. The next three competitive characteristics are tangibles, consistent personal skills and responsiveness. The ability of the indirect-patient strategy to win competition is affected much more by performance in speed and tangibles than performance in reliability and cost.

Using the QMSQS approach, the hierarchical structure of the evaluation of the performance of customised and indirect-patient service strategies can be constructed as indicated in Fig. 8.8. The level 0 of the structure is the overall performance of the service innovation strategies. The performance of the service innovation strategies depends on the line of the loan (the scenario) as indicated by level 1 of Fig. 8.8. There are three possibilities of the line of loan: low (pessimistic scenario), average (normal scenario) and high (optimistic scenario). Level 2 of the structure shows performance criteria. Based on the generic performance of service innovation strategy, the performance of the alternatives can be evaluated based on the criteria of reliability, responsiveness, tangibles, assurance and empathy. Finally, level 3 of the structure shows the alternative service innovation strategies which could be adopted.

We conducted a presentation to explain the concept of the QMSQS model to the management team of the company. It is very critical in this step to make clear to the management the concept of the pairwise comparison questionnaires used by the model, which ask, 'Comparing factor A to B, which one has a stronger effect on performance?' and 'How strong is that effect?' At the end of the presentation the research team asked the management team to start thinking about the problem that might be selected as the case study.

Evaluation of these alternative strategies is carried out level by level starting from the top level down to the lower levels. The first evaluation assesses the possibilities of scenarios occurring in the planning period. The second evaluation assesses the relative effects of each criterion on performance under a particular scenario.

For example, what are the relative effects of reliability, responsiveness, tangibles, assurance and empathy on performance if the line is low? The relative effects of each criterion on performance are not necessarily the same under different scenarios. The third evaluation assesses the performance of each alternative on each performance criterion. Finally, the overall performance of each alternative can be computed through the composition process as explained earlier.

Using the control model, the performance of customised and indirect-patient strategies can be evaluated as indicated in Fig. 8.8. From the evaluation, it can be seen that the performance of customised patient strategy (0.514) is better than the performance of indirect-patient strategy (0.486), given that the probability of line for low, average and high are 26.3 %, 26.6 % and 44.1 %, respectively.

8.5.6 System Dynamics Analysis of the Service Innovation

Management uses a set of hospital and non-hospital performance measures to monitor and control the operation of companies through a set of performances. As external environments change rapidly, the set of performance measures employed by companies should also change to reflect changes in the environment. That is, performance measures reported to the management should change as a result of changes in patients, competitors, internal improvement and so on. We proposed the use of SDMs to simulate both the macro level of the entire company with interrelationships to patients—which are shown in Fig. 8.9—and the micro level of a credit department—shown in Fig. 8.10—to see the individual tasks performed.

Changes in performance measures can be in the form of deleting, adding or replacing some performance measures with other performance measures or just changing the priority of some performance measures. A performance measure

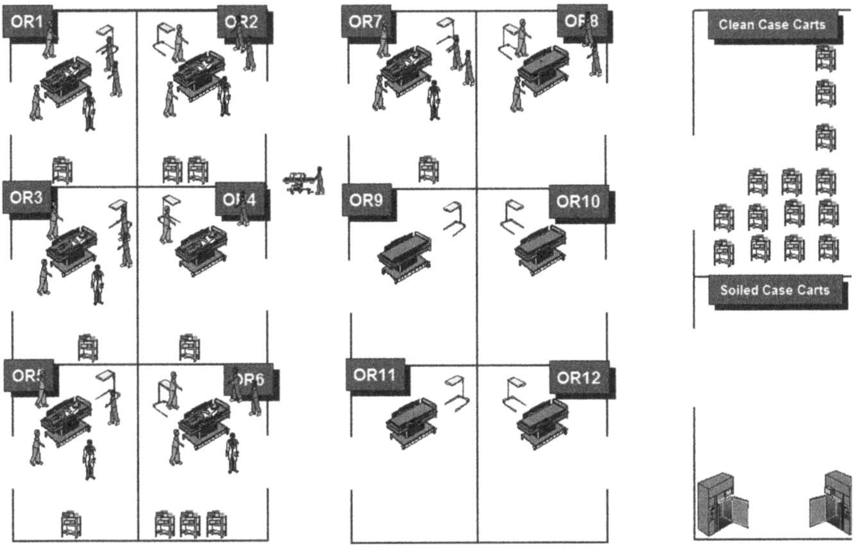

Fig. 8.9 System dynamic analysis of macro level

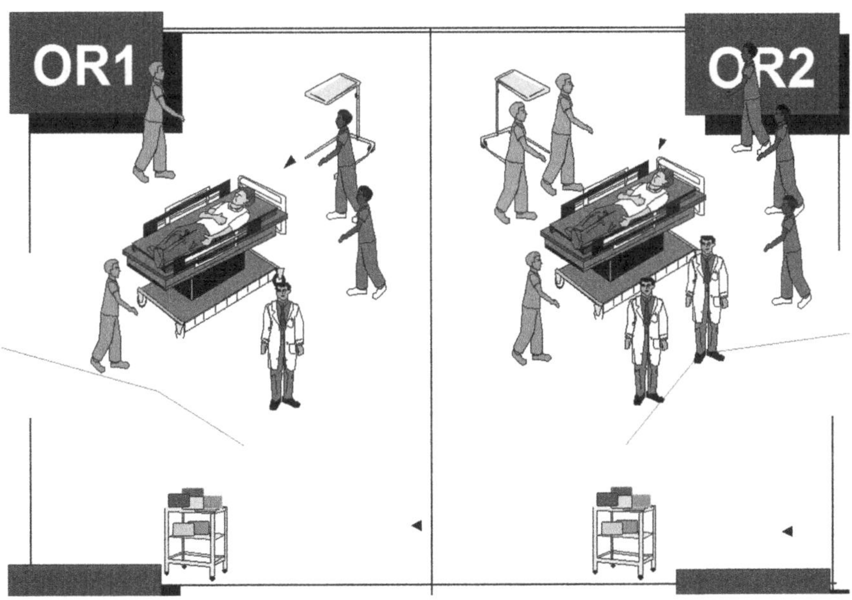

Fig. 8.10 System dynamic analysis of micro level

Table 8.3 Sensitivity analysis of service innovation indigenous management

Low	Normal	High	Cust.	Indirect	Strategy
0.263	0.266	0.441	0.514*	0.486	Customised
1.000	0.000	0.000	0.416	0.584*	Indirect
0.000	1.000	0.000	0.463	0.537*	Indirect
0.000	0.000	1.000	0.565*	0.435	Customised
0.414	0.000	0.586	0.500	0.500	Either
0.530	0.000	0.470	0.485	0.515*	Indirect

*Significantly different from zero at the P = 0.05 significance level

classified as high priority may move to other classes because of changes in the internal or external environments of the business. The QMSQS can cope with the dynamism through the what-if simulation analysis.

For example, for the service innovation strategy evaluation explained earlier, the actual line of loan cannot be known in advance. The judgement of the probability of an occurrence of low, average and/or high loan is based on the information available at the time of evaluation. The judgement may change some time later if more information is available. Based on the current judgement, the priority of customised strategy is better than the priority of indirect strategy. However, it is important to analyse further how the priority will change if the probability of demand level changes. Again the SDMs could be used to evaluate the sensitivity analysis. The results of such analysis, based on the model presented earlier, are illustrated in Table 8.3. If the probability of low line is 100 %, the performance of the indirect strategy will be better than the performance of the customised strategy. While, if the probability of high line is 100 %, the customised strategy will perform better than the indirect strategy.

Finally, if the probability of the occurrence of average line is 100 %, the performance of indirect strategy will be better than the performance of customised strategy. In general, if the probability of the occurrence of low line is greater than 43.3 %, the performance of indirect strategy will be better than the performance of customised strategy as indicated by Table 8.3. The sensitivity analysis can also be carried out on changes of the impacts of performance criteria on performance under different scenarios.

8.6 Discussion and Conclusion

8.6.1 Achievements and Benefits

An approach for quantifying the relationships between various factors affecting performance has been developed and demonstrated. The benefits of the QMSQS approach may be summarised as follows:

- Factors affecting performance can be identified, and then their effects can be quantified.

- Effects of multidimensional factors on performance can be aggregated into a single dimensionless unit (priority).
- Managers can be helped to quantify the level of impact of each factor on overall performance and therefore assisted in focusing improvement activities.
- The relationships between factors can be clearly identified and expressed in quantitative terms.
- Models can be easily altered to assist understanding the dynamic behaviour of factors affecting performance.
- A reduction in the number of performance measurement reports is facilitated.

An important benefit gained from the QMSQS approach is that the interaction of the factors can be clearly identified and expressed in quantitative terms. This identification will bring us one step forward in understanding the dynamic behaviour of factors affecting performance.

8.6.2 *Subjectivity vs. Objectivity of Approach*

People may feel that the technique used in the SDMs for quantifying the effects of factors on performance is very intuitive, subjective and very difficult to use in practice. However, through careful explanation of the concept of the approach, the authors have found that people can understand and implement it with little difficulty.

In a PMS a large number of multidimensional factors can affect performance. Integrating those multidimensional effects into a single unit can only be done through subjective, individual or group judgement. It is impossible to have objective measurements and scale systems for each different dimension of measurement that can facilitate objective value trade-off between different measures. Since the quality of service uses subjective measurement, the results may not be very accurate. However, this problem can be overcome by using group judgement rather than individual judgement. This will reduce the subjectivity of the judgement. The accuracy of the QMSQS can also be improved through experience.

8.6.3 *Practical Issues*

The example presented in the paper is highly simplified. In practice the evaluation will be more complicated as all important factors affecting the performance of service innovation strategy will need to be included in the model and the interactions among factors should be considered and agreed. Some potential problems might be encountered in applying the QMSQS method. The first relates to managers' hesitation in filling in the pairwise comparison questionnaires, particularly if the model is applied to model performance improvement. Performance improvement usually involves identification and quantification of a large number of factors affecting performance. Consequently, the number of pairwise comparison questionnaires will be enormous. Filling in all the questionnaires will be exhausting and time-consuming. However, this problem can be minimised through three approaches:

- Firstly the users, i.e. the management team, must be involved in the whole process. In the case study example presented in this chapter, the researchers helped the management team to build a model of their PMS using the cognitive mapping technique. This in turn heightened the team's awareness of the interaction between various factors affecting performance in their company.
- Secondly the model should be decomposed into several smaller models which are then distributed to groups of people who complete only a subset of the overall questionnaire.
- The use of the interactive software makes the implementation of the model much easier. In fact the QMSQS model is now being implemented at 'TCM' to prioritise 100 performance measures.

The second problem of the QMSQS application relates to getting a single judgement in pairwise comparison if more than one person is involved in filling in the questionnaires. Several discussions may be required to elaborate the real situation before a general consensus of the judgement of a particular problem can be achieved. Dynamic modelling is also an effective tool which could be used to elaborate the problem.

In summary, this chapter demonstrates the theoretical feasibility of using the QMSQS approach to implement suitable service innovation strategy through quantification of the relationships between performance measures and factors affecting quality of service.

Acknowledgements We would like to thank National Technology Support Program (2009BAH53B02), National Soft Science Planning (2011GXQ4K029) and National Natural Science Foundation of China (Grant No. 70831003).

References

Ahluwalia, S., & Offredy, M. (2005). A qualitative study of the impact of the implementation of advanced access in primary healthcare on the working lives of general practice staff. *BMC Family Practice, 6*, 39.

Atkinson, A. A., Waterhouse, J. H., & Wells, R. B. (1997). A stakeholder approach to strategic performance measurement. *Sloan Management Review, 38*, 25–37.

Ben-Tovim, D., Bassham, J. E., Bennett, D. M., Dougherty, M. L., Martin, M. A., & O'Neill, S. J. (2008). Redesigning care at the flinders medical centre: Clinical process redesign using "lean thinking". *Medical Journal of Australia, 188*(6), S27–31.

Bititci, U. S. (1995). Modelling of performance measurement systems in manufacturing enterprises. *International Journal of Production Economics, 42*, 137–147.

Bowen, D. E., & Youngdahl, W. E. (1998). "Lean" service: In defense of a production-line approach. *International Journal of Service Industry Management, 9*, 207–225.

Candido, C. J. F. (2005). Service quality strategy implementation: A model and the case of the Algarve hotel industry. *Total Quality Management and Business Excellence, 16*, 3–14.

Candido, C. J. F., & Morris, D. S. (2000). Charting service quality gaps. *Total Quality Management, 11*, S463–S472.

Candido, C. J. F., & Morris, D. S. (2001). The implications of service quality gaps for strategy implementation. *Total Quality Management, 12*, 825–833.

Chow, C. C., & Luk , P. (2005). A strategic service quality approach using analytic hierarchy process. *Managing Service quality, 15*(3), 278–289.

Dahlgaard, J. J., & Dahlgaard, S. M. (2006). Lean production, six sigma quality, TQM and company culture—A Critical Review. *The TQM Magazine, 18*, 263–281.

De Koning, H., Verver, J. P. S., Van den Heuvel, J., Bisgaard, S., & Does, R. (2006). Lean Six Sigma in healthcare. *Journal for Healthcare Quality, 28*, 4–11.

Den Boer, K. T., De Wit, L. T., Dankelman, J., & Gouma, D. J. (1999). Peroperative time-motion analysis of diagnostic laparoscopy with laparoscopic ultrasonography. *British Journal of Surgery, 86*, 951–955.

De Toni, A., & Tonchia, S. (2005). Definitions and linkages between operational and strategic flexibilities. *Omega-International Journal of Management Science, 33*, 525–540.

Dey, P. K., Hariharan, S., & Clegg, B. T. (2006). Measuring the operational performance of intensive care units using the analytic hierarchy process approach. *International Journal of Operations & Production Management, 26*, 849–865.

Dickson, E. W., Singh, S., Cheung, D. S., Wyatt, C. C., & Nugent, A. S. (2008). Application of Lean Manufacturing Techniques in the Emergency Department, *Journal of Emergency Medicine*.

Dobni, C. B., & Luffman, G. (2003). Determining the scope and impact of market orientation profiles on strategy implementation and performance. *Strategic Management Journal, 24*, 577.

Dye, R. A. (2004). Strategy selection and performance measurement choice when profit drivers are uncertain. *Management Science, 50*, 1624–1637.

Harding, J. A., & Popplewell, K. (2000). Simulation: An application of factory design process methodology. *Journal of the Operational Research Society, 51*, 440–448.

Hudson, M., Smart, A., & Bourne, M. (2001). Theory and practice in SME performance measurement systems. *International Journal of Operations & Production Management, 21*, 1096–1115.

Jimmerson, C., Weber, D., & Sobek, D. K. (2005). Reducing waste and errors: Piloting lean principles at IHC. *Joint Commission Journal on Quality and Safety, 31*, 249–257.

Johnson, C., Allen, R. H., Sonderman, T. A., & Wedgwood, I. D. (2004, 28 February). Attacking waste and variation hospital-wide: A comprehensive Lean Sigma Development Available: http://www.iienet.org/uploadedFiles/SHS/Lean%20Sigma%20Deployment%20Columbus%20Regional%20Hospital%20Charles%20Johnson.pdf.

Jones, D., & Mitchell, A. (2006). Lean thinking for the NHS. *National Health Service (NHS) Confederation Report, UK*.

Kaplan, R. S., & Norton, D. P. (2005). The balanced scorecard: Measures that drive performance. *Harvard Business Review, 83*, 172.

King, D. L., Ben-Tovim, D. I., & Bassham, J. (2006). Management and Quality Redesigning emergency department patient flows: Application of Lean Thinking to health care. *Emergency Medicine Australasia, 18*, 391.

Koota, P., & Takala, J. (1998). Developing a performance measurement system tor world-class distribution logistics by using activity-based costing and management: Case: Basic metal industries. *International Journal of Technology Management, 16*, 267–280.

Maier-Speredelozzi, V., Thompson, A., Hossfield, P., & Abby, S. (2005). *Applying lean principles to a continuing care patient dischage process*.

Moden, Y. (1993). *Toyota production system: An introduction to just-in-time* (2nd ed.). Norcross, GA: Industrial Engineering and Management Press.

Neely, A., Gregory, M., & Platts, K. (2005). Performance measurement system design—A literature review and research agenda. *International Journal of Operations & Production Management, 25*, 1228–1263.

Park, C., Occena, L. G., Goodwin, C., & Payne, A. (1998). Analysis of performance measures—A veterans home case study. *Journal of Nursing Administration, 28*, 28–35.

Rangone, A. (1996). An analytical hierarchy process framework for comparing the overall performance of manufacturing departments. *International Journal of Operations & Production Management, 16*, 104–119.

Reichhart, A. (2007). Lean distribution: Concepts, contributions, conflicts. *International Journal of Production Research, 45*, 3699–3722.

Saaty, T. L. (1980). The Analytic Hierarchy Process, McGraw Hill International.

Saaty, T. L., & Vargas, L. G. (2001). *Models, methods, concepts & applications of the analytic hierarchy process*. Boston: Kluwer Academic Publishers.

Shinohara, M. (2006). *European and Japanese Logistics Paradigms: An Explorative and comparative study of the dynamics of logistics management*. Thesis Erasmus University Rotterdam.

Taj, S., & Berro, L. (2006). Application of constrained management and lean manufacturing in developing best practices for productivity improvement in an auto-assembly plant. *International Journal of Productivity and Performance Management, 55*, 332–345.

Tolga Taner, M., Sezen, B., & Antony, J. (2007). An overview of Six Sigma applications in healthcare industry. *International Journal of Health Care Quality Assurance, 20*, 329–340.

Wegelius-Lehtonen, T. (2001). Performance measurement in construction logistics. *International Journal of Production Economics, 69*, 107–116.

Womack, J. P., & Jones, D. T. (1996). *Lean thinking*. New York, NY: Simon & Schuster.

Womack J. P., & Jones, D. T. (2003). *Lean Thinking: Banish Waste and Create Wealth in Your Corporation*: Free Press.

Young, T., Brailsford, S., Connell, C., Davies, R., Harper, P., & Klein, J. H. (2004). Using industrial processes to improve patient care. *British Medical Journal, 328*, 162–4.

Yu, B., Harding, J. A., & Popplewell, K. (2000). A reusable enterprise model. *International Journal of Operations & Production Management, 20*, 50–69.

Yurdakul, M., & Ic, Y. T. (2005). Development of a performance measurement model for manufacturing companies using the AHP and TOPSIS approaches. *International Journal of Production Research, 43*, 4609–4641.

Zhang, X., & Prybutok, V. R. (2004). An empirical study of online shopping: A service perspective. *International Journal of Services, Technology and Management, 5*, 1–13.

Chapter 9
Lean Thinking in Dementia Care Through Smart Assistive Technology: An Evaluation

Trudy Yuginovich and Jeffrey Soar

Abstract This chapter provides an analysis and evaluation of a community-based project trialling the use of smart assistive technologies (ATs) for people with dementia and their families. The 12-month project was funded by Home and Community Care (HACC) Queensland and conducted by Alzheimer's Queensland and the University of Southern Queensland in the North Brisbane and Toowoomba areas.

Participants in the project were selected on the basis of having a diagnosis or suspected diagnosis of dementia; live at home and be HACC eligible. In most cases they were service users of Alzheimer's Queensland respite centres, but some were referred from other services; all participants had expressed an interest in trialling AT. All participants were assessed by an Occupational Therapist, and then based on this assessment of individual need and functional capacity were prescribed individual items of AT.

AT prescribed included sensor mats, emergency call systems, robot vacuum cleaners, calendar clocks, bed occupancy and exit sensors, and personal amplifying devices. Depending on when the clients entered the study, the period of trial of equipment varied from 11 months to less than 1 month. Carers were required to complete a survey before and after a trial of the AT, as well as the option to participate in an interview and or focus group after the trial. Data was also collected via interviews with the project Occupational Therapists to gain their feedback on the strengths, weaknesses and general applicability of the AT for this group. Data was analysed using both qualitative and quantitative methods.

The challenges of caring for a person with Alzheimer's disease or other forms of dementia were identified by participants in this study as being the inability to stop worrying, feeling afraid all the time, feeling isolated and feeling vulnerable.

T. Yuginovich (✉) • J. Soar
School of Information Systems, Faculty of Business & Law,
University of Southern Queensland, West St., Toowoomba, QLD 4350, Australia
e-mail: jeffrey.soar@usq.edu.au; petertrud@bigpond.com

N. Wickramasinghe et al. (eds.), *Lean Thinking for Healthcare*, Healthcare Delivery in the Information Age, DOI 10.1007/978-1-4614-8036-5_9,

The main carer concerns were perceived as being the client falling, risk of fire and inability for the client to be left alone. Lack of sleep and inability to relax were identified as major issues for carers.

The most useful and successful types of AT were identified by respondents as being sensor mat with remote pager, bed exit sensor with interval timer and pager, the robotic vacuum cleaner and the hearing devices. Vacuum cleaners were seen as increasing independence and hearing devices improved communication.

Quantitative survey results found a significant reduction in the extent to which carers were worried about the client getting out of bed at night and falling following the implementation of AT. Qualitative results obtained in the focus groups and in-depth interviews then linked this decreased worried to improved carer sleep patterns. No difference was found in the ability of carers to leave the client alone at home as a result of the AT, nor any indication that AT made the clients feel safer. AT did not reduce their need for external support services (respite) and in-home care (housework and/or meals). Contrary to expectations, results also found that neither the levels of stress nor the frequency of stress chaptered by carers decreased significantly secondary to the introduction of AT. Finally, carers had perceived that using the AT would enable the client to remain home longer; however, this was not supported by the post-AT survey.

Carers noted that it did not take long for them to feel comfortable with the technology in the home.

All carers indicated both in surveys and interview that they felt comfortable to contact AQ at any time, but despite this training and support, when problems arose (such as persistent beeping by sensor mats or flat batteries), the carers indicated that they simply unplugged the AT and stopped using it.

Involvement in the selection of the type of AT to be used was important for carers who stated that they appreciated being able to identify their particular needs, to be listened to and to be provided with adequate and appropriate education upon receipt of the AT.

9.1 Introduction

Life expectancy of people in developed countries worldwide is continuing to increase (Currell et al. 2000), creating health implications, and places greater pressure on the community and residential facilities (Currell et al. 2000; World Health Organization 2005; Bayliss et al. 2007). As well as an ageing population, the incidences of people diagnosed with dementia have increased over the last decade and are predicted to continue to increase. The needs of this group of clients' places increased pressure in relation to care and financial costs on the aged care sector. As a result clients, carers and the government want older people to stay in their own home as long as possible (Currell et al. 2000; World Health Organization 2005; Darkins et al. 2008). One possible way to achieve this is through the use of assistive technology (AT) (McCreadie and Tinker 2005; Cowan and Turner-Smith 1999).

Assistive technologies (ATs) are key enablers for change in community aged care, by reducing the risks of adverse events for consumers and, ultimately, enabling persons to remain in their own homes longer, reduce costs and improve outcomes (McCreadie and Tinker 2005). They also have a role in promoting and maintaining a person's dignity, respect and independence (Faife 2007; Hagen et al. 2007). There is some evidence emerging internationally to suggest AT can provide care at lower cost, deliver consumer satisfaction, improve workforce productivity, better assist consumers in self-care and decrease hospital admissions (Glover et al. 2007). This is important in view of figures suggesting that in Australia, 9 % or 552,000 hospital admissions were found to be potentially avoidable, with almost one third of those occurring in the 75 years and over age bracket (Glover et al. 2007).

Limited information or research exists in relation to how smart assistive technology can assist clients with dementia to remain independent at home for longer. This literature review considered all primary studies that explored the lived experiences of consumers and health professionals in relation to use of assistive technologies in the community. Previous research (Hegney et al. 2006) found that the aged and community sector particularly those in rural and remote communities often do not have access to suitable internet infrastructure, support and training to assist them in their work.

Health professionals such as registered nurses, Occupational Therapists, social workers, carers and physiotherapists work in a field where there is a likelihood of a high level of adverse events, conditions and unmet needs of the frail aged needing support in the community (Soar and Youngjoon 2007). These adverse events include falls, difficulties in managing medications, incontinence, social isolation, fear of crime, depression, cognitive decline and associated challenges such as wandering and safety (Soar and Youngjoon 2007). Such issues are similarly highlighted by other researchers (McMillen and Soderberg 2002) who identified that the relationship between the approach that people take to their illness and the acceptance of using AT needs further study.

AT has been described as 'any device or system that allows an individual to perform a task that they would otherwise be unable to do, or increases the ease and safety with which the task can be performed (McCreadie and Tinker 2005; Cowan and Turner-Smith 1999)'. The terminology around AT can vary greatly and encompass a variety of specific equipment. Telecare for instance is an assistive technology that uses a combination of alarms, sensors and other equipment, connected to a response centre to support functional independence (Cook 2008; National Health System (NHS) 2009).

An example of AT is a bed occupancy sensor that can be used to monitor when a person gets out of bed at night and if they do not return within a certain period. Bed sensors can be linked with an automatic light sensor so that when the person gets out of bed, the light turns on. Similarly, door exit sensors will detect if someone opens the front door and movement detectors will provide an alert if the person then leaves their home at a time that might be inappropriate (Cook 2008; National Health System (NHS) 2009).

The power of AT is still under-recognised by physicians and other health providers (McIntosh et al. 2012; Bonner and Idris 2012; Bewernitz et al. 2009), and its potential as an aid to clients is underexploited. There are limits to the extent to which rehabilitation professionals can help to improve the skills of impaired people and the broader environments in which they live, and AT provides powerful means to overcome those limitations. In the USA, the effectiveness of Telecare has been demonstrated (Darkins et al. 2008) by the implementation of home Telecare which reduced hospital admissions by 19 %, hospital bed days by 25 % and readmissions by 25 %.

With nearly 14 % of people over age 71 diagnosed with some form of dementia and prevalence increasing to nearly 40 % of those over age 90 (Bewernitz et al. 2009), cognitive impairment is an important issue when considering supporting people living at home. As dementia progresses, it impacts a person's independent functions and can increase the burden on caregivers. Use of assistive devices can help individuals with dementia live more independently and safely. However, older individuals with cognitive impairment, visual, auditory or speech disabilities may have difficulties using AT because the devices are not designed to address their specific needs. The development of 'smart devices' has potential in assisting older adults with cognitive impairment (Bewernitz et al. 2009).

The application of AT for use in the home should be directed by the client as the key stakeholders, collectively and individually rather than the developers (Harris 2010). It is important to gain an insight into the experiences of the end user of AT in order to design technology which meets carer needs (Cohen-Mansfield and Biddison 2007). It must be noted that not everyone will benefit from or accept the new technological aids and devices and each individual's situation must be carefully assessed (Miskelly 2001; Murasa et al. 2008).

AT is most effective when provided early in the disease process and after careful assessment, the correct prescription and home-based follow-up training in how to use it. Research (Connell et al. 2008) also suggests that families and carers have an improved sense of confidence about older peoples' quality of life when they are provided with comprehensive Telecare and/or 'smart' technology. Overall, the technology can improve 'peace of mind' for older people and carers and may also improve safety, reduce hospitalisation, improve quality of life and enhance opportunities to remain at home, thereby deferring the need to move into residential care.

Despite current advances in the range of technology and networking capabilities in the home, AT and Telecare solutions have not been taken up as eagerly as might have been anticipated (Clark and McGee-Lennon 2011; Cornes and Weinstein 2005; Choi 2011). These barriers include lack of clear access and information points for people to learn about AT and be properly assessed and lack of follow-up home-based training and basic maintenance of technologies. Other barriers include poor design and unattractive appearance of aids and devices, compounding concerns related to self-image, feelings of stigma and denial about disability and ageing (Connell et al. 2008). Many stakeholders emphasised that the design of technologies often lacks consideration of older people's views, attitudes and tastes. Another significant barrier for older people is apprehension about the cost and affordability of assistive technologies.

Findings highlight the need to expand usage of and promotion of equal access to technologies that enable greater social and economic participation for people. Government funding of AT needs to move beyond a limited focus on functional needs and take responsibility for fully equipping clients' homes. Government and service systems are seen to be a constraining rather than an enabling force (Layton and Wilson 2009). These findings reveal that when sectors work together, they can provide quality, cost-effective support services that do reduce demands on staff at the same time as providing benefits to consumers.

Evaluating AT services to demonstrate quality or measure outcomes requires ethical obligation (DeRuyter 1995). The ethics involved in providing AT is not widely discussed (Zwijsen et al. 2011). However, recommendations were made that partnerships between industry, consumers and purchasers of the technology must be established and be long-term commitments (3–5 years at least) (Goodwin 2012). Partnership and long-term commitment will assist in developing AT which is user friendly, easy to manage, improve client outcomes and reduce carer burnout. Decision making about AT must respect the rights of individuals.

Despite some evidence indicating the validity of AT as a means of enhancing safety and reducing hospitalisation, uptake of the technology remains low in many places. Historically, user experiences have not been adequately explored. Some of the reasons included funding, policies, cost, invasion of privacy, lower educational attainment and fear of technology as some of the barriers. Other issues raised by the literature include benefits of AT and its associated ability to reduce hospitalisations and enabling people to remain in their own homes longer. Lack of inclusion of clients in decision making processes was repeatedly raised as an issue as was lack of user friendliness of some forms of AT. The ethics of decision making in relation to AT by practitioners was identified as an area that has had little overt discussion. For these reasons a need exists to further explore the experiences of those using the technology to better identify the benefits and issues of AT in the community.

9.2 Methodology

9.2.1 Objective

The primary objective of this project was to demonstrate the usability of smart assistive technologies for clients who have dementia and/or who are frail aged. The study aimed to identify evidence in relation to the experiences of carers of a person with dementia, over 65, living at home with AT. Alzheimer's Queensland's (AQ) aim for the project was to determine how using smart assistive technology might be of benefit (or detriment) to clients, their carers and families and what factors influence this. Smart assistive technology uptake was determined using a client-focused approach, in line with AQ's philosophy. The overall aims of implementing assistive technology into clients with dementia homes were to assess whether there were:

- Increased safety in the home whether living independently or with carers
- Decreased carer burden and anxiety

- Reduced need for in-home, residential or community care
- Reduced wandering
- Earlier chaptering of falls and/or injuries

9.2.2 *Method*

The impact of smart assistive technology uptake was determined using a client-focused approach based on Fourth Generation Evaluation (FGE) as the theoretic framework and methodology to answer the research questions posed. This involved the development, implementation and review of rigorous screening and assessment tools to ensure that clients are prescribed smart assistive technology that is appropriate to their individual needs and promotes the client's functional independence. FGE identifies stakeholders' claims and issues and then reaches a consensus about the phenomena (in this case, assistive devices and consumer satisfaction with outcomes) (Guba and Lincoln 2003). It encourages the use of multiple methods (in this case, focus groups, in-depth interviews and surveys) to accomplish the facilitation of stakeholder views by focus groups, semi-structured interviews or satisfaction surveys. It uses a constructivist inquiry method that is outcome oriented and includes the dynamic, human, political social, cultural and contextual elements (Guba and Lincoln 1989). It also contributes to the philosophy of community development and empowerment that underpins practice such as in the current study (Clendon 2003).

The study involved five phases: (1) AQ staff managed the project, (2) USQ developed the surveys whilst AQ utilised their current tools, (3) Tunstall provided a 2-day workshop to AQ staff and management, (4) ongoing service provision including screening and assessment of the appropriateness of using smart assistive technology for individual Home and Community Care (HACC) clients was provided throughout the study, (5) USQ collected data via focus groups (lasting about 2 h), surveys and in-depth interviews. Participants were invited to discuss issues and benefits or otherwise of the assistive devices they were using. Interviews were digitally recorded and transcribed with participant permission. The assessment process used ensured that the participant was looked at holistically (including all activities) which involved the technology and how it will impact within the context that the person lives.

9.2.3 *Data Collection*

9.2.3.1 Sampling and Recruitment

Inclusion Criteria

Carers and people with dementia living at home were invited to participate in the study. Clients and carers were selected by the Occupational Therapists (OTs) in the two centres. To ensure the quality of the service developed under the smart assistive technology project, the client must fall within the following criteria:

- Must live in Brisbane North or Darling Downs HACC regions
- Must have a diagnosis or suspected diagnosis of dementia
- Live at home
- Must be HACC eligible

Approximately 60+ clients with carers were screened and assessed as being suitable to trial the smart assistive technology. The final number that agreed to be involved in the project and provide feedback was 39 carers.

9.2.3.2 Data Collection and Limitations

Two surveys were developed (pretest, posttest) and were delivered to carers in each of the two locations. The second survey tool was delivered 1–11 months after the AT was provided. Data collected via the surveys was analysed using SPSS.

Thirty-nine participants over the 12 months were involved in the project. Data was collected in various formats, in two different locations and at three different periods in time. The results cannot be generalised across populations, based on the small sample and study findings. Researchers contacted each of these carers individually and offered them the opportunity to participate in an in-depth phone interview. This resulted in 15 people expressing willingness to be interviewed. (Interviews lasted about 45–70 min each.) An additional four carers participated in a focus group

9.2.3.3 Ethics

Ethics approval was obtained from the University of Southern Queensland ethics committee prior to commencing the study (approval number *H11REA111*). Prior to commencement each participant was provided with a plain language statement outlining the purpose of the study and a consent form.

9.3 Summary of Findings

Note. Key to following tables and figures: throughout this chapter, a response indicator of '98' indicates that there was no response by participants to the question asked.

Participants were surveyed 1–11 months after commencement of using the AT, to determine what the impact of the AT had been for them. The two samples yielded low response rates (survey 1 n-39): site 1 (*n*–13) and site 2 (n-26). Survey 2 yielded n-34 (site 1 n-13, site2 n-21). As a result the samples were joined to provide an overall sample of 39 respondents for survey 1 and 34 for survey 2. 59 % of carers

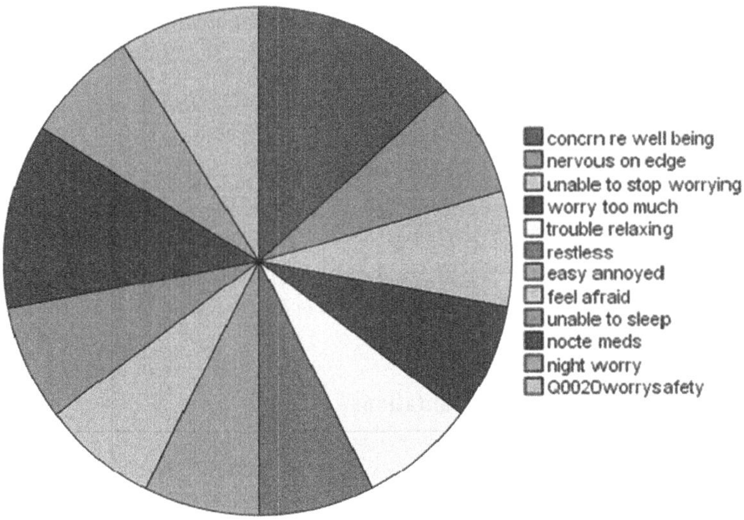

Fig. 9.1 Impact on carers

identified as being the spouse of the client, 87.2 % of carers are female, and the mean age of respondents is 65.5 years, ranging from 26 to 92 years. 84.6 % of respondents identified as being the main carer and 66.7 % stated they were the only carer. 56.4 % identified that they are unable to leave the client alone (Fig. 9.1). The types of AT used by carers included sensor mats, hearing devices, robotic vacuum cleaners and GPS watches. This AT had varying levels of success. 96.4 % of respondents stated that they received adequate information and preparation prior to using the AT, and 89.3 % stated that they had experienced positive outcomes by using the AT during the last 6 months. 78.6 % of respondents indicated that they felt comfortable troubleshooting the AT if problems arose (Fig. 9.2).

9.3.1 Impact of Caring for a Person with Dementia

The impacts of caring for a person with dementia were identified by participants as being primarily unable to stop worrying, feeling afraid all the time, inability to sleep and inability to relax (see Fig. 9.1). The main carer concerns about clients were perceived as being the clients falling, risk of fire and their inability to be left alone (see Fig. 9.4). One carer expressed that the major risk for them was flooding as a result of the client leaving taps running. 86 % of respondents (n-39) indicated high to very high levels of concern for the client, 61 % expressed very high concern for the safety of the client, 74.4 % indicated they are nervous and on edge, 33.3 % of respondents identified that they are unable to stop worrying, 48.7 % indicated they

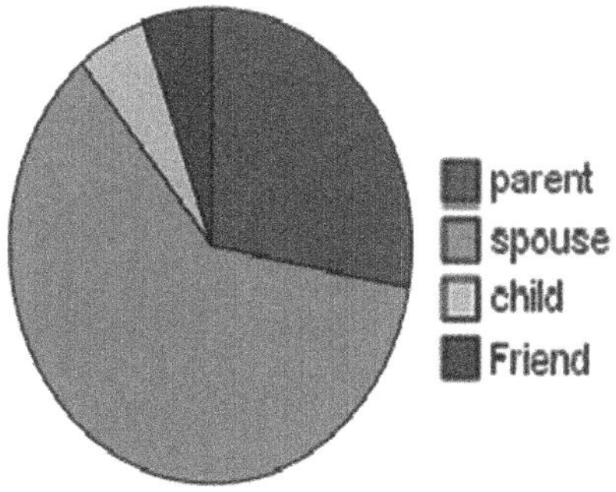

Fig. 9.2 Relationship between carer and client

believe that they worry too much, 48.7 % have trouble relaxing, 25.6 % stated they are restless, 61.5 % responded that they are easily annoyed, 30.8 % feel afraid, 56.4 % are unable to sleep, 69.2 % worry about the client getting out of bed at night, whilst 20.5 % indicate that they have been prescribed sleeping medications. Participants indicated that improvements as a result of using AT were of direct benefit for the carer and had little impact on the quality of life of the client with 59.3 % of respondents indicating they did not believe the client was really aware of or felt any safer as a result of AT being used.

9.3.2 Main Issues Identified

38.5 % of respondents indicated in survey 1 that they are able to leave the client alone at home, 63.9 % indicate that the client falls regularly, 47.2 % state the client wanders, 50 % indicate that the client gets lost, 27.8 % indicated the client is unaware of dangers such as fire. There was no statistical difference ($t=0.29$) in the ability of carers to leave client alone at home as a result of AT. Likewise, there was no significant increase in carer perceptions in the post-AT survey that using the AT would enable the client to feel safer. Additionally, 30 % indicated that they experienced nervousness for the person they cared for each day (Figs. 9.3 and 9.4).

There was no significant impact on carer need for sleeping medications as a result of using the AT with 20.8 % of respondents indicating that they continued to take sleeping medications compared with 21.1 % at survey 1.

Respondents were asked to rank their stress levels on a scale from 1 to 10 with 1 being no stress and 10 being maximum stress. No significant difference in carer-identified stress levels was noted between pre-AT and post-AT usage. These remained high with more than 50 % indicating they were experiencing high or very high levels of stress most of the time. This may be related to the disease progression and different stressors being placed on the carer (Fig. 9.5).

More than 30 % of carers indicated that they experience nervousness every day about the person they care for.

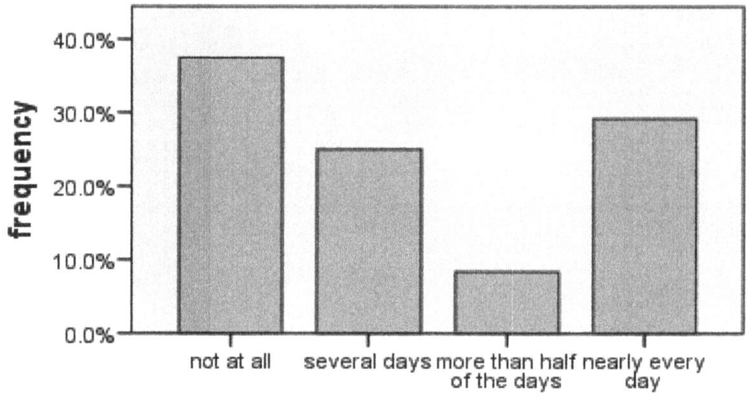

Fig. 9.3 Frequency of carer nervousness

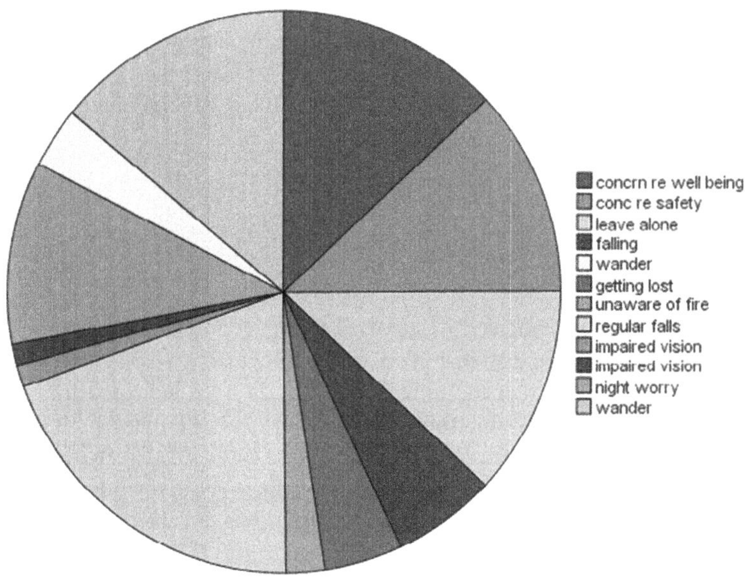

Fig. 9.4 Client issues

At survey 1, 80.5 % of respondents believed that using AT would enable them to feel less anxious, 73.1 % believe that using AT will let the client feel safer, whilst 88.5 % believe that using AT will enable the client to remain at home longer. On the other hand, 61.5 % of respondents do not believe that using AT will mean that the client will require less external support and care and 57.7 % do not believe that the use of AT will assist them with current issues.

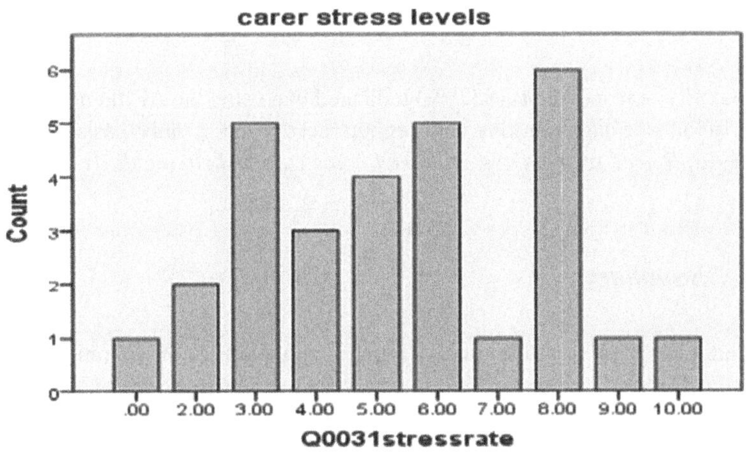

Fig. 9.5 Carer stress levels

Carers indicated that since using AT, they are less worried about the client getting out of bed at night and falling. Paired samples *t*-test indicated a statistically significant decrease in carer concern at night from survey 1 (−1.10, SD.89) to survey 2 (M–0.47, SD.89), $t = -5.06$, $p < 0.000$ two tailed. This was attributed to the use of the sensor mats beside the beds. This also contributed to their improved sleep patterns at night as evidenced by comments provided during focus groups and in-depth interviews (see Part V).

Finally, significant correlation (0.05 one-tailed) was noted between participants who believed that AT would assist them with their issues and that they would feel less anxious in survey 1. However, this was not identified in survey 2. Likewise, no correlation was noted between the use of AT and the ability to leave clients alone for a longer period of time. High correlation (Pearson's) was evident between the need to remind clients about medications and all forms of dementia was noted as was the need for the client to be reminded to go to toilet and requiring help getting out of chairs.

9.3.3 Understanding and/or Current Use of AT

35.9 % of respondents (n-39) stated they currently use AT, whilst 89.7 % stated they understand what is meant by AT. 7.7 % of respondents stated they use medication reminders, 5.1 % use smoke detectors (however, 92.3 % did not respond to this question), 1 respondent identified that they currently used GPS watches, only 7.7 % use sensor mats (nonresponse rate was 92.3 % to this question), and 20.5 % indicated that they use personal alarms.

9.3.4 Need for Outside Interventions

The majority of respondents (85.7 %) indicated that using the AT did not reduce the levels of outside interventions and support needed on a daily basis. Comments included *still need respite days, still need home care or help regularly.*

9.3.5 Summary

The findings (n–39) from the surveys mirror the findings of the literature review in that similar issues are presented especially in relation to worry and safety. The majority of respondents (59 %) identified that they were the spouse of the client and majority chaptered they were the only carer. The majority of respondents understood what is meant by AT prior to receiving it, and some were already using some of the technologies in their homes prior to the commencement of this project. Analysis of findings indicates that clients are willing to embrace the technology but are nervous about learning new systems and technologies.

The mean age of carers was 65.5 years; majority indicated that they are very stressed and unable to stop worrying about the person they care for. They also indicated that they have experienced this level of stress for up to 12 months in some cases. All carers indicated that the issues faced were the same, i.e. activities of daily living such as showering, dressing and toileting.

Wandering was a concern of carers due to risk of safety to the client. 57.7 % of respondents indicated that the implementation of bed sensor mats and door alarms assisted with minimising this concern. There was significant correlation between beliefs that the use of AT would enable clients to stay home longer, that the carer would feel less anxious and stressed and that the client would need less external care.

Feedback included the appearance of AT devices (e.g. GPS watches) was seen as being large and unattractive and of poor quality, fall detector systems not responsive, and pagers and sensor routing systems not always efficient to operate AT devices already in place. These reflect findings from the literature review. Despite these issues, analysis showed that carers believe that using the devices would improve the quality of their lives especially in relation to safety and ability to sleep and worry less. These findings were compared and only a slight reduction was noted.

Carers indicated that they felt that there would have been a greater impact of the AT if it was provided earlier in the dementia process. Overall though, positive results indicated a significant decrease in carer concerns about the client getting out of bed at night, and this was attributed to the use of the sensor mats besides beds or chairs. However, their overall stress levels did not decline. In some instances the high level of sensitivity of the sensor mats caused more stress for the carer due to an alarm that sounded when the client shifted.

Carers chaptered no significant impact of AT on individual clients as they appeared not to be aware of the presence of the technology. Carers did indicate that as a result of the AT, their sleep improved and, as such, were more able to cope at night and for a longer period of time. This enabled the client to remain home in some cases for a longer period of time although this was not clearly shown in the survey responses. Neither the levels of stress nor the frequency of stress chaptered by carers decreased significantly as a result of using the AT. 40 % of respondents using the AT rated their concern for the client as remaining very high and a further 32 % rating concern as being high. Carers overall chaptered that their anxiety levels had decreased through the use of the technology.

9.4 Qualitative Findings

The data analysis presented in this section of the chapter is a result of 21 interviews conducted by the researcher and recorded and transcribed by the researcher. Qualitative data was collected via in-depth interviews (n-15) and a focus group comprising carers (n-4) as well as in-depth interviews (n-2) of staff from AQ who were participating in the trial project. Experiences were based on 1 to 11 months experience of using the AT.

9.5 Carers Experience

Feedback from carers throughout the project varied depending on what their needs were, what equipment was trialled and the how far progressed the dementia was. Overall, carers chaptered a positive experience with using the technology.

All carers stated that they had been willing to try the technology and hoped that it would be beneficial for their specific needs. Comments were made such as:

> ... I definitely wanted to monitor her getting out of bed.... after the first few days I was quite happy and I rested. We agreed to try it for twelve months. One of her neighbours fell off a chair and spent hours alone until she was found... Mum told her she should get one of these... I'll try anything once. It's better than nothing.

Respondents indicated that it did not take long for them to feel comfortable using and trusting the AT. Most comments reflected that carers were able to use the technology immediately once they have been shown how to use it.

Additionally, all carers commented that their ability to adjust and cope with the technology was due to the high level of support provided by the staff, staff availability and the frequent opportunities provided for informal follow-up or the assistance offered when the client attended respite at the centres.

Upon application of the technology, carers chaptered success with the personal alarms, sensor mats, the robotic vacuum cleaner, hearing devices and PIR sensors.

Positive feedback was given from carers regarding the hearing device:

> It works alright! - It's unreal! I can put it under the TV and hear it all over the house-especially the State of origin!..
>
> Best invention ever made for someone like Bridget it saves my sanity!... we can watch TV and know.... It has made me less anxious yes!

Carers suggested that the AT is useful as an added means of support for them each day. In addition they are now more able to sleep at night knowing that the sensors will activate as needed. It was seen as being useful in maintaining their own confidence in their ability to keep their loved one at home for longer.

Carers utilising the bed exit sensor stated:

> Now that we have the sensor I no longer sleep on the floor in the hallway outside her room...
>
> ....Sleeping at night (and) not broken sleep.
>
> Yes (I am) able to sleep can hear mum get up and moving.....Yes absolutely!!

The major outcome or improvement noted by the carers was knowing that the AT was working 24 h per day and was not affecting the dignity of the client. This provided carers with extra confidence and a sense that they were no longer alone in the event of an unexpected situation. In turn, this enabled the carers to feel safe to leave the client unattended for short periods of time at home if they needed to go out shopping, church or other regular activities. This was seen as being beneficial for their own mental health as the carer role can socially isolate them from their own former contacts and support people in the community. Improved sleep and thereby an enhanced ability to cope with situations throughout each day was expressed as a significant outcome for most of the carers:

> Gives her more independence without us hovering... It's insurance to have it but not need to use it.. and; Mum feels better too.... and; .. just knowing she's awake- just putting her feet on the mat-just knowing she is awake.. my room is just across the way from her-knowing I'm close by. It's easy I could get there quickly.

Other responses included:

> Just confidence knowing that help will always be there [this was in response to the personal alarm].
>
> I don't have to do the actual work! [this was in response to the robotic vacuum cleaner].
>
> I started to sleep better myself- I wasn't alerted each time he moved. I always had broken sleep [this was in response to a bed sensor].

Many carers indicated that as a result of using the AT in the home, their personal stress and anxiety levels had decreased. The OTs indicated that this was particularly the case for carers who had experienced success using sensor systems and personal alarms for themselves. One client related it to reducing their vulnerability:

> One time last year I felt so vulnerable and I needed someone for support... It made me less anxious yes.

I think it certainly made me less anxious and more confident. I'm not usually away from him much. We do everything together mostly. I'm still anxious when I go to church but he can wear that thing around his neck, that alarm, and it will notify them if he falls.

> There's probably slightly less yelling and less stress now...

Not all carers felt less anxious. For some the presence of AT and the fact that it beeped frequently was such a source of extra stress that they simply removed the batteries so that they could have some peace:

> No it [my anxiety] increased because it [the mat] beeped all the time even if he changed position.

Alternative equipment was trialled to reduce the sensitivity of the equipment or the existing equipment was repositioned to improve effectiveness. In some cases this corrected the concerns. One staff member commented about the stress and anxiety in relation to the carer:

> Reduction in stress was very individual. I do think a majority (of carers) have had a reduction in stress... We provided an alarm for both of them as they both worried "what would happen if I had heart attack or fall and broke my hip". Her husband wouldn't know what to do even if she told him what to do. He couldn't follow the steps to dial 000 in an emergency...

One carer had quite a different experience, with the client 'out witting' the technology:

> I had it [mat sensor] going for five and a half months but she got out of the back of the bed! You have to have the bed next to the walls because she is clever and gets out on the opposite side of the bed... She only ever got out of one side of the bed her whole life until I got the mat and then she knew and she got out the other side!!

Without exception each participant in the focus group indicated that there was no impact on the person for whom they cared. The perception expressed by staff was that the benefit of the AT was primarily for carers and not the client:

> I think that it's very dependent on the client... who they are and what stage they are at. I know for one client in particular he was very aware that he was wearing the watch. He didn't like it, he only did it to please his wife... he didn't think he needed it but we did. He didn't mind wearing it...

9.6 Limitations of AT

The most anticipated, yet the most flawed device was the GPS watch. Carers chaptered that the fear of a client wandering away and becoming lost was a factor related to their stress and a large part of why they did not leave them alone. Unfortunately, feedback from all carers and staff in relation to both GPS watches trialled was negative. The quality of the products on the market in Australia did not meet the needs of the clients or carers. One carer advised that it was *too big, too bulky and the back kept falling off.*

Frustrations caused by poor design and size of the GPS watch far outweighed any perceived benefit that carers had hoped it may have provided.

Carers who were using the sensor mat identified that was useful, with some identifying that they felt it did prevent the client falling. However, it was not without its own difficulties. Some of these difficulties included the fact that the mat was so sensitive that every time the client moved their feet the alarm sounded; *it beeped all the time….* Another issue was that the batteries became low on charge and then the mat seemed to beep incessantly causing more anxiety for both the client and the carer. For example:

> I tried the bed mat but it kept going off whenever she moved. Eliza didn't like it. It upset her so I only used it for about a week… That was enough…

Other issues chaptered were with faulty or over sensitive equipment. Some comments included:

> We tried [sensor mats] for a few days but it was too awkward and got in the way and the first month was good… then the hiccups started… I tried for a while then after about ….. And then after about 3 months and then I gave up.

One issue that did occur was carers declining participation in the project with many finding the use of the word technology *too confronting I don't even own a computer.* Some carers had concerns about trying unfamiliar technology. These concerns are reflected throughout the current population with many having very little interaction with computer-based technology. It is anticipated that the baby boomer generation entering into the aged care sector will be more open and comfortable with using technology through phones and computers.

This lack of interaction with technology was taken into consideration when working with carers in determining what equipment may be suitable for their needs. Staff learnt over the duration of the project that it was easier to show a carer the technology first, rather than just discussing. This technique increased the uptake of the technology during the last 6 months of the project.

Timing of presentation of the AT to carers as part of the client care was seen as being an important part of the caring cycle by both carers and staff. One participant comment was that the AT should have been introduced earlier. Some carers believed that the client had progressed too far for the equipment to be of benefit.

Additionally, with the exception of one carer all identified that cost of AT would have been a major issue if they had to purchase the equipment and most people would not have bought it without trying it first. They wanted to know how it worked up front that. The reason given for cost being an issue was the fact that all other carers are pensioners with limited fixed incomes and the cost was seen as being too expensive and therefore prohibitive. This was reflected in comments such as:

> Definitely I would not have been able to buy one. Its way out of the budget, there no way we could afford it….

Whilst for this study the AT was freely provided, only one carer stated that they would have purchased the AT regardless of the cost to them stating that

> 'The benefit I get, I probably would buy it anyway'. and 'Not a money issue really I don't think… more an invasion of privacy and loss of control'.

Qualitative analysis of the transcripts from focus group and in-depth interviews with both carers and staff members engaged in the project indicated that the majority of carers have had positive experiences and outcomes when using the AT. Most carers indicated that they would recommend it to others. This is despite some initial apprehension on their part in relation to the fact that it is new, unfamiliar, that it is technology and therefore a large learning experience for them. The level of satisfaction was not linked to the level of prior education or ongoing support provided by staff but rather the level of intrusiveness into their daily routines and impact on their ability to sleep at night. All carers indicated that the improved awareness of movement by clients was a benefit for them providing an extra layer of support that reduced their feelings of vulnerability. People using the hearing devices stated that there was an improvement in communication ability and reduced frustration levels. Design issues were mentioned many times by carers as being a limitation for them and a barrier to the effectiveness of the AT.

9.7 Discussion of Findings

The overall aims of implementing assistive technology into clients with dementia homes were to assess whether there were:

- Increased safety in the home
- Decreased carer burden and anxiety
- Reduced need for in-home, residential or community care
- Reduced wandering
- Earlier chaptering of falls and/or injuries

9.7.1 Increased Safety in the Home

The findings (n–39) from the surveys mirrored the findings of the literature review in that similar issues are presented especially in relation to worry and safety. From the AT survey 61 % expressed very high concern for the safety of the client.

Carers chaptered varying levels of exhaustion, burnout, stress and anxiety. Through the provision of AT, there was some reduction in the levels of anxiety about client safety but not carer stress. Even with this reduction in anxiety regarding client safety, concerns for their loved one remained very high for many respondents. Carers did chapter a perceived enhancement in safety from the AT product, reduced carer stress and reduced carer fatigue.

Also, despite the issues related to appearance of AT, analysis showed that carers believe that using the devices would improve the quality of their lives especially in relation to safety and ability to sleep. This reflects findings from the literature review.

9.7.2 Decreased Carer Burden and Anxiety

The burdens of caring for people with dementia were identified by participants as being primarily their inability to stop worrying, feeling afraid all the time, feeling isolated and feeling vulnerable. Inability to sleep and inability to relax were also identified as major issues for the carers (see Fig. 9.2). Whilst the main carer concerns about clients were perceived as being the client falling, risk of fire and inability for the client to be left alone, one carer expressed that the major risk for them was flooding as a result of the client leaving taps running and that the AT had gone some way to improving the situation.

Carers indicated that they had expected that the technology was going to reduce their burdens and stress levels. This proved not to be the case for some. Post-AT burdens were identified by carers as actually being caused by needs in relation to activities of daily living, risks of clients falling, becoming lost and wandering rather than inconveniences for themselves (i.e. sheer workload imposed by client physical and cognitive condition). Carer issues were consistent across all participants, i.e. lack of sleep, continual worry, inability to stop worrying, frequency and levels of stress being experienced. Given that the majority of carers in this study are aged over 65 and female, this is not a surprising outcome and raises the further significant issue of carer burnout as often the carers are coping with various health issues of their own. This is a concern as carer stress levels remained greater than 5 out of a possible 10 for 65 % of carers post-AT.

Exhaustion and burnout was identified by carers as a constant daily battle. Whilst there was some reduction in the levels of anxiety about client safety (rather than carer stress), it was not in relation to ongoing carer concerns for their loved one which remained very high for many respondents. Some carers indicated that they were experiencing varying levels of exhaustion due to the non-stop nature of their burdens.

Frequent mention was made by carers about the social isolation they experienced whilst caring for their loved one. For some this was addressed in part when the client attended respite or when the carer was able to attend outings. However, it was evident from the conversations that even when undertaking such activities, a level of anxiety remained whilst they were separated from the client. Some younger carers indicated that they spent a large amount of time on the internet talking with friends. This was viewed by them as a *critical lifeline* and that social support system to assist with the social isolation was extremely important.

There was no statistical decrease in the levels or frequency of stress for carers. This may be explained due to the clients' dementia progresses which caused a functional decline increasing carer burden, anxiety and their need for further assistance with daily activities. Carers did chapter a perceived enhancement in safety from the AT product, reduced carer stress and reduced carer fatigue.

9.7.3 Reduced Need for In-Home, Residential and Community Care

Carers indicated (pre-AT survey and in interviews) that they believed that using the AT would enable the client to remain home longer; however, this was not supported by the post-AT survey. This may have been different had the technology been available earlier or the sample sizes been larger.

Using AT did not reduce carer need for external support services (respite), in-home care for housework and/or meals in some cases. One carer chaptered that she could see how the AT could be beneficial and would have been 2–3 years earlier for them. Carers also chaptered that whilst the AT may have reduced some of the burden, it would not reduce the external supports required as a personal alarm cannot assist with showering.

9.7.4 Earlier Chaptering of Falls/Injuries

Due to the short duration of the project, this aim was difficult to measure. However, the sensor mats were perceived as preventing falls by carers who stated that the mats gave them a sense of support and ability to sleep at night with the knowledge that should the client get out of bed, they (carers) would be immediately aware. This ensured the care was able to provide support with transfers and mobility when the client rose from bed, especially during the night.

9.7.5 Wandering

Likewise, due to the inefficiencies and design issues of the GPS watch, there was not an appropriate opportunity to assess whether or not the AT did effectively reduce wandering.

For some clients sensor mats (bed, chair or floor) were used as a means of preventing wandering as a carer would be alerted as soon as the client is up and moving. This may have decreased wandering but was difficult to assess through this project.

Wandering is not a universal symptom of dementia; therefore, with our small sample size any effect of the AT may not have been measurable. Ongoing development and research was identified as being required in this area.

9.8 Conclusion/Recommendation

The nature of this study (i.e. survey in-depth interviews, focus group of carers and staff) has provided a useful cross-sectional, triangulated view of perceptions of the effectiveness of AT to help in the care of people with dementia or other cognitive impairment. Carers indicated that they expected that the technology was going to reduce their burdens and stress levels and improve the quality of their own and their loved ones' life. This proved not to be the case for some. Whilst most indicated that they are sleeping better now, this appears not to have reduced the level or frequency of their stress nor the need for sleeping medications on the part of carers. The stress appears to be a direct consequence of carer's fear for the person they care for rather than the burden of their load. Post-AT, burdens were identified by carers in some cases as actually being caused by needs in relation to activities of daily living as well as the risks of clients falling, becoming lost and wandering rather than inconveniences for themselves (i.e. sheer workload imposed by client physical and cognitive condition of their loved one). Some carers also identified fear of what should happen should the carer become too frail.

Involvement in the selection of the type of AT to be used was important for carers who stated that they appreciated being able to identify their particular needs, to be listened to and to be provided with adequate and appropriate education upon receipt of the AT. Timing of the introduction of the AT for carers was noted as being an important factor in regard to the usefulness for carers. Despite this, carers expressed appreciation for the security that the AT presented for them. This was primarily related to the fact that if they needed to use it, they were able to do so and contact a service provider for help, and it was seen as a backup for them.

The most useful and successful types of AT were identified by respondents as being sensor mat with remote pager. The bed exit sensor with interval timer and pager were also identified as being beneficial, as was the robotic vacuum cleaner and the hearing devices. Mats were significant in enabling carers to obtain a better quality of rest at night and be better able to cope with demands during the days. Some carers indicated that the high level of sensitivity to movement by the mats caused them to buzz non-stop even if the client was only to change their position in the chair. In some cases this distressed carers to the point that they removed the batteries and only used the mats at night, with the result that there was a continued risk of daytime falls whilst ever the client was able to independently mobilise. Hearing devices and vacuum cleaners were seen as increasing independence and communication in the case of the hearing devices.

The small size of the sample limits the usability of these findings for the general target population. Having said this, the findings do reflect those in the wider literature in relation to carers and staff. The technology was seen by all as being relevant and useful even though the poor design of some technology caused more frustrations than actual help. Whilst this 12-month study has confirmed findings of the literature review that AT is seen as an acceptable and useful strategy to assist with caring for clients with various stages of dementia, it has also raised some issues that provide opportunity for further exploration.

Early in the project it was anticipated that integrated Tunstall monitored emergency call systems with automated/passive peripherals, i.e. door exit sensors and PIR sensors, would be heavily prescribed; however, there was very limited uptake of this equipment by clients and client families with dementia. Several possible explanations for this were put forward by the Occupational Therapists based on their observations and discussion with carers around the technologies. One explanation revolved around the nature of the system, specifically, to be effective the automated/passive systems (i.e. not reliant on the person pressing a personal alarm button to trigger an alert) required windows of time at least 4–5 h long, i.e. PIR movement sensors could trigger an alarm if a person did not move past the sensor between the hours of 7:30 and 12:30 am. Creating alarms for shorter windows was likely to result in too many false alarms, i.e. if the window was set to trigger an alert if the person did not move past the PIR sensor between the hours of 7:30 and 8:30, the client choosing to spend an extra long time doing their hair was likely to set off an alarm. Additionally, feedback from carers indicated that even with the Telecare technologies in place such as monitoring for lack of activity, flooding, fire, and falls, they didn't feel confident leaving the person with dementia alone for the longer periods of time. They advised the numerous risks which couldn't be controlled with technologies, e.g. person would become hungry but wouldn't be able to prepare food or person might sit in a low chair and not be able to get up. Additionally, many carers of clients with advanced dementia did not feel they could leave the person unsupervised even momentarily, let alone for extended periods, for these carers' simple unmonitored sensor mats were the best choice of technology.

Another explanation for the low levels of adoption of the Tunstall systems was that few clients living alone with dementia were referred to the programme. Those who were identified and approached refused to accept the technologies as they saw them as unnecessary. From their perspective they viewed themselves as at no particular risk for the kind of misadventure which would require such monitoring or assistance. The Occupational Therapists thought this may be due to a lack of insight into their own symptoms and thus their vulnerabilities, a common hallmark of the disease, for example, a client with dementia who was living alone and whose family was very concerned about her vulnerability to crime or becoming lost when leaving her unit. A Tunstall system would have allowed the family to be informed when the client exited the house and if she didn't return within a short period of time, i.e. longer than it would take for her to go to the mailbox. From such an alert, a family member could then travel to the local area to pick her up. However, the client refused on the grounds that she was in no way vulnerable and required no such assistance. The family determined it was not worth 'forcing it upon her'.

Potentially the window for client acceptance of such technologies is small and must occur before clients have lost their insight into the disease. Alternatively, for people living alone with dementia, systems with a less obvious physical presence in the home to which the person could object may be the answer. There are several such activity monitoring systems available overseas but not yet released in Australia. For example, NEC is releasing a system which works via a network of small unobtrusive sensors attached to electrical devices and doors. The sensors detect if appliances have been turned on and if doors on cupboards and fridges have been opened, et cetera; if patterns of use deviate from normal patterns, this information is transmitted via Wi-Fi to formal or informal carers. Where such monitoring technology is installed covertly and/or continued to be used covertly ethical issues of privacy must be considered.

The Occupational Therapists involved in the study noted high rates of AT abandonment, even in cases where the equipment was initially suitable and well accepted by the carer and or client. They advised that this was not surprising given the progressive nature of dementia, emphasising that carers often spoke about different 'phases' and that as symptoms changed AT needs changed. For example, sensor mats used to manage the risk of wandering may be very useful for a client who is highly mobile, but as their mobility deteriorates, this equipment may no longer be required. This suggests that an equipment loan scheme where equipment could be issued returned and new equipment issued could be a good approach.

Results found that carers' perceptions of concern for the person's safety and well-being remained high despite the implementation of AT. The Occupational Therapists postulated that this too might be a product of the progressive nature of dementia with deterioration in multiple areas of functioning, e.g. language, social skills, ability to independently attend to self-care tasks, continence, mobility and dexterity typical over the course of the project. Such deterioration generally increases the carer burden in terms of the level of assistance they must provide, thus resulting in an increase rather than decrease in the level of concern for safety and well-being. It may not be realistic to expect that AT can compensate for these types of decline.

Similarly, the progressive nature of the disease may explain why the carers chaptered no measurable decrease in stress after the implementation of the AT. The Occupational Therapists' impression was that the progression nature of dementia meant increasing levels of stress as the carers struggled to cope with the increasing demands for support, as well as trying to manage the grief and loss reactions normal for a person watching the decline of a loved one.

The survey used in this study was not subjected to any validity or reliability testing and as such has undetermined psychometric properties. The lack of measurable outcomes in several key area of study may be a result of flaws in the survey design. Consideration should be given to adopting a valid and reliable standardised assessment tool in future research.

The small size of the sample limits the usability of these findings for the general target population. Having said this, the findings do reflect those in the wider literature in relation to carers and staff. The technology was seen by all as being relevant and useful even though the poor design of some technology caused more frustrations than actual help. Whilst this 12-month study has confirmed findings of the literature review that AT is seen as an acceptable and useful strategy to assist with caring for clients with various stages of dementia, it has also raised some issues that provide opportunity for further exploration.

9.9 Recommendations

- Due to the small sample size, it is necessary to repeat the study with a larger cohort perhaps at state-wide level to overcome poor response rates coupled with the impact of client admission into residential care.
- Technology costs are prohibitive for many pensioners which may impact generally on user uptake. It would be useful to explore options for subsidies for carers of clients who are not DVA eligible to ensure wider access to AT. There is evidence, particularly overseas, on the benefits of AT implemented in the community for reducing hospital admissions and early admission into nursing homes and the cost benefits related to this. Ideally funding providing to organisation directly to be able to assess, purchase, implement, educate and monitor the technology would be of great benefit to this cohort of people. Additionally, AQ would recommend an equipment pool that could be utilised to hire equipment to clients/carers and reduce the cost of purchasing new equipment for people accessing this technology.
- From the study Alzheimer's Queensland will continue to seek financial assistance in continuing this project and for it to be implemented across all 4 HACC regions that their respite centres are based at. Additionally, they are implementing this technology into their respite centres and residential facilities to increase client/resident safety in these environments. Feedback to date has been positive.
- To create a Smart home in an actual home. AQ has identified one of their houses that can be converted into a Smart home not just using the equipment trialled but looking at a fully automated house for not just people with dementia but anyone with a disability. The aim will be that people will stay in this house as well as being a display centre for community carers/clients and service providers to see it in action in a real life situation.
- High rates of equipment abandonment were identified in the project. This result points to the need for more assertive follow-up from prescribers to ensure that the AT prescribed at one point in time continues to meet the client's changing needs as the disease progresses. An equipment loan scheme where equipment is issued and returned for reissue to others once no longer suitable is recommended.
- GPS tracking technologies were not properly trialled due to the poor quality of the product utilised. Better quality products were and are available on the market but none of those allowed carer to access the client location without accessing the Internet. Further trials of GPS technologies are warranted, particularly if AT with the following functionality can be sourced: smaller and more discrete to minimise risk of rejection from user, improved quality, improved ease of use and able to be used without accessing the Internet.
- Future research may need to recruit participants more widely and vigorously to identify people with dementia who are willing to adopt the Tunstall moni-

toring system technologies. It is likely that these will be people living alone and those in the very early stages of the disease who retain insight into their own deficits and vulnerabilities (or those vulnerabilities they are likely to develop as the disease progresses). Alternately, research may focus on trialling the new web-based activity monitoring systems being released in Japan and North America.
- Future research should utilise standardised assessment tools with proven reliability and validity to better detect the effect of AT on people with dementia and their carers.
- Due to the lack of knowledge of carers and service providers on what smart technology looks like, further education sessions are required. AQ is in the process of developing education sessions on this topic that would be presented locally, via video conferencing and webinars. Future funding to assist organisation with this education may assist in increasing the uptake of smart assistive technology nationally.

Acknowledgements The authors acknowledge the generous funding from the Queensland Department of Communities and the project support of Alzheimer's Queensland, Tunstall Healthcare and the University of Southern Queensland.

References

Bayliss, E., Bosworth, H., Noel, P., Wolff, J., Damush, T., & Mciver, L. (2007). Supporting self-management for patients with complex medical needs; recommendations for a working group. *Chronic Illness, 3*(2), 167–175.

Bewernitz, M. W., Mann, W. C., Dasler, P., & Belchior, P. (2009). Feasibility of machine-based prompting to assist persons with dementia. *Assistive Technology, 21*(4), 196–207.

Bonner, S., & Idris, T. (2012). Assistive technology as a means of supporting people with Dementia: A review. *Housing, Learning & Improvement Network (HLIN)*. J. Porteus, Housing, Learning & Improvement Network.

Choi, Y. M. (2011). Managing input during assistive technology product design. *Assistive Technology, 23*(2), 65–75.

Clark, J., & McGee-Lennon, M. (2011). A stakeholder-centred exploration of the current barriers to the uptake of home care technology in the UK. *Journal of Assistive Technologies, 5*(1), 12–25.

Clendon, J. (2003). Nurse managed clinics; issues in evaluation. *Journal of Advanced Nursing, 44*(6), 558–565.

Cohen-Mansfield, J., & Biddison, J. (2007). The scope and future trends of gerontechnology: Consumers' opinions and literature survey. *Journal of Technology in Human Services, 25*(3), 1–19.

Connell, J., Grealy, C., Olver, K., & Power, J. (2008). *Comprehensive scoping study on the use of assistive technology by frail older people living in the community*. Canberra: Department of Health and Ageing.

Cook, R. (2008). Introducing: Telehealth & telecare. *British Journal of Nursing, 12*(7), 307.

Cornes, M., & Weinstein, P. (2005). Managing assistive technology in hospice homecare: Implications for multi-disciplinary teams. *Journal of Integrated Care, 13*(6), 17–25.

Courtney, K. L., Demiris, G., Rantz, M., & Skubic, M. (2008). Needing smart home technologies: The perspectives of older adults in continuing care retirement communities. *Informatics in Primary Care, 16*(3), 195–201.

Cowan, D., & Turner-Smith, A. (1999). *The role of assistive technology in alternative models of care for older people*. London: The Stationery Office.
Currell, R., Urquhart, C., Wainwright, P., & Lewis, R. (2000). Telemedicine versus face to face patient care: Effects on professional practice and health care outcomes. *Cochrane Database of Systematic Reviews,* Issue 2 Art No, CD002098. doi:101002/14651858CD002098: Cochrane Database of Systematic Reviews 2000.
Darkins, A., Ryan, P., Kobb, R., Foster, L., Edmonson, E., Wakefield, B., et al. (2008). Care Coordination/Home Telehealth: The systematic implementation of health informatics, home telehealth, and disease management to support the care of veteran patients with chronic conditions'. *Journal of Telemedicine and e-Health, 14*(10), 1118–1126.
DeRuyter, F. (1995). Evaluating outcomes in assistive technology: Do we understand the commitment? *Assistive Technology, 7*(1), 3–8.
Faife, D. (2007). The role of assistive technology in achieving dignity, equality and respect. *Working with Older People: Community Care Policy & Practice, 11*(2), 20–23.
Glover, J., Page, A., Ambrose, S., & Hetzel, D. (2007). *Atlas of Avoidable hospitalisations in Australia: Ambulatory care-sensitive conditions*. Canberra: AIHW.
Goodwin, N. (2012). Telehealth and patient care: Challenges and Solutions A UK perspective. Healthcare IQ- a division of IOPC.
Guba, E., & Lincoln, Y. (1989). *Fourth generation evaluation*. Newbury Park, CA: Sage.
Guba, E., & Lincoln, Y. (Eds.). (2003). *Fourth generation evaluation* (2nd ed.). New York: Sage.
Hagen, I., Cahill, S., Begley, E., & Faulkner, J. P. (2007). "It gives me a sense of independence"—Findings from Ireland on the use and usefulness of assistive technology for people with dementia. *Technology and Disability, 19*(2–3), 133–142.
Harris, J. (2010). The use, role and application of advanced technology in the lives of disabled people in the UK. *Disability & Society, 25*(4), 427–439.
Hegney, D., Eley, R., Buikstra, E., Fallon, T., Soar, J., & Gilmore, V. (2006). Australian nurses access and attitudes to information technology—A national survey. In H. E. A. Park (Ed.), *The 9th international congress on nursing informatics*. Amsterdam, Netherlands: IOS Press, Nieuwe Hemweg 6B.
Layton, N., & Wilson, E. (2009). Re-conceptualizing disability and assistive technology: Australian consumers driving policy change. *Technology and Disability, 21*(4), 135–141.
McCreadie, C., & Tinker, A. (2005). The acceptability of assistive technology to older people. *Ageing & Society, 25*, 91–110. Cambridge University Press 91.
McIntosh, D., Gresham, M., Sarkodee, K., & Forbes, R. (2012). Empowering the Carer. Using Assisstive Technology to reduce the burden for carers of older Australians living in the community-Report summary. *H. care, Hammond Care*:11.
McMillen, A., & Soderberg, S. (2002). Disabled persons' experience of dependence on assistive devices. *Scandinavian Journal of Occupational Therapy, 9*(4), 176–183.
Miskelly, F. G. (2001). Assistive technology in elderly care. *Age and Ageing, 30*(6), 455–458.
Murasa, J. A., Stokes, E. K., & Cahill, V. (2008). Assistive technology in everyday living—A user survey of people with Parkinson's disease. *Technology and Disability, 20*(4), 271–282.
National Health System (NHS). (2009). Whole systems demonstrators—An overview of telecare and telehealth. UK Department of Health. http://dh.gov.uk/en/healthcare/longtermconditions/wholesystemdemonstrators.
Soar, J., & Youngjoon, S. E. O. (2007). Health and aged care enabled by information technology. *Annals of the New York Academy of Sciences, 1114*, 154–161.
World Health Organization. (2005). *Preventing chronic diseases: A vital investment*. Ottawa: Public health Agency of Canada.
Zwijsen, S. A., Niemeijer, A. R., & Hertogh, C. M. P. M. (2011). Ethics of using assistive technology in the care for community-dwelling elderly people: An overview of the literature. *Aging & Mental Health, 15*(4), 419–427.

Chapter 10
A Delphi Study on Developing a Conceptual Framework to Understand the Perception of Iranian Physicians Towards Electronic Health Records

Seyed Mohammad Seyedi Alavi and Khin Than Win

Abstract The aim of this study is to design a verified set of questions, which help the future studies to evaluate and identify factors, which might influence Iranian physician's perception towards EHR. Conceptual framework is developed and the Delphi method is used to analyse the validity of the questionnaire. Appropriateness of items in the framework was defined and validated through content validity index for items (I-CVI). In total, 18 questions have been modified from the first round of Delphi study. All items achieved CVI over 78 % for both confidence and importance for the second round with overall S-CVI of confidence and importance being 93 % and 92 %, respectively.

Keywords Electronic health record • Delphi study • Physician's perception • Attitude • Ease of use

10.1 Introduction

With information technology growing every day, the use of new technologies in our life is increasing. Hospitals and healthcare systems are not an exception as electronic health records (EHR) have been encouraged to be used in healthcare environment. It is envisioned that EHRs would transform our healthcare system by making it safer, more cost-effective and more efficient. However, hasty deployment of EHR may result in implementation failure or unintended consequences (Menachemi 2006; Ford et al. 2009). Introducing EHR to the hospitals requires changes to the workflow which affects the acceptance rate of physicians. The literatures which have investigated the clinical system implementation failure discovered the lack of adoption by users as a critical factor (Nancy Lorenzi and Riley 1995; Gans et al. 2005).

S.M.S. Alavi (✉) • K.T. Win
School of Information Systems and Technology, University of Wollongong,
Northfields Avenue, Wollongong, NSW 2522, Australia
e-mail: sallamir@gmail.com; win@uow.edu.au

N. Wickramasinghe et al. (eds.), *Lean Thinking for Healthcare*, Healthcare Delivery in the Information Age, DOI 10.1007/978-1-4614-8036-5_10,

In the Iranian hospital system, use of EHR has been minimum with majority still using paper-based information systems (Hajavi et al. 2005; Kazemi et al. 2009). Studied literatures (Maidani et al. 2006; Moghaddasi et al. 2006; MRC 2010) show us that EHR will be implemented in Iranian hospitals sooner or later. Physician's perception about the new technology does not depend entirely on its functionality, and their perception might be influenced by characteristics of users and social factors (Lowry 2002; Eschenburg et al. 2005; Morton and Wiedenbeck 2010). Previous studies have identified a lack of a user-centred approach as leading to increased costs (Johnson et al. 2005). In short, the failure of implementing EHR in hospitals could be attributed to developers who ignore users' needs and work processes in designing an EHR system (Winkelman and Leonard 2004). In order to provide a suitable and acceptable EHR system for healthcare professionals, it is essential for healthcare executives and EHR developers to recognize the acceptance, satisfaction and opinion of using such IT systems from an end-user perspective. Developing an acceptable EHR system for users is a challenging task for healthcare providers.

Therefore understanding perceptions of stakeholders on the development of EHR is an important aspect. The aim of this article is to design a verified set of questions which help the future studies to evaluate and weigh the factor which might influence physician's perception. Studies show that user's acceptance in different cultures requires different factors to be considered, and even the same factors might have different influences in different geographical position (Vanessa and Donald 1997; Al-Gahtani et al. 2007). Therefore determining these factors among Iranian physicians is essential as their culture and beliefs are different from other physicians, which have already been studied.

In general, there are a lot of benefits to be gained adopting a human-centred perspective in developing HIS or related software in healthcare, such as increasing working efficiency, ease of use and user satisfaction, decreasing medical errors and reducing both development time and establishment cost (Zhang 2005).

10.2 Developing a Conceptual Framework

A comprehensive literature review on factors, which might affect the acceptance of physicians, has been conducted. Literature stated that the user's perception about the new technology does not depend entirely on its functionality, and their perception might be influenced by characteristics of users and social factors (Lowry 2002; Eschenburg et al. 2005; Morton and Wiedenbeck 2010). Therefore, having a good knowledge about the influence of characteristics and social factors will facilitate successful adoption of EHR in the hospitals. There have been studies on the impact of attitudes towards EHR adoption, but the result which has been founded is not the same in all the cases. Some studies found "perceived usefulness" as the most important factor (Dansky et al. 1999); some found "computer experience" (van der Meijden et al. 2001); and the other researchers pointed to "training" as the most effective attitudes (Meade et al. 2009). The variety of the finding about the EHR adoption and studied literature proves that research on different culture will guide us to different findings, and user's acceptance in dissimilar cultures requires different factors to be considered (Vanessa and Donald 1997; Al-Gahtani et al. 2007).

Social factors that might influence the physician's use of EHR have been listed in Table 10.1.

Additional to social factors, there are a number of characteristics factors, which might influence the acceptance of the system. The "characteristics factors" include age, gender, experience with the system, EHR knowledge, new technology favourability, intelligence quotient, workplace, computer experience, specialty and years in practice.

10.2.1 User Acceptance Theories and Models

To gain better understanding of the influencing factors on EHR acceptance by physicians, several information system theories have been examined and similar elements from those have been coalesced and listed in Table 10.2.

After thorough literature review and analysis of factors that might influence the physician's acceptance of EHR and the information system theory, conceptual framework for physician's acceptance on EHR by Iranian doctors has been developed as described in Fig. 10.1.

10.3 Methodology

Article searched was conducted from ScienceDirect, Scopus, ProQuest, PubMed and Google Scholar. And as our research required well understanding of Iranian perception, we searched Persian electronic databases such as Sid, Magiran, Isu and Emodiran (2006–2011). Keywords used included "perception of physicians, electronic health record, user acceptance, and influence on acceptance".

The searches were conducted in February 2012. There was no time limit in the search. A total number of 1,462 articles have been found and been studied, 192 relevant articles were selected, and after thorough review, 72 articles have been selected for the study.

Delphi method is used in our study to evaluate the designed questionnaire. Delphi is a hybrid survey design that aims to reach agreement on important issues (Linstone and Turoff 1975). Use of the Delphi method for forecasting and issue identification/prioritization can be valuable in the early stages, particularly in selecting the topic and defining the research question(s) (Okoli and Pawlowski 2004). It has specific sequence of events: selection of an expert panel, designing the questions, generation of statements of opinion, reduction and categorization, rating, analysis and restatement (Mead and Moseley 2001).

Table 10.1 Social factors

Social factors	Related articles
Change in routine (workflow) In what degree EHR will change the everyday routine of physicians and work process	Miller et al. (1994); Overhage et al. (2001); Axtell et al. (2002); Ammenwerth et al. (2003); Ash and Bates (2005); Gans et al. (2005)
Third person access to EHR database How important it is for the physicians to keep the EHR database out of reach of third parties	Ammenwerth et al. (2003); Ash and Bates (2005); Bakhtiar (2007); Cherry et al. (2008)
Physician's autonomy How physician's autonomy after EHR implementation will be influenced	Edwards et al. (2002); Ford et al. (2005)
Doctor–patient relationship How physician's relation with patient will be influenced after EHR implementation	Charles et al. (1996); Friedman et al. (1999); Smith (2001); Morrissey (2004); Francis (2010)
Culture background How the culture of the physician might influence his decision in accepting or rejecting the system	Straub et al. (1997); Vanessa and Donald (1997); Walsham (2002); Lim (2004); Al-Gahtani et al. (2007); Teo et al. (2008); Guo (2009)
Physicians' involvement How important is the involvement of physicians	Ives and Olson (1984); Barki and Hartwick (1994); Harrison and Ralphs (2001); Doolan et al. (2002); Edwards et al. (2002); Kujala (2003)
Management support How supportive is the hospital manager after EHR implementation	MacEachern (1957); Lucas (1976); Robey (1979); Jarvenpaa and Ives (1991); Davis (1993); Garibaldi (1998); Al-Gahtani and King (1999); Purvis et al. (2001); Young et al. (2001); Chin (2003); Sharma and Yetton (2003); Ash et al. (2004); Griffith and White (2005); Lorenzi et al. (2009); Rouibah et al. (2009)
Training How well the training will be organized after the EHR implementation and how it influences the physicians' decision	Saarinen (1996); Brookstone (2004); Lapointe and Rivard (2006); Cherry et al. (2008); Lorenzi et al. (2009); Meade et al. (2009); Rouibah et al. (2009)
Benefits How beneficial (patient safety, economic benefits, faster process) physicians think that EHR is	Karahanna and Straub (1999); Eid (2009); Ming-Chi (2009); FanYun and Huang (2010); Nair (2011)

Table 10.2 User acceptance theories and factors[a]

Factors	Theories	Factors related
Performance expectancy: The degree to which an individual believes that using the system will help him/her to attain gains in job performance (Venkatesh et al. 2003)	TAM/TAM2	Perceived usefulness
	C-TAM-TPB	Economic benefits for hospital
	MM	Economic benefits for physicians
	MPCU	Number of patient they can visit
	UTAUT	Physicians autonomy
	DOI	Third-party access
		Doctor–patient relation
Effort expectancy: The degree of ease associated with the use of the system (Venkatesh et al. 2003)	TAM/TAM2	Perceived ease of use
	MPCU	Change in routine
	UTAUT	Physicians' involvement
	DOI	
Social influence: The degree to which an individual perceives that important others believe he or she use the new system (Venkatesh et al. 2003)	TAM/TAM2	Esteem factor
	C-TAM-TPB	
	TPB	
	MPCU	
	UTAUT	
	DOI	
	Theory of Reasoned Action (TRA)	
Facilitating conditions: The degree to which an individual believes that an organizational and technical infrastructure exists to support use of the system (Venkatesh et al. 2003)	C-TAM-TPB	Management support
	TPB	Training
	MPCU	
	UTAUT	
	DOI	
Characteristics elements: the characteristics factors, which might influence the decision of the users towards using or not using of the system	TPB	Gender
	UTAUT	Age
	DOI	Year in practice
	TAM/TAM2	Speciality
		IQ
		Technology favourability
		EHR knowledge
		EHR usage experience
		Culture background (religion strictness)
		Computer experience
		Workplace (private/public)

[a]*TAM* technology acceptance model, *C-TAM-TPB* combined technology acceptance model and theory of planned behaviour, *MM* motivational model, *MPCU* model of PC utilization, *UTAUT* unified theory of acceptance and use of technology, *DOI* diffusion of innovation

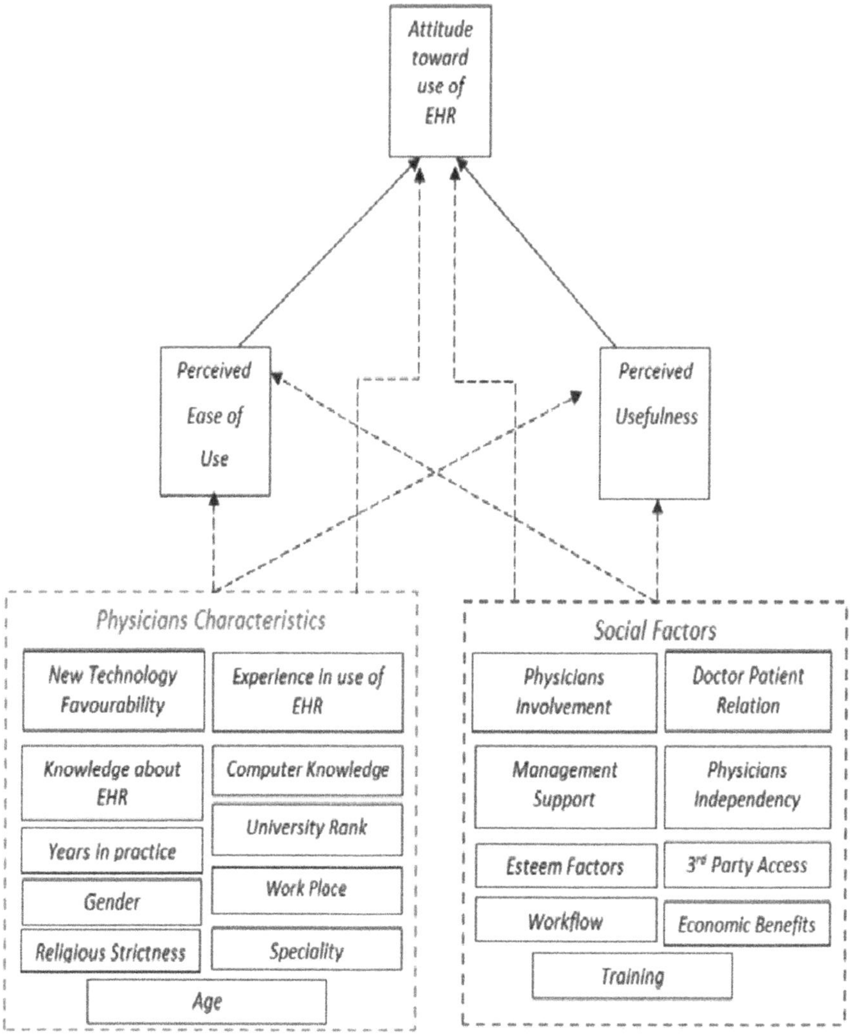

Fig. 10.1 Conceptual framework

Okoli (2004) mentioned that "The Delphi group size does not depend on statistical power, but rather on group dynamics for arriving at consensus among experts. Thus, the literature recommends 10–18 experts on a Delphi panel".

For a quantitative investigation, sampling issues are an important consideration. That is why, the number of professionals has been chosen from different areas to help us achieve better results. To fulfil the steps above, nine physicians, five information technology experts with background in health information system and five health informatics experts participated in our study. In other words, the ratio of participant (physicians vs. nonphysicians) was 0.9:1 (nine physicians and ten nonphysicians). Nonphysician participants were selected as they have been involved with the health information systems and with extensive knowledge in working together with physicians in different IT systems. Participants were asked to complete three main parts of the questionnaire. Firstly, participants evaluated the importance and confidence of each question by ranking on a 5-point scale. Secondly, their feedback on each question (e.g. wording, comprehension of the question) was obtained. Lastly, participants were encouraged to suggest opinions and suggestions within each indicator for further clarification. Participants are always anonymous to each other, but not to the authors. The responses are collected from all the participants and imported to the database anonymously; after analysing the first set, the next set of the questionnaire is distributed among the same participants who are known to the authors.

There are two sections, namely, "importance" and "confidence", in our questionnaire. In the importance section we asked the expert participants to rate each question from (1) No Judgment, (2) Unimportant, (3) Slightly Important, (4) Important and (5) Very Important. Participant may choose "No Judgment" when they feel that they have no knowledge to judge the item but, at the same time, feel that the appropriate individual (expert, decision-maker) should be able to provide an evaluation which they would prefer. So when the expert participant chooses "No Judgment", that question will not be considered. Second section (confidence) related to the reliability of each question. We follow the same rule for "No Judgment" and for the rest of the answers we rate "Unreliable", "Risky", "Acceptable" and "Certain". The value of I-CVI is an index to compute and express experts' opinion and proportion of agreement. For each item of a proposed instrument, taking a five-point scale, the value of the I-CVI is the summation of agreement, in the case of importance (4, Important; 5, Very Important divided by the total number of experts).

With the use of a quantitative approach, we have discovered the degree of consensus for each question by calculating content validity of importance and content validity of confidence. Content validity index for items (I-CVI) and content validity index for scales (S-CVI) were calculated, and questions were revised after the first round of responses and a survey was conducted based on a newer version of I-CVI and S-CVI. The level of defined importance guided us in keeping or removing the question, and the level of defined confidence showed us the questions which needed some modification. Qualitative approach provides a suggestion to revise wording and/or syntaxes of those questions which could be kept from results of content validity of importance. Thus it is vital to follow these steps to designing appropriate questions to evaluate factors affecting EHR acceptance in Iranian hospital. I-CVI of 0.78 (78 %) and S-CVI/Ave of 0.90 (90 %) are the determinate criteria for the study (Linstone and Turoff 1975).

10.4 Results

In the first round (round 1), 19 of 19 experts (100 %) responded to the questionnaire. As mentioned by Okoli et al. "Non-response is typically very low in Delphi surveys, since most researchers have personally obtained assurances of participation"

Table 10.3 CVI results for round 1 and round 2[a]

First round questions	Importance R1	Confidence R1
CH1	0.823529	0.9375
CH2	0.888889	1
CH3	0.947368	0.94737
CH4	0.294118	0.94444
CH5	0.833333	0.82353
CH6	0.176471	0.13333
CH7	0.611111	0.94444
CH8	0.888889	0.94444
CH9	0.947368	0.73684
CH10	0.823529	0.70588
CH11	0.833333	0.77778
CH12	1	0.89474
CH13	0.947368	1
TR-1	0.944444	0.94118
TR-2	0.944444	0.94118
TR-3	0.944444	1
WF-1	0.947368	0.94444
WF-2	1	0.94444
WF-3	0.894737	0.83333
WF-4	0.833333	0.88235
WF-5	0.944444	0.88235
IN-1	0.944444	0.76471
IN-2	0.947368	0.72222
SU-1	0.842105	0.88889
SU-2	0.947368	0.88889
SU-3	0.944444	0.94118
SU-4	1	0.94444
SU-5	1	0.94444
SU-6	0.789474	1
IND-1	0.944444	0.94118
IND-2	0.833333	0.82353
IND-3	0.823529	0.86667
IND-4	0.833333	0.8125
IND-5	0.882353	0.93333
DPR-1	0.833333	0.875
DPR-2	0.882353	0.93333
DPR-3	0.833333	0.8125
DPR-4	0.833333	0.8
GOV-1	0.842105	0.83333
GOV-2	0.888889	0.88235
GOV-3	0.842105	0.88889
GOV-4	0.894737	0.83333
EBH-1	0.947368	1
EBH-2	0.894737	0.61111
EBH-3	0.944444	0.58824
EBH-4	0.833333	0.70588

(continued)

Table 10.3 (continued)

First round questions	Importance R1	Confidence R1
EBH-5	0.888889	0.64706
EBH-6	0.888889	0.64706
EBH-7	0.947368	0.94444
EB-P-1	0.529412	0.5
EB-P-2	0.588235	0.82353
EB-P-3	0.666667	0.88235
EF-1	0.823529	0.8125
EF-2	0.842105	0.83333
EF-3	0.823529	0.8125
EA-1	1	0.94444
EA-2	0.842105	0.94444
EA-3	0.789474	0.94444
EA-4	0.842105	1
US-1	0.947368	0.88889
US-2	0.894737	0.94444
US-3	0.842105	0.88889
US-4	0.789474	0.83333
US-5	0.947368	0.94444
US-6	0.944444	1
US-7	1	1
AC-1	0.842105	0.70588
AC-2	1	1
AC-3	0.947368	0.72222
AC-4	0.894737	0.94444
AC-5	0.789474	0.83333
AC-6	1	1
Second round Q	*Importance R2*	*Confidence R2*
CH1	0.823529	0.941176
CH2	0.888889	1
CH3	0.944444	0.944444
CH4	0.9375	0.823529
CH5	0.944444	0.8125
CH6	0.888889	1
CH7	0.944444	1
CH8	0.944444	0.944444
CH9	0.833333	0.833333
CH10	0.833333	0.941176
TR-1	0.944444	0.882353
TR-2	0.944444	0.941176
TR-3	0.944444	0.941176
TR-4	0.944444	0.9375
WF-1	1	1
WF-2	0.888889	0.941176
WF-3	0.941176	0.941176
WF-4	0.944444	0.882353

(continued)

Table 10.3 (continued)

First round questions	Importance R1	Confidence R1
WF-5	0.941176	0.875
IN-1	0.944444	0.875
IN-2	0.833333	0.941176
SU-1	1	0.941176
SU-2	1	0.882353
SU-3	0.944444	0.941176
SU-4	0.944444	0.9375
SU-5	0.777778	1
SU-6	0.941176	1
IND-1	0.944444	1
IND-2	0.882353	1
IND-3	0.833333	0.823529
IND-4	0.9375	1
IND-5	0.833333	0.823529
DPR-1	0.882353	1
DPR-2	0.888889	0.9375
DPR-3	0.882353	1
DPR-4	0.944444	0.9375
GOV-1	0.941176	0.866667
GOV-2	0.944444	0.875
GOV-3	0.944444	0.875
GOV-4	1	0.882353
EBH-1	0.888889	0.823529
EBH-2	1	1
EBH-3	0.944444	1
EBH-4	0.941176	1
EBH-5	0.944444	0.941176
EBH-6	1	1
EBH-7	0.823529	0.875
EF-1	0.944444	0.941176
EF-2	1	0.866667
EF-3	0.8125	0.882353
EA-1	0.833333	0.941176
EA-2	0.875	0.823529
EA-3	1	0.882353
EA-4	0.888889	0.866667
EA-5	0.888889	0.941176
US-1	0.888889	1
US-2	1	0.941176
US-3	0.888889	0.941176
US-4	0.833333	0.941176
US-5	0.833333	0.941176
US-6	1	0.882353

(continued)

Table 10.3 (continued)

First round questions	Importance R1	Confidence R1
US-7	0.941176	0.823529
US-8	1	0.882353
US-9	0.888889	1
AC-1	0.944444	1
AC-2	0.944444	0.941176
AC-3	0.944444	1
AC-4	0.888889	0.941176
AC-5	1	0.941176
AC-6	1	0.823529

[a]*CH* characteristics, *TR* training, *WF* workflow, *IN* involvement, *SU* support, *IND* physicians independency, *DPR* doctor–patient relation, *GOV* government access, *EBH* economic benefits for hospital, *EB-P* economic benefits for physicians, *EF* esteem factor, *EA* ease of use, *US* usefulness, *AC* acceptance

Table 10.4 Results after the first round of Delphi study[a]

EL	NU	MO	RE	CR
CQ	10	4	3	6
TR	3	0	0	0
WF	5	0	0	0
IN	2	2	0	2
SU	6	0	0	0
IND	5	0	0	0
DPR	4	0	0	0
GOV	4	0	0	0
EBH	8	5	0	5
EB-P	3	1	3	3
EF	3	0	0	0
EA	4	0	0	0
US	7	0	0	0
AC	6	2	0	2

EL elements, *NU* number of questions, *MO* modify, *RE* removed, *CR* cumulative revise, *CQ* characteristic questions, *TR* training, *WF* workflow, *IN* involvement, *SU* support, *IND* physicians independency, *DPR* doctor–patient relation, *GOV* government access, *EBH* economic benefits for hospital, *EB-P* economic benefits for physicians, *EF* esteem factor, *EA* ease of use, *US* usefulness, *AC* acceptance

(Okoli and Pawlowski 2004). For the second round of this study, we have received 18 of 19 responses (close to 95 %). Nine physicians, four information technology experts and five health and informatics experts participated in our study. In other words, the ratio of participant (physicians vs. nonphysicians) was 1:1 (nine physicians and nine nonphysicians). The results were shown in Table 10.3. Questions with CVI less than 0.78 were either removed or revised accordingly as shown in Table 10.4.

In total, 18 questions have been modified from the first round of Delphi study. The questions that experts found unreliable or improvable have been modified for the second round. According to the feedbacks received, EA-1 "My interaction with the EHR will be clear and understandable (user-friendly)" has been split to EA-1 "EHR will be user-friendly (enjoyable to work with)" and "EHR software will have understandable symbols (icons)". The results from the additional responses from the suggestions and opinions further explained why CVIs of certain items were low in first round, for example, for question CH Q6, "If we value strictness toward religion from 1 to 5 (5 as highest strictness and 1 as the lowest strictness) how strict you consider yourself toward your religion?" This question has been commented by experts as inappropriate in this study due to its being a sensitive issue of religion, and the stakeholders would not like to reveal the truth. And for question EB PQ1, "With use of EHR, the hospital will be richer, thus they will increase my salary", the respondents commented that, "Salaries of physicians are fixed (in Iran) and that won't increase the salary", that opinion reflected why CVI 0.59 (importance) and 0.5 (confidence). As a result, this could be used to explain why the values of I-CVI in such questions are lower than 78 % in importance and confidence in round 1. All items achieved CVI over 78 % for both confidence and importance for the second round with overall S-CVI of confidence and importance being 93 % and 92 %, respectively.

After the second round, the questionnaires have been finalized as follows in Table 10.5.

10.5 Discussion and Conclusion

This research has created a survey, which defines current social and characteristics factors of the physicians and their perceptions towards use of EHR. Thus in the future studies, this survey might be used to weigh those factors and determine the influence of each of them in user acceptance.

Although user acceptance models have been tested in information system research, it has not been applied in Iranian physician's use of EHRs and identifying appropriate questionnaires for the physician's attitude of EHR. The purpose of this research was to design a proper questionnaire which helps researcher define attitude of Iranian physicians towards the use of EHR. To achieve that, important factors that could influence their attitudes have been identified. In addition expert's opinions on importance and confidence of the factors and the designed questions have been reviewed using Delphi method study that has defined a number of factors which might affect acceptance of EHR among Iranian physicians. Two rounds of experts' opinions have been obtained and analysed for appropriateness of these questions. Two rounds of study were conducted as the consensus was reached on expert opinions after the second round of the study. The study could be applied in another country with similar scopes (economic, religion, culture, etc.). This study will be the first step towards understanding Iranian's physician opinions on use of EHRs.

Table 10.5 Drs Preception

CH1	Gender
CH2	Age
CH3	How long have you been working in the healthcare field as a physician?
CH4	Which university you have been graduated from?
CH5	Do you use a personal computer (PC) or PC device (such as laptop or handheld device) to… (select all that apply)
CH6	On the whole, how sophisticated a computer user do you consider yourself?
CH7	If we don't consider money as an issue, when would you like to change your cell phone? (Choose as many as applicable)
CH8	In general when do you usually buy a new computer? (Choose as many as applicable)
CH9	How well you know EHR?
CH10	Have you ever used EHR?
TR-1	The training which I will receive will be well organized
TR-2	I will receive the training that I need to be able to understand all about EHR. (General concepts)
TR-3	I will receive the training that I need to be able to use the EHR. (How to work with it in real life)
TR-4	Overall I think my colleagues and I will learn whatever we need in those training
WF-1	EHR will help me to retrieve the information that I need easier
WF-2	EHR will help me insert the information into the database easier
WF-3	EHR will not make me confused in my daily routine
WF-4	EHR will help me visit more patients every day
WF-5	Overall EHR will enhance my everyday routine
IN-1	It is essential that physicians like me are involved in the implementation phase of EHR
IN-2	Involvement of the physicians like me during the EHR implementation phase will be effective for ensuring that the project is conducted properly
SU-1	The EHR implementation project is important to hospital top management that's why I think he/she will try his/her best to support me
SU-2	Management will introduce the EHR project to physicians effectively
SU-3	Management will do what he/she can to have a well-implemented EHR
SU-4	Management will provide me with the training that I need in order to use the EHR effectively
SU-5	I will have easy access to resources to help me in understanding and using the EHR
SU-6	Management expects me to use the EHR, that's why he requires me to learn EHR usage
IND-1	Using the EHR will increase the ability of a higher authority to control and monitor my clinical practices and decision-making
IND-2	Using the EHR may threaten my personal and professional privacy
IND-3	Using the EHR may result in legal or ethical problems for me
IND-4	Using the EHR may limit my independency in making clinical decisions or judgments
IND-5	Overall, I think using EHR will negatively affect my independency
DPR-1	The patient's confidence in the physician will likely be diminished if the patient sees the physician using computer-based technology as a diagnostic aid
DPR-2	Using the EHR will likely threaten the physician's credibility with his/her patients
DPR-3	Using the EHR will likely reduce the patient's satisfaction with the quality of healthcare he/she receives

(continued)

Table 10.5 (continued)

CH1	Gender
DPR-4	Overall, using the EHR will likely damage the doctor–patient interaction
GOV-1	Using the EHR will increase the government's ability to monitor my daily work
GOV-2	Using the EHR may threaten the information that I don't want to share with government
GOV-3	Using EHR allows the government to have an exact number of the patient that I will visit and arrange the tax that I should pay based on that
GOV-4	Overall, I do not feel comfortable as government may access to EHR database
EBH-1	With use of EHR the hospital may assist more patient
EBH-2	With use of EHR, the hospital will enhance the communication
EBH-3	Considering that saving lives will have economic benefits. I think EHR will assist in saving lives
EBH-4	Considering that better collaboration among physicians will have economic benefits I think EHR will improve collaboration among physicians
EBH-5	Considering better work process will save money. I think EHR will improve the work process
EBH-6	Considering better task distribution will save money. I think EHR will improve task distribution
EBH-7	Overall, use of EHR will have economic benefits for the hospital
EF-1	With use of EHR, I will feel special as I am doing something which other physicians are not doing
EF-2	Fewer errors in our hospital (as a result of EHR) will separate our hospital from the rest
EF-3	Overall I think if the society knows that we are using EHR, they see us more respectfully
EA-1	EHR will be user-friendly
EA-2	EHR will use understandable symbols
EA-3	Learning to use the EHR will be easy for me
EA-4	I expect to become skilled at using the EHR
EA-5	Overall, I expect the EHR will be easy for me to use
US-1	Using the EHR will improve the quality of my work in providing better patient care
US-2	I think EHR will help healthcare sections to provide better health services
US-3	Using the EHR will give me greater control over my work schedule
US-4	I think use of EHR will provide more effective patient care
US-5	Using the EHR will allow me to accomplish tasks more quickly
US-6	Using the EHR will allow me to accomplish more work than would otherwise be possible
US-7	Using the EHR will enhance my overall effectiveness in my job
US-8	Using the EHR will make my job easier to perform
US-9	Overall, I believe EHR is an effective tools for my profession
AC-1	The development and implementation of the EHR technology will support the physician in providing better patient care
AC-2	I will encourage the use of the EHR among my colleagues
AC-3	I think that using EHR should be compulsory in all the hospital
AC-4	I like to use EHR instead of the paper-based system
AC-5	I believe all physicians should learn to use the EHR effectively
AC-6	Overall, my attitude about EHR usage will be positive

References

Al-Gahtani, S. S., Hubona, G. S., et al. (2007). Information technology (IT) in Saudi Arabia: Culture and the acceptance and use of IT. *Information Management, 44*(8), 681–691.

Al-Gahtani, S. S., & King, M. (1999). Attitudes, satisfaction and usage: Factors contributing to each in the acceptance of information technology. *Behaviour and Information Technology, 18*(4), 277–297.

Ammenwerth, E., Mansmann, U., et al. (2003). Factors affecting and affected by user acceptance of computer-based nursing documentation: Results of a two-year study. *Journal of the American Medical Informatics Association, 10*(1), 69–84.

Ash, J. S., & Bates, D. W. (2005). Factors and forces affecting EHR system adoption: Report of a 2004 ACMI discussion. *Journal of the American Medical Informatics Association, 12*(1), 8–12.

Ash, J. S., Gorman, P. N., et al. (2004). Computerized physician order entry in U.S. hospitals: Results of a 2002 survey. *Journal of the American Medical Informatics Association, 11*(2), 95–99.

Axtell, C., Wall, T., et al. (2002). Familiarity breeds content: The impact of exposure to change on employee openness and well-being. *Journal of Occupational and Organizational Psychology, 75*(2), 217–231.

Bakhtiar, A. (2007). Ahmadinejad's achilles heel: The Iranian economy. *Payvand Iran News*. Retrieved August 6, 2011, from http://www.payvand.com/news/07/jan/1295.html

Barki, H., & Hartwick, J. (1994). Measuring user participation, user involvement, and user attitude. *MIS Quarterly, 18*(1), 59–82.

Brookstone, A. (2004). Electronic medical records: Creating the environment for change. *British Columbia Medical Journal, 46*(5), 233–235.

Charles, F., Southon, G., et al. (1996). Information technology in complex health services organizational impediments to successful technology transfer and diffusion. *Journal of the American Medical Informatics Association, 4*(2), 112–124.

Cherry, B., Carter, M., et al. (2008). Factors affecting electronic health record adoption in long-term care facilities. *Journal for Healthcare Quality, 30*(2), 37–47.

Chin, T. (2003). *Doctors pull plug on paperless system*. Retrieved September 17, 2011, from http://www.ama-assn.org/amednews/2003/02/17/bil20217.htm

Dansky, K. H., Gamm, L. D., Vasey, J., & Barsukiewicz, C. (1999). Electronic medical records: Are physicians ready?/Practitioner application. *Journal of Healthcare Management, 44*(6), 440–454; discussion 454–455.

Davis, F. D. (1993). User acceptance of information technology: System characteristics, user perceptions and behavioral impacts. *International Journal of Man-Machine Studies, 38*(3), 475–487.

Doolan, D., Bates, D., et al. (2002). The use of computers for clinical care: A case series of advanced U.S. sites. *American Medical Informatics Association*.

Edwards, N., Kornacki, M. J., et al. (2002). Unhappy doctors: What are the causes and what can be done? *British Medical Journal, 324*(7341), 835–838.

Eid, R. (2009). Extending TAM and IDT to predict the adoption of the internet for B-to-B marketing activities: An empirical study of UK companies. *International Journal of E-Business Research, 5*(4), 18.

Eschenburg, F., Lylykangas, J., et al. (2005). User acceptance: The BioSec approach. *Biometric Technology Today, 13*(7), 8–10.

FanYun, P., & Huang, K. (2010). Applying the technology acceptance model to the introduction of healthcare information systems. *Technological Forecasting and Social Change, 78*(4), 650–660.

Ford, E. W., Menachemi, N., et al. (2005). Predicting the Adoption of electronic health records by physicians: When will health care be paperless? *Journal of the American Medical Informatics Association, 13*(1), 106–112.

Ford, E. W., Menachemi, N., et al. (2009). Resistance is futile: But it is slowing the pace of EHR adoption nonetheless. *Journal of the American Medical Informatics Association, 16*(3), 274–281.

Francis, L. P. (2010). The physician-patient relationship and a National Health Information Network. *The Journal of Law, Medicine & Ethics, 38*(1), 36–49.

Friedman, C., Elstein, A., et al. (1999). Enhancement of clinicians' diagnostic reasoning by computer-based consultation. *Journal of the American Medical Association, 282*(19).

Gans, D., Kralewski, J., Hammons, T., & Dowd, B. (2005). Medical groups' adoption of electronic health records and information systems. *Health Affairs, 24*(5), 1323–1333.

Garibaldi, R. A. (1998). Computers and the quality of care—A clinician's perspective. *The New England Journal of Medicine, 338*(4), 259–260.

Griffith, J. R., & White, K. R. (2005). The revolution in hospital management. *Journal of Healthcare Management, 50*(3), 170–189.

Guo, C. (2009). *A cross cultural validation of perceptions and use of social network service: An exploratory study* (pp. 42–50). An exploratory study. M. S. University, ProQuest.

Hajavi, A., Azar, F., et al. (2005). Medical records standards in selected countries and Iran: A comparative study. *Institute of Health Record & Information Management, 46*(1).

Harrison, B., & Ralphs, D. (2001). How best to organise acute hospital services? *British Medical Journal, 323*(7324), 1305.

Ives, B., & Olson, M. H. (1984). User involvement and mis success: A review of research. *Management Science, 30*(5), 586–603.

Jarvenpaa, S. L., & Ives, B. (1991). Executive involvement and participation in the management of information technology. *MIS Quarterly, 15*(2), 205–227.

Johnson, C. M., Johnson, T. R., et al. (2005). A user-centered framework for redesigning health care interfaces. *Journal of Biomedical Informatics, 38*(1), 75–87.

Karahanna, E., & Straub, D. W. (1999). The psychological origins of perceived usefulness and ease-of-use. *Information & Management, 35*(4), 237–250.

Kazemi, A., Ellenius, J., et al. (2009). CPOE in Iran–A viable prospect?: Physicians' opinions on using CPOE in an Iranian teaching hospital. *International Journal of Medical Informatics, 78*(3), 199–207.

Kujala, S. (2003). User involvement: A review of the benefits and challenges. *Behaviour and Information Technology, 22*(1), 1.

Lapointe, L., & Rivard, S. (2006). Getting physicians to accept new information technology: Insights from case studies. *Canadian Medical Association Journal, 174*(11).

Lim, C. L. (2004). Race, multi-cultural accommodation and the constitutions of Singapore and Malaysia. *Singapore Journal of Legal Studies, 117–149.*

Linstone, H., & Turoff, M. (1975). *The Delphi method: Techniques and applications*. Reading, MA: Addison-Wesley.

Lorenzi, N. M., Kouroubali, A., et al. (2009). How to successfully select and implement electronic health records (EHR) in small ambulatory practice settings. *BMC Medical Informatics and Decision Making, 9*(1).

Lorenzi, N., & Riley, R. (1995). *Organizational aspects of health informatics: Managing technological change*. California: Springer.

Lowry, G. (2002). Modelling user acceptance of building management systems. *Automation in Construction, 11*(6), 695–705.

Lucas, H. C. (1976). *The implementation of computer-based models*. New York: National Association of Accountants.

MacEachern, M. T. (1957). *Hospital organization and management*. Chicago: Physicians' Record Co.

Maidani, Z., Safdari, R., et al. (2006). Comparative study on the establishment's approach to information management standards (E-Health). *Hormozgan Health Journal*, 167–172.

Mead, D., & Moseley, L. (2001). The use of the Delphi as a research approach. *Nurse Researcher, 8*(4), 4–23.

Meade, B., Buckley, D., et al. (2009). What factors affect the use of electronic patient records by Irish GPs? *International Journal of Medical Informatics, 78*(8), 551–558.

Menachemi, N. (2006). Barriers to ambulatory EHR: Who are 'imminent adopters' and how do they differ from other physicians? *Informatics in Primary Care, 14*(2), 101–108.

Miller, V. D., Johnson, J. R., et al. (1994). Antecedents to willingness to participate in a planned organizational change. *Journal of Applied Communication Research, 22*(1), 59–80.

Ming-Chi, L. (2009). Factors influencing the adoption of internet banking: An integration of TAM and TPB with perceived risk and perceived benefit. *Electronic Commerce Research and Applications, 8*(3), 130–141.

Moghaddasi, H., Hosseini, A., et al. (2006). A new model for the organizational structure of the medical records. *Perspectives in Health Information Management., 3*, 4.

Morrissey, J. (2004). CHW plans IT initiative. *Modern Healthcare, 34*(8), 16.

Morton, M. E. P. R., & Wiedenbeck S. (2010). EHR acceptance factors in ambulatory care: A survey of physician perceptions. *Perspectives in Health Information Management,* (1559–4122), 1–17.

MRC. (2010). *Evaluation of electronic health record in Iran*. Retrieved September 17, 2011, from http://www.majlis.ir/mhtml/index.php?newlang=english

Nair, S. V. (2011). *Benefits and security of electronic health record (EHR) use by pediatric staff: A technology acceptance model (TAM)-based quantitative study* (p. 112). Minnesota: School of Business and Technology, Capella University.

Okoli, C., & Pawlowski, S. D. (2004). The Delphi method as a research tool: An example, design considerations and applications. *Information Management, 42*(1), 15–29.

Overhage, M., Perkins, S., Tierney, W. M., & McDonald, C. J. (2001). Controlled trial of direct physician order entry: Effects on physicians. Time utilization in ambulatory primary care internal medicine practices. *Journal of the American Medical Informatics Association, 8*(4), 361–371.

Purvis, R. L., Sambamurthy, V., et al. (2001). The assimilation of knowledge platforms in organizations: An empirical investigation. *Organization Science, 12*(2), 117–135.

Robey, D. (1979). User attitudes and management information system use. *Academy of Management Journal, 22*(3), 527–538.

Rouibah, K., H. I. Hamdy, et al. (2009). Effect of management support, training, and user involvement on system usage and satisfaction in Kuwait. *Industrial Management & Data Systems, 109*(3), 338–356. Bingley: Emerald Group

Saarinen, T. (1996). An expanded instrument for evaluating information system success. *Information Management, 31*(2), 103–118.

Sharma, R., & Yetton, P. (2003). The contingent effects of management support and task interdependence on successful information systems implementation. *MIS Quarterly, 27*(4), 533–555.

Smith, R. (2001). Why are doctors so unhappy? *British Medical Journal, 322*(7294), 1073–1074.

Straub, D., Keil, M., et al. (1997). Testing the technology acceptance model across cultures: A three country study. *Information Management, 33*(1), 1–11.

Teo, T., Sing, C. C., et al. (2008). A cross-cultural examination of the intention to use technology between Singaporean and Malaysian pre-service teachers: An application of the technology acceptance model (TAM). *Educational Technology & Society, 11*(4), 265–280.

van der Meijden, M. J., Tange, H., et al. (2001). Development and implementation of an EPR: How to encourage the user. *International Journal of Medical Informatics, 64*(2–3), 173–185.

Vanessa, E., & Donald D. (1997). The role of culture in interface acceptance. In *Proceedings of the IFIP TC13 international conference on human-computer interaction*. London: Chapman Hall.

Venkatesh, V., Morris, M. G., et al. (2003). User acceptance of information technology: Toward a unified view. *MIS Quarterly, 27*(3), 425–478.

Walsham, G. (2002). Cross-cultural software production and use: A structurational analysis. *MIS Quarterly, 26*(4), 359–380.

Winkelman, W. J., & Leonard, K. J. (2004). Overcoming structural constraints to patient utilization of electronic medical records: A critical review and proposal for an evaluation framework. *Journal of the American Medical Informatics Association, 11*(2), 151–161.
Young, G. J., Charns, M. P., et al. (2001). Top manager and network effects on the adoption of innovative management practices: A study of TQM in a public hospital system. *Strategic Management Journal, 22*(10), 935–951.
Zhang, J. (2005). Human-centered computing in health information systems. Part 1: Analysis and design. *Journal of Biomedical Informatics, 38*(1), 1–3.

Chapter 11
Trying to Streamline Healthcare Delivery in Australia via the Personally Controlled Electronic Health Record (PCEHR)

Imran Muhammad, Say Yen Teoh, and Nilmini Wickramasinghe

Abstract Healthcare systems around the world are facing a number of challenges. Increasing focus is thus being placed on constructing appropriate healthcare reforms to address challenges and streamline healthcare services. One of the critical enablers in this reform is the adoption of an e-health solution. These e-health solutions are not only expensive and complex endeavours but also have far-reaching implications. Given that the implementation and adoption of these e-health solutions is so important; it is also vital to have an extensive evaluation and analysis of these systems with a theoretically informed lens. This then will serve to maximise and sustain the benefits of the proposed solution and realise its full potential for achieving superior healthcare delivery. To date the literature is void of such evaluations. Hence, this paper proffers the use of a sociotechnical systems (STS) analysis. The exemplar case study under consideration is that of the personally controlled electronic health record (PCEHR), the chosen e-health solution by the Australian government.

Keywords Healthcare • Healthcare delivery • Healthcare operations • Healthcare management • Personally controlled electronic health records (PCEHR) • e-Health • Electronic health record (EHR) • Sociotechnical system (STS)

I. Muhammad
School of Business IT & Logistics, RMIT University, GPO Box 2476, Melbourne, VIC 3001, Australia
e-mail: imran.muhammad@rmit.edu.au

S.Y. Teoh
HIRi and BITL, RMIT University, Melbourne, VIC, Australia
e-mail: sayyen.teoh@rmit.edu.au

N. Wickramasinghe (✉)
Epworth HealthCare & Department of BITL & HIRi, RMIT University, GPO Box 2476, Melbourne, VIC 3001, Australia
e-mail: nilmini.wickramasinghe@rmit.edu.au

N. Wickramasinghe et al. (eds.), *Lean Thinking for Healthcare*, Healthcare Delivery in the Information Age, DOI 10.1007/978-1-4614-8036-5_11,

11.1 Introduction

In today's fluid healthcare environment, governments and healthcare service providers are facing major challenges of waste reduction from paperwork, inventory to waiting-room delays and unnecessary surgical tools in trying to deliver quality healthcare services (Wickramasinghe et al. 2009). This is putting more pressure on governments and healthcare service providers while they are being asked to do more to provide patients, physicians, nurses, and administrators with a high quality and level of service with very limited resources (Womack and Jones 2003) to find ways to serve consumers as well as manage staggering costs of healthcare services (Wickramasinghe et al. 2009). This confluence of factors in turn necessitates policy makers and healthcare leaders to call for a redesign of the healthcare delivery system, a comprehensive system that can not only handle multispectral data and disparate information but also improve the flow of this information between key stakeholders (e.g. service providers, consumers, government agencies and healthcare managers) to improve health outcomes and quality of care (Mort et al. 2009), a competitive necessity.

Health information systems in general and e-health solutions more especially have the potential to transform the healthcare delivery system (Wickramasinghe and Schaffer 2010); and hence, we see the key role for e-health solutions on all healthcare reform agendas today (Wickramasinghe and Schaffer 2010; Mort et al. 2009; Car et al. 2008). However, transformation is not a straightforward proposition and is sometimes faced with many known and unknown hurdles. Reasons for this include that healthcare is not only an information-rich industry but also complex consisting of a web of players, in addition to being a culturally deep-rooted industry (Wickramasinghe and Schaffer 2010) where different human and non-human actors must interact in order to treat a patient.

The convolution of funding arrangements and interactions between different levels of service providers and consumers in healthcare service delivery in Australia is illustrated in Fig. 11.1.

Although there are many benefits of health information technology (Buntin et al. 2011; Devaraj and Kohli 2000; Goldzweig et al. 2009; Shekelle et al. 2006; Tang et al. 2006; Wu et al. 2006), but the transformation is difficult, the level of adoption and usage of such systems is generally low (Kaelber et al. 2008; Steinbrook 2008). Issues relating to the adoption and usage of such systems in healthcare environments are not just technical in nature but are multidimensional that include organisational, cultural, legal and social considerations as well (Ammenwerth et al. 2006; Catwell and Sheikh 2009; Cresswell et al. 2011; Lorenzi et al. 2009; DesRoches et al. 2008; André et al. 2008).

Furthermore, it is important to note that these interventions are to improve the healthcare service delivery by enhancing the process of delivery system and reducing the bottlenecks by introducing the value-added process improvements. One of the choices of studying the process improvements in service sectors is lean thinking approac. Lean thinking approach is thought as to generate positive results

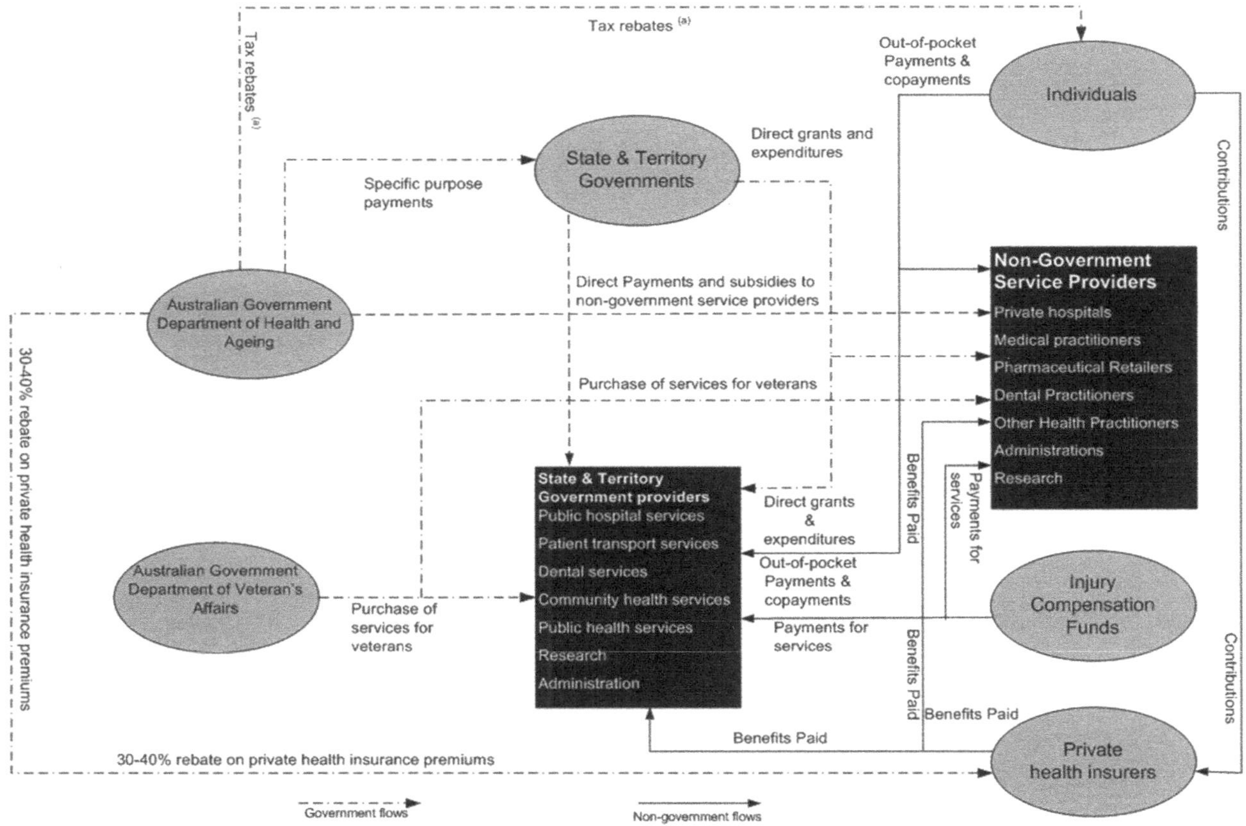

(a) The tax rebate is not an expense of the Australian Government Department of health and Ageing, but is a tax expenditure of the Australian Government.

Fig. 11.1 The structure of Australian healthcare system and its flow of funds (AIHW 2012, p. 4)

(Ben-Tovim et al. 2007; Fillingham 2007), but it is also argued that its implementation may lead to resistance because this approach tends to neglect the unique sociotechnical aspects of healthcare settings (Fillingham 2007). Recent literature on the implementation of technology-based change programmes in healthcare to streamline, the value-added process puts a lot of emphasis on the significance of the actors and their networks and the way they influence and have impact on the results of these interventions (Papadopoulos and Merali 2008, 2009; Wickramasinghe et al. 2009). Furthermore, a common theme is the call for more empirical and theoretical investigations in this respect (Bevir and Richards, 2009; Rhodes, n.d.; Greenhalgh et al., 2004; Cresswell et al. 2011).

To fully explore all issues pertaining to successful implementation, adoption and usage of e-health solutions and technologies for healthcare delivery, researchers have rightly argued that IT-based interventions in healthcare settings should be evaluated with theoretically informed techniques (Wickramasinghe and Schaffer 2010). One approach advocated in the literature is the application of a sociotechnical perspective-based evaluation of complex healthcare systems and IT-based interventions (Wickramasinghe et al. 2009; Yusof et al. 2007; Aarts et al. 2004) and also enriched by drawing on lean thinking (Papadopoulos 2011; Papadopoulos et al. 2011).

A sociotechnical perspective synthesises a powerful lens and serves to explain how to evaluate the implementation of complex technology-based interventions that have not only technical but also social and organisational dimensions (Latour, 1986, 2005; Law and Hassard, 1999; Callon, 1986). We propose that a sociotechnical perspective is theoretically rich enough to provide additional value in explaining the process of technology-based interventions built on lean thinking. Moreover, it helps researchers in their exploration of the emergence of social, cognitive, political and technical dimensions of the interactions and associations between different actors/actants. By combining such an analysis with the concepts of lean thinking, it becomes possible to further help in shaping the meaning and outcomes of such interventions and their far-reaching impacts for healthcare delivery and thereby assist in managing short-term coherence/consensus between the actors involved in the process.

The main focus of a sociotechnical perspective in this respect is to understand the nature of the relationship and interaction between two interrelated systems: a social system and a technical system in a given environmental context (Whetton and Georgiou 2010). The emphasis is to study the multidimensional impact of technology on people, organisations and tasks as well as the impact of social and people issues on technology design, adoption and use (Cresswell et al. 2011). For this reason, it is also important to understand the interrelationship and interactions of the two between each other (Coiera 2004). Thus, in order to develop a true assessment of the key barriers and facilitators of the PCEHR implementation and adoption, it is important to analyse this project through a sociotechnical lens which will serve to facilitate the capture of all key issues—technical and non-technical.

Hence, this paper proffers the merits of taking a sociotechnical system (STS) approach to evaluate the Personally Controlled Electronic Health Record (PCEHR) in the Australian context in an attempt to provide a rich analysis of all key issues and critical success factors necessary for its successful deployment. In so doing, this research in progress will also demonstrate the merits of an STS approach. Specifically, we will answer the research question how a sociotechnical perspective can facilitate a better understanding of the critical issues regarding e-health solutions development and successful deployment to streamline the healthcare delivery system in Australia. To answer this question, we will use an exploratory qualitative case study approach. We choose the exemplar case of the PCEHR in Australia, and as noted by Yin (1994) the use of an exemplar case is appropriate when investigating a novel, new phenomenon (Yin 1994). We subscribe to recognised qualitative data collection and analysis techniques including thematic analysis as discussed by Kvale (1996) and Boyatzis(1998). First we will discuss PCEHR, and then in the next section, we will discuss lean thinking and its role in streamlining healthcare delivery and why sociotechnical approach is important in evaluation of e-health systems.

11.2 The Personally Controlled Electronic Health Record

The terminology adopted in Australia for electronic record keeping and its e-health solution is known as the PCEHR which sits between individually controlled health records and healthcare provider health records (NEHTA and DoHA 2011; Fig. 11.2). Thus, the PCEHR has a shared use and mixed governance model (NEHTA and DoHA 2011; Fig. 11.2).

Specifically, the PCEHR is a person-centric secure repository of electronic health and medical records of individual's medical history that would act as a hub for linking hospital, medical and pharmaceutical systems using a patient unique identifier (NHHRC 2009, p. 134). One of its key features is that it captures information from different systems and presents this information in a single view to consumers and authorised service providers for better decision making about health and service delivery (NEHTA and DoHA 2011). This is a hybrid health information system that integrates web-based personal health records with a clinical electronic health record system and allows shared access to both consumers and healthcare providers based on a shared responsibilities and mixed governance model (Leslie 2011).

Fig. 11.2 The position of the PCEHR in the e-health solution spectrum

As we can see from the overview, the PCEHR is a person-centric system where technology is going to be implemented in a complex clinical and organisational environment and users are going to be different set of stockholders including healthcare service providers, healthcare managers, government bodies, healthcare pressure groups and most importantly patients.

Further, the PCEHR is a patient-centric system and is a model for essentially engaging patients in their healthcare and empowering them in this undertaking. The PCEHR utilises advances in technology most notably that of Web 2.0 which makes it possible to engage users by providing them interactive user interfaces. Hence, it also becomes important to understand the rules of interaction between users, tasks and technology, which is possible with a sociotechnical approach.

11.3 Lean Thinking in Healthcare

The concept of lean thinking has had its roots in Toyota Motors mainly focused on operations management since it gained widespread attention both in practice and academic (Womack et al. 2007) fields, including healthcare. Based on the Toyota model, lean thinking focuses on innovative techniques to reduce and eliminate waste by using available resources efficiently and effectively (Hines et al., 2004; Shah and Ward 2003). The underlying assumption that constitutes the principle of lean thinking is that organisations are made up of different processes and these processes need to be improved to streamline the services and these process improvements are linked with the concept of value, value stream (waste reduction), flow, pull and perfection (continuance improvements) through repeating processes (Papadopoulos et al. 2011).

11.3.1 Value

The value concept is the corner stone of the lean thinking paradigm. Lean thinking argues that each step in the process of service delivery should add some value for the customer. In the case of healthcare services, customers can be patients, physicians or administrators depending on what aspect of the process is under consideration. If a process is not adding any value, it should be eliminated or re-engineered depending on its importance and necessity (Campbell 2009).

Value is defined by Womack and Jones (2003, p. 75) as:

> the capability to deliver exactly the (customized) product or service a customer wants with minimal time between the moment the customer asks for that product or service and the actual delivery at an appropriate price

By understanding the needs of customers, the process steps in service delivery can be divided into two categories, that is, value adding and non-value adding.

A value-adding process helps to satisfy customer needs, while non-value-adding process does not satisfy customer needs and should be considered as waste. If process is not adding any value it should be eliminated or re-engineered depending on its importance and necessity (Campbell 2009).

For example, in the case of a GP consultation, a patient might have to go through different processes such as booking an appointment, waiting for his/her turn to see GP and filling out a patient medical history and health record form each time the patient visits their doctor. In this process, for a patient seeing the doctor is the important and value-adding activity, while waiting and filling up forms are wastages and those should be eliminated or minimised.

11.3.2 Pull

Pull has been described as the services needed to be provided in line with demand to support the creation of value (Bushell and Shelest 2002). Delivering services aligned with demand that means all needed resources, information and materials should be pulled towards the required places and time when it is needed without urgency or delay. Early or delayed availability of resources is a form of waste. For example, if the patient is ready to be discharged but the doctor is not available to sign him out or ambulance is not available to take the patient that would result in delays and thus waste of resources.

11.3.3 Flow

The next step is flow, where each patient worked with one unit at a time and passed on to the next step of the process without any delay (Jones and Mitchell 2006). The primary goal of the flow is to eliminate the need of queuing and batching in a given process that further eliminate multiple waiting times and interruptions. Flow will make sure the continuity of the process until it finishes. For example, to achieve best possible results and eliminate delays, it is important to have test results available to the doctor when he/she consults the patient.

11.3.4 The Value Stream

The value stream is a necessary step to successfully complete a process or service that can help to identify the waste within a process. A seamless flow to happen, an integrated value stream is needed to be designed and then efficiently managed. All steps required in the context of healthcare services from start to finish that add value need to be streamlined and integrated and thought of as one continuous process, keeping in mind the effect of each step on its preceding and following step to link them together seamlessly.

11.3.5 Perfection

A key principle in lean thinking is that a continued improvement in a process will lead to an enhanced process, and thus continuity in improvement (continuous improvement) should not stop at any time. The foundation of the idea of perfection is based on a notion of "continuous improvement through incremental change based on outcomes" (Tsasis and Bruce-Barrett 2008). By simplifying the process, a foundation can be created for the incremental and continues improvement in the process that would eventually lead to the improvement in the next process.

The lean thinking concept has been widely used in public services since the mid-2000. Reports are suggesting that lean in healthcare is mostly used in regard to process improvement methodologies; more and more literature is emerging to confirm this including that from the USA (57 %), the UK (29 %) and Australia (4 %) (Brandao de Souza 2009; Radnor 2010). Approaches based of lean principles focussed on process improvement in hospitals, and allied healthcare settings have been reported as very effective and the literature shows that there are tangible results in terms of cost and waiting-time reductions, improvement in quality of service and significant increases in consumer as well as service provider satisfaction (Silvester et al. 2004; Radnor and Boaden 2008). However, the use of lean principles in healthcare settings is currently archived through the application of simple tools in a single process such as one ward or section rather than covering the complete journey of a patient (Brandao de Souza 2009; Radnor 2010).

Most of the literature describes lean as a fixed object, very well designed and defined, but successful implementation depends on the degree of resistance from different actors (Walley et al., 2001; Proudlove et al. 2008). It is important here to note that the method of adoption and negotiation of lean by different actors in pursuit of their own programmes in healthcare is not recognised in literature very well at this time. Isolated and small-scale projects for streamlining healthcare services involving one or two wards might have less complexity whereas projects like the PCEHR, where a nationwide healthcare reform is initiated, need a more robust and theoretically informed lens along with process improvement techniques. Thus, we argue that a sociotechnical perspective is such a lens that can explore and help in understanding the dynamic associations between heterogeneous networks and actors associated with these networks. It further can explore emergent networks in shaping implementation and outcomes of a process improvement intervention drawing on lean thinking in a PCEHR implementation and use case.

11.4 Why Sociotechnical Approach

Modern healthcare systems are very complex and consist of many social and technical organs that are very deeply rooted, interrelated and interdependent (Wickramasinghe et al. 2009). The change in one aspect of the system can affect another aspect and can further increase the complexity of healthcare services (Wears and Berg 2005). The introduction of new technology would have implications in clinical roles and work processes and may enforce cultural changes (Coiera 2004; Ash et al. 2006; 2009) despite the fact that the user attitude and the use of technology is socially shaped (Coiera 2004). A sociotechnical approach views IT (information technology) systems and software as an active member of the organisation or an important factor in the social network of healthcare settings that continuously interact and cooperate with clinical teams, organisational routines and individual users (Wears and Berg 2005; Anderson and Aydin 2005).

A sociotechnical approach attempts to describe the characteristic or manner of an interaction or behaviour of competing systems, it further tries to explain the dynamics of the interaction between technology and the sociocultural environment where technology is going to be used (Whetton 2005). Purely techno-centric evaluations have been widely criticised because of their limitations (Whetton 2005; Berg 2003; Littlejohns et al. 2003). In addition, the sociotechnical approach involves a paradigm shift in the way we study the details of failures; it requires how to think beyond the poor system design and the perceptions about how to perform clinical tasks (Wears and Berg 2005; Aarts and Gorman 2007; Aarts et al. 2007). Thus, a sociotechnical approach emphasises an understanding that the very existence of technology is a part of social system and mediated by organisation considerations. In the case of the PCEHR, this approach would enable us to study also if technology can or cannot exist as an independent entity.

The application of such a sociotechnical perspective has been widely encouraged in healthcare settings to study the poor use and acceptance of information technology within healthcare settings (Coiera 2004; Whetton 2005; Berg 1999). The major challenge organisations are facing at the moment is to find ways to successfully incorporate health information systems into the work process and infrastructure of the organisations (Sittig 1994; Atkinson et al. 2001). One solution argued by Atkinson and his colleagues is to develop a sociotechnical research and development agenda to "undertake participative, multi-stakeholder problem solving within a healthcare context" (Atkinson et al. 2001, p. 1). Further Coiera again emphasised this by arguing that "if health care is to evolve at a pace that will meet the needs of society it will need to embrace this science of Sociotechnical design" (Coiera 2004, p. 1197).

Today's IT-based healthcare solutions such as the PCEHR are not stand-alone systems. On the contrary, they are purposed to work in a networked healthcare environment (Lubitz and Wickramasinghe 2006) whence implemented in one department or section of a hospital would not only be impacted by the other departments or sections (Georgiou et al. 2005; 2007) but may also be affected by external environmental factors such as health organisations, government and private funding bodies and regulators. This then becomes a complex healthcare environment and one in which we suggest that it is important to evaluate these systems at both micro and macro level to cover all internal and external issues.

11.4.1 Sociotechnical Issues Relating to the Development, Adoption, Implementation and Diffusion of (PCEHR) Technology

In Australian healthcare IT transformation, social issues have huge significance. Topics relating to individual privacy, health information security, ethics and legal issues have been extensively debated in different reports (Showell 2011). The breach of privacy and security of health information is a common concern among Australian consumers and health privacy advocates despite the fact that the draft (PCEHR Act 2011) emphasises the security and privacy of an electronic health record of individuals as well as any information that is protected by law. But in essence, the hard fact is that the language about the placement of the requirements and standards is vague and serves to add to the confusion and also raise many more concerns among users (Hoffinan and Podguski 2008). Furthermore, there are many policy issues involving development of standards to set security and access rules of the system (Hoffinan and Podguski 2008). In addition, a comprehensive process of consultation between PCEHR system users and system developers and implementation team is urgently needed and should be emphasised as key policy issues (Showell 2011).

Along with these privacy and policy issues, organisational issues, e.g. poor governance, organisational culture and poor management of the change process have also been reported. These issues can have damaging effect on e-health adoption and implementation (Hoffinan 2009; Greenhalgh and Stones 2010; Kennedy 2011; Bernstein et al. 2007). Further, these issues can aggravate the resistance to the change process and also complicate the diffusion of the PCEHR technology.

At the micro level, user acceptance (Frame et al. 2008; Agarwal and Prasad 1997), perceived ease of use (Al-Azmi et al. 2009), lack of knowledge about the system (Bath 2008; Elrod and Androwich 2009; Kaplan and Harris-Salamone 2009; André et al. 2008; Liu et al. 2011), lack of training, lack of stakeholder consultation (Showell 2011), lack of willingness to assimilate the technology into daily routines and processes (Cash 2008; Ross et al. 2010; Davidson and Heslinga 2007; Kaplan and Harris-Salamone 2009), conflict between system and user-embedded values (Cash 2008; Kaplan and Harris-Salamone 2009), complex and complicated user interfaces (Yusof et al. 2007) and conflict between physician activities and training schedules (André et al. 2008; Yusof et al. 2007; Kaplan and Harris-Salamone 2009) are some major concerns.

Lastly, in regard to technology, the lack of infrastructure, standards and protocols which in turn results in lack of interpretability and fragmented healthcare information systems which serve to further complicate a very complex situation (Davidson and Heslinga 2007; Hoffinan and Podguski 2008; Kralewski et al. 2010; Vitacca et al. 2009; HFMA 2006; Kennedy 2011; Trudel 2010). Pre-implementation and post-implementation vendor support is yet another key concern for organisations (Kralewski et al. 2010; Cohn et al. 2009; Kennedy 2011; Liu et al. 2011; Trudel 2010; Tang et al. 2006). Lack of financial resources to buy very expensive health information systems hardware and software for start-up and later on upgrades is also identified as a complex issue (Aarts and Koppel 2009; Ashish 2009; Bates 2005; Bath 2008; Weimar 2009; Kaplan and Harris-Salamone 2009). Lack of technical resources and experience with information technology implementation within healthcare settings is another problem faced by many (Torda et al. 2010; Trudel 2010; Liu et al. 2011; Kennedy 2011; André et al. 2008; Bath 2008; DePhillips 2007; Davidson and Heslinga 2007; McReavy et al. 2009). The accuracy of data obtained through the information system and its ability of sorting, querying and validating data in some cases is very poor and is considered as a big barrier for HIT (healthcare IT) adoption (Rosenbloom et al. 2006; Rosebaugh 2004; Kimaro and Nhampossa 2007).

Given the complex nature of the healthcare system, coupled with the challenges and barriers described above relating to the adoption and implementation of IT into healthcare contexts, the importance of conceptualising and framing the critical factors for evaluating the proposed PCEHR system cannot be overemphasised. Hence, the next section presents our initial conceptual model that attempts to capture all the key considerations as discussed above for further analysis.

11.5 Results: Initial Conceptual Model

Based on a comprehensive literature review (Wickramasinghe and Schaffer 2010; Aarts and Koppel 2009; Al-Azmi et al. 2009; Atkinson et al. 2001) and synthesis, five key considerations and factors were identified for the successful implementation and adoption of e-health solutions in general, namely financial, organisational, social, people and technological. These have facilitated the development of the proposed conceptual model as presented in Fig. 11.3. Specifically as the PCEHR has many similar aspects to e-health solutions implementation, it is logical to use these factors as the basis of our model. Naturally the specific study will test the validity of the proposed conceptual model.

This initial conceptual model serves to capture the important aspects of the barriers and facilitators for the prediction of the successful adoption and implementation of the PCEHR. The proposed model identifies a network of different actors interconnected to each other. Further it illustrates that a central issue with the evaluation of IT-based healthcare interventions is concerned with the complexity of the evaluation objects (Ammenwerth et al. 2003). For instance, the nature of the

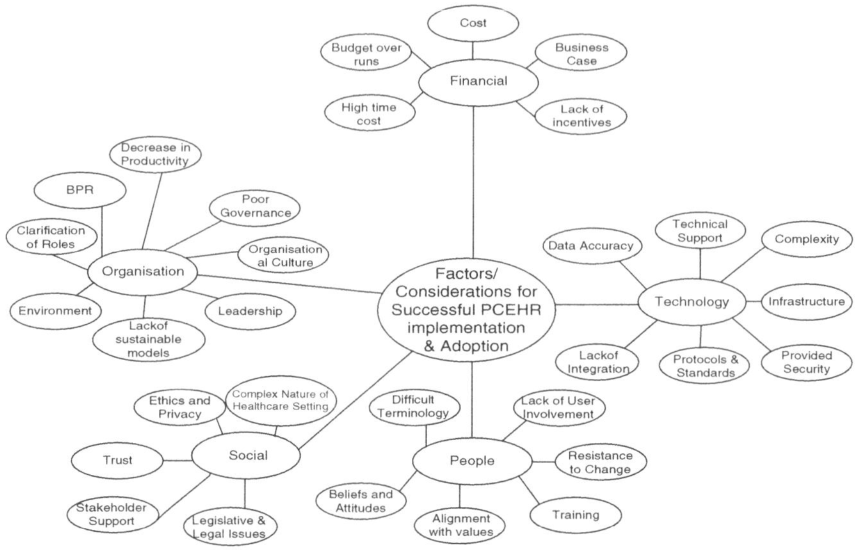

Fig. 11.3 Initial conceptual model

integration of health information systems with the culture and business process of healthcare organisations puts more emphasis on the evaluation methods and goes beyond the technology aspects of hardware and software that captures external and internal environmental factors as well as to understand the diverse nature of system effects in the healthcare settings (Ammenwerth et al. 2003). To study this complex network of interactions of humans with technology in organisations and certain individual levels, an STS perspective is indeed prudent (Cresswell et al. 2011).

We note that in the conceptual model (Fig. 11.3), it is possible to view these factors at different levels. In particular micro level issues (i.e. issues related to the individual user level), meso level issues(i.e. issues related to the organisational level) and macro level issues(i.e. issues related to the government level) dealing with policy regarding funding and privacy aspects; however, it is important to remember that the actual factors are relevant at all levels (micro, meso and macro) and together form a heterogeneous network as per actor-network theory (Latour 2005), and thus it is important at least initially to view them at the same level much like the way actants are all treated equally in ANT (Latour 2005).

In STS perspective ANT illustrates the networks of interactions and their relations. It further explains their composition, their development over time, their construction and maintenance, their durability and the way they compete with other networks (Law and Callon 1992; Latour 2005). ANT negates the existence of any phenomena in itself by taking the formative viewpoint that means it is created by actors in the process of ongoing associations (Latour 2005).

Furthermore ANT's stand is that during change process, to fully understand the occurrences of the associations and actors, all factors including human and non-human, social and technical need to be considered and evaluated by using same analytical lens (Alcadipani and Hassard, 2010; Muhammad, Teoh, & Wickramasinghe, 2012). The issues relating to human stakeholders and their associations concern with social aspects whereas issues that are important during lean projects such issues relating to documents, medical technologies, workshops, process improvements, record keeping and distributing are mostly linked with technical aspects.

It is important to note that the initial conceptual model is based on the first part of our study which consisted of a comprehensive literature review and document archival analysis. For the second part of our study, we will go forward with the qualitative data collection and thematic analysis of different emergent themes within the scope of Australian healthcare system and PCEHR development and adoption. This will serve the purpose test and then accordingly to revise the conceptual model and also uncover key issues regarding STS including people, process and technology issues as they relate to the PCEHR.

11.6 Discussion

IT-based interventions, to reform and streamline healthcare services for the improvement of health outcomes and the reduction of waste, based on lean thinking approaches, are increasing. Further, it is important to note here that typically these lean thinking approaches are composed of many components that work independently as well as interdependently. This in turn serves to make the success rates with these interventions difficult to measure and at times discouraging. Evaluations of failed systems have emphasised the need to use appropriate tools and techniques that can capture and explain the complex nature of healthcare service deliveries and their interactions with the new proposed technologies. Moreover, it is also important to evaluate these technologies with theoretically informed techniques that are sufficiently rich and robust in order to understand the barriers and facilitators that are critical for more successful outcomes.

An initial investigation into e-health solutions and their adoptions has indicated a need that developers and implementation teams should start focusing on social and organisational issues and shift away from the techno-centric obsession of "how the technical system can be made to work right". This has been confirmed by our initial analysis of the health information systems literature. Literature clearly outlines that failure in general is not just because of a poor understanding of technological issues but also and more importantly concerned with a lack of understanding and interest in organisational, cultural and social issues.

For example, a user-friendly interface and easy-to-learn system would not be adopted if the privacy and security concerns of the users could not be addressed at the same time poorly designed and complex information systems in healthcare settings where users have insufficient IT training would face real challenges of adoption. In addition, ignoring the existing organisational workflows and social interactions with the use of lean thinking methodology in redesigning the organisational process may hinder the implementation and adoption process which not only could generate waste but might have adverse effects on healthcare service outcomes. Therefore, the information system alone might not be the decisive factor but also the ability to incorporate lean thinking to improve and streamline complex healthcare services and processes. As the literature clearly shows, some tangible lean thinking results are in terms of cost and waiting-time reduction, improvement in quality of service and increases in consumer as well as service provider satisfaction (Silvester et al. 2004; Radnor and Boaden 2008).

The inherent complexities of the healthcare environment such as its organisational culture and social aspects and their interactions with newly introduced technology require the application of techniques and tools in order to better explain, explore and resolve critical issues and thereby realise the potential benefits of the technology solutions. Given this, our study proposes that the main focus of development and implementation teams should also consider linking the concept of value, value stream (waste reduction), flow, pull and perfection (continuance improvements) through repeating processes (Papadopoulos et al. 2011) and then map these concepts with the organisational work practices, teamwork and communication; organisational cultural issues; leadership role; user attitudes, perceptions, reactions and satisfactions; government role and governance; and stakeholder consultation at all stages of system development and adoption including policy formation, different kinds of financial issues, ethics and privacy issues.

In summary, this chapter proposes that a sociotechnical design coupled with lean thinking provides a well-thought-out, rich and rigorous approach to acknowledge the complexities of the healthcare environment and explain the interaction between a social system and a technology and thereby facilitate successful embracement of e-health solutions (Altman 1997; Atkinson et al. 2001; Coiera 2004). To further explore this topic, we intend to extend this study with a qualitative data collection phase. Specifically, we will identify key stakeholders in the PCEHR development, implementation and adoption and from this we will begin with identifying key informants and follow up with interviews to understand and validate the key factors and considerations for successful PCEHR implementations and adoptions as identified from the literature and presented in the above initial conceptual model.

It is important to note that the PCEHR has both similarities and differences to other e-health solutions noted in the literature. In particular it is a unique nationwide patient-centred e-health solution that has the potential to streamline and add value to healthcare delivery for all Australians. We are confident that our next phase of research will serve to confirm if this has been an appropriate approach.

11.7 Conclusion

Healthcare systems have always been complex systems; however now when they are integrated with information technology, this complexity appears to be increasing exponentially in contrast to the beliefs and expectations of policy holders and governments. The challenges are further complicated by the interaction of different human and non-human actors that alas mainly lead to failed technology-based healthcare interventions and implementations, thereby making failure rates surprisingly high and costly.

This makes it important to evaluate these interventions with theoretically informed techniques to enable a deeper understanding which could facilitate the successful implementations and adoptions of health information technology. As a starting point, we believe that an STS perspective can provide a solid foundation for a better understanding of these systems. Furthermore, such an analysis can also enhance our understanding by providing a mechanism to study the relationships between technology, organisation, people and social and financial factors that influence the success of e-health implementation and adoption. Moreover, we believe that a viable healthcare system can only be achieved if all of these considerations are jointly optimised. Our initial analysis and presented conceptual model for the PCEHR development in Australia to date shows that the process underlying the PCEHR development, implementation and adoption are inherently sociotechnical in nature. A sociotechnical approach of study therefore will allow more flexibility in system design and adoption. We are confident that this approach will be of benefit to both practitioners, for better design and implementations and researchers, for better evaluation. Therefore the contribution of this study is in the area of the application of sociotechnical perspective as a lens for the exploration of the different implications of the deployments of IT-based interventions based on lean thinking. In addition, this study begins to fill the gap in current lean or process improvement literature (Esain et al. 2008; Radnor 2010; Proudlove et al. 2008; Brandao de Souza 2009) and complement current literature on sociotechnical perspective focus on healthcare reforms and their applications of process improvements in the complex settings of Australian PCEHR case study (Muhammad, Teoh, & Wickramasinghe, 2012; Nicolini 2010). We do however acknowledge that sociotechnical theory does have shortcomings and suggest that to overcome these one should combine such an analysis with other theories such as actor-network theory and/or structuration theory. We conclude by calling for more confirmatory follow-up research in this vital area.

References

Aarts, J., Ash, J., & Berg, M. (2007). Extending the understanding of computerized physician order entry: Implications for professional collaboration, workflow and quality of care. *International Journal of Medical Informatics, 76*, S4–S13.

Aarts, J., Doorewaard, H., & Berg, M. (2004). Understanding implementation: The case of a computerized physician order entry system in a large Dutch University Medical Center. *Journal of the American Medical Informatics Association, 11*, 207–216.

Aarts, J., & Gorman, P. (2007). IT in health care: Sociotechnical approaches "To err is system". *International Journal of Medical Informatics, 76*(Suppl 1), 1–3.

Aarts, J., & Koppel, R. (2009). Implementation of computerized physician order entry in seven countries. *Health Affairs (Project Hope), 28*(2), 404–414.

Agarwal, R., & Prasad, J. (1997). The role of innovation characteristics and perceived voluntariness in the acceptance of information technologies. *Decision Sciences, 28*(3), 557–582.

Al-Azmi, S., Al-Enezi, N., & Chowdhury, R. (2009). Users' attitudes to an electronic medical record system and its correlates: A multivariate analysis. *The HIM Journal, 38*(2), 33–40.

Alcadipani, R., & Hassard, J. (2010). *Actor-Network Theory, organizations and critique: towards a politics of organizing. Organization, 17*(4), 419–435. doi:10.1177/1350508410364441.

Altman, R. B. (1997). Informatics in the care of patients: Ten notable challenges. *The Western Journal of Medicine, 166*(2), 118–122.

Ammenwerth, E., Gräber, S., Herrmann, G., Bürkle, T., & König, J. (2003). Evaluation of health information systems-problems and challenges. *International Journal of Medical Informatics, 71*(2–3), 125–135.

Ammenwerth, E., Iller, C., & Mahler, C. (2006). IT-adoption and the interaction of task, technology and individuals: A fit framework and a case study. *BMC Medical Informatics and Decision Making, 6*.

Anderson, J. G., & Aydin, C. E. (2005). *Evaluating the organizational impact of health care information systems*. New York: Springer.

André, B., Ringdal, G. I., Loge, J. H., Rannestad, T., Laerum, H., & Kaasa, S. (2008). Experiences with the implementation of computerized tools in health care units: A review article. *International Journal of Human-Computer Interaction, 24*(8), 753–775.

Ash, J. S., Sittig, D. F., Campbell, E., Guappone, K., & Dykstra, R. (2006). An unintended consequence of CPOE implementation: Shifts in power, control, and autonomy. *AMIA Annual Symposium Proceedings, 2006*, 11.

Ash, J. S., Sittig, D. F., Dykstra, R., Campbell, E., & Guappone, K. (2009). The unintended consequences of computerized provider order entry: Findings from a mixed methods exploration. *International Journal of Medical Informatics, 78*, S69–S76.

Ashish, K. (2009). Use of electronic health records in U.S. hospitals. *Medical Benefits, 25*(10), 4–9. doi:10.1056NEJMsa0900592.

Atkinson, C., Eldabi, T., Paul, R., & Pouloudi, A. (2001). Investigating integrated Sociotechnical approaches to health informatics. In *Proceedings of the 34th Hawaii international conference on system science* (pp. 1–10). IEEE Computer Society.

Australian Institute of Health and Welfare. (2012). Health expenditure Australia 2010–11. Health and welfare expenditure series no. 47. Cat. no. HWE 56. Canberra: AIHW

Bates, D. W. (2005). Physicians and ambulatory electronic health records. *Health Affairs, 24*, 1180–1189.

Bath, P. (2008). Health informatics: Current issues and challenges. *Journal of Information Science, 34*(4), 501.

Ben-Tovim, D. I., Bassham, J. E., Bolch, D., Martin, M. A., Dougherty, M., & Szwarcbord, M. (2007). Lean thinking across a hospital: Redesigning care at the Flinders Medical Centre. *Australian Health Review, 31*(1), 10–15.

Berg, M. (1999). Patient care information systems and health care work: A sociotechnical approach. *International Journal of Medical Informatics, 55*(2), 87–101.

Berg, M. (2003). *Health information management: Integrating information technology in health care work*. New York: Routledge.

Bernstein, M. L., McCreless, T., & Côté, M. J. (2007). Five constants of information technology adoption in healthcare. *Hospital Topics, 85*(1), 17–25.

Bevir, M., & Richards, D. (2009). Decentring policy networks: A theoretical agenda. *Public Administration, 87*(1), 3–14. doi:10.1111/j.1467-9299.2008.01736.x.

Boyatzis, R. E. (1998). *Transforming qualitative information: Thematic analysis and code development*. Thousand Oaks: Sage.

Brandao de Souza, L. (2009). Trends and approaches in lean healthcare. *Leadership in Health Services, 22*(2), 121–139.

Buntin, M. B., Burke, M. F., Hoaglin, M. C., & Blumenthal, D. (2011). The benefits of health information technology: A review of the recent literature shows predominantly positive results. *Health Affairs, 30*(3), 464–471.

Bushell, S., & Shelest, B. (2002). Discovering lean thinking at progressive healthcare. *The Journal for Quality and Participation*. Retrieved from http://www.highbeam.com/doc/1P3-141057351.html

Callon, M. (1986). Some elements of a sociology of translation: domestication of the scallops and the fishermen of St bricue bay.

Campbell, R. J. (2009). Thinking lean in healthcare. *Journal of AHIMA, 80*(6), 40–43.

Car, J., Anandan, C., Black, A., Cresswell, K., Pagliari, C., McKinstry, B., et al. (2008). *The impact of e-health on the quality & safety of healthcare: A systematic overview and synthesis of the literature, report*. Birmingham: NHS Connecting for Health Evaluation Programme.

Cash, J. (2008). Technology can make or break the hospital-physician relationship. *Journal of the Healthcare Financial Management Association, 62*(12), 104–109.

Catwell, L., & Sheikh, A. (2009). Evaluating e-health interventions: The need for continuous systemic evaluation. *PLoS Medicine, 6*(8), e1000126. doi:10.1371/journal.pmed.1000126.

Cohn, K., Berman, J., Chaiken, B., Green, D., Green, M., Morrison, D., et al. (2009). Engaging physicians to adopt healthcare information technology. *Journal of Healthcare Management/ American College of Healthcare Executives, 54*(5), 291.

Coiera, E. (2004). Four rules for the reinvention of health care. *BMJ, 328*(7449), 1197–1199.

Cresswell, K., Worth, A., & Sheikh, A. (2011). Implementing and adopting electronic health record systems: How actor-network theory can support evaluation. *Clinical Governance, 16*(4), 320–336.

Davidson, E., & Heslinga, D. (2007). Bridging the IT—Adoption gap for small physician practices: An action research study on electronic health records. *Information Systems Management, 24*(1), 15.

DePhillips, H. A. (2007). Initiatives and barriers to adopting health information technology: A US perspective. *Disease Management and Health Outcomes, 15*(1). Retrieved September 27, 2011, from http://ideas.repec.org/a/wkh/dmhout/v15y2007i1p1-6.html

DesRoches, C. M., Campbell, E. G., Rao, S. R., Donelan, K., Ferris, T. G., Jha, A., et al. (2008). Electronic health records in ambulatory care–A national survey of physicians. *The New England Journal of Medicine, 359*(1), 50–60. doi:10.1056/NEJMsa0802005.

Devaraj, S., & Kohli, R. (2000). Information technology payoff in the health-care industry: A longitudinal study. *Journal of Management Information Systems, 16*(4), 41–67.

Elrod, J., & Androwich, I. M. (2009). Applying human factors analysis to the design of the electronic health record. *Studies in Health Technology and Informatics, 146*, 132–136.

Esain, A., Williams, S., & Massey, L. (2008). Combining planned and emergent change in a healthcare lean transformation. *Public Money & Management, 28*(1), 21–26 (special issue on Lean in public services).

Fillingham, D. (2007). Can lean save lives? *Leadership in Health Services (Bradford, England), 20*(4), 231–241.

Frame, J., Watson, J., & Thomson, K. (2008). Deploying a culture change programme management approach in support of information and communication technology developments in Greater Glasgow NHS Board. *Health Informatics Journal, 14*(2), 125–139.

Georgiou, A., Westbrook, J., Braithwaite, J., & Iedema, R. (2005). Multiple perspectives on the impact of electronic ordering on hospital organisational and communication processes. *The HIM Journal, 34*(4), 130–134.

Georgiou, A., Westbrook, J., Braithwaite, J., Iedema, R., Ray, S., Forsyth, R., et al. (2007). When requests become orders–A formative investigation into the impact of a computerized physician order entry system on a pathology laboratory service. *International Journal of Medical Informatics, 76*(8), 583–591.

Goldzweig, C. L., Towfigh, A., Maglione, M., & Shekelle, P. G. (2009). Costs and benefits of health information technology: New trends from the literature. *Health Affairs, 28*(2), w282–w293.

Greenhalgh, T., Robert, G., Macfarlane, F., Bate, P., & Kyriakidou, O. (2004). Diffusion of innovations in service organizations: systematic review and recommendations. *Milbank Quarterly, 82*(4), 581–629.

Greenhalgh, T., & Stones, R. (2010). Theorising big IT programmes in healthcare: Strong structuration theory meets actor-network theory. *Social Science & Medicine (1982), 70*(9), 1285–1294.

HFMA, (2006). Overcoming barriers to electronic health record adoption: Results of survey and roundtable discussions conducted by the healthcare financial management association. Retrieved October 4, 2011, from http://mhcc.maryland.gov/electronichealth/mhitr/EHR%20 Links/overcoming_barriers_to_ehr_adoption.pdf

Hines, P., Holweg, M., & Rich, N. (2004). Learning to evolve: A review of contemporary lean thinking. *International Journal of Operations & Production Management, 24*(10), 994–1011.

Hoffinan, L. (2009). Implementing electronic medical records. *Communications of the ACM, 52*(11), 18–20. doi:10.114515927611592770.

Hoffinan, S. & Podguski, A. (2008). Finding a cure: The case for regulation and oversight of electronic health record systems. *Harvard Journal of Law and Technology, 22*(1). Retrieved from http://ssrn.com/abstract=1122426.

Jones, D., & Mitchell, A. (2006). *Lean thinking for the NHS*. London: NHS Confederation. Retrieved from https://www.ohsu.edu/ohsuedu/academic/som/radmedicine/upload/lean_thinking_for_the_nhs.pdf

Kaelber, D. C., Jha, A. K., Johnston, D., Middleton, B., & Bates, D. W. (2008). A research agenda for personal health records (PHRs). *Journal of the American Medical Informatics Association, 15*(6), 729–736. doi:10.1197/jamia.M2547.

Kaplan, B., & Harris-Salamone, K. D. (2009). Health IT success and failure: Recommendations from literature and an AMIA workshop. *Journal of the American Medical Informatics Association, 16*(3), 291–299.

Kennedy, B. L. (2011). Exploring the sustainment of health information technology: Successful practices for addressing human factors. Dissertation, Northcentral University. Arizona: Prescott Valley.

Kimaro, H., & Nhampossa, J. (2007). The challenges of sustainability of health information systems in developing countries: Comparative case studies of Mozambique and Tanzania. *Journal of Health Informatics in Developing Countries, 1*(1), 1–10.

Kralewski, J., Dowd, B. E., Zink, T., & Gans, D. N. (2010). Preparing your practice for the adoption and implementation of electronic health records. *Physician Executive, 36*(2), 30–33.

Kvale, S. (1996). *InterViews: An introduction to qualitative research interviewing*. London: Sage.

Latour, B. (1986). The Powers of association, in power, action and belief. (Vol. 32 SRC-GoogleScholar).

Latour, B. (2005). *Reassembling the social: An introduction to Actor-Network Theory*. Oxford: Oxford University Press.

Law, J., & Callon, M. (1992). The life and death of an aircraft: A network analysis of technical change. In W. E. Bijker & J. Law (Eds.), *Shaping technology/building society: Studies in sociotechnical change* (pp. 21–52). Cambridge, MA: MIT Press.

Law, J., & Hassard, J. (1999). Actor network theory and after Blackwell, Oxford, England., 1999 SRC-GoogleScholar.

Leslie, H. (2011). *Australia's PCEHR challenge|archetypical*. Retrieved from http://omowizard.wordpress.com/2011/08/30/australias-pcehr-challenge/

Littlejohns, P., Wyatt, J. C., & Garvican, L. (2003). Evaluating computerised health information systems: Hard lessons still to be learnt. *BMJ, 326*(7394), 860.

Liu, L. S., Shih, P. C., & Hayes, G. R. (2011). Barriers to the adoption and use of personal health record systems (pp. 363–370). In *Proceedings of the 2011 iConference*, Seattle.

Lorenzi, N., et al. (2009). How to successfully select and implement electronic health records (EHR) in small ambulatory practice settings. *BMC Medical Informatics and Decision Making, 9*, 15.

Lubitz, D., & Wickramasinghe, N. (2006). Healthcare and technology: The doctrine of network-centric healthcare. *International Journal of Electronic Healthcare, 2*, 322–344.

McReavy, D., Toth, L., Tremonti, C., & Yoder, C. (2009). *The CFO's role in implementing EHR systems: the experiences of a Florida health system point to 10 actions that can help CFOs manage the revenue risks and opportunities of implementing an electronic health record*. Retrieved December 16, 2011, from http://findarticles.com/p/articles/mi_m3257/is_6_63/ai_n35529545/

Mort, M., Finch, T., & May, C. (2009). Making and unmaking telepatients: Identity and governance in new health technologies. *Science, Technology & Human Values, 34*(1), 9–33.

Muhammad, I., Teoh, S. Y., & Wickramasinghe, N. (2012). *Why using actor network theory (ANT) can help to understand the personally controlled electronic health record (PCEHR) in Australia. International Journal of Actor-Network Theory and Technological Innovation, 4*(2), 44–60. doi:10.4018/jantti.2012040105.

NEHTA & DoHA. (2011). *Concept of operations: Relating to the introduction of a personally controlled electronic health record system*. Retrieved September 26, 2011, from http://www.yourhealth.gov.au/internet/yourhealth/publishing.nsf/Content/CA2578620005CE1DCA2578F800194110/$File/PCEHR%20Concept%20of%20Operations.pdf

NHHRC. (2009). *A healthier future for all Australians: National Health and Hospitals Reform Commission—Final report June 2009*. Retrieved August 11, 2011, from http://www.health.gov.au/internet/main/publishing.nsf/Content/nhhrc-report

Nicolini, D. (2010). Medical innovation as a process of translation: A case from the field of telemedicine. *British Journal of Management, 24*(4), 1011–1026.

Papadopoulos, T. (2011). Continuous improvement and dynamic actor associations: A study of lean thinking implementation in the UK National Health Service. *Leadership in Health Services, 24*(3), 207–227.

Papadopoulos, T., & Merali, Y. (2008). Stakeholder network dynamics and emergent trajectories of lean implementation projects: A study in the UK National Health Service. *Public Money & Management, 28*(1), 41–49 (special issue on Lean in public services).

Papadopoulos, T., & Merali, Y. (2009). Stakeholder dynamics during process innovation implementation in healthcare: Lean thinking in a hospital of UK National Health Service. *International Journal of Healthcare Technology and Management, 10*(4/5), 303–324.

Papadopoulos, T., Radnor, Z., & Merali, Y. (2011). The role of actor associations in understanding the implementation of lean thinking in healthcare. *International Journal of Operations & Production Management, 31*(2), 167–191.

Proudlove, N., Moxham, C., & Boaden, R. (2008). Lessons for lean in healthcare from using six sigma in the NHS. *Public Money & Management, 28*(1), 27–34 (special issue on Lean in public services).

Radnor, Z. J. (2010). *Review of business process improvement methodologies in public services*. London: Advanced Institute of Management.

Radnor, Z. J., & Boaden, R. (2008). Does lean enhance public services? Editorial. *Public Money & Management, 28*, 3–6.

Rhodes, J. (n.d.). Using actor-network theory to trace an ICT (Telecenter) implementation trajectory in an african women's micro-enterprise development organization. *Information Technologies & International Development, 5*(3), 1–20.

Rosebaugh, D. (2004). Getting ready for the software in your future. *Home Health Care Management Practice, 16*(3), 228–234. doi:10.1177108482230325 9877.

Rosenbloom, S. T., et al. (2006). Implementing pediatric growth charts into an electronic health record system. *Journal of the American Medical Informatics Association, 13*, 302–308.

Ross, S. E., Schilling, L. M., Fernald, D. H., Davidson, A. J., & West, D. R. (2010). Health information exchange in small-to-medium sized family medicine practices: Motivators, barriers, and potential facilitators of adoption. *International Journal of Medical Informatics, 79*(2), 123–129. doi:10.1016/j.ijmedinf.2009.12.001.

Shah, R., & Ward, P. T. (2003). Lean manufacturing: Context, practice bundles, and performance. *Journal of Operations Management, 21*(2), 129–149.

Shekelle, P. G., Morton, S. C., & Keeler, E. B. (2006). Costs and benefits of health information technology. *Evidence Report/Technology Assessment*, (132), 1.

Showell, C. M. (2011). Citizens, patients and policy: A challenge for Australia's national electronic health record. *Health Information Management Journal, 40*(2), 39–43.

Silvester, K., Lendon, R., Bevan, H., Steyn, R., & Walley, P. (2004). Reducing waiting times in the NHS: Is lack of capacity the problem? *Clinician in Management, 12*(3), 105–111.

Sittig, D. F. (1994). Grand challenges in medical informatics? *Journal of the American Medical Informatics Association, 1*(5), 412–413.

Steinbrook, R. (2008). Personally controlled online health data–The next big thing in medical care? *The New England Journal of Medicine, 358*(16), 1653–1656. doi:10.1056/NEJMp0801736.

Tang, P. C., Ash, J. S., Bates, D. W., Overhage, J. M., & Sands, D. Z. (2006). Personal health records: Definitions, benefits, and strategies for overcoming barriers to adoption. *Journal of the American Medical Informatics Association, 13*(2), 121–126. doi:10.1197/jamia.M2025.

Torda, P., Han, E. S., & Scholle, S. H. (2010). Easing the adoption and use of electronic health records in small practices. *Health Affairs (Project Hope), 29*(4), 668–675.

Trudel, M. C. (2010). *Challenges to personal information sharing in interorganizational settings: Learning from the Quebec Health Smart Card project*. London, ON: The University of Western Ontario.

Tsasis, P., & Bruce-Barrett, C. (2008). Organizational change through lean thinking. *Health Services Management Research, 21*(3), 192–198.

Vitacca, M., Mazzù, M., & Scalvini, S. (2009). Sociotechnical and organizational challenges to wider e-Health implementation. *Chronic Respiratory Disease, 6*(2), 91–97.

Walley, P., Watt, A., & Davies, C. (2001) A study of demand for emergency access health services in two UK health and social care communities. The University of Warwick, Coventry.

Wears, R. L., & Berg, M. (2005). Computer technology and clinical work. *JAMA: The Journal of the American Medical Association, 293*(10), 1261.

Weimar, C. (2009). Electronic health care advances, physician frustration grows. *Physician Executive, 35*(2), 8–15.

Whetton, S. (2005). *Health informatics: A sociotechnical perspective*. Melbourne: Oxford University Press.

Whetton, S., & Georgiou, A. (2010). Conceptual challenges for advancing the sociotechnical underpinnings of health informatics. *The Open Medical Informatics Journal, 4*, 221–224. doi:10.2174/1874431101004010221.

Wickramasinghe, N., Bali, R. K., & Lehaney, B. (2009). *Knowledge management primer*. Hoboken: Taylor & Francis.

Wickramasinghe, N., & Schaffer, J. (2010). *Realizing value driven e-Health solutions*. Washington, DC: IBM centre for the Business of government.

Womack, J. P., & Jones, D. T. (2003). *Lean thinking: Banish waste and create wealth in your corporation* (2nd ed. Revised (Exp Upd.)). London: Simon & Schuster Audio.

Womack, J. P., Jones, D. T., & Roos, D. (2007). *The machine that changed the world*. New York: Free Press.

Wu, S., Chaudhry, B., Wang, J., Maglione, M., Mojica, W., Roth, E., et al. (2006). Systematic review: Impact of health information technology on quality, efficiency, and costs of medical care. *Annals of Internal Medicine, 144*(10), 742–752.

Yin, R. K. (1994). *Case study research: Design and methods* (2nd ed.). Thousand Oaks: Sage.

Yusof, M., Stergioulas, L., & Zugic, J. (2007). Health information systems adoption: Findings from a systematic review. *Studies in Health Technology and Informatics, 129*, 262–266.

Chapter 12
Identifying Critical Issues for Developing Successful e-Health Solutions

Manuel Zwicker, Juergen Seitz, and Nilmini Wickramasinghe

Abstract As an industry, healthcare exhibits numerous contradictions, most notably with regard to its embracement of technology. On one hand, medical science is at the cutting edge with technology playing a key role in new techniques in oncology and cardiology as well as advances in various aspects of biomedical engineering. In contrast, healthcare delivery is a noted laggard with regard to its incorporation of technology. Current challenges which are impacting all members of the Organization for Economic Cooperation and Development (OECD) countries (including longer life expectancy, ageing population and technological changes) continue to exponentially affect rising health expenditures. Reducing these expenditures as well as offering effective and efficient quality healthcare treatment has now become a key priority on all healthcare agendas. Technology and automation in general have the potential to reduce these costs; hence, OECD countries are now looking at how to use information and communication technologies (ICT) in general and e-health solutions in particular to address these challenges and thereby enable superior healthcare delivery.

The following presents the key points and initial findings from an exploratory research in progress that is focused on uncovering critical issues for developing

M. Zwicker
Department of Business IT and Logistics (BITL), RMIT University, GPO Box 2476, Melbourne, VIC 3001, Australia
e-mail: manuel.zwicker@gmx.de

J. Seitz
Department of Business Information Systems, DHBW Heidenheim, Marienstrasse 20, 89518, Heidenheim, Germany
e-mail: seitz@dhbw-heidenheim.de

N. Wickramasinghe (✉)
Epworth HealthCare & Department of BITL & HIRi, RMIT University, GPO Box 2476, Melbourne, VIC 3001, Australia
e-mail: nilmini.wickramasinghe@rmit.edu.au

N. Wickramasinghe et al. (eds.), *Lean Thinking for Healthcare*, Healthcare Delivery in the Information Age, DOI 10.1007/978-1-4614-8036-5_12,

successful e-health solutions in two OECD countries: Australia and Germany. Additionally, in this research we focus on the principles of lean thinking and six sigma as well as lean six sigma. We also discuss how these approaches can be used to reduce the weaknesses and threats of Australia's and Germany's e-health solutions by using the TOWS analysis tool.

Keywords e-Health • e-Health card (eHC) • Electronic health record (EHR) • Electronic health professional card (HPC) • Electronic prescription (e-prescription) • Personally controlled electronic health record (PCEHR) • Australian healthcare system • German healthcare system • Lean thinking • Six sigma • Lean six sigma

12.1 Background

Healthcare industries continue to be at the forefront of agendas globally. Between 1970 and 1997 the average percentage of gross domestic product (GDP) on healthcare by members of the Organization for Economic Cooperation and Development (OECD) countries rose from about 5 % to roughly 8 % (Huber 1999). Since 2000, total spending on healthcare in these countries has been rising faster than economic growth, which has resulted in an average ratio of health spending to GDP of 9.0 % in 2008. Challenges including technological changes, longer life expectancy and population ageing serve to push health spending up further. Hence, such a growing health spending creates a significant cost pressure for several countries (OECD 2010a).

Reducing these expenditures as well as offering effective and efficient quality healthcare treatment is a priority worldwide. Technology and automation in general have the potential to reduce these costs (Abd Ghani et al. 2010). Moreover, the use of information and communication technologies (ICT) in e-health solutions in particular appears to be the key to respond to these challenges (Wickramasinghe and Schaffer 2010).

Given that the current situation is no longer feasible, we are witnessing a focus by all OECD countries on developing new healthcare reforms where a key role is played by ICT most especially e-health solutions. Hence, this chapter presents the key points and initial findings from our research in progress exploratory study which serves to uncover critical issues for developing successful e-health solutions. Specifically, we use a multiple case study analysis to examine the e-health solution developments in the OECD countries Australia and Germany. Additionally, we focus on the principles of lean thinking and six sigma as well as lean six sigma and discuss how these approaches can be used to reduce the weaknesses and threats of Australia's and Germany's e-health solutions. This is done with the use of the TOWS analysis tool.

12.1.1 Literature Review

In order to realise the aims and objectives of this research, it is necessary first to summarise the germane issues of NCHO (network-centric healthcare operations) as it provides the logical framework for all successful e-health solutions (von Lubitz and Wickramasinghe 2006). In addition, it is necessary to discuss the different types of healthcare systems and to define e-health.

12.1.1.1 Network-Centric Healthcare

The doctrine of NCHO has been defined as "unhindered networking operations within and among the physical, information, and cognitive domains that govern all activities conducted in healthcare space based on free, multidirectional flow and exchange of information without regard to the involved platforms or platform systems, and utilising all available means of ICCTs to facilitate such operations" (von Lubitz and Wickramasinghe 2006, p. 334; Jamshidi 2009).[1]

The confluence of three domains is critical to the success of NCHO (Wickramasinghe and Schaffer 2010; von Lubitz and Wickramasinghe 2006): (1) information domain contains all elements, which are required for generation, storage, dissemination/sharing, manipulation of information and in addition its transformation and dissemination/sharing as knowledge in all its forms; (2) physical domain encompasses the structure of the entire environment healthcare operations intended to influence indirectly or directly (political environment, fiscal operations, patient and personnel education, etc.); and (3) cognitive domain relates to all human factors, which affect operations—education, training, experience, motivation and intuition of individuals involved in the relevant activities.

Based on this information, it is important to look at a healthcare information grid. This grid allows a full and hindrance-free sharing of information among the individual domains and their constituents as well as among constituents across the domains. Moreover, the grid forms the basis for the overarching IT architecture and infrastructure needed to support any e-health solution. The grid must typically consist of an interconnected matrix of ICT systems and capabilities (communication platforms, data collection, etc.) and associated processes like knowledge and information storage, people (healthcare providers, etc.) and agencies (governmental and non-governmental organisations) at a local, national or international level, so as to achieve such a function (Wickramasinghe et al. 2007).

As noted in the literature (Wickramasinghe et al. 2007; Porter and Teisberg 2006; von Lubitz and Wickramasinghe 2006), it is essential to position the healthcare organisation and the e-health initiative in view of external pressures and present

[1] The abbreviation ICCT stands for information, computer and communication technologies.

trends. In order to achieve this, it is vital to take a network-centric perspective and to design an e-health solution to support NCHO (von Lubitz and Wickramasinghe 2006). The critical success factor here is not the technology per se rather the macro understanding of the need to design suitable technology-enabled solutions (Wickramasinghe and Schaffer 2010).

12.1.1.2 Different Healthcare Systems

Healthcare systems can be thought of as traversing a continuum (Wickramasinghe et al. 2007; Porter and Teisberg 2006; von Lubitz and Wickramasinghe 2006). On one side of the continuum, we have a healthcare system that is primarily predicated on private healthcare (e.g. the US healthcare system) while on the other side, a healthcare system that is mainly based on a public healthcare system (e.g. the United Kingdom healthcare system), and then finally in the middle a variety of 2-tier healthcare systems.

For the purposes of this study, a 2-tier healthcare system is defined as a system, where, in addition to a guaranteed public health insurance, a private healthcare system exists, which can have a substitutive or complementary function, and different factors like income and job status, which may or may not influence the classification of an enrollee (ArticlesBase.com 2009).

Specifically, this chapter focuses on the Australian healthcare system and the German healthcare system as exemplars of 2-tier healthcare systems in OECD countries. At this time, both are in the process of not only developing new healthcare reforms but also designing and developing e-health solutions to improve their respective healthcare delivery systems. Table 12.1 summarises the relevant key facts of the Australian and German healthcare systems.

12.1.1.3 e-Health

For the purposes of this chapter, the term "e-health" will be used as defined by WHO: "a new term used to describe the combined use of electronic communication and information technology in the health sector" or as "the use, in the health sector, of digital data-transmitted, stored and retrieved electronically for clinical, educational and administrative purposes, both at the local site and at a distance" (WHO 2005).

As discussed in the literature, e-health is the main driver for three significant changes within the healthcare environment (Maheu et al. 2001): (1) patients to become better informed, (2) patients to become more active and empowered in their healthcare, and (3) healthcare to become more efficient.

Based on this, Table 12.2 serves to summarise key e-health developments to date in Australia and Germany.

Table 12.1 Summary of key facts of the German and Australian healthcare systems

Theme	Australia	Germany
Healthcare expenditure	2007: total expenditure on health 8.5 % of GDP: US$3,353 per capita (OECD 2010b)	2009: total expenditure on health 11.6 % of GDP (2.1 % higher than the average ratio of the OECD countries); US$4,218 per capita (OECD countries spent on average US$3,223 per capita) (OECD 2011)
Healthcare system structure	The healthcare system consists of public and private components. The public health insurance under Medicare is funded by taxation. Enrollees have the possibility to use subsidised medical services and pharmaceuticals as well as free of charge hospital treatment according to their status as a public health enrollee. Besides Medicare, Australian patients have the possibility to use, in addition, a private health insurance, which gives, e.g. patients access to dental services and hospital treatment as a private patient (The Commonwealth Fund 2010)	(1) Healthcare actors: enrollees, service providers (medical doctors, pharmacists, hospitals) and cost units (health insurance companies). Around 70.23 million people of around 82.14 million inhabitants have public health insurance. Around 8.62 million people use a private health insurance. 319,697 medical doctors, 2,087 hospitals and 21,602 pharmacies (BMG 2009). 195 health insurance companies (146 public (GKV-Spitzenverband 2012) and 49 private (Verband der privaten Krankenversicherung e. V. 2011) health insurance companies). (2) Health insurance is compulsory for all citizens. Depending on factors like income, job status, etc. enrollees have either public and/or private health insurance (The Commonwealth Fund 2010)
Financing of the healthcare system	Healthcare system is financed by (The Commonwealth Fund 2010): (1) National health insurance: Medicare (compulsory and administered by the government); Medicare is funded in large part by general revenues and partly by a 1.5 % levy based on taxable income; depending on the income of an individual or family the amount of levy can change; in 2007 till 2008, the governments funded 69 % of all health expenditures, while 43 % came from the Federal and 26 % from State or Territory governments. (2) Private insurance: 7.6 % of total health spending can be contributed to the private health insurance; since 1999, the Australian government has supported private health insurance by giving enrollees a rebate of 30 % of private health insurance premiums; the government's rebate increases for elderly; in mid of 2009, 44.6 % of Australia's population had a private hospital insurance; private health insurance is in Australia community-rated ("everyone pays the same premium for their health insurance") (Australian Government 2012); nonprofit as well as for-profit insurers. (3) Out-of-pocket spending: in 2007 till 2008, 16.8 % of health expenditures were out-of-pocket spending; e.g. dental services and copayments on medical fees	(1) Public health insurance companies are autonomous, non-profit-oriented and nongovernmental bodies, which are regulated by law. This system is financed by premiums charged as a percentage of the gross wages up to a threshold. Based on the facts of July 2009, the employee contributes 7.9 % of their gross wage, while the employer adds 7.0 % on top of the gross wage, which is in total a premium of 14.9 % of each individual's gross wage. Dependents like kids and spouses without income are also included (The Commonwealth Fund 2010). (2) Private health insurance is taking mainly a substitutive function. This private health insurance scheme is covering two groups, who are mostly exempt from public health insurance (The Commonwealth Fund 2010): civil servants and people with high incomes

Table 12.2 Key e-health issues in Australia and Germany

Theme	Australia	Germany
Background	(1) Problem with Australia's healthcare system: the usage of ICT is very low (Pearce and Haikerwal 2010). A comparison of health information technologies between developed countries: Australia's system was ranked in the middle—its use of modern electronic solutions for communication and information exchange within the health systems was low (Jha et al. 2008). (2) National E-Health Transition Authority Limited (NEHTA): founded by the Australian Commonwealth, State and Territory governments in July 2005; plays an important role in order to achieve a higher level of electronically collecting and securely exchanging healthcare information (NEHTA 2012a)	The gematik (Gesellschaft für Telematikanwendungen der Gesundheitskarte mbH), which is an organisation founded on January 11, 2005, has been charged with the aim to implement the German e-health card (eHC) and the necessary telematics infrastructure (gematik 2012a)
e-Health strategy	NEHTA's strategy (NEHTA 2012b): deliver, operationalise and enhance the essential foundations required; coordinate the progression of priority e-health initiatives; manage the delivery of key components of DOHA's (Department of Health and Ageing) PCEHR Programme; accelerate national adoption of e-health; lead the further progression of e-health in Australia	eHC: will change healthcare delivery in Germany; concept allows several new functions; will lead to a more connected healthcare system

e-Health functions	(1) Personally controlled electronic health record (PCEHR): an individual electronic health record (EHR) of a patient; summarises key medical information of a patient from different systems centrally; only the patient or authorised healthcare providers will have access to the PCEHR; information of a PCEHR will support healthcare providers in their decisions and treatments; it will be also possible for a patient to add own information to his/her PCEHR (NEHTA 2012c). Benefits of this solution are, e.g. higher level of quality of care; time savings through a faster availability of health information; better communication between healthcare actors (NEHTA 2012d). (2) To realise the PCEHR, the Australian government allocated around $466 million over 2 years in the 2010 budget (Pearce and Haikerwal 2010)—overall Australians will support the idea of an individual electronic health record, but they have concerns about data security and privacy. Eighty percent want that participation is voluntary and most of the Australians want that Federal government will manage this implementation (NEHTA 2008). (3) NEHTA is also working on e-communications in practice (NEHTA 2012e): e-Diagnostic Imaging; e-Pathology; e-Discharge Summaries; e-Referrals; e-Medication Management. (4) Electronic prescription: developing a national electronic prescription system (NEHTA 2012f). (5) For using e-health services, it is essential to have a Healthcare Identifiers (HI) Service. The HI Service includes identifiers, which are unique 16-digit reference numbers (The Royal Australian College of General Practitioners 2010): Individual Healthcare Identifier (IHI); Healthcare Provider Identifier—Individual (HPI-I); Healthcare Provider Identifier—Organisation (HPI-O). (6) Identifiers allow to identify a healthcare individual at the point of care uniquely and consistently and to connect healthcare data of an individual within a healthcare context (NEHTA 2010)	(1) Functions of the eHC are divided into two category groups: administrative functions, which are compulsory for all card owners; medical functions, which are optional for the card holders (Barmer GEK Krankenkasse 2012). (2) Storage of information about the insurance agreement and the necessity of additional payments (compulsory): data will be stored on the eHC respectively on a server and can be updated, e.g. during every consultation of a doctor through an online process. Storage of data about the care provider and personal information about the enrollee. Each enrollee will become a lifelong valid insurance number, which will be printed on the eHC. Each eHC will be equipped with a personal photo of the enrollee. Through this lifelong valid insurance number and the personal photo the eHC is well protected against misusage (gematik 2012b). (3) Insurance coverage for enrollees within the European Union (compulsory): requirement is that the appropriate countries have a social agreement among each other. The back side of the eHC is perfect as identity card for the European Health Insurance Card (EHIC) (European Commission 2012). (4) Electronic prescriptions (e-prescription): compulsory for all involved healthcare actors in Germany; possible to remove the approximately 600–700 million paper-based prescriptions and to process these transactions electronically; necessary signature of the doctor will be generated electronically with the aid of the electronic health professional card (HPC) (Die gesetzlichen Krankenkassen 2007). (5) Storage of personal health data about the enrollees (optional): examples are documentation of medicine and storage of an emergency data record of the enrollee in case of emergency; due to the medicine documentation it is possible to avoid interdependencies between the individual drugs (gematik 2012c); the emergency data should help the emergency doctor to medicate purposefully and effectively, because patient's allergies and chronic illnesses can take into consideration through the therapy (ZTG 2010). (6) Electronic health record (EHR): With this optional EHR it is possible to have access to the entire patient's data. For example, the EHR can include information about medications, past medical history and radiology reports. The patient's data can be accepted, processed and attended centrally (GVG 2004)

12.2 Initial Results and Preliminary Findings

In order to uncover critical issues for developing successful e-health solutions, we embarked upon an exploratory, multiple case study research subscribing to the directives of Kvale (1996), Boyatzis (1998) and Yin (1994). Our analysis is being conducted at two levels macro and micro in both Australia and Germany (see Fig. 12.1).

Moreover, we are targeting exemplar case studies as per recommendations of Yin (1994)—where it is noted that exemplar case studies are a particularly good source for uncovering new, novel issues and insights especially, when nothing or little is known about a phenomenon at the time. Thus for Australia we choose a public and a private hospital and in Germany we focus on a typical German hospital. This is appropriate because the basic rollout of the German eHC is targeting only enrollees of public health insurance companies to date, and because these enrollees typically cannot utilise services of a private hospital which will be paid through their public health insurance companies, this study takes only a public hospital in Germany into consideration.

In addition, in order to get an in depth understanding of key issues, we are currently performing extensive qualitative data analysis predominantly in the form of over 50 unstructured interviews of key factors including medical practitioners, nurses and IT specialists in the respective hospitals. Further, triangulation is being achieved by in depth examination of critical documents and the application of a survey instrument to a wider target group including enrollees and/or users of the system. Questions are primarily focused on the respective national e-health solution, the transferability of e-health solutions as well as the idea of a global e-health solution.

While conducting thematic analysis, key themes and subthemes were developed. The themes were chosen based on literature including key aspects of NCHO and a socio-technical perspective while emergent themes were derived from the data such as "lack of awareness" which became a very key emergent theme especially in the Australian context.

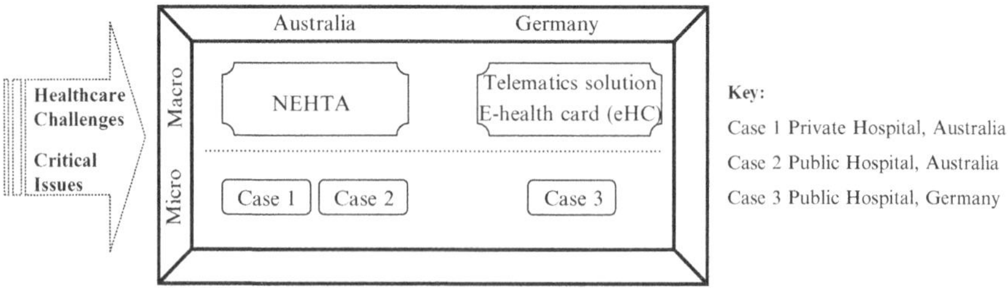

Fig. 12.1 Schematic of study design

From Table 12.3 it is important to highlight that both solutions try to establish national e-health solutions to cut costs and provide high-quality care. However, the German e-health solution to date appears to integrate all the web of healthcare players, while the Australian e-health solution is struggling to bring together a fragmented healthcare delivery system. This important finding also indicates that while both as planned subscribed to the principles of NCHO, it would appear at this stage that the German e-health solution is on track to be realising a NCHO while the Australian solution is struggling in this regard.

From an initial analysis of the unstructured interviews conducted to date, we find that most of the concerns are related to the theme of people issues, including confusion between the different stakeholders regarding the end solution and how it is in fact beneficial and useful, to at times not even being aware of its existence and how they will need to interact—e.g. with the PCEHR in Australia, the solution developed by NEHTA—key stakeholders including medical providers and pharmacists as well as citizens are confused about their role regarding interacting with this system; while in Germany, strong concerns by medical professionals have served to halt the initial design and development of the e-prescribing module.

In addition, we find process issues appear to date to be more problematic in the Australian context but this is partly due to the fact that the Australian healthcare delivery system is and has been historically complex and fragmented. Thus, this finding indicates that redesigning of this system before the implementation of the PCEHR might be prudent. Finally, in both countries technical concerns while prevalent appear to be at this point the least problematic.

12.3 Lean Thinking, Six Sigma and Lean Six Sigma

This section will give an overview about lean thinking, six sigma and lean six sigma as well as how these approaches can improve e-health solutions.

Lean thinking is an approach of managing an organisation with the goal to improve effectiveness and efficiency and also the quality of products and services. The approach was originally developed in the automotive industry at Toyota. There are several principles of lean thinking which organisations have to follow in order to achieve a lean enterprise (International Technology Centre and National Research Council Canada 2004):

- Definition of value precisely from the end customers' perspective, in terms of a specific product or service, with specific capabilities, offered at an explicit price and time
- Identification of the entire value stream for each product or service and eliminate unnecessary process steps
- Making of the remaining value-creating steps flowing
- Designing and providing products or services depending on customers' needs and requests
- Pursuing of perfection

Table 12.3 SWOT analysis of e-health to date in Australia and Germany

Theme	e-Health in Australia	e-Health in Germany
Strengths	First step for the fragmented structure to become a more coordinated system → in the context of its possibilities this approach should lead to a better information exchange, cost and time savings and higher quality of care	The German eHC connects all healthcare stakeholders nationally → better information exchange, cost and time savings and higher quality of care (mhplus Krankenkasse 2011; vdek 2012)
Weaknesses	(1) Costs; (2) Time schedule uncertain to attain; (3) Still underlying fragmented system → healthcare information exchange is difficult respectively not possible between different stakeholders	(1) High implementation costs of approximately 1.7 billion Euros and 150 million Euros running costs a year (Scheer 2009); (2) Time schedule: the implementation of the eHC does not meet the deadline for several times → several decision-makers
Opportunities	(1) Possibility for health information exchange with other countries; (2) First step for a healthcare information exchange between different stakeholders worldwide and is consistent with NCHO; (3) Australia's e-health solution is a first step to develop a national e-health solution → doctrine of NCHO	(1) Possibility for health information exchange with other countries; (2) First step for a healthcare information exchange between different stakeholders worldwide and is consistent with NCHO; (3) Contribution to life savings; (4) Potential to reduce health expenditures; (5) Extending scope of healthcare delivery
Threats	(1) Several decision-makers; (2) New laws from the government means maybe changes in the e-health solution; (3) Data security and data protection; (4) Information overload of a patient → doctor can lose overview and lose time; (5) Doctors need more time for documentation; (6) Acceptance by Australians is questionable; (7) Australia's e-health solution has still a complex structure because of different systems → therefore higher risk for succeed superior healthcare delivery; (8) Australians are concerned of costs	(1) A big range of decision-makers; (2) New law changes from the government; (3) Data security and data protection; (4) Information overload of a patient → doctor can lose overview and lose time; (5) Doctors need more time for documentation; (6) Acceptance by Germans is questionable

Lean thinking means the following benefits (Joint Commission on Accreditation of Healthcare Organizations 2008):

- By involving all stakeholders in the problem-solving process valuing diversity
- Information sharing between employees, which leads to a cross-functional understanding, process awareness and less rework
- Identification of process steps where waste occurs in order to promote implementation of solutions immediately
- Giving employees an increased feeling of empowerment and control
- Encouraging of team spirit

The six sigma approach is defined as "a systematic and statistically based process to reveal defects in performance, driven by customer specifications. Six Sigma methodologies aim to reduce the variation in clinical and business processes which give rise to long cycle times, high cost and poor outcomes" (Lazarus and Novicoff 2004). To achieve true "six sigma" levels, it is necessary to produce acceptable quality over 99.99 % of the time (Lazarus and Novicoff 2004).

It is important to notice that lean thinking and six sigma complement each other.

Benefits of six sigma and lean six sigma are (Go Lean Six Sigma 2012):

- Increases revenue
- Decreases costs
- Improves efficiency
- Develops effective people/employees

The five basic phases of six sigma and lean six sigma are (Go Lean Six Sigma 2012):

- Define: problem definition and definition of customer requirements
- Measure: description of the process in order to proceed data collection
- Analyse: investigation and identification of problem reasons
- Improve: implementation of a fix for problem solving
- Control: sustainment of the improvements

Lean thinking and six sigma are not only approaches which can be used in the manufacturing industries; they also are able to lead to contributions in the healthcare sector. Lean six sigma can help, e.g. to increase the time, which care providers can spend with their patients, reduce paperwork and reduce waiting times (Go Lean Six Sigma 2012).

George (2003) focuses especially on lean six sigma in the service industry. He mentions an example, where Stanford Hospital and Clinics' application of the approach of lean thinking and six sigma leads to a situation, where they could deliver higher quality of care with lower costs. In addition, they could regain market share from their local competitors (George 2003).

Lean Six Sigma for services has the potential to maximise shareholder value by improvement of customer satisfaction, cost reduction, quality improvement, process speed increase and maximised return on invested capital. The combination of lean thinking and six sigma is required because (George 2003):

- Lean thinking does not use statistics to control processes.
- Lean thinking is necessary for dramatic changes and therefore improvement of processes. Six sigma alone cannot reduce process speed extraordinarily and cannot reduce the invested capital.
- Both approaches together enable the reduction of the costs of complexity.

12.4 Discussion

In this section, we will use the TOWS analysis tool and discuss how lean thinking, six sigma and lean six sigma in the e-health context can help to minimise the weaknesses and threats from the SWOT analysis in Sect. 12.2.

The following Table 12.4 shows the TOWS matrix instrument. It is important to note that the TOWS analysis is used here on a national scale and not originally intended and normally used on a company level. Therefore, the TOWS analysis has needed an adaption.

The explanations of the four strategies are (Koontz and Weihrich 2008; Weihrich 1982; 1999):

- SO Strategy: take advantage of opportunities by using the strengths
- WO Strategy: defeat weaknesses to take advantage of opportunities
- ST Strategy: avoid or deal with the treats by using the own strengths
- WT Strategy: minimisation of weaknesses as well as threats

Based on these facts and our purpose to reduce the weaknesses and threats of Australia's and Germany's e-health solutions through lean thinking, six sigma and lean six sigma, we will concentrate our discussion on the WT Strategy (Mini–Mini).

Weaknesses and threats minimisation:

- *Costs* (Australia and Germany): Lean Six Sigma for services has the potential to reduce costs (George 2003). This is very important, because the costs of an e-health solution implementation but also running costs can also have a negative impact on the *acceptance* (Australia and Germany) of the e-health solution. It is important to note that the e-health solution can also reduce costs by its nature, but if processes are not adapted and not well connected or cannot interact with each other, costs will rise. For example, if an e-prescription solution will be used to reduce paper costs, e.g. between a doctor and a pharmacist, but for invoicing a printed prescription in a later process step is requested, benefits

Table 12.4 TOWS matrix (adapted from Koontz and Weihrich (2008), Weihrich (1982), Weihrich (1999))

	Strengths	Weaknesses
Opportunities	SO strategy: maxi–maxi	WO strategy: mini–maxi
Threats	ST strategy: maxi–mini	WT strategy: mini–mini

like paper saving will be abolished. This is exactly what we also know from the principles of lean thinking, where unnecessary process steps should be eliminated to reduce costs.

- *Time schedule* (Australia and Germany): Australia and Germany have problems with the e-health implementation to attain their time schedule, because there are among other things different opinions/requirements between the different e-health stakeholders, which were not addressed adequately, because they were not involved enough in the development. When we consider the principles of lean thinking, it is important to design the e-health solution on customers' needs and requests (International Technology Centre and National Research Council Canada 2004); therefore, it is important to look on the care providers' needs, patients' need, etc. If this principle is accounted, the *acceptance* (Australia and Germany) will rise, because all the *several decision-makers* (Australia and Germany) will be included and therefore all the e-health stakeholders will benefit from the e-health solution. But this means also that Australia has to bow out of the idea of an *underlying fragmented system* meaning *a complex structure*, because only a national e-health solution can connect the different e-health stakeholders and allow that the health information is fast available where and when needed, which will result in *succeed superior healthcare delivery*. Of course, if the *several decision-makers* (Australia and Germany) are included in the development and implementation of an e-health solution, this can be seen as a risk, e.g. resulting in a longer *time schedule* (Australia and Germany), but therefore it is important to look on the lean thinking principle and define value precisely from the end customers' perspective (care providers, patients, etc.) in terms of a specific service, with specific capabilities, offered at an explicit price and time (International Technology Centre and National Research Council Canada 2004). If this is accounted, the situation is clear for every stakeholder from the very beginning. In the first moment it takes more time, but the overall decision process is faster, because stakeholders were included early and have therefore not the feeling of segregation and have a more open mind for the interests of others. This fact will also help in Australia, because *Australians are concerned of costs* and therefore it is important to involve them and show them the costs they will be confronted with but also the benefits. The encouragement of team spirit is here overall a very important point, which is a benefit of lean thinking (Joint Commission on Accreditation of Healthcare Organizations 2008).
- *New laws from the government* (Australia and Germany): This threat can be minimised through involvement of all stakeholders as lean thinking is provided (Joint Commission on Accreditation of Healthcare Organizations 2008). By considering this, the government could avoid to introduce laws or law changes that will be completely against the other stakeholders.
- *Data security and data protection* (Australia and Germany): This threat cannot be overcome with a guarantee, because there is always a risk of hacker attacks, etc. But this threat can be minimised through the basic phases of six sigma and lean six sigma, which means that potential problems are defined and measured

and problem reasons are analysed, improved and controlled (Go Lean Six Sigma 2012). The continuous improvement process is here important.

- *Information overload of a patient, which means that doctor can lose overview and lose time* (Australia and Germany): As we know, lean six sigma can help to reduce paperwork and reduce waiting times (Go Lean Six Sigma 2012). In addition, the lean thinking principle of designing and providing services depending on customers' needs and requests (International Technology Centre and National Research Council Canada 2004) can help here, so that the right information is at the right time at the right place.
- *Doctors need more time for documentation* (Australia and Germany): Lean six sigma can help to increase the time, which care providers can spend with their patients and reduce paperwork (Go Lean Six Sigma 2012). This time can be spent on the detailed documentation of health information of a patient and can therefore minimise this threat. This can at the same time help to increase the *acceptance* (in Australia and Germany) within the care providers, because they have not additional overtime and also patients will be more open to an e-health solution, if this solution does not mean that the doctor has less time for treatment decisions then. Lean Six Sigma for services has the potential to maximise shareholder value by improvement of customer satisfaction (George 2003).

As we have seen, lean thinking, sig sigma as well as lean six sigma have the potential to minimise weaknesses and threats resulting of an e-health solution respectively an e-health solution development and implementation. What we have also seen in our discussion is that weaknesses and threats can depend on each other. It is important to note that these principles do not help if the stakeholders are not showing the required willingness.

12.5 Conclusion

All OECD countries are currently being confronted with rising healthcare expenditures and focusing on healthcare reform enabled through ICT use as a panacea. e-Health appears to be the solution of choice for all these countries as they respond to the key healthcare challenges. This makes it vital to understand the critical issues for developing successful e-health solutions; an area the literature has been mute on to date. Thus, our study has tried to shed light on this by embarking on a deeper examination of the Australian and German e-health developments, two OECD countries that have respectively 2-tier healthcare systems and are currently embarking upon e-health initiatives and healthcare reforms to address the key healthcare challenges. Our preliminary findings have already uncovered many interesting points of note. Specifically, the SWOT analysis has demonstrated that the construction of e-health solutions is a challenging endeavour, and thus appropriate facilitators must be identified in order to realise a successful vision and thereby by achieve better healthcare outcomes. Moreover, it serves to identify that realising a network-centric healthcare solution is not at all an easy task. In addition, it serves to raise the question about the transferability of e-health solutions especially within similar healthcare systems, e.g. Australia and Germany. Other preliminary findings from our case study data at the micro level of analysis serve to indicate that while indeed a socio-technical perspective is important and people, process and technology considerations must be addressed in developing successful e-health solutions, it appears that the people issues especially given the existence of multiple-stakeholders in healthcare contexts appear to be a major barrier to success. Without a doubt e-health in some shape or form represents the future for healthcare delivery. Based on our analysis to date, it is possible to make the following recommendations: (1) For Australia: NEHTA should try to bring the different stakeholders together, increase the general awareness and understanding related to the PCEHR as well as make the healthcare delivery system itself less fragmented; (2) For Germany: the government together with the key stakeholders and organisations need to work together to ensure high acceptance by the citizens; (3) There are potential lessons to be learnt from other industries such as banking that can and should be applied into both settings; (4) International bodies such as the United Nations and/or World Health Organization should take the lead in developing global protocols and policies regarding e-health solutions; in this way, increasing the likelihood of appropriate network-centric healthcare solutions resulting; and (5) Given the importance of e-health today, as well as its growing importance in the future, it may be prudent for the development of a new international organisation that solely focuses on key e-health considerations including security and privacy aspects as well as standards and protocols.

In addition, we have used the TOWS analysis matrix and have shown how the lean thinking, six sigma and lean six sigma approaches can help to minimise the weaknesses and threats of Australia's and Germany's e-health solutions. This can help them for the success of their e-health solutions, which is very important based on the fact that e-health can lead to superior healthcare delivery.

The limitations of our study are mainly concerned with the possibility of information loss through translation (English vs. German) and the fact that the key stakeholders in the respective countries do not have exactly similar roles, responsibilities and tasks with regard to the design and implementation of the proposed e-health solution.

We close by calling for more research into this context and note that we are confident that at the conclusion of our study we will be able to shed light on: (1) How to find better strategies so that countries can fight against their weaknesses and threats which in turn will result in superior healthcare delivery; (2) How countries can focus on a national and even a worldwide e-health solution, which is the idea of NCHO; and (3) Key considerations regarding the issue of the transferability of e-health solutions between countries.

References

Abd Ghani, M., Bali, R., Naguib, R., Marshall, I., & Wickramasinghe, N. (2010). Critical issues for implementing a Lifetime Health Record in the Malaysian Public Health System. *International Journal of Healthcare Technology and Management (IJHTM), 11*(1/2), 113–130.

ArticlesBase.com—mcmillan. (2009). *Two-tier health care.* Retrieved February 21, 2012, from http://www.articlesbase.com/health-articles/twotier-health-care-1020480.html

Australian Government—Department of Health and Ageing. (2012). *Private health insurance.* Retrieved February 21, 2012, from http://www.health.gov.au/internet/main/publishing.nsf/Content/health-privatehealth-consumers-glossary.htm

Barmer GEK Krankenkasse. (2012). *Die neue elektronische Gesundheitskarte: Macht Gesundheit einfach sicher.* Retrieved February 21, 2012, from https://www.barmer-gek.de/barmer/web/Portale/Versicherte/Leistungen-Services/Leistungen-Beitraege/Multilexikon_20Leistungen/Alle_20Eintr_C3_A4ge/Gesundheitskarte.html?w-cm=CenterColumn_tdocid

BMG—Bundesministerium fuer Gesundheit. (2009). *Daten des Gesundheitswesens 2009.* Retrieved February 21, 2012, from http://www.bmg.bund.de/uploads/publications/BMG-G-09030-Daten-des-Gesundheitswesens_200907.pdf

Boyatzis, R. E. (1998). *Transforming qualitative information: Thematic analysis and code development.* Thousand Oaks: Sage.

Die gesetzlichen Krankenkassen. (2007). *Das elektronische Rezept.* Retrieved February 21, 2012, from http://www.g-k-v.de/gkv/fileadmin/user_upload/Projekte/Telematik_im_Gesundheitswesen/2.1.7_das_elektronische_rezept.pdf

European Commission. (2012). *The European health insurance card.* Retrieved February 21, 2012, from http://ec.europa.eu/social/main.jsp?catId=559

gematik—Gesellschaft für Telematikanwendungen der Gesundheitskarte mbH. (2012a). *gematik—Über uns.* Retrieved February 21, 2012, from http://www.gematik.de/cms/de/gematik/gematik_1.jsp

gematik—Gesellschaft für Telematikanwendungen der Gesundheitskarte mbH. (2012b). *Versichertenstammdaten.* Retrieved February 21, 2012, from http://www.gematik.de/cms/de/egk_2/anwendungen/verfuegbare_anwendungen/versichertendaten/versichertendaten_1.jsp

gematik—Gesellschaft für Telematikanwendungen der Gesundheitskarte mbH. (2012c). *Anwendungen der eGK.* Retrieved February 21, 2012, from http://www.gematik.de/cms/de/egk_2/anwendungen/anwendungen_1.jsp

George, M. L. (2003). *Lean six sigma for service: How to use lean speed and six sigma quality to improve services and transactions.* New York: McGraw-Hill.

GKV-Spitzenverband. (2012). *Alle gesetzlichen Krankenkassen.* Retrieved February 21, 2012, from http://www.gkv-spitzenverband.de/ITSGKrankenkassenListe.gkvnet

Go Lean Six Sigma. (2012). *The basics of Lean Six Sigma.* Retrieved August 29, 2012, from http://www.goleansixsigma.com/wp-content/uploads/2012/02/The-Basics-of-Lean-Six-Sigma-www.GoLeanSixSigma.com_.pdf

GVG—Gesellschaft für Versicherungswissenschaft und—gestaltung. (2004). *Managementpaper Elektronische Patientenakte.* Retrieved February 21, 2012, from http://ehealth.gvg-koeln.de//cms/medium/676/MP_ePa_050124.pdf

Huber, M. (1999). Health expenditure trends in OECD countries 1970-1997. *Health Care Financing Review, 21*(2), 99–117.

International Technology Centre and National Research Council Canada. (2004). *Principles of lean thinking: Tools & techniques for advanced manufacturing.* Retrieved August 29, 2012, from http://www.itc.mb.ca/downloads/resources_by_topic/princ_lean%20thinking/PrinciplesofLeanThinkingRevD2004.pdf

Jamshidi, M. (2009). *System of systems engineering: Innovations for the 21st century.* Hoboken, NJ: Wiley.

Jha, A. K., Doolan, D., Grandt, D., Scott, T., & Bates, D. W. (2008). The use of health information technology in seven nations. *International Journal of Medical Informatics, 77*, 848–854.

Joint Commission on Accreditation of Healthcare Organizations. (2008). *Advanced lean thinking: Proven methods to reduce waste and improve quality in health care*. Oakbrook Terrace: Joint Commission Resources.

Koontz, H., & Weihrich, H. (2008). *Essentials of management: An international perspective* (7th ed.). New Delhi: Tata McGraw-Hill.

Kvale, S. (1996). *InterViews: An introduction to qualitative research interviewing*. London: Sage.

Lazarus, I. R., & Novicoff, W. M. (2004). *Six Sigma enters the healthcare mainstream: Six Sigma proves its staying power in a crowded field of performance improvement alternatives*. Retrieved August 29, 2012, from http://www.creative-healthcare.com/pdf/SixSigma.pdf

Maheu, M. M., Whitten, P., & Allen, A. (2001). *E-Health, telehealth, and telemedicine: A guide to start-up and success*. San Francisco: Jossey-Bass.

mhplus Krankenkasse. (2011). *Infos zu Vorteilen bei der eGK*. Retrieved August 26, 2011, from http://www.mhplus-krankenkasse.de/1228.html

NEHTA—National E-Health Transition Authority Limited. (2008). *Quantitative survey report*. Retrieved February 21, 2012, from http://www.nehta.gov.au/component/docman/doc_downlod/585-public-opinion-poll-iehr

NEHTA—National E-Health Transition Authority Limited. (2010). *Healthcare identifiers service: Implementation approach*. Retrieved February 21, 2012, from http://www.nehta.gov.au/component/docman/doc_download/1139-healthcare-identifiers-implementation-approach

NEHTA—National E-Health Transition Authority Limited. (2012a). *Delivering E-Health's foundations*. Retrieved February 21, 2012, from http://www.nehta.gov.au/media-centre/nehta-news/416-delivering-e-healths-foundations

NEHTA—National E-Health Transition Authority Limited. (2012b). *The National E-Health transition authority strategic plan refresh*. Retrieved February 21, 2012, from http://www.nehta.gov.au/about-us/strategy

NEHTA—National E-Health Transition Authority Limited. (2012c). *What is a PCEHR?* Retrieved February 21, 2012, from http://www.nehta.gov.au/ehealth-implementation/what-is-a-pcher

NEHTA—National E-Health Transition Authority Limited. (2012d). *Benefits of a PCEHR*. Retrieved February 21, 2012, from http://www.nehta.gov.au/ehealth-implementation/benefits-of-a-pcehr

NEHTA—National E-Health Transition Authority Limited. (2012e). *e-Communications in practice*. Retrieved February 21, 2012, from http://www.nehta.gov.au/e-communications-in-practice

NEHTA—National E-Health Transition Authority Limited. (2012f). *Electronic transfer of prescription (ETP) release 1.1 draft*. Retrieved February 21, 2012, from http://www.nehta.gov.au/media-centre/nehta-news/704-etp-11

OECD. (2010a). *Growing health spending puts pressure on government budgets*. Retrieved July 29, 2011, from http://www.oecd.org/document/11/0,3343,en_2649_34631_45549771_1_1_1_37407,00.html

OECD. (2010b). *OECD health data 2010*. Retrieved June 6, 2011, from http://stats.oecd.org/Index.aspx?DatasetCode=HEALTH

OECD. (2011). *Gesundheitsdaten 2011—Deutschland im Vergleich*. Retrieved February 21, 2012, from http://www.oecd.org/dataoecd/15/1/39001235.pdf

Pearce, C., & Haikerwal, M. C. (2010). E-health in Australia: Time to plunge into the 21st century. *The Medical Journal of Australia, 193*(7), 397–398.

Porter, M., & Teisberg, E. O. (2006). *Redefining health care: Creating value-based competition on results*. Boston: Harvard Business School Press.

Scheer, A. -W. (2009). *BITCOM-Pressekonferenz E-Health*. Retrieved February 21, 2012, from http://www.bitkom.org/files/documents/BITKOM_Praesentation_E-Health_PK_04_03_2009.pdf

The Commonwealth Fund. (2010). *International Profiles of health care systems*. Retrieved February 21, 2012, from http://www.commonwealthfund.org/~/media/Files/%20Publications/Fund%20Report/2010/Jun/1417_Squires_Intl_Profiles_622.pdf

The Royal Australian College of General Practitioners. (2010). *Model healthcare community*. Retrieved February 21, 2012, from http://www.racgp.org.au/scriptcontent/ehealth/201002MHC_Handout.pdf

vdek—Verband der Ersatzkassen e. V. (2012). Fragen und Antworten zur elektronischen Gesundheitskarte (eGK). Retrieved February 21, 2012, from http://www.vdek.com/presse/Fragen_und_Antworten/faq_egk.pdf

Verband der privaten Krankenversicherung e. V. (2011). *Zahlen zur privaten Krankenversicherung*. Retrieved February 21, 2012, from http://www.pkv.de/zahlen/

von Lubitz, D. K. J. E., & Wickramasinghe, N. (2006). Healthcare and technology: The doctrine of network centric healthcare. *International Journal of Electronic Healthcare, 2*(4), 322–344.

Weihrich, H. (1982). The TOWS matrix–A tool for situational analysis. *Long Range Planning, 15*(2), 54–66.

Weihrich, H. (1999). Analyzing the competitive advantages and disadvantages of Germany with the TOWS matrix—An alternative to Porter's model. *European Business Review, 99*(1), 9–22.

WHO—World Health Organization (2005). *What is e-health?* Retrieved February 21, 2012, from http://www.emro.who.int/his/ehealth/AboutEhealth.htm

Wickramasinghe, N., Bali, R. K., & Tatnall, A. (2007). Using actor network theory to understand network centric healthcare operations. *International Journal of Electronic Healthcare, 3*(3), 317–328.

Wickramasinghe, N., & Schaffer, J. L. (2010). *Realizing value driven e-Health solutions*. Washington, DC: IBM Center for the Business of Government, Improving Healthcare Series.

Yin, R. K. (1994). *Case study research: Design and methods* (2nd ed.). Thousand Oaks: Sage.

ZTG—Zentrum für Telematik im Gesundheitswesen GmbH. (2010). *Notfalldaten*. Retrieved August 26, 2011, from http://www.egesundheit.nrw.de/content/elektronische_gesundheitskarte/infos_fuer_aerzte/e3380/index_ger.html

Chapter 13
Applying the Principles of KM to Effect Streamlined Healthcare Operations: A Malaysian Case Study

Sou Wei Wong and Nilmini Wickramasinghe

Abstract In 1997, Malaysia that has vowed to be a developed country with a national program called "Vision 2020" and as part of its plan to achieve this goal was to improve the health sector. There is not much time left before the year "2020" is reached, and it would appear that at the current condition the country's public healthcare is, the goal of effective and affordable healthcare will never be achieved unless significant changes are made to the plan to improve the healthcare sector.

The following proposes to develop a knowledge strategy based on Zack's (The strategic management of intellectual capital and organisational knowledge, Oxford University Press, Oxford, pp. 255–276, 2002) model to encapsulate the knowledge flow and create a strategic framework for mapping knowledge within the organization internally and externally.

While unable to control economic factors that deter the Malaysian government from providing more funding to improve the facilities or medical technology of its hospitals, with knowledge management strategies such as the ones that are produced using the proposed methodologies can help achieve effectiveness and most importantly competitive advantage that is sustainable.

Keywords Knowledge management • Affordable healthcare • Effective healthcare • Strategic knowledge gap

---

S.W. Wong (✉)
School of Business IT and Logistics, RMIT University,
GPO Box 2476, Melbourne, VIC 3001, Australia
e-mail: s3179796@student.rmit.edu.au

N. Wickramasinghe, Ph.D., M.B.A.
Epworth HealthCare & Department of BITL & HIRi, RMIT University,
GPO Box 2476, Melbourne, VIC 3001, Australia
e-mail: nilmini.wickramasinghe@rmit.edu.au; nilmini.work@gmail.com

N. Wickramasinghe et al. (eds.), *Lean Thinking for Healthcare*, Healthcare Delivery in the Information Age, DOI 10.1007/978-1-4614-8036-5_13,

13.1 Healthcare System in Malaysia

In Malaysia, the healthcare system uses a two-tier system which is very similar to Australia's system with a number of subtle differences. In a two-tier system, healthcare is provided by both the private and government institutions. According to Sulaiman (2011), the Malaysian government subsidizes up to almost 98 % of all health services in the public health sector. The Malaysian government, however, does not provide any subsidy for private healthcare to its citizens although it regulates it to ensure cost and quality control.

In Australia, although it has the same two-tier system as Malaysia, the Australian government has a system called Medicare, funded by income tax that provides from as much as 75 to 100 % subsidy for various types of health services in the public sector as well as a Pharmaceutical Benefits Scheme that also subsidizes prescription medicine. In addition to that, the Australian government encourages people who can afford private health insurance by reducing the cost of the plans and increased benefits.

In 2007–2008, the Australian government spent about 9.1 % of GDP on healthcare which amounts to AUD$103.6 billion or USD$2,874 per capita, whereas the Malaysian government spends about 4 % of GDP equivalent of AUD$4.1 billion or USD$400 per capita. The Malaysian government has been heavily criticized for not providing adequate affordable healthcare services for its citizen and instead choosing to privatize healthcare.

Less wealthy Malaysians who cannot afford treatment at private hospitals are forced into long waiting lists at public hospitals, and those private health hospitals that have continued to expand and now have excess capacity are attracting patients from abroad which is also known as "Health Tourism." The Malaysian government is also known to outsource some healthcare services from its public hospitals to private hospitals.

13.2 Knowledge Management

Knowledge management (KM) is a current management technique that is aimed at solving business challenges to increase efficiency and efficacy of core business processes while simultaneously incorporating continuous innovation. The premise for the need for knowledge management is based on a paradigm shift in the business environment where knowledge is central to organizational performance (Drucker 1993, 1999; Davenport and Prusak, 2000).

Knowledge management offers organizations many tools, techniques, and strategies to apply to their existing business processes. Given that healthcare is an information-rich industry, it therefore lends itself to benefit from an application of KM tools, techniques, and strategies in order to effect superior healthcare outcomes.

13.3 Hospital Background

To illustrate the benefits of adopting and applying a knowledge management strategy, an exemplar case study of Mary Hospital is presented. Yin (1994) notes the benefits of such an approach. Mary Hospital is a general hospital located in Miri, Sarawak, in East Malaysia. There are a total of 21 hospitals across the state with Mary Hospital being the largest and only general hospital, three district hospitals with specialist services, 15 district hospitals without specialist services, and two special institutions. Mary Hospital and three other hospitals in the state are the only known public hospitals to provide emergency care services.

Each of these hospitals offers a distinctive specialist services, and specialists from each of four hospitals including Mary Hospital travel to other hospitals to conduct clinic and training sessions. Mary Hospital offers the widest range of specialist services compared to the others. There are also psychiatric clinics across the state but not in Mary Hospital and two other hospitals. Despite this, psychiatrists from Mary Hospital and the two other hospitals regularly visit these clinics. An organization chart was obtained from the hospital's official website and is shown in Fig. 13.1.

It is important to note that most of the staff including doctors and nurses employed at Mary Hospital are still junior employees and therefore less experienced and skilled.

According to Mary Hospital's website, the main objective of the hospital is to provide a clean and healthy environment that will help patients recover with a combination of effective treatment and good care under a systematic and organized approach.

13.4 Strategic and Knowledge Gap

The first step of Zack's approach is to identify the core competency knowledge of the organization and compare it against its competitors. Mary Hospital's core competency is the patient care and medical practice and is said to possess only core knowledge that allows the organization to operate and try to compete against its competitors. Mary Hospital's competitors are private hospitals which possess advanced knowledge and Mary Hospital is described as a "Laggard" to its competitors (Fig. 13.2).

The next step in Zack's approach involves the use of a SWOT analysis to identify any knowledge or strategic gaps (Fig. 13.3).

The SWOT analysis (Table 13.1) clearly reveals a knowledge gap in Mary Hospital, this knowledge gap exists in the form of know-how, there is a lack of specialists in the hospital which meant patients had to be referred to another hospital in a different city or region for treatment, and this has resulted in inefficiency by allowing the severity of the patient's disease to develop and lower the chances of a full recovery.

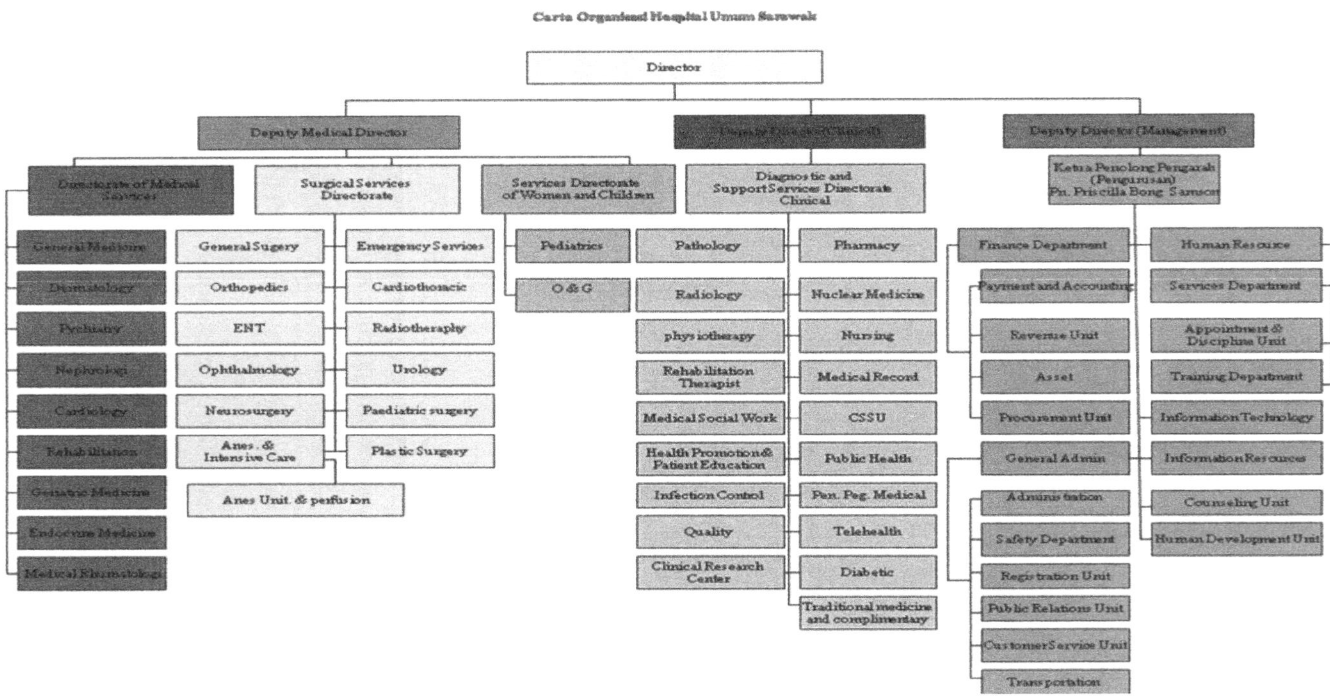

Fig. 13.1 Mary Hospital organization chart

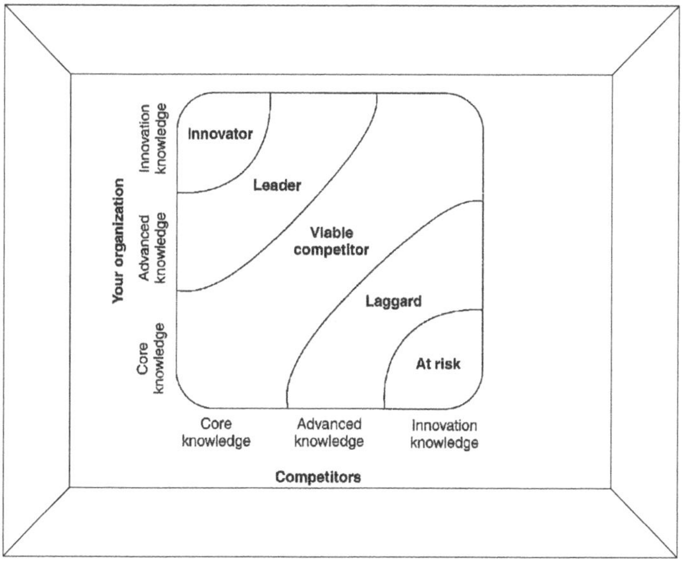

Fig. 13.2 Comparing knowledge levels (adapted from Zack 2002)

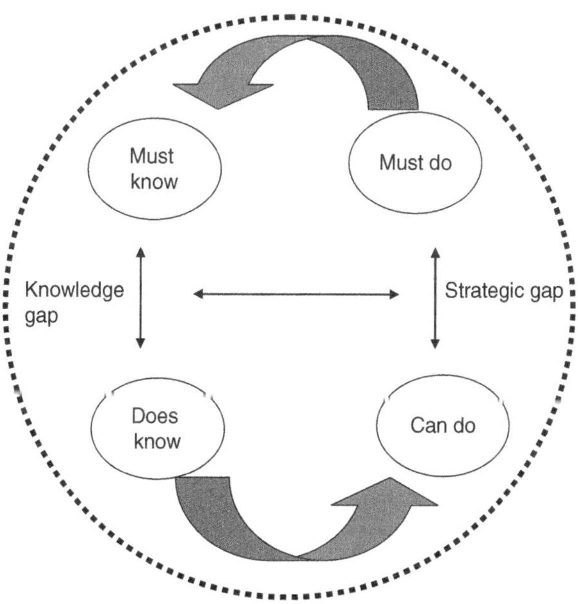

Fig. 13.3 Knowledge and strategy gap (adapted from Zack 2002)

Table 13.1 SWOT analysis

Strengths	*Weakness*
• Sole provider of healthcare services to patients who cannot afford to pay large sums of money for private healthcare • Also provider of specialized healthcare services not found in other public hospitals in the region	• Lack of specialist—treatment of certain diseases and only available in large cities • Lack of skilled staff • Waiting times too long in hospital • Shortage of doctors and nurses • Poor facilities and healthcare quality
Opportunity	*Threats*
• Being an efficient central health hub in the State with all the specialist and healthcare services required by patients	• Perception of better healthcare quality in private hospitals • People are forced to look for alternate treatment elsewhere due to no treatment availability for patient's disease

There is also a shortage of skilled staff that is able to operate the latest healthcare technologies which meant the hospital could not upgrade its facilities until the expertise required in its staff is obtained. Another weakness found during the SWOT analysis was currently there is not enough staff in the hospital to attend to patients, which eventually leads to excessive waiting times for patients which is fairly common in Malaysian public hospitals.

Some of these weaknesses are in agreement with Sulaiman (2011). Sulaiman (2011) stated that currently in Malaysia, there is a mismatch in supply and demand where 75 % of all admissions are in government hospitals but only about 25 % of the total number of specialist work in these hospitals. Sulaiman (2011) added that this has resulted in poorer healthcare quality and long waiting times.

Threats to Mary Hospital are due to competitors—private hospitals that are able to attend to patients with very little time and use the best medical technology which is a lot superior to the technology and facilities used in Mary Hospital. Despite its strength of Mary Hospital to offer the widest range of specialist services in the public healthcare in the region, it is also a weakness as well as a threat. Not all possible specialists are available in the entire state, and patients are forced to look for treatment elsewhere such as in West Malaysia or the neighboring country, Brunei, should the disease become too serious and the patient requires immediate treatment.

13.5 Flow of Patient

In Malaysia, there are three main institutions that a patient would go to for medical or health services; it is either a public hospital (an example would be Mary Hospital) or a private hospital and lastly a traditional health institution. A private hospital would be defined as a medical center practicing Western health practices, whereas a traditional health institution is said to practice traditional means of treatment which can range from a variety such as acupuncture (Fig. 13.4).

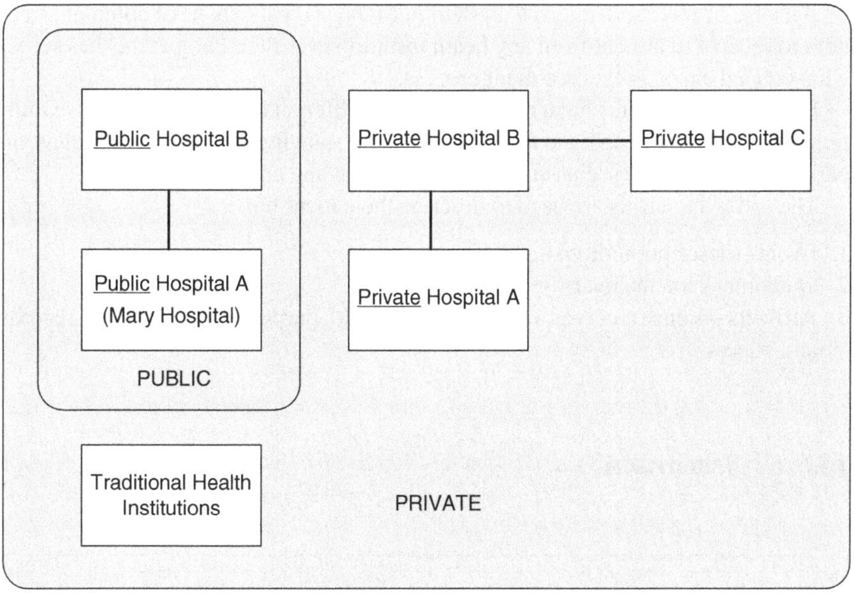

Fig. 13.4 Private and public health sector Malaysia

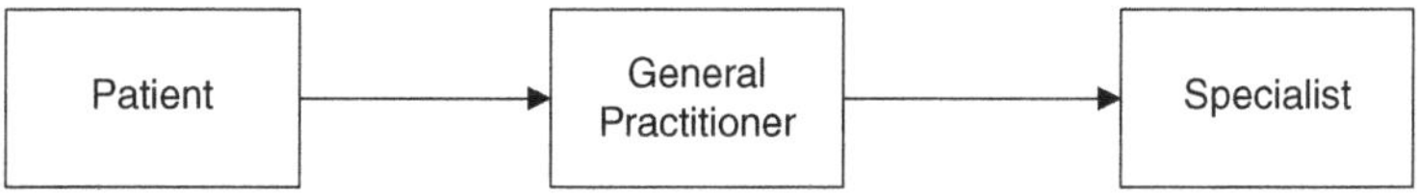

Fig. 13.5 Patient referral in Australia

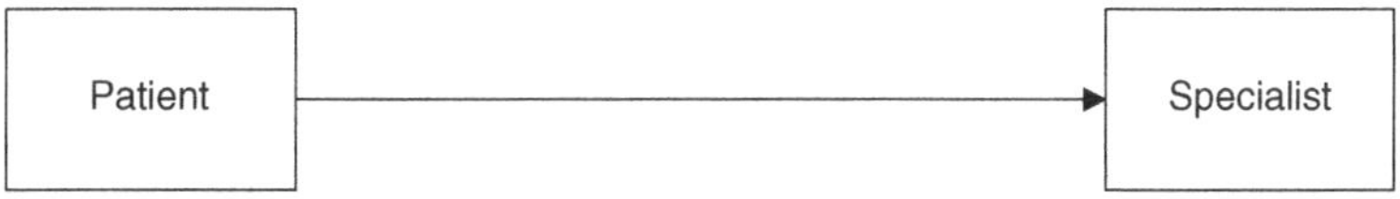

Fig. 13.6 "Self" patient referral in Malaysia

In Australia, the typical process that a patient would undergo is to visit a General Practitioner (GP) first to diagnose his/her health problems and be referred to a specialist if required.

This process is true in many countries including Malaysia where access to specialists is controlled by a national system of referrals but many patients have managed to bypass the first step of visiting a GP and directly to a specialist, usually in the private sector (Figs. 13.5 and 13.6).

Because of this "self-referral" system in Malaysia, patients have complete freedom to receive treatment from any heath institutions of their choice; this has somewhat created chaos in the treatment process.

For example, patients have multiple visits to different doctors and can have multiple prescriptions. In order to have a better understanding of the flow of Malaysian patients, two example scenarios have been created and are examined.

The following terms are used to describe the patient flow:

1. Event—description of visit
2. Outcome—conclusion of visit
3. Artifacts—items received or collected for KM purposes, i.e., medical records and papers

13.5.1 Scenario A

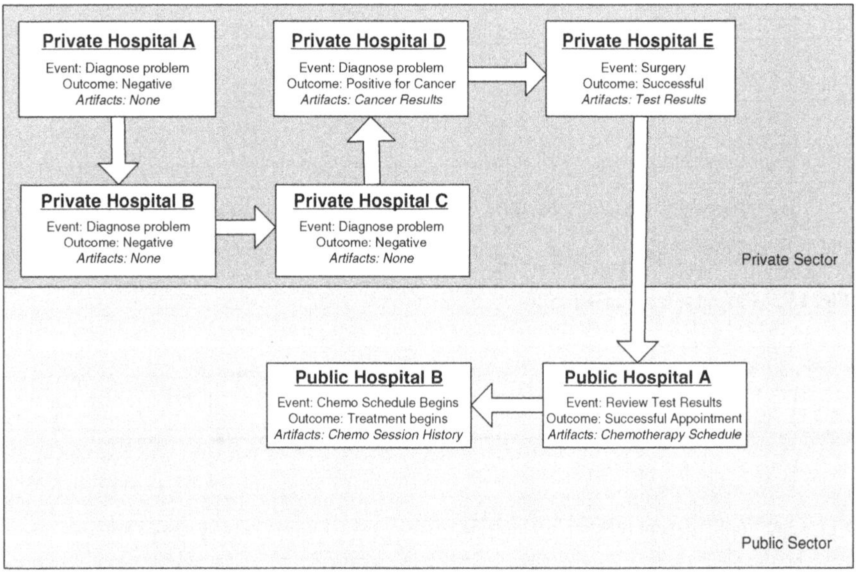

13.5.1.1 Description

In this scenario, a patient has voluntarily visited a Private Hospital A to diagnose the pain in various regions of her body; diagnoses at three private separate hospitals were negative until a visit to a fourth hospital that she was diagnosed with cancer. However because the fourth hospital did not have the facilities to conduct surgery operations, the patient was asked to visit a fifth hospital, where she had her surgery and waited for her test results. Upon receiving her surgery results, she visited Public Hospital A to review her test results so treatment could be scheduled. The patient had been assigned to receive chemotherapy treatment at another public hospital because Public Hospital A did not have chemotherapy treatment. The choice of switching back from a private hospital to public hospital was entirely based on the financial situation of the patient. Furthermore, due to limited number of staff that was available to the hospital, the patient had to wait a further 3 weeks for her first scheduled treatment to begin.

13.5.1.2 Analysis

From a KM-perspective point of a view, the author is in opinion that there are many opportunities to preserve tacit and explicit knowledge that will aid the entire patient flow process. For instance, based on scenario A, the first four visits to private hospitals were completely related to diagnosis, but no artifacts were used or communicative tool utilized between the four hospitals to capture explicit knowledge such as patient body temperature and patient blood pressure. The patient was forced to undergo the same standard diagnosis process at every visit. This is important because the first visit to "Private Hospital A" may be when the patient first realized the problem; therefore, any explicit knowledge regarding the patient's status or description of pain will be at most accurate before the problem complicates itself. The author believes that this explicit knowledge of the patient's initial status will greatly benefit the patient and doctors, especially for a disease such as cancer where discovering earlier stages of cancer will increase the chances of removing it dramatically.

13.5.2 Scenario B

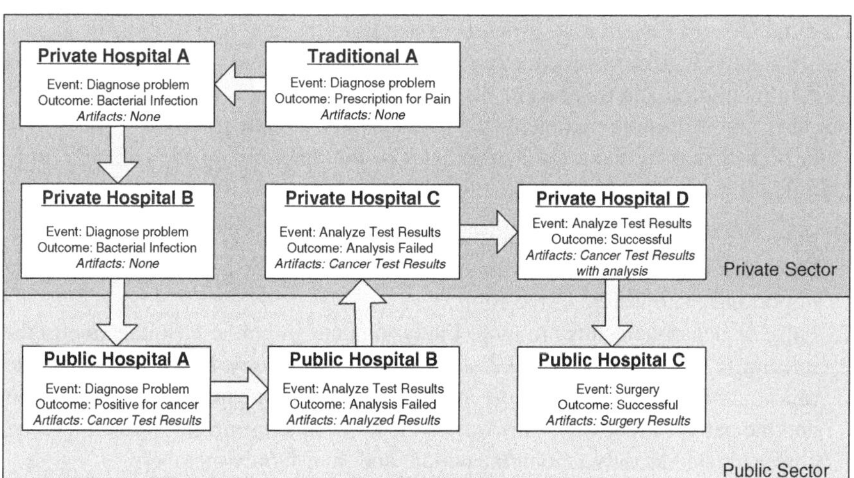

13.5.2.1 Description

Scenario B describes about a patient who has initially approach a traditional doctor to first inquire about her problem. Traditional Doctor A provides her with some prescription, but because the pain continued, she had decided to check her problem with other hospitals. From "Private Hospital A," the patient was diagnosed with bacterial infection and given antibiotics. However, as the pain continued, the patient went to a "Private Hospital B" and the outcome of the diagnosis was the same as the previous "Hospital A." The patient had finally decided to visit a hospital in the public sector, "Public Hospital A," and was finally diagnosed with cancer. The patient had to be reassigned to another "Public Hospital B" because "Public Hospital A" did not have the doctors who could analyze the cancer results. In "Public Hospital B," the analysis failed and the same outcome was achieved at a visit to another "Private Hospital C." Finally in "Private Hospital D" that the doctor was able to confirm the patient's cancer status and refer her for surgery.

13.5.2.2 Analysis

The patient flow in scenario B is very similar to scenario A, the pattern observed is that patients are constantly treated by a number of different doctors, and there are collaborations between the hospitals except when a linear process occurs such as seen in scenario B where the patient requires the initial test results in order for it to be analyzed and tested further. And the second analyzed results were required in order to proceed with a surgery operation in another hospital. In this type of patient flow, patients take a risk whenever they approach a new doctor or hospital; at each different hospital visits, the patient has a higher risk of a loss in follow-up of things such as radiology test results and can lead to missing fatal diagnoses.

Also, the scenario has shown that in the end, the patient has her surgery in Public Hospital C; even though it is sufficient to just have the analyzed test results to conduct the surgery, doctors do not have access to any records of the patient's past medical condition and treatments; also this sometimes leads to repeating diagnostics tests and instituting treatments the patients have already used.

In both scenarios, there are inaccuracies in the diagnosis of the patient's problem; this is due to two factors:

1. Inconsistencies in terms of reporting because of variability among different hospitals in radiological scan's calibration, the radiographer's experience, and most importantly knowledge of the context.
2. False or negative results are more likely to occur in public hospitals due to the inferiority of the specialist's skill and medical technology. Doctors are forced to repeat similar diagnostic tests to confirm results which cause delay in diagnosis and the patient's recovery. This wastes the hospital's resources as well as creates confusion and anxiety among the patient and their family members.

13.6 KM-Based Approach

Using Nonaka's SECI model (Ichijo and Nonaka 2007) of knowledge categorization and conversion model, it is assumed that knowledge flows through:

1. Socialization—sharing tacit knowledge with others using mental models or similar tools
2. Externalization—tacit to explicit by collective reflection or journal
3. Internalization—explicit to tacit by repeatedly doing things
4. Combination—combining all existing and new explicit knowledge by networking (Fig. 13.7)

Based on this assumption of knowledge flow, recommendations are created using three infrastructures that support knowledge management: technology infrastructure, operational infrastructure, and cultural infrastructure. The first recommendation is to exploit the current and existing knowledge that public hospitals like Mary Hospital have. This can be done in a number of ways. Because it is understood that in Malaysia, healthcare staff including doctors and nurses have a preference to leave the public sector and join the private sector due to the number of reasons discussed before. It is important to understand that whenever a senior staff leaves an organization, the senior staff leaves with all the knowledge he/she has gained in the organization if the organization has no mechanisms to capture this knowledge. The organization has to create new policies to ensure that knowledge does that leave in such manner; this can be done by forcing staff members to give a minimum of 3 months prior notice before leaving a position so the organization can prepare a

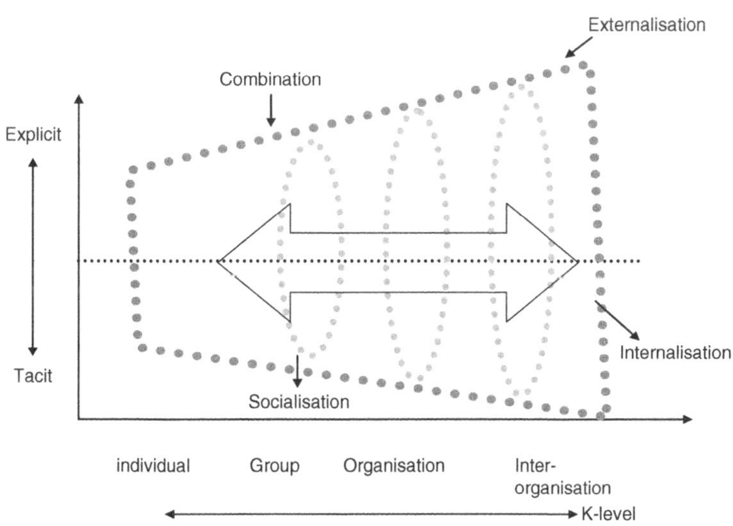

Fig. 13.7 Nonaka SECI model (adapted from Holsapple and Joshi 1999)

replacement and organize a means of "Knowledge Transference." This is also an opportunity for the organization to mentor junior staff members through many ways such as apprenticeship or "war stories." This ensures that there is tacit knowledge transfer between leaving staff members and existing staff members.

The second recommendation will be a technology-based recommendation that will support not only the first recommendation but as well as existing operations. The second recommendation is to implement a content management system within the organization to share knowledge among different departments. Even though the flow of patient data is not entirely clear between departments in the organization, it is critical that both explicit and tacit knowledge is established and stored consistently within one hospital before it is further passed on. Content management for KM is more than just databases; the three important aspects of the content management system to be considered are document management, types and formats as well as version control have to be considered for consistency; records management, to record metadata in transactions and such; and, finally, Web content management for any content hosted on Web servers. This recommendation allows the first recommendation to store all the tacit and explicit information regarding patients and operations skills knowledge and can be shared between the entire hospitals in a consistent manner. Examples of some content management system that can be considered for Mary Hospital are intranets, repositories, portals, and knowledge bases.

The third recommendation is an extension of the second recommendation; once the second recommendation has been implemented and consistency of patient and know-how (tacit) knowledge is created and preserved, Mary Hospital can implement a collaboration knowledge technology such as an EXTRANET to collaborate with other hospitals which can be either private or public. However, it should also be closely monitored that the other hospitals follow the same standards used and established to avoid variation in knowledge transferences. This recommendation is a direct response to two of the problems discussed before, that is, the inconsistency of diagnoses of patient and lack of senior and specialist in the public sector. This enables doctors between hospitals to discuss the patient's disease more efficiently and effectively as other doctors can communicate and follow-ups of test results can be done better. Alternative technologies are also available to Mary Hospital if the hospital does not have the budget to implement a content management system that requires its own IT platform and infrastructure such as Cloud Computing.

The final recommendation is not necessarily a realistic possibility in public hospitals such as Mary Hospital where staff already do not have enough time to attend to patients however if any how possible would benefit the hospital in the long term. The final recommendation is to have an After Action Review (AAR) approach similarly to a project-based AAR where doctors and nurses can reflect on the process of patient flow from the very beginning to the treatment and ongoing care after treatment. This can nurture a culture of self-assessment and critical thinking of individual staff members. Eventually, the learning process can become a policy and good practice when dealing with similar patterns of patient flow in the future.

13.7 Discussion

This exploratory case study served to illustrate the benefits of incorporating a KM strategy in order to examine how to develop an appropriate plan that will enable effective, efficient, and appropriate healthcare delivery to ensue. In particular it is possible to understand how KM strategies assist to enable a suitable redesign that not only subscribes to lean principles but also supports value-driven healthcare operations to ensue. This in turn then enables the realization of a healthcare value proposition of excellence in access, quality, and value.

13.8 Conclusions

Although a KM strategy can potentially resolve some of the problems currently existing in the healthcare sector in Malaysia, in order to achieve excellent healthcare services delivery for the people, the Malaysian government should rethink its overall strategy in healthcare to resolve some of these issues. The Malaysian government can perhaps look to another healthcare system such as the Australian healthcare framework as a guide in this process. A few examples of what approaches the Malaysian government can do are listed below:

1. A referral system that General Practitioners can use to refer patients to specialists/emergency departments or private hospitals. This is because, even in the presence of a KM strategy and KM tools are in place, the lack of a General Practitioner's input in filtering and streamlining of patients means emergency departments are congested with even patients with minor, nonurgent medical ailments. This finally results in longer waiting times while the overworked medical staffs are already overwhelmed with patients and leading to poorer overall performance and efficiency.
2. A system of collaboration of GP with community healthcare services (district nursing, maternal child care nurses, psychiatry services), hospital specialist/allied health, and such in providing patient's care. This system should also not discriminate between public and private institutions.
3. Transparency and accountability—ensure that even healthcare providers at the bottom of the medical hierarchy can make a complaint or give opinions on processes, operations, and such. This allows the inspection of these mistakes and can improve patient's healthcare delivery. Furthermore, doctors should be promoted based on merit rather than social status. This will restrict the influence of drug companies and ensure doctors are truly competent and ethical in terms of practice.
4. Compulsory registrations of all health practitioners that include pharmacists and alternative therapists. This means the quality or standards of competency are controllable and penalize members with unsafe practices.

Clearly a KM strategy is not a panacea for designing and developing healthcare delivery solutions which fit a value proposition of excellence in access, quality, and delivery of care. We strongly contend, however, that a KM strategy is indeed a necessary (albeit not sufficient) key factor in order to ensure that superior healthcare delivery ensues. Moreover, a KM strategy support and is consistent with lean thinking principles.

References

Davenport, T. H., & Prusak, L. (2000). What do we talk about when we talk about knowledge. In *Working knowledge: How organisations manage what they know* (pp. 1–24). Boston: Harvard Business School Press.

Drucker, P. (1993). *Post-capitalist society*. New York: HarperCollins.

Drucker, P. (1999, October). Beyond the information revolution. *The Atlantic Monthly,* 47–57.

Holsapple, C. W., & Joshi, K. D. (1999). Description and analysis of existing knowledge management frameworks. *Proceedings of the Annual Hawaii International Conference on System Sciences (HICSS' 99)*, IEEE Computer Society.

Ichijo, K., & Nonaka, I. (2007). *Knowledge creation and management*. Oxford: Oxford University Press.

Sulaiman, H. 2011. Healthcare Information Systems assimilation The Malaysian experience Doctoral dissertation available at http://researchbank.rmit.edu.au/eserv/rmit:160123/Sulaiman.pdf accessed Jan 2012.

Yin, R. (1994). *Case study research: Design and methods* (2nd ed.). Newbury Park: Sage.

Zack, M. H. (2002). Developing a knowledge strategy. In C. W. Choo & N. Bontis (Eds.), *The strategic management of intellectual capital and organisational knowledge* (pp. 255–276). Oxford: Oxford University Press.

Chapter 14
Remaking Rosa Medical Center: A 5-Step Approach to Transitioning with Lean

Mohamed Abouzahra and Joseph Tan

Abstract The strategic goal of implementing Lean in organizations is to streamline processes, which further involves a linking of the enterprise to its network of suppliers and distributors. In this chapter, the case of Rosa Medical Center in lean healthcare management is used to illustrate how the different lean concepts may be contextualized in a healthcare setting for a multi-provider polyclinic. The discussion follows a step-by-step approach, focusing on identifying and eliminating specific sources of waste in the value stream. Increasingly, this strategy has been applied to healthcare organizations, although the inherent differences between healthcare and manufacturing systems must be judiciously considered. We further review different points of criticism to lean thinking and attempt to provide insights on how these challenges may be addressed.

Keywords Lean • Waste • Muda • Value stream • Perfection • Customer pull • Value creation

Key Questions

1. What are the main obstacles facing the implementation of the suggested changes in Rosa Medical Center (RMC)?
2. Can you think of more improvements for the RMC case?
3. If we incorporate radiology and lab in the value chain, how would that affect the flow in RMC?
4. Compare the types of waste "muda" in RMC and in your organization; can the same principles be applied to reduce your organization's waste?

M. Abouzahra (✉) • J. Tan, Ph.D.
Degroote School of Business, McMaster University, Hamilton, ON, Canada
e-mail: abouzamm@mcmaster.ca; An9188@gmail.com

N. Wickramasinghe et al. (eds.), *Lean Thinking for Healthcare*, Healthcare Delivery in the Information Age, DOI 10.1007/978-1-4614-8036-5_14,

5. What additional levels can be added to RMC pull system to maximize efficiency?
6. If we examine the payers (e.g., insurance companies) as the main customer for RMC, how would that affect the lean implementation?

14.1 Introduction

Over the decades, rapid escalation of healthcare costs has hampered many countries in providing affordable, accessible, timely, and quality health care. In the United States, for example, up until 2010, healthcare costs have already come close to $2.6 trillion, or almost 16 % of its Gross National Product (GDP). In Canada, healthcare spending may not have grown so quickly; even so, Canada has spent approximately $200 billion on health care based on 2011 data released by the Canadian Institute for Health Information (CIHI).

Despite the overwhelming healthcare cost escalation in developed countries such as the United States and Canada, the quality of care and the sustainability of needed services and programs are still being criticized, and indeed, of growing concerns. Often, the long-term failures to meet the demands of accessible, affordable, and available high quality care services delivery are seen to be the result of several key factors. These include, among others: (a) the use of disparate systems, thereby making timely exchange of critical health-related information among multiple care providers difficult, if not impossible (e.g., Ben-Tovim et al. 2007; Tan and Payton 2010); (b) unnecessary and redundant work that many healthcare provider organizations may be directed, and continued, to perform (e.g., Hayward and Hofer 2001; Kim et al. 2010; Falan 2012); and (c) the fact that much of the limited resources and patient care time spent on work was actually not adding values, if any, to the patient and/or the payer of such services, specifically, the government and/or insurance companies that are funding or cofinancing the system (e.g., Revere and Black 2003; Nelson-Peterson and Leppa 2007). Put simply, a lot of "waste" remains hidden in healthcare processes, and yet only limited efforts, if any, have been concentrated on eliminating such waste in the last several decades (e.g., Falan 2012).

Fortunately, major efforts on waste elimination have been well publicized and these efforts, sometimes called quality improvement (QI) programs, have since been cleverly applied and/or used to overhaul organizational processes in non-health care-related industries, especially the manufacturing industry (e.g., Walton 1986; Crosby 1979; Juran 1988). In fact, various QI methodologies that have been applied successfully in the manufacturing industry were also quickly and beneficially adopted by many other industries such as transportation, material management and inventory supply chains, as well as banking. Until fairly recently, the healthcare industry appeared to have blindly ignored the benefits of QI implementation efforts and their potentials towards reducing medical errors and improving clinical treatment efficiencies. The rationale for such attitudes among care providers may perhaps be traced to the nature of medical services, which, unlike more easily automated manufacturing processes, involves higher order human interactions and ethics, including (a) an overwhelming number of sensitive and ethical issues, touching on patient privacy and confidentiality, individual rights of patients and care providers, and human emotion; (b) a change of complex workflow practices and habits of care providers and specialists that, understandably, cannot be easily changed; and (c) the fact that health care is an attempt to save human lives and/or to achieve a higher quality of life for the patient.

Today, we are better at tracking potential waste and integrating nonmanufacturing processes for very complex systems such as health care, including the need to better structure medical services and intuitive work habits of care practitioners. Moreover, a more informed and highly educated patient population will often translate also into greater pressures among competing care provider organizations to vie for better quality of care services delivery. Finally, greater awareness of the power of advancing technologies and the willingness for governments as well as other healthcare and business partners to invest in and better understand the potential automation of health-related processes have pushed the adoption of more intelligent interfaces, the implementation of QI strategies, and the deployment of less error-prone, interoperable e-health systems. Evolving socio-political, economic, technological, and cultural factors have also resulted in worthwhile attempts to more ably apply QI programs for healthcare services delivery in a more systematic and integrated fashion.

Given that many healthcare organizations, as well as care providers and patients alike, suffer unnecessary loss of time and money on non-value adding processes such as unneeded duplication, retrieval, waiting, repeated sorting, transporting, and storing of paper-based medical records, the benefits of adopting QI techniques cannot be overly emphasized. In some instances, delays in the transmission of accurate patient care records in fast changing healthcare environments can lead to grave consequences such as increased morbidity and mortality. Hayward and Hofer (2001) reported, for example, that 22.7 % of hospital deaths were considered as possibly avoidable had QI techniques been adopted and/or implemented. Of these, 6 % of the deaths reported were rated as certainly or probably preventable. As well, Shen and Hsia (2011) concluded that lengthy periods of ambulance diversion due to overcrowding emergency departments would lead to higher mortality rates among patients with time-sensitive conditions. Other more recent studies such as Kim et al. (2010) also concluded that hospital staff spent approximately 7 % of their time travelling and about 67 % of their time in activities not directly related to patient care. In terms of applying advancing QI methodologies for health care, Revere and Black (2003), for example, presented an interesting study of combining Six Sigma and total quality management (TQM) in a framework that enables healthcare organizations to utilize the benefits of both methodologies without incurring much environmental change. Other examples of successful QI programs in healthcare management systems include Finders Medical Center (Ben-Tovim et al. 2007), and Virginia Mason Hospital and Medical Center (Nelson-Peterson and Leppa 2007). Altogether, these studies demonstrate that there are grave consequences arising from wasting healthcare resources, and that, to date, there is an overriding need to eliminate waste in order to provide patients with a higher quality of life, thereby ensuring that their care would be more effective and more efficiently delivered.

The objective of this chapter is to provide the readers, via the backdrop of an illustrative case study, with an overview of lean thinking in terms of its evolution, a conceptualization of the five steps needed to guide the application of lean thinking strategies for healthcare organizations, and a review of waste definition in the context of "Lean." Embedded in the discussion will therefore be a review of the Lean philosophy and its development, followed by the articulation of a framework for the purpose of transitioning healthcare organizations to lean. More importantly, the articulated 5-step conceptual framework will be further used to illustrate the remaking of a "Leaner" Rosa Medical Center (RMC), a multi-provider polyclinic. Additionally, an attempt will be made to provide insights as to how objections to lean thinking and how different challenges facing the implementation of lean management may be addressed. Finally, the major issues associated with the Lean evolution and future implementation directions for lean health care will conclude the chapter presentation.

Prior to reviewing the lean concepts, we introduce here the case on remaking RMC, as it will be used throughout our chapter discussions to illustrate the various lean management concepts.

14.2 Remaking Rosa Medical Center: A Case Study

Located in Riyadh, Saudi Arabia, the RMC is a multi-provider polyclinic (a medical center composed of multiple clinics). Essentially, the RMC comprises 25 clinics rendering services in most medical specialties, including a comprehensive laboratory and a radiology department. Close by the RMC is a pharmacy that also serves many of Rosa's patients; this pharmacy is not inside Rosa, but within walking distance of about 100 m.

On average, up to 300 patients a day may be serviced at the RMC. Patients are not required to make appointments, but are served on a first-come-first-served basis. During the weekdays, a majority of patient visits occur between 5 and 9 p.m. (closing time). Ninety-five percent of these patients are medically insured, who will be expected to co-pay a stipend of about 20 % of the service fees for what they would have been charged per visit with an upper limit of what is equivalent to $40. The remaining 5 % of Rosa's patients pay privately for the treatment services rendered.

In our analysis, as discussed throughout this chapter, we will only consider the typical scenario where patients come to one of the RMC clinics, receive a prescription, and go on to the pharmacy to fill the prescription. To simplify our case example even further on the application of the 5-step framework of lean thinking that is presented later, we will also assume that patients do not need any lab or radiology examinations.

How does "Lean" apply in the Rosa's case? In order to make sense of "Lean" strategies and the 5-step framework for implementing "Lean," it is important for us to trace back to the origin as well as development of the "Lean" concepts.

14.3 The "Lean" Evolution

To date, many theories, operational frameworks, and QI techniques have been advanced on how best to eliminate waste and to improve the quality of service delivery. Some modern approaches relating to such QI techniques include Six Sigma (e.g., Coronado and Antony 2002), TQM (e.g., Powell 1995), and Lean Thinking (e.g., Ohno 1988), all of which focus on understanding the needs of customers and optimizing workflow processes in the organization to meet those needs in an effort to reduce waste and achieve higher system efficiencies. More specifically, lean management is a philosophy aimed at eliminating waste in the organization's value producing processes leading to a "lean" workflow with no waste limiting its efficiency (Womack and Jones 1997). As such, "Lean" appears to be a relevant philosophy for remaking organizations such as RMC to become more patient-centered as well as payer-centered as its conceptualization mainly focuses on "what the customer values"—for this reason, it will be the primary focus of this contribution.

The genesis of "lean thinking" may be traced decisively to the Japanese automotive industry. Specifically, in the 1950s, under the leadership of Taiichi Ohno (Liker 2004), the Toyota Company focuses "lean thinking" on ways to eliminate waste (or "muda" when expressed in Japanese) among processes throughout the different workflows in a typical car manufacturing system (Ohno 1988). This philosophical perspective led Toyota to take on a prominent leadership role in the automotive industry while further empowering the company to produce high quality cars cheaper than many other car producers. Lean thinking, encapsulated within the Toyota Production System (TPS), remained more or less a secret of Toyota up until the 1980s. In 1990, the Toyota enterprise model was unveiled with the release of "The machine that changed the world" (Womack et al. 1990), thereby popularizing the term "lean production."

Although lean thinking started as a manufacturing QI technique, it soon expanded to other production and service industries such as hospitality, information technology (IT), and, eventually, health care. Started as a focused activity on cutting waste from various manufacturing processes, "lean thinking" was often referred to as a "shop-floor" perspective (Womack and Jones 1997). This is not surprising given the nature of the automotive industry in which such thinking has been deeply rooted. By the 1990s, however, the view on "lean thinking" had broadened, and by 1996, we soon witnessed the evolution of the first principles of lean thinking, that is, when "value" was first connected to "customer requirements" and was no longer focused on "shop-floor" or manufacturing requirements (Simons and Taylor 2007).

Today, lean thinking has strategically evolved into an enterprising concept where all efforts of the enterprise are now directed towards creating value for the "customer" with the intent of eliminating all identifiable sources of waste (Womack and Jones 1996). Placed in the context of the RMC enterprise, we may correctly predict that a "lean" paradigm shift represents a continuous effort to transform various medical servicing and delivery processes currently used or have been systematized in RMC towards a state of "perfection" through the gradual elimination of "waste." At this junction, it is therefore important for us to better understand the "Lean" paradigm shift through the 5-step framework for crafting a "Lean" Enterprise.

14.4 Framework for Crafting a "Lean" Enterprise

From an enterprise management perspective, integrating five logically sequenced steps (Ohno 1988; Womack et al. 1990; Womack and Jones 1997; Liker 2004) can eventually lead to an organizational-wide "lean" system. These steps are ordered in a logical fashion in order to achieve a systematic analysis of the different business processes as well as focusing on the issues that prevent the overall workflow servicing and processing from integrating efficiently and seamlessly. Together, the steps will aid the organizational system(s) in value creating processes as well as undergo various types of process waste elimination in any lean thinking project.

As depicted in Fig. 14.1, these five important steps include: (1) specifying value; (2) identifying the value stream; (3) creating flow; (4) creating a pull system; and (5) perfection. Together, these steps form an integrated framework that will be used to guide the discussions in our illustrative RMC case presented earlier. For the moment, our focus will be to describe each of the individual steps more fully and how they should link seamlessly into each other.

14.4.1 Step 1: Specifying Value

The first step in this framework is to specify "value." Basically, this entails a careful attempt to identify the value provided to customers, regardless if this value is linked to a product and/or a service. Briefly, "value" should be specified in terms of *specific products and/or services to be provided to customers at a specific time based on a specific pricing*. Therefore, components of specifying values include *product, time, and price* so that the "value" is well defined.

The critical point is that "value" should be defined exclusively from the perspective of the customers. Not only will a specific definition of "value" simplify the process of identifying the value stream but it will also aid to analyze waste. When setting "values" for an enterprise, a common mistake is to base these values upon seemingly influencing factors such as the governance structure of the enterprise or the technology used, while forgetting to focus on the customer's perspectives, particularly those of the primary customer. This mistake will then lead to an inaccurate value stream and to the failure of lean thinking implementation. If health insurance companies, for example, are considered the overriding key stakeholders, the value provided by the Rosa enterprise may tend to favor these companies on the expense of their patients, to whom quality services should, in fact, be rendered, as they are the true primary customers. Such a mistake will eventually lead to a failure in providing the quality services needed throughout RMC.

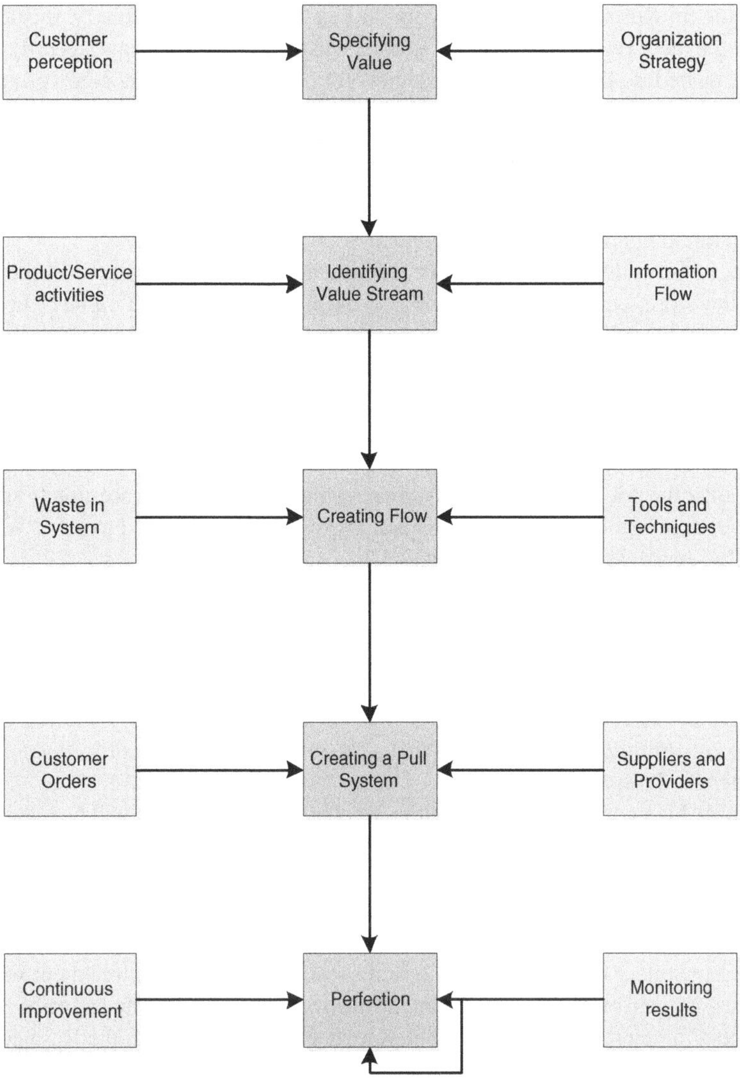

Fig. 14.1 Framework of lean thinking

14.4.1.1 Specifying Value for RMC: Step 1

In the RMC context, there are two major groups of "customers" served by the Rosa enterprise: (1) the patient who often is the primary customer interacting directly with the polyclinic service delivery system and (2) the government organizations and/or insurance companies ultimately responsible in paying for the care. Inadvertently, a key question for RMC is: "Who are Rosa's customers for which 'value' is to be specified?" Resolving this question will be critical in order to specify the value for Rosa polyclinic in any initial Lean analysis. Accordingly, it is argued that while these two main groups of external customers for Rosa have specific needs to be satisfied by the RMC lean strategies, for example, insurance companies need accurate and timely case reporting of all claims whereas patients are seeking to be served professionally, patients represent the largest customer population. Therefore, we will choose to focus only on the patient group to further simplify our analysis and to provide the readers a better understanding of how the different components of lean thinking apply in this very context.

The initial follow-up question for lean management to be realized in the Rosa case, therefore, centers on identifying "what is patient-centered value?" In other words, what specifies the quality of Rosa's healthcare services as reflected essentially by the healthcare value upheld by Rosa's patients? While several past attempts have been made to define value in health care (Young and McClean 2008; Gray 2007), most studies focused on definitions that were unrelated to the value perceived by patients (Ellis and Wittington 1993). As it is important in Lean thinking to consider the perspective of the customer (or patient) in order to accurately specify value (Jimmerson et al. 2005), we cannot overemphasize the need to ask: "What is the value expected by Rosa's patients?"

As mentioned, patients want to be treated efficiently, effectively, safely, and, as much as possible, comfortably. Also, the price of servicing the patients forms a key part of value specification. Therefore, these prices should be carefully specified to match the level of service provided and the payment capabilities of the visiting patients. In the RMC case, it is reasonable then for us to specify the "value" as *delivering affordable, efficient, effective, safe, and as much as possible, comfortable treatment to Rosa patients.*

Affordable treatment ensures that the fee charged to the patient will be reasonable and equitable when compared relatively to what other providers will charge for the same servicing. Efficient and effective care means that the patients will receive adequate treatment and proper care for their needs and that these services are to be administered quickly without unnecessary delays (Sirio et al. 2007). Safe and comfortable treatment means that patients can expect to receive such treatment without unnecessary pain or suffering, while medical errors are eliminated and adverse effects reduced (Jimmerson et al. 2005). Therefore, a specific example in the Rosa context would be that a patient visiting one of Rosa's specialty clinics suffering from acute flu syndromes can expect to receive timely and accurate treatment that will help cure her illness in the shortest possible time without adverse side effects or medication errors, and without putting her into unnecessary pain or financial hardship.

14.4.2 Step 2: Identifying the Value Stream

The next step is "value stream" identification. This step is defined as taking note of all the actions that are required to bring a product and/or a service from concept into the hands of customers. It includes designing the product, information flow (for processing, ordering, and delivering), and, finally, transferring the product from its raw material stage to the actual product.

Once the value stream is created, it can be used to differentiate between required actions to complete the product, and waste or "muda" of type 1 and type 2 clusters, which will be discussed in a separate section. Indeed, value stream represents a new way to look at creating a product. Instead of looking at the product from a manufacturing or production viewpoint, the product is analyzed based on the value it creates for the customers, who would, in turn, provide the enterprise with insights of the actions required to improve this value.

Apparently, the value stream should not be bounded by the enterprise, but can and, in fact, should cross the enterprise boundaries to other enterprises in the production chain. For example, in a hospital setting, providers of prescriptive medicine and medical supplies should be considered as parts of the value stream. This consideration is essential because the enterprise requires the value added by other parties in the supply chain in order to succeed in creating value to the customer(s).

The inclusion of external enterprises calls for new ways of thinking and communications within the enterprise and among different enterprises. It also mandates transparency in communications to facilitate coordination in creating value for customers. For example, a hospital must establish strong communication channels with all of its providers in order to identify its value stream(s) accurately.

In our RMC setting, the value stream may be considered as the different steps patients undergo to receive treatment. Of course these steps will vary as the type of patient changes (for example, inpatients or outpatients) and, therefore, there could be several value streams to be incorporated within the same healthcare enterprise.

14.4.2.1 Identifying the Value Stream for RMC: Step 2

Once the initial step of specifying value is ascertained, the value stream, or the sequence of steps required to create, order, and deliver the value, must now be clearly identified.

As noted, our assumption for RMC patients is that they do not need any lab or radiology examinations, just prescription drugs. Therefore, in order to identify the value stream accurately, we must also understand the different types of waste and on how such waste can and should be eliminated. For this reason, we will sidestep at this point to redirect our attention on how "waste" is viewed in "Lean" before stepping back to continue our discussion on the value stream for the RMC case.

14.4.3 *Defining "Waste" in Lean*

As the main focus of lean management is to eliminate waste, it is important to define the concept of "waste" as a critical component of the lean philosophy. Briefly, "waste" (or "muda") may be defined as *any sort of activities that uses resources but produces no practical added value* (Jimmerson et al. 2005). This understanding emphasizes "Lean" management in practice and the key focus of "Lean" when related activities have to be managed.

Many types of waste have been identified in different industries. However, only seven of these types have been widely accepted and popularly applied in different industries. Details of each of these types of waste were originally described in "The machine that changed the world" (Womack et al. 1990) and have been studied in many lean implementation cases across various industries (Levinson and Rerick 2002). A brief review of these seven types of waste that are also relevant and applicable to the healthcare industry, and, more specifically, to the RMC case, is provided below:

1. *Defects*: Such waste should not be limited to just end-product defects, but include, among others, processing defects, data entry defects, and any type of defect that requires rework. Within the RMC context, examples of "defects" could be any medication "errors" as well as the generation of incorrect and/or unclear reports.
2. *Overproduction*: Such waste includes the production of goods and/or services at a rate greater than their rate of use or consumption; in other words, overproduction will result in the creation of unwanted or unneeded products, thereby cumulating waste. Examples in the RMC context would include the act of dispensing medicine at a rate greater than what would be needed for the patients, or ordering unnecessary tests such as performing too many lab tests.
3. *Inventories*: Such waste is tightly linked to overproduction as it concerns storing the overproduced inventories, which ultimately consume valuable space and resources, due to their lack of instant market demands. Such waste also includes the overproduction of batched goods that must be stored before going out to market, or serving as inputs into the next production phase. In the RMC context, improper drug inventory management in anyone of its clinics would be an example of (waste in) inventories. The possibility that certain medicine will become dated and/or damaged due to lengthy storage is another follow-up example of (waste in) defects.
4. *Overprocessing*: Such waste involves performing unnecessary steps to complete a task and/or repeating the same step multiple times without gaining any new value. For example, entering the same information in different forms and generating unusable or unused reports would be wasteful. In the RMC context, generating unnecessary reports and/or ordering duplicate tests on patients is an obvious example of (waste in) overprocessing.
5. *Human motion*: Such waste involves the unnecessary movements of employees and/or customers while getting their work done. For instance, unnecessary time and effort may be spent by a worker who needs to go into the warehouse to get a required part and/or customers having to move between different counters for specific customer services. Examples of such waste in the RMC context could be the time and effort it takes for nurses and/or physicians to move between the different wards and the time and effort it takes for patients to go from a clinic to a lab or the pharmacy.

6. *Transportation*: Such waste accounts for unnecessary movement of material, information, and/or equipment. For instance, moving products along a production line or moving paperwork between offices may be costly as well as incur more problems in the process, such as moving the requested paperwork into the wrongly intended destinations. In the RMC context, this sort of waste includes moving patient documents and/or moving medical equipment between different service providers located in different RMC clinics.
7. *Waiting*: Such waste is one of the most recurring types of waste as it concerns the unnecessary time lost and expenses arising from waiting such as a care provider waiting for information requested from a customer and/or the transfer of such information from another department. Similarly, for the customer to have to wait to be serviced could be expensive over the long run. In the RMC context, patients usually suffer from this type of waste in overcrowded clinics.

Evidently, a key goal of lean thinking is to eliminate waste even though not all types of waste can be eliminated immediately and/or easily from the system. As part of a value generating process, specific type of waste may be simply warranted, begging a further analysis of the nature of waste. For instance, owing to the lack of specialists, it may be absolutely necessary for patients to have to wait in order to be serviced by one of the few specialists who are able to consult on the patients' particular illness(es); therefore, a classification of waste according to the capability to eliminate this waste may be further articulated as follows (Womack and Jones 1997):

Type 1 waste: A cluster of waste that adds no value to the customer but is needed in the value delivery process. Its elimination, therefore, requires some replanning and analysis; for example, the time patients will need to spend while waiting for their radiology reports adds no value to these patients. Yet, this waiting is a necessary part of the existing treatment care process. In order to eliminate this waiting, the workflow process will have to be redesigned.

Type 2 waste: A cluster of waste that adds no value and is unnecessary in the delivery process in that it can be eliminated directly, if so desired. For instance, forcing patients to repeat registration at different counters and/or for them to provide duplicate data at different places in the same healthcare system can be eliminated quite easily without losing any value that is of significance.

14.4.3.1 Continue with Identifying the Value Stream for RMC: Step 2

Figure 14.2 charts the value stream for the RMC case.

As patients arrive at the main polyclinic reception, their ID and insurance cards are examined and they are offered an appointment slip. Then, as the patients stand in line, their ID cards are being copied using a copier as per regulations and for future reference. After getting back their original IDs, the patients then go onto the cashier to prepay for the service(s) they are requesting. As shown in the figure, there are two separate main reception counters—one copier and one cashier.

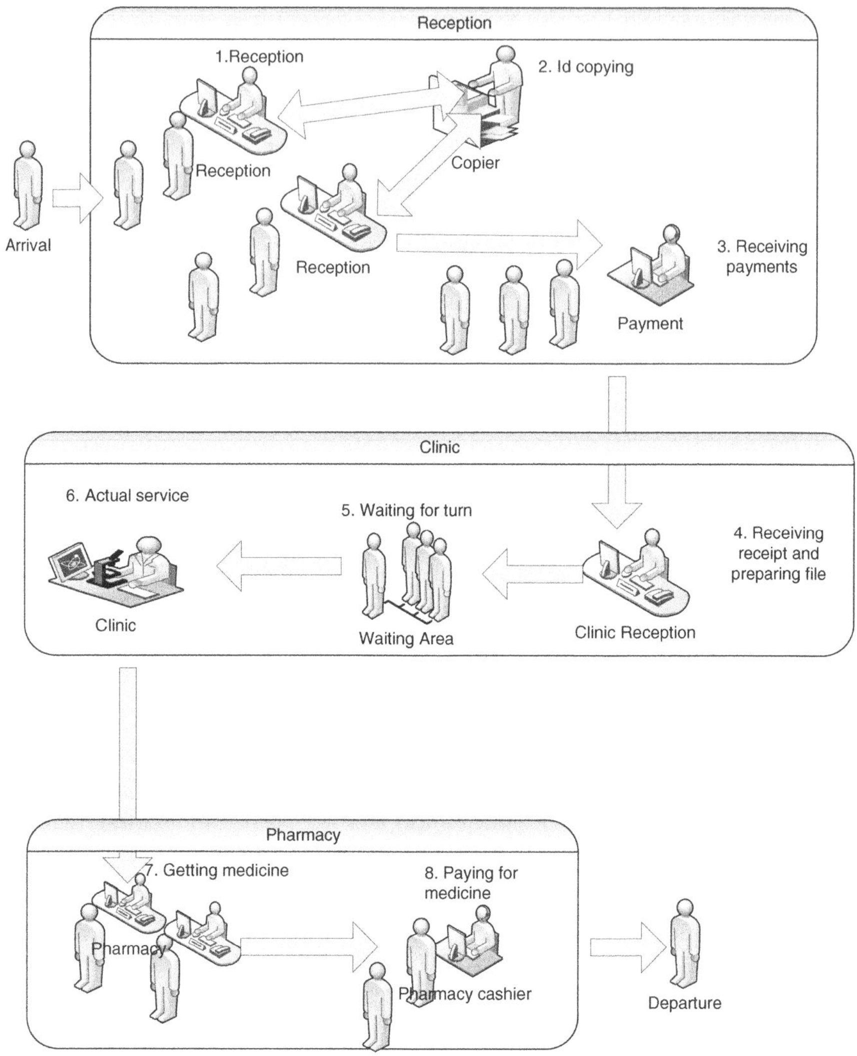

Fig. 14.2 Identifying value stream at the Rosa Medical Center

The next step for the patients is to proceed to the individual clinic reception where they would provide their appointment slip, and then wait in a designated waiting area until the appropriate physician is ready to serve them. Once the nurse calls for a patient, he/she enters the clinic, receives a prescription (in most cases), and then walks all the way to the pharmacy to have the prescribed medicine filled.

At the pharmacy, patients again wait their turns, get the medicine, and then wait for a final time at the pharmacy cashier to pay for the medicine. Notice that there are two servers and one cashier at the pharmacy. Although the pharmacy has an

Table 14.1 Time spent by patients in the system

Activity	Patient time as measured (in minutes)
1. Reception	5
2. Copying of ID cards	3
3. Receiving payment	9
4. Receiving receipt and preparing file	5
5. Waiting for turn	20
6. Actual service	12
7. Filling prescription (including walking to pharmacy)	25
8. Paying for medication	12

automated accounting system, prescription ordering is still done manually. It is often the case that the delivery of medicine is delayed. If patients do not find their prescribed medicine in the pharmacy, they are advised to visit an external pharmacy to receive their prescriptions.

In order to examine the total time patients spend and/or waste in the Rosa polyclinic, we measured the time spent by the pediatric clinic patients at different steps in the workflow. These measurements have been sampled over 5 successive working days from 6 to 9 p.m. We chose a single clinic to simplify measurements and to obtain a simple yet accurate view of "waste" in the study clinic. The number of patients throughout our study period over 5 days averages ten patients.

Table 14.1 shows the average time spent by patients in the RMC polyclinic system—patients were observed over 5 days from 5 to 9 p.m. These measurements represent the time spent in each step of the value stream. We collected these data by observing the time spent by patients in each activity of the value stream and calculating their average service time.

Based on this analysis, RMC patients expended an average of 91 min for a single visit in the system, with more than an hour (60 min) waiting for the desired service or moving between locations without receiving any service.

This observation highlights two challenges for remaking RMC. The first challenge is how the arrangement of the current value stream contradicts the RMC service value as we have defined earlier. Specifically, it would be much more efficient and effective to move the functions of the main reception (Steps 1–3) to the clinic reception. This would, in fact, decrease the time spent in the system significantly, improving the comfort of patients and create a more efficient system to enhance customer satisfaction and royalty.

Nonetheless, when the RMC polyclinic management was asked about the reason they chose the current system arrangement, they replied instead that centralizing administration and accounting simplified their management tasks and decreased errors in patient handling. This is a very common mistake from a failure to clarify and identify the value stream as advocated in "Lean." Instead of specifying value from the customer side, the RMC management chooses to look at it from a very different perspective, resulting in an inefficient and ineffective system that is probably causing the Rosa polyclinic to lose a number of unsatisfied customers. As patients enter RMC, they do not really care about the complexity of management procedures, nor how the Rosa clinic management wants to handle the accounting procedures. On the contrary, these patients are more concerned about not receiving their treatment on a timely fashion and having to waste over an hour to be served. This will eventually cause increasing dissatisfaction among patients as the lengthy waiting time may have adverse consequences on some patients who are faced with time-sensitive deteriorating conditions.

The second challenge is that this discussion of the identifying RMC value stream can only be limited to considering the time impact of servicing patients from a single clinic. As observed, the nature of "Lean" analysis can be much more involved and complex, which is beyond the scope of this chapter's contribution given that it requires a comprehensive understanding of all potential sources of waste and efforts to eliminate such waste. In the following section, we therefore discuss the different types of waste inherent in the current RMC system and spell out efforts that can be aimed at decreasing or eliminating such waste.

14.4.3.2 Types of Waste at RMC

With a more transparent understanding of the current value stream of the RMC system, several types of waste "muda" may be readily identified, including:

1. *Overproduction*: The RMC system produces a lot of paperwork that does not add any value to the customer. For example, the copies taken of ID and insurance cards every time a patient returns to the clinic when it can be easily stored and communicated electronically. Similarly, the appointment slip could also have been sent electronically to the clinic. In the near future, with the US Centers for Medicare & Medicaid Services moving towards mandating US hospitals to show "meaningful use" of electronic medical records (EMRs) to be eligible for federal incentives, such waste could be easily trimmed from US hospitals.
2. *Overprocessing*: There is significant waste of this sort in the RMC case; for example, patient information including demographic and visit history information is processed both at the main reception and at the clinic reception. Unifying the location of processing the same information can easily and quickly improve the uptake of the system.
3. *Inventories*: The main source of inventory as presented in our RMC case is the prescription medication ordered by the nearby pharmacy. The pharmacy orders its required supplies in batches without continuous inventory monitoring. This batch processing has two consequences: (a) the unavailability of some needed prescription drugs and the abundance of other unneeded medicine and (b) the expiry of unused medication, causing the pharmacy to waste unused inventories.
4. *Human motion*: In the current RMC value stream, patients are directed to move redundantly from the main reception to the clinic reception; then from the clinic

waiting area to the clinic; and then about 100 m to the pharmacy. For RMC patients in general, and for those suffering particularly from movement-related pain, this workflow contradicts patient perceived value of receiving treatment without undergoing unnecessary pain or suffering. The unnecessary movement can and should be eliminated to improve patient experience.

5. *Waiting*: RMC patients have to wait in many queues: (a) in main and clinic receptions for registration, documents checking and photocopying, service prepayment, and to hand over their appointment slips; (b) in the waiting room area; and (c) in the pharmacy. All these waiting periods do not add value to the patients and can and/or need to be eliminated. In the next section, we will examine some techniques and modifications in the workflow to decrease this waiting time.

Clearly, there is a lot of waste at RMC. This waste decreases the efficiency and efficacy of the system, and does not add value to the patient (customer). In fact, this waste decreases the value provided to patients and increases their suffering instead of relieving it. Therefore, the next logical step is to try to eliminate such waste in an attempt to improve the value added to the patients and to improve system performance as a whole.

14.4.4 Step 3: Creating Flow

Creating flow is a step towards eliminating waste from the value stream so as to form a new continuous flow with no waste, no batch processing, and no queues (Hines et al. 2004). Creating a flow usually requires the enterprise to rethink all of its actions, to extend this thinking behind and beyond its borders, and to come up with new tools and techniques to create the "flow."

In order to do this, the enterprise should focus on the product and/or service itself and the value it provides, while ignoring the boundaries within the enterprise such as departments, functions, and job descriptions. This step is essential in removing obstacles and creating a continuous stream. The final step in creating a flow is to deploy new tools and innovative techniques that replace traditional ones so that producing services or goods can proceed continuously. For example, deploying benchmarking (Camp 1989) and other operation research (OR) techniques as means to eliminating waste in emergency rooms (ERs), which will eventually lead to greater ER efficiency, thereby positively affecting the mortality rate due to overcrowded ERs. A noteworthy example is the effort of Great Ormond Street Hospital for Children to benchmark the Ferrari handover procedures in formula one races in order to decrease mortality rates while moving patients for surgery to the ICUs. These efforts have resulted in decreasing patient errors from 30 % before the study to only 10 % following the study (Catchpole et al. 2007).

Apparently, creating flow also will have a positive impact on the organization employees as a whole. It will not only provide them with a clear goal but also enable them to have a deeper understanding of the entire system. Such an exercise is touted, in fact, to improve employees' satisfaction (Kim 1984), decrease their turnover rates, and further increase their dedication to work. Therefore, creating flow may also be considered as a contributing factor to evolving a learning organization (DeWayne 1993; Garvin 1985), an essential component of enterprise success in the twenty-first century.

14.4.4.1 Creating a Flow for RMC: Step 3

This brings us to the next significant step to implementing lean thinking in RMC. The aim of creating a flow is to eliminate different types of waste and to make the service (treatment) provided to patients flow seamlessly from start to finish.

In order to create an improved flow (or workflow), there are several basic steps that need to be considered. The first one is to keep our focus on the service provided (comfortable and safe treatment in the RMC case) at all times. This must be our primary objective. The second basic step is to think of the RMC system with no boundaries, that is, above and beyond its internal boundaries. Our goal here is to create a "flow"; arguably, therefore, all obstacles hindering that flow should be eliminated, including clinics, departments, and functions. The final step is to redesign and/or restructure the value stream and to think of deploying the appropriate tools and intelligent techniques to eliminate waste in the system.

When these steps are analyzed at the RMC polyclinic, the first functions that need to be broken down (eliminated) and put back together are the various receptions and the cashier. These various RMC service stations offer unnecessary and wasteful functions. Therefore, in remaking RMC, an important action to take is to combine the varying redundant functions into a single location, most appropriately and beneficially to the customer, at the study clinic.

To uptake this change successfully, accounting and administrative training must now be provided to the clinic receptionists in order for them to handle incoming patients (customers) properly. With this change, the nurse at the clinic reception will now receive patients, set their appointments, and collect payments for the services to be rendered. More specifically, each respective RMC clinic reception will now handle only the patients coming to this particular clinic, resulting in serving fewer patients and thus less overall waiting for RMC patients (or customers).

Another positive result from this simple change is that the time patients will now spend waiting before being examined is decreased because the time for administrative tasks performed at the main reception counters is subtracted from the waiting time and the clinic waiting will include patient processing time. This step will also eliminate the need for an appointment slip since it is the clinic reception that creates the appointment and admits patients to the clinic. Evidently, a seemingly very small change in the system, which requires only minimum resources and training, can and has resulted in a huge and impactful improvement in system efficiency. Such a change represents essentially the core of "lean" thinking in particular and QI in general.

Another beneficial change in the RMC system that can be implemented for "Lean" is to replace the copying process by an electronic means to store respective patient ID and insurance cards. This is a more difficult change as it involves changing the regulations set by insurance companies and installing a new RMC enterprise information system (IS) such as a customer relation management (CRM) system (Tan and Payton 2010). However, if patients register themselves the first time, then the clinic receptionist just needs to check their cards in every visit instead of copying their ID cards. This will also eliminate the copying time, paper, as well as purchasing or renting the copying machines. Other viable solutions can also be implemented such as using wireless cards to identify patients, and/or even using of convenient R-codes readable from many mobile devices, which will further decrease processing times. Once the need for improvement is clear, the options are virtually unlimited.

Before exploring the pharmacy issues, we can speculate on gains arising from simplifying the RMC registration system. As the various queues rechannel into a single queue (at the clinic), the revised wait time for RMC patients can now be estimated. Assume that the clinic queue is a standard M/M/1 queue (Gross et al. 2008) we can calculate the waiting time to be around 24 min. This shows that the waiting time for patients until they are being served at the clinic has now reduced a significant 43 % in total wait time, from a previously noted 42–24 min!

Now, we will shift focus to the pharmacy. One major problem patients face here is the distance between the pharmacy and the RMC clinic. Naturally, one solution is to bring the pharmacy closer to the patients, but how? The solution to this challenge has been implemented many times in retail and production industries, that is, having a small local facility (localized pharmacy) inside the RMC close to the clinics. Patients can now go to this local pharmacy to get their prescription filled instead of walking all the way to the main pharmacy. The local pharmacy holds small quantities of different types of prescription medicine and whenever it is about to run out of a medication, the medicine is fetched from the main pharmacy. This approach will save space and the pharmacy can guarantee that any medicine in the main pharmacy can also be made available at the local pharmacy with a small delay in the worst case. Linking the clinic to the pharmacy by an e-prescription system will also help to decrease the wait time at the pharmacy as the prescribed medicine can be prepared at the pharmacy even before patients arrive. Allowing the pharmacists to handle patients from delivering prescription to payments can also eliminate the wait time at the pharmacy cashier.

Figure 14.3 shows the value stream following Step 3, the "flow" creation. As clearly observed, the number of procedures in the value stream is now four instead of eight, which means a 50 % decrease in steps required on top of the decrease in wait time and motion. This level of process simplification (50 % or more) is typical in "Lean" remaking and should be one of the goals when implementing "Lean" strategies.

To create the flow, waste in delivery and information flow was eliminated or decreased by thinking of the system as one stream with no regard to departmental or functional boundaries. Clearly, huge and impactful savings can be gained with seemingly simple changes and without incurring a lot of expenses. Therefore, the goal should always be first to "exploit the system" or make the most of the system before even trying to buy expensive tools or install complex automated systems.

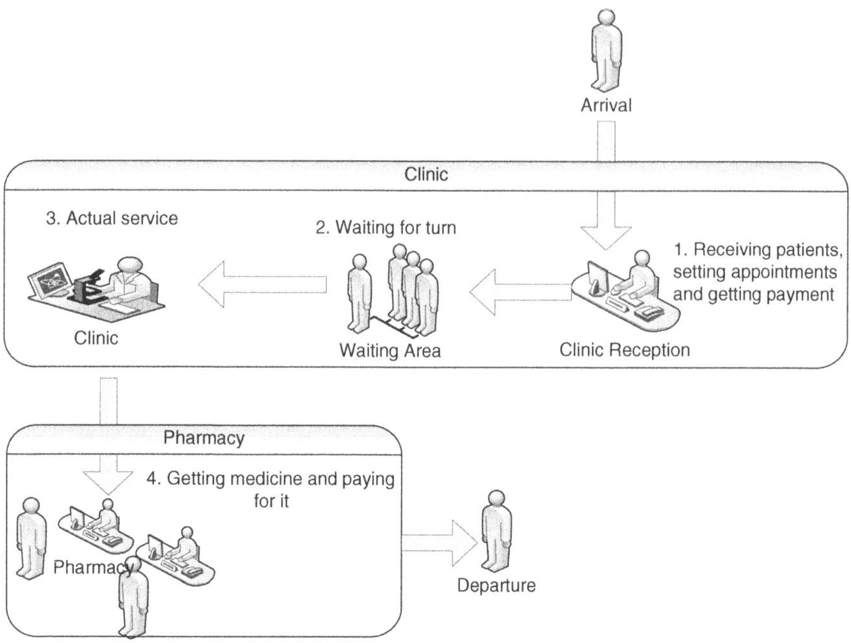

Fig. 14.3 Value stream after creating flow

14.4.5 Step 4: Creating a Pull System

Pull in lean thinking can be defined as not providing a product or a service until "it is requested by the customer" (Womack and Jones 1997). This definition is not limited to the enterprise boundaries, but should extend to include the entire value stream from the production of raw material to the distribution of the product to customers. Such a step is only possible after the flow has been created (Step 3) as creating the "flow" greatly reduces the production time, which is essential for the pull system to succeed.

Like all previous steps, service pulling requires transparency in communications and the open collaboration among all parties in the value stream. Without such a transparency, the pull system is reduced to the boundaries of the enterprise. For instance, when implementing a just-in-time (JIT) inventory as a part of its pull system (Ansari and Modaress 1990), an enterprise will push inventory to its supplier in the value chain if no coordination has been established. With proper coordination, however, the supplier will adjust its production according to the needs of the enterprise and will have no wasteful inventory.

For a hospital setting, creating a pull system for medical supplies requires the complete collaboration between the hospital and its suppliers so as to (1) understand the usage and consumption rates of the supplies and (2) build suitable procedures in order to supply exactly what the hospital needs and no more. This may indeed involve integrating inventory IT/IS of suppliers with those of the hospital's so as to notify suppliers of any shortages and immediate changes to the hospital's needs. Creating such a pull system is likely to decrease the inventory size needed for the hospital to keep its supplies from expiring, and at the same time providing it with just enough supplies to serve its customers.

To illustrate, if a hospital uses 500 blood bags per week, then the supplier should provide this amount to the hospital weekly which will enable the hospital to serve patients and limit its inventory of blood bags. Of course, the supplier must be able to supply additional bags in an emergency or if conditions change unexpectedly, which entails the complete collaboration between the hospital and suppliers of blood bags.

14.4.5.1 Pulling the Service for RMC: Step 4

Pulling means that a product or service is not produced until it is "required by the customer"; it is the most difficult step in "Lean" as it crosses the border of the local system and requires collaboration with providers in the supply chain. A supply chain is the system of entities responsible for moving a product or a service from suppliers to customers. This chain can extend from manufacturing to distribution, and sometimes from natural resources transformation to customers (Womack and Jones 1996). For prescription medicine supplies in the RMC case, we can consider the supply chain to be the manufacturer, the distributor, and the pharmacy filling the prescription drugs to the patients. In the RMC case, the clinics service itself does not offer an opportunity to explain how pulling works; however, the pharmacy provides us with the ability to examine this next step.

While trying to create a "flow" as discussed in the last section, a simple pull system between the local and main pharmacy was suggested and can be created. The local pharmacy keeps a little amount of the most commonly ordered and demanded prescription drugs. When the pharmacy inventories begin to run out of a particular medication, or when a patient orders an "out-of-stock" medication, this needed supply is brought from the main pharmacy in small quantities. This means that patients are actually "pulling" the medicine from the pharmacy. This pull process helps the local pharmacy to keep a variety of routinely ordered prescriptions in a relatively small space so as to satisfy patients' needs on a daily basis. However, only the medication that is available in the main pharmacy is available in the local pharmacy, which makes it important to expand this "pull" system to include even larger-scale pharmaceutical suppliers.

In the current RMC setting, the inventory of the local as well as main pharmacy is still not related to the way RMC patients tend to demand prescription medication on a routine basis. The pharmacy requests a prescription drug when this medicine is almost out and it receives the medication order whenever the distributor is able to deliver. This means that there will be times when the pharmacy has a large quantity of one medicine and at times when the pharmacy lacks a supply of that medicine

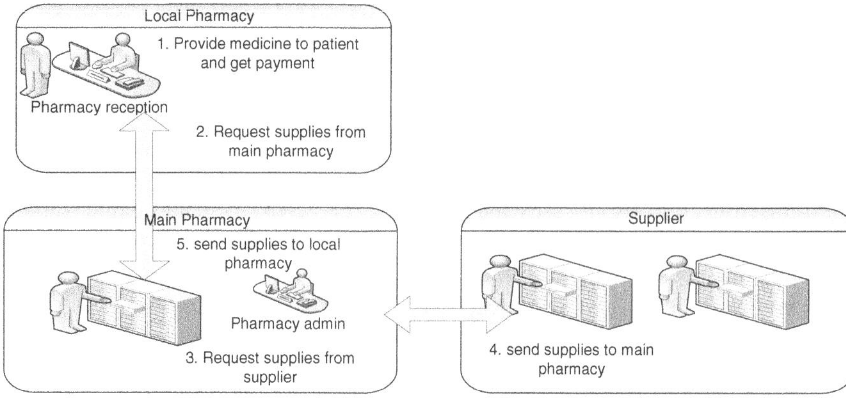

Fig. 14.4 Pulling medicine at the pharmacy supply chain

altogether. For example, the pharmacy can order a large batch of Azithromycin. This medicine will occupy space in the inventory and, due to the lack of clever inventory control and monitoring, the pharmacy either may find its inventory of Azithromycin expired or may not order a new quantity until it runs completely out of the medicine. This situation will obstruct the ability of the pharmacy to plan its purchases and inventory and at the same time will decrease the value that would be provided to patients (customers).

One way to resolve this challenge is to create a 3-step pull system between the large-scale medicine supplier, the main pharmacy, and the local pharmacy. Figure 14.4 shows this triple pull relation. To get the best result from such a pull system, it should be extended to all rings in the supply chain including manufacturers. However, adding medicine manufacturers to our case is likely to add more levels of complexity. Thus, we choose to limit the pull system to the three steps described below.

Figure 14.4 shows the collaborative mechanisms of the "pull" system:

1. First, patients typically get their prescription drug filled from the local pharmacy.
2. If a prescription medication is about to be exhausted and/or is not found at the local pharmacy, the local pharmacy will request a supply from the main pharmacy to cover the requirements for a specified period of time (for example, 2 h or more).
3. If this medicine is about to run out in the main pharmacy, the main pharmacy will in turn order the medicine to cover its requirements for a longer period of time (for example, 48 h or more) from the supplier. This step requires a very active collaboration between the main pharmacy and its suppliers to establish the order–supply mechanism. For example, the main pharmacy may agree to send requests daily, and the pharmacy supplier commits to restock the medicine in no more than 48 h. This agreement is crucial for the success of the pull system.

4. The supplier then sends the medicine to the main pharmacy for restocking in the agreed time.
5. The main pharmacy sends the medicine to the local pharmacy.

The above "pull" system positions the local pharmacy to be responsive to RMC patient needs. By keeping small quantities of medicines, the pharmacy is able to keep a larger variety of medicines, allowing it to serve more patients and decreasing situations where patients have to wait longer than usual to have their prescribed medicine filled. Again, the importance of collaboration across the supply chain is stressed. The pull system should extend from the local pharmacy all the way up to the manufacturer.

To summarize, creating the "pull" system provides the following benefits:

1. Patients will find the medicine they need either without delay or with very little delay
2. The pharmacy will not accumulate inventory, which takes up space and may lead to expiry of unused stocks of some drugs or the lack of space to store other medicine
3. The pharmacy and the distributor will always have timely information about the medicine that is needed, which will facilitate satisfying these needs

14.4.6 Step 5: Perfection

After completing all previous steps, the value and the value stream will become clear to the enterprise, and new types of waste may appear in the new value stream. This provides the enterprise with an opportunity to refine its product further and to move towards "perfecting" that product. Perfection is an endless process, as it recycles following modifications made to the value stream, and the surfacing of new improvement ideas targeted for further implementation. Therefore, perfection is, in and of itself, an unattainable goal; but it keeps the focus on the product and results in a continuous loop to improve its value, which in turn improves the efficiency and inherent value of the enterprise as a whole.

The RMC case will further clarify the idea of "perfection" and how it can improve healthcare enterprise efficiency and inherent value.

14.4.6.1 Perfection for RMC: Step 5

QI and lean thinking represent an endless journey of improvement. Hence, once the RMC polyclinic engages in the cycle of identifying value, specifying value stream, and creating a flow and a pull system, it starts moving into perfecting its system.

Once this cycle is clearly understood, new ways to improve the value emerge naturally. By involving other parties in the supply chain, all the participating entities can work together to improve the value provided to patients (customers). Note that while “perfection” can be pursued infinitely, most of the time, this is clearly and practically infeasible due not only to limited resources, but time commitment that can be invested into the perfection process.

In the RMC case, for example, the local pharmacy was created to be closer to the patients so as to save them time and unnecessary efforts. This solution can be extended to eliminate more of the wait time at the pharmacy by preparing the medicine for patients once their prescription is sent via an e-prescription system to the pharmacy, and/or the medicine can even be delivered to the patients without having them to visit the pharmacy.

Similarly, an alternative to enhancing the RMC registration system is to automate the clinic reception with the use of several self-registration terminals or kiosks that would accept ID cards and insurance cards, check them, and charge patients automatically for the visit. This will improve the service rate for patients and further decrease their wait time. New techniques can also be employed to decrease or eliminate the wait time in the waiting area, for example, by deciding to adopt an accurate appointment system and by providing some form of incentives to motivate patients to use such a system.

When an enterprise gets lured into understanding the value, the value stream, as well as creating flow and pull systems, it will be able to find endless opportunities to further transition the system into “Lean.”

14.5 Case Summary

The RMC case was used to clarify the different principles of “Lean,” starting with identifying the value required from the system along the patient’s point-of-view of providing an affordable, safe, efficient, effective, and comfortable treatment regimen. Then, the value stream was identified focusing on those steps required to create the value that would benefit the patients (customers). Different types of waste can be identified, and new techniques can often be innovated to eliminate such waste.

As a result of the efforts to create a “flow,” we see that the RMC stream value identification process significantly reduces the treatment delivery steps from eight to four, thereby eliminating most of the waste in the system. Moreover, a 3-way “pull” system in the pharmacy supply chain has been suggested to result in improving its inventory system as well as its service to RMC patients. Finally, we noted that to seek further improvements in the system is indefinitely possible if RMC chooses to reach “perfection.” This, in and of itself, is an everlasting process as RMC keeps the focus on identifying new opportunities for transitioning into “Lean.”

Altogether, the RMC case illustrates how “lean” management, if properly conceived and applied, can result in enhancing an organization’s performance, increasing its inherent value to its patients (customers), and enabling it to survive in a dynamic and customer-oriented market.

14.6 Conclusion

In this chapter, the "Lean" management concepts were introduced against the backdrop of the RMC case. In the RMC case, the application of a 5-step "Lean" framework was used to illustrate how to achieve "Lean" for a healthcare enterprise, demonstrating specifically the role that lean thinking can play in improving the quality of healthcare services delivery with a focus on the patient's perspective. Types of waste may differ among healthcare organizations, as well as the environments in which these organizations survive and/or thrive; however, under all circumstances, the 5-step framework of "Lean" can still be effectively applied, especially if it is cleverly integrated into redesigning the current processes of more complex organizations such as health care.

An important lesson to take home while designing a lean project is the change management component of this project. Change will never be easy as it will require a lot of dedication and training at different levels to attain the desired "lean" goals. However, once the project is initiated, there may not seem to be an ending cycle of QI possibilities, and the results are often worth the efforts.

In earlier sections, we presented the benefits of lean thinking, and noted how such thinking can significantly improve the efficiency and effectiveness of an enterprise. Does this, in fact, suggest that lean thinking is the magical answer to many quality challenges and all performance issues faced by today's healthcare organizations? Practically, and especially for complex healthcare systems, the truth is far from that—"Lean" is not a panacea.

14.6.1 Lean Thinking Criticisms

Despite its many benefits, "Lean" thinking has many shortcomings that can obstruct the success of its implementation in many cases. These problems stem typically from the lengthy process to implement "Lean" (e.g., Young and McClean 2008).

Some of lean thinking shortcomings include:

1. *Lack of sensitivity to human aspects*—Lean thinking, because of its history, focuses mainly on improving the workflow with little or no concern to the people who are actually doing the work. For most healthcare organizational settings, improving the value stream may cause healthcare professionals as well as knowledge workers to become overworked and overloaded. This aspect needs to be considered while developing a "Lean" strategy for health care. The availability of adequate resources and a careful consideration for the workload and work habits of healthcare professionals should form parts of a strategic focus in the "Lean" healthcare transitioning strategy.
2. *Inability to cope with variability*—In order to plan a pull system in "Lean," customer demand should be stabilized and continuous (Hines et al. 2004).

Demand variability represents a real obstacle in implementing "Lean"; in the event of high variability, agile techniques (Weber and Wild 2005) have been proposed to cater to more flexible and coping systems.

3. *Difficulty of obtaining buy-in from particular stakeholder groups*—As "Lean" requires the involvement of all entities in identifying the value stream, it is necessary to get buy-in from even those entities, who may not be highly motivated to change. Indeed, it is difficult for certain stakeholders to observe the benefits of "Lean" for them. Such difficulties can often be overcome through extensive training, workshops, and orientation to the people involved in the value stream. Nonetheless, it is important for different stakeholders to know how implementing "Lean" will benefit them personally in the long run.

   Healthcare providers and distributors should be involved in "Lean" orientation and training in order to buy into taking part in implementing "Lean." Successful lean implementations in health care usually involve huge investments in staff training and the need to guide these knowledge workers to realizing the benefits of lean thinking. North Western Memorial hospital "Lean" implementation is one such success story (Graban and Prachand 2010).
4. *High cost associated with lean implementation*—Lean projects must necessarily involve many parties and require changes in many parts of the organization. In our RMC case, the entire workflow of the polyclinic had to be reengineered. This definitely requires significant resources and budget to be sustained for a long time as it is usually uncertain how long a lean project will last. Therefore, it is always better to implement "Lean" strategically as illustrated in the RMC case, and to start by a specific set of goals instead of attempting to improve all value streams at once.

14.6.2 Future Directions for Lean

The main purpose of specifying a strategy is to set direction for the enterprise, and to transform this direction into shorter term goals, initiatives, and projects to execute the strategy (e.g., Evered 1983). In order to incorporate "Lean" thinking into the strategy, an enterprise should focus its efforts on a few, specific "Lean" goals (for example, creating a flow for some of its products). The next step is to create selectively impactful projects to achieve these goals, dedicate enough resources to execute these projects, and finally to set measurable targets for those projects. This process is known as policy deployment (e.g., Lee and Dale 1998), and usually goals are set via this approach.

Specifically, if a hospital strategy is to improve the service provided to its patients, then more specific goals should be articulated such as "decreasing wait times by 50 % in emergency rooms" or "decreasing time spent in ICU rooms by 40 % after operations." After these goals are articulated, "Lean" projects can be initiated for each of these goals where different lean processes are studied and applied. Once the desired results are attained, new goals can then be set.

In summary, "Lean" thinking is a very promising and influential QI approach that has extended behind its original shop-floor mentality to a more strategic focus and from a manufacturing perspective to a wider perspective benefitting wide ranging industries. As competition increased, in the current state of slow economic growth worldwide, we believe that now is the time to think "Lean." Important lessons have been learned and there is always room for more. After all, it takes a village, including academic researchers, practitioners, policymakers, vendors, and administrators to successfully transition a healthcare enterprise into "Lean," satisfying all current and future customers (i.e., patients, payers, and other stakeholders).

References

Ansari, A., & Modaress, B. (1990). *Just-in-time purchasing*. New York, NY: The Free Press.

Ben-Tovim, D., Bassham, J., Bolch, D., et al. (2007). Lean thinking across a hospital: Redesigning care at the Flinders Medical Centre. *Australian Health Review, 31*, 10–15.

Camp, R. C. (1989). *Benchmarking: The search for industry best practices that lead to superior performance*. Milwaukee, WI: ASQ/Quality Resources.

Catchpole, K. R., et al. (2007). Patient handover from surgery to intensive care: Using Formula 1 pit-stop and aviation models to improve safety and quality. *Pediatric Anesthesia, 17*(5), 470–478.

Coronado, R. B., & Antony, J. (2002). Critical success factors for the successful implementation of Six Sigma projects in organizations. *The TQM Magazine, 14*(2), 92–99.

Crosby, P. B. (1979). *Quality is free: The art of making quality certain*. New York: McGraw-Hill.

DeWayne, K. (1993). The fifth discipline: The art and practice of the learning organization: Book review. *Consulting Psychology Journal: Practice and Research, 45*(4), 31–32.

Ellis, R., & Wittington, D. (1993). *Quality assurance in healthcare, a handbook*. London: Edward Arnold.

Evered, R. (1983). So what is strategy? *Long Range Planning, 16*(3), 57–72.

Falan, S. L. (2012). Leading change in healthcare: Transforming organizations using complexity, positive psychology and relationship-centered care. *International Journal of Healthcare Information Systems and Informatics (IJHISI), 7*(2), 59–62.

Garvin, D. A. (1985). *Building a learning organization*. Org Dev & Trng, 6E (Iae), 274.

Graban, M., & Prachand, A. (2010). Hospitalists: Lean leaders for hospitals. *Hospital Medicine, 5*, 317–319.

Gray, J. A. M. (2007). *How to get better value healthcare*. Oxford: Offox Press.

Gross, D., Shortle, J. F., Thompson, J. R., & Harris, C. M. (2008). *Fundamentals of queuing theory* (Series in probability & statistics 4th ed.). New York: Wiley.

Hayward, R. A., & Hofer, T. P. (2001). Estimating hospital deaths due to medical errors preventability is in the eye of the reviewer. *Journal of the American Medical Association, 286*(4), 415–420.

Hines, P., Holweg, M., & Rich, N. (2004). Learning to evolve: A review of contemporary lean thinking. *International Journal of Operations and Production Management, 24*, 994–1011.

Jimmerson, C., Weber, D., & Sobek, D. K. (2005). Reducing waste and errors: Piloting lean principles at intermountain healthcare. *Joint Commission Journal on Quality and Patient Safety, 31*(5), 249–257.

Juran, J. M. (1988). *Juran on planning for quality*. New York, NY: The Free Press.

Kim, C. S., et al. (2010). Hospitalist time usage and cyclicality: Opportunities to improve efficiency. *Journal of Hospital Medicine, 5*(6), 329–334.

Kim, J. S. (1984). Effect of behavior plus outcome goal setting and feedback on employee satisfaction and performance. *Academy of Management Journal, 27*(1), 139–149.
Lee, R. G., & Dale, B. G. (1998). Policy deployment: An examination of the theory. *International Journal of Quality & Reliability Management, 15*(5), 520–540.
Levinson, W. A., & Rerick, R. A. (2002). *Lean enterprise: A synergistic approach to minimizing waste*. Milwaukee, WI: ASQ Press.
Liker, J. (2004). *The Toyota way: 14 principles from the world's greatest manufacturer*. New York: McGraw Hill.
Nelson-Peterson, D., & Leppa, C. (2007). Creating an environment for caring using lean principles of the Virginia mason production system. *Journal of Nursing Administration, 37*, 287–294.
Ohno, T. (1988). *Toyota Production System, beyond large scale production*. Portland, OR: Productivity Press.
Powell, T. C. (1995). Total quality management as competitive advantage: A review and empirical study. *Strategic Management Journal, 16*(1), 15–37.
Revere, L., & Black, K. (2003). Integrating Six Sigma with total quality management: A case example for measuring medication errors. *Journal of Healthcare Management, 48*(6), 377–391.
Shen, Y.-C., & Hsia, R. Y. (2011). Association between ambulance diversion and survival among patients with acute myocardial infarction. *Journal of the American Medical Association, 305*(23), 2440–2447.
Simons, D., & Taylor, D. (2007). Lean thinking in the UK red meat industry: A systems and contingency approach. *International Journal of Production Economics, 106*(1), 70–81.
Sirio, C., Segel, K., Keyser, D., Harrison, E., Lloyd, J., & Weber, R. (2007). Pittsburgh regional healthcare initiative: A systems approach for achieving perfect patient care. *Health Affairs, 22*(5), 157–165.
Tan, J., & Payton, F. (2010). *Adaptive health management information systems: Concepts, cases, & practical applications*. Gaithersburg, MD: Aspen Publishers.
Walton, M. (1986). *Quality and me: Lessons from an evolving life* (pp. 138–139). New York: Penguin Group.
Weber, B., & Wild, W. (2005). *Towards the agile management of business processes*. New York: Springer.
Womack, L., & Jones, D. (1996). *Lean thinking: Banish waste and create wealth in your corporation*. New York: Simon & Schuster.
Womack, J., & Jones, D. (1997). *Lean thinking*. London: Simon& Schuster.
Womack, J. P., Jones, D. T., & Roos, D. (1990). *The machine that changed the world*. New York: Rawson Associates.
Young, T., & McClean, S. (2008). A critical look at lean thinking in healthcare. *Quality & Safety in Health Care, 17*, 382–386.

Chapter 15
Lean Thinking and Customer Focus: Patient Centered Perspectives on Hospital Quality

Anke Simon and Nilmini Wickramasinghe

Abstract *Objectives*: In order to be able to make a differentiated choice between healthcare providers, people require information about their quality. An understanding of patient needs and preferences is crucial in providing helpful information regarding hospital quality. This study is the first comprehensive investigation in this field in Germany, focused on patient involvement in, and preferences for, information on hospital quality.

Methods: A patient involvement scale was developed to measure the subjective interest in hospital information. To analyse what particular information on hospital quality patients prefer a relatively new variant of choice experiment a Best–Worst Scaling (BWS) task was integrated into the questionnaire. Goodness of fit tests show good constructs quality. A total of 276 respondents participated including hospital patients and healthy persons (response rate 71 %, representative sample regarding the variables age, gender and social class).

Results: The analysis showed a high involvement in information regarding hospital quality. A second-order confirmative factor analysis revealed three reliable components: general importance of information (0.70), need of certainty (0.85) and need of participation (0.57). In the measurement of information preferences (35 attributes/ quality indicators), patients rated indicators of structure quality as the most important attributes. Information about process quality was moderately relevant from the

---

A. Simon
Baden-Wuerttemberg Cooperative State University, Stuttgart, Germany

N. Wickramasinghe, Ph.D. (✉)
Epworth HealthCare & Department of BITL & HIRi, RMIT University, GPO Box 2476, Melbourne, VIC 3001, Australia
e-mail: nilmini.wickramasinghe@rmit.edu.au

N. Wickramasinghe et al. (eds.), *Lean Thinking for Healthcare*, Healthcare Delivery in the Information Age, DOI 10.1007/978-1-4614-8036-5_15,

patients' point of view. Objective results of outcome quality were more important for patients than subjective quality indicators. We identified two patient clusters (two-step cluster analysis): outcome-orientated and service-orientated patients.

Conclusion: Both the assessment of patient involvement in hospital quality information and the measurement of patient preferences in order to rank patients' perception provide important insights into information needs of patients. The BWS experiment is useful to investigate patient preferences, particularly in research designs with a larger number of items and a focus of the relative ranking of complete attributes (not just levels within attributes).

15.1 Introduction

Ultimately healthcare delivery must provide benefits to the patient else no matter how good it is if the patient is not satisfied to a large extent the process has not realized its goal. Today, there is growing concern globally about the lack of patient centeredness in many healthcare contexts such as inpatient and outpatient care. One way to address this and simultaneously ensure heightened quality of care is to embrace and incorporate various aspects of lean thinking. The following then serves to illustrate how a patient-centric perspective can be combined with lean thinking principles to facilitate the delivery of better quality, patient-centered healthcare delivery.

15.2 Lean Thinking and Hospital Quality

Lean thinking (often called "Lean") is a quality improvement technique that has been implemented with great success in many industries especially in the manufacturing area. Notable examples include Toyota and Boeing Integral to the principles and practices of a lean approach is to enable high quality and effective and efficient process to ensue and eliminate all waste. Globally, healthcare delivery especially in the OECD countries is facing a tremendous cost pressure. Faced with escalating healthcare costs, governments are forced to re-examine how it might be possible to deliver quality healthcare that is also effective and efficient. Such a scenario appears the perfect context for trying to apply Lean thinking principles to facilitate a superior state. And thus we witness the application of lean principles and practices into various healthcare contexts. To do this successfully, it is necessary to understand and at times refine for the nuances of healthcare. Given that at its core Lean thinking is founded on a process management philosophy which has its roots in manufacturing and technology, it is also appropriate in today's healthcare environments as healthcare is currently embracing various forms of IS/IT and e-health solutions.

15.3 Value

A significant component of Lean thinking is the concept of value: the theoretical concept of value, the measurement of value, and the tangible processes behind delivering value (Majdi 2012). In trying to create and/or increase value a key aspect of Lean thinking is concerned with the elimination of seven key wastes (Caldwell 2005; Cross 2009). The seven wastes of Lean thinking translated into healthcare include (Caldwell 2005; Cross 2009) (1) overproduction (e.g. ordering of duplicate tests), (2) wasting time (e.g. patients waiting for treatments), (3) waste of stock on hand (e.g. medications and other items that are stored but not used and then must be disposed of), (4) waste of movement (e.g. time spent walking from one location to another), (5) waste of defective products (e.g. misinformation or recording of wrong information on patient record), (6) waste in transportation (e.g. moving patient unnecessarily) and waste in processing (e.g. duplication of forms and redundant capture of information).

Thus, a core principle of Lean thinking is that the elimination of waste is required in order to achieve both real and potential value. Further, the recovering of this value can present itself in the form of saved costs or other tangibles. Another key concept in Lean thinking is being customer focused which is especially relevant to healthcare and today has even led to the development of consumer health informatics (Manos et al. 2006; Thrall 2008; Toyota Manufacturing Kentucky, Inc 2003; Toyota Motor Corporation 2009; United States Army 2009). However at its simplest level a patient-centric perspective must be considered at all times when applying Lean thinking to healthcare contexts. If this is the case, then patient satisfaction translates easily into high quality, reduction of errors and the realizing of quality healthcare outcomes (Gabow et al. 2008) and hence Lean thinking dictates that processes and methods must be efficiently optimized with the needs of patients in mind in order for organizations to be fully effective.

Another important aspect in Lean thinking is the identification of waste through root cause analysis (Majdi 2012). Root cause analysis in Lean involves the 5-Whys approach (Majdi 2012; Toyota Manufacturing Kentucky, Inc 2003; Toyota Motor Corporation 2009; United States Army 2009), i.e. a systematic method that rapidly identifies root causes and aides in determining the relationship between multiple root causes.

The following is an example of a 5-Whys exercise used in a hypothetical hospital setting (Majdi 2012):

(Q1) Why are patients being diverted to neighbouring hospitals?

(A1) Because wait times for our hospital are exceeding industry norms.

(Q2) Why are our wait times exceeding industry norms?

(A2) Because patient volume is exceeding capacity.

(Q3) Why is patient volume exceeding capacity?

(A3) Because not enough hospital beds are available.

(Q4) Why are not enough hospital beds available?

(A4) Because hospital patients are not being discharged efficiently.

(Q5) Why are hospital patients not being discharged efficiently?

(A5) Because ER staff is not following best practices for proper discharge.

> In this example, waste in the throughput process comes from incorrect processing. Once hospital management determines the root cause they can implement further training, ensure compliance with existing standards, or eliminate other barriers. In this case the hospital might consider implementing a training program to ensure that ER staff is following best practices for patient discharge. The hospital might also conduct additional 5-Whys analyses to uncover other problem as. Once root causes of waste are uncovered, the elimination of waste or other related action plans can be executed. (Majdi 2012)

We apply root cause analysis and the ideas of Lean thinking in the following sections to be able to understand patient needs and preferences in order to design a high quality, value adding healthcare setting.

15.4 Study Design

The objective of the study presented here is to understand the current state of information needs on hospital quality, and to provide a descriptive picture of the present situation from the subjective perspective of consumers. Furthermore, the aim of the investigation is to analyse and validate the usability of the implemented measures.

We developed a multidimensional approach (Fig. 15.1). Our comprehensive concept includes the measurement of information involvement, information preferences, various influence factors and consumer clusters. The study results presented and discussed here focus on the information involvement and information preferences on hospital quality. A detailed description of the study protocol and the complete results has been published elsewhere (Simon 2010).

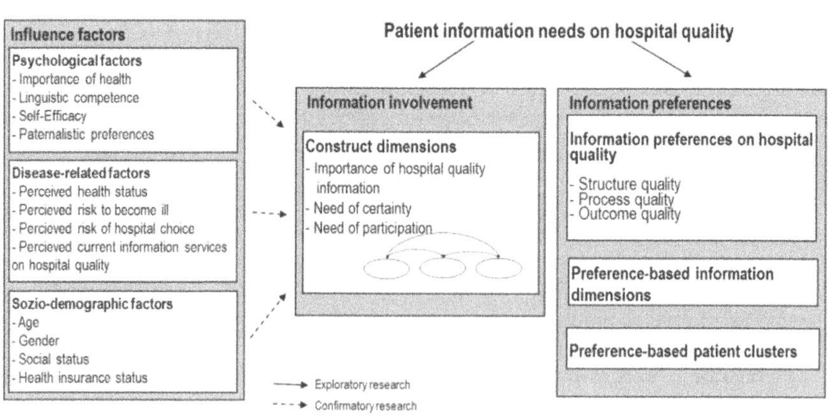

Fig. 15.1 Study design

15.5 Methods

15.5.1 Participants and Data Collection

The exploratory cross-sectional study included current patients of a mayor hospital as well as normal inhabitants of the State of Baden-Wurttemberg (latter named in the presented study as *potential patients*). We selected participants according to the following inclusion criteria: 18 years or older, willing to participate in the study, physically and mentally able to participate.

Regarding the subgroup of hospital patients, we covered all clinical departments but excluded intensive care as well as palliative care wards due to ethical concerns. The recruitment of normal citizens (potential patients) was based on various areas of normal live, i.e. employees of a company, members of a protestant church community, catholic student association and consumers of a fitness studio. The study was conducted in January, February and March 2008.

15.5.2 Questionnaire

We developed a multi-topic questionnaire with an embedded choice-based experiment. The measurement tools were administered as self-reported paper-and-pencil questionnaires.

15.5.2.1 Involvement Scale

A literature search revealed sufficient and often used involvement measurements for consumer goods (exemplarily Zaichkowsky 1994; Laurent and Kampferer 1985; Jain and Srinivasan 1990) but failed to identify a validated instrument specifically addressing the information involvement on hospital quality or other health-related information.

The review of existing involvement theories and literature in health science and information behaviour guided the composition and content of the new measure. We followed the theoretical assumption regarding involvement as a multidimensional construct rather than simple direct measures (Laurent and Kampferer 1985; Simon 2010, p. 103f). After a pre-test the final involvement scale comprised ten items on three a priori defined dimensions: (general) importance, need of certainty and need of participation. The items were to be rated on a five-point Likert-scale. The original version of the involvement questionnaire is available from the author on request.

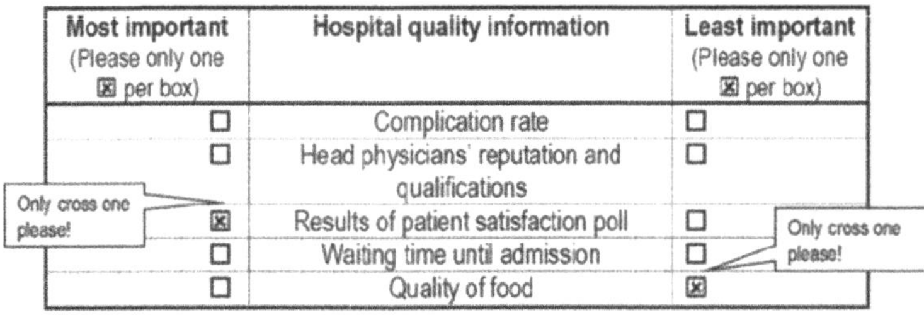

Fig. 15.2 BWS task example: when considering hospital quality information, among the five attributes shown here, which is the most and least important?

15.5.2.2 Best–Worst Scaling

Over the last 2 decades, choice or trade-off experiments already well known in market research have also become a popular method in healthcare research for eliciting patient, consumer and community preferences. A relatively new variant of choice-based experiments the BWS task, grounded in random utility theory (Flynn et al. 2007; Marley and Louviere 2005), has recently gained popularity in health service research. In surveys employing standard rating scales or importance scales usually respondents find it very easy but they do tend to deliver results which indicate that everything is *quite important*. BWS tasks forces participants to make choices between options. One example is shown in Fig. 15.2. The task consists of a list of item sets (boxes). In each task, respondents were simply asked to identify the most and least important item.

The BWS task has been shown to be less cognitively demanding than choosing between complete profiles, an important aspect considering hospital patients. Moreover the BWS experiment can provide information on the relative ranking of complete attributes (second study question) not just levels within attributes which is not available in standard discrete choice experiments.

In the study presented here, our aim was to design and administer a BWS experiment to analyse information preferences on hospital quality from the subjective perspectives of patients.

First of all, we conducted a comprehensive search to identify potential attributes on hospital quality based on the data sources of pubmed and manual search (1997–2007). In total 29 information services on hospital quality, i.e. internet portals, reports and benchmark publication in Germany and other countries could be found. A detailed overview as synopsis is published elsewhere (Simon 2010).

An iterative content analysis (Mayring 2000) was conducted to identify 35 potentially relevant quality indicators (Table 15.1). According to the theory of information economics based on the principles of asymmetric information and quality uncertainty affecting the consumer information search behaviour, we separated all identified attributes on hospital quality in search, experience and credence qualities (Nelson 1970; Darby and Karni 1973; Adler 1996). We included all indicators associated with search qualities (features and characteristics can be evaluated before

Table 15.1 Hospital quality information—35 BWS items

Age of physicians	Professional qualifications of nursing staff/care personnel—qualification, training, competence, expertise
Availability of a patient advocate/patient representative in the hospital, who can be contacted in case of problems and questions	Professional qualifications of the doctors—qualification, training, competence, expertise
Availability of diagnostic technologies—e.g. equipment in the operating theatre, X-ray, laboratory	Quality accreditation of the hospital by independent institutions—quality accreditation as a kind of seal of approval, comparable with the TÜV or Stiftung Warentest
Comfort in patient rooms—e.g. number of beds per room, telephone, TV, toilet	Quality of food—e.g. number of menus available, opportunity of free choice and compilation for the patient
Cooperation between the hospital and other health service partners—e.g. with the treating doctor/family doctor, other hospitals, rehabilitation	Rate of complications—proportion of patients, who had complications during the treatment (e.g. infections after operation, unexpected side effects of medication)
Cooperation with self-supporting groups	Rate of recommendations of practicing doctors—e.g. survey of general physicians, family doctors and specialists once a year, where they would be treated themselves or family members
Costs for additional/optional services—e.g. treatment by head/senior physician, single room or double room, additional room service	Rate of unplanned re-admissions—proportion of patients who had to be hospitalized again
Distance from home/access to the hospital	Reputation and qualification/expertise of the chief/head physician
Efficiency/effectivity—use of cost-effective treatment methods for the same quality of treatment	Research activities—research of new interventions and treatment methods as well as publications of the results in medical journals
Evaluation results of the hospital by/through self-supporting groups—e.g. evaluation of the hospital by/through self-help groups by an annual survey (experienced, active patients)	Results of consumer/patient satisfaction surveys—e.g. anonymous evaluation of the hospital through/by patients after discharge by a satisfaction questionnaire, usually using school grades from 1 to 5
Hospital facilities—e.g. cafeteria, shop, library, prayer room, smoking room, park	Sanitation and hygiene—e.g. hygiene standard
Length of the distances within the hospital—ways to walk in and between the hospital buildings	Size of the hospital—e.g. number of beds, number of special departments
Mortality rate—proportion of patients, who died during the treatment	Specialized treatment options and services—specialization on certain diseases, range of services, outpatient treatment possibilities, alternative therapy offerings, etc.
Number and type of medical malpractice/treatment errors—medical malpractice/errors with serious/severe consequences for the patient	Success rate—proportion of patients with good treatment success (e.g. healing, restoration of performance/physical capacity, pain reduction, improvement of condition)

(continued)

Table 15.1 (continued)

Number and type of patient complaints	Time management during the treatment—morning wake-up times, frequency and duration of contacts with the doctor, number of patients per employee, on-time delivery of diagnostic- and treatment activities
Number of patients (already been) treated with my disease/illness	Waiting time during the treatment—e.g. at the admission, waiting time before the X-ray or ECG, at the discharge
Number or frequency of specific/certain medical interventions or specific treatment methods—e.g. number of bypass operations on the heart per year	Waiting time for admission to the hospital—waiting time in weeks from the statement/finding, that hospitalization is necessary until admission
Personal, individual reports/letters/stories of patients about events and experiences in the hospital (e.g. published on the internet)	

purchase or consumption) and excluded attributes related to experience qualities (quality or features are difficult to observe in advance) or credence qualities (whose utility impact is merely impossible for the consumer to ascertain).

A BWS design was computer-based created with 21 sets, five items per set, three item iterations and three BWS versions, fulfilling well the criteria of frequency balance, orthogonality, connectivity and positional balance (Cohen 2003; Chrzan and Patterson 2006). The BWS tasks were incorporated into a paper-and-pencil questionnaire. An introduction text was provided to present the participants the hypothetical offer of a new information service on hospital quality. A short description as well as an included clear example made them familiar with the experiment. A list with all quality indicators are presented as appendix in case additional explanations were needed (Table 15.1).

The original version of the BWS tasks is available from the authors on request.

15.5.3 Statistical Analysis

Descriptive statistics, reliability analysis, exploratory factor analysis (EFA), *t*-test and two-step cluster analysis were performed with the Statistical Package for the Social Sciences (SPSS), version 16.0. Structure equation model and second-order confirmatory factor analysis (CFA) was computed in AMOS, version 16.0. The software MaxDiff by Sawtooth, version 2.0, was used to create orthogonal BWS designs. A hierarchical Bayes model was estimated to compute the preference structure. Utility (preference) scores were calculated. Significance was set at 5 % level ($p<0.05$).

15.6 Results

15.6.1 Study Population

433 questionnaires could be distributed. 307 participants answered the questionnaire; a very good response rate of 71 % was achieved (Table 15.2). Not all questionnaires could be included in the analysis mainly because of incomplete answers. The effective sample size consists of 276 cases (64 %). Expectantly the drop out quote in the subgroup of hospital patients was higher (15 %) than the rate of incomplete questionnaires within the subgroup of healthy participants (4 %).

Chi-square tests were conducted to analyse statistically significant differences between study sample and population data. Expected values were derived from the population data for each demographic variable. The study sample was representative regarding the variables age (l^2 8.088, d*f* 4, $p<0.05$), gender (l^2 2.595, d*f* 1, $p<0.05$) and social class (l^2 5.786, d*f* 2, $p<0.05$). Private insured patients were slightly overrepresented.

15.6.2 Information Involvement on Hospital Quality

15.6.2.1 Factor Analysis

First, an EFA (principal components) was performed including the ten items dealing with (general) importance, need of certainty and need of participation. Kaiser's rule was used to extract components with an eigenvalue greater than 1. The a priori defined three involvement dimensions fit very well the components derived from EFA considering item-component loadings of >0.40 as significant. The highly significant Bartlett test and a Kaiser-Meyer-Olkin (KMO) value of 0.820 (as well as very good KMO values regarding each item) showed an excellent goodness of fit. A varimax-rotation revealed three factors with eigenvalues >1 explaining 67.5 % of the total variance. The factor *need of certainty* accounts for 27.41 % of the variances followed by the factors *importance* (21.76 %) and *need of participation* (18.36 %).

Second, a CFA was performed. We employed the aspiration levels by Homburg and colleagues including global and local goodness of fit statistics (Homburg et al. 2008, p. 288).

Table 15.2 Participation rate

	Distributed questionnaires	Participated	Completed questionnaires
Hospital patients	193	167	142
Potential patients	240	139	134
Total	433	306	276

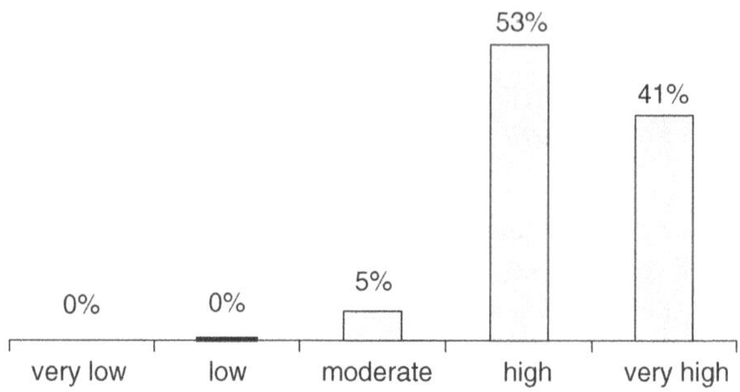

Fig. 15.3 Distribution of information involvement

Fig. 15.4 Second-order CFA

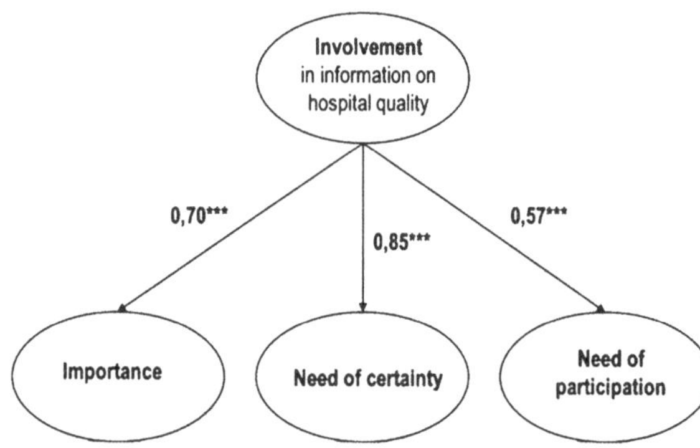

Table 15.3 shows the result of the CFA as well as related psychometric properties. The model fitted the data very well. Furthermore a high discriminant validity of the three involvement scale factors based on the Fornell-Larcker criterion was found. Finally to examine the content validity of the developed involvement scale, we used a direct involvement measurement adapted by Zaichkowsky (Zaichkowsky 1994). We found significantly high correlations between the two scales (® coefficient 0.71, $p<0.001$).

15.6.2.2 Descriptive Results and Second-Order CFA

Figure 15.3 describes the distribution of information involvement on hospital quality within the participants. The vast majority show a high and very high involvement in information on hospital quality. The mean values of the two subgroups were compared using a *t*-test and a Kolmogorov-Smirnov test. We identified no significant differences between the two subgroups of participants (hospital patients and healthy participants).

We conducted a second-order CFA to find out more about the motivation or reason behind the information involvement (Fig. 15.4). The model fits the empiric date

Table 15.3 CFA and psychometric properties of the involvement scales

Involvement construct with three dimensions							
Goodness of fit							
l^2/df	84.625/32	CFI	0.95				
		GFI	0.95	(0.99)			
RMSEA	0.077	AGFI	0.91	(0.98)			
	Indicator reliability	C.R.	Item-to-total correlation	Cronbach alpha	Variance explained (EFA)	Factor-reliability	DEV
Factor 1: Importance							
Information on hospital quality is very important to me	0.72	9.44	0.71				
I'm really very interested in information on hospital quality	0.67	9.40	0.67	0.79	0.70	0.81	0.74
I couldn't care less about information on hospital quality	0.35	*	0.53				
Factor 2: Need of certainty							
Information on hospital quality provides certainty whether the hospital will meet my needs	0.53	*	0.63				
Information on hospital quality provides help for orientation between different alternative hospitals and treatment options	0.65	12.36	0.72	0.85	0.69	0.85	0.66
Information on hospital quality helps me to better understand my doctor's advice about the right hospital	0.53	11.32	0.65				
Information on hospital quality helps me to make an informed decision about the right hospital	0.67	12.52	0.76				
Factor 3: Need of participation							
The decision about the right hospital should be a shared decision between patient and doctor	0.44	*	0.45				
I would like to have real influence when it comes to choose the right hospital	0.31	6.28	0.45	0.65	0.59	0.65	0.51
I would like to participate in the decision about the right hospital	0.42	6.58	0.48				

ML-estimation/()–ULS-estimation
*Reference indicator

well ($p<0.001$). Besides the general importance of hospital information and the willingness for participation, surprisingly, the need of certainty showed the highest factor loadings. We conclude that the need of certainty—just to know whether the hospital might be good, outstanding or low performing—is highly important. And besides the other factors, a good predictor for the participants' information involvement on hospital quality. Our results reflect common theories of coping. Typically individuals in stressful situations use two types of coping mechanism: problem-orientated and emotion-orientated coping strategies. Literature findings indicate that in stressful events related to health problems individuals seek predominantly information to maintain their intra-psychic balance (Pakenham 1999; Vitaliano et al. 1990; Taylor 2003). Our results related to hospital quality indicate that even in case individuals with less interest in actively shared decision making nonetheless might be very interested in information on hospital quality to improve their certainty as a factor of intra-psychic well-being.

15.6.3 Information Preferences on Hospital Quality

The subjective priority scores for the 35 information items on hospital quality are presented in Table 15.4. First a count analysis is performed on the BWS data. The relationship between the square root of the ratio (most count divided by least count) and the most counts appear to be linear with an R^2 of 84 %. This result confirms the possibility of using the BW ratio as an estimate of the position attributes on the scale of importance. This is consistent with the international literature on the BWS method.

Second the BWS data are analysed with probability model (estimated by hierarchical Bayes method). The percent certainty value of 0.564 and the mean root likelihood of 0.507 showed a sufficient goodness of fit. We found a strong linear relationship between the hierarchical Bayes (HB) estimates and the (most–least) score with an R^2 of 98 %. The HB analysis provided a ranking list as well as utility scores. First we conducted a ranking over all utility scores. The top ten information preferences on hospital quality consist of:

1. Physicians' qualifications
2. Specialized treatment options and services
3. Nurses' qualifications
4. Availability of diagnostic technologies
5. Sanitation and hygiene
6. Treatment success rate
7. Number of treated patients (with a certain disease)
8. Quality accreditations from independent institutions
9. Number and frequency of certain diagnostic and therapeutic treatments
10. Head physicians' reputation and qualifications

Table 15.4 Information preferences on hospital quality—BWS results

		Total counts			Calculated		
Nr.	Item	Most	Least	Most–least	Sqrt (most/least)	HB score	Rang HB score
1	Mortality rate	58	159	−101	0.60	1.663	25
2	Number and type of medical malpractice/treatment errors	177	45	132	1.98	4.034	12
3	Success rate	252	45	207	2.37	4.658	6
4	Rate of complication	153	59	94	1.61	3.812	13
5	Rate of unplanned re-admissions	64	199	−135	0.57	1.947	22
6	Efficiency/effectivity	23	305	−282	0.27	0.830	32
7	Evaluation results of the hospital by/through self-supporting groups	37	262	−225	0.38	1.243	29
8	Results of consumer/patient satisfaction surveys	103	127	−24	0.90	2.550	19
9	Rate of recommendations of practicing doctors	199	93	106	1.46	3.796	14
10	Number and type of patient complaints	91	208	−117	0.66	1.898	23
11	Quality accreditation by independent institutions	310	55	255	2.37	4.455	8
12	Personal, individual reports/letters/stories of patients	79	278	−199	0.53	1.563	26
13	Professional qualifications of the doctors	552	2	550	16.61	5.566	1
14	Reputation and qualification/expertise of the chief/head physician	236	65	171	1.91	4.235	10
15	Professional qualifications of nursing staff	342	10	332	5.85	5.149	3
16	Age of physicians	17	411	−394	0.20	0.398	35
17	Research activities	112	133	−21	0.92	2.739	17
18	Specialized treatment options and services	447	17	430	5.13	5.242	2
19	Availability of medical technologies	291	21	270	3.72	5.005	4
20	Number of patients (already been) treated with my disease/illness	271	70	201	1.97	4.483	7
21	Number or frequency of certain medical interventions or treatment methods	249	36	213	2.63	4.380	9
22	Distance from home/access to the hospital	78	261	−183	0.55	1.743	24
23	Size of the hospital	22	396	−374	0.24	0.516	33
24	Availability of a patient advocate/patient representative	36	298	−262	0.35	1.050	30
25	Cooperation with self-supporting groups	25	264	−239	0.31	0.906	31

(continued)

Table 15.4 (continued)

		Total counts			Calculated		
Nr.	Item	Most	Least	Most–least	Sqrt (most/least)	HB score	Rang HB score
26	Costs (out of pocket) for additional/optional services	57	211	−154	0.52	1.423	28
27	Quality of food	59	225	−166	0.51	1.507	27
28	Hospital facilities	180	28	152	2.54	4.048	11
29	Comfort in patient rooms	73	150	−77	0.70	2.120	21
30	Waiting time until admission	134	111	23	1.10	3.197	16
31	Length of the distances within the hospital	16	420	−404	0.20	0.436	34
32	Cooperation between the hospital and other health service partners	119	133	−14	0.95	2.550	20
33	Time management during the stay	176	122	54	1.20	3.341	15
34	Waiting time during the stay	119	116	3	1.01	2.636	18
35	Sanitation and hygiene	201	10	191	4.48	4.879	5

On the opposite site of the ranking with clearly low priority can be found the attributes *age of physicians, length of the distances within the hospital, hospital size* and *efficiency/effectivity* of the hospital.

Second we identified all information items above average mean utility score (2.709) and categorized them according to the quality dimensions by Donabedian in structure, process and outcome quality (Donabedian 1980).

Over all information on structure quality was highly important for the participants (Fig. 15.5). Within all structural items, qualification of physicians and nurses as well as health service characteristics has the highest priority score. Less relevant were comfort attributes, i.e. patient rooms or food quality.

Information on process quality was moderately relevant. The most important here was information about *sanitation and hygiene* followed by *time management during the stay* and *waiting time until admission* (Fig. 15.6).

We analysed also outcome quality preferences and found clear but highly different opinions (Fig. 15.7). Interestingly the respondents prefer strongly objective information, i.e. success rates, accreditation results, information on medical incidents or complication rates to subjective quality indicators. The preference analysis showed clearly if patients have the chance to get these information they are less interested in subjective indicators like results of consumer satisfaction surveys or narrative patient stories. The most relevant attribute within the information on subjective quality was the recommendation rate of GPs.

As mentioned before, we addressed two subgroups of participants—hospital patients and potential patients (normal citizens). In the third step of our investigation, we analysed significant differences with a *t*-test. The comparison is shown in (Table 15.5). We found only a few significant differences between both subgroups

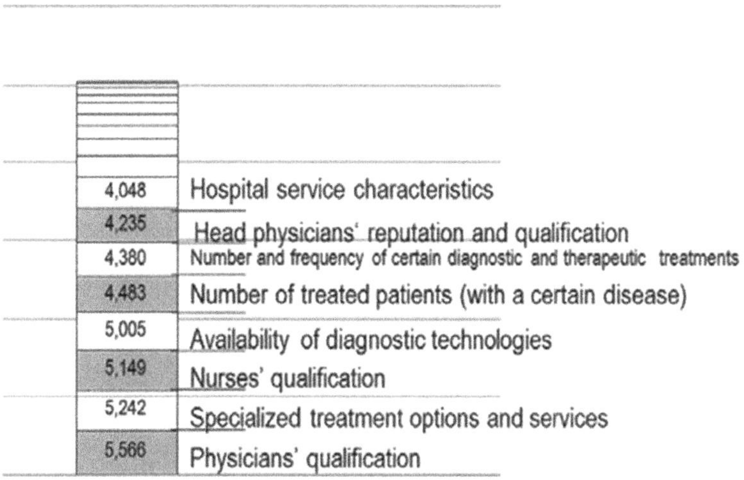

Fig. 15.5 Information preferences on structure quality. HB/utility scores in reverse order

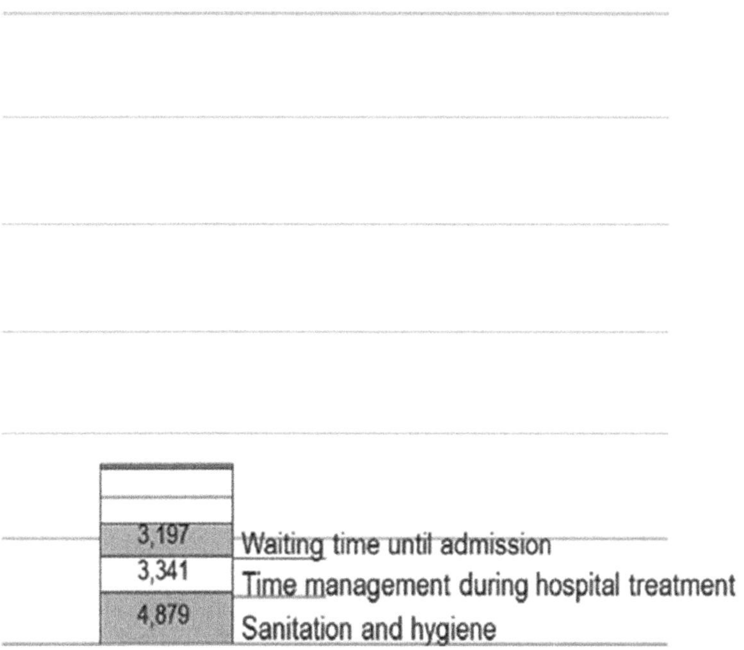

Fig. 15.6 Information preferences on process quality. HB/utility scores in reverse order

(7 of 35 items). Hospital patients prefer significantly more information about the reputation and qualification of the head physician, research activities, time management during the stay, waiting time for admission and the hospital's efficiency and effectivity. Potential patients are more interested in information about patient complaints and the results of quality accreditations.

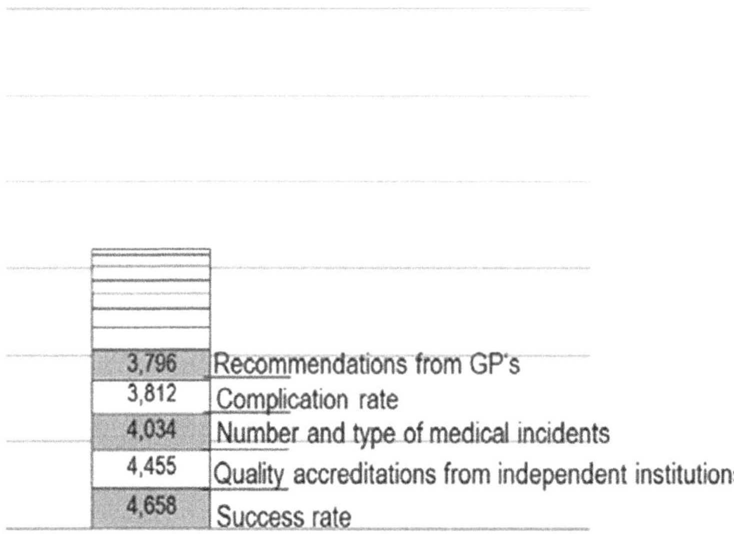

Fig. 15.7 Information preferences on outcome quality. HB/utility scores in reverse order

Table 15.5 Significant differences between the two subgroups of participants

Item nr.	Quality indicator	HB score hospital patients	HB score potential patients	*t*
6	Efficiency/effectivity	1.006	0.658	3.271
10	Number and type of patient complaints	1.653	2.138	−2.600
11	Quality accreditation by independent institutions	4.177	4.726	−3.613
14	Reputation and qualification of the head physician	4.529	3.949	3.242
17	Research activities	3.074	2.412	3.728
33	Time management during the treatment	3.653	3.037	2.913
34	Waiting time for admission to the hospital	3.013	2.267	3.550

In the fourth step of our BWS study, we summarized all most preferred quality information (mean utility score above average 2.709) and ended up with a total of 70 % information preferences on hospital quality:

- Structure quality 38 %
- Process quality 11 %
- Outcome quality 21 %

That means 70 % of patient information preferences could already be meet if the most relevant information for patients would be provided sufficiently.

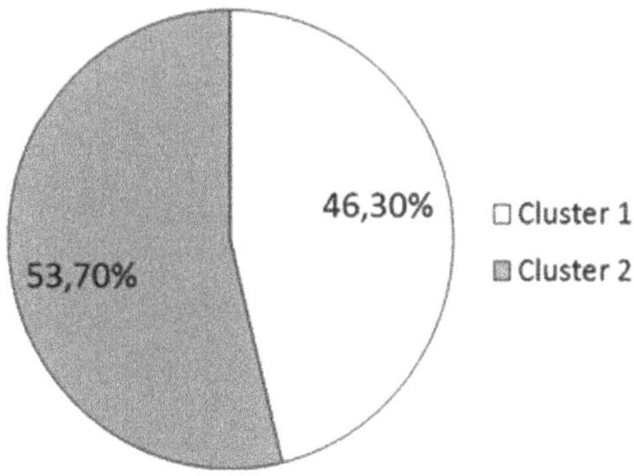

Fig. 15.8 Cluster size

15.6.3.1 Preference-Based Patient Clusters

Data clustering is a method that can group classes of objects with similar characteristics. Clustering is often confused with classification, but there is a major difference between them, namely, when classifying, the objects are assigned to pre-defined classes, whereas in the case of clustering, those classes must be empirically defined too.

The algorithm of the two-step analysis groups the observations in clusters, using the approach criterion. The procedure uses an agglomerative hierarchical clustering method. Compared to classical methods of cluster analysis, the two-step method employed here offers several advantages, i.e. the optimal number of clusters can be determined automatically (based on empirical evidence). Therefore the common practice of a priori defined clusters often related to merely hypothetically content-based grouping can be avoided (Jensen 2008, p. 349ff).

All 35 utility scores (HB estimates) regarding patients' information preferences were included. First, we choose Akaike information criterion (AIC) to determine the number of clusters. The results obtained using Bayesian information criterion (BIC) are not different from those obtained with AIC. No outliners were to handle with.

The lowest AIC coefficient indicated a maximum of six clusters, according to the two-step algorithm, the optimal number of clusters is two, because the largest ratio of distances showed clearly two clusters.

As shown in Fig. 15.8 nearly half of the study population belongs to each of both clusters. Moreover we found significant differences in various information preferences (Fig. 15.9). In cluster one (named by *outcome-orientated patients*) respondents preferred clearly more objective as well as subjective outcome quality indicators, i.e. incident rates, complication rates, unplanned re-admission, patient complaints or results of consumer satisfaction surveys. In contrary participants with higher priority for hospital service and performance attributes, i.e. waiting time until admission, comfort in patient rooms, waiting time during the stay and distance to the hospital were grouped in cluster two (named therefore by *performance-orientated patient type*).

Additionally we used other variables of the questionnaire to describe the two patient clusters further. Outcome-orientated respondents showed significantly less

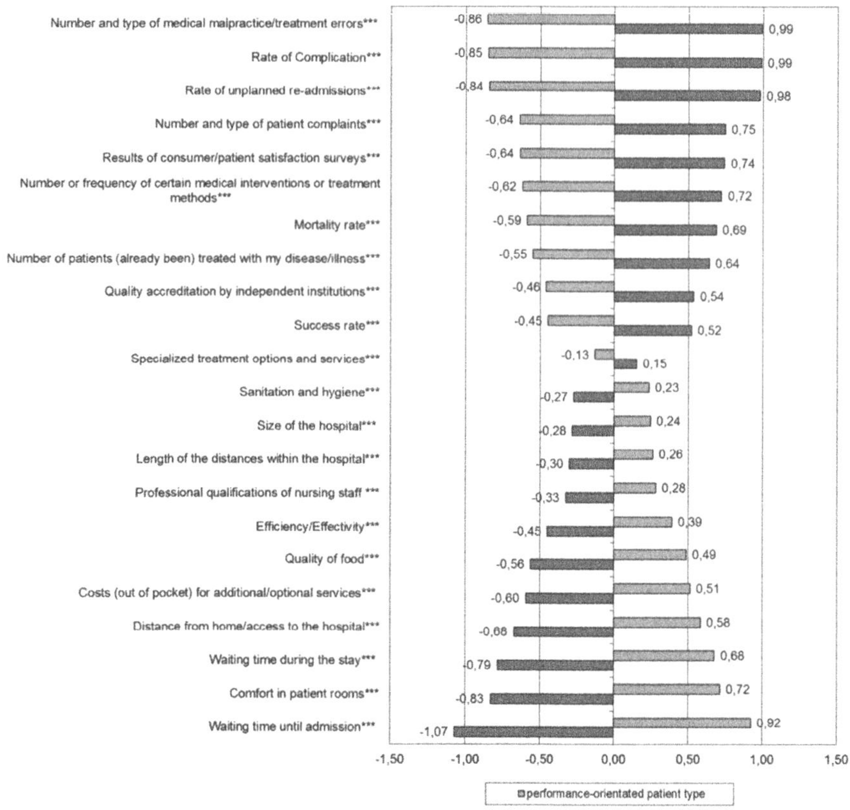

Fig. 15.9 Two-step clustering results—significant preference score differences. ***t-test, Mann–Whitney U-test $p<0.001$

paternalistic preference (e.g. tendency to follow doctor's advice without any questioning) (F 8.504, $p<0.05$) and found current information services on hospital quality less sufficient (F 6.611, $p<0.05$) than performance-orientated participants. Among the cluster one patients' information involvement is even higher (F 18.330, $p<0.001$) as well as the perceived risk of hospital choice (F 5.386, $p<0.05$) compared with the second patient cluster. Outcome-oriented respondents tend to be rather private insured (F 4.870, $p<0.05$) and have a higher social status (F 17.525, $p<0.001$).

15.7 Conclusion

We have presented here the results of the first comprehensive study in the research field of consumers' information needs on hospital quality.

Summarizing, the assessment of information involvement in hospital quality provides important insights into information needs. The analysis shows a high consumer involvement in information regarding hospital quality. Besides the general importance and the need of participation, the need of certainty turned out to be the strongest predictor.

The research also demonstrates how choice-based experiments can be used to provide estimates of the importance of quality information. The BWS task used forced respondents to discriminate between the quality indicators on offer, unlike rating scales. Moreover it turned out to be less cognitively demanding than other choice-based tasks, therefore well applicable on hospital patients.

The empirical results revealed that within 35 attributes/quality indicators, patients rated indicators of structure quality as the most important information. Information about process quality was moderately relevant from the patients' point of view. Objective results of outcome quality were more important for patients than subjective outcome indicators. The cluster analysis showed evidence for two significantly distinguished types of respondents: patients with more interest for information on outcome quality and patients with higher preferences to information on performance quality.

The findings can subsequently be used by patient information services to improve the information supply regarding hospital quality. Current information services on hospital quality, i.e. Internet portals should be tailored. Further, from the perspective of lean thinking the study goes to show how patients perspectives on service quality is also a necessary consideration in trying to examine waste and design and develop appropriate flows of patients and resources so that quality healthcare delivery can ensue.

15.8 Limitations

The present study exhibits some limitations. The cross-sectional design of the study and the relatively small sample size may limit the interpretation of our data. Due to the lack of research on consumers' information needs on hospital quality, further studies should follow based on larger samples. Moreover the information involvement scale as well as the BWS design could also be useful for further investigations on different types of health-related patient information (i.e. information flyer about medication or treatment options as well as information websites). We welcome participatory efforts.

References

Adler, J. (1996). *Informationsökonomische Fundierung von Austauschprozessen. Eine nachfragerorientierte Analyse*. Wiesbaden: Gabler.

Caldwell, C. (2005). A high quality of care. *Industrial Engineer, 37*, 44–48.

Chrzan, K., & Patterson, M. (2006). *Testing for the optimal number of attributes in MaxDiff questions*. Sawtooth Software, research paper series. Retrieved from http://www.sawtoothsoftware.com

Cohen, S. H. (2003). *Maximum difference scaling. Improved measures of importance and preference for segmentation*. Sawtooth Software, research paper series. Retrieved from http://www.sawtoothsoftware.com
Cross, C. S. (2009). *Lean reaches rural hospital*. Institute of Industrial Engineers. Retrieved March 2, 2009, from http://www.iienet2.org/Details.aspx?id=10808
Darby, M., & Karni, W. (1973). Free competition and the optimal amount of fraud. *Journal of Law and Economics, 14*, 67–88.
Donabedian, A. (1980). *The definition of quality and approaches to its assessment*. Michigan: Health Administration Press.
Flynn, T. N., Louviere, J. J., Peters, T. J., et al. (2007). Best-worst scaling: What it can do for health care re-search and how to do it. *Journal of Health Economics, 26*(8), 661–677.
Gabow, P. A., Albert, R., Kaufman, L., Wilson, M., & Eisert, S. (2008). Picture of health: Denver health uses 5S to deliver quality, safety, efficiency. *Industrial Engineer, 40*(2).
Homburg, C., Klarmann, M., & Pflesser, C. (2008). Konfirmatorische Faktorenanalyse. In A. Herrmann, C. Homburg, & M. Klarmann (Eds.), *Handbuch Marktforschung. Methoden, Anwendungen, Praxisbeispiele* (pp. 271–303). Wiesbaden: Gabler.
Jain, K., & Srinivasan, N. (1990). An empirical assessment of multiple operationalizations of involvement. *Advances in Consumer Research, 17*, 594–602.
Jensen, O. (2008). Clusteranalyse. In A. Herrmann, C. Homburg, & M. Klarmann (Eds.), *Handbuch Marktforschung. Methoden, Anwendungen, Praxisbeispiele* (pp. 305–372). Wiesbaden: Gabler.
Laurent, G., & Kampferer, J.-N. (1985). Measuring consumer involvement profiles. *Journal of Marketing Research, 2*, 41–53.
Majdi, C. (2012). *Lean methodology in health care quality improvements*. Retrieved from http://transitionconsultants.com/articles/19-lean-methodology-in-health-care-quality-improvement on 01082012
Manos, A., Sattler, M., & Alukal, G. (2006). Make healthcare lean. *Quality Progress, 39*(7), 24–30.
Marley, A. A. J., & Louviere, J. J. (2005). Some probabilistic models of best, worst and best-worst choices. *Journal of Mathematical Psychology, 49*(6), 464–480.
Mayring, P. (2000). *Qualitative Inhaltsanalyse. Grundlagen und Techniken*. Weinheim: Springer.
Nelson, P. (1970). Information and consumer behavior. *Journal of Political Economy, 74*(2), 311–329.
Pakenham, K. I. (1999). Adjustment to multiple sclerosis: Application of a stress and coping model. *Health Psychology, 18*, 383–392.
Simon, A. (2010). *Der Informationsbedarf von Patienten hinsichtlich der Krankenhausqualität. Eine em-pirische Untersuchung zur Messung des Involvements und der Informationspräferenzen*. Wiesbaden: Gabler Verlag/Springer Fachmedien Wiesbaden GmbH.
Taylor, S. E. (2003). *Health psychology*. Boston, MA: McGraw-Hill.
Thrall, T. H. (2008). Best practices in quality and patient safety. *Hospitals & Health Networks, 82*(7), 25–38.
Toyota Manufacturing Kentucky, Inc. (2003). *The Toyota production system*. Retrieved March 10, 2009, from http://www.toyotageorgetown.com
Toyota Motor Corporation. (2009). *Toyota production system*. Retrieved February 2, 2009, from http://www.toyota.co.jp/en/vision/production_system/
United States Army. (2009). *Lean six sigma*. Retrieved February 17, 2009, from http://www.army.mil/ArmyBTKC/focus/cpi/tools3.htm
Vitaliano, P. P., Maiuro, R. D., Russo, J., Katon, W., DeWolfe, D., & Hall, G. (1990). Coping profiles associated with psychiatric, physical health, work, and family problems. *Health Psychology, 9*, 348–376.
Zaichkowsky, J. L. (1994). The personal involvement inventory: Reduction, revision, and application to advertising. *Journal of Advertising, 23*(4), 59–70.

Part III
Macro Issues

1.1 Introduction

In recognition of the fact that healthcare operations span macro and micro aspects the next two sections focus respectively on important macro and micro aspects within healthcare delivery where principles of lean thinking can be applied to greatly enhance current operations and practice. Specifically, the chapters that make up this section focus on various lean thinking applications in healthcare from a macro perspective. Important aspects of system of systems thinking and network centric operations are also introduced to facilitate a better understanding and appreciation of various macro level aspects.

Chapter 16 "Applying a System of Systems" by Wickramasinghe and Chalasani introduces the concept of system of systems thinking to healthcare.

Chapter 17 "The Role for a Healthcare System of Systems Approach Coupled with Collaborative Technologies to Provide Superior Healthcare Delivery" by Wickramasinghe et al. illustrates the issues of a system of systems perspective using the context of collaborative technologies to facilitate healthcare delivery for AI/AN populations.

Chapter 18 "The Role of a Disruptive Pervasive Technology Solution to Facilitate Better Healthcare Delivery to Native American Patients" by Chalasani et al. further examines the context of Native American patients and the benefits of pervasive technology solutions in this context.

Chapter 19 "Improving Healthcare Service Quality and Patients' Life Quality Through Mobile Technologies: The Case of Diabetes self-management" by Hill et al. examines the benefits of mobile solutions to address the chronic disease diabetes.

Chapter 20 "Designing Enabling Regulatory Frameworks to Facilitate the Diffusion of Wireless Technology Solutions in Healthcare" by Troshani et al. examines the need to address healthcare regulatory frameworks in order to facilitate appropriate delivery of care and service.

Chapter 21 "The Role of Online Social Networks in Consumer Health Informatics: An Example of the Implicit Incorporation of Lean Principles" by Durst et al. provides an introduction into the role for on-line social networks to facilitate and promote healthy behaviours.

Chapter 22 "Supporting preventative healthcare with persuasive services" by Hamper and Mueller focuses on the benefits of supporting preventative healthcare and the technologies that might assist in this.

Chapter 23 "Using Technology Solutions to Streamline Healthcare Processes for Nursing: The Case of an Intelligent Operational Planning Support Tool(IOPST) Solution" by Wickramasinghe et al. provides an in depth discussion of nursing care and the importance of lean thinking principles and technology solutions to support care in this complex and often chaotic healthcare domain.

Chapter 24 "Using an e-health strategy to facilitate the design and development of effective healthcare processes" by Di Francesco and Wickramasinghe evaluates the benefits of developing an appropriate e-health strategy.

As can be seen, the chapters that make up this section cover a range of topics all of which have significance and importance to healthcare delivery today. More importantly, they serve to highlight key areas where the principles of lean thinking can effect better operations and enable value driven healthcare to ensue.

Chapter 16
Applying a System of Systems Approach to Healthcare

Suresh Chalasani and Nilmini Wickramasinghe

Abstract Many challenges in today's twenty-first century such as the energy crisis regarding fossil fuels and the financial crisis require new approaches and management techniques. System of systems and system of systems engineering have presented themselves as key approaches to address problems related to complex, dynamic systems and how best to manage them effectively and efficiently. Healthcare systems are complex and currently facing several challenges. The following chapter serves to explore the application of a system of systems approach to healthcare, i.e., a healthcare system of systems (HSoS). Specifically, a HSoS is defined as a collection of independent, large-scale complex, distributed systems. HSoS exhibit operational and managerial independence, geographic distribution, and evolutionary development. Furthermore, a HSoS perspective is imperative in order to realize network-centric healthcare operations, as the chapter discusses.

Keywords Healthcare systems • Managed care systems • Hospitals • Critical care • Network-centric healthcare operations • Patient centric

---

S. Chalasani
MIS Department, School of Business and Technology, University of Wisconsin-Parkside, 900 Wood Rd, Kenosha, WI 53141–2000, USA
e-mail: chalasan@uwp.edu

N. Wickramasinghe, Ph.D., M.B.A. (✉)
Epworth HealthCare & Department of BITL & HIRi, RMIT University, GPO Box 2476, Melbourne, VIC 3001, Australia
e-mail: nilmini.work@gmail.com

N. Wickramasinghe et al. (eds.), *Lean Thinking for Healthcare*, Healthcare Delivery in the Information Age, DOI 10.1007/978-1-4614-8036-5_16,

16.1 Introduction

Healthcare systems are inherently complex in nature and address the needs of several stakeholders in healthcare management. Key stakeholders in the healthcare industry include patients, physicians, nurses, hospitals, healthcare organizations, pharmacies, government regulatory and licensing agencies, and government funding agencies. These stakeholders make up what is known as the Web of healthcare players, see Fig. 16.1 (Wickramasinghe and Schaffer 2010). The interests of these key stakeholders are not always aligned and serve to translate into a myriad of business rules that in turn lead to heterogeneity in healthcare delivery and management. Often it is because of these competing goals that many challenges face healthcare delivery today (Wickramasinghe et al. 2012).

A "patient-centric" approach to healthcare delivery is universally agreed to the objective for healthcare delivery and requires that at all times the patients' needs and interests are the number one priority (Wickramasinghe and Schaffer 2010; Wickramasinghe et al. 2012). Patient-centric healthcare, however, is simple in concept but difficult to implement in practice due to the complex nature of independent systems that govern healthcare (Wickramasinghe et al. 2012). One approach to facilitate the realization of patient-centric healthcare delivery is to apply the concept of a system of systems (SoS) approach (Jamshidi 2009). Specifically, the idea of SoS has been adapted to healthcare by Kotov (1997), who has defined a healthcare system of systems (HSoS) as a collection of independent, large-scale complex, distributed systems (Jamshidi 2009). In addition, we note that HSoS exhibit several key characteristics of a general system of systems as suggested by Sage and Cuppan (Jamshidi 2009; Sage and Cuppan 2001). In particular, they exhibit operational and managerial independence. For example, hospitals, clinics, and organizations such as HMOs may work together but also work independently of each other. In a similar fashion, government funding agencies such as Medicare/Medicaid and physicians and hospitals work independently of each other. Moreover, all these organizations are geographically distributed. It is possible that a patient who resides in Little Rock needs to be treated at the Cleveland Clinic or even overseas. Further, all healthcare

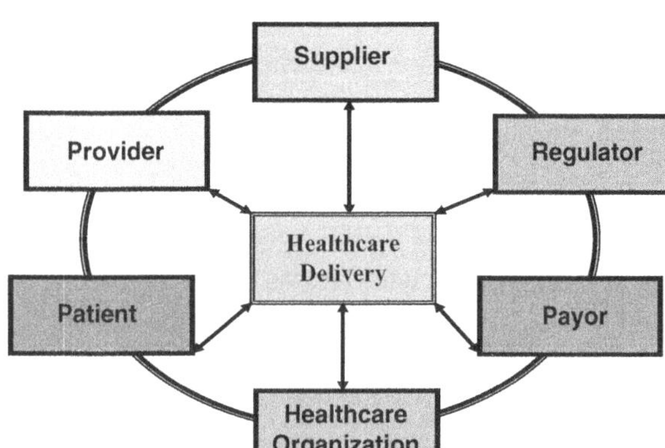

Fig. 16.1 Web of players (adapted from Wickramasinghe and Schaffer 2010)

systems exhibit evolutionary development since they change continuously in response to government regulation, advances in medical technology, and new developments including natural disasters or even bioterrorism and thus must cope with large-scale catastrophic events.

In this chapter, we first discuss healthcare systems and how these fit the definition of general system of systems. We discuss different components of the HSoS and their characteristics before presenting the concept of network-centric healthcare and how it relates to a system of systems approach.

16.2 Background

System of systems has become a widely accepted term for describing complex systems in recent years (Jamshidi 2009; Kotov 1997; Sage and Cuppan 2001). Table 16.1 provides a useful summary of key definitions from the system of systems literature (Jamshidi 1996, 2009; Kotov 1997; Sage and Cuppan 2001; Proceedings of the IEEE International Symposium on System of Systems 2006; Carlock and Fenton 1999).

A closer examination of these definitions shows that they relate as well into healthcare contexts. In fact, significant amount of research has been done into healthcare systems (Luskasik 1998). Moreover, Madni, for example, has designed smart reconfigurable wireless sensor networks for SoS applications (Wickramasinghe and Geisler 2006; Madni 2006).

Table 16.1 System of systems definitions

Definition number	Description
1	SoS exists when there is a presence of a majority of the following: operational and managerial independence, geographic distribution, emergent behaviors, and evolutionary development (Jamshidi 2009; Kotov 1997; Sage and Cuppan 2001)
2	SoS are large-scale concurrent and distributed systems that are composed of complex systems (Jamshidi 1996)
3	Enterprise SoS engineering is focused on coupling traditional systems engineering activities with enterprise activities of strategic planning and investment analysis (Jamshidi 2005; Carlock and Fenton 2001)
4	SoS provides a method to pursue development, integration, as well as enhance performance (Jamshidi 2009)
5	SoS engineering relates to the integration of systems into system of systems that ultimately contribute to evolution of the social infrastructure (Keating et al. 2003)

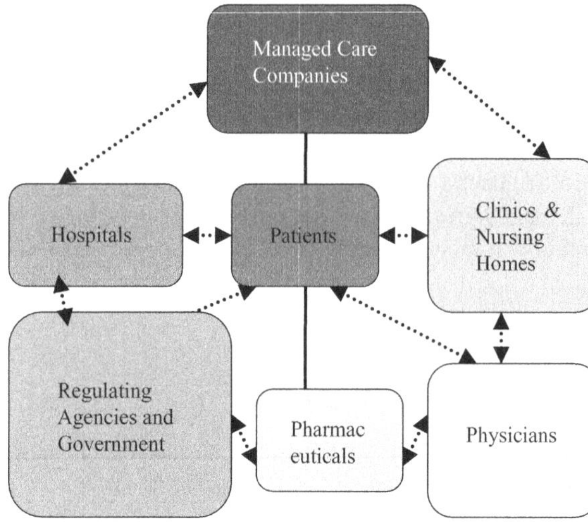

Fig. 16.2 Different systems that are part of HSoS (adapted from Jamshidi 2009)

16.3 Healthcare System of Systems

In this chapter, HSoS are assumed to be composed of systems that include several of the Web of players as shown in Fig. 16.1. Figure 16.2 serves to depict this for a typical US healthcare context which would include Managed care companies, hospitals, clinics, physicians, governmental agencies, and programs such as Medicare and Medicaid that all work together to serve and support patients. Table 16.2 provides definitions for these terms. Table 16.3 serves to identify the key properties of healthcare systems based on Sage and Cupan's definition of HSoS (Sage and Cuppan 2001).

16.4 Network-Centric Healthcare

The previous sections have served to introduce the approach of SoS as a way to realize patient-centric healthcare delivery. Given that today IS/IT (information systems and information technology) play a key role in all operations including healthcare delivery, it is essential to also look at NCHO (network-centric healthcare operations) in order to effectively and efficiently design and develop superior patient-centric healthcare solutions.

As discussed by Von Lubitz and Wickramasinghe (Getzen and Allen 2007; Von Lubitz and Wickramasinghe 2006a, b; Von Lubitz et al. 2006), network-centric healthcare operations are conducted at the confluence of three critical domains, namely, informational, physical, and cognitive (refer to Table 16.4). In essence these domains serve to cumulatively capture and then process all critical information and data so that effective and efficient value-driven healthcare operations may ensue.

Table 16.2 Key terms in a US healthcare SoS

Term	Description
Managed care companies	Managed care companies have become popular in the last decade primarily because of their efforts to contain medical costs. PPOs (preferred provider organizations) and HMOs (Health Maintenance Organizations) are examples of managed care companies. Managed care companies employ a variety of techniques to contain costs including gate-keeping (requiring mandatory authorization for hospitalization), capitation (payment of a fixed amount per member per month), and generic drug substitution for brand name drugs (Ramamurthy et al. 2007). A variety of information systems exist within managed care companies to enroll patients, maintain their claim records, audit claims, and track physician services
Hospitals	Hospitals are financed by a variety of sources including payments from managed care companies, Medicare, and Medicaid programs. DRG (diagnosis related group) payments reimburse the hospitals based on the diagnosis and treatment. Hospital care in the USA is characterized by technologies for diagnosis and treatment to electronic maintenance of patient health records
Physicians	Groups of physicians often practice together serving patient needs. Physician groups work with managed care companies via insurance contracts, utilize hospitals for in-patient care, and work with governmental agencies such as Veteran's Administration hospitals, Medicare, and Medicaid programs. Physicians utilize a number of technologies and information systems to diagnose and monitor patient's health status
Clinics	Clinics are utilized by physician groups for treating outpatients. Clinical information systems are utilized for managing patient health records to scheduling patient visits and billing managed care organizations for patient visits
Governmental agencies	Governmental agencies provide oversight of physicians, clinics, hospitals, and nursing homes. Special units exist for dealing with veterans health and for administering programs such as Medicare and Medicaid

Underlying a network-centric perspective for healthcare is the philosophy of a process perspective to knowledge management. Within the evolving field of knowledge management, the two predominant perspectives regarding knowledge generation are a people-centric perspective and a technology-centric perspective (Wickramasinghe 2006; Wickramasinghe and von Lubizt 2007, p. 17). Specifically, a people-oriented perspective draws from the work of Nonaka as well as Blacker and Spender (Wickramasinghe and von Lubitz 2007; Nonaka and Nishiguchi 2001; Nonaka 1994; Newell et al. 2002). Central to this perspective of knowledge creation is that knowledge is created by people and that new knowledge or the increasing of the extant knowledge base occurs as a result of human cognitive activities and the effecting of specific knowledge transformations [ibid]. In contrast, a technology-driven perspective to knowledge creation is centered around the computerized technique of data mining and the many mathematical and statistical methods available to transform data into information and then meaningful knowledge (Wickramasinghe and von Lubitz 2007; Adriaans and Zaninge 1996; Becerra-Fernandez and Sabherwal 2001; Award and Ghaziri 2004).

Table 16.3 Healthcare systems properties (adapted from Jamshidi 2009)

Property	Description
Operational and managerial independence	It is clear that each individual system—from managed care systems to governmental systems—exists on its own independent of the other systems. Together, they serve the patient needs, while operating independently. In addition, each has its managerial independence with the management structure ranging from governmental management to private sector management
Geographical distribution	Healthcare systems are inherently distributed with no central organizational structure. Clinical systems, hospital systems, and regulatory systems are dispersed geographically
Evolutionary development	Healthcare systems undergo evolutionary development. For example, pharmaceutical companies bring new drugs to the market after years of research, while hospital technologies are evolving to incorporate sensor-based monitoring of in-patients
Emergent behavior	An example of emergent behavior is to track the quality of care using the data from the individual systems such as the clinical systems and the hospital systems. For example, insurance companies such as the United Health certify physicians on whether they meet the quality standards based on national averages on quality care obtained from information on physician treatment of patients across the nation

Table 16.4 The three domains in network-centric healthcare (adapted from Jamshidi 2009; Getzen and Allen 2007; Von Lubitz and Wickramasinghe 2006a, b; Von Lubitz et al. 2006)

Domain	Description
Physical	Encompasses the structure of the entire environment healthcare operations intend to influence directly or indirectly, e.g., elimination of disease, fiscal operations, political environment, and patient and personnel education
Information	Contains all elements required for generation, storage, manipulation, dissemination/sharing of information, and its transformation and dissemination/sharing as knowledge in all its forms. It is here that all aspects of command and control are communicated and all sensory inputs gathered
Cognitive	Relates to all human factors that affect operations, such as education, training, experience, political inclinations, personal engagement (motivation), "open-mindedness," or even intuition of individuals involved in the relevant activities

In contrast to both of these approaches, a process perspective to knowledge creation not only combines the essentials of both the people-centric and technology-centric perspectives but also emphasizes the dynamic and on-going nature of the process. A critical feature of a process-centered knowledge generation is that it is grounded in the pioneering work of Boyd and his OODA Loop, a conceptual framework that maps out the critical process required to support rapid decision making and extraction of critical and germane knowledge (Wickramasinghe and von Lubitz 2007; Boyd 1987).

Currently, key challenges regarding healthcare delivery (Wickramasinghe and Schaffer 2010; Wickramasinghe et al. 2012) include: (1) cost effectiveness, i.e., less costly than traditional healthcare delivery; (2) functionality and ease of use, i.e., they should enable and facilitate many uses for physicians and other healthcare users by combining various types and forms of data as well as be easy to use; and (3) they must be secure. One of the most significant legislative regulations in the USA is the Health Insurance Portability and Accountability Act (HIPAA) (Von Lubitz and Wickramasinghe 2006c). Given the nature of healthcare and the sensitivity of healthcare data and information, it is incumbent on governments not only to mandate regulations that will facilitate the exchange of healthcare documents between various healthcare stakeholders but also to provide protection of privacy and the rights of patients. Moreover, irrespective of the type of healthcare system, i.e., whether 100 % government driven, 100 % private, or a combination thereof, it is clear that some governmental role is required to facilitate successful e-health initiatives.

A network-centric perspective to healthcare delivery also serves to underscore the inextricable connection and intertwining of e-health and e-government which to date has rarely been researched let alone acknowledged. Furthermore, for such an approach to become adopted successfully it requires governments to develop policies and protocols which will in turn facilitate its usability. We identify four key areas that will have an important impact on the development of the necessary policies and protocols as IT education, morbidity, cultural/social dimensions, and world economic standing (Wickramasinghe and Schaffer 2010; Wickramasinghe et al. 2012).

16.5 Health Information Grid

The backbone of network-centric healthcare operations is the HIG (Healthcare Information Grid), a set of interconnected Web enabled information networks with intelligence capabilities that support the seamless transferring of all necessary data and information to the point of care so that the physician (or decision maker) is always making decision based on the best possible data, information, and knowledge (Fig. 16.3).

Specifically the nodes on the grid (circles at various grid intersections in Fig. 16.3) represent the portal entry to the grid and various systems that capture, store, and then transmit data and information as depicted in Fig. 16.3. The power of this interconnected system is that at all times current data and information are accessible to all decision makers no matter where they are located; hence decision makers are supported with relevant information and germane knowledge anywhere anytime, unlike in most healthcare systems which are platform centric in design and hence information chaos results which leads to volumes of irrelevant and more often erroneous data which in turn lead to suboptimal or poor quality decision making.

The HIG provides the technology backbone for network-centric healthcare delivery. However, for the HIG to function as intended, various protocols and procedures must be developed at a global level. Without such standardization even the simplest of functions such as the exchange of documents and other procurement information, connectivity, and e-commerce-enabled benefits become problematic while the

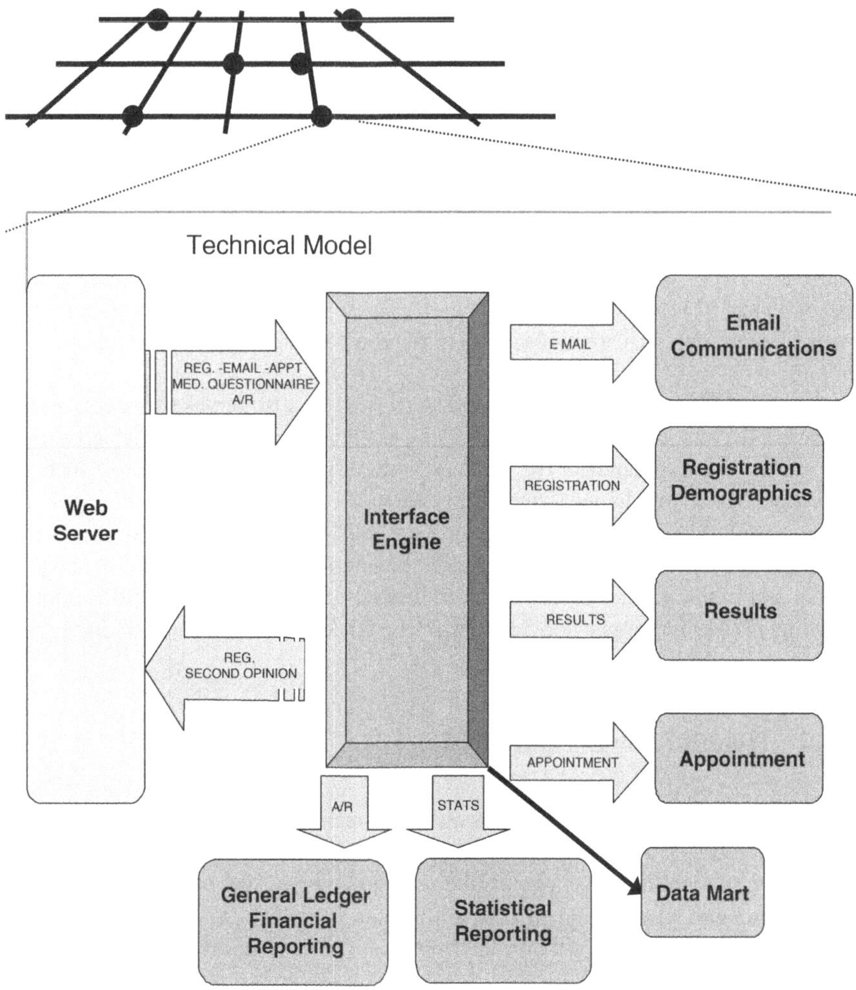

Fig. 16.3 Schematic of the HIG (adapted from Jamshidi 2009; Madni 2006)

critical goal of decreasing information asymmetry becomes unattainable. Unfortunately, standardization is woefully lacking in too many areas of healthcare let alone e-health. We indicate below two key areas that must be addressed.

(a) *Information communication technology (ICT) architecture/infrastructure*: The generic architecture for most e-health initiatives is similar to that required by the HIG. However this infrastructure which is made up of diverse technologies—phone lines, fiber trunks and submarine cables, T1, T3 and OC-xx, ISDN, DSL as well as satellites, earth stations and teleports—must be available globally.

A sound technical infrastructure is an essential ingredient to the undertaking of e-health. Such infrastructures should also include telecommunications, electricity, access to computers, number of Internet hosts, number of ISPs (Internet Service Providers), and available bandwidth and broadband access. To offer a good multimedia content and thus provide a rich e-health experience, one would require a high bandwidth. ICT considerations are undoubtedly one of the most fundamental infrastructure requirements.

In addition, networks and telecommunications are a vital piece of the infrastructure for Internet access. One of the pioneering countries in establishing a complete and robust e-health infrastructure is Singapore which is in the process of wiring every home, office, and factory up to a broadband cable network which will cover 98 % of Singaporean homes and offices (Health Insurance Portability and Accountability Act (HIPPA) 2001; APEC 2001; Asia Pacific Foundation 2002).

(b) *Security and trust*: Consumers are also concerned about a number of dimensions of trust: for example, trust in the security of value passed during electronic transactions with organizations that are "virtual" in a disconcertingly ineffable way and trust in the privacy of personal data arising from electronic transactions (Asia Pacific Foundation 2002; Roquilly 2002; Fjetland 2002; Ghosh and Swaminatha 2001; Panagariya 2000).

In addition, ethical concerns are inevitably related to healthcare operations. The notion of the governmental bodies having ready access to healthcare information of the citizens is among the major concerns in the USA, and similar-reservations are also voiced in Europe. The possibility of security breaches, similar to those that recently affected millions of credit card customers in the USA, demands a very stringent layer of protective layers that will assure prevention of commercial misuse of healthcare data.

When we overlay Fig. 16.2 with Fig. 16.3 what we see is that the model of network-centric healthcare operations describes and supports the different systems that comprise the HSoS. Hence network-centric healthcare mandates the conceptualization of healthcare as system of systems.

More recently, Porter and Tiesberg (2006) note that the problem with the US healthcare system is that it is engaged in zero-sum competition. This means that the Web of players compete with each other. Porter recommends that healthcare be redefined to encourage, as in other industries, positive sum competition. In so doing, it will be possible for all actors in the Web of healthcare to benefit and most importantly for healthcare to be value driven and patient centric. However Porter falls short of describing a model that can enable this to take effect. Healthcare is a knowledge-rich environment where data and information are critical for diagnosis and then the consequent prescription of the appropriate healthcare treatment. In today's Information Age clearly ICTs play an integral role in enabling the correct data and information to reach the decision maker when and where it is required.

However given the complex nature of healthcare operations the careful design of ICTs in healthcare is crucial. The proposed system of systems model coupled with the ideas of network-centric healthcare appears to hold the key.

16.6 Conclusions

As both USA and Europe move forward on their respective agendas to incorporate e-health and electronic medical records or computerized patient records, the concept of healthcare systems of systems becomes more important if we are to fully realize the benefit of ICT use in healthcare delivery. In the context of network-centric healthcare operations it becomes a strategic necessity. Moreover, if the full potential of such solutions is to be ever realized it is critical that the principles of lean thinking are embraced and healthcare processes are streamlined, effective, and efficient. We close therefore with a strong call for more research in this area as it relates to healthcare.

References

Adriaans, P. & Zaninge, D. (1996). Data Mining Addison-Wesley, New York.

A report prepared for Asia Pacific Foundation (2002). Available at http://www.apfoundation.org/. Accessed on January 2011.

APEC. (2001). *The new economy and APEC*. Report to the Economic Committee of APEC. http://www.diw.de/deutsch/produkte/veranstaltungen/docs/apec-report.html

Award, E., & Ghaziri, H.(2004). Knowledge Management Prentice Hall, New Jersey.

Becerra-Fernandez, I., & Sabherwal, R. (2001). *Organisational Knowledge Management J. of MIS 18*(1), 23–55.

Boyd, J (1987). A discourse on winning and losing. Available at http:// www.danford.net. Accessed on January 2011.

Carlock, P. G., & Fenton, R. E. (2001). System of systems (SoS) enterprise systems for information-intensive organizations. *Systems Engineering, 4*(4), 242–261.

Carlock, P., & Fenton, R. (1999). Agency level systems engineering for systems of systems, systems and info. *Technology Review Journal, Spring/Summer*, 99–110.

Fjetland, M. (2002). Global commerce and the privacy clash. *The Information Management Journal, 36*(1), 54–58.

Getzen, T. E., & Allen, B. H. (2007). *Healthcare economics*. New York: Wiley.

Ghosh, A. K., & Swaminatha, T. M. (2001). Software security and privacy risks in mobile E-commerce. *Communications of the ACM, 44*(2), 51–58.

Health Insurance Portability and Accountability Act (HIPPA). (2001, May). *Privacy compliance executive summary*. Protegrity. Available at https://www.cms.gov/Regulations-and-Guidance/HIPAA-Administrative-Simplification/HIPAAGenInfo/downloads/HIPAALaw.pdf. Accessed on January 2012

Jamshidi, M. (1996). *Large-scale systems: Modeling, control, and fuzzy logic*. Upper Saddle River, NJ: Prentice Hall TR.

Jamshidi, M. (2005). System-of-systems engineering—A definition. *IEEE SMC 2005*, Big Island, Hawaii. URL: http://ieeesmc2005.unm.edu/SoSE_Defn.htm

Jamshidi, M. (2009). *System of systems engineering*. Hoboken, NJ: Wiley.

Keating, C., et al. (2003). System of systems engineering. *Engineering Management Journal, 15*(3), 36–45.
Kotov, V. (1997). *Systems of systems as communicating structures*. Hewlett Packard Computer Systems Laboratory Paper HPL-97-124, pp. 1–15.
Luskasik, S. J. (1998). Systems, systems of systems, and the education of engineers. *Artificial Intelligence for Engineering Design, Analysis, and Manufacturing, 12*(1), 55–60.
Madni, A. M. (2006). Smart configurable wireless sensors and actuators for system of systems (SoS) applications. *Proceedings of the IEEE SMC International Conference on System of Systems Engineering*, Los Angeles, April 2006.
Newell, S., Swan, J., & Scarborough, H. (2002). Knowledge Management Palgrave Macmillian, New York.
Nonaka, I., (1994). Knowledge Management, Oxford University Press, Oxford.
Nonaka, I., & Nishiguchi, T, (2001). Knowledge Emergence Oxford University Press, Oxford.
Panagariya, A. (2000). E-commerce, WTO and developing countries. *The World Economy, 23*(8), 959–978.
Porter, M., & Tiesberg, E. (2006). *Redefining health care*. Boston: Harvard Business School Press.
Proceedings of the IEEE International Symposium on System of Systems, April 2006, Los Angeles, CA. Available at http://ieeexplore.ieee.org/xpl/mostRecentIssue.jsp?punumber=10995. Accessed on January 2012
Ramamurthy, H., Prabhu, B. S., Gadh, R., & Madni, A. M. (2007). Wireless industrial monitoring and control using a smart sensor platform. *IEEE Sensors Journal, 7*, 611–618.
Roquilly, C. (2002). Closed distribution networks and E-commerce: Antitrust issues. *International Review of Law, Computers & Technology, 16*(1), 81–93.
Sage, A. P., & Cuppan, C. D. (2001). On the systems engineering and management of systems of systems and federations of systems. *Information, Knowledge, Systems Management, 2*(4), 325–345.
Von Lubitz, D., & Wickramasinghe, N. (2006a). Healthcare and technology: The doctrine of network centric healthcare. *International Journal of Electronic Healthcare (IJEH), 4*, 322–344.
Von Lubitz, D., & Wickramasinghe, N. (2006b). Network centric healthcare: Applying the tools, techniques and strategies of knowledge management to create superior healthcare operations. *International Journal of Electronic Healthcare (IJEH), 4*, 415–428.
Von Lubitz, D., & Wickramasinghe, N. (2006c). Key challenges and policy implications for governments and regulators in a network centric healthcare environment. *International Journal of Electronic Government, 3*(2), 204–224.
Von Lubitz, D., Yanovsky, G., & Wickramasinghe, N. (2006). Network centric healthcare operations: The telecommunications structure. *International Journal of Networking and Virtual Organizations, 3*(1), 60–85.
Wickramasinghe, N. (2006). Knowledge Creation: A meta-Framework. *International Journal of Innovation and Learning, 3*(5), 558–573.
Wickramasinghe, N., Bali, R. K., Kirn, S., & Sumoi, R. (2012). *Critical issues in developing sustainable e-health solutions*. New York: Springer.
Wickramasinghe, N., & Geisler, E. (Eds.). (2006). *Proceedings of the Fifth International Conference on the Management of Healthcare and Medical technology*, Chicago, IL, August 2006.
Wickramasinghe, N., & Schaffer, J. (2010). *Realizing value driven e-health solutions*. Washington, DC: IBM Center for the Business of Government.
Wickramasinghe, N., & von Lubitz, D. (2007). *Knowledge-Based Enterprise: Theories and Fundamentals*. Idea Group, Hershey.

Chapter 17
The Role for a Healthcare System of Systems Approach Coupled with Collaborative Technologies to Provide Superior Healthcare Delivery

Nilmini Wickramasinghe, Suresh Chalasani, and Sridevi Koritala

Abstract Healthcare delivery in the United States exists at varying levels. The Cleveland Clinic, Johns Hopkins, Kaiser, and the Mayo Clinic are noted for typically providing world class care. However, there also exist several instances of inferior delivery of care, mostly as a result of inefficient and ineffective processes which in turn result in poor access and low quality. One segment of the community that continues to suffer from issues pertaining to poor access and low quality is the American Indians and Alaska Natives (AI/AN) population. Such a situation is clearly untenable, especially given the plethora of tools, techniques, technologies, and tactics afforded by today's knowledge economy. In this chapter, we proffer a model incorporating a system of systems approach in order to streamline process flows and thereby provide better healthcare delivery to Native American patients. We note that while this chapter specifically focuses on the case study of Native American patients we strongly urge for the incorporation of a system of systems perspective in all areas of healthcare delivery.

This chapter has been adapted from an earlier version presented at the 2012 HICSS Conference, 4–7 Jan 2012, Maui.

N. Wickramasinghe, Ph.D., MBA (✉)
Epworth HealthCare & Department of BITL & HIRi, RMIT University,
GPO Box 2476, Melbourne, VIC 3001, Australia
e-mail: nilmini.wickramasinghe@rmit.edu.au

S. Chalasani
MIS Department, School of Business and Technology, University of Wisconsin-Parkside,
900 Wood Rd, Kenosha, WI 53141-2000, USA
e-mail: chalasan@uwp.edu

S. Koritala
Lakeshore Medical Clinic, 2000 E Layton Ave Suite 100, Saint Francis, WI 53235, USA
e-mail: sridevi.koritala@aurora.org

N. Wickramasinghe et al. (eds.), *Lean Thinking for Healthcare*, Healthcare Delivery in the Information Age, DOI 10.1007/978-1-4614-8036-5_17,

Keywords Healthcare delivery • Native American patient care • Knowledge management • Healthcare information systems • Healthcare system of systems • Intelligence continuum

17.1 Introduction

The Indian Health Service (IHS), an agency within the Department of Health and Human Services, is responsible for providing federal health services to American Indians and Alaska Natives (AI/AN). The provision of health services to members of federally recognized tribes grew out of the special government-to-government relationship between the federal government and Indian tribes. This relationship, established in 1787, is based on Article I, Section 8 of the Constitution, and has been given form and substance by numerous treaties, laws, Supreme Court decisions, and Executive Orders. The IHS is the principal federal healthcare provider and health advocate for Indian people, and its goal is to raise their health status to the highest possible level. The IHS currently provides health services to approximately 1.5 million AI/AN who belong to more than 557 federally recognized tribes in 35 states (http://www.ihs.gov/PublicInfo/PublicAffairs/Welcome_Info/IHSintro.asp). While most IHSs are provided on or near reservations, approximately 1 % of the budget is used to provide services to Indian people living in urban areas, even though most recent census data shows the majority of Native Americans are urban. Clients of the Urban Indian program commonly experience barriers in accessing basic health services due to a multiplicity of reasons mostly connected with poor data, bad information, and minimal knowledge. Figure 17.1a, b provides a schematic of the current system. As can be seen from these figures, healthcare delivery to this segment is provided through a complex network structure. It is for this reason that we contend that such a situation can benefit from the application of the intelligence continuum and a system of systems approach (Wickramasinghe and Schaffer 2006).

17.2 The Intelligence Continuum

Healthcare delivery is a data-rich environment (Moghimi et al. 2012). Thus, scholars have noted that to successfully operate in such a context it is beneficial to embrace the tools and techniques of today's knowledge economy; such as data mining and knowledge management (KM). To effectively and efficiently apply the techniques of data mining and strategies of knowledge management to healthcare, Wickramasinghe and Schaffer developed the intelligence continuum model (Wickramasinghe and Schaffer 2006). Succinctly stated, the intelligence continuum (IC) is a collection of key tools, techniques, and processes of today's knowledge economy (Fig. 17.2b); i.e., including but not limited to data mining, business intelligence (BI)/analytics, and knowledge management. Taken together it represents a

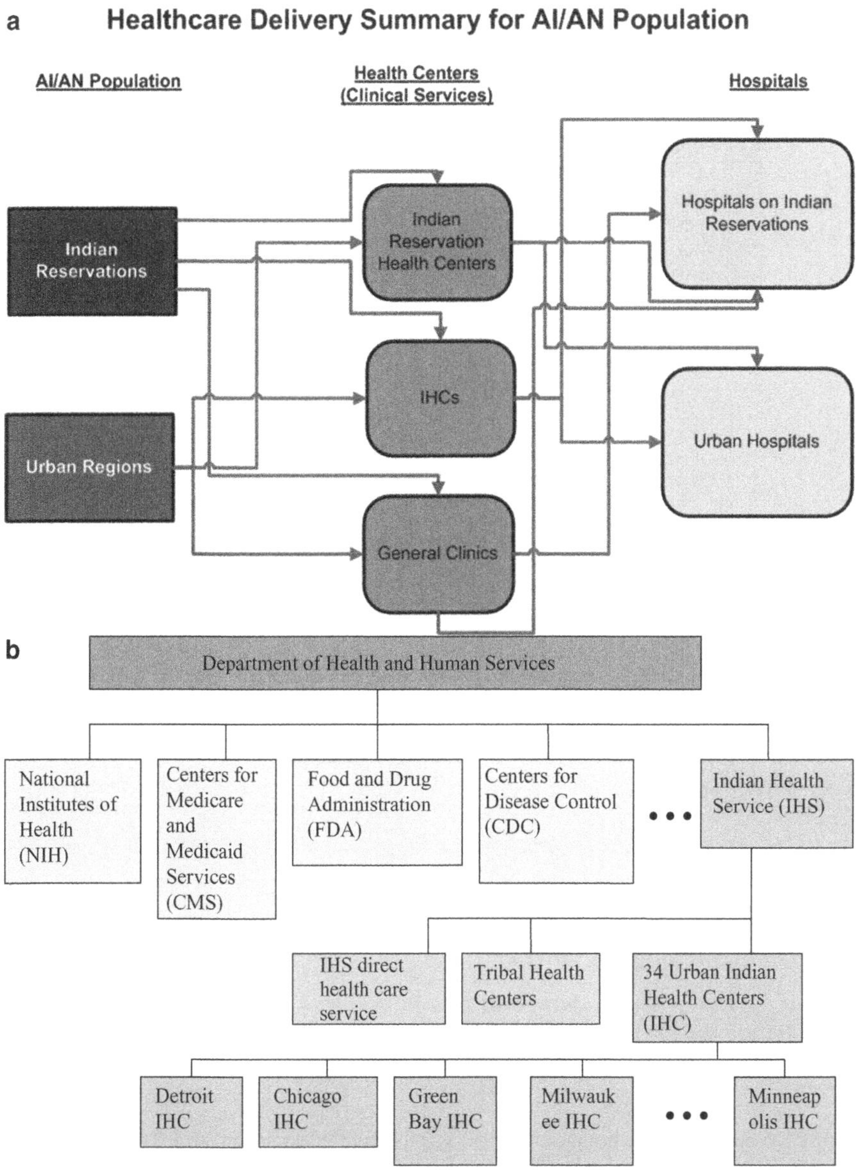

Fig. 17.1 (**a**) Health delivery summary for AI/AN population. (**b**) The role of Indian Health Centers in the Department of Health and Human Services (HHS) [adapted from (http://www.ihs.gov/PublicInfo/PublicAffairs/Welcome_Info/IHSintro.asp; Anonymous 2005a, b, c, d; Wickramasinghe et al. 2011; http://www.glitc.org; http://naaccr.org; Knutsen et al. 2005; Cunningham 1993)]

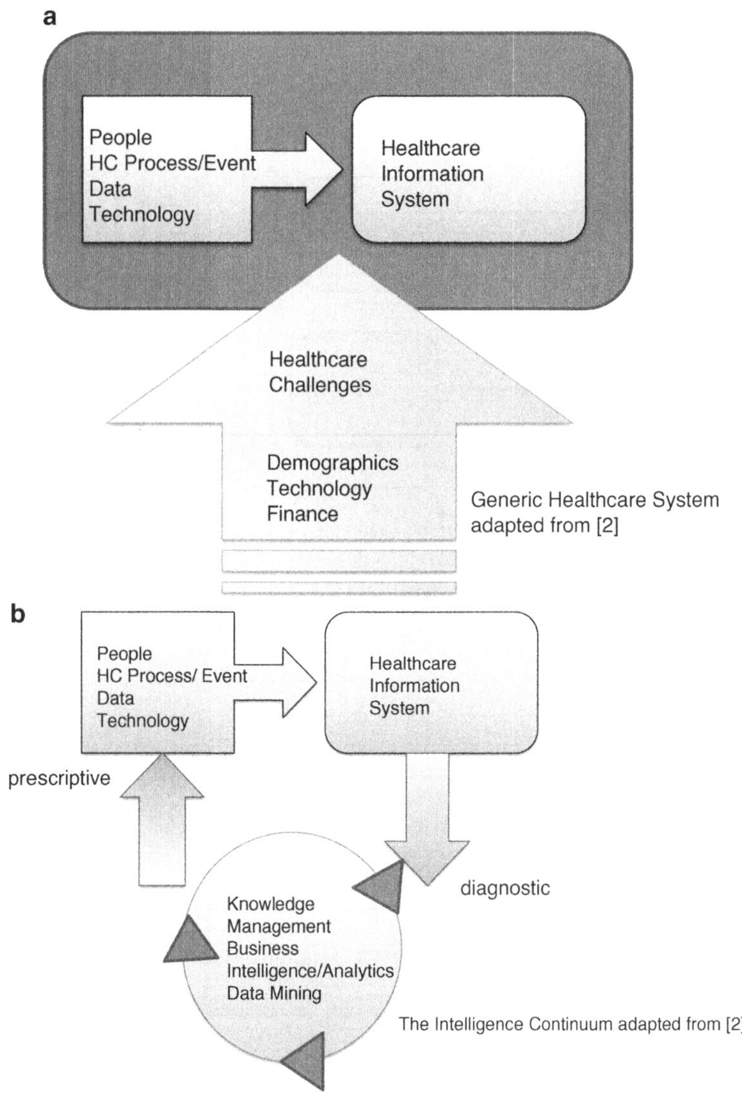

Fig. 17.2 (**a**) The generic healthcare system adapted from Wickramasinghe and Schaffer (2006). (**b**) The intelligence continuum adapted from Wickramasinghe and Schaffer (2006)

very powerful system for refining the data raw material stored in data marts and/or data warehouses and thereby maximizing the value and utility of these data assets for the creation of superior outcomes and processes.

An understanding of the role of the intelligence continuum begins with an examination of a generic healthcare information system (Fig. 17.2a). The important aspects in this generic system include the socio-technical perspective; i.e., the people, processes, and technology inputs required in conjunction with data as a key input. The combination of these elements comprises an information system and in any organization multiple such systems could exist. To this generic system, we add the healthcare challenges; i.e., the challenges of demographics, technology, and finance.

In order to address these challenges a closer examination of the data generated by the information systems and stored in the larger data warehouses and/or smaller data marts is necessary. In particular, it is important to make decisions that invoke the intelligence continuum; apply the tools, techniques, and processes of data mining, business intelligence/analytics, and knowledge management, respectively. On applying these tools and techniques to the data generated from healthcare information systems, it is first possible to diagnose the "as is" or current state processes in order to make further decisions regarding how existing processes should be modified and thereby provide appropriate prescriptions to enable the achievement of a better future state; i.e., improve the respective inputs of the people, process, technology, and data so that the system as a whole is significantly improved.

Components of the intelligence continuum: The intelligence continuum is a collection of key tools, techniques, and processes of today's knowledge economy; i.e., including but not limited to data mining, business intelligence/analytics, and knowledge management.

As can be seen from Fig. 17.2, data mining, business intelligence/analytics, and knowledge management form the key components of the intelligent continuum so they will now be discussed briefly in turn.

Data mining: Due to the immense size of the data sets, computerized techniques are essential to help physicians as well as administrators understand relationships and associations between data elements. Data mining is closely associated with databases and shares some common ground with statistics since both strive toward discovering structure in data. However, while statistical analysis starts with some kind of hypothesis about the data, data mining does not. Furthermore, data mining is much more suited to deal with heterogeneous databases, data sets, and data fields, which are typical of data in medical databases that contain numerous types of text and graphical data sets. Data mining also draws heavily from many other disciplines, most notably machine learning, artificial intelligence, and database technology.

Data mining, then, is the nontrivial process of identifying valid, novel, potentially useful, and ultimately understandable patterns from data (Wickramasinghe and Schaffer 2006; Moghimi et al. 2012; Von Lubitz et al. 2006; Von Lubitz and Wickramasinghe 2006; Cios 2001; Fayyad 1996). Clinicians accomplish these tasks daily in their care of patients using their own "personal CPU"; however, the enormous amounts and divergent sources of information coupled with time constraints limit any clinician's ability to fully examine all issues. Data mining algorithms are used on databases for model building or for finding patterns in data. When these patterns are new, useful, and understandable, it leads to knowledge discovery (Fayyad 1996).

Business intelligence/analytics: Another technology-driven technique, like data mining, connected to knowledge creation is the area of business intelligence and the now newer term of business analytics. The business intelligence (BI) term has become synonymous with an umbrella description for a wide range of decision-support tools, some of which target specific user audiences (Wickramasinghe and Schaffer 2006; Moghimi et al. 2012; Von Lubitz et al. 2006; Von Lubitz and Wickramasinghe 2006; Cios 2001). At the bottom of the BI hierarchy are extraction and formatting tools which are also known as data-extraction tools. These tools collect data from existing databases for inclusion in data warehouses and data marts. Thus the next level of the BI hierarchy is known as warehouses and marts. Because the data come from so many different, often incompatible systems in various file formats, the next step in the BI hierarchy is formatting tools; these tools and techniques are used to "cleanse" the data and convert it to formats that can easily be understood in the data warehouse or data mart. Next, tools are needed to support the reporting and analytical techniques. These are known as enterprise reporting and analytical tools. OLAP (online analytic process) engines and analytical application-development tools are for professionals who analyze data and do business forecasting, modeling, and trend analysis which are some examples. Human intelligence tools form the next level in the hierarchy and involve human expertise, opinions, and observations to be recorded to create a knowledge repository. These tools are at the very top of the BI hierarchy and serve to amalgamate analytical and BI capabilities along with human expertise. Business analytics (BA) is a newer term that tends to be viewed as a subset of the broader business intelligence umbrella and specifically focuses on the analytic aspects within BI (Wickramasinghe and Schaffer 2006).

Knowledge management: Knowledge management is aimed at solving the current business challenges to increase efficiency and efficacy of core business processes while simultaneously incorporating continuous innovation (Wickramasinghe 2006). Broadly speaking, knowledge management involves four key steps of creating/generating knowledge, representing/storing knowledge, accessing/using/reusing knowledge, and disseminating/transferring knowledge (Wickramasinghe and Schaffer 2006). The captured knowledge can take the form of either tacit knowledge (know how) or explicit knowledge (know what); furthermore, it is possible to transform tacit knowledge to explicit knowledge and vice versa by invoking specific knowledge transformations (Wickramasinghe and Schaffer 2006). In the context of AI/AN populations both tacit and explicit knowledge are essential to facilitate patient-centric superior healthcare delivery thereby making KM an integral component to facilitating better healthcare delivery in this context. Furthermore, it is the strategies of KM that become particularly important in ensuring that at all times relevant data, pertinent information, and germane knowledge permeate systems and the extant knowledge base continually grows in a meaningful and useful fashion.

The concept of intelligence continuum then can be applied to several healthcare issues related to the Native American population. However, to ensure that the full benefits of such an approach are realized it is necessary to take a system of systems perspective. To facilitate such an understanding and the appreciation of such an approach it is thus necessary to first discuss the web of healthcare players and how a system of systems approach fits into the healthcare context. From this we will then discuss several case vignettes to illustrate the prudence of such an approach to be adopted in the specific context of the AI/AN population.

17.3 Brief Background of the Healthcare System in the United States

The healthcare system in the United States is inherently complex in nature and serves to address the needs of several stakeholders (Getzen and Allen 2007). Key stakeholders include patients, providers (including physicians and nurses), healthcare facilities (such as hospitals and clinics), pharmacies, governmental agencies, funding agencies, payers (including insurance companies and employers), federal and state regulators, and funding agencies. Taken together they form the web of healthcare players (Wickramasinghe and Schaffer 2006). Interests of these key stakeholders translate into multiple business rules that lead to heterogeneity in healthcare delivery and management. Some of the major processes and systems used by the web of healthcare players are briefly described below.

Managed care companies: Managed care companies have become popular in the last decade primarily because of their efforts to contain medical costs. PPOs (preferred provider organizations) and HMOs (health maintenance organizations) are examples of managed care companies. Managed care companies employ a variety of techniques to contain costs including gate-keeping (requiring mandatory authorization for hospitalization), capitation (payment of a fixed amount per member per month), and generic drug substitution for brand name drugs (Zuckerman et al. 2004). A variety of information systems exist within managed care companies to enroll patients, maintain their claim records, audit claims, and track physician services.

Hospitals: Hospitals are financed by a variety of sources including payments from managed care companies and Medicare and Medicaid programs. DRG (diagnosis-related group) payments reimburse the hospitals based on the diagnosis and treatment. Hospital care in the United States is characterized by technologies for diagnosis, treatment to electronic maintenance of patient health records.

Physicians: Groups of physicians often practice together serving patient needs. Physician groups work with managed care companies via insurance contracts, utilize hospitals for inpatient care, and work with governmental agencies such as Veteran's Administration hospitals and Medicare and Medicaid programs. Physicians utilize a number of technologies and information systems to diagnose and monitor patient's health status.

Clinics: Clinics are utilized by physician groups for treating outpatients. Clinical information systems are utilized for managing patient health records to scheduling patient visits and billing managed care organizations for patient visits.

Governmental agencies: Governmental agencies provide oversight of physicians, clinics, hospitals, and nursing homes. Special units exist for dealing with veterans health and for administering programs such as Medicare and Medicaid.

Based on the above discussion, we next describe how healthcare systems fit into the definition of system of systems (Wickramasinghe et al. 2007; Kotov 1997; Sage and Cuppan 2001; HICSS-43; Carlock and Fenton 2001; Keating et al. 2003; Luskasik 1998). Healthcare systems exhibit the following properties.

Operational and managerial independence: It is clear that each individual system—from managed care systems to governmental systems—exists on its own independent of the other systems. Together, it serves the patient needs, while operating independently. In addition, each has its managerial independence with the management structure ranging from governmental management to private sector management.

Geographical distribution: Healthcare systems are inherently distributed with no central organizational structure. Clinical systems, hospital systems, and regulatory systems are dispersed geographically. The negative effects of geographical separation of healthcare systems, even though an impediment, can be alleviated by technology mediation.

Evolutionary development: Healthcare systems undergo evolutionary development. For example, pharmaceutical companies bring new drugs to the market after years of research, while hospital technologies are evolving to incorporate sensor-based monitoring of inpatients. Again myriad technologies ranging from mobile technologies to electronic health records (EHRs) help evolutionary development.

Emergent behavior: An example of emergent behavior is to track the quality of care using the data from the individual systems such as the clinical systems and the hospital systems. For example, insurance companies such as the United Health certify physicians on whether they meet the quality standards based on national averages on quality care obtained from information on physician treatment of patients across the nation. As another example, The Affordable Care Act signed into law by president Obama in March 2010 consists of dozens of individual changes, or provisions (The Affordable Care Act 2010). Each of these provisions has an impact on the web of healthcare players. Healthcare systems are exhibiting emergent behavior to respond to the changes mandated by this law.

Based on this discussion, it can be seen that healthcare is complex and can be categorized as system of systems. In the next section we explore the role of technology in healthcare system of systems (HSoS).

17.4 Collaborative Technologies in Healthcare

Table 17.1 shows the rise of healthcare expenditures in the United States from 2000 to 2009 (latest available data is for 2009). Healthcare expenses have increased from \$1.4 billion in 2000 to \$2.5 billion in 2009, while their share as a percentage of GDP increased from 13.8 % in 2000 to 17.6 % in 2009. Further, the following is noted by the centers for Medicare and Medicaid services report on US healthcare expenditures (Healthcare Expenditures 2009):

- Shares of total national health spending financed by businesses (21 %), households (28 %), governments (44 %), and other private sponsors (7 %) have remained relatively steady over time. Between 2008 and 2009, however, the federal government share increased significantly (from 24 to 27 %), while the state and local government shares declined (from 17 to 16 %).
- In 2009, health spending by households decelerated, growing 0.2 % in 2009 compared to 5.4 % in 2008. Health spending by state and local governments declined 1.3 % and health spending by private businesses declined 0.5 % in 2009.
- Hospital spending increased 5.1 % to \$759.1 billion in 2009 compared to 5.2 % growth in 2008. Growth in 2008 and 2009 was much slower than the trend between 1999 and 2007, when spending increased an average of 7.2 % per year. The slower growth in 2009 was influenced by decelerating private health insurance spending and slower price growth. Partially offsetting these factors was an increase in Medicaid spending, as Medicaid enrollment increased considerably in 2009.
- Physician and clinical services: Spending on physician and clinical services increased 4.0 % in 2009 to \$505.9 billion, a deceleration from 5.2 % growth in 2008. Slower growth in the use and intensity of services in 2009 was partially offset by increasing prices.

Table 17.1 Healthcare expenditures

	2000	2005	2009
National health expenses (in billions)	\$1,378	\$2,021	\$2,486
US population in millions	283	296	307
GDP in billions	\$9,952	\$12,638	\$14,119
National health exp. share of GDP	13.8	16	17.6
Per capita national health expenses	\$4,878	\$6,827	\$8,086
Annual percent change			
US population	1	0.9	0.9
Gross domestic product	6.4	6.5	−1.7

Source: Centers for Medicare & Medicaid Services, Office of the Actuary, National Health Statistics Group; U.S. Department of Commerce, Bureau of Economic Analysis; and U.S. Bureau of the Census

It should also be noted that the WHO predicts the US healthcare expenditure to increase to 20 % of GNP by 2020 if unchecked (http://www.who.int/en/). To reduce healthcare expenses, technology mediation can play a significant role. For example, mobile technologies to monitor chronic diseases (Wickramasinghe et al. 2011; HICSS-44) can enable pervasive monitoring, thereby enabling patients to receive feedback on the readings related to chronic diseases (e.g., blood glucose readings for diabetes). This in turn may facilitate superior control of chronic diseases, reduce patient visits to hospitals, and thus contribute to controlling healthcare expenses.

Technology-mediated collaboration appears to be worthy goal in order to address these escalating costs and deliver superior healthcare, and is currently being used in limited settings in the HSoS (HICSS-44; HICSS-43; Weiss and Blake June 2011). However, its widespread use in HSoS across different players requires overcoming of significant barriers. In the next section, we consider several scenarios/cases of this ontology and discuss how the collaboration is taking place now or can take place in future. We also indicate the significant benefits and barriers for these scenarios.

17.5 Collaborative Technologies to Facilitate Different Processes in HSoS

Scenario 1: Use of collaborative technologies by clinicians to communicate diagnosis information to patients.

Currently, the most prevalent means of communicating

Diagnosis information based on laboratory testing is by telephone. The results are either communicated by telephone or the patient is asked (via phone conversation) to come in for a follow-up visit to discuss the findings and lab results. A future process could use email and/or mobile devices for communicating diagnoses. However, barriers to adopting new technologies include the following:

- Clinician time and effort
- Risk of communicating without using any kind of security, encryption

There are currently no incentives for physicians to communicate via email. They are not reimbursed by payers/patients for communicating results via email; this is very similar to them not being compensated for returning patient phone calls and providing prescription refills. This fact is reflected in a recent survey's findings by CompTIA (Weiss and Blake June 2011): only 21 % of the responding physicians mentioned that they allow patients to email or text health-related questions, 12 % said they email appointment reminders, and only 5 % said they text appointment reminders. Also, abnormal test results and bad news in terms of diagnosis are best discussed face-to-face rather than via email. Also, communication via mobile devices will require additional mechanisms to comply with HIPAA regulations. In fact, the providers need to demonstrate to HIPAA (in case of an audit) that there are mechanisms to ensure integrity of data. Thus, technologies such as email and text messages may have a role in communicating routine diagnosis information to patients, while FTF communication is the significant mode of communication for abnormal test results.

Scenario 2: *Communication of prescription information from clinician to pharmacy*. This scenario involves communication between two key players of HSoS—providers/clinicians and pharmacies. The following discussion assumes that the ontology is further extended for communicating prescription information accurately between providers and pharmacies. Currently, prescription information is communicated by the clinicians to pharmacies by hand-written prescriptions, telephone, or fax. However, as EHRs get implemented at a sustained pace, prescription orders are electronically communicated using the Computerized Physician Order Entry (CPOE) component of EHRs. EHRs is the most commonly accepted term for software with a full range of functionalities to store, access, and use patient medical information. EHRs contain longitudinal electronic record of patient health information generated by one or more encounters in any care delivery setting. CPOE is an automated order entry system that captures physicians' instructions regarding the care of their patients. It is often implemented as a component of the EHR. It must be able to communicate orders to other connected systems within the EHR. Barriers to implementing EHRs include the following:

- Confusion due to complexity
- Cost of implementation
- Lack of standardization
- Lack of motivation in creating interoperability
- Uncertainties about the direct benefits
- Significant changes to clinical processes

EHRs allow direct sourcing and capturing of patient data. Hence, benefits of implementing EHRs include:

Direct patient care, continuing patient care, research, improving legal compliance, cutting costs, improving patient safety, and providing decision support.

In fact, to demonstrate the meaning use of EHRs for federal incentives, 15 core objectives need to be met by the healthcare facility implementing the EHRs. One of these 15 core objectives is related to providing the CPOE functionality of EHRs (Weiss and Blake June 2011).

Core objective: Use CPOE for medication orders directly entered by any licensed healthcare professional who can enter orders into the medical record per state, local, and professional guidelines.

With the increased prevalence of EHRs, CPOE may become the predominant mode of communication for prescriptions in future years. In the next section, we apply these concepts to healthcare delivery for Native American patients.

17.6 Applying SoS and the IC to Healthcare Delivery in Native American Population

In fiscal year (FY) 2006 (http://www.ihs.gov/PublicInfo/PublicAffairs/Welcome_Info/IHSintro.asp; Anonymous 2005a, b; Wickramasinghe et al. 2011), Urban Indian health is funded at $33 million. Urban Indian health organizations also typically leverage funding in order to maximize service provision. IHS provides about half of all funding available to these organizations. Other major funding agencies include Medicaid, state and local programs, and other federal programs separate from IHS. Services provided vary from outreach, referral, and case management to comprehensive care, including: ambulatory medical care; dental services; community education (health education, transportation, patient advocacy); alcohol and substance abuse prevention, treatment and counseling; AIDS and STD information; mental health counseling; and social services.

Some of the key issues related to Native American health as identified by Wickramasinghe et al. (2007) include the following:

- Barriers to quality healthcare due to factors such as poverty and lack of insurance.
- Misclassification of Native Americans as either Whites or Hispanics. This misclassification leads to unreliable data on the incidence of diseases (such as cancer) in the Native American population, which in turn leads to misconceptions about the immunity of Native Americans to diseases such as cancer.
- Lack of cultural awareness on the part of physicians.
- Limited federal funding. IHS funding from federal government was approximately $33 million for FY 2006, which translates to $210 per user. In contrast, the per capita national health expenses were $7,198 in 2006 (see Table 17.1).
- Disparity between funds allocated to IHSs on reservations versus the IHSs in urban regions. Most recent census data from 2000 showed that 61 % of the Native Americans live in urban regions. However, only 1 % of the budget is allocated to Native American health services in urban regions.

While some of these issues require policy changes from the federal government for their resolution, other issues can be resolved by effective management of data and knowledge related to Native Americans. For example, funding the Indian Health Centers (IHCs) adequately can be accomplished by congressional action during budget negotiations. However, data required to track the health issues of Native American population can be accomplished by using information systems that can effectively capture specific data relevant to Native American population. Nevertheless before the tools, techniques, technologies, and tactics of knowledge management can be successfully applied it is first useful to conceptualize this context as a HSoS.

17.7 Collaborative Technologies and System of Systems Approach for Healthcare Delivery to AI/AN Population

Given the barriers such as limited funding to IHCs and poverty of AI/AN population, it is difficult to utilize the full extent of collaborative technologies for AI/AN population. Underfunding of IHCs may dissuade providers (physicians, nurses) to communicate with patients using technologies such as email and mobile devices. Further, IHCs may not have fully implemented EHRs that facilitate seamless communication among providers, hospitals, pharmacies, and other key players in HSoS. In this section, we take the example of cancer diagnosis in Native American patients and describe the current process versus the desired process using collaborative technologies for AI/AN patients. We selected cancer because it is often misreported in AI/AN population, thus making cancer incidence rates in AI/AN population appear lower than the actual incidence rates (Anonymous 2005a). Figure 17.3 shows a simple process for cancer diagnosis in AI/AN population. In this process, communication of information, diagnosis, and data occurs between primary care physician (PCP), specialist, patient, and the stage agencies tracking cancer (if cancer is

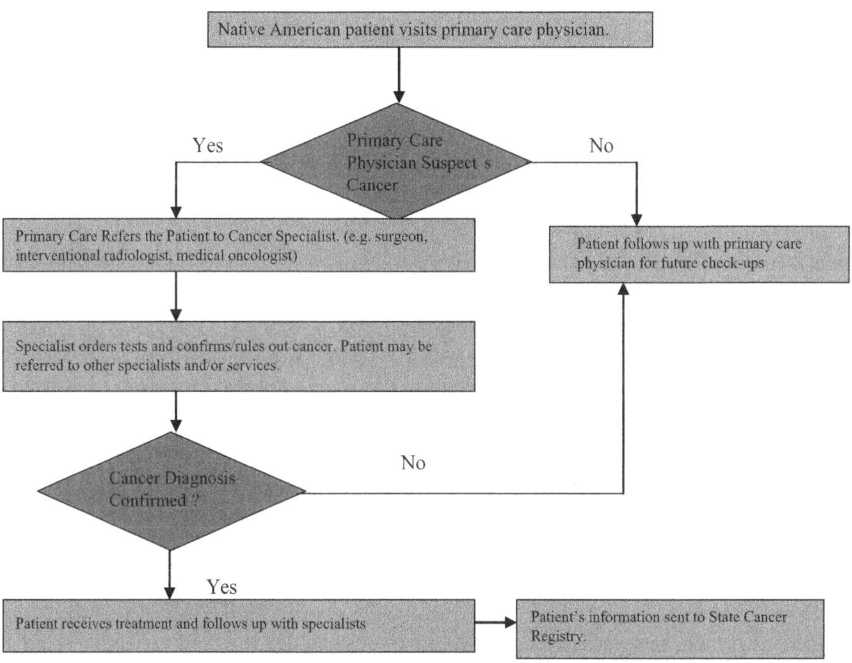

Fig. 17.3 A simplified process for cancer diagnosis and tracking AI/AN cancer patients

diagnosed in the patient). The current process for this communication is paper-based and manual. For example, the specialist reports are delivered to PCP by paper and the communication of diagnosis to the patient occurs face-to-face. By applying the ontology in Table 17.2, it is possible to utilize EHRs and mobile devices for communication involving the PCP and the specialists. Similarly, it is possible to utilize web-portals to communicate cancer diagnosis to state agencies. The key barriers such as lack of EHR implementations can be overcome if better funding and governmental incentives are provided to the IHCs.

17.8 Concluding Remarks

Few would disagree that healthcare delivery in the United States is currently at a crossroads. Costs are escalating and quality is too often a growing concern. In order to address effective and efficient patient-centric healthcare delivery, it is necessary to focus on how to provide value. In the Information age this is only feasible by embracing technology to enable superior healthcare delivery.

One of the areas where healthcare delivery is embarrassingly inadequate in the United States is the delivery of care to AI/AN segments of the community. The preceding has served to proffer an approach that serves to rectify this untenable situation. Specifically we have proposed the adoption of a system of systems conceptualization coupled with the introduction of the intelligence continuum in order to systematically and appropriately apply the tools, techniques, technologies, and tactics of the knowledge economy to this context.

By introducing the intelligence continuum model, it is possible to generate better data and information which then can be extracted and utilized to support enhanced decision making to facilitate superior diagnosis and thereby better treatment. An added benefit of the IC model is that it is continuous and hence the extant knowledge base is always built upon with each iteration so that the future state is always better than the current state in terms of having more data and information from which to make critical decisions. Moreover, the IC model also captures and utilizes vital tacit and explicit knowledge.

Providing quality healthcare for all Americans is a priority on the government's agenda. In order to realize this vision for the AI/AN segment of the community, it is imperative that pertinent data and relevant information are appropriately analyzed in order to support the necessary and consequent decision making required. This can only occur if a rigorous and systematic approach is adopted making it an imperative to take a system of systems approach coupled with the IC as the preceding has described. Only then will it be possible to provide the necessary patient-centric quality healthcare that is incumbent on the US healthcare system for AI/AN segments of the community. In closing we note that the system of systems approach coupled with the IC model is also appropriate for any/all areas of healthcare operations and encourage researchers to further investigate appropriate opportunities.

References

Anonymous. (2005a). Wisconsin's Comprehensive Cancer Control Plan 2005–2010. *State of Wisconsin Report.*

Anonymous. (2005b). Community Health Data Profile: Minnesota, Wisconsin & Michigan Tribal Communities 2005. *Great Lakes EpiCenter.*

Anonymous. (2005c). Community Health Profile Milwaukee 2005. *Great Lakes EpiCenter Epidemiology Project Report.* http://www.glitc.org.

Anonymous. (2005d). NARCH Cancer Surveillance Project: Improving American Indian Cancer Surveillance an Data Reporting in Wisconsin. *Gerald L. Ignace Indian Health Center Report.*

Carlock, P. G., & Fenton, R. E. (2001). System of systems (SoS) enterprise systems for information-intensive organizations. *Systems Engineering, 4*(4), 242–261.

Cios, K. J. (Ed.). (2001). *Medical data mining and knowledge discovery.* Heidelberg: Physica-Verlag.

Cunningham, P. J. (1993). Access to care in the Indian Health Service. *Health Affairs, 12*(3), 224–233.

Epidemiology Project Report. Retrieved December, 2010, from http://www.glitc.org.

Fayyad, U., Piatetsky-Shapiro, G., & Smyth, P. (1996). From data mining to knowledge discovery: an overview. In U. Fayyad, G. Piatetsky-Shapiro, P. Smyth, & R. Uthurusamy (Eds.), *Advances in knowledge discovery and data mining.* Menlo Park, CA: AAAI Press/The MIT Press.

Getzen, T. E., & Allen, B. H. (2007). *Healthcare economics.* Hoboken, NJ: Wiley.

Healthcare Expenditures. (2009). Retrieved December, 2010, from http://www.cms.gov/NationalHealthExpendData/.

Keating, C., Rogers, R., Unal, R., Dryer, D., Sousa-Poza, A., Safford, R., Peterson, W., Rabadi, G., (2003). System of systems engineering. *Engineering Management Journal, 15*(3), 36–45.

Knutsen, K., et al. (2005). Cancer Information Resources: Preferences among health professionals serving American Indian communities in Minnesota, Wisconsin, and North Dakota. *Spirit of Eagles, University of Wisconsin Comprehensive Care Center Report.* March 2005.

Kotov, V. (1997). *Systems of systems as communicating structures.* Hewlett Packard Computer Systems Laboratory Paper HPL-97-124 (pp. 1–15).

Luskasik, S. J. (1998). Systems, systems of systems, and the education of engineers. *Artificial Intelligence for Engineering Design, Analysis, and Manufacturing, 12*(1), 55–60.

Moghimi, H., Zadeh, H., Schaffer, J., & Wickramasinghe, N. (2012). Incorporating intelligent risk detection to enable superior decision support: The example of orthopaedic surgeries. *Health and Technology.* doi:10.1007/s12553-011-0014-z.

North American Association of Central Cancer Registries (NAACCR) Washington Reports. Retrieved December, 2010, from http://naaccr.org.

Papers in the session "Technology Mediated Collaborations in Healthcare," in HICSS-44. http://www.hicss.hawaii.edu.

Papers in the session "Technology Mediated Collaborations in Healthcare," in HICSS-43. http://www.hicss.hawaii.edu.

Sage, A. P., & Cuppan, C. D. (2001). On the systems engineering and management of systems of systems and federations of systems. *Information, Knowledge, Systems Management, 2*(4), 325–345.

The Affordable Care Act. (2010). Retrieved December, 2010, from http://www.healthcare.gov/.

The Indian Health Service (IHS) Web-site. Retrieved December, 2010, from http://www.ihs.gov/PublicInfo/PublicAffairs/Welcome_Info/IHSintro.asp.

Von Lubitz, D., & Wickramasinghe, N. (2006). Networkcentric healthcare: Applying the tools techniques and strategies of knowledge management to create superior healthcare operations. *International Journal of Electronic Healthcare, 4*, 415–428.

Von Lubitz, D., Yanovsky, G., & Wickramasinghe, N. (2006). Networkcentric healthcare operations: The telecommunications structure. *International Journal of Networking and Virtual Organizations, 3*(1), 60–85.

Weiss, G. G., & Blake, G. (June 2011). Email and your patients: Too risky & time consuming, or an idea whose time has come? *Medical Economics, 88*(11), 22–33.
WHO. Retrieved December, 2010, from http://www.who.int/en/.
Wickramasinghe, N. (2006). Knowledge creation: A meta-framework. *International Journal of Innovation and Learning, 3*(5), 558–573.
Wickramasinghe, N., Chalasani, S., Bali, R., & Kumar, P. (2007). Applying the intelligence continuum for better healthcare delivery of Native American Patients. *International Journal of Biomedical Engineering and Technology, 1*(2), 172–189.
Wickramasinghe, N., & Schaffer, J. (2006). Creating knowledge driven healthcare processes with the intelligence continuum. *International Journal of Electronic Healthcare, 2*(2), 164–174.
Wickramasinghe, N., Chalassani, S., & Goldberg, S. (2011). Wireless diabetes for Native Americans. *Hawaii International Conference on System Sciences (HICSS)*, (pp. 4–7).
Zuckerman, S., Haley, J., Roubideaux, Y., & Lillie-Blanton, M. (2004). Health service access, use, and insurance coverage among American Indians/Alaska Natives and Whites: What role does the Indian health service play? *American Journal of Public Health, 94*(1), 53–59.

Chapter 18
The Role of a Disruptive Pervasive Technology Solution to Facilitate Better Healthcare Delivery to Native American Patients

Suresh Chalasani, Steve Goldberg, and Nilmini Wickramasinghe

Abstract Chronic diseases are increasing exponentially and by their very nature and definition mean that no cure is in sight. One such chronic disease is diabetes. The WHO has described diabetes as a silent epidemic given the current number of sufferers and future projections of increased number of individuals who are expected to contract diabetes. While globally the numbers of diabetic sufferers are alarming, in some segments of the community there is significant overrepresentation due to many factors including ineffective and inefficient healthcare delivery processes. The following proffers a disruptive, pervasive technology solution as a way to not only facilitate superior care for diabetic patients but also enable needed healthcare delivery process redesign.

Keywords Pervasive technology • mHealth • Diabetes • Knowledge management e-Health • Process redesign • Native American healthcare

---

An earlier version of this material was presented at the 2011 HICSS conference, 4–7 Jan, Kuai, Hawaii.

S. Chalasani
MIS Department, School of Business and Technology, University of Wisconsin-Parkside, 900 Wood Rd, Kenosha, WI 53141-2000, USA
e-mail: chalasan@uwp.edu

S. Goldberg
INET International Canada, 131 Glen Crescent, Thornhill, ON, Canada, L4J 4W4
e-mail: sgoldberg@inet-international.com

N. Wickramasinghe (✉)
Epworth HealthCare & Department of BITL & HIRi, RMIT University, GPO Box 2476 Melbourne, VIC 3001, Australia
e-mail: nilmini.wickramasinghe@rmit.edu.au

N. Wickramasinghe et al. (eds.), *Lean Thinking for Healthcare*, Healthcare Delivery in the Information Age, DOI 10.1007/978-1-4614-8036-5_18,

18.1 Introduction

Many have noted that the United States has an unparalleled capacity to treat, especially in the context of trauma and infectious diseases (Gibbons et al. 2010). However, and sadly, the US healthcare system too often fails to provide appropriate and adequate healthcare delivery to many groups of the population including urban communities, and low income individuals, leading to one of the worst paradoxes of the US healthcare system as noted in the key note address at the International Conference on Urban Health, Baltimore, 31 Oct–2 Nov 2007.

While some of the critical issues necessary to address this untenable situation require policy changes from the federal government for their resolution, we believe many of the issues can be resolved through the prudent application of pervasive technology solutions coupled with the effective application of the techniques and tactics of knowledge management.

To illustrate this, we focus on one segment of the community that continues to suffer from inferior healthcare delivery; namely American Indians and Alaska Natives (AI/AN). We present the case for the benefits of using a pervasive wireless monitoring solution for enabling superior healthcare delivery for Native American diabetic sufferers as an example of how a pervasive technology solution that utilizes the tools, techniques, tactics, and technologies of knowledge management can in fact provide a sustainable and far reaching solution to the current situation.

The rest of this chapter is organized as follows. Section 18.2 presents background on critical issues regarding healthcare delivery and the access models for healthcare delivery to AI/AN population. Section 18.3 discusses the problem of diabetes in the AI/AN population. Section 18.4 presents the pervasive wireless solution and discusses the key success factors of the solution strategy. Section 18.5 describes how the INET framework is being applied to diabetes care for AI/AN population. Section 18.6 provides a discussion of key issues, directions for future research, and any limitations. Finally Sect. 18.7 presents the conclusions.

18.2 Background: Essential Elements of the Structure of AI/AN Healthcare Delivery

The Indian Health Service (IHS), an agency within the Department of Health and Human Services, is responsible for providing federal health services to AI/AN. The provision of health services to members of federally recognized tribes grew out of the special government-to-government relationship between the federal government and Indian tribes. This relationship, established in 1787, is based on Article I, Section 7 of the Constitution, and has been given form and substance by numerous treaties, laws, Supreme Court decisions, and Executive Orders. The IHS is the principal federal healthcare provider and health advocate for Indian people and its goal is to raise their health status to the highest possible level. The IHS currently provides health services to approximately 1.5 million AI/AN who belong to more than

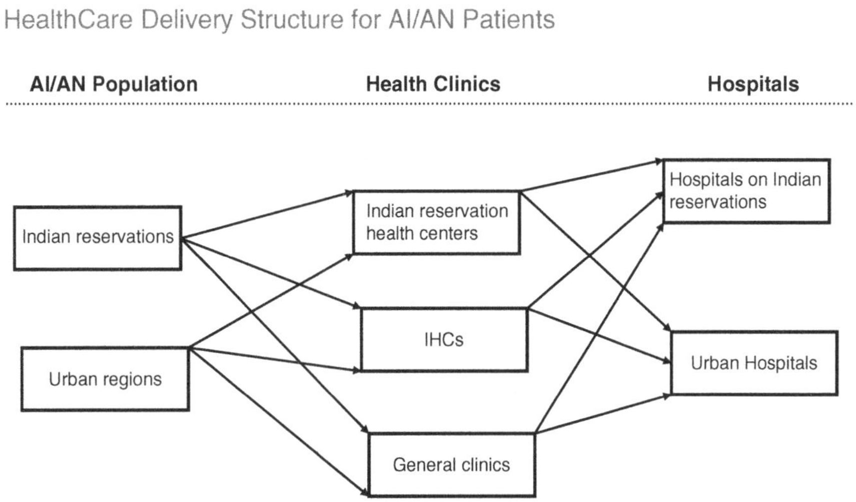

Fig. 18.1 Healthcare delivery to AI/AN population

557 federally recognized tribes in 35 states (the IHS web site). Most IHSs are provided on or near reservations and approximately 1 % of the budget is used to provide services to Indian people living in urban areas; however, most recent census data shows the majority of Native Americans are urban. Hence, clients of the Urban Indian program commonly experience significant barriers in accessing basic health services. Figure 18.1 summarizes the healthcare delivery for AI/AN population.

IHS funds a total of 34 Urban Indian health organizations to reduce barriers to access in urban areas. In fiscal year 2006, Urban Indian health was funded at $33 million. Urban Indian health organizations also typically leverage funding in order to maximize service provision. IHS provides about half of all funding available to these organizations. Other major funding agencies include Medicaid, state and local programs, and other federal programs separate from IHS.

Resource limitations may compel some eligible persons to go outside of the IHS system to receive healthcare (Cunningham 1993). In terms of access to healthcare, AI/AN had less insurance coverage and worse access and utilization than Whites. Over half of low income uninsured AI/AN did not have access to the IHS (Zuckerman et al. 2004; Lautenschlager and Smith 2006; Sequist et al. 2005; Cullen 2001; Parker et al. 2004; Hays 2003).

To address this problem we embarked upon a research study to investigate how a pervasive technology solution might ameliorate this significant problem. We chose to adopt a case study approach since, as noted by several researchers, a case study approach is suitable when trying to answer a "how" or "why" question, especially in an exploratory research context, as is the case with our chosen study (Yin 1994; Kavale 1996; Boyatsis 1998). The chosen case was that of investigating the application of a pervasive wireless solution; namely the use of a cell phone for facilitating superior monitoring of AI/AN patients suffering from diabetes.

18.3 Diabetes in AI/AN Population

The world diabetes population is expected to increase by 76 % from 159 million in 2000 to 236 million in 2025 and thus diabetes has been called a silent epidemic by the WHO (http://www.who.int/en/). While globally the situation regarding diabetes is problematic, for the AI/AN population in particular, it is even worse not only because the prevalence of diabetes is overrepresented in this segment of the community but more especially given the existing inadequate healthcare delivery structures in place. According to United States Census 2000, an estimated 2,447,989 AI/AN people live in the United States. Studies of diabetes among AI/AN population by several researchers (Acton et al. 2002; Burrows et al. 2000; Miller et al. 2004; Ogunwole 2006) concluded the following:

1. In the span of 8 years from 1990 to 1997, prevalence of diabetes among AI/AN population increased by 30 % to 65,000. In contrast, prevalence in US population increased by 14 %.
2. Prevalence of diabetes in AI/AN population increased with age for both men and women. Diabetes prevalence is more in AI/AN women than in men.
3. The increase in prevalence for AI/AN population less than 45 years is 10 times as much the increase in the general population for the same age group.
4. The AI/AN diabetic population are younger than the US diabetic population.
5. 110,814 or 14.9 % of AI/AN aged 20 years or older and receiving care from IHS have diabetes.
6. At the regional level, diabetes is least common among Alaska Natives (8.2 %) and most common among American Indians in the southeastern United States (27.8 %) and southern Arizona (27.8 %).
7. On average, AI/AN are 2.3 times more likely to have diabetes as non-Hispanic whites of similar age.
8. Diabetes among American Indian youth (ages 15–19) has increased 106 % between 1990 and 2001.

The above observations indicate that diabetes in AI/AN populations is not only reaching an epidemic proportion but also an example that serves to underscore a totally untenable situation with regard to acceptable quality of care. This makes it a most suitable case for illustrating the benefits of a pervasive technology solution, DiaMonD, to provide a cost-effective superior healthcare solution.

18.4 DiaMonD: A Pervasive Wireless solution

Containment of cost and yet offering the highest quality healthcare has become a global priority for healthcare delivery (Wickramasinghe and Schaffer 2010). In such an environment prevention and/or early detection becomes critical since initiatives

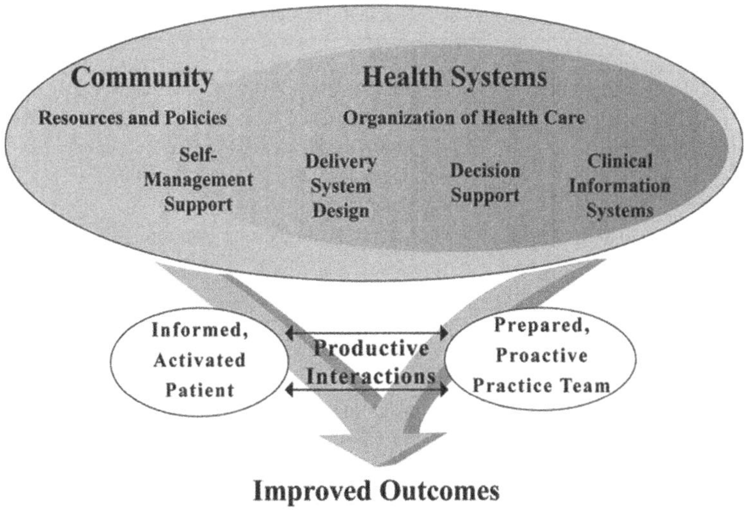

Fig. 18.2 Chronic disease care model (adapted from Rachlis 2006)

that prevent the occurrence of a disease help to circumvent costly healthcare interventions, while initiatives that detect early the occurrence of a disease usually enable better control of this disease and thereby less costly healthcare interventions. Moreover, in both instances quality is high since the patient is subjected to less invasive healthcare interventions and can enjoy a higher quality of life.

This is especially relevant in the context of chronic disease. Chronic diseases such as diabetes, asthma, or hypertension if detected early can be contained and the sufferers from these diseases can continue to lead full and high quality lives. Conversely, if these diseases are not well managed, sufferers can develop more complicated healthcare problems and life for such patients becomes less than satisfactory. By its very definition, there is no likely cure for sufferers of chronic diseases; hence, critical to effective chronic disease management is regular monitoring of an informed patient who takes responsibility for managing his/her wellness (Wickramasinghe and Goldberg 2009). As identified by Rachlis (2006) a chronic disease care model requires the interaction and coordination of numerous areas (Fig. 18.2). In particular, it requires the interaction of four key components of the healthcare system including self-management support, delivery support, decision support, and clinical information systems and support from the community at large (see Table 18.1). Taken together, this provides a conducive environment for productive interactions between an informed and activated patient and a prepared and proactive healthcare team. Moreover, this was the basis for the development of DiaMonD, a pervasive wireless diabetic solution.

Table 18.1 Components of Chronic Care Model (Rachlis 2006)

Component	Description
Organization of health system	• Leadership in chronic disease management (CDM) • Goals for CDM • Improvement strategy for CDM • Incentives and regulations for CDM • Benefits
Self-management support (SMS)	• Assessment and documentation of needs and activities • Addressing concerns of patients • Effective behavior change interventions
Decision support system (DSS)	• Evidence-based guidelines • Involvement of specialists in improving primary care • Providing education for CDM • Informing patients about guidelines
Delivery system design (DSD)	• Practice team functioning • Practice team leadership • Appointment system • Follow-up • Planned visits for CDM • Continuity of care
Clinical information systems (CIS)	• Registry • Reminders to providers • Feedback • Information about relevant subgroups of patients needing services • Patient treatment plans
Community	• Linkages for patients to resources • Partnerships with community organizations • Policy and plan development

18.4.1 The DiaMonD Solution

DiaMonD—diabetes monitoring device—is a pervasive technology solution to provide superior healthcare for sufferers of diabetes. The solution incorporates software that facilitates the ubiquitous monitoring of an individual's diabetes, thereby, contributing to diabetes self-management. The solution is grounded in trying to support key components of a chronic disease care model (Table 18.1). INET International Inc.'s research (Goldberg 2002a, b, c, d, e; Wickramasinghe and Goldberg 2003, 2004, 2007) starts with a 30-day e-business acceleration project in collaboration with many key players in hospitals, such as clinicians, medical units, administration, and I.T. departments. Together, they follow a rigorous procedure that refocuses the traditional 1- to 5-year SDLC into concurrent 30-day projects to accelerate healthcare delivery improvements. At completion, an e-business acceleration project delivers a scope document to develop a handheld technology application (HTA) proof-of-concept specific to the unique needs of a particular environment. The proof-of-concept is a virtual lab case scenario which operates

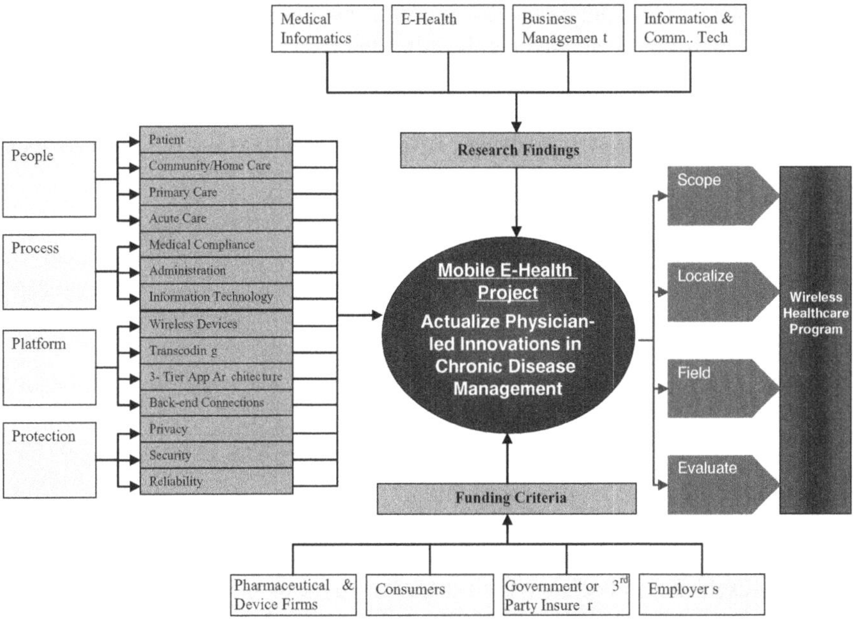

Fig. 18.3 INET model (adapted from Wickramasinghe and Goldberg 2009)

within a mobile Internet (wireless) environment by working with hospitals and technology vendors. The final step is the collection of additional data with clinical HTA trials consisting of 2-week hospital evaluations.

The INET web-based model (Fig. 18.3) provides the necessary components to enable the delivery framework to be positioned in the best possible manner so it can indeed facilitate enacting the key components of the chronic disease model successfully (Table 18.1).

The model is positioned to suit the complex nature of healthcare environments by iteratively, systematically, and rigorously incorporating lessons learnt data to healthcare processes for ensuring superior healthcare delivery. This manner not only maximizes the value of past data and organizational learning but also makes processes amendable as complex needs and requirements evolve.

It is important to note that in the INET web-based model the three key areas of risk, namely people, processes, and technology, are minimized through the use of pervasive technology, which we believe is a unique benefit of the INET solution. Specifically, since the proposed solution is an application that is compatible with any mobile phone or wireless device (e.g., a PDA), data transfers occur between patients and providers on a well-vetted model. Therefore, the learning curve for patients is minimal as they are likely to be in possession of mobile devices.

What makes this model unique and most beneficial is its focus on enabling and supporting all areas necessary for the actualization of ICT initiatives in healthcare. By design, the model identifies the inputs necessary to bring an innovative chronic disease management solution to market. These solutions are developed and implemented through a physician-led mobile e-health project. This project is the heart of the model that bridges the needs and requirements of many different players into a final (output) deliverable, a "Wireless Healthcare Program." To accomplish this, the model is continually updated to identify, select, and prioritize the ICT project inputs that will:

- Accelerate healthcare system enhancements and achieve rapid healthcare benefits. The model identifies key healthcare system inputs with the four Ps, namely (1) People that deliver healthcare, (2) Process to define the current healthcare delivery tasks, (3) Platform used in the healthcare technology infrastructure, and (4) Protection of patient data.
- Close the timing gaps between information research studies and their application in healthcare operational settings.
- Shorten the time cycle to fund an ICT project and receive an adequate return on the investment.

These 4 Ps were chosen after discussions with various healthcare professionals as to the areas they believed were critical inputs for any model. These categories are mutually exclusive and collectively exhaustive based on the views of experts consulted. In applying the DiaMonD solution to any particular context of diabetes sufferers it is necessary to consider the scope or extent of the diabetes problems in this context, the specific contextual features such as demographics, as well as current processes in place to treat patients so that the application will be tailored to this population; hence, "localize" is an important aspect in the delivery framework. In addition, it is important to understand the make-up of the care team or field and finally results need to be evaluated.

Thus, the delivery framework helps to make the solution applicable to any context of diabetes patients which is an essential consideration given that diabetes cuts across all areas of the community. Together the components of the model will help in actualizing physician-led solution for the management of chronic diseases in general and of diabetes in particular. To successfully implement the INET web-based model described above, it was necessary to have an appropriate methodology. Based on this need, the adaptive mapping to realization methodology (AMR) was developed (Fig. 18.4) (Wickramasinghe and Goldberg 2007). The idea of the methodology was to apply a systematic rigorous set of predetermined protocols to each business case and then to map the post-prior results back to the model. In this way, it was possible to compare and contrast both a priori and post-priori findings. From such a comparison, first a diagnosis of the current state was made; then prescriptions were derived for the next business case. Hence, each pilot study incorporated the lessons learnt from the previous one and the model was adapted in real time.

By applying the tools and techniques of today's knowledge economy as presented in the intelligence continuum (IC), it is possible to make the AMR methodology into a very powerful knowledge-based systems development model (Wickramasinghe and Goldberg 2007). The IC was developed by Wickramasinghe and Schaffer (2006) to enable the application of tools and technologies of the

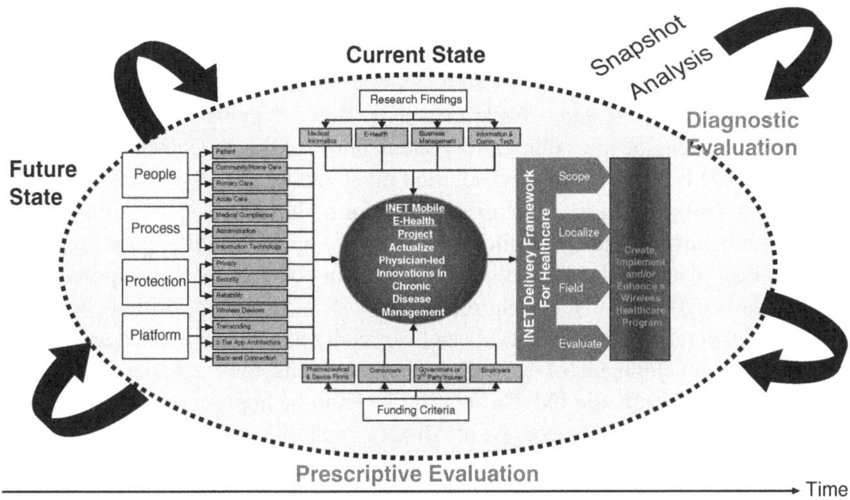

Fig. 18.4 AMR methodology (adapted from Rachlis 2006)

knowledge economy to be applied to healthcare processes in a systematic and rigorous fashion, thereby ensuring superior healthcare delivery. The collection of key tools, techniques, and processes that make up the IC include, but are not limited to, data mining, business intelligence/analytics, and knowledge management (Wickramasinghe and Schaffer 2006).

Taken together, they represent a very powerful system for refining the raw data stored in data marts and/or data warehouses, thereby maximizing the value and utility of these data assets for any organization. To maximize the value of the data generated through specific healthcare processes and then to use this to improve processes, IC techniques and tools must be applied in a systematic manner. Once applied, the results become part of the data set that are subsequently reintroduced into the system and combined with other inputs of people, processes, and technology to develop an improvement continuum.

Thus, the IC includes the generation of data, the analysis of these data to provide a "diagnosis," and their reintroduction into the cycle as a "prescriptive" solution. In this way, the IC is well suited to the dynamic and complex nature of healthcare environments and ensures that the future state is always built upon the extant knowledge-base of the preceding state. Through the incorporation of the IC with the AMR methodology we then have a knowledge-based systems development model that can be applied to any setting, not necessarily to chronic disease management. The power of this model is that it brings best practices and the best available germane knowledge to each iteration and is both flexible and robust.

Given the uniqueness of this approach it was necessary to develop this model from the beginning rather than look at other existing models. This was done by trying to understand key criteria from various stakeholders such as patients, healthcare professionals, and hospital personnel and sort this information into a coherent whole. This was an iterative process which involved many and multiple discussions with the various stakeholders until all parties were agreed; the model captured the essential elements as discussed in detail in Goldberg (2002a, b, c, d, e).

To date, directional data (Wickramasinghe and Goldberg 2007) has already shown the benefits of this solution in various pilot studies in Canada. We believe that DiaMonD is a most beneficial solution given the huge and growing impact of diabetes. In particular, it is very cost effective for both patients and healthcare providers. We believe that as more pilot studies are conducted in different settings this will add data that will show the full and far reaching benefits of the proposed solution. What is certain is that current methods for treating patients with diabetes are unwieldy, generating significant costs, not especially patient-centric and doing little to stem the development of secondary complications thus a better solution is required. At this stage, the INET's solution looks to be appropriate in general and especially well suited to the context of AI/AN population.

Thus, DiaMonD represents a pervasive technology-enabled solution, which, while not exorbitantly expensive, can facilitate the superior monitoring of diabetes (Fig. 18.5). The proposed solution enables patient empowerment by way of enhancing self-management. This is a desirable objective because it allows patients to become more like partners with their clinicians in the management of their own

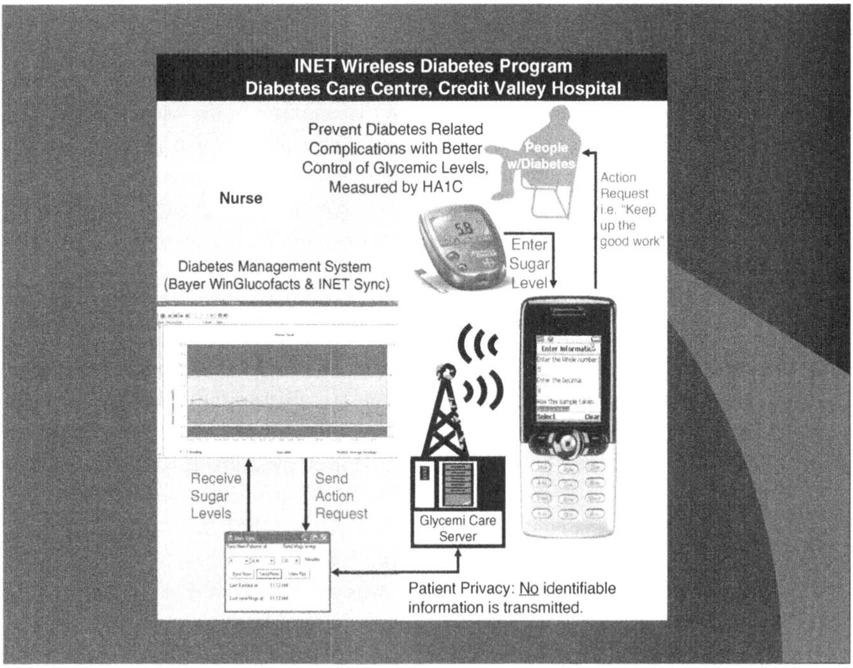

Fig. 18.5 Logical design of the DiaMonD solution (adapted from Rachlis 2006)

healthcare (Opie 1998; Radin 2006) by enhancing the traditional clinical-patient interactions (Mirza et al. 2008). Figure 18.5 provides the DiaMonD solution schematic; the process steps in monitoring diabetes using the DiaMonD approach are outlined below.

1. Each patient receives a blood glucose measurement unit.
2. Patient conducts the blood glucose test and enters the blood glucose information into a handheld wireless device (Blackberry, iPhone, or other PDAs).
3. The blood glucose information is transmitted to a Glycemic Care Center whose servers store the data related to the patient. Patient's handheld device uniquely identifies the patient for recording the blood glucose data.
4. The blood glucose information of the patient is reviewed using a web-based application by the clinical staff (physician/nurse).
5. Feedback on glucose levels is transmitted back to the patient's handheld device. Feedback examples include complimenting the patient when glucose levels are normal or asking the patient to come for a follow-up appointment when the levels are out of norm.

18.5 AI/AN and DiaMonD

When we simply apply the Chronic Care Model (Rachlis 2006) to diabetic sufferers in AI/AN populations, there is failure in almost all dimensions primarily due to limited funding which in turn leads to poor leadership in IHCs for chronic disease management. However, as has been discussed, regular monitoring of diabetes is a necessary part to controlling this particular chronic disease and keeping it from evolving into more complicated healthcare problems. This makes the DiaMonD solution especially important in this context. Figure 18.5 serves to highlight the importance of maintaining appropriate levels of blood sugar (HA1C). Even a 1 % sustained reduction in the HA1C levels can significantly reduce the risk of other potentially fatal events such as heart attack and stroke (Stratton 2000).

As identified earlier in Sects. 18.2 and 18.3 the problems resulting in inadequate healthcare delivery for AI/AN diabetic patients are concerned with poor resources which in turn lead to access barriers, and infrequent or no monitoring of their diabetic condition. The solution outlined by the above process addresses the following barriers to better diabetes care in AI/AN population:

- (Barrier to access) AI/AN patients have better connectivity to the clinical staff through the mobile device and their blood glucose levels are readily monitored by the staff.
- (Regular monitoring) Since the system requires pre- and post-fasting blood sugars to be transmitted this can be done routinely without the patient having to make physical visits for this data and information to be received.
- (Physician availability) Physicians can monitor the patients remotely without the need to be present in the clinic.

It is also important to note that the solution is simple enough to be supported on any cell phone which significantly reduces the cost for the patient. Moreover, as the charge is only for transfer of data, most data plans cover this in their free minute packages and hence again the cost to the patient is minimal and not an extra charge onto of regular services they may have with their cell phone. It is important to note that a recent study conducted by cellular news (WHO 2002) shows that cell phone usage by AI/AN segments of the community is not significantly low as compared to whites and is growing rapidly. Further confirmation to us that large scale adoption of pervasive technology solutions for facilitating healthcare based on cell phones such as DiaMonD will be successful.

18.6 Discussion

The preceding has served to proffer the benefits of the application of a pervasive technology solution, DiaMonD, to address and ameliorate a currently untenable solution; namely the gross inadequacy of healthcare delivery to the AI/AN population.

This was done by firstly providing the background to the current state of healthcare delivery for this segment of the community and especially highlighting the situation in the context of diabetes a chronic disease that is a significant healthcare issue globally. We then presented the research question and underscored the need for a case study approach.

The pervasive technology solution proposed was the application of DiaMonD the software solution developed by INET Intl. to be used on cell phones while the case study reported represents a work in progress and at this stage we have identified the AI/AN patient population and are working with the clinic to move forward.

This solution has many unique aspects including its rapid and tailored design and development, its grounding in the tools and techniques of knowledge management which enable the solution at all times to leverage from the extant knowledge to always ensure it is providing latest best practices, and the low cost yet high quality monitoring solution that is provided to the diabetic sufferer anytime and anywhere. In the context of AI/AN population this is especially important with regard to also building upon evidence-based medicine where much lower representation of AI/AN statistics currently exists. Thus the contributions of this study are numerous and far reaching and fall into two key areas as follows:

Benefits to the AI/AN community

The proposed solution:

1. Enables low income AI/AN patients with diabetes to better control this disease and thereby lead more normal lives. This is particularly important since 75–85 % of healthcare spending is on chronic disease management and the number of people suffering from diabetes in the United States is growing exponentially.

2. Enables AI/AN patients with diabetes to be continuously educated and mentored. This will serve to control their diabetes and in turn play a significant role in limiting the progress of the disease which can lead to unpleasant and costly medical complications.
3. Serves to address a part of the community that desperately needs help, the underinsured and low income. Being both underinsured and low income, diabetics in AI/AN and Hispanic communities tend not to steadily monitor their condition nor do they tend to subscribe to healthy lifestyles.
4. The long-term impact of diabetes and the medical complications are both costly in terms of healthcare will have a positive impact on decreasing healthcare costs and increasing productivity of members of the society.
5. Will enable integration of mobile health data from diabetes monitoring into the existing electronic health record (EHR) systems, thus enabling the healthcare team to provide overall higher quality of care for this segment of the population.

Implications for healthcare and IS research:

The proposed solution:

1. Provides a systematic and rigorous solution strategy to take and IS/IT application in healthcare from idea to realization in a rapid fashion.
2. Underscores the importance of sustained and cost-effective IT solutions for healthcare.
3. Provides a sound example for the need to incorporate the tools and techniques of knowledge management (via the IC) to provide superior solutions that continually build on extant knowledge in order to at all times provide the latest and best practice recommendations.
4. Underscores the need to at all times consider the web of healthcare players when developing any healthcare solution.
5. Offers an example of how technology can be used to increase healthcare equality as well as support superior healthcare delivery.
6. The proposed solution supports the continuum of care recommended by the WHO in the treatment and management of chronic diseases (Fig. 18.6) (WHO 2002).

As noted this is a research in progress. We are confident that on the completion of the pilot study we shall have strong directional data to continue larger wide scale testing of the DiaMonD solution. We also plan to expand the study to include other types of chronic diseases such as asthma and hypertension. At this stage we believe a major limitation is getting access to necessary data not only takes time but given the structure of the AI/AN healthcare delivery system as a whole is an arduous and at times difficult task which in turn creates delays in moving forward with the study.

Fig. 18.6 Innovative care for chronic conditions framework (ICCC) (adapted from the WHO 2002)

18.7 Conclusions

In the current context healthcare delivery especially in the United States is in need of fundamental redesign (http://www.cellular-news.com/story/15627.php; Porter and Tiesberg 2006). The focus on cost containment also necessitates a shift to prevention rather than cure. This is particularly important in the case of chronic diseases such as diabetes.

Diabetes is the fifth-deadliest disease in the United States. Since 1987 the death rate due to diabetes has increased by 45 %, while the death rates due to heart disease, stroke, and cancer have declined. The total annual economic cost of diabetes in 2002 was estimated to be $132 billion. Direct medical expenditures totaled $92 billion and comprised $23.2 billion for diabetes care, $24.6 billion for chronic diabetes-related complications, and $44.1 billion for excess prevalence of general medical conditions. Indirect costs resulting from lost workdays, restricted activity days, mortality, and permanent disability due to diabetes totaled $40.8 billion. The per capita annual costs of healthcare for people with diabetes rose from $10,071 in 1997 to $13,243 in 2002, an increase of more than 30 %. In contrast, healthcare costs for people without diabetes amounted to $2,560 in 2002. One out of every 10 healthcare dollars spent in the United States is spent on diabetes and its complications. As discussed in Sect. 18.3, the AI/AN population is particularly vulnerable to diabetes.

The DiaMonD solution is indeed applicable to all segments of the community and moreover actually offers the possibility of a global solution to more effective and efficient monitoring of diabetes and support of superior self-management and care for patients suffering from diabetes. However, the goal of this chapter was to particularly focus on a segment of the community that is too often forgotten and continually faces poor quality healthcare delivery, the AI/AN population. For this community the DiaMonD solution represents the possibility for enjoying a significantly higher level of care and thereby also ensuring a high quality of life. Given the percentage of AI/AN population affected by diabetes this in and of itself is important. However, this study attempts to go further to show that in general pervasive technology solutions might offer the answer for significantly increasing quality of care for urban and low income segments of the population. The disparity of healthcare delivery in the United States is a very tragic paradox of the US healthcare system and we believe that this research serves as a big first step in trying to address this conundrum. In closing, we urgently call for more research in this critical area.

References

Acton, K., Burrows, N., Moore, K., Querec, L., Geiss, L., & Engelgau, M. (2002). Trends in diabetes prevalence among American Indian and Alaska Native children, adolescents and young adults. *American Journal of Public Health, 92*(9), 1485–1490.

Boyatsis, R. (1998). *Transforming qualitative information*. Thousand Oaks: Sage.

Burrows, N., Geiss, L., Engelgau, M., & Acton, K. (2000). Prevalence of diabetes among Native Americans and Alaska Natives 1990–1997. *Diabetes Care, 23*(12), 1786–1790.

Cellular News. http://www.cellular-news.com/story/15627.php

Cullen, T. (2001). Standards and the computerized patient record. *IHS Primary Care Provider., 26*(4), 58–59.

Cunningham, P. J. (1993). Access to care in the Indian Health Service. *Health Affairs, 12*(3), 224.

Gibbons, M., Bali, R., & Wickramasinghe, N. (2010). *Perspectives of knowledge management in urban healthcare*. New York: Springer.

Goldberg, S. (2002a). Building the evidence for a standardized mobile internet (wireless) environment in Ontario, Canada. January Update, Internal INET Documentation, Ontario, Canada, INET.

Goldberg, S. (2002b). HTA Presentation rendering component summary. Internal INET documentation, Ontario, Canada, INET.

Goldberg, S. (2002c). HTA presentational selection and aggregation component summary. Internal INET Documentation, Ontario, Canada, INET.

Goldberg, S. (2002d). HTA quality assurance component summary. Internal INET documentation, Ontario, Canada, INET.

Goldberg, S. (2002e). Wireless POC device component summary. Internal INET documentation, Ontario, Canada, INET.

Hays, H. (2003). The IHS electronic health record project. *IHS Primary Care Provider, 28*(11), 233–236.

Kavale, S. (1996). *Interviews*. Thousand Oaks: Sage.

Lautenschlager, L., & Smith, C. (2006). Low-income American Indians' perceptions of diabetes. *Journal of Nutrition Education and Behavior, 38*(5), 307–315.

Miller, D. R., Safford, M. M., & Pogach, L. M. (2004). Who has diabetes? Best estimates of diabetes prevalence in the department of Veterans Affairs based on computerised patient data. *Diabetes Care, 27*(Suppl. 2), B10–B21.

Mirza, F., Norris, T., & Stockdale, R. (2008). Mobile technologies and the holistic management of chronic diseases. *Health Informatics Journal, 14*(4), 309–321.
Ogunwole, S. U. (2006). *We the people: American Indians and Alaskan Natives in the United States*. Census 2000 Special Reports, Issues Feb. Retrieved December, 2009, from http://www.census.gov/population/www/socdemo/race/censr-28.pdf.
Opie, A. (1998). Nobody's asked me for my view: Users' empowerment by multidisciplinary health teams. *Qualitative Health Research, 18*, 188–206.
Parker, J. D., Schenker, N., Ingram, D. D., Weed, J. A., Heck, K. E., & Madans, J. H. (2004). Bridging between two standards for collecting information on race and ethnicity: An application to Census 2000 and vital rates. *Public Health Reports, 119*(2), 192–205.
Porter, M., & Tiesberg, E. (2006). *Re-defining health care delivery*. Boston: Harvard Business Press.
Rachlis, M. (2006). *Key to sustainable healthcare system*. Retrieved February, 2008, from http://www.improveingchroniccare.org.
Radin, P. (2006). To me, it's my life: Medical communication, trust, and activism in cyberspace. *Social Science & Medicine, 6*, 591–601.
Sequist, T. D., Cullen, T., & Ayanian, J. Z. (2005). Information technology as a tool to improve the quality of American Indian health care. *American Journal of Public Health, 95*(12), 2173–2179.
Stratton, I. (2000). UKPDS. *British Medical Journal, 321*, 405–412.
WHO. (2002). *Innovative care for chronic conditions: Building blocks for action: Global report*. Geneva: Noncommunicable Diseases and Mental Health, World Health Organization.
WHO. http://www.who.int/en/
Wickramasinghe, N., & Goldberg, S. (2003). The wireless panacea for healthcare. In *Proceedings of 36th Hawaii International Conference on System Sciences*. Hawaii, 6–10 January, IEEE.
Wickramasinghe, N., & Godlberg, S. (2004). How M = EC^2 in Healthcare. *International Journal of Mobile Communications, 2*(2), 140–156.
Wickramasinghe, N., & Goldberg, S. (2007). Adaptive mapping to realisation methodology (AMR) to facilitate mobile initiatives in healthcare. *International Journal of Mobile Communications, 5*(3), 300–318.
Wickramasinghe, N., & Goldberg, S. (2009). The S'ANT approach to facilitate a superior chronic disease self-management model. *IJANTTI, 1*(4), 21–34.
Wickramasinghe, N., & Schaffer, J. (2006). Creating knowledge driven healthcare processes with the intelligence continuum. *International Journal of Electronic Healthcare, 2*(2), 164–174.
Wickramasinghe, N., & Schaffer, J. (2010). *Realizing value driven e-health solutions*. Washington, DC: IBM Center for The Business of Government.
Yin, R. (1994). *Case study research* (2nd ed.). Thousand Oaks: Sage.
Zuckerman, S., Haley, J., Roubideaux, Y., & Lillie-Blanton, M. (2004). Health service access, use, and insurance coverage among American Indians/Alaska Natives and Whites: What role does the Indian health service play? *American Journal of Public Health, 94*(1), 53–59.

Chapter 19
Designing Enabling Regulatory Frameworks to Facilitate the Diffusion of Wireless Technology Solutions in Healthcare

Indrit Troshani, Steve Goldberg, and Nilmini Wickramasinghe

Abstract Pervasive e-health solutions are emerging as a solution to address key challenges faced in healthcare delivery including escalating costs and the exponential increase of chronic diseases. However, existing regulatory regimes appear to be one of the key stumbling blocks in trying to successfully diffuse these proven superior technology solutions. This is largely due to the fact that they are ill-equipped for dealing with them. The following exploratory study serves to investigate institutional regulatory factors that can impact the adoption of such pervasive solutions. These factors are important as they can shape both the nature of these solutions and their diffusion trajectory. In particular it is argued that co-regulation, a mixture of direct monitoring and intervention of regulators through legislation and complete industry self-regulation, can be an effective approach especially in view of the complex and dynamic nature of this industry. Co-regulation can minimize monitoring costs and enhance compliance. A case vignette is provided to illustrate these points.

Keywords e-Health • Pervasive healthcare • Wireless in healthcare • Regulation • Co-regulation

---

This chapter is adapted from a paper "Adoption of Pervasive e-Health Solutions: The Need for an Appropriate Regulatory Framework" by Troshani, Goldberg, and Wickramasinghe presented at the 2012 AMCIS Conference, Seattle, USA, Aug 9–12.

I. Troshani (✉)
University of Adelaide Business School, 10 Pulteney Street Level,
Adelaide, SA 5005, Australia
e-mail: indrit.troshani@adelaide.edu.au

S. Goldberg
INET International Canada, 131 Glen Crescent, Thornhill, ON, Canada L4J 4W4
e-mail: sgoldberg@inet-international.com

N. Wickramasinghe, Ph.D., MBA
Epworth HealthCare & Department of BITL & HIRi, RMIT University,
GPO Box 2476, Melbourne, VIC 3001, Australia
e-mail: nilmini.wickramasinghe@rmit.edu.au

N. Wickramasinghe et al. (eds.), *Lean Thinking for Healthcare*, Healthcare Delivery in the Information Age, DOI 10.1007/978-1-4614-8036-5_19,

19.1 Introduction

Pervasive e-health constitutes the use of digitally enabled technologies to facilitate and enhance the exchange of clinical, administrative, informational, educational, and transactional data ubiquitously in healthcare settings (Holliday and Tam 2004). Examples of pervasive e-health solutions include telemedicine and telecare services, virtual reality, computer-assisted surgery, mobile monitoring systems (e.g., for the electronic management of chronic diseases), electronic medical records management, including digital imaging and archiving systems, and electronic prescribing (Ferraud-Ciandet 2010). Taken together, pervasive e-health solutions have the potential to generate enormous efficiencies and services quality as well as to reduce medical errors (Anderson 2007).

Delivering pervasive e-health solutions effectively requires the integration of diverse technological and organizational resources which typically cannot be found within individual organizations. The knowledge necessary for developing and deploying these solutions may involve several heterogeneous stakeholders that are often embedded in various technological, economic, and social settings (Holliday and Tam 2004). To succeed, these stakeholders must interact with each other while complying with institutional requirements including legal and societal requirements that balance their diverging interests, motivations, and needs (Kluge 2007; Troshani and Rao Hill 2009). These requirements constitute a regulatory regime which can operate at industrial, national, or international levels and can influence, direct, limit, or prohibit any activity undertaken by stakeholders operating in the pervasive e-health solutions industry (Holliday and Tam 2004; Ooijevaar 2010).

Given the nature of healthcare and the sensitivity of healthcare information, it is typically incumbent upon regulatory and legislative government authorities to set up regulatory regimes and mandate their use (Huang et al. 2010). Generally, these regimes can facilitate the exchange of healthcare data and information amongst various healthcare stakeholders while also providing protection of patient rights including privacy. Credible and transparent regulatory rules can boost much needed investments in the pervasive e-health solutions industry, promote public confidence and the development of innovative and affordable pervasive e-health solutions, and stimulate industry research and development efforts (Kluge 2007). However, regulation can also impact the industry in a negative way. Increasing the regulatory compliance burden for stakeholders can increase the overall cost of operation which can impede the development and deployment of pervasive e-health solutions by acting as a barrier, and thus hampering pervasive e-health innovations (Ooijevaar 2010).

It is not until particular pervasive e-health solutions have been commercialized that their originators realize the problems that they pose to patients in particular and more broadly to society (MacInnes 2005). Therefore, "one needs to be concerned with societal, legal, and general economic factors" (MacInnes 2005, p. 7) when a service technology has reached a minimum standard of performance and reliability. This is a stage that is generally overlooked. That is, answers are needed for potential legal, societal, and general economic concerns that pervasive e-health solutions may introduce (Goggin and Spurgeon 2005; MacInnes 2005; Parente 2000).

Even though regulation has been attracting the attention of policy makers as e-health matures, regulatory regimes around the globe are ill-equipped and moving slowly for dealing with these technologies (Ooijevaar 2010). In fact, there are growing concerns in extant literature that regulatory agencies have failed to keep abreast with developments in the pervasive e-health realm (Goldsmith 2000). Yet, extant research also shows that regulatory issues including legal barriers have been identified as a major force in the development and deployment of pervasive e-health solutions (Holliday and Tam 2004; Min et al. 2007). In fact, because extant policy frameworks that are inherited from specific national and international settings are "not well-placed to deal with contemporary communications technologies that blur the boundaries among these" (Goggin and Spurgeon 2005, p. 181), pervasive e-health solutions may not always fit within traditional healthcare regulation models (Ooijevaar 2010). For example, while in some regulatory regimes there may be legal obstacles that influence the reimbursement structures and payments when treatments are carried out in the e-health realm, in others there are limitations that mandate physical face-to-face physician–patient consultation thereby restricting the use of corresponding emerging e-health opportunities (Holliday and Tam 2004). These examples suggest that regulation can shape the form pervasive e-health solutions will (or will not) take (Ooijevaar 2010; Parente 2000).

This chapter attempts to answer the key research question "why do current regulatory regimens fail to facilitate e-health solution adoption and what can/should be done to address such barriers?" To address this we first leverage extant literature by using the institution-based view as a tool to investigate how regulation can affect the adoption of pervasive e-health solutions. Then, we illustrate with a case vignette and finally present an institutional regulatory framework that we argue is suitable to facilitate the adoption of the plethora of pervasive e-health solutions today.

19.2 Institution-Based View

The institution-based view suggests that institutions interact with organizations or networks of organizations by indicating which choices can be acceptable and supportable; that is, institutions reflect "humanly devised constraints that structure human interaction" (North 1990, p. 3). These constraints take the shape of "regulative, normative, and cognitive structures and activities that provide stability and meaning to social behavior" (Scott 1995, p. 33). In providing constraints and establishing the "rules of the game" (Peng et al. 2009, p. 64) institutional frameworks can help minimize uncertainty in the environment in which organizations operate. Institutional frameworks can comprise both formal and informal constraints. While formal constraints are regulatory, and thus coercive in nature, and include laws (e.g., economic liberalization), regulations (e.g., regulatory regime), and political rules (e.g., transparency and/or corruption), informal constraints include socially accepted norms of behaviors that are entrenched in culture, ethical standards, and ideology (North 1990; Peng et al. 2009; Scott 1995).

In healthcare all stakeholders operate within the boundaries of a regulated environment (Peng et al. 2008, 2009). In extant literature both formal and informal aspects of the institutional context have been taken for granted and have been assumed away as "background" (Peng et al. 2008, p. 922) conditions (Barney et al. 2001). Further research is required examining the interactions between institutions and organizations in healthcare, particularly in contexts where pervasive e-health solutions are emerging and growing (Kluge 2007; Ooijevaar 2010). Understanding of these interactions and the institutional context is important, particularly in complex knowledge-intensive settings, such as healthcare and e-health, as it can help deepen current understanding concerning ensuing strategic behaviors of stakeholders. Institutional settings can create a conducive (or restrictive) atmosphere that determines an organization's behavior in its market. It follows that the development of pervasive e-health solutions may be better understood with a full examination of the institutional setting where organizations interact in attempts to achieve their objectives. In this chapter, we focus on the formal aspects of the institution-based view in the healthcare industry with particular reference to pervasive e-health. These aspects are encapsulated in a regulatory regime which is "a form of public policy" (Wilks 1996) that includes monitoring and intervention in order to remedy any form of perceived social injustice (Benoliel 2003).

19.3 Regulatory Issues

This section discusses prominent relevant regulatory issues including privacy, quality of online health content, and access to development resources.

19.3.1 Privacy

Privacy regulation as it pertains to pervasive e-health solutions needs to establish that special security measures are undertaken by healthcare providers to ensure that patient information is not inadvertently disclosed or leaked to or even shared with any stakeholder without the patient's explicit agreement (Boulding 2000). Such obligation of healthcare providers that holds personal identifiable health information to protect a person's privacy is commonly referred to as confidentiality (Lumpkin 2000). That is, holders of personal identifiable health information can only share such information on the basis of fair information practices and established regulation (Lumpkin 2000).

Another important concept related to privacy and confidentiality is that of security which concerns the extent to which "information can be stored with access limited to those who are authorized" (Lumpkin 2000). With security, personal identifiable health information needs to be protected while in storage (e.g., in a hard-disk drive or backup devices) or in transit from one location to another via networked computers or the Internet (i.e., being emailed). Whether in storage or in transit health information needs to be protected against vulnerabilities (e.g., hacker attacks) using technologies such as encryption which have been proven to help achieve confidentiality, authentication, and message integrity (Lumpkin 2000). For example, public key infrastructure and certification authorities which commonly use public key cryptography to encrypt and decrypt mobile transmissions and authenticate both patients and healthcare providers.

Ironically, the same information practices which provide value to both patients and healthcare providers also cause privacy concerns. Some of these concerns include: the type of information that can be collected about patients and the ways in which it will be protected; the stakeholders and entities that can access this information and their accountability; and the ways in which the information will be used. In healthcare settings, where pervasive e-health solutions are used, a trusting environment can be encapsulated in perceived credibility (Lin and Wang 2005). Evidence shows that there is a significant direct relationship between perceived credibility and the intention to adopt pervasive e-health solutions (Lin and Wang 2005).

19.3.2 Quality of Online Health Content

Online health content quality concerns websites that provide medical advice or distribute medical information or healthcare education to patients ubiquitously (Bodkin and Miaoulis 2007; Houston et al. 2003). Patients demand and can have both synchronous and asynchronous access to scientific evidence, online doctors, educational materials, support groups, and online counseling (Cudore and Bobrowski 2003; Paris and Ferranti 2001). Typically online health content sites offer free information concerning disease treatments, wellness, and lifestyle management programs. Quality health content is important because well-informed patients can become productive participants and take responsibility in their healthcare and treatment regimen. There are, however, growing concerns that this information might be incomplete, incorrect, biased, or even misleading since the sites that offer it often rely heavily on sponsorship and advertising revenues from sponsoring organizations such as pharmaceutical companies or even private hospitals (Eysenbach 2000).

While there are debates in the literature supporting both forms of outright government regulation and industry self-regulation, there is general agreement that the perceived quality of online health content can impact on patient trust which can, in turn, adversely affect patient's confidence in these websites and their intentions to interact with them. This suggests that some form of regulation that attempts to rate content quality is necessary (Huang et al. 2010). Whether implemented by government regulators, industry associations, or third party accreditation agencies, online health content quality should be measured against quality assurance and compliance criteria that are set by credible and authoritative bodies that aim at filtering content for compliance and quality assurance before it is made publicly available (Terry 2002).

19.3.3 Access to Development Resources

Government organizations and industry associations can also facilitate the regulation of pervasive e-health solutions by assisting with knowledge development and deployment, subsidies, and standardization.

Knowledge development. The creation of technical and business knowledge underlying the development of pervasive health content and services is essential for the success of emerging areas such as e-health. Currently, while evidence suggests that many e-health content providers have exhibited a huge interest for distributing e-health content electronically via the Internet or mobile channels, the knowledge concerning the ways that such content can be adequately formatted is limited (King et al. 1994).

Knowledge deployment. Once built, development knowledge and technical know-how needs to be deployed and this is important not only for building awareness amongst stakeholders but also for showing them how e-health business models operate. Government organizations and industry associations could become proactive in undertaking additional knowledge deployment measures including education and training. These measures can help pervasive e-health service developers acquire the necessary knowledge and learn about the ways that they can format and structure e-health content and services for various channels (e.g., mobile), and to distribute to patients.

Subsidies. Often governments, industry associations, and other powerful players in the market may provide subsidies to players in emerging industries such as e-health which can help fund innovative pervasive e-health solutions, and research and development initiatives (King et al. 1994).

Standardization. It involves developing standards or local practices that can be adopted by all stakeholders involved in the provision of pervasive e-health solutions and limiting the use of other options (King et al. 1994; Lyytinen and Damsgaard 2001). Lack of industry standards can make the development of pervasive e-health solutions prohibitively costly.

19.4 DiaMonD: Case Vignette

Chronic diseases are generally incurable diseases, and are said to be the greatest threat to the nation's health and to its health delivery system (Geisler and Wickramasinghe 2009; Bali et al. 2013). There are five major chronic diseases: cardiovascular diseases (hypertension, heart disease, congestive heart disease), strokes, asthma, cancer, and diabetes (some add a sixth chronic disease, arthritis). These chronic diseases account for 83 % of healthcare expenditure in the general population (AIHW 2010).

The focus of this case vignette is on the chronic disease of diabetes. Diabetes is characterized by high levels of blood glucose, resulting from defects in the production of insulin. Regular monitoring of diabetes is a necessary part of controlling the disease and keeping it from becoming life threatening. To effectively and efficiently monitor diabetic patients, there is a role for wireless technologies. They can provide the means to enable affordable superior monitoring anywhere and anytime, thereby allowing the patient to enjoy a quality lifestyle (Rachlis 2006).

19.5 The DiaMonD Solution

INET International Inc., a technology company from Canada, has developed a workable system which connects handheld devices to a stationary center and which allows for the transfer of medical data. This system provides the medical provider with the capability to interface with patients by their use of a cellular telephone. We call this pervasive e-health solution the DiaMonD (diabetes monitoring device) solution

The DiaMonD solution is anchored in the use of a specially equipped cell phone and the installation of a secure wireless application that allows patients to monitor glucose levels and to immediately transfer the data to their care provider (Goldberg 2002a, b, c). The physician or nurse uses a handheld device such as a PDA (Personal Digital Assistant) which is connected to a wireless network to confidentially access, evaluate, and act on the patient's data.

Moreover, the solution calls for the patient to enter readings from the glucose monitor into the special cell phone. This requires the ability to read the data from the monitor and to input the numbers into the cell phone. In the past, INET considered the possibility of the direct reading of the glucose monitor into the special cell phone by utilizing Bluetooth technology. However, the company soon discovered that this significantly limited the pervasiveness of the technology since currently there are very few glucose monitors with embedded Bluetooth technology. The important issue to remember is that the INET approach is based on using cell phone technology that the patient is already using and is familiar with its features; that is, a truly pervasive solution.

Following the success of this solution in Canada, the authors attempted to investigate the possibilities of implementing this solution into the Australian healthcare context (Wickramasinghe et al. 2011; Goldberg 2002a, b, c). The Australian healthcare system is not dissimilar to that in Canada; it has both a government-supported system and a private healthcare model. In addition, it also has state and federal jurisdictions. Figure 19.1 captures schematically the key aspects of the Australian healthcare delivery system.

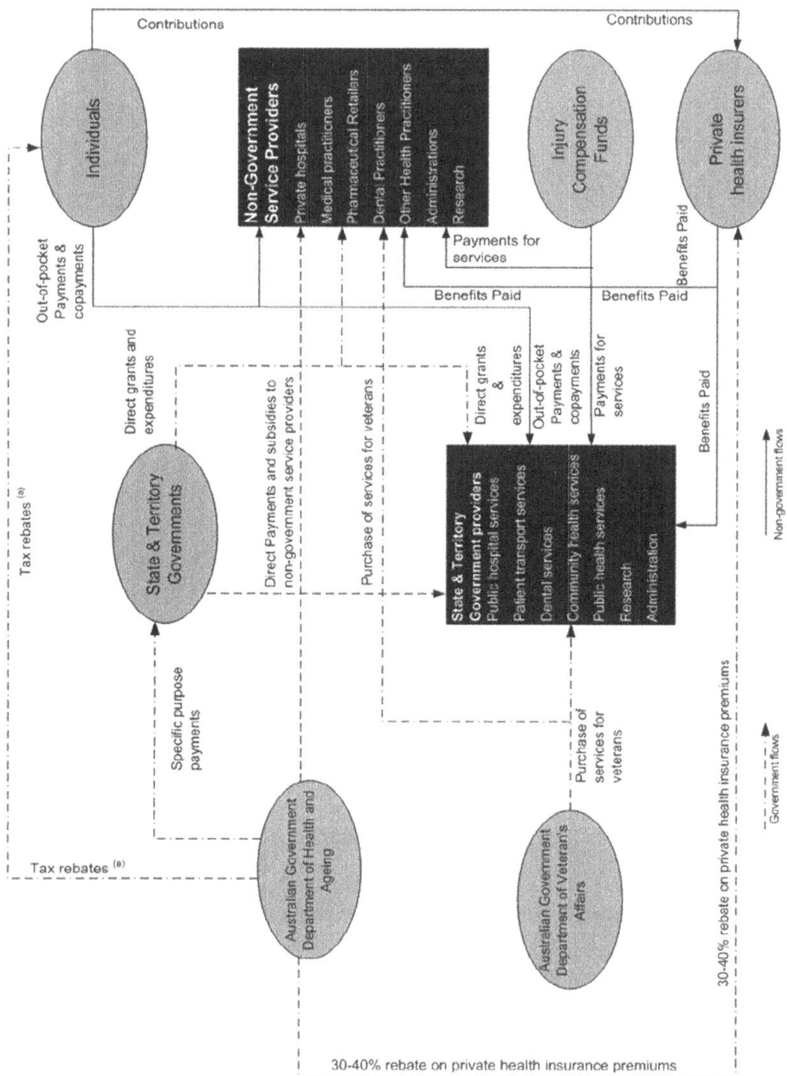

(a) The tax rebate is not an expense of the Australian Government Department of health and Ageing, but is a tax expenditure of the Australian Government.

Fig. 19.1 The structure of Australian healthcare system (adopted from AIHW 2010)

19.6 Case Study Findings

Based on our exploratory case study research which subscribes to the recommendations of Yin (2003), several key emergent themes have become apparent with regard to the successful adoption of the DiaMonD solution into the Australian healthcare context. First, given the complex nature and structure of the healthcare delivery system in Australia, at present there exists no clear method to identify how the adoption of a wireless device can assist in providing medical advice that can be coded. Currently, such advice is coded as a consultation in a GP (general practitioner or primary care office). If a service or intervention cannot be coded then it cannot be billed which in turn means that all medical professionals connected to offering/supporting this application do not get reimbursed, while the less efficient and lower quality solutions of the GP visit do bring a set level of reimbursement. Moreover, if such an intervention cannot be coded, regulations and protocols surrounding duty of care and appropriate use cannot be established. Thus what our interim data is showing is that irrespective of how appropriate a pervasive e-health technology solution might be, if the regulatory framework cannot incorporate its existence and use, it is a huge barrier to its adoption. The situation becomes even further complicated when one adds the role of private versus public healthcare insurance. We note that in Canada, INET International Inc. has succeeded in getting the Canadian government to reimburse citizens who use a pervasive e-health solution such as DiaMonD to support their diabetes care. This is further evidence for us that a changed regulatory framework is an essential critical success factor for the adoption and large scale embracement of such pervasive e-health solutions.

19.7 An Institutional Framework for Pervasive e-Health Solutions

An institutional regulatory setting is generally implemented by organizations with legislative powers, such as regulatory bodies. These regulate the context in which pervasive e-health solutions are developed, deployed, and used. It is vital for such a framework to be well understood by all stakeholders that operate in a healthcare system. An institutional framework can provide regulatory certainty and predictability which is essential for all healthcare stakeholders. However, for emerging technology solutions in healthcare such as the pervasive e-health solutions, regulatory authorities typically have to deal with a multitude of heterogeneous networked stakeholders. Furthermore, as pervasive e-health solutions are dynamic and still undergoing rapid changes, regulatory definitions become a moving target which implies that regulators should constantly acquire industry-specific knowledge over time (Tallberg et al. 2007). Consequently, the institutional regulatory context in the domain of pervasive e-health solutions can become extremely complex and

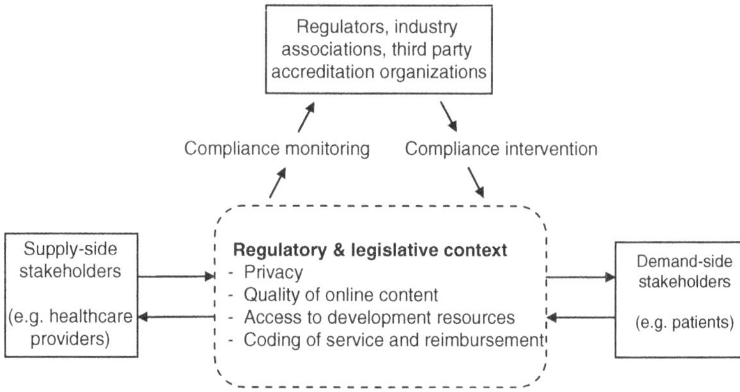

Fig. 19.2 Institutional regulatory framework for pervasive e-health solutions

achieving regulatory certainty may be an elusive or even unrealistic undertaking (Fisher and Harindranath 2004).

We argue that a co-regulation approach should be adopted for regulating pervasive e-health solutions. Accordingly, co-regulation represents close collaboration between regulatory bodies, including government organizations, industry associations, and third party accreditation bodies, and the e-health industry in terms of a mixture of direct monitoring and intervention through legislation, on the one hand, and complete self-regulation, on the other. There is no direct regulation, nor is there pure self-regulation. Regulatory bodies can provide the e-health industry with some parameters concerning the regulatory issues discussed in the previous section in which key problems are to be solved. It is, subsequently, the responsibility of the e-health industry to work out the details that best suit the specific technologies used and business models adopted. The role of the regulator is, thus, to allow the industry to apply its own codes in the first instance and to monitor the effectiveness and enforcement of those codes.

The diagram in Fig. 19.2 integrates the regulatory issues discussed previously with the notion of co-regulation to form the proposed institutional regulatory framework for the pervasive e-health solutions industry. This constitutes a contribution to the existing body of knowledge as it provides an integrative view of regulatory issues concerning the emerging pervasive e-health solutions industry. Figure 19.2 also shows that the institutional regulatory framework operates via compliance monitoring and intervention. First, monitoring may be implemented by establishing suitable reporting mechanisms. Second, intervention should only occur in cases of compliance violations or market failure.

With co-regulation, the e-health industry is empowered to take responsibility for participating in the development of its own regulation. Three major benefits emerge with this approach: first, regulation costs are likely to be significantly reduced; second, compliance is likely to occur naturally, and, therefore, regulation in itself is likely to be perceived to be less restrictive and onerous than in traditional regulation models; third, industry-driven co-regulation also has the advantage to ensure that it is likely to remain appropriate and be responsive to changing market conditions and technology development and capable of delivering timely and transparent outcomes. Taken together, these advantages are likely to promote business activity, market integrity, and patient confidence in emerging pervasive e-health solutions.

19.8 Discussion and Conclusion

This chapter set out to answer the research question "why do current regulatory regimens fail to facilitate e-health solution adoption and what can/should be done to address such barriers?" To answer this question we first drew on existing literature. This not only served to provide the motivation and highlight the critical need but also assisted us in developing the appropriate themes for our exploratory case study research. In addition, we have presented our initial research findings from our research in progress case study, the DiaMonD solution. As noted by Yin (1994) such an approach of focusing on an exemplar case study is most prudent and appropriate for trying to uncover critical issues pertaining to a new phenomenon. While the research still continues, the findings to date clearly underscore the significant barrier posed by regulatory frameworks that have been designed before the development of pervasive e-health solutions and therefore are both archaic and inflexible to accommodate the potential and possibilities afforded to healthcare delivery by such solutions. We have subsequently discussed a proposed framework that provides the foundations for an appropriate regulatory structure. We argue that these encompass the interests of the main stakeholders operating in the e-health industry and given its dynamic and complex nature co-regulation is the most effective approach to minimize costs and enhance compliance.

We believe that this framework is the first of its kind, and, thus, it contributes to the existing body of knowledge which can be employed by both academics and practitioners alike. First, it can be invaluable to stakeholders in the pervasive e-health solutions industry in helping them improve their understanding of the institutional factors that enhance or constrain their positions in their value chain and industry. A deeper understanding of such factors can help stakeholders in many ways in the following: (1) Achieving a valuable competitive advantage. Stakeholders that exhibit compliance with regulatory rules that benefit e-health service users may achieve their trust more effectively than those who do not. (2) Providing stakeholders the opportunity to "achieve knowledge on legal issues, to stay away from legal areas in which processes are unclear, and to avoid related risks" (Kijl et al. 2005, pp. 66–67) which decreases potential transaction costs (Kijl et al. 2005). (3) Helping avoid unbalanced legal rights amongst stakeholders which can severely threaten businesses by causing otherwise innovative business practices to be illicit (Kijl et al. 2005). Second, regulatory and legislative influences can have direct implications on how pervasive e-health solutions and related business practices are designed and how they operate at organizational, industrial, and institutional levels. Further, these influences can determine the nature of pervasive e-health solutions that can be offered and their diffusion trajectories amongst end-users or patients (MacInnes 2005).

Without a doubt, creating a solid institutional regulatory context in the fast evolving pervasive e-health solutions industry is an extremely difficult task. There are many reasons for this, including the highly complex nature of the networks and stakeholder relationships required to provide pervasive e-health solutions as well as the constantly evolving underlying technologies. However, we close by noting that healthcare will never be able to enjoy the full power and potential of pervasive e-health solutions until this key issue is addressed and we close by calling for both scholars and practitioners alike for further research in this area.

References

AIHW. (2010). *Australia's Health 2010: The twelfth biennial health report of the Australian Institute of Health and Welfare*. Canberra: AIHW.

Anderson, J. G. (2007). Social, ethical and legal barriers to e-health. *International Journal of Medical Informatics, 76*(5–6), 480–483.

Bali, R. K., Troshani, I., & Goldberg, S., Wickramasinghe, N. (Eds.). (2013). *Pervasive health knowledge management* . New York: Springer.

Barney, J. B., Wright, M., & Ketchen, D. J. J. (2001). The resource-based view of the firm: Ten years after 1991. *Journal of Management, 27*, 625–641.

Benoliel, D. (2003). Cyberspace technological standardization: An institutional theory retrospective. *Berkeley Technology Law Journal, 18*(4), 1259–1339.

Bodkin, C., & Miaoulis, G. (2007). eHealth information quality and ethics issues: An exploratory study of consumer perceptions. *International Journal of Pharmaceutical and Healthcare Marketing, 1*(1), 27–42.

Boulding, M. E. (2000). Self-regulation: Who needs it? *Health Affairs, 19*(6), 133–139.

Cudore, B. A., & Bobrowski, P. E. (2003). How effective are healthcare web sites for marketers? *Marketing Health Services, 23*(3), 37–41.

Eysenbach, G. (2000). Towards ethical guidelines for e-health: JMIR theme issue on eHealth Ethics. *Journal of Medical Internet Research, 2*(1), 1–7.

Ferraud-Ciandet, N. (2010) Privacy and data protection in ehealth: A comparative approach between South African and French legal systems. In P. Cunningham & M. Cunningham (Eds.), *IST-Africa 2010 Conference Proceedings*.

Fisher, J., & Harindranath, G. (2004). Regulation as a barrier to electronic commerce in Europe: The case of the European fund management industry. *European Journal of Information Systems, 13*(4), 260–272.

Geisler, E., & Wickramasinghe, N. (2009). *The role and use of wireless technology in the management and monitoring of chronic diseases*. Washington, DC: IBM Center for The Business of Government.

Goggin, G., & Spurgeon, C. (2005). Mobile message services and communications policy. *Prometheus, 23*(2), 181–193.

Goldberg, S. (2002a). Building the evidence for a standardized mobile internet (wireless) environment in Ontario. January Update, Internal INET Documentation, Ontario, INET.

Goldberg, S. (2002b). HTA presentational selection and aggregation component summary. Internal INET Documentation, Ontario, INET.

Goldberg, S. (2002c). Wireless POC device component summary. Internal INET documentation, Ontario, INET.

Goldsmith, J. (2000). How will the Internet change our health system? *Health Affairs, 19*(1), 148–156.

Holliday, I., & Tam, W.-K. (2004). E-health in the East Asian tigers. *International Journal of Medical Informatics, 73*(11–12), 759–769.

Houston, T. K., Sands, D. Z., Nash, B. R., & Ford, D. E. (2003). Experiences of physicians who frequently use email with patients. *Health Communication, 15*(4), 515–525.

Huang, W., Seitz, J., & Wickramasinghe, N. (2010). *Manifesto for e-health success*. Paper presented at the 14th Pacific Asia Conference on Information Systems.

Kijl, B., Bouwman, H., Haaker, T., & Faber, E. (2005). *Dynamic business models in mobile service value networks: A theoretical and conceptual framework (FRUX/D2.2-II)*. Delft, The Netherlands: TU Delft.

King, J. L., Gurbaxani, V., Kraemer, K. L., McFarlan, F. W., Raman, K. S., & Yap, C. S. (1994). Institutional factors in information technology innovation. *Information Systems Research, 5*(2), 139–169.

Kluge, E.-H. W. (2007). Secure e-health: Managing risks to patient health data. *International Journal of Medical Informatics, 76*(5–6), 402–406.

Lin, H., & Wang, Y. (2005). Predicting consumer intention to use mobile commerce in Taiwan. In W. Brookes, E. Lawrence, R. Steele, & E. Chang (Eds.), *International conference on mobile business, July 11–13*. Sydney: IEEE.

Lumpkin, J. R. (2000). E-health, HIPAA, and beyond. *Health Affairs, 19*(6), 149–151.

Lyytinen, K., & Damsgaard, J. (2001). What's wrong with the diffusion of innovation theory: The case of a complex and networked technology. In *Proceedings of IFIP 8.6*. Banff, Canada.

MacInnes, I. (2005). Dynamic business model framework for emerging technologies. *International Journal of Services, Technology and Management, 6*(1), 3–19.

Min, S. D., Lee, B. W., Yoon, S. W., Lee, Y. B., Kim, J. K., Lee, M., et al. (2007). Actual condition of Korean e-health: What do enterprisers want for developing e-health industry? In *Proceedings of 9th International Conference on e-Health Networking, Application and Services*.

North, D. C. (1990). *Institutions, institutional change, and economic performance*. Cambridge, MA: Harvard University Press.

Ooijevaar, J. R. (2010). *The influence of national healthcare regulation on e-health business models: An exploratory comparative case study of four European healthcare markets*. University of Twente.

Parente, S. T. (2000). Beyond the hype: A taxonomy of e-health business models. *Health Affairs, 19*(6), 89–102.

Paris, J., & Ferranti, J. (2001). The changing fact of medicine: Health care on the internet. *Journal of Perinatology, 21*(1), 34–39.

Peng, M. W., Sun, S. L., Pinkham, B., & Chen, H. (2009). The institution-based view as a third leg for a strategy tripod. *Academy of Management Perspectives, 23*(3), 63–81.

Peng, M. W., Wang, D. Y. L., & Jiang, Y. (2008). An institution-based view of international business strategy: A focus on emerging economies. *Journal of International Business Studies, 39*(5), 920–936.

Rachlis, M. (2006). *Key to sustainable healthcare system*. Retrieved June 21, 2008, from http://www.improveinchroniccare.org

Scott, W. R. (1995). *Institutions and Organizations*. Thousand Oaks, CA: Sage.

Tallberg, M., Hämmäinen, H., Töyli, J., Kamppari, S., & Kivi, A. (2007). Impacts of handset bundling on mobile data usage: The case of Finland. *Telecommunications Policy, 31*(10/11), 648–659.

Terry, N. (2002). Regulating health information: A US perspective. *British Medical Journal, 324*(7337), 602–605.

Troshani, I., & Rao Hill, S. (2009). Linking stakeholder salience with mobile services diffusion. *International Journal of Mobile Communications, 7*(3), 269–289.

Wickramasinghe, N., Troshani, I., Rao, S., Hague, W., & Goldberg, S. (2011). A transaction cost assessment of a pervasive technology solution for gestational diabetes. *International Journal of Healthcare Information Systems and Informatics, 6*(4), 60–75.

Wilks, S. (1996). Regulatory compliance and capitalist diversity in Europe. *Journal of European Public Policy, 3*(4), 536–559.

Yin, R. K. (1994) *Case study research: Design and methods.* London: Sage Publication.

Yin, R. K. (2003). *Case study research: Design and methods.* Beverley Hills: Sage.

Chapter 20
Improving Healthcare Service Quality and Patients' Life Quality Through Mobile Technologies: The Case of Diabetes Self-management

Sally Rao Hill, Indrit Troshani, Steve Goldberg, and Nilmini Wickramasinghe

Abstract Chronic diseases such as diabetes often require lifestyle adjustment and sometimes lifelong medical care especially when patients are not admitted to hospitals. In this context, self-management becomes pivotal. Anecdotal evidence suggests that using wireless technologies to facilitate self-management, in particular, is increasing adherence and even treatment outcome in chronic disease management. However, it is not clear if and how using wireless technology solutions also improves patients' service quality perception concerning their healthcare. The objective of this chapter is to address this shortcoming in existing literature and propose a service quality framework for wireless solutions in healthcare settings.

Keywords Wireless technology • Self-management • Healthcare service quality • Satisfaction • Quality of life

20.1 Introduction

Chronic diseases such as diabetes can have considerable social, human, and economic impact and tackling these requires solutions that substantially enhance the existing fragmented and uncoordinated capacity for effective prevention, early detection, and management (Victorian Government 2007 #17). Diabetes is one of

S. Rao Hill • I. Troshani (✉)
University of Adelaide Business School, 10 Pulteney Street, Adelaide, SA 5005, Australia
e-mail: sally.raohill@adelaide.edu.au; indrit.troshani@adelaide.edu.au

S. Goldberg
INET International Canada, 131 Glen Crescent, Thornhill, ON, Canada, L4J 4W4

N. Wickramasinghe, Ph.D., MBA
Epworth HealthCare & Department of BITL & HIRi, RMIT University,
GPO Box 2476, Melbourne, VIC 3001, Australia

N. Wickramasinghe et al. (eds.), *Lean Thinking for Healthcare*, Healthcare Delivery in the Information Age, DOI 10.1007/978-1-4614-8036-5_20,

the leading chronic diseases affecting Australians and its prevalence continues to rise (ref DiabetesAustralia 2008 #30). Recent statistics show that for every person diagnosed with diabetes, it is estimated that there is another who has yet to be diagnosed which doubles the number of diabetes sufferers {ibid}.

Further, research shows that there are several deficiencies and gaps in the information provided by the existing system for monitoring diabetes in Australia (Dixon 2006 #16). The most notable include: First, data collected in hospitals are episode-based rather than patient-based which makes it difficult to determine statistics concerning individual admissions, re-admissions, and treatment patterns. Second, there is lack of data on incidence and prevalence by diabetes type that can help reliably assess the magnitude of the problem. Also, diabetes trend information across the population is sparse. Third, the accuracy of recording data in administrative data sets, such as hospital morbidity, mortality, and general practice data, is uncertain. Fourth, clinical management information is derived from uncoordinated and fragmented data collections that are not representative of the entire population of diabetes patients which makes comparison, analysis, and trend identification difficult. Finally, information is necessary for improving services and maintaining the quality of life of diabetes patients.

20.2 Technology-Facilitated Self-management

As there is no cure for diabetes, non-medical approaches are used jointly with medical approaches, so that patients with this disease can have a life which is as normal as possible. Such treatment strategies require effective and ongoing lifestyle management, together with meticulous attention and monitoring by both patients and healthcare professionals (Britt et al. 2007). To be successful, patients need to be both informed and active in their treatment regimen (AIHW 2007, 2008). Moreover, effective self-management which involves active participation of diabetes patients is a key strategy for managing their condition and reaching improved treatment outcomes is an essential critical success factor (Colagiuri, Colagiuri, and Ward 1998; Poulton 1999; Rasmussen, Wellard, and Nankervis 2001; Wellard, Rennie, and King 2008). However, self-management is time-consuming and requires significant self-discipline (Russell, Churl Suh, and Safford 2005) and support strategies such as assessment, goal-setting, action-planning, problem-solving, and follow-up (ICIC 2008). In addition, because effective self-management may require patient interaction with various healthcare professionals, including diabetes physicians, general practitioners, diabetes educators, dieticians, and community nurses (Knuiman, Welborn, and Bartholomew 1996), difficulties can arise when diabetes patients encounter problems ranging from making appointments to needing to travel to many locations (Zigbor and Songer 2001; Van Eyk and Baum 2002; Wellard, Rennie, and King 2008). Given both the importance and complexity of applying self-management effectively for both prevention and early detection of diabetes, there are increasing calls for further research to facilitate self-management (Wellard, Rennie, and King 2008).

There is evidence suggesting that technology-facilitated telemedicine can help patients improve both their self-management (Balas et al. 2004) and their relationship with healthcare professionals (Bodenheimer et al. 2002; Downer et al. 2006). These technologies can be considered as self-service technologies (SSTs) as they include interfaces that enable customers to produce a service without or with little direct service employee involvement (Meuter et al. 2000). This phenomenon has been coined as person-to-technology service delivery (Dabholkar 1996). In the case of diabetes, driven by the appropriate software, a diabetes monitoring device (DiaMonD) using pervasive mobile technology can be used to improve diabetes self-management. Using a standardized mobile Internet (wireless) environment, this device can improve patient outcomes with immediate access to patient data which can result in better clinical management at the point of care.

Much of the extant research in the area of SST has focused on the predictive factors concerning adoption of SSTs. For example, attitudinal theory and technology adoption theory are used to examine consumers' intention of using SSTs (Meuter et al. 2003, 2005; Bobbitt and Dabholkar 2001). While Bobbitt and Dabholkar (2001) provide a framework which considers consumer attitude and external and situational influences, Meuter et al. (2005) categorize factors that influence the SST adoption into innovation characteristics and adopter characteristics which are moderated by adopter's technology readiness to explain consumer trials of SSTs. Variations of the technology adoption model have also been used to explain why some consumers adopt SSTs while others do not. For example, relative advantage and capacity to adopt are combined with perceived risk to predict consumers' willingness to use SSTs (Walker and Johnson 2006). In addition, Meuter et al. (2002) found that technology anxiety was a better predictor of self-service usage than demographic characteristics such as age and gender across a variety of service settings and SSTs. Factors such as voluntariness (Walker and Johnson 2004) and, technology readiness (Lanseng and Andreassen 2007) have also been identified as the antecedents of SST adoption and usage. Further, the need for interpersonal interaction (Dabholkar 1996) and the enjoyment experienced while interacting and playing with technology may reduce consumers' need for interacting with service staff, and, thus, influence consumer attitudes towards using SSTs. In addition, Dabholkar and Bagozzi (2002) found that the need for interaction, self-efficacy, novelty seeking, and self-consciousness were significant moderators of attitude towards SSTs.

20.3 Health Service Quality

Quality in healthcare is currently at the forefront of professional, political, and managerial attention, primarily because it is seen ultimately as an approach to achieving better health outcomes for consumers. In this context, service quality in healthcare is of paramount importance. Service quality is a well-established construct in the service marketing literature. Perceived service quality is defined as the overall attitude towards a service (Parasuraman et al. 1988). Over the past 2 decades, service quality theory and practice have received considerable attention from academics and practitioners alike because service quality in many service-oriented organizations is considered to be a source of sustainable competitive advantage.

Service quality is a multidimensional phenomenon. To measure it, Parasuraman et al. (1988) developed a generic 22-item instrument which is known as SERVQUAL. It is based on the notion of a gap between what customers expect in terms of service quality from the providers of a service and their assessment of the actual performance of that particular service (Bebko 2000). The SERVQUAL instrument items capture how consumers differentiate performance on five dimensions of service quality, namely, tangibility, reliability, responsiveness, assurance, and empathy.

Many researchers have argued that given the nature of the service quality construct (especially with respect to the number of dimensions), it is highly likely that dimensions may vary and might be industry-specific. A major concern with the SERVQUAL instrument raised by many researchers concerns its dimensional structure. Thus, the universality of SERVQUAL's five dimensions has been questioned (Buttle 1996; Cronin and Taylor 1992). Shortcomings concerning convergent and discriminant validity have also been noted (Buttle 1996). It has also been argued that a performance-only measure, such as SERVPERF, explains more of the variance in an overall measure of service quality than does SERVQUAL (Cronin and Taylor 1994). However, despite the concerns over the validity of the instrument, Buttle (1996) argues that it is still a useful tool for the measurement of service quality and it continues to be widely used because of its adaptability to varying researchers' needs.

In the past decade, researchers and companies have also sought and found evidence about the profit consequences of service quality. Service quality is known to contribute to market share and customer satisfaction (Zeithaml 2000). The impact of service quality on profit and other financial outcomes of the organization has received much interest and attention (Rust, Zahorik, and Keiningham 1995). One of the key interests on service quality for both academics and practitioners has been because of the positive relationship between service quality and consumers' behavioural intentions. This fact was supported by several studies (e.g. Bitner 1990; Fornell 1992; Parasuraman et al. 1991a, b). Bitner (1990) suggested that a high level of service quality will lead to service loyalty while Parasuraman et al. (1991a, b) found a positive and significant relationship between customers' perceptions of service quality and their willingness to recommend a service provider. Fornell (1992) noted that high quality leads to high levels of customer retention which in turn are strongly related to profitability. Olorunniwo et al. (2006) found service quality to be an important driver of behavioural intentions.

In addition, Bolton and Myers (2003) investigated the determinants of price elasticity and concluded that service quality influenced price elasticity. The results of the study indicate that customers who receive more responsive service are less price-sensitive than customers who receive less responsive service. Also, customers are more tolerant of price changes and less apt to defects to alternative suppliers when they experience highly reliable service. Customers who receive more assurance or empathy from service representatives over time are less price-sensitive than customers who receive less assurance. Zeithaml et al. (1996) offered a conceptual model of the impact of service quality on particular behaviours. Their study found that service quality is positively associated with willingness to pay more. Regardless of the debate over the order of service quality and satisfaction relationship, researchers generally agree that service quality is closely linked with customer satisfaction. Considerable scholarly effort has been devoted to improve our practical understanding of such important service constructs as service quality and satisfaction (Cronin and Taylor 1992; Brady and Robertson 2001).

20.4 Technology-Based Self-service Evaluation

The benefits associated with self-service have been well documented in service marketing literature. However much of this research has been conducted in the areas of financial services sector. For example, in the banking context, SSTs are associated with increased reliability, assurance, and responsiveness dimensions of SERVQUAL (Zhu et al. 2002). Kelley et al. (1990) also stated that involving customer participation will eventually enhance service quality and customer satisfaction as it gives more control to customers. That is, customer evaluations of service encounters, including both technical and functional aspects of the service, and of service satisfaction may well affect the quality of life experienced by individuals.

Research concerning SST outcomes is relatively scant. It is generally agreed that the provision of IT-based service options, in and of itself, does not guarantee customer satisfaction. In fact, IT-based services or more generally technology-based self-services (TBSSs) can affect customer perceptions of service quality either positively or negatively. Studies have been conducted to explore the gaps between retailer's value offering and customers' perceptions based on qualitative data combined with personal experience and observations (Anitsal and Paige 2006). Further studies examined service quality perceptions in TBSS in relation to service participation, service environment, and support provided by service employees (Anitsal and Paige 2006).

Amongst all TBSSs, e-service, defined as web-based service or an interactive service that is delivered on the Internet, has gained much attention in recent years due to its pervasiveness and its ability to provide consumers with a superior experience with respect to the interactive flow of information (Santos 2003). Recent work on e-service quality has focused on developing scale measurements. For example, Wolfinbarger and Gilly (2003) developed 14-item eTailQ scale for retailing online. They grouped these 14 items into four dimensions labelled web site design, fulfilment/reliability, security/privacy, and customer service. Ho and Lin (2010) developed a multiple-item scale for measuring Internet banking service quality. Based on the service quality dimensions based on traditional delivery channels, these studies added dimensions such as web design, information provision (Ho and Lin 2010), security, and support (Santos 2003) that are specific to the web context. Zeithaml, Parasuraman, and Malhotra (2000, 2002) developed e-SERVQUAL for measuring e-service quality through a three-stage process using exploratory focus groups and two phases of empirical data collection and produced seven dimensions, namely, efficiency, reliability, fulfilment, privacy, responsiveness, compensation, and contact. They further developed a multiple-item scale (E-S-QUAL) for measuring the service quality delivered by web sites on which customers shop online (Parasuraman et al. 2005). They argue electronic service quality is not unidimensional, rather it is multifaceted, including dimensions, such as ease of use, privacy/confidentiality, reliability, and site design.

20.5 DiaMonD: A TBSS for Diabetes Self-management

A SST like DiaMonD is well-suited to facilitate required diabetes monitoring behaviours due to its pervasive nature and relative ease of accessibility which is considered a source of satisfaction for users or consumers (Meuter et al. 2000). DiaMonD is likely to be easy to use and useful for both diabetes patients and healthcare professionals. As shown in Fig. 20.1, the solution requires diabetes sufferers to input their glucose (HA1C) readings systematically via a simple user interface before sending them for processing. In fact, the manner in which DiaMonD operates

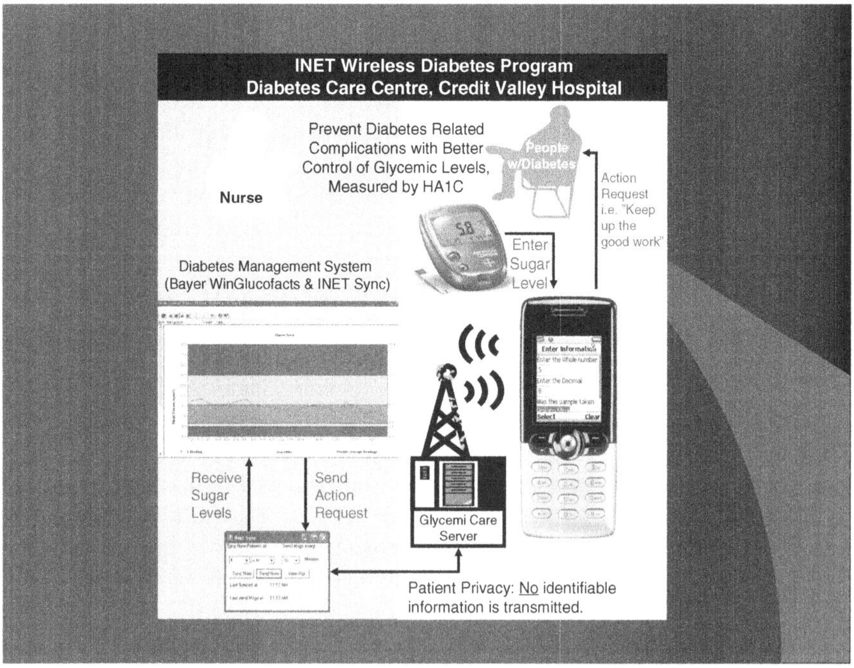

Fig. 20.1 ICT support for diabetes (Wickramasinghe and Goldberg 2006)

is very similar to Short Message Service (SMS) applications which are renown for their popularity (Mackay and Weidlich 2007; O'Doherty et al. 2010; Oh et al. 2008). It is, therefore, anticipated that diabetes sufferers will find the solution easy to use and useful as also supported in preliminary studies and assessments in previous trials both in the United States and Canada (Wickramasinghe and Goldberg 2004; 2007; Wickramasinghe, Goldberg, and Bali 2008). Additionally, as research evidence from the United States and Canada and preliminary anecdotal evidence from Australia show, healthcare professionals that have used the proposed solution have indicated that the functionality that concerns them (Fig. 20.1) is also easy to use and useful (Wickramasinghe and Goldberg 2004, 2007; Wickramasinghe, Goldberg, and Bali 2008). That is, the solution enables healthcare professionals to both monitor diabetes trends and interact with patients relatively easily, inexpensively, and pervasively.

From the patients' viewpoint, operating the proposed solution entails a mobile handset and a data plan. Current evidence shows that in many countries worldwide mobile penetration rates exceed 100 % (Netsize 2009). Evidence also shows increasing trends of usage of mobile data services suggesting that a growing number of mobile phone users are subscribed to mobile data plans (Netsize 2009). The proposed mobile diabetes self-management solution has been designed to run on all mobile handsets which diabetes patients are likely to already have in their possession. Similar arguments can be made for healthcare professionals and their organization. It is anticipated that aside from software upgrades in existing servers and corresponding license fees, upgrades to new computer hardware are not necessary. Hence this solution requires minimal expense to all concerned.

The interaction frequency between diabetes patients and healthcare providers using the proposed mobile solution will be high, though dictated by the treatment regimen that healthcare professionals prescribe to patients. For example, some patients may be required to send their glucose readings to their healthcare professional 6 times daily, i.e. 3 times daily before and after each meal, while other patients may be required to fulfil different patterns. We argue that interaction frequency is not only a means of maximizing cost efficiencies but also a way of strengthening and complementing long-term patient–healthcare professional relationships thereby improving the overall quality of healthcare services offered. Thus, DiaMonD constitutes a TBSS solution which, while not exorbitantly expensive, can facilitate superior self-management and monitoring of diabetes. Further, it can enable patient empowerment by way of enhancing traditional clinical-patient interactions (Mirza, Norris, and Stockdale 2008) and therefore potentially result in improved service quality perceptions in healthcare outcomes (Opie 1998; Radin 2006).

20.6 TBSS Constructs

The literature on TBSS quality is scant. Thus, we reviewed primarily the e-service quality literature and information system adoption literature about how users form quality perceptions. As discussed below, this review revealed a number of dimensions which are in line with those included in the SERVQUAL model. Extensions to these dimensions are also proposed.

Ease of use is one of the most prevalent constructs in technology adoption models which can be described as "the degree to which a person believes that using a particular mode would be free of effort" (Davis 1989, p. 320). The impact of perceived ease of use on user's intentions to adopt a technology is well documented (Davis 1989; Taylor and Todd 1995; Venkatesh and Davis 2000; Venkatesh 1999). Simply put, the lesser effort is needed when using a particular innovation, the more likely it is to be adopted. Ease of use will not only save consumers' effort but it will also reduce social risk (e.g. they may fear looking stupid if they struggle to use it) (Dabholkar 1996).

Reliability is the dependability and accuracy of service performance. The importance of reliability in traditional service delivery is well documented (Zeithaml and Bitner 2000). With a high level of perceived risk often involved in TBSSs, consumers may be concerned about the reliability of new service delivery options. For example, server down time in the delivery of web-based services may influence the overall service quality of an online retailer. Similarly, self-checking kiosks at airports may temporarily have mechanical problems.

Speed of delivery is crucial in a technology-driven economy. TBSSs are expected to provide faster service delivery than face-to-face services. Consumers prefer to perform the service themselves if it reduces delivery time (Lovelock and Young 1979). This is because unoccupied time feels longer than occupied time (Maister 1985). Thus slow service delivery affects our overall perceptions of service quality. Although no direct bearing of speed on service quality was found in a study on TBSS fast-food ordering options (Dabholkar 1996), perceived speed of delivery in Internet banking services was found to have a positive effect on perceived service quality (Shamdasani et al. 2008)

Assurance refers to security, privacy, and recovery aspects when TBSSs fail. With little human interaction, consumers often feel a sense of risk when they use TBSSs. The privacy dimension in E-S-QUAL developed by Parasuraman et al. (2005) corresponds to assurance. Customer perceptions of security are one of the key elements of TBSS transactions (see Grewal and Dharwadkar 2002; Montoya-Weiss et al. 2003).

Enjoyment is one of the intrinsic motivators for technology adoption and may be used to gauge service quality by some consumers. Playfulness or fun and aesthetic value gained by participating in service experiences satisfy pleasure-oriented or hedonic needs and operate outside extrinsic motivations (Mathwick et al. 2002; Moon and Kim 2001). In fact, some consumers enjoy playing with machines and may prefer self-service options. Perceived enjoyment is one of the most important types of user needs (Anckar and D'Incau 2002). Thus, a TBSS is more likely to be adopted when it looks like something that would be enjoyable.

Perceived control refers to the extent of control that consumers feel they have over service processes or outcomes. A sense of control is essential to satisfactory experience with any type of service delivery (Guiry 1992). Perceived behavioural control is an individual's belief about the "presence or absence of requisite resources and opportunities" (Ajzen and Madden 1986). With TBSSs, an increased level of perceived control increases the expected value of the service (Dabholkar 1996).

In regard to self-service, Dabholkar (1996) developed two alternative service quality models concerning consumer perceptions of service quality. Although the direct relationship between service quality and behavioural intention posited by Dabholkar (1996) has gained support (Zeithaml et al. 1996), the impact of such options on customer perceptions towards overall service quality as measured by the traditional SERVQUAL dimensions of service quality is unclear. For example some researchers found that TBSSs have a direct impact on the SERVQUAL dimensions and an indirect impact on customer satisfaction (Zhu et al. 2002) while others found TBSSs are directly linked with customer satisfaction (Meuter et al. 2000; Yen 2005), commitment (Beatson et al. 2006), and loyalty (Selnes and Hansen 2001).

20.7 Service Quality Perception, Patient Satisfaction, and Quality of Life

Service evaluation research mainly centres on the concept of service quality and satisfaction. A large body of literature links service quality and service satisfaction. Much of this work is based on Parasuraman, Zeithaml, and Berry's seminal work developing a model of service quality (Parasuraman et al. 1985, 1991a, b), which has been built on by many other authors. Although various authors investigating this area have identified service quality either as an antecedent (Bhat 2005; Cronin and Taylor 1992; Oh 1999) or as an outcome of satisfaction (Bitner 1990; Oliver 1981; Bolton and Drew 1991), currently the dominant view has been to identify service quality as an antecedent to or mediator of satisfaction (Dabholkar et al. 2000; Sivadas and Baker-Prewitt 2000; Brady and Robertson 2001).

Using a pervasive mobile technology solution such as DiaMonD in chronic disease self-management may not only contribute to service quality perception but indeed also contribute to the life quality of the patient as these technologies are designed to save consumers' time and effort and improve their quality of life. Recent service marketing literature recognizes the centrality of quality of life to marketing. Lee and Sirgy (2004) suggested that quality of life is a new paradigm following a succession of previous paradigms including sales and profit, competition, customer satisfaction, and relationship marketing. Dagger and Sweeney (2006) argue that it is in the services context that quality of life may be most relevant as an outcome of the consumption process. Customer evaluations of services and service satisfaction may well affect the quality of life experienced by users of the service. Quality of life is defined as the wellbeing, happiness, and life satisfaction of individuals. That is,

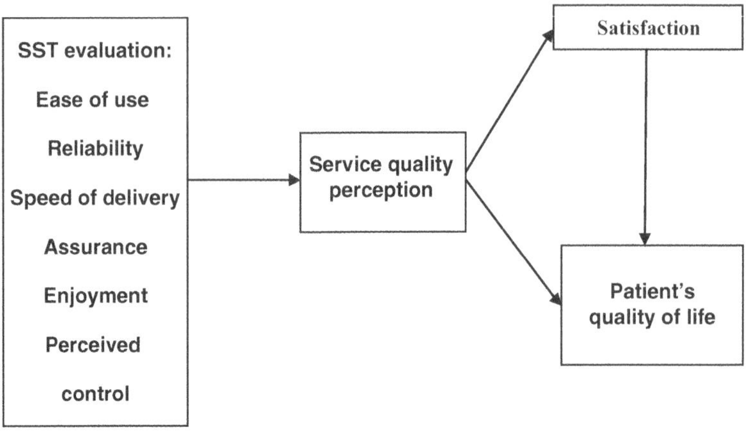

Fig. 20.2 Antecedents and factors that impact service quaulity perceptions

quality of life is a subjective, individual, experiential concept. In the limited marketing and HR literature quality of life is often used interchangeably with that of life satisfaction, utility, and wellbeing (Endres 1999) and can be conceptualized as an overall measure or as a measure based on experiences in a variety of domains, such that the greater the satisfaction with various life domains, including personal health, consuming, work, family, and leisure, the greater the satisfaction with life in general (Lee et al. 2002; MacFadyen 1999; Sirgy 2001). Thus overall, quality of life reflects the culmination of an individual's subjective evaluation of his or her current life circumstances. Given the healthcare care context of the present study and the identification of health as the most significant component of quality of life (Giles 1987), we define quality of life as a sense of overall wellbeing and we argue that DiaMonD can contribute towards improving it (Fig. 20.2).

20.8 Implications and Conclusions

The implications of this research are highly relevant to the healthcare industry. Service quality perceptions constitute an important catalyst for improving the quality healthcare particularly in the context of chronic diseases where interactions between patients and healthcare providers are frequent. Thus, improving service quality perceptions should constitute a key component of healthcare providers' strategies. There are, thus, two main practical implications from this research that may be useful to practitioners. The functionality of novel wireless technology solutions such as DiaMonD needs to be aligned with the SERVQUAL dimensions proposed in this study if patients' service quality perceptions concerning their healthcare are to be positively enhanced. Knowledge and appreciation of the importance of these dimensions may help healthcare providers to both design new services or enhance existing ones in order to improve patients' quality of life.

This chapter has set out to underscore the importance of service quality and quality of life perceptions of patients with regard to the use of technologies especially wireless technologies in healthcare. Wireless technologies have been widely adopted in various industries and now are becoming more prevalent in healthcare. Thus, we believe the implications of our research are particularly important and far reaching as healthcare actors look to embrace more technology-enabled solutions to facilitate superior healthcare delivery and we close by calling for more research in this area.

References

AIHW, (2007). National Indicators for Monitoring Diabetes: Report of the Diabetes Indicators Review Subcommittee of the National Diabetes Data Working Group: AIHW cat. no. CVD 38. Canberra: AIHW.

Aihw, (2008). Diabetes: Australian Facts 2008, Australian Institute of Health and Welfare, Canberra.

Ajzen, I., & Madden, T. J. (1986). Prediction of goal-directed behavior: Attitudes, intentions, and perceived behavioral control. *Journal of Experimental Social Psychology, 22*, 453–474.

Anckar, B., & D'incau, D. (2002). Value creation in mobile commerce: Findings from a consumer survey. *Journal of Information Technology Theory and Application, 4*, 43–64.

Anitsal, I., & Paige, R. C. (2006). An exploratory study on consumer perceptions of service quality in technology-based self-service. *Services Marketing Quarterly, 27*, 53–67.

Balas, E. A., Krishna, S., Kretschmer, R. A., Cheek, T. R., Lobach, D. F. & Boren, S. A. (2004). Computerized knowledge management in diabetes care. *Medical Care, 42*(6), 610–621.

Beatson, A., Coote, L. V., & Rudd, J. M. (2006). Determining consumer satisfaction and commitment through self-service technology and personal service usage. *Journal of Marketing Management, 22*(7/8), 853–882.

Bebko, C. P. (2000). Service intangibility and its impact on consumer expectations of service quality. *Journal of Services Marketing, 14*(1), 9–26.

Bitner, M. J. (1990). Evaluating service encounters: The effects of physical surroundings and employee responses. *Journal of Marketing, 54*(2), 69–82.

Bobbitt, L. M., & Dabholkar, P. A. (2001). Integrating attitudinal theories to understand and predict use of technology-based self-service. *International Journal of Service Industry Management, 12*(5), 423–450.

Bodenheimer, T., Lorig, K., Holman, H. & Grumbach, K. (2002). Patient self-management of chronic disease in primary care. Journal of American Medical Association (JAMA), 288(19), 2469–2475.

Bolton, R. N., & Drew, J. H. (1991). A multistage model of customers' assessments of service quality and value. *Journal of Consumer Research, 17*(4), 375.

Bolton, R. N., & Myers, M. B. (2003). Price-based global market segmentation for services. *Journal of Marketing, 67*(3), 108–128.

Brady, M. K., & Robertson, C. J. (2001). Searching for a consensus on the antecedent role of service quality and satisfaction: An exploratory cross-national study. *Journal of Business Research, 51*(1), 53–60.

Britt, H., Miller, G. C., Charles, J., Pan, Y., Valenti, L., Henderson, J. et al. (2007). General Practice Activity in Australia 2005-06, Cat. no. GEP 16. Canberra: AIHW.

Buttle, F. (1996). SERVQUAL: Review, critique, research agenda. *European Journal of Marketing, 30*(1), 8–32.
Colagiuri, S., Colagiuri, R. & Ward, J. (1998). National Diabetes Strategy and Implementation Plan. Canberra: Diabetes Australia.
Cronin, J. J., & Taylor, S. A. (1992). Measuring service quality: A reexamination and extension. *Journal of Marketing, 56*, 55–68.
Cronin, J. J., Baker, J. T. L., & Hawes, J. M. (1994). An assessment of the role performance measurement of power-dependency in marketing channels. *Journal of Business Research, 30*(3), 201–210.
Dabholkar, P. A. (1996). Consumer evaluations of new technology-based self-service options: An investigation of alternative models of service quality. *International Journal of Research in Marketing, 13*(1), 29–51.
Dabholkar, P. A., & Bagozzi, R. P. (2002). An attitudinal model of technology-based self-service: Moderating effects of consumer traits and situational factors. *Journal of the Academy of Marketing Science, 30*(3), 184–201.
Dabholkar, P. A., Shepherd, C. D., & Thorpe, D. I. (2000). A comprehensive framework for service quality: An investigation of critical conceptual and measurement issues through a longitudinal study. *Journal of Retailing, 76*(2), 139–173.
Dagger, T. S., & Sweeney, J. C. (2006). The effect of service evaluations on behavioral intentions and quality of life. *Journal of Service Research, 9*(1), 3.
Davis, F. D. (1989). Perceived usefulness, perceived ease of use, and user acceptance in information technology. *MIS Quarterly, 13*(3), 319–340.
DiabetesAustralia. (2008). Diabetes in Australia. Retrieved from http://www.diabetesaustralia.com.au/Understanding-Diabetes/Diabetes-in-Australia/.
Dixon, T. & Webbie, K. (2006). The National System for Monitoring Diabetes in Australia (AIHW Cat. No. CVD 32). Canberra: Australian Institute of Health and Wealfare.
Downer, S. R., Meara, J. G., Da Costa, A. C. & Sethuraman, K. (2006). SMS text messaging improves outpatient attendance. Australian Health Review, *30*(3), 389–396.
Fornell, C. (1992). A national customer satisfaction barometer: the Swedish experience. *Journal of Marketing, 56*, 6–21.
Giles, R. H. (1987). Systems ecology, marketing and quality of life. In A. Coskun & A. Samli (Eds.), *Marketing and the quality-of-life interface*. New York: Quorum Books.
Grewal, R., & Dharwadkar, R. (2002). The role of the institutional environment in marketing channels. *Journal of Marketing, 66*(3), 82–97.
Guiry, M. (1992). Consumer and employee roles in service encounters. *Advances in Consumer Research, 19*(1), 666–672.
Ho, C. T. B., & Lin, W. C. (2010). Measuring the service quality of internet banking: Scale development and validation. *European Business Review, 22*(1), 5–24.
ICIC. (2008). Improving Chronic Illness Care: The Chronic Care Model. Retrieved from http://www.improvingchroniccare.org/indix.php?p=The_Chronic_Care_Model&s=2.
Knuiman, M. W., Welborn, T. A. & Bartholomew, H. C. (1996). Self-reported health and use of health services: a comparison of diabetic and nondiabetic persons from a national sample. *Australian and New Zealand Journal of Public Health, 20*(3), 241–247.
Lanseng, E. J., & Andreassen, T. W. (2007). Electronic healthcare: A study of people's readiness and attitude toward performing self-diagnosis. *International Journal of Service Industry Management, 18*(4), 394–417.
Lee, D. J., & Sirgy, M. J. (2004). Quality-of-life (QOL) marketing: Proposed antecedents and consequences. *Journal of Macromarketing, 24*(1), 44.
Lee, D. J., Sirgy, M. J., Larsen, V., & Wright, N. D. (2002). Developing a subjective measure of consumer well-being. *Journal of Macromarketing, 22*(2), 158.
Lovelock, C. H., & Young, R. F. (1979). Look to customers to increase productivity. *Harvard Business Review, 57*(3), 168–178.

MacFadyen, A. J. (1999). Well-being. In P. E. Earl & S. Kemp (Eds.), *The Elgar companion to consumer research and economic psychology*. Cheltenham: Edward Elgar.

Mackay, M. M. & Weidlich, O. (2007, March 2007). Australian Mobile Phone Lifestyle Index, 3rd Edition, Australian Interactive Media Industry Association (AIMIA), Mobile Content Industry Development Group (MCIDG). Retrieved 8 April, 2007, from http://www.aimia.com.au/mobile.

Maister, D. H. (1985). The psychology of waiting lines. In J. A. Czepiel, M. Solomon, & C. S. Surprenant (Eds.), *The service encounter* (pp. 113–123). Lexington, MA: Lexington Books.

Mathwick, C., Malhorta, N. K., & Rigdon, E. (2002). The effect of dynamic retail experiences on experiential perceptions of value: An internet and catalogue comparison. *Journal of Retailing, 78*, 51–60.

Meuter, M. L., Ostrom, A. L., Roundtree, R. I., & Bitner, M. J. (2000). Self-service technologies: understanding customer satisfaction with technology-based service encounters. the Journal of Marketing, 50–64.

Meuter, M. L., Bitner, M. J., Ostrom, A. L., & Brown, S. W. (2005). Choosing among alternative service delivery modes: An investigation of customer trial of self-service technologies. *Journal of Marketing, 69*(2), 61–83.

Meuter, M. L., Ostrom, A. L., Bitner, M. J., & Roundtree, R. (2003). The influence of technology anxiety on consumer use and experiences with self-service technologies. *Journal of Business Research, 56*(11), 899–906.

Mirza, F., Norris, T. & Stockdale, R. (2008). Mobile technologies and the holistic management of chronic diseases. *Health Informatics Journal, 14*(4), 309–321.

Montoya-Weiss, M., Voss, G. B., & Grewal, D. (2003). Determinants of online channel use and overall satisfaction with a relational, multichannel service provider. *Journal of the Academy of Marketing Science, 31*(4), 448–458.

Moon, J.-W. & Kim, Y.-G. (2001). Extending the TAM for a World-Wide-Web context. *Information & Management, 38*(4), 217–230.

Netsize. (2009). Netsize Guide 2009 Edition: Mobile Society and Me: When worlds combine. Levallois-Perret: Netsize.

O'Doherty, K., Rao Hill, S., Mackay, M. M. & McPherson, J. (2010). Mobile Data Service usage and preference: an investigation of Australian consumers. *International Journal of Mobile Communications, 8*(1), 106–127.

Oh, S., Yang, S., Kurnia, S., Lee, H., Mackay, M. M. & O'Doherty, K. (2008). The characteristics of mobile data users in Australia. *International Journal of Mobile Communications, 8*(2), 217–230.

Oliver, R. L. (1981). Measurement and evaluation of satisfaction process in retail setting. *Journal of Retailing, 57*, 25–48.

Olorunniwo, F., Hsu, M. K., & Udo, G. J. (2006). Service quality, customer satisfaction, and behavioral intentions in the service factory. *Journal of Services Marketing, 20*(1), 59–72.

Opie, A. (1998). Nobody's asked me for my view: users' empowerment by multidisciplinary health teams. *Qualitative Health Research, 18*, 188–206.

Parasuraman, A., Berry, L. L., & Zeithaml, V. A. (1991a). Refinement and reassessment of the SERVQUAL scale. *Journal of Retailing, 67*(4), 420–450.

Parasuraman, A., Berry, L. L., & Zeithaml, V. A. (1991b). Understanding customer expectations of service. *Sloan Management Review, 10*, 39–48.

Parasuraman, A., Zeithaml, V. A., & Berry, L. L. (1985). A conceptual model of service quality and its implications for future research. *Journal of Marketing, 49*, 41–50.

Parasuraman, A., Zeithaml, V. A., & Berry, L. L. (1988). SERVQUAL: A multiple-item scale for measuring consumers perceptions of service quality. *Journal of Retailing, 64*(1), 12–37.

Parasuraman, A., Zeithaml, V. A., & Malhotra, A. (2005). Es-Qual: A multiple-item scale for assessing electronic service quality. *Journal of Service Research, 7*(3), 213.

Poulton, B. C. (1999). User involvement in identifying health needs and shaping and evaluating services: is it being raised? *Journal of Advanced Nursing, 30*(6), 1289–1296.

Radin, P. (2006). To me, it's my life: medical communication, trust, and activism in cyberspace. *Social Science & Medicine, 6*, 591–601.
Rasmussen, B., Wellard, S. & Nankervis, A. (2001). Consumer issues in navigating health care services for type I diabetes. *Journal of Clinical Nursing, 10*, 628–634.
Russell, L. B., Churl Suh, D. & Safford, M. M. (2005). Time requirements for diabetes management: too much for many? *The Journal of Family Practice, 54*(1), 52–56.
Rust, R. T., Zahorik, A. J. & Keiningham, T. L. (1995). Return on quality (ROQ): making service quality financial accountable. *Journal of Marketing, 59*(2), 58–70.
Santos, J. (2003). E-Service quality: A model of virtual service quality dimensions. *Managing Service Quality, 13*(3), 233–246.
Selnes, F., & Hansen, H. (2001). The potential hazard of self-service in developing customer loyalty. *Journal of Service Research, 4*(2), 79.
Shamdasani, P., Mukherjee, A., & Malhotra, N. (2008). Antecedents and consequences of service quality in consumer evaluation of self-service internet technologies. *Service Industries Journal, 28*(1), 117–138.
Sirgy, M. J. (2001). Handbook of quality-of-life research: An ethical marketing perspective (Vol. 8): Springer.
Sivadas, E., & Baker-Prewitt, J. (2000). An examination of the relationship between service quality, customer satisfaction and store loyalty. *International Journal of Retail and Distribution Management, 28*(2), 73–82.
Taylor, S., & Todd, P. A. (1995). Understanding information technology usage: A test of competing models. *Information Systems Research, 6*(2), 144–176.
Van Eyk, H. & Baum, F. (2002). Learning about interagency collaboration: Trialling collaborative projects between hospitals and community health services. *Health and Social Care in the Community, 10*(4), 262–269.
Venkatesh, V. (1999). Creating favourable user perceptions: Exploring the role of intrinsic motivation. *MIS Quarterly, 23*(2), 239–260.
Venkatesh, V., & Davis, F. D. (2000). A theoretical extension of the technology acceptance model: Four longitudinal field studies. *Management Science, 46*(2), 186–204.
Victorian government. (2007). Diabetes Prevention and Management: A Strategic Framework for Victoria 1007–2010, Victorian Government, Department of Human Services, Melbourne.
Walker, R. M. (2006). Innovation type and diffusion: an empirical analysis of local government. *Public Administration, 84*(2), 311–335.
Walker, R. H., & Johnson, L. W. (2004). Managing technology-enabled service innovations. *International Journal of Entrepreneurship and Innovation Management, 4*(6), 561–574.
Wellard, S. J., Rennie, S. & King, R. (2008). Perceptions of people with type 2 diabetes about self-management and the efficiency of community based services. *Contemporary Nurse, 29*(2), 218–226.
Wickramasinghe, N., & Goldberg, S. (2004). How M=EC2 in healthcare, *International Journal of Mobile Communications, 2*(2), 140–156.
Wickramasinghe, N., & Goldberg, S. (2007). Adaptive mapping to realisation methodology (AMR) to facilitate mobile initiatives in healthcare, *International Journal of Mobile Communications, 5*(3), 300–318.
Wickramasinghe, N., Goldberg, S. & Bali, R. (2008). Enabling superior m-health project success: a tri-country validation. *International Journal of Services and Standards, 4*(1), 97–117.
Wolfinbarger, M., & Gilly, M. C. (2003). Etailq: Dimensionalizing, measuring and predicting etail quality. *Journal of Retailing, 79*(3), 183–198.
Yen, H. R. (2005). An attribute-based model of quality satisfaction for internet self-service technology. *Service Industries Journal, 25*(5), 641–659.
Zeithaml, V. A. (2000). Service quality, profitability, and the economic worth of customers: What we know and what we need to learn. *Journal of the Academy of Marketing Science, 28*(1), 67–86.
Zeithaml, V. A., Berry, L. L., & Parasuraman, A. (1996). The behavioural consequences of service quality. *Journal of Marketing, 60*, 31–46.

Zeithaml, V. A., Parasuraman, A., & Malhotra, A. (2000). Conceptual Framework for understanding e-service quality: Implications for future research and managerial practice.

Zeithaml, V. A., Parasuraman, A., & Malhotra, A. (2002). Service quality delivery through web sites: a critical review of extant knowledge. *Journal of the Academy of Marketing Science, 30*(4), 362–375.

Zigbor, J. C. & Songer, T. J. (2001). External barriers to diabetes care: addressing personal and health systems issues. *Diabetes Spectrum, 14*, 23–28.

Zhu, F. X., Wymer, W., & Chen, I. (2002). It-based services and service quality in consumer banking. *International Journal of Service Industry Management, 13*(1), 69–90.

Chapter 21
The Role of Online Social Networks in Consumer Health Informatics: An Example of the Implicit Incorporation of Lean Principles

Carolin Durst, Janine Viol, and Nilmini Wickramasinghe

Abstract Consumer health informatics is a relatively new and rapidly expanding area within the field of medical informatics. Central to this discipline is the importance of providing information and support to individuals (consumers) so that they can be empowered and take a central role in their own health and well-being.

The rapidly increasing prevalence of obesity is a phenomenon often referred to as the "obesity epidemic" (Obesity: preventing and managing the global epidemic. Report of a WHO Consultation. WHO Technical Report Series 894, WHO, Geneva, 2000). Literature suggests social networks to be one of the most important dimension of people's social environment that may enable or constrain the adoption of health-promoting behaviors (e.g., The New England Journal of Medicine, 357:370–379, 2007; Social Science & Medicine (1982), 63:1011-1022, 2006). Using data collected in qualitative interviews and via a Facebook application, this research in progress provides first insights on the relationship between online social connections, health-related behaviors, and body weight.

An outlook is given on how the use of online social networks may facilitate appropriate health-related behaviors in the context of obesity.

C. Durst (✉) • J. Viol
Institute of Information Systems, University Erlangen-Nürnberg,
Lange Gasse 20, 90403 Nürnberg, Germany
e-mail: carolin.durst@wiso.uni-erlangen.de; janine.viol@wiso.uni-erlangen.de

N. Wickramasinghe Ph.D., MBA
Epworth HealthCare & Department of BITL & HIRi, RMIT University, GPO Box 2476,
Melbourne, VIC 3001, Australia
e-mail: nilmini.wickramasinghe@rmit.edu.au

N. Wickramasinghe et al. (eds.), *Lean Thinking for Healthcare*, Healthcare Delivery in the Information Age, DOI 10.1007/978-1-4614-8036-5_21,

21.1 Introduction

Consumer health informatics is arguably the most rapidly expanding area within medical informatics and is playing a key role in paving the way for healthcare delivery in today's twenty-first century (Eysenbach 2000). Central to this discipline is the goal to provide consumers the information and support required in order that they can make informed choices and be empowered to take a central role in their own health and wellness regimen (Eysenbach 2000). Moreover, consumer health informatics has been able to develop due to advances in various technologies especially Web 2.0. Web 2.0 technologies are nowadays applied in various areas, such as education, traveling, dating, or job seeking (BVDW 2010). In the context of healthcare, Health 2.0 applications combine health data and health information with (patient) experience through the use of ICT (Bos et al. 2008). Embracing patient-centered health informatics, Health 2.0 applications may become an effective self-care information and disease self-management tool in the future. Given that consumer health informatics in general and Web 2.0 technologies in particular have the potential to provide consumers with information and support needed to make appropriate choices that can have a positive impact on the health and well-being, we decided to investigate this more closely by examining the impact of using online social networks to foster healthier lifestyles in the context of obesity.

21.2 Background

Obesity has become an issue of grave global concern. Today there exist more than one billion overweight adults out of which at least 300 million are medically obese (WHO, 2011). Since 1980 obesity has more than doubled worldwide. Once thought to be a disease linked to people from high-income countries, nowadays, obesity is also a serious problem for people in urban settings in low- and middle-income countries. Not only is obesity in and of itself problematic, but it also leads to various secondary disorders such as diabetes, heart diseases, and cancer (MedStar Physician Partners/MedStar Family 2007; WHO, 2011), which add more burdens to healthcare delivery, its costs, and likelihood of recovery (Wickramasinghe et al. 2012). The future looks even more bleak given that approximately 43 million children under the age of five in 2010 have been diagnosed as being medically overweight which indicates that the projections are likely to be even higher regarding obese adults within the next years (WHO, 2011). It is evident that the far-reaching impact of obesity is not only on individual health outcomes but also on the economy of healthcare delivery for countries. For example, in the USA, the medical costs of obesity were estimated to be as high as $147 billion per year in 2008. This number is equal to about 9 % of all medical spending (Finkelstein et al. 2009). By 2030, costs attributable to obesity are projected to account for 16–18 % of total US healthcare costs (Wang et al. 2008).

The causes of obesity are multifaceted and result from a confluence of several factors. Individual medical conditions may determine a person's susceptibility to gain weight but cannot explain the dramatic increase in the number of obese people worldwide (WHO 2000). Changes in individual behaviors leading to an increased intake of high-caloric foods and a decrease of physical activity are suggested to be a key contributor to the global obesity epidemic (WHO; Huffman 2011).

Individual behaviors, preferences, and lifestyle choices are subject to social and environmental influences. Moreover, social networks have been identified as one of the most important dimensions of people's social environment that may enable or constrain the adoption of many behaviors including health-promoting behaviors (McNeill et al. 2006).

Previous studies have focused on the spread of obesity within traditional (offline) social networks (e.g., Christakis and Fowler 2007; Cohen-Cole and Fletcher 2008; Fowler and Christakis 2008). As ideas, behaviors, and trends are passed on within people's social environment, a person-to-person spread of obesity within social networks has been suggested (Christakis and Fowler 2007).

In today's IT Age, we are seeing that social media have proved to be powerful in shaping opinions, behaviors, and affecting different areas of public life (Wefing 2012). Recent examples include the 2009 "Twitter Revolution" in Iran as well as the revolution in Tunisia and Egypt at the beginning of 2011 where social media played an important role in organizing the protest movement (von Rohr 2011). During the riots in England in August 2011, rioters communicated using social media application to incite looting and violence (Schone 2011). Yet, Twitter and Facebook were used to spread information on the riots and to organize clean-up operations in the affected areas, too (Polke-Majewski 2011).

The dramatic growth of electronic (online) social networks has resulted in blurring the boundaries between the real and virtual world (BVDW 2010). Deeply embedded in people's daily life, online social connections may—just as "real-world contacts"—shape people's opinions and possibly exert influence on their health-related behaviors (Ma et al. 2010).

Given that online social networks are becoming more important in people's daily lives, it is reasonable to hypothesize that online social network might also impact the adoption of health-related behaviors. Thus, this chapter focuses on the analysis of the relationship between people's online social connections, their health-related behaviors, and their body weight.

21.3 Literature Review

This chapter aims to understand the association between a person's online social network and his or her health status and in doing so also uncovers the existence of the incorporation of lean principles, albeit implicitly.

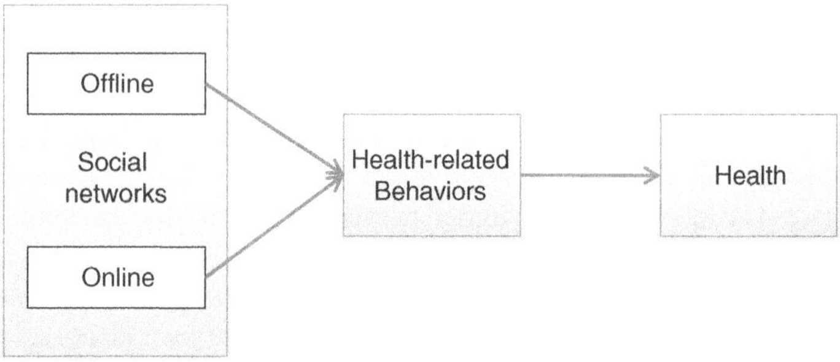

Fig. 21.1 Association between offline or online social networks, social capital, and health

Providing the theoretical background for this research, the following sections examine contributions dealing with the association between offline or online social networks, an individual's health-related behavior, and health (see Fig. 21.1).

A social network "consists of a finite set or sets of actors and the relation or relations defined on them" (Wasserman and Faust 1994, p. 20). Most commonly, social relationships are categorized into strong and weak ties (Kneidinger 2010). Tie strength is determined by the amount of time, the emotional intensity, the intimacy (mutual confiding), and the reciprocal services which characterize the tie (Granovetter 1973). According to Granovetter (1973), *strong ties* are intimate bonds between family members or close friends which are maintained regularly and permanently. Tending to be concentrated in particular groups, they are of informal nature and occur between network members with a shared social identity. Contrary, *weak ties* emerge as non-intimate bonds between acquaintances. Maintained infrequently and inconsistently, weak ties may be formal contacts and are more likely to link members of different small groups (Rostila 2011). Weak social ties are more likely to generate informational support, whereas informal and strong social ties are associated with the provision of emotional support (Rostila 2011).

Regarding the spread of obesity in large social networks, Christakis and Fowler (2007) provide three explanations for the collective dynamics of obesity.

- Homophily (selection) which is defined as the tendency of people to associate with people who are similar to them. The homophily argument is supported by, e.g., Bahr et al. (2009) who found that people with similar BMIs cluster together into groups within a social network.
- Confounding (contextual influences) which may occur when people share attributes or "jointly experience unobserved contemporaneous events" (Christakis and Fowler 2007) and results in simultaneous weight gain.
- Induction (endogenous social effect) which refers to a person-to-person spread of behaviors and traits.

According to Christakis' and Fowler's (2007) study, the susceptibility of a person to become obese increases when close members in the social network become obese.

The chance of becoming obese is positively correlated with the closeness and strength of the relationship. Though the design and findings of their study have been criticized (e.g., in Cohen-Cole and Fletcher 2008), a number of papers support their line of argument. Talking about epidemic diseases in social networks, Gershenson (2011) distinguishes between communicable diseases transmitted through, e.g., bacteria and viruses, such as influenza and HIV, and noncommunicable diseases, e.g., cancer and diabetes, that—by definition—cannot be transmitted. However, he acknowledges that the spread of ideas and behaviors as well as contagious trends and habits provides a powerful substitute for physical mechanisms to spread diseases and result in a so-called social infection. Thus, the risk factors for noncommunicable diseases, e.g., overweight and obesity, are spread across social networks. Having modeled the diffusion of health-related behaviors in a case study, Madan et al. (2010) found that health-related behaviors of peers correlate and a literature review by Hammond (2010) examining the relationship between social influence and obesity points to social influence and social network structures being important factors in obesity.

According to Arnaboldi et al. (2011), online social networks exhibit a high similarity to offline social relationships as they offer similar functionalities as unmediated spaces. They display people's (extended) offline social network and are primarily used to maintain and reinforce existing offline relationships (Boyd and Ellison 2007). Social network sites are applications that allow users to build a semi-public or public profile within a bounded system, to create explicit linkages to other users, and to communicate by sharing information or sending messages between each other. Organized around people, social network sites are structured as egocentric networks with the individual at the center of their personal network (Boyd and Ellison 2007; Kaplan and Haenlein 2010). Social network sites, online communities, and forums connect individuals with similar interests. Having studied a health online social network for 6 months, Ma et al. (2010) found out that the users' weight changes correlated positively with the number of their friends and their friends' weight-change performance. The study revealed that the online influence and its propagation distance appear to be greater than in real-world social networks (Ma et al. 2010).

Taking into account the findings from Christakis' and Fowler's (2007) study as well as the implications of the empirical study of health online social networks, this chapter seeks at analyzing the relationship between a person's online social network and his or her corresponding health status.

21.4 Research Design

This research has adopted a mixed methodology consisting of qualitative and quantitative components. In order to analyze the relationship between online social networks and health, a large dataset containing personal network data and information on health-related behaviors is required.

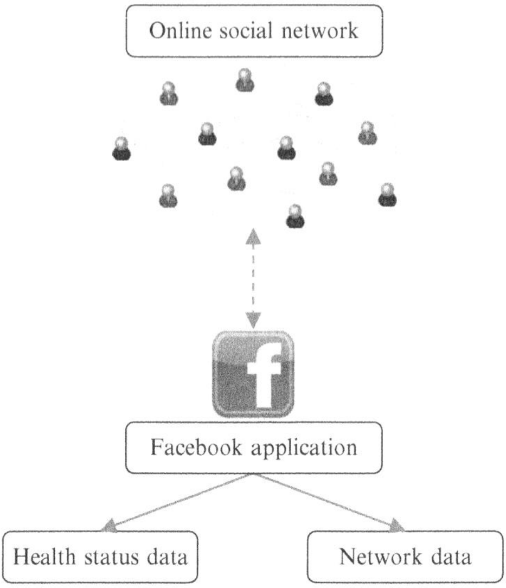

Fig. 21.2 Data collection logic via the Facebook application

Generic social networks are broadly diffused and allow access to profiles of people with different health status ranges. Using data from a generic social network site, such as Facebook, in the subsequent data collection and analysis enables the comparison of social network structures of normal weight people and obese people. Therefore, Facebook is selected as the data source in this study.

The network data collection process via Facebook requires an application that accesses user profiles via the Facebook API. The development of an application in the area of fitness and sports would enable simultaneous collection of health data (see Fig. 21.2).

The design is a crucial success factor for the usage of the application and consequently determines the number of user profiles collected using the application. It is hoped that a well-designed and playful application will trigger viral network effects and spread fast within the online social network. The requirements for an appealing application were elicited by conducting 15 explorative interviews.

Having analyzed the interviews, the Facebook application will be designed and implemented (Sect. 21.6). Preliminary analyses of the online social networks of the interviewees will provide first insights regarding the relationship between online social connections and health (Sect. 21.7).

Once the Facebook application is established and distributed within the community, a quantitative study will be conducted as a next step. Observing and analyzing the online social networks of the participating users, the application is suitable for longitudinal data collection and may be used to offer services fostering positive health-related behaviors or to promote behavior change in the future.

21.5 Qualitative Study

Using a qualitative approach including explorative interviews with 15 study participants, this study pursues two objectives: The first objective of the interviews is to obtain insights concerning causes and influences for weight gain as well as weight loss in the "real life." Referring to Christakis and Fowler (2007), a particular focus concentrates on the relationship between social connections and health-related behaviors. It is hoped that the findings can support the interpretation of the social network analysis and the statistical analysis later on. Second, the study seeks to identify relevant design implications for the Facebook application.

This will be done based on interviews with persons dealing or having dealt with weight issues as described in the following sections.

21.5.1 Sampling

Using a purposeful sampling approach (Flick 2009, pp. 122), the interviewees were selected based on the criterion to currently experience problems with overweight and obesity or to have experienced weight issues in the past. Moreover, the interviewees were required to currently engage in activities in order to lose weight or to have substantially reduced their body weight in the past. Being member of Facebook was a third requirement. Table 21.1 gives a short overview of the interviewees.

To be able to explore potential gender-specific differences, the sample included eight women, aged between 21 and 29, as well as seven men, aged between 24 and 39. All of the female interviewees were recruited with the help of a gym specialized in fitness for women. The male interviewees are contacts of friends and acquaintances of the authors. The interviewees were contacted via Facebook and email and received an information sheet including a project description prior to the interview.

The 15 interviews, each of which lasted between 41 and 67 min, were conducted over a period of 3 weeks in August 2011. Interviews with all female participants and four out of seven male participants were conducted during face-to-face meetings. The remaining three interviews were conducted by telephone or Skype.

21.5.2 Data Collection

An interview guideline (Hopf 2007, p. 351) composed of six parts addressing different areas, such as the weight gain process and weight loss motivation, was developed to prepare for the interviews. Subsequently, the data was collected conducting

Table 21.1 Overview of the interviewees

Interviewee	Age	Sex	Occupation	Marital status
1	29	f	Student, journalist	Single
2	26	f	Dental assistant	Single
3	28	f	Dental assistant	Engaged
4	26	f	Works in the public sector	In a relationship
5	26	f	Sales assistant, works freelance as a educationalist	Single
6	21	f	Management assistant in office communication	Single
7	24	f	Management assistant in office communication	Single
8	22	f	Student, waitress	Single
9	24	m	Hairdresser	Single
10	24	m	Media designer	Single
11	39	m	Real estate agent	Married
12	23	m	IT technician	Single
13	24	m	Student	Single
14	39	m	Senior manager	Married
15	35	m	Senior manager	Single

semi-structured interviews composed of open-ended questions. Dealing with the very delicate and personal topic of obesity, this method provides several advantages (Hopf 2007, p. 350): Exploratory interviews left room for spontaneous questions and allowed for in-depth exploration of the relationship between the interviewees' personal traits, social environment, and their motivation to lose weight, for instance. Interacting directly with the interviewee, it was easily possible to control the interview's flow, to avoid misunderstandings, to shift the interview's focus to particularly interesting aspects, or to neglect certain areas of interrogation if the interviewee did not seem comfortable with the questions. Open-ended questions were advantageous as the interviewees had to make answers based on their personal experiences (Flick 2009, p. 156).

The interviews were conducted by a single interviewer and transcribed along the interview guideline using the software F4.[1]

21.5.3 Data Analysis

The data coding was supported by the qualitative data analysis software NVivo.[2] Using Mayring's approach of inductive category building (2000), free nodes with respect to, e.g., the interviewees' family and friends' environment, reasons for weight gain, and motivation to lose weight were created while going through the interview material. Following this process resulted in 154 free nodes at the end of the first stage of coding. An example for a free node coding in "boredom eating" is "[...] when you are bored, you sometimes have food even when you are not hungry"

[1] http://www.audiotranskription.de/f4.htm.

[2] http://www.qsrinternational.com/products_nvivo.aspx.

Table 21.2 Example tree node coding

	Tree nodes	Number of references
Eating as a redirection activity	Boredom eating	McNeill et al. (2006)
	Comfort eating	BVDW (2010)
	Food as a reward	McNeill et al. (2006)
	Stress eating	MedStar Physician Partners/MedStar Family (2007)

(Interviewee 13). To eliminate redundant nodes, some free nodes were deleted or merged in a next step. Afterwards, the free nodes were classified into categories and organized into tree nodes. Table 21.2 shows a sample of tree node coding.

Concluding the coding procedure, the remaining redundancy was removed by merging some more tree nodes into other nodes which led to a final number of 131 nodes.

21.5.4 Findings and Implications for the Facebook Application

This section presents key findings regarding the (1) causes and influencing factors for the interviewees' weight gain, (2) aspects of the interviewees' social environment keeping up the motivation to lose weight, as well as the (3) connection between Facebook and health-related behaviors. Design implications for the Facebook application are derived according to these categories:

1. Firstly, isolation or a lack of friends can be identified as a reason for weight gain. Being an outsider in her class, Interviewee 3 did not have many friends and therefore spent a lot of time sitting at home rather than engaging in activities outside. Secondly, changes in the interviewees' living circumstances have been found to coincide with weight gain in several cases. The start of a different life stage or entering a new situation often had an impact on the interviewees' health-related behaviors irrespective of specific personal relationships. On the one hand, e.g., moving out from home to start university or a job was often related to increased sedentary behavior due to more desk work. On the other hand, the interview participants engaged less than before in physical activity due to school sport and previous memberships in sports clubs ceasing to exist and generally having less time for sports due to new responsibilities:

   > I did not have to do school sports nor the 20 minutes daily walk to school anymore. I went to university by car, had virtually no physical activity and ate rather more than less than before. The food in the university canteen was not particularly healthy and sitting in the library did not really help to lose weight [...]. (Interviewee 11)

Moving to a new place may also coincide with a lack of friends at the beginning and less physical activity than before as in the cases of Interviewees 9 and 10. Addressing the issue of changed living circumstances and isolation, a Facebook application dealing with fitness and sports activities could work as a "sports club on the go." Changed living circumstances, like moving house, may matter less than before if users of the application can do sports virtually with their friends.

2. The majority of the interviewees reported the experience of a key moment that triggered their personal motivation. Having experienced this key moment that incited the weight loss process, the interviewees' personal motivation, social environmental factors, and living circumstances played an important role in keeping up the motivation to lose weight. Intrinsic motivation is clearly found to be the most important aspect when talking about keeping up the motivation to lose weight. Explicit ways to keep motivated include realistic goal setting. Goals may refer to, e.g., the improvement of sports results (Interviewee 14), reaching a certain weight at a certain point of time in the future such as the beginning of the holidays (Interviewee 2) or to decreasing the size (e.g., Interviewees 4 and 6). Set by the interviewees themselves, reaching these targets can be compared with reaching milestones in a project and was found to be associated with a great feeling of satisfaction for the interviewees. Setting goals seems to be a particularly feasible strategy for disciplined and ambitious individuals (Interviewee 14).

Interviewee 7 mentioned that she had had a bad conscience when she went to the gym only once due to a lack of time in a particular week. The strategy of setting goals on the one hand and experiencing a bad conscience on the other hand shows that the interviewees developed the will and to some extent an internal pressure to practice healthy behaviors since the inception of the weight loss process. Features like goal setting and the tracking of sports activities should thus be implemented in the Facebook application.

Regarding the interviewees' social environment, role models, social pressure, social control, emotional and informational support, and recognition were found to reinforce the ongoing motivation to lose weight. For instance, social pressure emerged implicitly when the interviewees compared themselves with others or were competing with others in their social environment.

> In the gym, I met many sportive and body-conscious people who have now become friends. Even if I don't aim for a six pack, which some of my friends have, it does motivate me. (Interviewee 9)

Explicitly, social pressure was created through key people, e.g., friends who did sports together with the interviewees and "pushed them" (e.g., Interviewees 8, 9, and 14). A more original and impersonal form of pressure was created by coaches in the gym and received particularly well by, e.g., Interviewee 8 who admitted a lack of self-discipline:

> I need a coach, I am used to having a coach. I've always had someone who told me 'Do that exercise again'. This is why I really like the gym. Because I have coaches who don't care if it hurts and tell me to do it again. I need a good kick up the backside.

Moreover, control, e.g., in the form of "friendly teasing," appears to be another factor emerging from people's environment.

The interviewees received different types of support from their social networks. Close friends and mothers were mentioned as a source of *emotional support* (e.g., Interviewees 1, 5, and 6). Doctors, nutritional consultants, and coaches were important to obtain *informational support* (e.g., Interviewees 11 and 15).

Finally, compliments and appraisal support made the interviewees feel more attractive and recognize their success which is related to *weight loss effects*. This can be identified as another factor keeping up the interviewees' motivation:

> Recognition is definitely the best motivator for me. Also, I wear different colors than black now and I don't mind going to the swimming pool anymore. And I feel that people perceive me as more competent at work [...]. (Interviewee 4)

Therefore, the integration of an award system and features enabling the comparison with other users are recommended to be implemented within the Facebook application.

3. The interviewees used Facebook every day and had between 80 and 500 contacts in their friends list. Generally speaking, the interviewees did not link Facebook with their health-related behaviors or body weight. Yet, it was indicated that Facebook could be used to create implicit or explicit pressure which may then influence the interviewees' health-related behaviors as in the case of Interviewee 14:

> I use several social network sites, e.g. [...] Facebook. I started to tell people that I was going to do the Iron Man when I had a body weight of 130 kg. I did this to create pressure on me. The more people knew about it, the higher the pressure on me to do it. I did successfully accomplish the Iron Man [...]. (Interviewee 14)

A Facebook application focusing on sports activities was suggested to be feasible to promote positive health-related behaviors:

> My friends do sports, too, and that motivates me to engage in physical activity as well. A Facebook application could reinforce competition: 'Hey, I did more than you; I was faster [...]'. Yeah, I guess it could promote physical activity and make people develop fighting spirit. (Interviewee 10)

The statement of Interviewee 10 was, e.g., supported by Interviewee 9 who acknowledged that "no one wants to be at the bottom of the league." As suggested in the previous section, the integration of elements such as comparison and competition with other users in the application may be a way to keep people's motivation up.

21.6 Calorie Cruncher Application

Based on the findings and implications derived from the qualitative study, the Facebook application "Calorie Cruncher" has been developed. The user of this application can "crunch" calories or consume calories and share their activities with their friends.

When first using the application, (new) users need to create a profile by filling in information related to their health status (see Fig. 21.3).

Afterwards, users can add new activities that can be either physical activities (crunching) or food-consuming activities. This feature supports the idea of

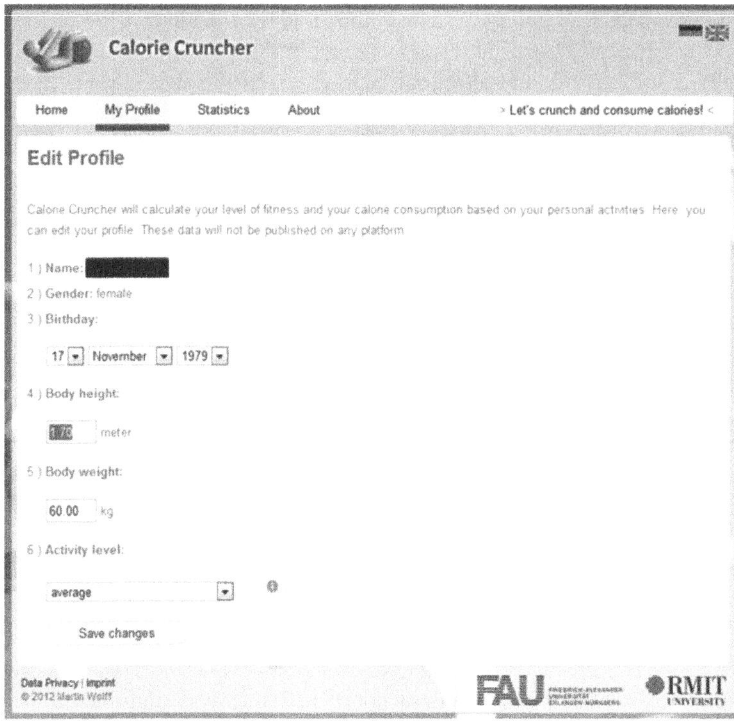

Fig. 21.3 User registration for Calorie Cruncher application

comparison and competition as the users' friends can see these activities and vice versa (see Fig. 21.4). According to behavior change theory, competition against others fosters the commitment to change (Prochaska et al. 2008). Also, goal setting can be motivating when the individual defines goals in order to achieve personal progress.

Providing statistics about the user's activities and BMI measures, the Calorie Cruncher application enables the monitoring of the user's activities over time as well as personal goal setting.

Achievements or rewards are used to motivate individuals in a playful way. Rewards can either be monetary or virtual, like vouchers and virtual points. The award system used in the Calorie Cruncher application compares the calorie consumption across all users. If a user "crunches" more calories than the other members of the Calorie Cruncher community, he or she can become "the cruncher of the day" and win a golden medal.

The application collects data on the health status of the user, tracks the activities, and monitors the BMI over time. Additionally, information on the users' online social network—including profile information, network information, and indicators for the communication within the social network—is retrieved (see Table 21.3).

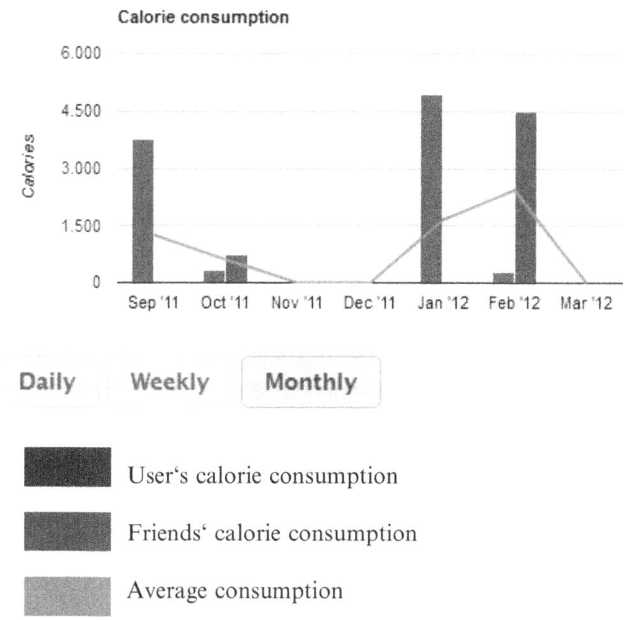

Fig. 21.4 Statistics on calorie consumption

Table 21.3 Data collected via the Calorie Cruncher application

Health status	Profile information	Communication	Network information
• Body height • Body weight • Activity level • Health-related behavior	• User ID • Gender • Birthday • Work and education history • Hometown • Current location • Activities and interests	• Status updates • Checkins • Likes • Picture tags • Wall posts	• Friends' user IDs

Once a reasonable number of users are reached, the collected data allows the analysis of the network structure, network ties, and network members. Hence, Christakis' and Fowler's (2007) findings regarding the spread of obesity in large social networks can be investigated in an online social network context.

21.7 Preliminary Social Network Analysis

For the preliminary social network analysis, a 25-year-old female with a class 1 obesity BMI (Interviewee 7) and a 24-year-old male with a normal BMI (Interviewee 12) were selected from the interview sample (see Table 21.4).

The objectives of this analysis were:

1. Testing the data extraction and reliability of the Calorie Cruncher application
2. Revealing features of the basic composition of the collected dataset
3. Learning how to analyze and interpret the dataset
4. Derive lessons learned for the quantitative study

Both interviewees provided self-reported general information on their Facebook friends (see Table 21.5).

The general structure of the chosen Facebook profiles is very similar: Both interviewees are connected to most of their "real-world" friends on Facebook. They met only very few Facebook friends online, and the interviewees stated that only few of their Facebook friends are close friends. Looking at the answers concerning the homogeneity of the Facebook network, it can be assumed that both networks are rather homogeneous regarding the first language, ethical background, and the level of education.

The datasets of their personal Facebook networks and profile information were extracting using the Calorie Cruncher application. Table 21.5 shows selected statistical information on the networks of Interviewee 7 and Interviewee 12.

Table 21.4 Selected interviewees for the preliminary social network analysis

	Interviewee 7	Interviewee 12
BMI	31.60	23.87
Sex	f	m
Age	25	24

Table 21.5 General information on the Facebook networks of the Interviewees 7 and 12

Questions	Interviewee 7	Interviewee 12
How many of your Facebook friends did you meet online?	Few	Few
How many of your friends in the "real world" are connected to you on Facebook?	Most	Most
How many of your Facebook friends are close friends?	Few	Few
How many of your Facebook friends speak the same first language as you?	Most	Most
How many of your Facebook friends have the same ethical background as you?	Most	Most
How many of your Facebook friends have the same level of education as you?	Most	Most

Table 21.6 Preliminary social network analysis

	Interviewee 7		Interviewee 12	
Measures	All friends	Close friends	All friends	Close friends
Density	0.076	0.190	0.076	0.225
Number of friends	131	28	224	23
Gender distribution (%)	F: 62	F: 93	F: 43	F: 50
	M: 36	M: 7	M: 56	M: 50

Considering the interviewees' overall personal networks (all friends), the network density which equals the total number of ties divided by the total number of possible ties (Abraham et al. 2009) was calculated using the social network analysis software UCInet (Table 21.6).[3] Showing the extent to which actors in a network are connected to each other, the network density is an ambiguous number. For instance, a very densely connected network may limit the access to nonredundant sets of resources. Also, depending on the characteristics of densely connected ties, network level density may positively or negatively affect health-related behaviors (Borgatti et al. 1998; Lakon et al. 2008).

The overall network density is 0.076 for both interviewees which indicates a rather loosely connected network. Interviewee 7 has 131 Facebook friends of which 62 % are female and 36 % are male. In comparison, the network of Interviewee 12 counts 224 friends of which 43 % are female and 56 % are male.

Both interviewees stated that they are connected to most of their "real-world" friends on Facebook, but only a few of those online friends are considered close friends. Due to ties in online social networks being indistinguishable with respect to their strength (Lewis et al. 2008), it is important to identify meaningful relations. This can be done by creating interaction graphs displaying actual interaction between users, such as wall posts and comments (Wilson et al. 2009), for instance. In order to distinguish meaningful relations in the interviewees' networks, we identified those friends who had created at least two posts on the interviewees' Facebook wall within the last 1,000 feed entries and are currently on the interviewees' Facebook friends list. The network of close friends of Interviewee 7 is displayed in Fig. 21.5, and the network of Interviewee 12 is displayed in Fig. 21.6, respectively.

The network of Interviewee 7 counts 28 close friends, and its density is equal to 0.19. Interestingly, 26 of these 28 close friends are female which indicates a strong interaction of Interviewee 7 with other female friends. The only two male friends are very isolated from all other network members. Besides Interviewee 7 herself, nodes a, b, c, d, and e are very well connected to other nodes in the network. Being possibly able to act as brokers or gatekeepers, these nodes seem to play an important role and should be analyzed in more detail in the continuation of this study.

Counting 23 nodes, the network of close friends of Interviewee 12 is slightly smaller than the network of Interviewee 7. Compared to the network of Interviewee 7,

[3] https://sites.google.com/site/ucinetsoftware/home.

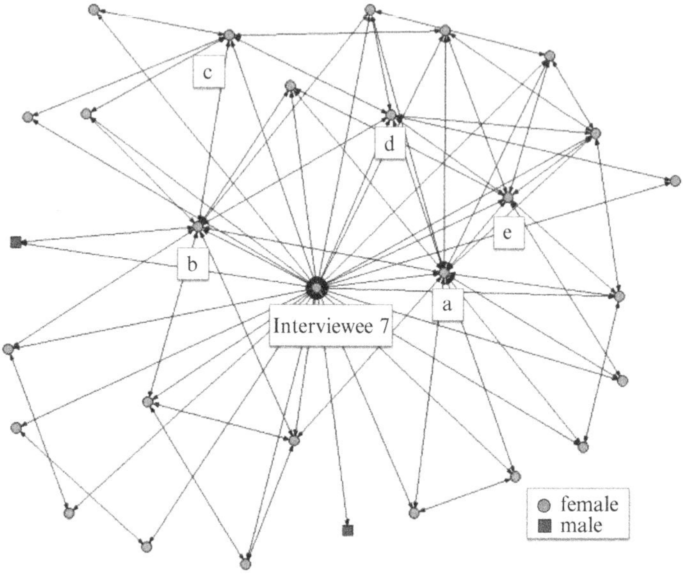

Fig. 21.5 Egocentric network of Interviewee 7 displaying close friends

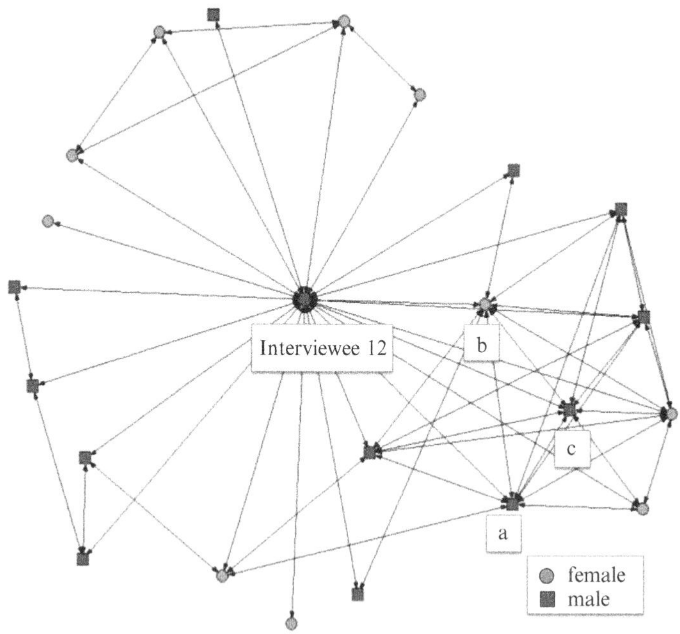

Fig. 21.6 Egocentric network of Interviewee 12 displaying close friends

the network of Interviewee 12 has a more balanced gender distribution and a higher density of 0.225. Again, there are several very well connected nodes (a, b, and c) and a few isolated notes which should be considered in more detail in future studies.

21.8 Lessons Learned and Next Steps

Lessons learned and next steps can be identified with regard to (1) the employed Facebook application Calorie Cruncher, (2) the data collection, as well as the (3) social network analysis:

1. The Calorie Cruncher application performed well within the pilot study. In a next step, the test users will be surveyed to analyze the application's usability and identify areas for improvement.
2. Only a very small number of participants took part in this exploratory pilot study, and only two cases were considered in more detail. To detect causal relationships and generalizable results, the continuation of this study will look at a larger sample. Yet, being dependent on the viral spread of the application, a convenient sampling approach may remain a limitation in future studies.
3. The preliminary analysis of the personal Facebook networks of Interviewee 7 and Interviewee 12 was conducted manually and, thus, on a very high level. Once we are able to, e.g., count the number of exchanged wall posts and comments for all study participants in an automated way, this research will analyze interactions in more detail and provide more precise results regarding the participants' strong ties. Using the profile information and the health status of these strong ties, the network homogeneity could be analyzed in a next step. Additional network measures, such as network constraint, clustering coefficient, and cliques, could provide better insights into the network structure and enable the analysis of the impact of different relationships on health-related behavior and body weight (Moore 2010). The collection of longitudinal data could be used to test for phenomena like induction and homophily in online social networks (Christakis and Fowler 2007).

The exploration of the social aspects of obesity and effect of obesity propagation through the ubiquitous use of electronic social networks will help facilitate appropriate health-related behaviors in the context of consumer healthcare informatics using innovative communication technologies. Findings from our research will inform the development of possible online intervention strategies.

The area of CHI is growing and evolving. Without question this is an important area, and there is a growing and key role here for online social networks to facilitate and support superior healthcare outcomes and foster appropriate healthcare behaviors. Our study has served to try to open the door to this possibility and illustrate the possible benefits in the context of obesity, a growing healthcare concern globally.

Given that the current healthcare delivery has failed to provide cost-effective and quality care to citizens especially in the case of chronic disease management such as diabetes and obesity, it would appear that new methods and paradigms for redesigning healthcare delivery are essential. In today's Information Technology Age, clearly technology in general and the role for online social networks in particular will grow. From the preceding it can be seen that the design of such online social network type solutions and applications incorporate albeit implicitly many of the principles of lean thinking and by doing so serve to streamline workflow, create value, and facilitate the correct information going to the correct people at the correct time. We believe that the more such technology solutions incorporate principles of lean thinking and related theories and concepts, the more benefit and value they will deliver and thus we close by calling for more research in this key area.

References

Abraham, A., Hassanien, A. E., & SnáSel, V. (2009). *Computational social network analysis: Trends, tools and research advances*. Dordrecht: Springer.

Arnaboldi, V., Passarella, A., Tesconi, M., & Gazze, D. (2011). Towards a characterization of egocentric networks in online social networks. Retrieved from cnd.iit.cnr.it

Bahr, D. B., Browning, R. C., Wyatt, H. R., & Hill, J. O. (2009). Exploiting social networks to mitigate the obesity epidemic. *Obesity (Silver Spring, Md.), 17*, 723–728.

Borgatti, S. P., Jones, C., & Everett, M. G. (1998). Network measures of social capital'. *Connections., 21*, 27–36.

Bos, L., Marsh, A., Carroll, D., Gupta, S., & Rees, M. (2008). Patient 2.0 empowerment. In H. R. Arabnia & A. Marsh (Eds.), *Proceedings of the 2008 international conference on Semantic Web & Web Services* (pp. 164–167), Las Vegas.

Boyd, D. M., & Ellison, N. B. (2007). Social network sites: Definition, history, and scholarship. *Journal of Computer-Mediated Communication, 13*, 210–230.

BVDW. (2010) Social Media Kompass 2010/2011. Fachgruppe Social Media im Bundesverband Digitale Wirtschaft (BVDW) e.V., Düsseldorf.

Christakis, N. A., & Fowler, J. H. (2007). The spread of obesity in a large social network over 32 years. *The New England Journal of Medicine, 357*, 370–379.

Cohen-Cole, E., & Fletcher, J. M. (2008). Is obesity contagious? Social networks vs. environmental factors in the obesity epidemic. *Journal of Health Economics, 27*, 1382–1387.

Eysenbach, G. (2000). Consumer health informatics. *BMJ, 320*, 1713–1716.

Finkelstein, E. A., Trogdon, J. G., Cohen, J. W., & Dietz, W. (2009). Annual medical spending attributable to obesity: Payer-and service-specific estimates. *Health Affairs (Project Hope)., 28*, w822–w831.

Flick, U. (2009). *An introduction to qualitative research*. London: Sage.

Fowler, J. H., & Christakis, N. A. (2008). Estimating peer effects on health in social networks: A response to Cohen-Cole and Fletcher; Trogdon, Nonnemaker, Pais. *Journal of Health Economics., 27*, 1400.

Gershenson, C. (2011). Epidemiology and social networks. *Sociological Methods, 22*(1), 199–200.

Granovetter, M. S. (1973). The strength of weak ties. *The American Journal of Sociology, 78*, 1360–1380.

Hammond, R. A. (2010). Social influence and obesity. *Current Opinion in Endocrinology, Diabetes, and Obesity, 17*, 467–471.

Hopf, C. (2007). Qualitative interviews—ein Überblick. In: U. Flick, E. von Kardoff, & I. Steinke, I. (Eds.), *Qualitative Forschung: Ein Handbuch* (pp. 349–360). Reinbek bei Hamburg: Rowohlt Taschenbuch Verlag.
Huffman, S. K. (2011). BMI changes in Russian adults: The role of lifestyles and spousal relationships. Agricultural and Applied Economics Association, 2011 Annual Meeting, Pittsburgh, Pennsylvania. Accessed September 22, 2011, Available at: http://ageconsearch.umn.edu/bitstream/102653/2/HuffmanAAEA2011.pdf.
Kaplan, A. M., & Haenlein, M. (2010). Users of the world, unite! The challenges and opportunities of Social Media. *Business Horizons., 53*, 59–68.
Kneidinger, B. (2010). *Facebook und Co.* Wiesbaden: VS Verlag für Sozialwissenschaften.
Lakon, C. M., Godette, D. C., & Hipp, J. R. (2008). Network-based approaches for measuring social capital. In I. Kawachi, S. V. Subramanian, & D. Kim (Eds.), *Social capital and health* (pp. 63–81). New York, NY: Springer.
Lewis, K., Kaufman, J., Gonzalez, M., Wimmer, A., & Christakis, N. A. (2008). Tastes, ties, and time: A new social network dataset using Facebook.com. *Social Networks., 30*, 330–342.
Ma, X., Chen, G., & Xiao, J. (2010). Analysis of an online health social network. In: *IHI' 10* (pp. 297–306), Arlington.
Madan, A., Moturu, S. T., Lazer, D., & Pentland, A. S. (2010). Social sensing. In Wireless Health 2010 on—WH '10 (p. 104). New York: ACM Press. doi:10.1145/1921081.1921094.
Mayring, P. (2000). Qualitative Inhaltsanalyse. *Forum Qualitative Sozialforschung/Forum: Qualitative Social Research, 1*(2): Art. 20.
McNeill, L. H., Kreuter, M. W., & Subramanian, S. V. (2006). Social environment and physical activity: A review of concepts and evidence. *Social Science & Medicine (1982), 63*, 1011–1022.
MedStar Physician Partners/MedStar Family. (2007). *Clinical guidelines on the identification, evaluation, and treatment of overweight and obesity in adults*. Retrieved September 6, 2011, from http://www.medstarfamilychoice.com/documents/guidelines/obesity.pdf.
Moore, S. (2010). Social networks, social capital and obesity: A literature review. In L. Dubé, A. Bechara, A. Dagher, A. Drewnowski, J. Lebel, P. James, & R. Y. Yada (Eds.), *Obesity prevention* (pp. 673–685). San Diego: Academic Press.
Polke-Majewski, K. (2011). *Cameron hat kein digitales Problem, sondern ein soziales*. Retrieved from http://www.zeit.de/politik/ausland/2011-08/grossbritannien-krawalle-cameron-twitter-facebook-scial-media/komplettansicht
Prochaska, J. O., Redding, C. A., & Evers, K. E. (2008). The transtheoretical model and stages of change. In K. Glanz, B. K. Rimer, & K. V. Viswanath (Eds.), *Health behavior and health education: Theory, research, and practice* (pp. 1–552). San Francisco, CA: Jossey-Bass.
Rostila, M. (2011). A resource-based theory of social capital for health research: Can it help us bridge the individual and collective facets of the concept? *Social Theory & Health., 9*, 109–129.
Schone, M. (2011). *London riots: Blame Twitter—or BlackBerry Messenger?* Retrieved from http://abcnews.go.com/Blotter/london-riots-blame-twitter-blackberry-messenger/story?id=14255618
von Rohr, M. (2011). *Die Revolution, die keine war*. Retrieved from http://www.spiegel.de/spiegel/0,1518,742430-3,00.html
Wang, Y., Beydoun, M. A., Liang, L., Caballero, B., & Kumanyika, S. K. (2008). Will all Americans become overweight or obese? Estimating the progression and cost of the US obesity epidemic. *Obesity., 16*, 2323–2330.
Wasserman, S., & Faust, K. (1994). *Social network analysis: Methods and applications*. Cambridge: Cambridge University Press.
Wefing, H. (2012). Wir! Sind! Wütend! Die Zeit, 3–5.
WHO. (2000). *Obesity: Preventing and managing the global epidemic. Report of a WHO Consultation. WHO technical report series 894*. Geneva: WHO.

WHO. (2011) World health statistics 2011. Available at http://www.who.int/whosis/whostat/2011/en/accessed dec 2012.
Wickramasinghe, N., Bali, R., Goldberg, S., & Troshani, I. (Eds.). (2012). *Pervasive health knowledge management*. New York: Springer.
Wilson, C., Boe, B., Sala, A., Puttaswamy, K. P. N., & Zhao, B. Y. (2009). User interactions in social networks and their implications. In: *Proceedings of the fourth ACM European conference on Computer systems—EuroSys '09* (p. 205). New York: ACM.

Chapter 22
Supporting Preventive Healthcare with Persuasive Services

Andreas Hamper and Tino Müller

Abstract National healthcare systems are increasingly supporting preventive measures to prevent diseases or lower their severity in order to avoid eventual high costs of acute medical treatment. Compared to other medical treatments, the effectiveness of preventive measures highly depends on patients' participation and compliance over a long period of time. Since patients cannot be monitored 24 h per day, the effectiveness of preventive care depends on the compliance how well patients follow the preventive behavior in their daily life.

The chapter at hand provides an overview which services have a highly positive impact on the user rating in mobile preventive applications. It shows how an application should be designed in order to be accepted by the user. In order to support preventive behavior, persuasive mobile technology has been applied in various projects.

In a first step, a classification framework is built by summarizing distinct persuasive services developed in research projects. The extracted categories are used as a basis to review existing mobile applications. As a result, a summary of existing mobile applications and their included persuasive services is generated. Based on the evaluation of the applications, the influence of distinct persuasive services on the acceptance is analyzed. The knowledge is used to build persuasive applications that contain services which are leading to a higher acceptance.

Keywords Persuasive services • Persuasive mobile applications • Mobile solutions • User acceptance

A. Hamper (✉) • T. Müller
Institute of Information Systems, University Erlangen-Nürnberg, Lange Gasse 20, 90403 Nürnberg, Germany
e-mail: andreas.hamper@fau.de

N. Wickramasinghe et al. (eds.), *Lean Thinking for Healthcare*, Healthcare Delivery in the Information Age, DOI 10.1007/978-1-4614-8036-5_22,

22.1 Introduction

Healthcare systems are facing challenges in multiple fields. Traditionally, curative treatment of diseases is the main focus. Besides that, rehabilitation, care, and prevention are important fields to prevent the appearance of diseases or lower their severity (W. H. Organization 2006). Healthcare in general aims at fostering health and quality of life. A successful healthcare intervention may lead to an improved individual health state as well as to avoidance of costs for future treatment (Cohen et al. 2008). The creation of healthcare services is closely linked to the patient as every measurement has a direct impact on the patient. Whereas curative treatment is often limited in the time span and under supervision of professional doctors, prevention is a long-term process that is primarily conducted by the patient in the daily life. Therefore, successful preventive care highly depends on the patients support and compliance. If the patient is working together with professional doctors on preventive measures, a large number of chronically diseases could be prevented.

During the 1990s, a long-term study examines causes of deaths in the United States. The authors reveal that about half of all deaths occurred in the year 2000 can be attributed to a limited number of largely preventable behaviors and exposures. The top three causes of death are tobacco, poor diet, and physical inactivity as well as alcohol consumption (see Fig. 22.1).

The authors of the study emphasize the need to establish a more preventive orientation in healthcare (Mokdad et al. 2004). This includes all activities designed to improve personal and public health (Miller 2002), for instance, the promotion of a healthy lifestyle, immunization campaigns, preventive examinations, and general education on diseases, but also the suppression of harmful factors in the environment (Bürger 2003).

Most interventions are realized by statutory health insurances through education aimed to achieve a behavioral change. Today, these interventions are limited in number and scope. This is because the budget for intervention programs is quite low and hence limits the channels of health promotion and disease prevention. Many programs are unidirectional and focus primarily on education and enlightenment (e.g.,

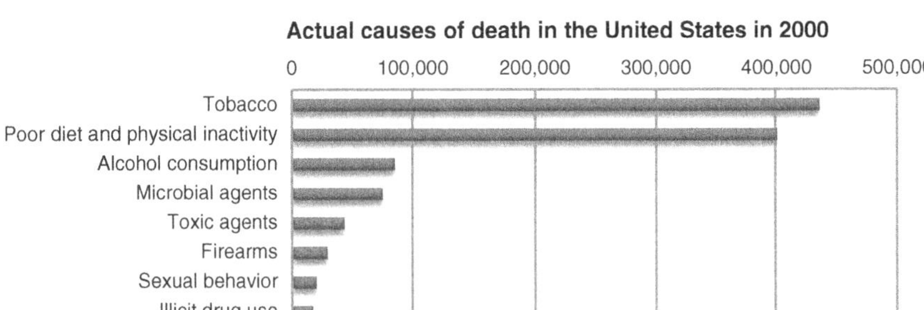

Fig. 22.1 Actual causes of death in the United States in 2000 (*Source*: Own illustration, adapted from (Mokdad et al. 2004))

through print campaigns) (GKV-Spitzenverband 2012). However, many of the previously mentioned causes of death are prevailingly preventable through an individual's behavioral change. Unlike curative medical treatment, prevention depends on the interplay of medical professionals and compliant patients. In the process of preventive treatment, medical advices from professionals have to be performed by patients on a regular basis which requires them to change their behavior and old habits.

An important characteristic of behavior change is persuasion, while an actor sends a persuasive message to another actor in order to reinforce, change, or shape attitudes or behaviors (Oinas-Kukkonen and Harjumaa 2009).

22.2 Persuasive Services in Preventive Healthcare

Traditionally, this is established by human-to-human communication (e.g., group therapies, counseling sessions) or mediated communication (e.g., media campaigns). Personal fitness coaching is a well-established form of human-to-human persuasion, but it is also too expensive to be applied broadly. But as new technologies are arising, there are possibilities through web, mobile, and other ambient technologies to establish human–computer interaction (HCI), which may also be persuasive (Oinas-Kukkonen and Harjumaa 2009)—in the following referred to as persuasive technology, a term coined by Fogg (1999).

Consequently, mobile software systems can be used to support an individual's behavior change towards a healthier life in order to prevent or delay medical treatments. As mobile devices—especially smartphones—are emerging and providing a large number of applications, it is of interest which applications are available that support preventive behavior.

A deep insight into these applications can reveal s that are used to increase motivation and support the behavior change process. As there is little known about applications focusing on disease prevention and health promotion, this research examines the state-of-the-art mobile applications in preventive healthcare. Recommendations derived from these findings should help developers to build and improve mobile applications.

22.2.1 Behavior Change in Preventive Healthcare

Preventive interventions are always aimed to eliminate the causes of a disease by reducing risk factors (GKV-Spitzenverband 2010). According to Leppin (2007), two basic approaches are distinguished:

- Behavior-oriented prevention
- Condition-oriented prevention

Behavior-oriented prevention addresses the individual or groups of individuals and tries to reduce risk-taking behaviors. It includes, for instance, the promotion of a healthy lifestyle, immunization campaigns, and screenings (e.g., early cancer diagnosis, information campaigns) (Bürger 2003), whereas condition-oriented prevention focuses on changes within the environment (e.g., ecologic, social, economic, and cultural) of individuals. It includes, for instance, ergonomic measures at the workplace, flexible working hours, obligational air bags in cars, or the prohibition of hazardous construction materials (Leppin 2007). To achieve preventive measures in both behavior- and condition-oriented prevention, three different methods are denoted:

- Educational techniques
- Normative-regulatory techniques
- Economic incentive or punishment systems

Educational techniques refer primarily to enlightenment, consultation, and self-assessment trainings. Therefore, these measures focus on motivation and one's judgment, while normative-regulatory techniques are enforced by regulations and laws (e.g., mandatory seat belt wearing, ban of smoking, or the drunk-driving limit). In addition, the third method tries to change or influence certain behaviors by providing economic incentive or punishment systems. Famous examples are the ongoing price increase of taxes on cigarettes in order to change the consumer behavior or the possibility of getting incentives for being physically active (e.g., through lower insurance charges) (Leppin 2007).

Industrialized nations are experiencing a change from short-term to cost-intensive long-term diseases (Singh 2008). Most of these diseases are attributed to negative behaviors in the past, such as a lack of physical activity, poor nutrition, tobacco use, or excessive alcohol consumption (Centers for Disease Control and Prevention 2009).

It is necessary to encourage individuals to take responsibility (e.g., improving knowledge, changing attitudes and behaviors) for their own health and well-being (Mattila et al. 2010), which is one of the main goals in primary prevention. Most of the existing measures are aimed to encourage behavior change (Jepson et al. 2010), as this has been recognized as an effective approach (Willet 2002).

Anyway, the maintenance of behavior changes is difficult and challenging. For instance, only 20 % of obese people succeed in long-term weight loss maintenance (Wing and Phelan 2005). Therefore, the following section deals with behavior change theory and the factors that influence an individual's behavior.

Behavior change in general is a difficult, complex, and a long-term process. Many behaviors are deeply integrated into people's daily lives, whereas even a small change in daily routines may have an impact on various different things, forcing an individual to restructure his priorities. Especially when individuals try to adapt to new fragile habits, there are many factors of influence, which may lead to relapse and setbacks (Klasnja et al. 2011):

- Internal factors (e.g., getting injured or sick, having a busy period at work, disliking healthy foods or sports)
- Social factors (e.g., spouses, friends, or coworkers preferring unhealthy foods)
- Logistical factors (e.g., possibilities to shower and lock up the bike when cycling to work)
- Environmental factors (e.g., bad weather conditions for doing sports)

In order to achieve long-term sustainability in adapting new habits, it is important to integrate strategies to reinforce motivation—intrinsically and extrinsically—along the process of change (Bielik et al. 2012). To derive matching strategies, a deeper insight into the process of behavior change is necessary.

Nowadays, new technologies enable different ways of communication through the Internet, mobile devices, and other ambient technologies, which may also be persuasive or foster motivation (Oinas-Kukkonen and Harjumaa 2009). Consequently, it might be possible to use software systems to change an individual's behavior towards a healthier lifestyle. Therefore, the next section introduces the field or persuasive technology, referring to computer systems designed to change people's attitudes or behaviors (Fogg 2003a, p. 1).

22.2.2 Persuasive Services to Support Behavior Change

The usage of technology influences the user behavior, regardless of this was intended by the developer of the IT system or is an unexpected side effect of the usage. Persuasion means the influence of beliefs, attitudes, intentions, motivations, or behaviors (Wood 2000). No matter what individuals are doing—shopping, watching television, or just talking with friends—persuasion and its influence are all around. Technology is used to influence individuals by sending persuasive messages in order to motivate people to purchase, donate, vote, or act (Ijsselsteijn et al. 2006).

The spread of powerful mobile devices such as smartphones facilitate an easy and fast way to reach users and foster the occurrence of interpersonal and mass communication (Oulasvirta et al. 2012) by creating, accessing, and sharing information in new ways (Oinas-Kukkonen 2010a). Traditionally persuasion is defined as "human communication designed to influence the autonomous judgments and actions of others" (Simons et al. 2001). Persuasive technology pursues the same objective by computer–human persuasion. It is distinguished from computer-mediated persuasion, e.g., persuasion through discussion forums, e-mail, instant messages, blogs, or social network systems (Oinas-Kukkonen and Harjumaa 2008).

B. J. Fogg—a pioneer in persuasive systems design—defines persuasive technology as "a computing system, device, or application intentionally designed to change a person's attitudes or behavior in a predetermined way" (Fogg 1999). A similar but more precise definition is proposed by Oinas-Kukkonnen (2010b). According to him, persuasive technology (or a behavior change support system (BCSS), respectively) is defined as "an information system designed to form, alter, or reinforce attitudes or behaviors or both without using coercion or deception" (Oinas-Kukkonen 2010b). Fogg describes six distinct advantages of modern technology over human persuaders (Fogg 2003a): Technology

- Is more persistent than humans
- Enables anonymity
- Accesses and manages huge amounts of data

- Uses many modalities to influence
- Scales easily
- Is ubiquitous

One of the most successful mobile technologies is the smartphone. Because of convincing functionalities and reasonable costs, the penetration rate of smartphones rises constantly (Klasnja et al. 2011). According to Gartner (2012), approximately 1,774 million mobile devices (including smartphones) are sold in 2011. 472 million or 31 % of mobile communication device sales account for smartphones. These numbers state that especially the market of smartphones is booming.

Smartphones are personal and pervasive devices (Arteaga et al. 2010). Due to persistent network connectivity, smartphones are called always-on devices (Mattila et al. 2010). They are ubiquitous and offer the possibility to interact with the user anywhere and at any time (Arteaga et al. 2010). This enables mobile devices to intervene at the opportune moment for persuasion as proposed by Fogg (2003a). They can determine the user's physical location, typical routine, the time of day, goals for the day, and current tasks (Fogg 2003a).

Moreover, smartphones provide additional technological services. They run powerful operating systems (Abroms et al. 2011)—comparable to personal computers—and offer the possibility to install third-party applications, so-called apps. They come along with built-in sensors (e.g., GPS, accelerometer, camera, microphone, compass), which allow the device, for instance, to track the user's position or to send push messages. Furthermore, modern smartphones are able to integrate external sensor technology (Arteaga et al. 2010), like heart rate sensors and sensors for running or cycling (WahooFitness 2012; Zephyr Technology 2012).

According to several investigations and studies, smartphones are suggested as promising platforms for preventive healthcare. Recent studies focus on:

- Physical activity (Ahtinen et al. 2010; Arteaga et al. 2010; Buttussi et al. 2006; Chuah and Sample 2011; Munson and Consolvo 2012)
- Nutrition (Breton et al. 2011; Grimes et al. 2010; Kim et al. 2010; Pollak et al. 2010)
- Addiction (Abroms et al. 2011; Backinger and Augustson 2011; Graham et al. 2006)
- Healthy sleep (Bauer et al. 2012)

Smartphones are used to support positive health-related behavior. Fogg (2003a) conducted the study "Mobile Health Applications" looking at different services of 72 healthcare applications for PDAs, mobile phones, and pagers (Fogg 2003a). All the identified applications intend to change individuals' health-related behaviors. Looking at the applications from a behavior change perspective, the services did not support behavior change strategies sufficiently. Services were mainly used to track certain behaviors and to calculate data, e.g., calories or indices like the body mass index. Furthermore additional information is provided via the application including articles, charts, or definitions. Fogg (2003a) concludes that there is a major opportunity for health applications in the future due to the technological development of mobile devices (Fogg 2003a).

Smartphones combine and enhance the services of PDAs, mobile phones, and pagers. Trends like social sharing or gamification provide room for innovative health applications—more motivating and more persuasive.

The next chapter presents recent projects in which predominantly mobile technology is utilized to reach preventive goals (e.g., encouraging towards more physical activity). Thereby, the focus is on services that are used in recent persuasive technologies to support the process of health behavior change.

22.3 Market Analysis of Mobile Applications

To characterize mobile applications, an overview of the latest research projects supporting positive health behavior change through persuasive technology is given. The focus is on services that help individuals during the process of behavioral change.

In a first step, Sect. 22.3.1 describes recent projects in preventive healthcare. Secondly, relevant services are summarized and discussed. The identified services are used to construct the characterization framework afterwards. Section 22.3.2 describes the usage of the identified services in real application that can be downloaded from the application distribution platforms. Thereafter, the impact of the existence of certain services on the user rating is analyzed.

22.3.1 Characterization of Mobile Applications

In this study, eight recent projects were examined, whereas each project utilizes various services which support individuals to achieve a healthier lifestyle. The projects focus primarily to encourage physical activity but also to support weight loss or achieving better dietary habits. Services derived from these projects are summarized in Table 22.1.

Table 22.2 shows the usage of services inside the examined projects.

In order to provide a clear overview, the services are consolidated in four categories. Table 22.3 shows the four categories: education, feedback, gamification, and social interaction with the corresponding services. Each category is discussed below.

22.3.1.1 Education

The bases of most health preventive interventions are education and knowledge building (Jepson et al. 2010). Educational programs provide *information* about the negative health issue and try to increase the awareness for the need in behavior change. Therefore, they aim to foster learning and awareness raising. For instance, Move2Play provides an educational component to teach its users the fundamentals of a healthy lifestyle (Bielik et al. 2012). In contrast, RunWithUs uses a marketing tool to encourage users to jogging or doing other sports (Gil-castiñeira et al. 2011).

Table 22.1 Feature description

Education	
Information	General information about behavioral risks, for example, susceptibility to poor health outcomes or mortality risk in relation to the behavior (McLean et al. 2003)
Risk illustration	Information about the benefits and costs of action or inaction, focusing on what will happen if the individual does not perform the desired behavior (McLean et al. 2003)
Instructions	Instructions comprise specific information on what to do and how to perform a behavior. It includes a clear action plan to overcome the behavioral risk (Abraham and Michie 2008)
Feedback	
Tracking	Tracking refers to the recording of one or several parameters (e.g., diet, weight, sleep, stress, smoking, alcohol) and storing the data into log files (Ahtinen et al. 2010)
Analysis	Analysis services provide reasonable information and help to reflect about the user's past behavior (Consolvo et al. 2009)
Goal setting	Goal setting is the process of defining what to achieve, it concerns a valued, future end state (Shilts et al. 2004) and involves solely specific goals (e.g., losing 4 kg of weight) (Abraham and Michie 2008) instead of general goals (e.g., doing more sports)
Coaching	Coaching refers to context aware personalized virtual agents that provide the user with feedback (Den Akker et al. 2011). Feedback can either be visual or audible
Prompting	Prompts remind users to perform desired behaviors (Campbell and Chau 2010; Pollak et al. 2010), including times of day or elements of contexts
Gamification	
Points	Points are important for driving motivation. They are a numerical value and can be used as rewards and status indicators, but also to unlock further content or purchase virtual goods. In gamification, earning points is the primary reward mechanism (Bunchball Inc. 2010)
Levels	Levels refer to different classes. They signify the accomplishment of a milestone and often indicate status or participation in certain actions (Bunchball Inc. 2010). They inform users about their progress and serve as markers (Zichermann and Cunningham 2011). Additionally, levels are frequently used to indicate the difficulty
Challenges	Challenges provide the user with tasks, quests, or missions to accomplish. They are most often based on actions that are traceable and give players directions for what to do (Zichermann and Cunningham 2011). After reaching a milestone or completing a challenge, users are rewarded with visible trophies, badges, or achievements. Whereas the visibility of rewards is of importance to foster recognition by others (Bunchball Inc. 2010)
Virtual goods	Virtual goods are intangible nonphysical items. In game design, they are used to increase participation and engagement. For instance, earned points can be used to purchase virtual items (e.g., decorations) for self-expression and comparison among others (Bunchball Inc. 2010)

Leaderboards	Leaderboards or "high-score tables" are defined as ordered lists to make simple comparisons. Usually they comprise a score beside a name, whereas the score defines the position within a list (Zichermann and Cunningham 2011). Leaderboards are the primary mechanisms to foster competition by the indication of one's own rank in comparison to the position of others (e.g., friends) (Bunchball Inc. 2010)
Gifts	Gifting is a powerful retention mechanic. Receiving a gift from others ties the user to the application (e.g., Farmville) (Bunchball Inc. 2010)
Social interaction	
Intern infrastructure Extern infrastructure	A social networking infrastructure provides the basis for a group of people to exchange information. Providers of applications can either run an own platform or use interfaces to connect with externally operated platforms (e.g., Twitter or Facebook)
Identity management	Representation of an individual's identity by name, interests, and other content, dependent on the field of application (Far 2010)
Relationship management	Relationship management refers to friending and the possibility to administrate own contacts (Koch et al. 2007)
Social communication	Communication services provide means to exchange information with others, either synchronous or asynchronous (Ashley and Soren 2003)
Social sharing	Sharing services provide the possibility to share resources (e.g., knowledge, information, multimedia data) at an online social network with a group of people, privately or publicly (Vogel 2011). Sharing services can be implemented synchronously and asynchronously

Source: Own illustration

Table 22.2 Services of persuasive technologies

Project	Year	Services
Houston	2006	Tracking, analysis, goal setting, prompting, social communication, social sharing, challenges, leaderboards
Fish'n'Steps	2006	Tracking, analysis, goal setting, social communication, social sharing, levels, challenges
UbiFit Garden	2008	Tracking, analysis, goal setting, prompting, challenges
Mobile Mentor	2010	Tracking, analysis, goal setting, coaching, prompting
Fitness Tour	2011	Tracking, analysis, goal setting, identity management, social sharing, challenges
RunWithUs	2011	Information, tracking, analysis, goal setting, coaching, identity management, relationship management, social communication, social sharing, points, leaderboards
iDetective	2011	Tracking, analysis, goal setting, coaching, points, levels, challenges
Move2Play	2012	Information, tracking, analysis, goal setting, coaching, identity management, relationship management, social communication, social sharing, points, levels, challenges, virtual goods, leaderboards

Source: Own illustration

Table 22.3 Consolidated services of persuasive technologies

Education	Feedback	Gamification	Social interaction
Information	Tracking	Points	(Infrastructure)
(Risk illustration)	Analysis	Levels	Identity management
(Instructions)	Goal setting	Challenges	Relationship management
	Coaching	Virtual goods	Social communication
	Prompting	Leaderboards	Social sharing
		(Gifts)	

Source: Own illustration
Features given in brackets are not used in the described research projects, but they are found to be important when examining preventive mobile applications. They are mentioned in the subsequent discussion

However, educational services are not restricted to information and background knowledge. The category rather involves *instructions* or material focusing on *risk illustration*. Instructions tell the user how to perform desired behaviors, whereas risk illustration highlights health consequences due to a specific behavior.

22.3.1.2 Feedback

Each of the previously mentioned projects provides some form of feedback to inform the user about his individual progress. Therefore, smartphones are used to measure activities or actions of individuals. Derived from the collected data, applications can provide context-based services. Based on the earlier findings, the following services are identified and assigned to this category.

The services *tracking and analysis* are often closely coupled and refer to self-monitoring and self-observation, which is a core concept of many behavioral programs (Foreyt and Goodrick 1993; McLean et al. 2003) and a key method in the cognitive behavioral therapy (Ahtinen et al. 2010). It is defined as the recording of one or several parameters (e.g., diet, weight, physical activity, sleep, stress, smoking, and alcohol consumption) and storing the data into log files (Ahtinen et al. 2010). The records provide reasonable information (e.g., by graphical and textual analysis) and help to reflect the user's past behavior (Consolvo et al. 2009).

In primary prevention, *goal setting* is an often utilized and suggested technique to support health behavior change (McLean et al. 2003; Medynskiy et al. 2011), especially for nutrition and physical activity-related change interventions (Shilts et al. 2004). Most of the interventions rely on the Goal Setting Theory proposed by Locke and Latham (Locke and Latham 1990, 2002).

Coaching refers to context aware virtual agents that provide the user with personalized feedback (Den Akker et al. 2011) and is distinguished from prerecorded static videos. Especially in the area of physical activity, virtual coaching is an often addressed and discussed feature (Bielik et al. 2012; Buttussi et al. 2006; Den Akker et al. 2011; Fogg 2003b). For instance, virtual coaches offer information on the user's current status (e.g., speed, time, calories burned) and give directions for navigation or assistance on certain tasks (Ahtinen et al. 2010).

According to Consolvo et al. (2009), *prompting* is an effective strategy for positive behavior change. Prompts remind users to perform desired behaviors (Campbell and Chau 2010; Pollak et al. 2010). Fogg (2009) describes prompting as triggers that tell people to perform a behavior. They are noticed and associated with a target behavior and happen in an opportune moment, when the user is both motivated and able to perform the desired behavior (Fogg 2009).

22.3.1.3 Gamification

Gamification is a term which originated in the digital media industry in 2008 (Deterding et al. 2011), while others state the term already evolved in 2004 (Gamification Wiki 2011). Nevertheless, it became more frequently used around 2010 (Deterding et al. 2011; Gamification Wiki 2011).

At its roots, gamification is defined as the incorporation of game mechanisms in nongame contexts (Bunchball Inc. 2010; Deterding et al. 2011; Groh 2012; Zichermann and Cunningham 2011). The goal is to incorporate game mechanics and dynamics to make nongame products, services, or applications more enjoyable, motivating, or engaging to use (Deterding et al. 2011).

Table 22.4 illustrates a list of game mechanics and dynamics presented by Bunchball Inc. (2010) and Zichermann and Cunningham (2011). As the terms—game mechanics and game dynamics—are closely related, they are often used synonymously and interchangeably. Hereby, game mechanics are the functioning components that are used to get a meaningful response, whereas game dynamics refer to the aspects that create an engaging user experience, namely, human desires (Bunchball Inc. 2010; Zichermann and Cunningham 2011).

Table 22.4 Game mechanics and game dynamics

Game mechanics	Game dynamics
Points	Reward
Levels	Status
Challenges	Achievement
Virtual goods	Self-expression
Leaderboards	Competition
Gifts	Altruism

Source: Own illustration, adapted from (Bunchball Inc. 2010)

According to Bunchball Inc. (2010), gamification has the ability to build a highly motivational user experience by the integration of these mechanisms into a website, business service, or online community (Deterding et al. 2011)—individually or altogether. In healthcare, the use of game mechanisms may be used to motivate individuals to perform desired behaviors.

22.3.1.4 Social Interaction

Another method to promote healthy behaviors is the incorporation of social interaction as it is known to be effective in helping individuals to achieve positive health behavior changes (Consolvo et al. 2006; Lin et al. 2006). According to Heaney and Israel (2008), social support is defined as the "aid and assistance exchanged through social relationships and interpersonal transactions." Social support is always intended to be supportive and helpful, distinguishing it from negative interactions (Heaney and Israel 2008). On the contrary, influence through social pressure or peer pressure refers to the theory of social facilitation. The theory states that people perform better when other people are present, either participating or observing (Aiello and Douthitt 2001).

Within the investigated projects, competition (i.e., social pressure) and cooperation (i.e., social support) among groups of people are established by providing them tools for social interaction, either internally implemented (e.g., own social networking infrastructure) or externally implemented (e.g., interfaces to existing social networks). These tools provide users means to present themselves (e.g., identity management), to connect with other people (e.g., relationship management), to communicate (e.g., personal messages, chat, discussion boards), or to share progress and achievements among each other.

22.3.2 The Impact of Persuasive Services on the User Acceptance

The characterization of applications from research projects and the identification of persuasive services in them lead to the question, which of these services are the most effective when used in healthcare applications? In addition to the results of the individual project, the effectiveness of the persuasive services in existing applications on the market needs to be quantified. Smartphones allow to install applications via mobile distribution platforms (Holzinger et al. 2010), most frequently offered by the developer and vendor of an operating system (e.g., Apple, Google). The mobile distribution platforms also provide a rating system, where the user can rate the application on a 5-star Likert scale. As acceptance and impact of these mobile applications cannot be measured directly, the user rating is used as a replacement for the acceptance of the overall application.

A sample of 952 applications available for download[1] at the Apple App Store and Google Android Market is the basis for the market analysis. The applications have been selected from the category of Health and Fitness. Each application is reviewed by the information available at the store's online webpage (i.e., general description of the developer with a list of services, user reviews, and screenshots).

In the following, the linear regression analysis is used to examine the relationship between applications' characteristics and the user rating. The objective is to identify characteristics and combinations of characteristics that influence the user rating of mobile applications.

As the user rating is a critical value, it is necessary to improve its precision and explanatory power. Therefore, the sample of preventive applications is limited to applications that are rated at least 300 times[2] by users (votes ≥300). Additionally, applications within the category of other measures are excluded as they barely inherit services. The size of the investigated sample is now limited to 137 applications. Figure 22.2 illustrates the selection of the study sample for the multivariate results.

22.3.2.1 Impact of Individual Characteristics on the User Rating

Table 22.5 shows the results of the linear regression test. Herein, each characteristic (independent variable) is examined in its relationship towards the user rating[3] (dependent variable).

Two values are of special interest: *b*- and *p*-value. The *p*-value states whether there is a significant relationship between the examined variables or not. In this work, a usual significance level of 0.05 (5 % level) is chosen (Backhaus et al. 2010; Nagel and Hatzinger 2009). The regression coefficient or unstandardized coefficient b represents the effect of the independent variable (service) on the dependent variable (user rating) by average, ceteris paribus. As the variables are measured with the same scale, it is allowed to use the size of the regression coefficient as a measurement of importance in comparison to the other calculated regression coefficients within a group (Backhaus et al. 2010). A comparison of coefficients across groups is not possible.

[1] Downloaded in February 2012.

[2] Number of votes is set high in order to eliminate biased user ratings.

[3] The user rating is given on a scale from 1 point (poor) to 5 points (excellent).

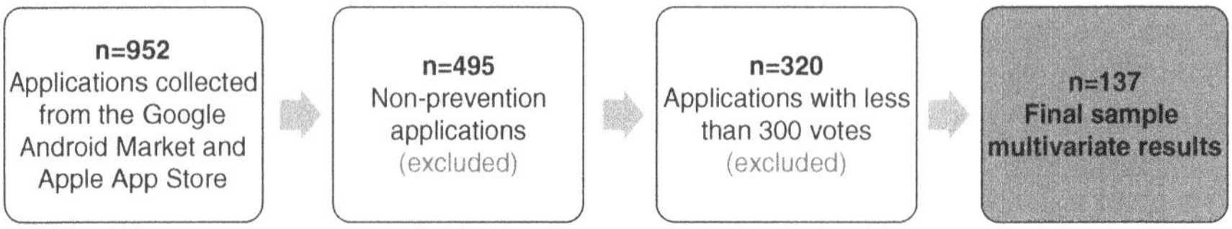

Fig. 22.2 Selection of the study sample for the multivariate results (*Source*: Own illustration)

Table 22.5 Results of the linear regression analysis on the coherence between characteristics and the user rating

	Total	
Average rating	3.91	
Number of applications n	137	
Characteristics	**b**	**p-value**
Education	0.288	0.024
Information	0.021	0.905
Risk illustration	-0.006	0.984
Instructions	0.202	0.115
Feedback	0.022	0.916
Tracking	0.289	0.090
Analysis	0.000	1.000
Goal setting	0.317	0.012
Coaching	0.569	0.000
Prompting	0.251	0.287
Gamification	0.614	0.000
Points	0.400	0.453
Levels	0.463	0.016
Challenges	0.602	0.001
Virtual goods	-	-
Leaderboards	0.578	0.033
Gifts	-	-
Social interaction	0.468	0.000
Intern infrastructure	0.413	0.008
Extern infrastructure	0.488	0.000
Identity management	0.396	0.014
Relationship management	0.398	0.024
Social communication	0.432	0.011
Social sharing	0.488	0.000

Source: Own illustration

The significant results are highlighted in the table, while green-shaded values constitute a positive relationship (i.e., characteristic leads by average to an increase of the rating) and red-shaded values illustrate a negative relationship (i.e., characteristic leads by average to a decrease of the rating). Missing values signify that one of the examined variables is a constant. This is either the case when a characteristic is not available in any application or available in all applications within the examined sample. It is important to keep in mind that individual characteristics may reveal a significant relationship, while a category as a whole may not lead to a significant result and vice versa. The given values of categories (e.g., education, feedback) and subcategories (e.g., tracking, goal setting) consider all applications that implement at least one characteristic within the respective category or subcategory. For instance, the b- and p-value of the category education are calculated by considering all applications that implement at least one of the given characteristics within the category (e.g., information, risk illustration, or instructions).

The significant results are summarized below. In a first step, the effect of characteristic categories towards the user rating is presented. Secondly, the investigation focuses on individual characteristics and their influence on the user rating.

22.3.2.2 Impact of Characteristic Categories on the User Rating

The table shows the impact of characteristic categories on the user rating. The given value in the table represents the unstandardized regression coefficient b and therein the change of the rating by average (ceteris paribus) when characteristics within the respective category are available in applications. Missing values denote that there is no significant relationship between the given category as a whole and the user rating.

Results covering the sample ($n = 137$) reveal that especially gamification services and social interaction services lead to a remarkable increase of the user rating. If applications incorporate gamification services, the user rating increases by 0.614 points on average. The adherence of social interaction services increases the rating by 0.468 points.

22.3.2.3 Impact of Individual Characteristics on the User Rating

The table also shows the impact of individual characteristics on the user rating. The interpretation is similar to the interpretation of the categories.

Across all examined applications, characteristics having the strongest influence on the user rating are the game mechanics challenges (0.602 points) and leaderboards (0.578 points). These characteristics are leading by a large margin to other characteristics as illustrated in Fig. 22.3.

The possibility to share content on social networking platforms like Twitter of Facebook seems to be another important functionality for users. On average, these services lead to an increase by 0.488 points of the rating. Services that give feedback and provide the user with personalized status messages improve the rating by 0.486 points, whereas personalized instructions enhance it at an average by 0.482

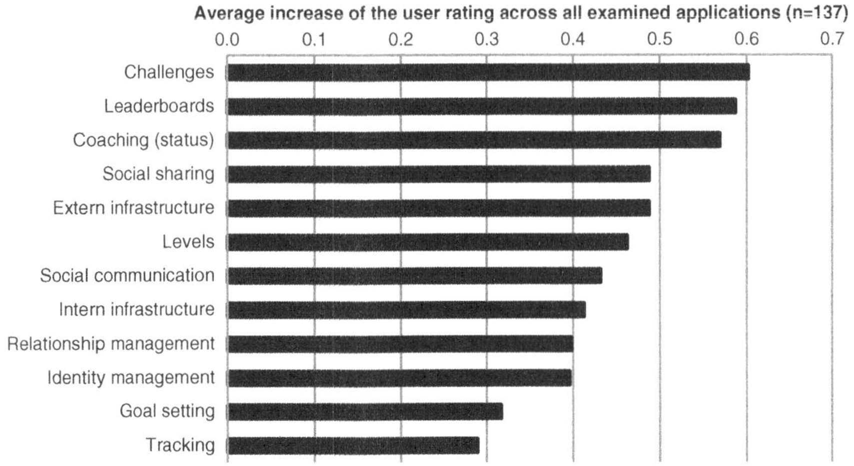

Fig. 22.3 Impact of individual characteristics on the user rating across all examined applications (*Source*: Own illustration)

points. Especially services of social interaction increase the average user rating. Each given feature in the category of social interaction is significant (p-value $\leq$0.05) in its coherence with the rating. Sharing (0.488 points) and social communication (0.432 points) lead approximately to a similar increase by average. The potential to manage own contacts (0.398 points) or to present oneself (0.396 points) increases the rating a little less. Other characteristics that yield a significant result are levels (0.463 points) as well as self-set goals (0.319 points) and automatic tracking (0.267 points).

22.4 Conclusion and Discussion

The previously conducted analysis examined the coherence between characteristics and the user rating. The results reveal several characteristics that increase the rating remarkably when implemented in mobile applications.

Future application development should incorporate services within the given categories, as illustrated in Table 22.6. These services have been shown to be successful in preventive applications.

Many applications focus on activity or behavior tracking. Users most frequently rate applications higher that enable automatic activity assessment via sensor technology. It is assumed that automatic tracking is more convenient for users, increases the usability, and leads to more accurate data than manual tracking. Developers should think about how existing technologies can be used in different ways.

Table 22.6 Recommended services in preventive mobile applications

Education	Feedback	Gamification	Social interaction
	Tracking	Levels	(Infrastructure)
	Goal setting	Challenges	Identity management
	Coaching	Leaderboards	Relationship management
			Social communication
			Social sharing

Source: Own illustration

Additionally, the opportunities and effects of goal setting need to be considered. In applications, especially the use of self-set goals has proved to be successful. Goals give directions, provide motivation, and lead to higher self-efficacy when achieved—all of these aspects are crucial in behavior change programs.

Actually, there exist many applications that provide the user with tools for self-observation. For instance, users can log and analyze their physical activity or nutritional intake. Nevertheless, many of these applications do not provide personalized performance feedback or guidance (e.g., information on the appropriate type and amount of activity reflecting users' individual needs). It has been found that applications are rated better when they include services providing personalized assistance or herein called coaching (e.g., depicting current status/progress, guiding towards goals). This includes, for instance, individually adjusted exercise plans or diet plans and instructions depending on the user's current state in order to achieve these plans. As the given services increase the rating considerably, it is recommended to include them in mobile applications.

No matter which prevention category is examined, whether it is physical activity, nutrition, or addiction, the use of social interaction services consistently leads to a higher user rating when implemented in mobile applications. Most users seem to like services that enable possibilities to share content (e.g., social networking status messages, goals, and achievements) among others. It is assumed that social interaction services increase overall application usage and lead to a higher commitment due to the provision of access to more dynamic content. Referring to Oulasvirta et al. (2012), quick access to dynamic content may increase overall application usage because of the strength of checking habits.[4] This opportunity can be intelligently leveraged to increase the commitment of users to an application (e.g., application is integrated into users' everyday activities) (Oulasvirta et al. 2012). Exchanging information (e.g., personal messages and discussion forums) with like-minded people may provide social support, recognition, and further motivation to achieve a positive health behavior change.

[4] Checking habit = brief, repetitive inspection of dynamic content quickly accessible on smartphones (e.g., quick access to rewards like social networking, communications, and news) (Oulasvirta et al. 2012, January).

Besides social networking mechanisms, it is recommended to make use of game mechanisms. Applications implementing these services are frequently rated better by users. Developers should primarily focus on the following game mechanics: challenges, leaderboards, and levels. Challenges provide users with tasks to accomplish and give them goals and the feeling they are working towards something (e.g., challenging friends on a running route, collecting physical activity points to unlock achievements, completing goals to earn awards) (Bunchball Inc. 2010). Leaderboards are used to enable comparisons (e.g., how am I doing against myself or friends) (Zichermann and Cunningham 2011). They track and display desired actions, using competition to drive motivation (Bunchball Inc. 2010). Levels inform users about their progress and serve as markers, so that users know where they are in a gaming experience (e.g., current level of physical activity) (Zichermann and Cunningham 2011). These mechanisms are often used in combination and can be seen as important reinforcing factors to raise people's motivation. They should be used accordingly.

Furthermore, it is suggested to combine social interaction services and gamification services. According to gamification design principles, the use of achievements, badges, or trophies is more successful when being visible to others. Zichermann and Cunningham (2011) state "The more public the achievement, the more valuable it is to players,…" (Zichermann and Cunningham 2011). For that reason, it is important to provide a platform where users have the possibility to show their achievements in order to receive recognition and support by others (e.g., trophy case, user profile that displays their achievements) (Bunchball Inc. 2010).

22.4.1 Feature Composition Referring to the Kano Model of Customer Satisfaction

Referring to the Kano model of customer satisfaction, services can be assigned to categories to derive further recommendations for concept development. The categories are named *basic services*, *performance services*, and *excitement services* as shown in Fig. 22.4 (Bieger 2007). Each category is described and presented below.

It is important to keep in mind that the categorization of services is not evidence based (i.e., Kano survey). It is a suggestion by the author according to the description of the Kano model and the results of the multivariate analysis.

22.4.1.1 Basic Services

Basic services are fundamental and expected by users. The absence or poor performance of these services results in dissatisfaction, whereas the inclusion of these services provides diminishing returns in terms of customer satisfaction. The importance of basic services is only realized by users when they are lacking (Reinecke and Janz 2006). Manual tracking (e.g., manual recording of actual behavior) and data analysis (e.g., statistics/history, graphs/charts, and calculators) can rank among

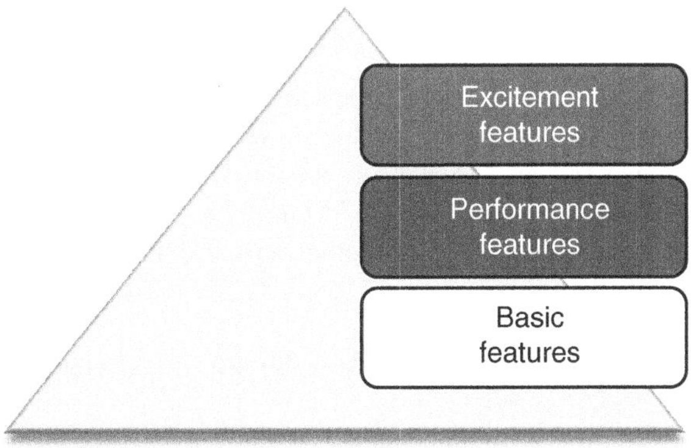

Fig. 22.4 Categories referring to the Kano model of customer satisfaction (*Source*: Own illustration, adapted from Bieger (2007, p. 192))

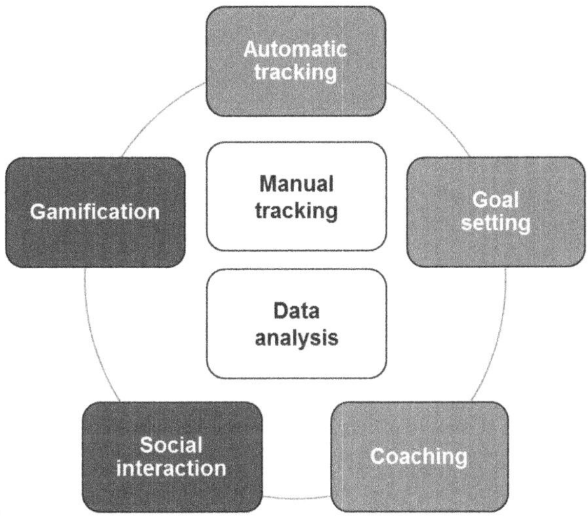

Fig. 22.5 Recommended feature composition referring to the Kano model of customer satisfaction (*Source*: Own illustration)

basic services as illustrated in Fig. 22.5. They are standard in most preventive applications and need to be available. As they are expected, their availability does not lead to a significant increase of the user rating.

22.4.1.2 Performance Services

Performance services improve user satisfaction remarkably when implemented. In contrast, the absence or weak performance of these services leads to a decrease in user satisfaction (Bieger 2007). When applications are advertised, the advertising material is closely tied to performance services. Automatic tracking, goal setting, and coaching can be assigned to this category.

22.4.1.3 Excitement Services

Excitement services provide benefits that are unexpected. They distinguish applications from competing products and arouse enthusiasm. A slight improve in performance can lead to a disproportional user satisfaction (Reinecke and Janz 2006). Services that provide the opportunity to interact with others and game mechanisms (e.g., challenges, levels, and leaderboards) can be assigned to this category.

22.4.1.4 Recommendations for Successful Healthcare Applications

It is highly recommended for preventive healthcare applications to implement basic services, such as manual tracking and data analysis (e.g., statistics/history, graphs/charts, and calculators).

To reduce the user's effort of entering data and to make applications generally more supportive of self-monitoring, developers should consider performance services (e.g., automatic tracking, goal setting, and coaching). Although applications provide automatic data acquisition, the possibility of manual tracking should be maintained in order to provide users means to not rely on automatic tracking mechanisms.

Excitement services are suggested to differentiate one's application from competitors, e.g., tools to interact with others and game mechanisms enabling playful experiences.

Interesting areas for future research include the development of a deeper understanding of important services for the users. It might be of interest how individuals rate the services independently. A survey regarding these services can be helpful to validate the findings in this work. As there is known little about the users of the previously examined applications, the survey may also answer the question whether users are, e.g., technology enthusiasts, athletes, or individuals interested in prevention.

Disease prevention using persuasive technology offers considerable opportunities for preventive healthcare and should be developed accordingly. Hereby, especially preventive measures for which few applications exist should further be addressed in mobile applications. Most of the examined applications do not make use of services that have been found to have a positive influence on the user rating. Being considered an important facilitator of preventive care, development efforts should focus on these services.

References

Abraham, C., & Michie, S. (2008, May). A taxonomy of behavior change techniques used in interventions. *Health Psychology: Official Journal of the Division of Health Psychology, American Psychological Association, 27*(3), 379–387.

Abroms, L. C., Padmanabhan, N., Thaweethai, L., & Phillips, T. (2011, March). iPhone apps for smoking cessation: A content analysis. *American Journal of Preventive Medicine, 40*(3), 279–285.

Ahtinen, A., Huuskonen, P., & Häkkilä, J. (2010). Let's all get up and walk to the north pole: Design and evaluation of a mobile wellness application. *Proceedings of the 6th Nordic Conference on Human-Computer Interaction* (pp. 3–12). New York: ACM.

Aiello, J. R., & Douthitt, E. A. (2001). Social facilitation from triplett to electronic performance monitoring. *Group Dynamics: Theory, Research, and Practice, 5*(3), 163–180.

Arteaga, S. M., Kudeki, M., Street, W. I., & Woodworth, A. (2010). Mobile system to motivate teenagers' physical activity. *Proceedings of the 9th International Conference on Interaction Design and Children* (pp. 1–11).

Ashley, J., & Soren, K. (2003). Synchronous and asynchronous communication tools. *Executive update online*.

Backhaus, K., Erichson, B., Plinke, W., & Weiber, R. (2010). *Multivariate Analysemethoden: Eine anwendungsorientierte Einführung* (Vol. 2010, p. 583). Berlin: Springer.

Backinger, C. L., & Augustson, E. M. (2011, March). Where there's an app, there's a way? *American Journal of Preventive Medicine, 40*(3), 390–391.

Bauer, J. S., Consolvo, S., Greenstein, B., Schooler, J., Wu, E., Watson, N. F., et al. (2012) ShutEye: Encouraging awareness of healthy sleep recommendations with a mobile, peripheral display. *Proceedings of the 30th International Conference on Human Factors in Computing Systems*. New York: ACM.

Bieger, T. (2007). *Dienstleistungs-Management: Einführung in Strategien und Prozesse bei persönlichen Dienstleistungen* (p. 354). Stuttgart: UTB.

Bielik, P., Tomlein, M., & Barla, M. (2012). Move2Play: An innovative approach to encouraging people to be more physically active. *Proceedings of the 2nd ACM SIGHIT International Health Informatics Symposium* (pp. 61–70). New York: ACM.

Breton, E. R., Fuemmeler, B. F., & Abroms, L. C. (2011, September 13). Weight loss—There is an app for that! But does it adhere to evidence-informed practices? *Translational Behavioral Medicine, 1*, 1–7.

Bunchball Inc. (2010, October). Gamification 101: An introduction to the use of game dynamics to influence behavior. Retrieved December, 2012, from http://www.bunchball.com/.

Bürger C. (2003). *Patientenorientierte Information und Kommunikation im Gesundheitswesen* (p. 415). New York: DUV.

Buttussi, F., Chittaro, L., & Nadalutti, D. (2006). Bringing mobile guides and fitness activities together: A solution based on an embodied virtual trainer. *Proceedings of the 8th International Conference on Human Computer Interaction with Mobile Devices and Services*. New York: ACM.

Campbell, C., & Chau, S. (2010). Mobile Mentor: Weight management platform. *Proceedings of the 2010 International Conference on Intelligent User Interfaces* (pp. 409–410). New York: ACM.

Centers for Disease Control and Prevention. (2009). The power of prevention: Chronic disease... the public health challenge of the 21st century.

Chuah, M., & Sample, S. (2011). Fitness Tour: A mobile application for combating obesity. *Proceedings of the Mobile Health 2011 Conference*. New York: ACM.

Cohen, J. T., Neumann, P. J., & Weinstein, M. C. (2008). Does preventive care save money? Health economics and the presidential candidates. *The New England Journal of Medicine, 358*(7), 661–663.

Consolvo, S., Everitt, K., Smith, I., & Landay, J. A. (2006). Design requirements for technologies that encourage physical activity. *Proceedings of the 24th International Conference on Human Factors in Computing Systems* (pp. 457–466).

Consolvo, S., McDonald, D. W., & Landay, J. A. (2009). Theory-driven design strategies for technologies that support behavior change in everyday life. *Proceedings of the 27th International Conference on Human Factors in Computing Systems* (pp. 405–414). New York: ACM.

Den Akker, H., Moualed, L. S., Jones, V. M., & Hermens, H. J. (2011). A self-learning personalized feedback agent for motivating physical activity. *Proceedings of the 4th International Symposium on Applied Sciences in Biomedical and Communication Technologies*. New York: ACM.

Deterding, S., Khaled, R., Nacke, L. E., & Dixon, D. (2011). Gamification: Toward a definition. *Proceedings of the 29th International Conference on Human Factors in Computing Systems* (pp. 12–15). ACM, New York.

Far, S. M. (2010). *Social software in Unternehmen: Nutzenpotentiale und Adoption in der innerbetrieblichen Zusammenarbeit* (p. 268). BoD—Books on Demand. ACM, New York.

Fogg, B. J. (1999). Persuasive technologies. *Communications of the ACM, 42*(5), 26–29. ACM, New York.

Fogg, B. J. (2003a). *Persuasive technology: Using computers to change what we think and do* (p. 283). San Francisco, CA: Morgan Kaufmann.

Fogg, B. J. (2003). Computers as persuasive social actors. *Persuasive Technology: Using Computers to Change What We Think and Do* (pp. 89–120). Amsterdam: Morgan Kaufmann.

Fogg, B. J. (2009). A behavior model for persuasive design. *Proceedings of the 4th International Conference on Persuasive Technology.*

Foreyt, J. P., & Goodrick, G. K. (1993). Evidence for success of behavior modification in weight loss and control. *Annals of Internal Medicine, 119*(7), 698–701.

Gamification Wiki. (2011). *Gamification*. Retrieved December 10, 2011, from http://gamification.org/wiki/Gamification

Gartner. (2012). *Gartner says worldwide smartphone sales soared in fourth quarter of 2011 with 47 percent growth.* Retrieved March 14, 2012, from http://www.gartner.com/it/page.jsp?id=1924314

Gil-castiñeira, F., Cid-vieytes, N., Conde-lagoa, D., & Javier, F. (2011). RunWithUs: A social sports application in the ubiquitous oulu environment. *Proceedings of the 4th IEEE International Conference on Computer Science and Information Technology* (pp. 195–204). ACM, New York.

GKV-Spitzenverband. (2010). *Leitfaden Prävention.* Berlin Springer, Hamburg.

GKV-Spitzenverband. (2012). *Präventionsbericht 2011.* Germany: Essen.

Graham, C., Benda, P., Howard, S., Balmford, J., Bishop, N., & Borland, R. (2006). 'heh—keeps me off the smokes…': Probing technology support for personal change. *OZCHI 2006* (pp. 221–228). ACM, New York.

Grimes, A., Kantroo, V., & Grinter, R. E. (2010). Let's play!: Mobile health games for adults. *Proceedings of the 12th ACM International Conference on Ubiquitous Computing* (pp. 241–250). ACM, New York.

Groh, F. (2012). Gamification: State of the art definition and utilization. *Proceedings of the 4th Seminar on Research Trends in Media Informatics* (pp. 39–46). ACM, New York.

Heaney, C. A., & Israel, B. A. (2008). Social networks and social support. In K. Glanz, B. K. Rimer, & K. V. Viswanath (Eds.), *Health behavior and health education: Theory, research, and practice* (pp. 189–210). San Francisco, CA: Jossey-Bass.

Holzinger, A., Dorner, S., & Födinger, M. (2010). Chances of increasing youth health awareness through mobile wellness applications. *Proceedings of the 6th Symposium of the WG HCI&UE of the Austrian Computer Society* (pp. 71–81).

Ijsselsteijn, W., De Kort, Y., Midden, C., & Eggen, B. (2006). Persuasive technology for human well-being: setting the scene. *Proceedings of the 1st International Conference on Persuasive Technology* (pp. 1–5). ACM, New York.

Jepson, R. G., Harris, F. M., Platt, S., & Tannahill, C. (2010, January). The effectiveness of interventions to change six health behaviours: A review of reviews. *BMC Public Health, 10*, 538.

Kim, S., Schap, T., Bosch, M., Maciejewski, R., Delp, E. J., Ebert, D. S., et al. (2010). Development of a mobile user interface for image-based dietary assessment. *Proceedings of the 9th International Conference on Mobile and Ubiquitous Multimedia* (pp. 1–7). ACM, New York.

Klasnja, P., Consolvo, S., & Pratt, W. (2011). How to evaluate technologies for health behavior change in HCI research. *Proceedings of the 29th International Conference on Human Factors in Computing Systems* (pp. 3063–3072). ACM, New York.

Koch, M., Schlosser, A., & Richter, A. (2007). Produkte zum IT-gestçtzten Social Networking in Unternehmen. *Wirtschaftsinformatik, 49*(6), 448–455.

Leppin, A. (2007). Konzepte und Strategien der Krankheitsprävention. In A. Leppin (Ed.), *Lehrbuch Prävention und Gesundheitsförderung* (pp. 31–40). Springer Hamburg.

Lin, J. J., Mamykina, L., Lindtner, S., Delajoux, G., & Strub, H. B. (2006). Fish'n'Steps: Encouraging physical activity with an interactive computer game. *Proceedings of the 8th ACM International Conference on Ubiquitous Computing* (pp. 261–278). ACM, New York.

Locke, E. A., & Latham, G. P. (1990). *A theory of goal setting & task performance* (p. 413). Englewood Cliffs, NJ: Prentice Hall.

Locke, E. A., & Latham, G. P. (2002, September). Building a practically useful theory of goal setting and task motivation: A 35-year odyssey. *American Psychologist, 57*(9), 705–717.

Mattila, E., Korhonen, I., Salminen, J. H., Ahtinen, A., Koskinen, E., Särelä, A., et al. (2010, March). Empowering citizens for well-being and chronic disease management with wellness diary. *IEEE Transactions on Information Technology in Biomedicine: A Publication of the IEEE Engineering in Medicine and Biology Society, 14*(2), 456–463.

McLean, N., Griffin, S., Toney, K., & Hardeman, W. (2003, September). Family involvement in weight control, weight maintenance and weight-loss interventions: A systematic review of randomised trials. *International Journal of Obesity and Related Metabolic Disorders: Journal of the International Association for the Study of Obesity, 27*(9), 987–1005.

Medynskiy, Y., Yarosh, S., & Mynatt, E. (2011). Five strategies for supporting healthy behavior change. *Proceedings of the 29th International Conference on Human Factors in Computing Systems* (pp. 1333–1338). ACM, New York.

Miller, R. E. (2002). *Epidemiology for health promotion and disease prevention professionals* (p. 457). Routledge, New York.

Mokdad, A. H., Marks, J. S., Stroup, D. F., & Gerberding, J. L. (2004, March). Actual causes of death in the United States, 2000. *Journal of the American Medical Association, 291*(10), 1238–1245.

Munson, S. A., & Consolvo, S. (2012). Exploring goal-setting, rewards, self-monitoring, and sharing to motivate physical activity. *6th International Conference on Pervasive Computing Technologies for Healthcare*. ACM, New York.

Nagel, H., & Hatzinger, R. (2009). *Schnelleinstieg in SPSS* (Vol. 1, p. 352). Auflage: Pearson Studium.

Oinas-Kukkonen, H. (2010a). Behavior change support systems: A research model and agenda. *Proceedings of the 5th International Conference on Persuasive Technology* (pp. 4–14). ACM, New York.

Oinas-Kukkonen, H. (2010b). Behavior change support systems: The next frontier for web science. *Proceedings of the Second International Web Science Conference*. ACM, New York.

Oinas-Kukkonen, H., & Harjumaa, M. (2008). Towards deeper understanding of persuasion in software and information systems. *Proceedings of the 1st International Conference on Advances in Computer-Human Interaction* (pp. 200–205). ACM, New York.

Oinas-Kukkonen, H., & Harjumaa, M. (2009). Persuasive systems design: Key issues, process model, and system features. *Communications of the Association for Information Systems, 24*(28), 485–500.

Oulasvirta, A., Rattenbury, T., Ma, L., & Raita, E. (2012, January). Habits make smartphone use more pervasive. *Personal and Ubiquitous Computing, 16*(1), 105–114.

Pollak, J., Gay, G., Byrne, S., Wagner, E., Retelny, D., & Humphreys, L. (2010, July). It's time to eat! Using mobile games to promote healthy eating. *IEEE Pervasive Computing, 9*(3), 21–27.

Reinecke, S., & Janz, S. (2006). *Marketingcontrolling: Sicherstellen von Marketingeffektivität und-effizienz* (p. 516). Stuttgart: W. Kohlhammer.

Shilts, M. K., Horowitz, M., & Townsend, M. S. (2004). Goal setting as a strategy for dietary and physical activity behavior change: A review of the literature. *American Journal of Health Promotion: AJHP, 19*(2), 81–93.

Simons, H. W., Morreale, J., & Gronbeck, B. E. (2001). *Persuasion in society* (p. 440). Thousand Oaks, CA: Sage Publications.

Singh, D. (2008). How can chronic disease management programmes operate across care settings and providers? Available at http://www.euro.who.int/__data/assets/pdf_file/0009/75474/E93416.pdf. Accessed Dec 2012.

Vogel, A. (2011). *Der Buchmarkt Als Kommunikationsraum: Eine Kritische Analyse Aus Medienwissenschaftlicher Perspektive* (p. 387). Gabler Wissenschaftsverlage, Sprigner, Hamburg.
W. H. Organization. (2006). *World health statistics 2006*. ACM, New York.
WahooFitness. (2012). *Fitness sensors*. Retrieved January 26, 2011, from http://www.wahoofitness.com/Products/Products.asp
Willet, W. C. (2002). Balancing life-style and genomics research for disease prevention. Retrieved March 16, 2012, from http://snhs-plin.barry.edu/cell-biology/Science Complex Diseases/Science—Willett 296 (5568) 695 Balancing life style and Genomics Res.htm
Wing, R. R., & Phelan, S. (2005, July). Long-term weight loss maintenance. *The American Journal of Clinical Nutrition, 82*(1 Suppl), 222S–225S.
Wood, W. (2000, January). Attitude change: Persuasion and social influence. *Annual Review of Psychology, 51*, 539–570.
Zephyr Technology. (2012). *Consumer HxM*. Retrieved January 26, 2012, from http://www.zephyr-technology.com/consumer-hxm
Zichermann, G., & Cunningham, C. (2011). *Gamification by design: Implementing game mechanics in web and mobile apps* (p. 208). O'Reilly Media, Boston.

Chapter 23
Using Technology Solutions to Streamline Healthcare Processes for Nursing: The Case of an Intelligent Operational Planning Support Tool (IOPST) Solution

Nilmini Wickramasinghe, Bridie Kent, Fatemeh Hoda Moghimi, Malte Stien, Lemai Nguyen, Bernice Redley, Nyree Taylor, and Mari Botti

Abstract Identifying the value stream relating to healthcare processes primarily focuses around diagnosing and treating patients coupled with removing waste. This is now becoming a key priority for many healthcare organisations globally, yet remains an area that is significantly under researched especially with regard to nursing. Lean thinking, as a method to redesign processes in order to improve outcomes has been used with success especially in the manufacturing sector, and now, given the importance of identifying and creating value in healthcare processes, is becoming of increasing interest within various healthcare contexts. In this chapter, we discuss how lean thinking as a management approach, with focuses on operational aspects, can be used to facilitate effective and efficient nursing care. We illustrate with the example of an Intelligent Operational Planning Support Tool (IOPST) solution.

Keywords Lean thinking • Nursing care • Value stream • Intelligent operational system

---

N. Wickramasinghe (✉)
Epworth HealthCare & Department of BITL & HIRi, RMIT University,
GPO Box 2476, Melbourne, VIC 3001, Australia
e-mail: nilmini.wickramasinghe@rmit.edu.au

B. Kent • L. Nguyen • B. Redley • N. Taylor • M. Botti
Epworth Research Institute, 185-187 Hoddle, St. Richmond, VIC 3121, Australia
e-mail: bridie.kent@deakin.edu.au; lemai.nguyen@deakin.edu.au; bernice.redley@deakin.edu.au; nytlr95@gmail.com; bridie.kent@deakin.edu.au

F.H. Moghimi
School of Business IT and Logistics, RMIT University, GPO Box 2476,
Melbourne, VIC 3001, Australia
e-mail: moghimi87@gmail.com

M. Stien
SmartWard Pty Ltd, Canberra, Australia
e-mail: malte.stien@smartward.com.au

N. Wickramasinghe et al. (eds.), *Lean Thinking for Healthcare*, Healthcare Delivery in the Information Age, DOI 10.1007/978-1-4614-8036-5_23,

23.1 Introduction

Lean design is an emerging influence in healthcare. The central notions of value-added care and process improvement are most applicable and relevant for today's healthcare processes plagued by waste and inefficiency (Capuano et al. 2004; Institute for Healthcare Improvement 2010). Hence, applying "lean" into healthcare services has become one of the most visible recent trends in the services industry (Holm and Ahlstrom 2010; Jones and Mitchell 2006; Guimarães and De Carvalho 2012). Scarce but important review articles (Young and Mc Clean 2008; Winch and Henderson 2009; Souza 2009; Mazzocato et al. 2010; Sobek and Lang 2010; Guimarães and De Carvalho 2012) present the deployment extension of lean thinking in healthcare. All these reviews however, seem to be surgical in scope presenting only success cases under a tool and technique view (also called the "hard" side) and narrow in extension, not trying to cover different contexts of healthcare (the "soft" side).

The purpose of this chapter is to address a key void and begin to examine the benefits of lean deployment in nursing care contexts. Specifically, to answer the question: how can lean thinking, as a management approach with focuses on operational aspects, facilitate a better understanding of—and thereby create superior—nursing care contexts.

23.2 Background

Nursing care has a profound impact on the ultimate success of a healthcare intervention (Institute of Management 2012). However, given the pressure facing healthcare including escalating costs, impacts of technology, changes in disease profile and the increase of chronic diseases and the emphasis on quality care, nursing care also needs to be examined and redesigned to be effective and efficient. We believe this can be done in a systematic fashion by understanding the key dynamics and roles of nurses, understanding the benefits of lean thinking in such contexts and then investigating how a specific technology solution might be the catalyst for such a redesign.

23.2.1 *Nursing Care Current Situation*

Nursing care is typically complex and chaotic. Specifically, it is important to identify two broad areas in which nurses play a key role: (1) at the macro level—during the patient journey nurses are integral especially with regard to information management during the patient journey especially at the points of admission, handover and discharge. (2) At the micro level—where the nurse plays a major role in all components of the nursing process which is an iterative cycle of care focussing on the patient, their care needs and the environment (Barach and

Johnson 2006). In order to bring some order and structure to nursing care contexts, IT has been introduced in more recent years in many hospitals to support nurses in their daily work and try to help coordination of care activities (Hannah et al. 2005). This in turn has led to several evaluation studies that have focused on the effects of nursing information systems on different criteria such as the quality of nursing information processing (Ammenwerth et al. 2011), nursing documentation (Larrabee 2001; Nahm and Poston 2000), time needed for certain tasks (Marasovic et al. 1997), user satisfaction (Langowski 2005; Lee et al. 2008) or patient outcome (Currell and Urquhart 2003).

Moreover, quite a few studies examine the introduction of computerised decision support systems into nursing care contexts. Dowding et al. (2009) explore how technology and nursing need to have an aligned approach marrying nursing clinical experience with supportive or reflective technology design. This approach should reflect the most appropriate aspects of nursing care to suit the needs of the clinical environment. In addition, Kirkley and Rewick (2003) highly recommend that the introduction of technology into the clinical setting should extend from a nursing perspective and state outcomes such as improved patient safety and a more coordinated approach to nursing workflow to assist with the management and delivery of quality nursing care. Hence, it would appear prudent for nursing systems not only to be improved through using a systematic approach to enhance nursing care safety and quality but also to design such systems to fit with local clinical practices.

Finally, a strong common theme (Cornell et al. 2010) that recurs in the literature is the potential benefit of using lean thinking in order to improve the patient's journey and ensure effective, efficient and appropriate care is delivered by the nursing team.

To address these issues, this study highlights the importance of the deployment of lean approaches in nursing care contexts in order to improve the processes of care provided by nursing staff using an Intelligent Operational Planning Support Tool (IOPST) solution.

23.2.2 Key Aspects of Lean Thinking

Lean thinking embodies a set of design principles that guide organisational processes and enable them to become more and more effective and efficient, continuously improving service delivery, systematically reducing all forms of waste and ultimately contributing positively to society (Crawford 2008). With its roots in Deming's transformational system of management, the preceding captures the full ethos of the term lean (Crawford 2008).

A key concept in lean thinking is "value". Value is defined as the capability to deliver exactly the (customised) product or service a customer wants with minimal time between the moment the customer asks for that product or service and the actual delivery at an appropriate price (Womack and Jones 2003). Table 23.1 presents examples of values and wastes in healthcare contexts.

Table 23.1 Value and waste examples in healthcare (adapted from Kujala et al. 2006)

Lean thinking	Application in healthcare
Value adding time	Diagnostic and care time: • Diagnostic time (collecting and analysing clinical information) • Active care time (clinical interventions) • Passive care time (under observation, no interventions) WT • Positive WT (patients' condition is likely to improve without interventions)
Non-value adding time (waste)	Diagnostic and care time: • Superfluous time (not needed diagnostics, observations or interventions) • Administrative time WT • Passive WT (no change in patients' condition is expected) • Negative WT (patients' condition is likely to deteriorate)

In addition, the key principles of lean thinking are summarised as follows (Ben-Tovim et al. 2007):

- Specify the value desired by the customer
- Identify the value stream for each product or service providing that value and challenge all the wasted steps
- Make the product or service flow continuously
- Introduce pull between all the steps where continuous flow is impossible
- Manage towards perfection so that the number of steps and the amount of time and information transfer needed to serve the customer continually fall

For completeness, the evolution of lean thinking is summarised in Table 23.2:

Womack and Jones (2003) concisely capture the key elements of lean thinking and more specifically the components that need to be focused on in order to be a lean enterprise (Fig. 23.1). In particular, they point out that a lean enterprise consists of five elements: a product development process, a supplier management process, a customer management process, an overarching enterprise management process and a production process from order to fulfilment. Each of these processes is tailored for the organisation in question and is designed to perform in a consistent way despite the ups and downs of business or political life.

23.2.3 Toyota Production System

The benefits of applying lean thinking and lean principles were probably first best evidenced when applied at Toyota, later to be called the Toyota Production Systems (TPS) (Blach and Miller 2008). Fundamental to the approach was the design of equipment to stop automatically and call attention to problems immediately so that quality was not compromised. Such a system is predicated on jidoka or the intelligent use of people and technology as well as the possibility to halt the system at the first sign of an abnormality thus ensuring high quality. Another essential aspect is the elimination of muda or wastes, i.e. any activity, service or supply that consumes

Table 23.2 The evolution of lean thinking (adapted from Liker 2004; Joosten et al. 2008)

	Key developments of lean thinking			
Time line	1980–1990	1990–Mid 1990	Mid 1990–1999	2000+
Focus on approach	Production cell and line	Shop-floor	Value stream	Value system
	Highly prescriptive, using lean tools	Highly prescriptive, imitating lean organisations	Prescriptive, applying lean principles	Integrative, using different management instruments
Industry sector	Automotive-vehicle assembly	Automotive-vehicle and component assembly	Manufacturing in general—often focused on repetitive manufacturing	High and low volume manufacturing, extension into service sectors
Typical activity in this phase	Application of JIT—techniques, 5s, kanban	Emulation of successful lean organisations training and promotion, TQM	Improving flow; process-based improvements, collaboration in the supply chain	Improving customer value to improve organisational alignment. Decrease variability

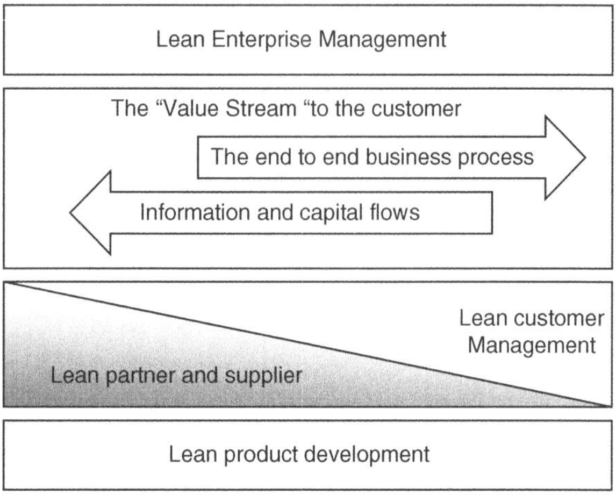

Fig. 23.1 Essentials of Womack and Jones's model (adapted from Womack and Jones 2003)

time, money or other resources and creates no or little value. Over the 80s Boeing applied the lean principles and TPS ideas to effect significant improvements including 45–75 % increases in productivity, 25–55 % cost reductions and 60–90 % throughput increases. At essence then at the heart of lean is the elimination of waste and the focus on quality outputs. These two aspects are critical to healthcare as they try to provide effective, efficient and efficacious healthcare delivery to patients.

23.3 Applying Lean to Nursing Care Contexts

To understand the application of lean thinking to healthcare and how to apply the TPS into healthcare contexts it is necessary to first identify the seven wastes in healthcare (Blach and Miller 2008) which include

1. Overproduction (e.g. ordering of duplicate tests)
2. Wasting time (e.g. patients waiting for treatments)
3. Waste of stock on hand (e.g. medications and other items that are stored but not used and then must be disposed of)
4. Waste of movement (e.g. time spent walking from one location to another)
5. Waste of defective products (e.g. misinformation or recording of wrong information on patient record)
6. Waste in transportation (e.g. moving patient unnecessarily)
7. Waste in processing (e.g. duplication of forms and redundant capture of information)

Generally, to address the wastes and inefficient processes a catalyst, usually in the form of a technology solution, is introduced into the system. This technology solution by its very disruptive nature affords all the opportunity to not only examine existing processes but also work to redesign and reengineer existing processes to

Table 23.3 Using the seven flows to improve performance (adopted from Blach and Miller 2008)

Flows	Improvement target
1. Patient flow	Provide patients with one location for all needs. Reduce patient travel and movement by 50 %
2. Clinician flow	Reduce clinicians' travel by 30 % at one site so they can be more attentive to patients' need
3. Medication flow	Reduce inventory and number of storage locations by 50 %. This results in significant reduction in movement
4. Supply flow	Reduce storage locations and inventory by 50 %, and greatly reduce movement of supplies
5. Information flow	Rely less on electronic information and more on personal contact with patients
6. Equipment flow	Use 25 % less equipment for the same volume of patients
7. Flow of process engineering	Reduce number of instruments used by 25 % for the same volume of patients by eliminating duplication and minimising movement of instruments

ensure efficient and effective as well as efficacious process ensue. Inextricably connected to the wastes in lean thinking are the seven flows (Blach and Miller 2008). Table 23.3 depicts these flows as they relate to healthcare contexts.

23.4 Case Study: IOPST Solution

Yin (1994) notes that useful approach to illustrate critical issues or key point is via an exemplar case study. To illustrate the potential benefits that lean thinking and lean principles can bring to nursing care we now present the case of the IOPST solution. IOPST is a new, unique nursing information system being designed and developed in Australia to be used at the point of care in both private and public hospitals. Information such as patient details, assessment and observation notes, care plans, treatment details, prescriptions and test results is currently handwritten in hospital wards in Australia. The developers envisage that this IOPST system will replace the paper-based nursing documentation in hospital acute wards. The system will be located at the patient's bedside and is designed to enable nursing staff to document key information, retrieve and share the documented information with other nursing, medical and allied health professionals to provide safe, continuous and high quality care for the patients in the ward. With its built-in intelligence, the system aims to evaluate, filter and process clinical data to ensure the quality of data entry, to support nursing decision making, to provide alerts and prompts to prevent treatment errors such as errors or omissions in medication administration, to improve nursing information access (real time and flexibility) and quality (accuracy and legibility), reduce time collecting information from multiple sources. Clearly then, not only does such a system represent a disruptive technology solution, but it can also serve as a catalyst from a lean perspective, in order to reexamine nursing processes to identify possibilities for eliminating waste, enhancing flows and thereby creating value.

Thus, an application of lean thinking perspectives (Womack and Jones 2003) in the context of nursing work in the example of the IOPST solution then would focus on the following:

1. Specify value from the customer's perspective: safe and high quality care, patient's well-being always considered and patient satisfaction maximised.
2. Identify all the steps in the value stream for the product or service (care service provision) and challenge those steps that do not create value. In general, the nursing process includes assessment, nursing diagnostic, planning of care, implementation and evaluation (Gardner 2003). Two steps of admission and discharge are added to include the arrival and departure of the patient to—and from—the care service. Based on the description of nursing process (Gardner 2003) and previous research into nurses' information needs and behaviours, the information tasks associated with each step are identified (see Table 23.4). Value creation and potential waste is also highlighted in another column.
3. Make the value-creating steps occur in flow continuously. In this project, system's capabilities are explored to enable a continuous flow of value adding steps (refer to Table 23.4).
4. Implement the pull system: system's capabilities will be pulled towards value creation along the value stream.
5. Repeat the process until a value is maximised with no waste. The before (pre-system) state is examined. The system will be introduced and evaluated through cycles of the above steps.

23.5 Discussion and Conclusions

First, it is important to examine how/why IOPST solution addresses the seven wastes as follows:

1. Overproduction
   - Duplication of data entry (e.g. assessments by multiple clinicians) is avoided through storage of and access to patient data in a single location
   - Real-time communication of investigations ordered, performed and results to avoid unnecessary repeated tests
   - Activities can be recorded real time for communication to the team to inform multiple caregivers simultaneously
   - Avoiding missed care can reduce the need for additional activities
2. Wasting time
   - Nurse can perform multiple functions at the bedside instead of leaving the patient to complete documentation or access information required to inform decision making
   - Reduce time searching for information—only if the user interface facilitates this—high face validity is needed and should be familiar by replicating what

Table 23.4 Patient journey, before & after using IOPST

Before						
Patient journey	Value creation from the patient's view	Nursing information behaviours	Value creation of nurses' information behaviours	Current wastes		
Patient admission	Patient is admitted into the care value chain Timely	Nurse collects information from different sources and in multiple formats • Verbal from patient and carer (family) • Verbal and written from previous care settings such as emergency department, operating theatre or another ward • Written from different health professionals e.g. Medical, allied health, general practitioner, specialist, community health • Written referral letters	Collected patient and clinical information will support problem identification (Kujala et al. 2006)	Waiting time (2): Nurse waits for information and searching multiple separate information sources e.g. paper-based documents, recorded by different disciplines. Nurse enters same information in multiple locations e.g. paper-based forms Waste of movements (4): Information often not located in single place- Time walking from one location to another to collect information. Looking for missing or misplaced information Waste of defective products (5): Human error in transcription resulting in inaccurate or lost information Waste in processing (7): Time and cognitive load to check, ensure accuracy and completeness of information from multiple sources and in multiple formats (paper, verbal, digital) Duplicating existing information e.g. transcribing from one form to another or information already available in another format Potential for error in data duplication and mismatches		

(continued)

Table 23.4 (continued)

Before						
Patient journey	Value creation from the patient's view	Nursing information behaviours	Value creation of nurses' information behaviours	Current wastes		
		• Medications the patient may have with them • Patient held records e.g. chronic disease plan Record patient information gathered from multiple other sources				
Handover at transfer of responsibility and accountability for patient care (ACSQH 2005) (e.g. change of shift, change of location)	Transfer of comprehensive patient information between clinicians to support safe ongoing care	All patient care information recorded accurately Care delivery and planning information up to date	Patient information required for ongoing care delivery is transferred between clinicians when responsibility and accountability for ongoing care is transferred	Overproduction (1): Duplication of existing information by creating notes to support verbal handover communication at transfer of care Waiting time (2): Delay in handover as information is gathered from multiple locations Waste of movements (4): Time spent locating required information from multiple sources and forms, and in the creation of duplicated information in a written form for handover Waste of defective products (5):		

				New information gathered during the handover process e.g. new problem or risk identification, problem solving or new solutions are often not stored or retained in the system Waste in processing (7): Patient care information collected at handover is stored on the nurse (e.g. on paper in pocket) and is potentially lost to the system		
Discharge	Patient's departure with improved health/ satisfaction	Collecting information from multiple sources. Documenting discharge	Information about patient's health outcome and follow up plan upon discharge	Waiting time (2): Waiting time to collect and read information from different paper forms/sources. Documentation time (administrative time)		

(continued)

Table 23.4 (continued)

After						
Patient journey	Value creation from the patient's view	Nursing information behaviours	Value creation of nurses' information behaviours	Waste reduction i.e. value created by IOPST	Waste introduced or remaining	Idealistic vision
Patient admission	Patient is admitted into the care value chain	Use the IOPST to link information from different clinicians and locations (such as patient, ED notes, medical or allied health staff, GP referral letters, family, medications, investigations and results) to a single source Document patient's information and clinical information from other sources into IOPST	Collected patient and clinical information will support accurate problem identification (Kujala et al. 2006)	Waiting time reduced (2) Reduce time to document information —use common text, checklists and pre-populated data field (Reduced Administrative time) Waste of movements (4): Access all information in single location —near the patient—Expected reduction of time walking from one location to another to collect information that can be retrieved from other systems that are integrated with IOPST Expected removal of waste of defective products (5): Reduce data collection if cross-linked information reduces duplication and risk of human error during transcription Missing information or inaccurate information can be validated and detected by IOPST Illegible information due to hand writing —removed Better information quality	Remaining Waiting time (2) Nurse waiting for information from other information systems not integrated with IOPST. Remaining Waste of movements (4): Time walking from one location to another to collect information not in IOPST. Introduced waiting time to log in and use IOPST, especially if the system has low responsiveness or not available. (this is repeated in other processes)	Patient information linked to populate the system. All these wastes are expected to be eliminated. Duplication is reduced as the system evolves and improves.

				Expected reduction of waste in processing (7): Multiple users can access the same information at the same time Decision support for common situations Reduced time and cognitive load because IOPST provides support to check and ensure accuracy and completeness of information from different sources and in multiple formats (different forms, verbal, digital). Potential data duplication and mismatches can be reduced/eliminated	System may be slow Enough hardware for the number of users Multiple users at the same time	
Handover at transfer of care	There is timely, relevant and structured clinical handover that supports safe patient care (ACSQHC 2011)	Nurses use the IOPST to guide and support verbal handover communication at transfer of care Nurses cross-check accuracy and content of information at transfer of care and update the system real-time	Patient information required for ongoing care delivery is transferred between clinicians when responsibility and accountability for ongoing care is transferred Nurses have documented evidence of clinical handover processes (ACSQHC 2011)	Remove overproduction (1) Clinicians access IOPST to access handover information to support verbal handover communication at transfer of care avoiding duplication of existing information Reduce waiting time (2) expected reduction of time required to prepare information for handover Remove waste of movements (4): Nurses can access the most up to date information from care records real time at the bedside to support verbal handover communication Reduce waste of defective products (5): New information gathered during the handover process e.g. new problem or risk identification, problem solving or new solutions can be entered real-time and retained in the system for ongoing care Remove waste in processing (7):		Up to date handover specific information is readily accessible to clinicians at the point of transfer of care new information gathered at transfer of care is recorded real time and immediately available on the system to guide ongoing care

(continued)

Table 23.4 (continued)

After						
Patient journey	Value creation from the patient's view	Nursing information behaviours	Value creation of nurses' information behaviours	Waste reduction i.e. value created by IOPST	Waste introduced or remaining	Idealistic vision
				Avoid loss of information collected at handover and not stored in the patient care record		Organisations have documentation of clinical handover processes in place (ACSQHC 2011)
Discharge	Patient's departure with improved health/ satisfaction	Collecting information from multiple sources Documenting discharge	Information about patient's health outcome and follow up plan upon discharge	Waiting time (2): Waiting time to collect and read information from different paper forms/sources Documentation time (administrative time)	Remaining waiting time (2): Waiting time to collect and read information from different paper forms/ sources Documentation time (administrative time)	Eliminated because information is available in the system Greatly reduced (for example, still has to do following up)

nurses already to in the first instance. Once nurses are engaged in using the system a process of change can be used to transition nurses work to a state of increased efficiency—expecting that initially it may take longer
- Single entry point—links all clinicians involved in patient care—no need to gather information from other documents or clinicians
- Nurse in charge can overview workload on the entire ward and reallocate or redistribute resources to priority activities

3. Waste of stock on hand

- Avoid costs for printing and storage of paper forms in multiple locations
- IOPST can replace multiple documents stored in multiple locations—at the bedside, nurses station—reduce requirement for storage locations
- Potential to link to inventory management to request and replace stock for patient activities

4. Waste of movement

- Geographical co-location of the device with the patient will increase time spent with the patient and reduce nurses unnecessary movement around the ward to search for the care records
- A single unit can provide access to information on multiple patients without the need for the nurse to enter the patient room—this allows for more efficient work planning and prioritisation of work
- Clinicians can access patient information from anywhere reducing need to travel to the patient unnecessarily

5. Waste of defective products

- Increase the accuracy of information, reduce misinformation if all data is stored and accessed from one location
- Standard forms and checklists can be used to reduce variation and improve compliance with recommended practices
- Single source of patient information for all clinicians reduces risk of misinformation over multiple verbal or written communications

6. Waste in transportation

- Electronic access to information—no need to retrieve patient notes
- Can identify location of the patient at any point in time

7. Waste in processing

- Link information typically recorded in multiple locations to a single point to avoid redundant capture of information through duplication of data entry and duplication of forms
- Reminders in the system to prompt activities in real time or at the best time
- Misinformation can be corrected and linked to all care records

The final state with the full scale implementation of the IOPST solution is yet to occur however it is envisaged to be an organisation-wide system (Fig. 23.2).

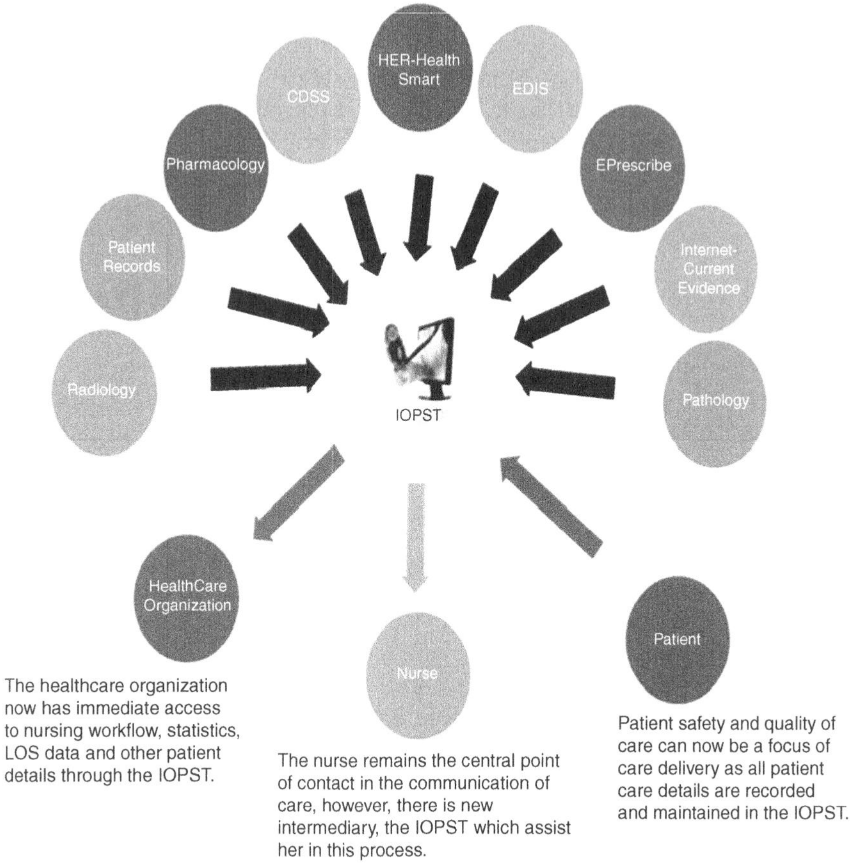

Fig. 23.2 Envisaged IOPST solution as an organisation-wide system

What this figure does underscore is that the current careful balancing act the nurse must perform to juggle the delivery of safe and quality patient care with the mindfulness of efficient and effective patient throughput through the hospital system will be impacted by the ability to access and receive more information with the introduction of the computer system (IPOST). Hence, we expect an increase in pressure on the nurse initially as she/he adapts to the world of the new technological system as well as maintaining this delicate balance. This could result in a perceived possible decrease in values of the system initially. However, over time once nurses have adapted to using the new system to manage care delivery more effectively, increase in safety and quality of care as well as efficiency in the coordination of patient throughput is expected. The ultimate goal is to decrease pressure on the nurse and increase the perceived value of the IOPST to the nurse.

Initial results from the early stages of a longitudinal study to introduce a disruptive technology solution into a nursing context, coupled with the literature (Tables 23.4 and 23.5) suggest that introducing an IOPST may serve as a catalyst to embrace

Table 23.5 Nursing process before & after using IOPST

Before						
Nursing process	Value creation from the patient's view	Nursing information behaviours	Value creation of nurses' information behaviours	Current wastes		
Assessment	Assessment and decision making time; passive care time (Kujala et al. 2006)	Locate the correct form to record each type of information Collect information based on physical assessment, observation and patient interview Documenting assessment results using the required forms	Patient can communicate about their health problems/concerns Information about the patient's health problem and risks is collected Assessment results are recorded to support problem identification	Waiting time (2): Hand writing information into documents (administrative time) Waste of defective products (5): Missing assessment steps/results or recording inaccurate, invalidated, incomplete results. Illegible hand written information Waste in processing (7): Time and cognitive load to source and interpret information from multiple sources Validate by cross-checking information from multiple sources and locations for accuracy, factuality, relevance Identify and correct mismatches in data		
Problem identification	Diagnostic time; passive care time (Kujala et al. 2006)	Accessing and retrieve all available information Integrate, interpret, analyse and synthesise the data Document the patient problems to inform care planning	Clarify patient's actual and potential problems Identify actual and potential clinical risks Identify interventions to meet care needs and avoid harm	Waiting time (2): Time to access information require to support decisions (for example diagnostic systems) Waste of movements (4): Time to access knowledge/expertise to interpret data Waste of defective products (5): Risk of making a wrong judgement		

(continued)

Table 23.5 (continued)

Before						
Nursing process	Value creation from the patient's view	Nursing information behaviours	Value creation of nurses' information behaviours	Current wastes		
		Locate additional information required for decision making in complex situations	Make decisions to prepare a plan for care Collaborate with other clinicians for shared problem solving of complex problems Access to expert advice, guidance on best practice	Waste in processing (7): Time and cognitive load to interpret, analyse and synthesise assessment results Waste in processing (7): Errors in documenting the diagnosis. Illegible handwriting		
Planning of care	Patient contribution to care plan that is acceptable to patient values and preferences Passive care time (Kujala et al. 2006)	Use clinical decision making (knowledge and experience) to plan care: set goals and prioritise activities, specify interventions and regime Document the care plan Create a feasible schedule for care delivery in collaboration with the patient and other carers	Set patient goals, desired outcome of care Create a care plan appropriate to meet the patient's health needs and preferences Safety checks to minimise clinical risks Collaborate with other clinicians for to deliver complex care	Waste of movements (4): Time to access knowledge/expertise to develop an appropriate care plan Waste of defective products (5): Care plan not matched to patient needs or available resources Waste in processing (7): Errors in documenting the care plan. Illegible handwriting Waiting time (2) Time to document care plan in paper (administrative time)		

Interventions	Health needs are met Harm and errors are avoided Care delivery uses evidence based best practices Timely interventions Active care time (Kujala et al. 2006)	Identify, analyse, interpret and deliver interventions in the care plan Document interventions and note response or change Modify interventions to individual patient characteristics, preferences and the environmental context context Verbal exchanging of information with other nurses, medical and allied health during ward rounds (Ballard 2006)	Knowledge of best practices to deliver care Care delivery is in compliance with policies, protocols and guidelines Nurse practical skill to deliver interventions Flexibility to adapt to change in patient and environmental factors Adapt to individual patient needs and preferences	Waste in processing (7): Mistiming of interventions in relation to other care activities Waste of defective products/care service (5): Mistakes, accidents, errors, incorrect care and discontinuity of care Omission of care Commission errors Waiting time (2) due to process inefficiency Waste of movements (4): Time walking from one location to another—looking for equipment needed to deliver care Time to contact different staff involved in care in order to collect information from them		
Evaluation	Patient care is measured. Passive care time	Reassessment Collect and analyse patient information, evaluate for change and interpret findings in relation to patient goals Searching for previous assessment results, noting and documenting changes Evaluating, revising and updating care plan	Continuous evaluation of care is conducted to obtain information about patient's response, change in the patient's condition and to inform revision of the care plan as needed	Waiting time (2): Documentation time using the assessment forms (administrative time) Waste of defective products (5): Missing (re)assessment steps/results or recording inaccurate, invalidated, incomplete results. Illegible information due to hand writing Waste in processing (7): Time and cognitive load to interpret and validate to ensure accuracy, factuality, relevance, and completeness of information from interviewing patient and from physical (re)assessments Possible mismatches in assessment results (data)		

(continued)

Table 23.5 (continued)

After						
Nursing process	Value creation from the patient's view	Nursing information behaviours	Value creation of nurses' information behaviours	Waste reduction i.e. value created by IOPST	Waste introduced or remaining	Idealistic vision
Assessment	Assessment and diagnostic time; passive care time (Kujala et al. 2006)	Searching for assessment forms Collecting information based on physical assessment, and observations, and interviews with patient Documenting assessment results into the forms	Patient can communicate about their health problems/concerns Information about the patient's health problem and risks is collected Assessment results are recorded to support nursing diagnosis	Waiting time (2) Reduced waste of defective products (5): Record patient information in one location that is linked to all information sources Missing assessment steps/results or recording inaccurate, invalidated, incomplete results to be validated and detected by IOPST Illegible information due to hand writing will be eliminated, hence better information quality Reduced Waste in processing (7): Time and cognitive load to interpret and validate to ensure accuracy, factuality, relevance, and completeness of information from interviewing patient and from physical assessment. → certain data can be validated by the system Possible mismatches in assessment results (data) → will be validated by IOPST	Introduced waiting time (2): Documentation time logging in and navigating the system to find the assessment forms in IOPST (administrative time) Introduced waste in processing (7): time to log in and navigate the system to find and use the assessment forms in IOPST (administrative time)	

Problem identification	Diagnostic time; passive care time (Kujala et al. 2006)	Searching for assessment results Accessing and retrieving assessment results Integrating, interpreting, analysing and synthesising the assessment results Documenting the diagnosis	Patient's actual or potential problems that can be responded to through nursing interventions are described Diagnosis to support the planning of care	Waiting time (2): Reduced Waste of movements (4) Select the combination of information to view specific to decision making Reduced Time to access knowledge/expertise to perform a nursing diagnosis can be reduced if IOPST provides help and access to Knowledge base Reduced Waste of defective products (5): single source of information can reduce error Reduced Risk of making a wrong judgement Reduced Waste in processing (7): Expected reduction of errors in documenting the diagnosis Eliminated Illegible handwriting. → better information quality	Remaining waiting time (2): Time to access other systems (for example diagnostic systems) Remaining Waste of movements (4) Time to access knowledge/expertise to perform a nursing diagnosis Remaining Waste of defective products (5): Risk of making a wrong judgement Remaining Waste in processing (7): Time and cognitive load to interpret, analyse and synthesise assessment results Remaining Waste in processing (7): Expected reduction of errors in documenting the diagnosis	Eliminated. Positive waste Greatly reduced Greatly reduced Positive waste Systematic fidelity Greatly reduced

(continued)

Table 23.5 (continued)

After						
Nursing process	Value creation from the patient's view	Nursing information behaviours	Value creation of nurses' information behaviours	Waste reduction i.e. value created by IOPST	Waste introduced or remaining	Idealistic vision
Planning of care	Passive care time (Kujala et al. 2006)	Using admission information and assessment results to plan care: setting and prioritising goals, identifying interventions Documenting the care plan	Appropriate care plan to enable safe and quality care that would address the patient's health problems	Reduced waste of movements (4): Time to access knowledge/expertise to develop an appropriate care plan if IOPST provides access to knowledge base (references) Communication of same plan to all clinicians involved in care Reduced waste of defective products (5): Reduced risk of making a wrong judgement—can this be validated by IOPST? Minimised waste in processing (7): Errors in documenting the care plan can be validated by IOPST illegible handwriting will be eliminated Removed waiting time (2): Time to document care plan in paper (administrative time)	Remaining waste of movements (4): Time to access knowledge/expertise to develop an appropriate care plan Remaining waste of defective products (5): Risk of making a wrong judgement Remaining waste in processing (7): *Semantic* errors in documenting the care plan Introduced Waiting time (2): Time to log in, navigate IOPST and document care plan using IOPST	Positive waste Increased value and decreased pressure Greatly reduced Greatly reduced Greatly reduced

Interventions	Active care time (Kujala et al. 2006)	Accessing, retrieving, and interpreting the initial and updated care plan Documenting the interventions and noting changes Documenting handover (pocket) notes and verbally exchange of handover notes. (Ballard 2006) Verbally exchanging of information with other nurses, medical and allied health during ward rounds and shifts. (Ballard 2006)	Clinical information enables safe and quality care. Patient's health is improved as informed interventions are carried out	Minimised waste in processing (7): Data duplication and mismatch between formal clinical notes, the care plan, and verbal exchange of handover note and observation notes between nurses (Ballard 2006) can be validated and detected by IOPST. Missing information or inaccurate post-hoc documentation, or lack of time to document. → Some can be addressed through real-time documentation Reduced waste of defective products/care service (5): Mistakes, accidents, errors, missed care, and discontinuity of care → can be reduced through the system reminders, alerts, information provision (charts), and validation Reduced Waste of movements (4): Reduced time walking from one location to another to collect information because it's not available in IOPST	Remained waste in processing (7): Missing information or inaccurate post-hoc documentation, or lack of time to document Remained waste of defective products/care service (5): Mistakes, accidents, errors, missed care, and discontinuity of care that are more difficult to avoid Remained waiting time (2) due to process inefficiency Remaining waste of movements (4): Time walking from one location to another or contacting different staff involved in care in order to collect information from them	Greatly reduced because of increased time Unavoidable Reduced Greatly reduced Reduced

(continued)

Table 23.5 (continued)

After						
Nursing process	Value creation from the patient's view	Nursing information behaviours	Value creation of nurses' information behaviours	Waste reduction i.e. value created by IOPST	Waste introduced or remaining	Idealistic vision
Evaluation	Patient care is measured. Passive care time	Documenting continuous observations and reassessments Searching for previous assessment results, noting and documenting changes Evaluating, revising and updating care plan	Care continuous evaluation is conducted to obtain information about changes and to support care plan revision as needed	Reduced Waiting time (2): Reduced documentation time using the assessment forms (administrative time) Minimised waste of defective products (5): Missing (re)assessment steps/results or recording inaccurate, invalidated, incomplete results will be validated and detected by IOPST Illegible information due to hand writing will be eliminated Waste in processing (7): Cognitive load to interpret and validate to ensure accuracy, factuality, relevance, and completeness of information from interviewing patient and from physical (re)assessments will be supported by IOPST Possible mismatches in assessment results (data) will be validated and detected by IOPST	Introduced waiting time (2) to log in, navigate and use the forms in IOPST Remaining waste of defective products (5): Eliminated Remaining waste in processing (7): Time and cognitive load to interpret and validate to ensure accuracy, factuality, relevance, and completeness of information from interviewing patient and from physical (re)assessments Introduced waiting time (2) to log in, navigate and find patient's history, timeline, clinical notes…	Greatly reduced Greatly reduced Positive waste greatly supported because all information is in one spot Reduced

lean thinking principles in nursing work processes; to decrease or eliminate wastes, create optimal work flows and increase value.

In closing however, we express caution. While clearly the IOPST solution has the potential to provide numerous benefits and possibilities to facilitate reengineering of nursing work processes, we also note that nursing care is not just complex, it is also chaotic and unpredictable; and hence, any technology solution must be flexible and robust enough to adapt to rapidly changing situations to support nursing care. To date this has been a key barrier and stumbling block for the use of technology in nursing work, and future studies are needed to test if the IOPST can meet this challenge.

References

Ammenwerth, E., Rauchegger, F., Ehlers, F., Hirsch, B., & Schaubmayr, C. (2011). Effect of a nursing information system on the quality of information processing in nursing: An evaluation study using the HIS-monitor instrument. *International Journal of Medical Informatics, 80*, 25–38.

Australian Commission on Safety and Quality in Health Care (ACSQHC). (2005). *Clinical handover and patient safety literature review report*. Canberra: Australian Government.

Australian Commission on Safety and Quality in Health Care (ACSQHC). (2011). *National safety and quality health service standards*. Sydney, NSW: Australian Commission on Safety and Quality in Health Care.

Ballard, E. C. (2006). Improving information management in ward nurses' practice. *Nursing Standard, 20*(50), 43–48.

Barach, P., & Johnson, J. K. (2006). Understanding the complexity of redesigning care around the clinical microsystem. *Quality & Safety in Health Care, 15*(1), i10–i16.

Ben-Tovim, D. I., Bassham, J. E., Bolch, D., Martin, M., Dougherty, M., & Szwarcboard, M. (2007). Lean thinking across a hospital: Redesigning care at the Flinders Medical Centre. *Australian Health Review, 31*(1), 10–15.

Black, J., & Miller, D. (2008). *The Toyota way to healthcare excellence* (p. 106). American College of Healthcare Executives Management Series, New York.

Capuano, T., Bokovoy, J., Halkins, D., & Hitchings, K. (2004). Work flow analysis. *Journal of Nursing Administration, 34*(5), 246–256.

Cornell, P., Herrin-Griffith, D., Keim, C., Petschonek, S., Sanders, A. M., D'Mello, S., et al. (2010). Transforming, nursing workflow, part 1. *The Journal of Nursing Administration, 40*(9), 366–373.

Crawford, J. (2008). *An introduction to lean thinking*. Touchpoint Ltd. Retrieved September 2012, from http://www.touchpointchange.co.uk/Lean%20Thinking%20Introduction%20TPC.pdf

Currell, R., & Urquhart, C. (2003). *Nursing record systems: Effects on nursing practice and health care outcomes*. Oxford: The Cochrane Library, Update Software.

Dowding, D., Mitchell, N., Randell, R., Foster, R., Lattimer, V., & Thompson, C. (2009). Nurses' use of computerised clinical decision support systems: A case site analysis. *Journal of Clinical Nursing, 18*, 1159–1167.

Gardner, P. (2003). *Nursing process in action*. Clifton Park: Thomson, Delmar Learning.

Guimarães, C., & De Carvalho, J. C. (2012). Lean healthcare across cultures: State-of-the-art. *American International Journal of Contemporary Research, 2*(6), 187–206.

Hannah, K. J., Ball, M. J., & Edwards, M. J. (2005). *Introduction to nursing informatics* (3rd ed.). New York: Springer.

Holm, J., & Ahlstrom, T. (2010). Lean, a tool set or a mind set? A healthcare case study. In C. M. Guimarães & J. C. de Carvalho (Eds.), *Modelling value contributions to management science* (pp. 313–328). New York: Springer.

Institute for Healthcare Improvement. (2010). *Transforming care at the bedside*. Retrieved March 4, 2010, from www.ihi.org/IHI/Programs/StrategicInitiatives/TransformingCareAtTheBedside.htm

Institute of Management. (2012). *The future of nursing*. Washington, DC: National Academy of Science.

Jones D., & Mitchell A. (2006). *Lean thinking for the NHS, a report commissioned by the NHS federation*. Retrieved September 2012, from http://www.leanuk.org/downloads/health/lean_thinking_for_the_nhs_leaflet.pdf

Joosten, T. C. M., Bongers, I. M. B., & Meijboom, B. R. (2008). Care programmes and integrated care pathways. *International Journal of Health Care Quality Assurance, 21*, 472–486.

Kirkley, D., & Rewick, D. (2003). Evaluating clinical information systems. *The Journal of Nursing Administration, 33*(12), 643–651.

Kujala, J., Lillrank, P., & Kronstrom, V. (2006). Time-based management of patient processes. *Journal of Health Organization and Management, 20*, 512–524.

Langowski, C. (2005). The times they are a changing: Effects of online nursing documentation systems. *Quality Management in Health Care, 14*(2), 121–125.

Larrabee, J. (2001). Evaluation of documentation before and after implementation of a nursing information system in an acute care hospital. *Computers in Nursing, 19*(2), 56–65.

Lee, T. T., Mills, M. E., Bausell, B., & Lu, M. H. (2008). Two-stage evaluation of the impact of a nursing information system in Taiwan. *International Journal of Medical Informatics, 77*(10), 698–707.

Liker, J. (2004). *The Toyota way—14 Management principles from the world's greatest manufacturer*. New York, NY: McGraw-Hill.

Marasovic, C., Kenney, C., Elliott, D., & Sindhusake, D. (1997). A comparison of nursing activities associated with manual and automated documentation in an Australian intensive care unit. *Computers in Nursing, 15*(4), 205–211.

Mazzocato, P., Savage, C., Brommels, M., Aronsson, H., & Thor, J. (2010). Lean thinking in healthcare: A realist review of the literature. *Quality & Safety in Health Care, 19*, 376–382.

Nahm, R., & Poston, I. (2000). Measurement of the effects of an integrated, point-of-care computer system on quality of nursing documentation and patient satisfaction. *Computers in Nursing, 18*(5), 220–229.

Sobek, D. K., & Lang, M. (2010). Lean healthcare: Current state and future directions. In A. Johnson & J. Miller (Eds.), *Proceedings of the 2010 industrial engineering research conference*, Cancun, MX.

Souza, B. U. (2009). Trends and approaches in lean healthcare. *Leadership in Health Services, 22*(2), 121–139.

Winch, S., & Henderson, A. J. (2009). Making cars and making health care: A critical review. *Medical Journal of Australia, 191*(1), 28–29.

Womack, J. P., & Jones, D. T. (2003). *Lean thinking: Banish waste and create wealth in your corporation* (2nd ed. Revised (Exp Upd.)). Simon & Schuster Audio.

Yin, R. (1994). *Case study research*. Thousand Oaks: Sage.

Young, T., & Mc Clean, S. (2008). A critical look at lean thinking in healthcare. *Quality & Safety in Health Care, 17*, 382–386.

Chapter 24
Using an e-Health Strategy to Facilitate the Design and Development of Effective Healthcare Processes

Raphael Di Francesco and Nilmini Wickramasinghe

Abstract The recent discussions and adoptions of e-health, and more specifically e-health solutions, within Australia and internationally can also be thought of as a catalyst for improving quality and safety, managing risk and controlling runaway cost in health care. e-Health, as defined by the World Health Organisation (WHO), is a combination of information and communication technologies in the health sector. The ultimate goal of e-health is to strengthen health systems, support delivery of high quality care, improve people's health and monitor public health (http://www.who.int/topics/ehealth/en/); thus it is also integrally connected with process improvement and hence the principles of lean thinking and six sigma are relevant in this context. The following looks at what Epworth HealthCare (Epworth) could adopt in order to embrace a complete e-health solution that is consistent with its expansion and redevelopment programme as well as the goal to provide the hospital with state-of-the-art facilities into the future. As noted in the literature, such an examination of a large-scale project represents a unique opportunity to implement digital clinical systems, which underpin redesigned workflow and processes to achieve improvements in standards, performance, quality of clinical care, safety and reduce risks. The case study thus outlines a proposed plan that focuses on developing an all encompassing e-health strategy to support the hospital's healthcare strategic plan and the goals set by the Epworth board (We note that this material is not necessarily representative of any plan that Epworth HealthCare will or plan to undertake. Rather, it is based on a project conducted by Raphael Di Francesco under the supervision of Prof. Nilmini Wickramasinghe. Moreover, the chapter is used solely for educational purposes and is in no way suggesting poor practice and/or improper management.).

R. Di Francesco • N. Wickramasinghe (✉)
Epworth HealthCare & Department of BITL & HIRi, RMIT University,
GPO Box 2476, Melbourne, VIC 3001, Australia
e-mail: nilmini.wickramasinghe@rmit.edu.au

N. Wickramasinghe et al. (eds.), *Lean Thinking for Healthcare*, Healthcare Delivery in the Information Age, DOI 10.1007/978-1-4614-8036-5_24,

Keywords e-health • Healthcare • PCEHR • KM • Knowledge management • Strategy definition • Strategic planning process • SWOT • TOWS • Six sigma

24.1 Introduction

Australia has been a relative laggard with regards to embracing the full potential of e-health, to date especially when compared to countries like Denmark, Norway and Singapore. Throughout Australia, some hospitals and healthcare centres are more invested than others with respect to technology initiatives to support and enable healthcare delivery. However, with the PCEHR going live as of July 2012 it is likely that this will change and interest in e-health will grow. The Australian healthcare environment is thus poised to stride forward into the next great frontier of e-health. At this time, many hospitals are evaluating how an e-health solution might be realised in their specific context. This chapter provides an analysis of what such an e-health solution might look like for Epworth HealthCare (Epworth), a private tertiary healthcare organisation in Melbourne, Australia. As a provider of acute medical, surgical and rehabilitation services, Epworth HealthCare, like other healthcare organisations today, is considering how it could improve healthcare services to facilitate superior healthcare delivery. The aim of this chapter is to determine what aspect(s) of e-health should be embraced in order to ensure the improvement of healthcare delivery. Further, the chapter will note why it behoves any healthcare organisation to consider principles of lean and six sigma in conjunction with the embracement of any e-health solution.

24.1.1 Chapter Objective

Epworth HealthCare is contemplating how best to embrace an effective and appropriate e-health solution. A first key step and critical success factor then becomes an assessment of a possible e-health solution and how this might/could fit with a strategic plan as the hospital decides how best to move forward. Hence, the following provides a possible e-health strategy and its plan which has as one of its core aims to improve and make clinical information more accessible, auditable, accurate and in support of an improved quality of care. The proposal also aims to examine how key knowledge management (KM) tools and principles can be applied in order to assist Epworth HealthCare to achieve its strategic goals.

This e-health strategy analysis then encompasses:

1. *A possible strategic analysis*, including the internal and external state of the hospital
2. *A possible strategic objective* that articulates a strategic intent for the hospital
3. *e-Health strategy definition*, which details possible strategic actions and priorities

24.1.2 Project Scope

The scope of this chapter includes:

- A review of Epworth's vision and goals
- An assessment of the current e-health services (what works and what could be improved)
- An identification of internal strengths and weaknesses
- An identification of possible opportunities and threats
- Development of a competitive advantage in matching strengths to identified opportunities
- Addressing any possible weaknesses and external threats
- Identifying possible strategy options
- Alignment with proposed objectives
- A suggested proposal of an e-health strategy and plan

The scope excludes:

- The e-health strategy and plan implementation
- The e-health strategy plan implementation costs
- The evaluation and control of the proposed e-health and plan strategy

24.1.3 Background

Epworth was established in 1920 by the Methodist Church as a community hospital. Through development and acquisition, Epworth has grown to encompass seven hospitals in the Melbourne Metropolitan area and is now Victoria's largest not-for-profit private healthcare group, renowned for excellence in diagnosis, treatment, care and rehabilitation. Over the years, Epworth has demonstrated leadership in acute healthcare delivery and rehabilitation. It is the first healthcare organisation to adopt surgical robotics in Australia and the first private hospital in Australia to perform cardiac surgery. Recently, to ensure it maintains its leadership position and also continues to meet the increasing healthcare requirements and treatment standards, the Board has adopted a strategy of expansion and redevelopment. The strategy aims to meet the needs of patients, staff and doctors by delivering 'world class' physical facilities and equipment. Due to the size of the strategic project and the investment required, two key challenges emerge:

Firstly, the management of the timing and budgeting; if not managed appropriately could represent a serious risk to the hospital

Secondly, Epworth's ability to maintain continuity of current service quality and performance might be challenged while progressing with the project

Fig. 24.1 The six phases of the strategic planning process

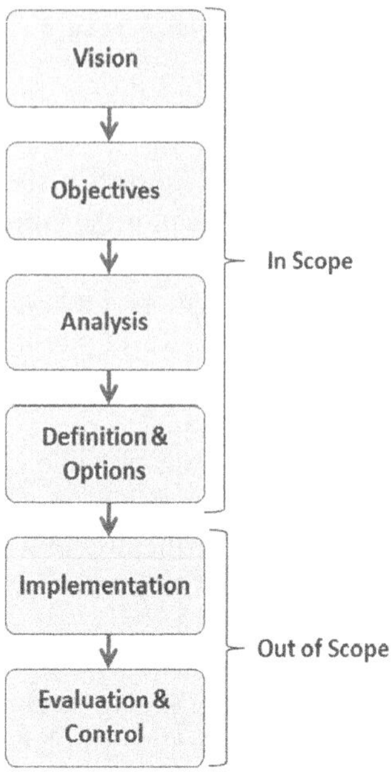

24.1.4 e-Health Strategy Project Processes

The development of the proposed e-health strategy will be based on two key processes:

1. The strategic planning process
2. The analysis approach process

24.1.5 Strategic Planning Process

While a common strategic planning process usually has six phases, the scope of this project only includes the first four phases of this process (Fig. 24.1), which were agreed by all project stakeholders.

Each of the phases of the strategic planning process has a purpose, deliverables and use tools as depicted in Fig. 24.2.

24.1.6 e-Health Strategy Analysis Key Informants

For completeness, Appendix A provides a schematic of the organisational structure while Appendix B provides the details of the actions taken to collect the information

	Vision	Objectives	Analysis	Definition & Options	Implement-ation	Evaluation & Control
Purpose	1. Understand what the organisation wants to be and when.	1. Confirm scope, objectives & deliverables; 2. Identify participants & their decision & input rights; 3. Define tasks, timing, roles, responsibilities & check points;	1. Identify internal Strengths & weaknesses; 2. Reveal opportunities and threats.	1. Develop a competitive advantage in matching strengths to identified opportunities; 2. Address weaknesses and external threats.	Out of Scope	Out of Scope
Deliverable	1. Business Vision Statements	1. Scope, objectives and deliverables; 2. Definition of tasks, timing, roles, responsibilities and check points;	1. Internal strengths & weaknesses 2. Internal & External environments	1. Strategy options; 2. Assumptions; 3. Strategy options evaluation 4. Identification and & resolution of key issues 5. Selected strategy; 6. Agreed objectives; 7. Resource allocation		
Tools	1. Stakeholders 2. Business Strategy	1. Stakeholders 2. PPT	1. SWOT 2. PPT 3. Five Forces	1. TOWS		

Fig. 24.2 *Source*: Adapted from Collins, J. & Porras, J. 'The Business Vision and Company Mission Statement'. 1996

required for the internal and external analysis, the responsibilities of the key informants and what were the deliverables that were used for the e-health strategy development.

24.2 Analysis Approach

It is important that a systematic and thorough analysis approach is structured and designed. The adopted approach conforms to current and recommended management techniques as well as making use of key analysis tools (Fig. 24.3).

24.2.1 Analysis Approach Process

The analysis approach process adopted includes:

1. Review the current e-health strategy.
2. Identify key hospital needs, duplication of effort, inconsistencies in practices, inefficiencies in business processes, opportunities for improved policies and/or procedures and any major issues and risks.
3. Propose a strategy to manage business operations knowledge and processes aligned with business needs, plans and governance.
4. Propose a strategy that enables the use of business operations knowledge and processes as a key strategic input for Epworth HealthCare.

Fig. 24.3 Analysis approach

The following approach was used to align the e-health operations knowledge and processes strategy with business needs, plans and governance requirements. In addition to this, key aspects of lean thinking most notably waste and inefficiencies were identified and ways and means for the e-health solution to resolve and/or address these issues were at all times investigated:

1. The 'internal analysis' identified strengths and weaknesses.
2. The 'external analysis' identified opportunities and threats.
3. The Strengths, Weaknesses, Opportunities and Threats (SWOT) analysis provided a structured summary of the most significant aspects of the internal and external analysis (strength and weakness) findings, and of the external analysis findings in order to summarise the internal and external analysis (opportunity and threat) findings.
4. The Threats, Opportunities, Weaknesses and Strengths (TOWS) analysis was used to identify strategy options, set clear assumptions, evaluate strategy options, identify and resolve key issues, select a strategy, and agree on objectives.

24.2.2 Internal Analysis

The internal analysis component consisted of four process workshops used to collect business information:

1. Executive interviews to understand Business and IT objectives

   (a) Collect existing business and IT documents (vision, mission, strategy, etc.)
   (b) Document the organisation's objectives and timing (current business plan)

2. Executive interviews to identify clinical IT decisions and their distribution across roles

   (a) Identify the major clinical IT decisions that are being made in the business; and
   (b) Identify who is deciding on what.

3. Individual and group discussions to assess the extent of IT alignment with clinical requirements/maturity model

   (a) Document the current organisation's level of maturity.

4. Assessment of what is, and what is not, working in the clinical environment

   (a) People

      - Resources
      - Skills and experience
      - Communication and management style

   (b) Process

      - Identify key clinical processes and gaps
      - Identify the extent to which the clinical strategy initiatives are dependent on IT (executive interviews)
      - Service availability
      - Operations services efficiently, effectiveness
      - Service levels

   (c) Technology

      - Identify key clinical IT applications and gaps
      - Identify the current state of the e-health information access and sharing with regard to complexity, aligned with business needs and compatibility between systems:

        – On-sites
        – Between sites
        – Off-sites (doctors, patients and others)

   (d) Security

      - Identify the current state of data protection, service continuity and recoverability.

24.2.2.1 Internal Analysis Tool

The tool used is called 'PPTS' People, Process, Technology and Security.

24.2.3 External Analysis

The external analysis component consists of a process model used to better understand the context in which the hospital operates.

1. Assessment of the influence of market five forces (Porter 2008)
    (a) Understand the nature of competition in the healthcare industry
    (b) Determine the national industry position of the hospital
    (c) Understand the competitive rivalry and healthcare industry growth
    (d) Understand the industry attractiveness
        - Industry core (key players)
        - Potential industry entrants
        - Substitutes or alternative health services
            – Not-for-profit hospitals
            – Public hospitals
            – Day care hospitals
            – Technology as a substitute to private hospital care (e.g. e-health)
        - Reduction in need/demand for private health services
    (e) Understand role and influence of suppliers
        - Medical practitioners
        - Consumable medical supplies
        - Medical equipment
    (f) Understand influence of buyers (patients).

24.2.3.1 External Analysis Tool

The tool used is Porter's five forces (Porter 2008).

24.2.4 SWOT Analysis Findings Summary

The SWOT analysis provided a succinct summary of the internal analysis and external analysis findings.

24.2.5 Assumptions and Premises

In developing this analysis, several assumptions have been made:

- The data gathered on Epworth HealthCare for analysis purposes are accurate.

- Epworth HealthCare is currently meeting their regulatory and compliance requirements—no compliance or other political issues were considered in the analysis of Epworth HealthCare.
- Epworth HealthCare has sufficient liquidity and managerial support to implement the changes recommended in this report.

24.3 Analysis Findings

Based on data collected and the use of various management tools, key findings at an internal and external level emerged.

24.3.1 Internal Analysis

Key aspects of the internal assessment are now presented.

24.3.1.1 Vision, Objective and Priorities

Epworth vision 'Achieving the Next Quantum Leap' in healthcare service, reach and capability, is facilitated by the 2009–2012 strategic framework.

The strategic framework supports Epworth's triple horizon. Figure 24.4 summarises the key elements that form the 2009–2011 strategic plan.

The five key principles which are diagrammatically represented in Fig. 24.5 support Epworth's strategic plan and specifically focus on the following:

1. The financial strength and stewardship of resources
2. The modern infrastructure and physical facilities
3. The integrated information systems and technology
4. The effective governance
5. The targeted marketing and business development

These principles aim to: facilitate Epworth's changes related to the recent acquisitions and building redevelopment; secure the current excellent patient satisfaction and clinical outcomes during the changes; and ensure the success of Epworth's strategic intent.

24.3.1.2 Strategic Goals

Priorities

There are several key strategic goal priorities which focus on continuing to:

STRATEGIC INTENT (Our consistent purpose)	**For Epworth HealthCare to be, and to be recognised as a pre-eminent provider of acute surgical, medical, obstetrics and rehabilitation services within Australia's health sector**
STRATEGIC PRIORITY AREAS (Prime areas of focus)	**Setting the Standard in Patient Service and Care** Providing a total experience of quality care and consistent high level of service for patients **Excellence In Core Clinical Services** Delivering excellence in clinical services supported by the establishment of Epworth HealthCare as a teaching organisation **Epworth's People: Leaders in their Fields** Partnering with leading medical specialists and becoming an 'employer of choice' for staff **Growing Reach in Service Provision** Building on existing services to maximise clinical and geographic growth opportunities
CORE ENABLERS (How we deliver it)	Financial Strength Wise: Stewardship of Resources Modern and Renewed Infrastructure and Physical Facilities Integrated Information Systems and Technologies Effective Governance Targeted Marketing and Business Development

Fig. 24.4 Epworth 2012 strategic framework

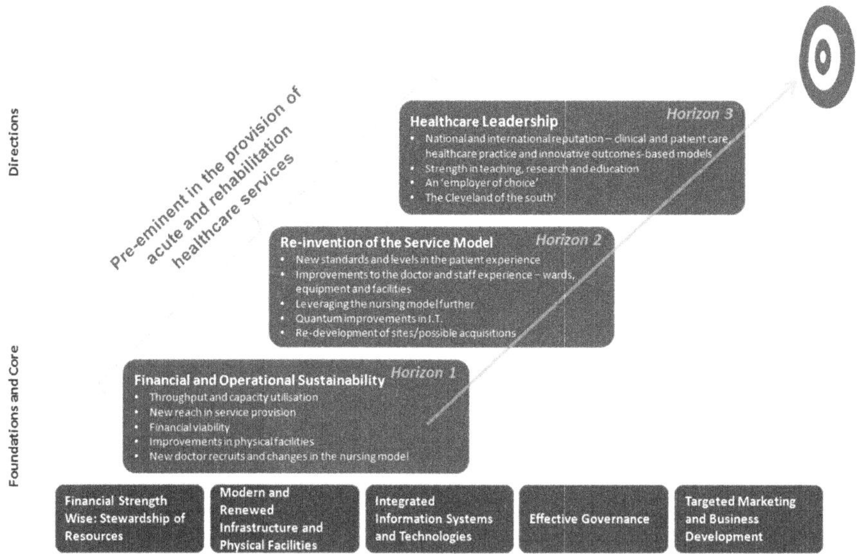

Fig. 24.5 *Source*: Adapted from Epworth Strategic Plan—Principles (2011)

1. Be a leading private hospital group in Victoria.
2. Provide a total experience of quality care for patients.
3. Deliver a consistently high level of service to patients.
4. Create a profile that attracts and retains high calibre doctors and staff in all areas.

5. Establish and promote Clinical Institutes.
6. Develop Epworth as a Teaching Hospital.
7. Instill a clinical culture based on evidence and outcomes.
8. Build a long term and effective research programme.

Core Enablers

There are several key core enabler goals which include and continue to:

1. Achieve financial performance outcomes in line with industry best practice.
2. Ensure an effective treasury function that allows ECH to meet all its obligations as they fall due.
3. Optimise fundraising opportunities through Epworth Medical Foundation (EMF).
4. Undertake major rebuilding and redevelopment programmes where/when required.
5. Refurbish, where required, existing facilities to create more attractive, functional and sustainable facilities across each Epworth campus.
6. Ensure state-of-the-art facilities, instrumentation and equipment.
7. Provide robust, efficient and standardised information systems to meet business needs.
8. Enable a dynamic and integrated information management environment.
9. Ensure that risks are identified and strategies implemented to manage all areas of potential risk.
10. Increase Epworth's reputation and recognition in target markets.
11. Build market knowledge and relationships across the health sector.
12. Identify and grow business development opportunities in line with the organisation's strategic intent and goals.

24.3.1.3 Clinical Systems Alignment/Requirements

The analysis of the clinical systems alignment/requirements showed while Epworth HealthCare has developed a strategic vision, teaching hospital strategy and business strategy, it now needs to further refine and develop a suitable clinical strategy that supports the organisation strategy with respect to clinical information systems and e-health in general with a forward looking focus (Fig. 24.6).

24.3.2 What Is Working and What Requires Improvement

Epworth clinical systems were reviewed through four key dimensions: effectiveness, efficiency, alignment and growth (Fig. 24.7). The following figure summarises the findings.

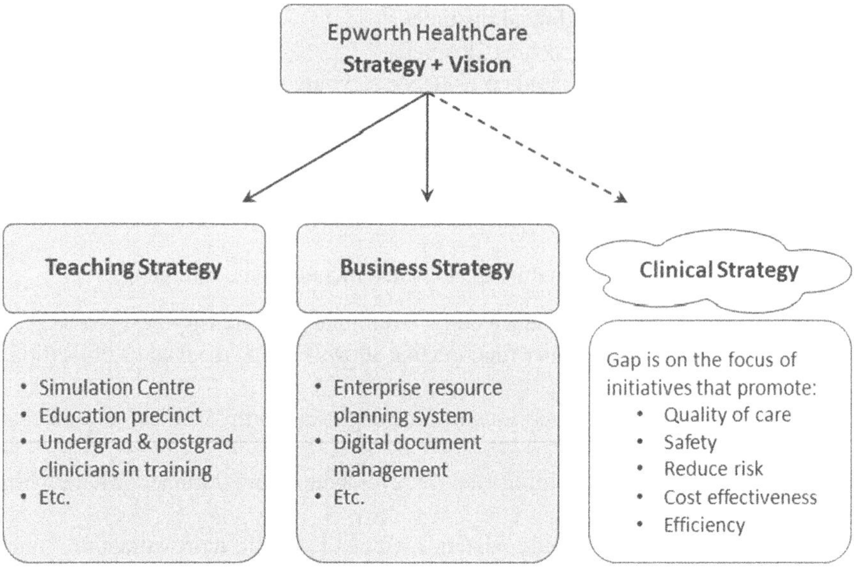

Fig. 24.6 Clinical strategy alignment

	Effectiveness	Efficiency	Alignment	Growth / Scalability
Process	× Localised e-health processes. × Limited input on information captured electronically. × With the exception of one hospital, the medical record is only available in paper format. × Information is only available on-site.	✓ SLA with the business. ✓ Good governance practices.	✓ KPIs for business service delivery defined. × Quality of care is measured, however tools to measure is limited. × Limited tools available to assess process performance in general. ✓ Formal change management process including business approval (ITIL).	× IT clinical decision system at infancy stage. × No central management or strategy of knowledge.
Technology	✓ Resilient and redundant Data Centre infrastructure (telecommunication, SAN, backup, archiving, virtualisation...).	× Localised e-health solutions. × Limited focus on establishing a consolidated healthcare ICT solution architecture. × Limited integration of healthcare solutions and of patient's records.	× With the exception of one hospital which is able to provide a scanned copy of the Medical Record post discharge, the Medical Record is only available in paper format. × These records are only available and can only be accessed on site.	× Limited use of IT technology to provide a secure access of patient's medical records anytime (as soon as available) and from anywhere (outside of the hospital) for care providers.
People	✓ Focussed on project delivery. ✓ Great technical skills and capabilities. × Limited internal service agility.	× Lack of agility in the IT service delivery.	× Insufficient visibility of IT achievements. × No e-health strategy.	× Governance and leadership of IT requires strengthening. × Limited direction and priorities given to IT in relation to e-Health.
Security	✓ Secured system environments (firewall project in progress). ✓ Elaborated data protection (clustering, backup, archiving and sites' replication). ✓ Successfully tested (yearly) Disaster Recovery (DR) plan and processes. The DR plan focuses on restoring systems after a disaster and is closely related to the BC plan	× Limited IT and business co-ordination for Business Continuity (BC) situations. The BC plan is initiated when the ability to conduct business operation is impacted. Systems may or may not be impacted in which case DR would occur concurrently.	× Limited integration of Business and IT BC plan and procedures.	✓ Established information security systems.

Fig. 24.7 People, process, technology and security analysis. *Source*: Adapted from Molla (2008)

It is important to note here that such an analysis must be taken in the context of the healthcare industry in Australia. As noted earlier, Australia has yet, to date, to embrace e-health in a significant fashion and is, when compared to countries like Denmark and Norway, an e-health laggard. In such a context the analysis presented in Fig. 24.7 is consistent with the state that the country is at with respect to e-health adoption. In fact, in many areas Epworth might even be thought to be at the higher echelons with regard to IS/IT adoption and use. However, if the goal is to develop a complete e-health solution, clearly Fig. 24.7 highlights areas on which focus must be given. In addition, it is useful to note that Fig. 24.7 also highlights a good foundation on which to develop and build such an enterprise wide e-health solution.

24.3.3 External Analysis

24.3.3.1 Influence of Market Forces

This analysis method considers the opportunities and threats presented by the five dimensions illustrated in Fig. 24.8.

Note: the below icons have been used to represent the current the state of business risk.

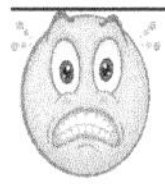
Increased risk to Epworth

Decreased risk to Epworth

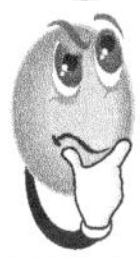
Risk neutral to Epworth

24.3.3.2 Threat of New Entrants and Substitution

The power against substitutes and new entrants may come from adopting a pioneering and innovative culture, retaining the best staff and emphasising the hospital reputation (Perrott and Hughes 2005). However, high capital costs; the difficulty in finding and building new hospitals in locations close to viable markets;

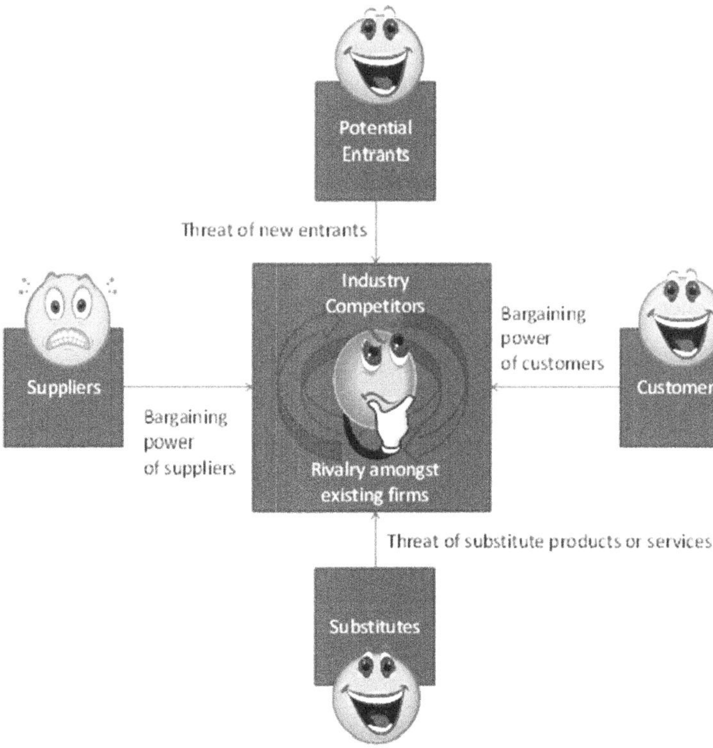

Fig. 24.8 Porter's five forces analysis summary. *Source*: Adapted from Harvard Business School (2005)

and the recruitment of nursing and hospital staff that suffers from a critical shortage represents a formidable hurdle for potential new entrants to the industry (AHWAC 2010; Perrott and Hughes 2005).

24.3.3.3 Bargaining Power of Suppliers

e-Health can give a competitive advantage through supplier integration with resulting cost-efficiencies. This variable has the potential to be most critical for members of the 'for profit' private hospital industry in managing viable hospital units. Individual organisations rely on key groups to supply quality and timely services and products to the various hospital locations.

Medical practitioners—Having a strong network of referring doctors is a fundamental prerequisite to viability and success. Case studies show that without the support of doctor groups this can lead to serious underperformance of both individual hospitals and company groups in the healthcare industry.

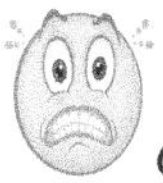*Consumable medical supplies*—e-Health can give competitive advantage through supplier integration with resulting cost-efficiencies (Mitchell and Cottrill 2002).

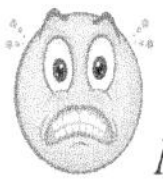*Medical equipment*—Over time the health industry has become increasingly dependent on advancing technology by way of high capital cost equipment. This equipment has been used for diagnostics and treatment of medical conditions with limited suppliers; subsequently, creating limited opportunity for competitive buying. In summary, the suppliers have the potential to impact on industry players in a negative way. Even if this influence is not activated, they hold a latent power which can be used in negotiating conditions of supply to industry members (Perrott and Hughes 2005).

24.3.3.4 Bargaining Power of Buyers/Patients

e-Health has the potential to significantly facilitate the development of the public health value proposition. This development has the potential to improve the quality of care and subsequently the quality of life (World Health Organisation 2004).

However, the ability of buyers/patients in isolation to impact on industry players in a negative way to shareholder interests or assets and returns is low (Mitchell and Cottrill 2002).

24.3.3.5 Intensity of Rivals

e-Health can facilitate the differentiation from the competition by emphasising the brand or reputation. e-Health can also be a medium through which inefficiencies and costs can be reduced, facilitating the access to a competitive advantage (Mitchell and Cottrill 2002).

24.3.3.6 Threat of Substitute Products or Services

The substitutes of health products or services as well as the threat and influence are shown in Fig. 24.9.

Substitute Products or Services	Threat	influence
Not for profit hospitals	Medium to high	Hospital location
Public hospitals	Low to medium	Type of service
Day care hospitals	Medium	Type of service and location
Technology as a substitute to private hospital care	Low	
Reduction in need/demand for health services	Nil	

Fig. 24.9 Five forces approach to the Australian private hospital industry (Perrott and Hughes 2005)

	Helpful	Harmful
Internal Origin	**Strengths**	**Weaknesses**
	• Resilient and redundant Data Centre infrastructure; • Established information systems security; • Formal change management practices including business approval (ITIL); • Great technical IT skills, project delivery capabilities and governance practices; • Agreed service levels and KPIs; and • Successfully tested (yearly) DR plan and processes.	• Silo-ed e-Health information systems and data; • Few specific e-health and Knowledge Management (KM) strategies; • Limited direction and priorities given to IT in relation to e-Health; • No e-health strategy; • Limited integration of healthcare solutions and of patient's records; • Limited use of IT technology to provide a secure access of patient's medical records anytime (as soon as available) and from anywhere (remote/mobile) for care providers; and • Limited IT and business co-ordination for Business Continuity (BC) situations.
External Origin	**Opportunities**	**Threats**
	• Be a key 'early' player in the PCEHR NEHTA initiative • Lead the improvement of standards, performance, quality of clinical care, safety by implementing digital clinical systems; and • Lead the implementation of digital clinical systems (as part of the hospital expansion and redevelopment program).	• Inability to meet healthcare services needs and expectations of Australian's patients, clinicians, hospital staffs and key stakeholders; • inability to provide cost effective healthcare service for Australians • Inability to address pressure/stress of the hospital clinicians and staffs; and • Not being prepared / ready to integrate with NEHTA 's PCEHR.

Fig. 24.10 SWOT analysis findings. *Source*: Adapted from Humphrey, A., 'SWOT Analysis', 2004

Based on these findings, a combined threat of substitutes impacting on industry players in a negative way to shareholder interests, assets or returns is low. Consequently, this element is favourable to industry members. Moreover, the power against new products or services may be obtained by adopting a pioneering and innovating approach to health services and retaining the best staff (Mitchell and Cottrill 2002).

24.3.4 SWOT Analysis Findings

The SWOT analysis provides a structured summary of the most significant aspects of the internal analysis (strength and weakness) findings and external analysis (opportunity and threat) findings (Fig. 24.10).

24.4 e-Health Strategic Objectives

The following strategic objectives were identified for Epworth HealthCare through the analysis approaches detailed in Sect. 24.4 of this report. The e-health strategy and implementation approach examined below directly support these objectives:

- Facilitate and support the hospital strategic plan to attain the goals set by the Epworth board
- Continuously improve and make clinical information more accessible, auditable, accurate and in support of an improved quality of care
- Continuously improve standards, performance, quality, safety, effectiveness, efficiency and reduce risks of clinical care

24.5 e-Health Strategy Definition

There exist many possible definitions of an e-health strategy. What is important is that the chosen definition is consistent with the goals and objectives of the specific organisation and is synergistic with other strategies and plans.

24.5.1 Strategy Alternatives (TOWS Analysis)

The following quadrant diagram depicts the four e-health strategy alternatives that are possible for Epworth (Fig. 24.11).

24.5.1.1 SO: Maxi–Maxi

Based on the findings of the TOWS's matrix Strength Opportunities (SO) quadrant, the 'Maxi–Maxi' strategy offers a strategy option that is very well aligned with: Epworth vision, Epworth 2012 Strategic Framework and the 2009–2011 strategic plan and objectives. It will also enable the delivery of the agreed critical success factors.

24.5.1.2 WO: Mini–Maxi

Similarly to the 'Maxi–Maxi' strategy option, the 'Mini–Maxi' strategy offers a proposed strategy option that is well aligned with the needs of Epworth and its future direction (Fig. 24.12).

	External Opportunities (O) 1. Be a key 'early' player in the PCEHR NEHTA initiative 2. Lead the improvement of standards, performance, quality of clinical care, safety by implementing digital clinical systems; and 3. Lead the implementation of digital clinical systems (as part of the hospital expansion and redevelopment program).
Internal Strengths (S) 1. Resilient and redundant Data Centre infrastructure; 2. Established information systems security; 3. Formal change management practices including business approval (ITIL); 4. Great technical IT skills, project delivery capabilities and governance practices; 5. Agreed service levels and KPIs; and 6. Successfully tested (yearly) DR plan and processes.	**SO - Maxi-Maxi strategy** use **strengths** to maximize **opportunities** 1. Use the already established ICT foundations and the hospital expansion and redevelopment program as an opportunity to implement integrated e-health solutions; 2. Use the well established ICT foundation , the Great technical IT skills, the project delivery capabilities and the good governance practices to implement leading e-health solutions aligned with the NEHTA PCEHR initiative. 3. Use the existing intranet and internet (WEB) infrastructure as delivery tools to provide secure access to hospital's e-health service anytime anywhere; 4. Use the existing infrastructure, health information knowledge bases to build knowledge sources for care providers and patients; 5. Use the already established ICT infrastructure to facilitate the centralisation and the information flows between hospitals to improve care planning, coordination and decision making at the point of care; and 6. Use the good change management practices to facilitate the implementation and adoption of e-health solutions.
Internal Weaknesses (W) 1. Silo-ed e-Health information systems and data; 2. Few specific e-health and Knowledge Management (KM) strategies; 3. Limited direction and priorities given to IT in relation to e-Health; 4. No e-health strategy; 5. Limited integration of healthcare solutions and of patient's records; 6. Limited use of IT technology to provide a secure access of patient's medical records anytime (as soon as available) and from anywhere (remote/mobile) for care providers; and 7. Limited IT and business co-ordination for Business Continuity (BC) situations.	**WO - Mini-Maxi strategy** minimise **weaknesses** by taking advantage of **opportunities** 1. Minimise W1, 2, 3, 4 and 5 by prioritising the implementing of digital clinical systems aligned with the NEHTA PCEHR initiative; and 2. Minimise the lack of a KM strategy by centralising, improving business process standards and process management.

Fig. 24.11 TOWS matrix 1/2. *Source*: Adapted from Mind Tools (2008)

	External Threats (T) 1. Inability to meet healthcare services needs and expectations of Australian's patients, clinicians, hospital staffs and key stakeholders; 2. inability to provide cost effective healthcare service for Australians; 3. Inability to address pressure/stress of the hospital clinicians and staffs; and 4. Not being prepared / ready to integrate with NEHTA 's PCEHR.
Internal Strengths (S) 1. Resilient and redundant Data Centre infrastructure; 2. Established information systems security; 3. Formal change management practices including business approval (ITIL); 4. Great technical IT skills, project delivery capabilities and governance practices; 5. Agreed service levels and KPIs; and 6. Successfully tested (yearly) DR plan and processes.	**ST - Maxi-Mini strategy** use **strengths** to minimize **threats** 1. Use the well established ICT foundation and the Great technical IT skills and project delivery capabilities to establish compatibility between the Epworth ICT and the NEHTA PCEHR architecture.
Internal Weaknesses (W) 1. Silo-ed e-Health information systems and data; 2. Few specific e-health and Knowledge Management (KM) strategies; 3. Limited direction and priorities given to IT in relation to e-Health; 4. No e-health strategy; 5. Limited integration of healthcare solutions and of patient's records; 6. Limited use of IT technology to provide a secure access of patient's medical records anytime (as soon as available) and from anywhere (remote/mobile) for care providers; and 7. Limited IT and business co-ordination for Business Continuity (BC) situations.	**WT - Mini-Mini strategy** minimise **weaknesses** and avoid **threats** 1. Rationalise healthcare efficiency's key issues to reduce pressure/stress of the hospital clinicians and staffs; and 2. Extend deployment of effective existing e-health solutions across all hospitals to improve quality of healthcare services and increase safety of patients.

Fig. 24.12 TOWS matrix 2/2. *Source*: Adapted from Mind Tools (2008)

24.5.1.3 ST: Maxi–Mini

The Strengths and Threats (ST) quadrant focuses on utilising the skilled hospital IT resources and the well established ICT infrastructure to achieve the hospital goals. However, this fails to address most of the identified weaknesses. Moreover, it fails

Objectives	Use strengths to maximise opportunities	Minimise weaknesses by taking advantage of opportunities	Use strengths to minimise threats	Minimise weaknesses and avoid threats
Facilitate and support the hospital strategic plan to attain the goals set by the Epworth board	√	√		
Improve and make clinical information more accessible, auditable, accurate and in support of an improved quality of care	√	√		√
Improve standards, performance, quality, safety, effectiveness, efficiency and reduce risks of clinical care.	√	√	√	√

Fig. 24.13 Business objectives against e-health strategy options

to meet the e-health objectives, most of the e-health critical success factors, and it does not support the hospital's vision and strategic plan.

24.5.1.4 WT: Mini–Mini

The Weaknesses and Threats (WT) quadrant is concerned with defensive strategy. This can be implemented to minimise current service issues and to 'buy-time' in order to implement a strategy that—at the appropriate time—will meet all the strategy objectives and critical success factors. Like the 'Maxi–Mini' strategy option, the 'Mini–Mini' strategy option, fails to meet the e-health objectives and most of the e-health critical success factors, and does not support the hospital vision and strategic plan.

24.5.2 Strategy

To determine which of the four strategy options—resulting from the TOWS analysis—provides the most benefits and will best support Epworth HealthCare's mission and vision, each of the TOWS strategy option has been assessed against the business objectives and the agreed critical success factors. When there is a match between the option and the objective or the critical success factors, a point is given to the strategy option. The strategy that offers the highest score is considered the best option. The figures below show these results (Figs. 24.13 and 24.14).

Based on the business objectives and on the outcome of the TOWS analysis, the recommended e-health strategy is to use strengths to maximise opportunities by applying the following principles.

Critical success factors	Use strengths to maximise opportunities	Minimise weaknesses by taking advantage of opportunities	Use strengths to minimise threats	Minimise weaknesses and avoid threats
Facilitate and support the business strategy and goals	√	√		
Increase patient, clinicians, hospital staffs and key stakeholders satisfaction	√	√		√
Develop superior quality of care	√			
Facilitates clinical decisions	√			
Reduces clinical risks	√	√	√	√
Provides enterprise wide e-health solutions	√	√		

Fig. 24.14 Critical success factors against strategy options

SO - Maxi-Maxi strategy
use **strengths** to maximize **opportunities**

1. Use the already established ICT **foundations** and the hospital expansion and redevelopment program as an opportunity to implement e-health solutions;
2. Use the already established ICT infrastructure to facilitate the centralisation of information and the **information sharing** between hospitals to improve care planning, coordination and decision making at the point of care;
3. Use the existing intranet and internet infrastructure as **delivery tools** to provide secure access to hospital's e-health services anytime anywhere;
4. Use the existing infrastructure, health information knowledge bases to build **knowledge sources** for care providers and patients;
5. Use the good **change management** practices to facilitate the implementation and **adoption** of e-health solutions; and
6. Use the well established ICT foundation , the Great technical **IT skills**, the **project delivery capabilities** and the good **governance practices** to implement leading **e-health solutions** aligned with the NEHTA PCEHR initiative.

Fig. 24.15 Proposed e-health strategy principles

24.5.3 Strategy Principles

The following principles demonstrate how the e-health strategy could help Epworth to meet its business goals (Fig. 24.15).

24.6 Strategy Recommendations

The utilisation of technology in most hospital activities suggests that the e-health strategy directly impacts the hospital's competitive advantage. It is expected that the following proposed recommendations will impact on the competitive

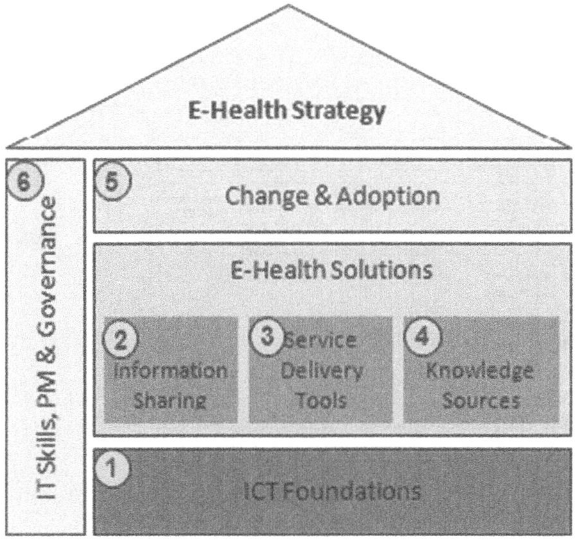

Fig. 24.16 Proposed e-health strategy blocks/principles. *Source*: Adapted from National e-health strategy work streams

advantage of Epworth by incrementally changing the activities themselves or by making possible new configurations of the value chain (Porter 2006). Moreover, it is noted that as the Australian healthcare scene changes and becomes more e-health reliant then the adoption of an e-health strategy will be a competitive necessity not a competitive advantage per se. Consequently, the strategy recommendations developed, if implemented, will serve to benefit healthcare providers and patients (see diagram below). These recommendations aim to enable a value-based competition on health plans, healthcare provider and patients (Porter 2006).

The proposed strategy is made of six blocks that directly relate to the e-health strategy principles (Fig. 24.16).

To implement the proposed e-health strategy, the following recommendations concerning processes, technologies and people are made:

24.6.1 Processes

- The proposed e-health strategy will be implemented by means of programmes, budgets and procedures.
- Use the hospital Internet and Intranet for knowledge sharing dissemination of corporate and business information.
- Streamline operation standard and processes by improving policies and procedures.

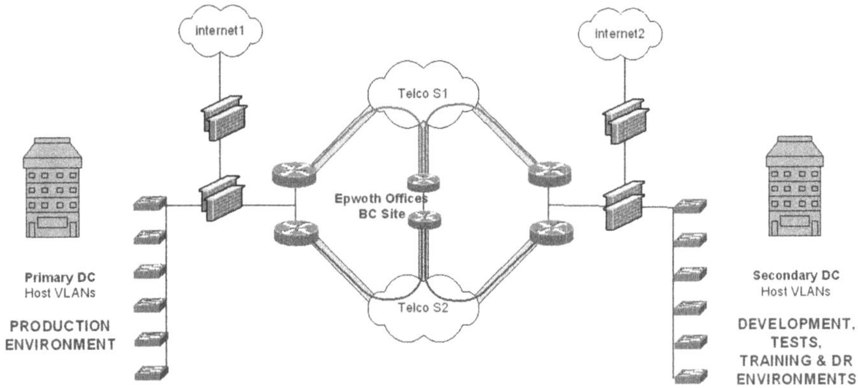

Fig. 24.17 e-health systems architecture

24.6.2 *Technologies*

1. The proposed e-health systems architecture (Fig. 24.17) is the first block (ICT foundations) of the proposed strategy. It encompasses elements from the e-health strategy recommendations as well as the network communication changes required for the strategy elements implementation. Its simplified design—which has no single point of failure—offers the foundation for a secure 24/7 operation.
2. Use the current hospital Intranet as a repository tool for the business knowledge and processes management.
3. Provide secure access, anytime, anywhere, to hospital knowledge for hospital staff, doctors and ICT support resources via devices such as desktops, iPhone and iPads.

24.6.3 *People*

1. The e-health strategy implementation will involve the hospital's resources and skills, and the great Epworth project delivery capability to achieve agreed objectives.
2. Business units will be empowered and responsible for keeping their knowledge repository up-to-date.

24.7 Strategy Implementation and Evaluation

To be successful, any strategy implementation needs to be supported by a project plan structured around the e-health strategy recommendations. The implementation project will benefit from both the business stakeholders support and an agreed budget.

The project activities will have to comply to change management and governance requirements. Once implemented it is important that Epworth has the capability to measure the ongoing performance of the e-health strategy and the impact of the recommended e-health strategy changes. It is suggested that Epworth uses the Boyd's Observe, Orient, Decide, and Act (OODA) loop concept to ensure that the proposed strategy still meets the defined e-health objectives, delivers the critical success factors and enables Epworth to achieve its goals (Von Lubitz and Wickramasinghe 2006). Measuring its performance not only assists in the guidance and implementation of future strategy and capacity planning, but can have more immediate benefits in providing early warning indicators for issues, and improving the business–IT relationship.

24.7.1 Implementation

The selected strategy will be implemented by means of programmes, budgets and procedures. The implementation will involve the organisation's resources and motivation of the staff to achieve objectives.

24.7.2 Implementation Key Activities

The implementation of the proposed e-health strategy has 11 key activities:

1. Agreement on a strategy
2. Consolidation of infrastructure and management
3. Establish e-health infrastructure and standards
4. Establish operations processes
5. Establish information sharing
6. Establish delivery tools
7. Establish knowledge sources
8. Manage change and adaptation
9. Manage IT skills, project management and governance
10. Implementation of e-health systems
11. Handover to ongoing management

24.7.3 e-Health Strategy Road Map

To achieve the e-health strategic objectives and to facilitate a continuity of service and reduce the risks during the transition, the following phases and timing are proposed (Fig. 24.18).

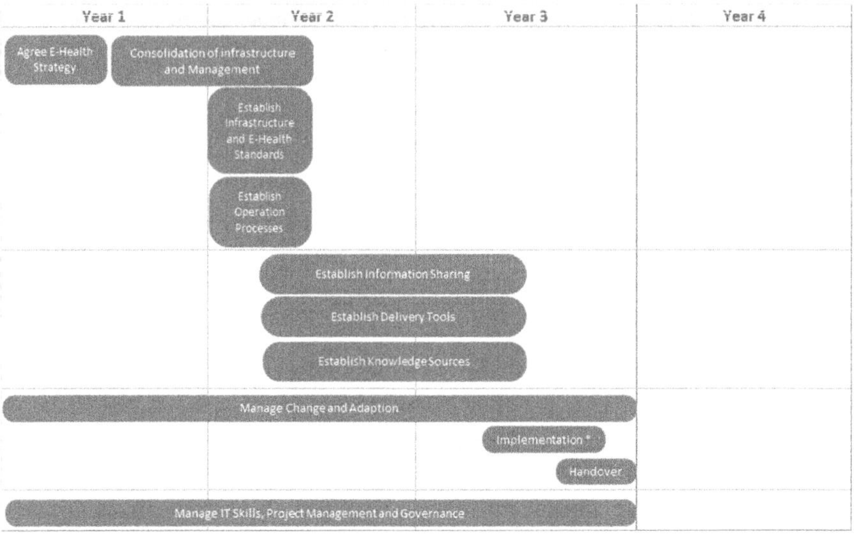

Fig. 24.18 e-health strategy road map. *Asterisk*: The implementation may appear ambitious but is doable if all key success factors are in place or else conservative duration for implementation would be 2.5 years and by then it is likely the window of opportunity to realise the full competitive advantage may be lessened

24.8 Conclusions

This chapter sets out to illustrate a systematic and careful approach to developing and designing an appropriate e-health strategy. In so doing, it has also served to illustrate how the principles of lean thinking and six sigma are also relevant, most especially, but not limited to the fact that the embracement of an e-health solution necessitates redesign of processes and an opportunity to reduce wastes and streamline patient and information flows to ensure effective, efficient high quality, value-driven healthcare delivery ensues.

Aligned with Epworth's vision and objectives, the proposed e-health strategy uses strengths to maximise opportunities. To ensure that the e-health strategy meets its objectives and critical success factors, it is recommended to implement the proposed six e-health strategic principles. These e-health strategic principles are supported by a number of recommendations encompassing ICT people, process and technology.

Finally, the analysis process of the strategic planning process has revealed a number of Knowledge Management (KM) gaps in processes, technologies and people. These gaps directly affect the effectiveness, efficiency, hospital growth, development and operation's cost. The proposed knowledge management tools (Intranet and Internet) will be particularly suited to provide the storage and access mediums to the hospital operation, support and patients knowledge management. The proposed KM tools deal with the creation, acquisition, integration, distribution and application of knowledge to improve the operation effectiveness and competitive advantage, and permit to provide the right information to the right people at the right time from any location.

Ultimately the success of any strategy is in its realisation and thereby its ability to achieve stated goals, but in order to achieve this, an imperative is to follow a systematic analysis as the preceding has documented.

24.9 Case Study Questions for Discussion

1. How and what would be the significant changes if one was developing an e-health strategy for a public healthcare organisation?
2. What elements are missing from this strategy recommendation and how might one set about accessing this information? If you have time, try to compile some of this information and incorporate it into the recommended strategy to see how things might change.
3. What are the important people/process/technology considerations that become apparent when considering the embracement of an appropriate e-health solution?
4. How is it possible to achieve the appropriate level of goal alignment when embarking upon such a project?

Acknowledgements The authors wish to acknowledge the support and assistance they received from Jenny O'Brien, Susan Wardle and Alan Kinkade of Epworth HealthCare in compiling this chapter.

Appendix A: Structure of the Organisation

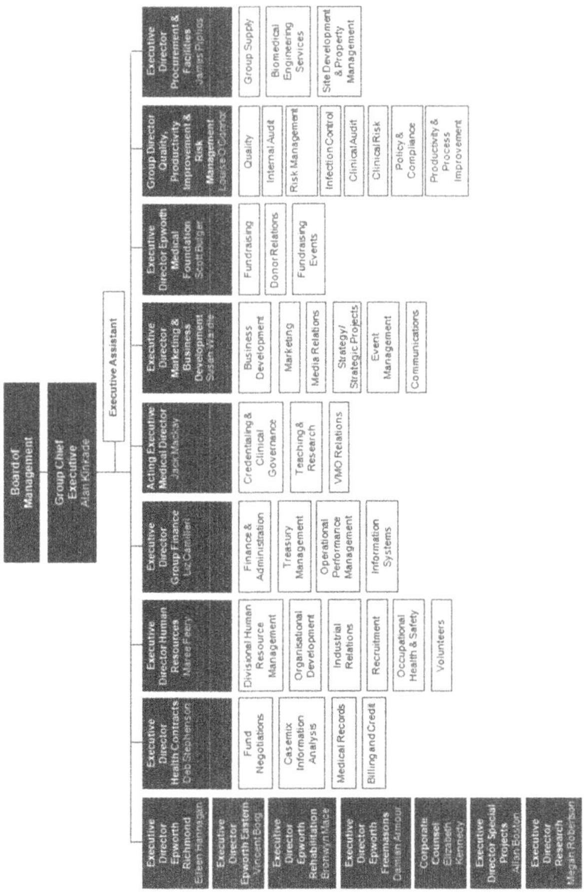

Appendix B: Interview Question Protocol

Section	Action	Who	When	Deliverables format
1	Understand Business and IT objectives	Chief Clinical Information Officer		
1.1	Collection of existing business and IT documents (vision, mission, strategy, etc.)	As above		*Vision document *Mission document *Business and IT Strategies documents
1.2	Collection of Epworth objectives and timing (current business plan) documents	As above		*HealthCare 2010 Annual Report
2	Identify clinical IT decisions distribution across roles	Chief Clinical Information Officer		
2.1	Identification of the major clinical IT decision that are being made in the business	As above		Answers
2.2	Identification of who is deciding on what	As above		Answers
3	Assess the extent of IT alignment with clinical requirements/maturity model	Chief Clinical Information Officer		
3.1	Collection of employee survey	As above		Survey results document
3.2	Documentation of the current organisation level of maturity	As above		Answers
4	Assess of what is, and what is not, working in the clinical environment	Exec Director Group Finance (Operational Performance Management)		
4.1	*People (ref to PPTS form)*			
4.1.1	Resources	As above		Answers
4.1.2	Skills and experience	As above		Answers
4.1.3	Communication and management style	As above		Answers
4.2	*Process (ref to PPTS form)*			
4.2.1	Identification of key clinical processes and gaps	As above		Answers/documents

(continued)

(continued)

Section	Action	Who	When	Deliverables format
4.2.2	Identification of to what extend the clinical strategy initiatives are dependent on IT	As above		Answers
4.2.3	Service availability (Collection of IT service reports)	As above		Monthly IT Service Reports (past 12 months)
4.2.4	Operations services efficiently, effectiveness	As above		Reports
4.2.5	Service levels (Epworth service level agreement)	As above		Reports
4.3	*Technology (ref to PPTS form)*			
4.3.1	Identification of key clinical IT applications and gaps	As above		Answers/documents
4.3.2	Current state of the e-health information access and sharing complexity, aligned with business needs and compatibility between systems	As above		Answers
4.3.2.1	On-sites	As above		Answers
4.3.2.2	Between sites	As above		Answers
4.3.2.3	Off-sites (Doctors, patients and others)	Doctors		Answers
4.4	*Security (ref to PPTS form)*			
4.4.1	Current state of data protection, service continuity and recoverability	Group Director Quality Productivity, Improvement and Risks		DR & BC last year reports/ Answers

References

Australian Health Workforce Advisory Committee (AHWAC). (2010).

Harvard Business School. (2005). *Strategy: Create and implement the best strategy for your business* (pp. 2–28). Boston: Harvard Business School Press.

Humphrey, A. (2004). *SWOT analysis: SWOT analysis method and examples*. Retrieved August 2, 2011, from http://www.businessballs.com/swotanalysisfreetemplate.htm#SWOT%20analysis%20inventors,%20origins%20and%20history%20of%20SWOT%20analysis

Mind tools. (2008). SWOT Analysis Discover New Opportunities. Manage and Eliminate Threats. from http://www.mindtools.com/pages/article/newTMC_05.htm

Mitchell, J., & Cottrill, A. (2002). *Improving your competitive advantage through e-health strategy*. In The Australian financial review 4th annual health congress, Australia.

Molla, A. (2008). *Lecture 4: IT strategy analysis I*. INTE1030: Information Technology Strategy. Melbourne: RMIT University.

Perrott, B., & Hughes, R. (2005). *A five forces approach to the Australian private hospital industry*. Interview with Patrick Grier, Australia.
Porter, M. (2006). *Value-based competition in health care*. Pennsylvania: Leonard Davis Institute of Health Economics.
Porter, M. (2008). *Competitive strategy*. New York: Free Press.
Von Lubitz, D., & Wickramasinghe, N. (2006). Network centric healthcare: Outline of entry portal concept. *International Journal of Electronic Business Management, 4*(1), 16–28.
World Health Organisation. (2011). *e-Health*. Retrieved October 10, 2011, from http://www.who.int/topics/ehealth/en/
World Health Organisation. (2004). e-*Health* (p. 1). Executive Board EB115/39, 115th Session 16, Provisional agenda item 4.13.

Part IV
Micro Issues

1.1 Introduction

Probably one of the most critical micro level issues where the principles of lean thinking can best be applied to healthcare is concerned with value stream mapping. To illustrate, this section provides three chapters that highlight this perspective.

Chapter 25 Value Stream Mapping in Lean Healthcare: A brief Introduction and Application by Dohan et al. serves to introduce the concept of value stream mapping.

Chapter 26 Using Value Stream Mapping to Improve Processes in a in a Urology Department by Gonzalez et al. illustrates an application of value stream mapping in the context of a urology department.

Chapter 27 A Technology Mediated Solution to Reduce Healthcare Disparities by Wickramasinghe et al. also explores the impact of adding value via a technology solution.

Although a relatively small section, these three chapters focus on the key topic of value stream mapping for healthcare and thus provide an in depth analysis on a critical aspect of lean thinking in healthcare contexts.

Chapter 25
Value Stream Mapping in Lean Healthcare: A Brief Introduction and Application

Michael S. Dohan, Ted Xenodemetropoulos, and Joseph Tan

Abstract The Lean approach espouses the elimination of sources of waste throughout a process, so that only value-added activities that address the desires of the customer should be implemented. Originating in manufacturing, Lean has been applied to healthcare, being used to address waste in this sector, for the benefit of patients and other healthcare actors. A central technique for identifying sources of waste is value stream mapping. This technique involves the creation of diagrams that depict workflow and its associated waste, and future state processes with waste reduced or eliminated, all occurring within an overarching series of activities that sees process improvements implemented. This chapter highlights the creation and use of value stream maps (VSMs) in the context of a Lean Healthcare initiative. A case example proposes current state and future state VSMs for medical coding and billing processes, which entail the capture of patient encounter information by the physician for the purpose of receiving remuneration from a healthcare system payer.

Keywords Value stream maps • Lean Healthcare • Medical coding and billing

---

This paper contains material from Agarwal et al. (2012).

M.S. Dohan, Ph.D. (ABD)
DeGroote School of Business, McMaster University, Hamilton, ON, Canada

Faculty of Business Administration, Lakehead University, Thunder Bay, ON, Canada

T. Xenodemetropoulos, M.D., F.R.C.P. (C)
Division of Gastroenterology, Department of Medicine, McMaster University, Hamilton, ON, Canada

J. Tan, Ph.D. (✉)
DeGroote School of Business, McMaster University, Hamilton, ON, Canada
e-mail: An9188@gmail.com

N. Wickramasinghe et al. (eds.), *Lean Thinking for Healthcare*, Healthcare Delivery in the Information Age, DOI 10.1007/978-1-4614-8036-5_25,

25.1 Introduction

Applying the Lean Healthcare approach for the improvement of healthcare systems entails the elimination of waste throughout a given process. Value stream mapping is a technique in Lean Healthcare that is used for identifying these sources of waste and redesigning processes with waste reduced or eliminated. It involves sketching diagrams representing healthcare processes, including details on methods of how they are requested, tasks involved in the fulfillment of that request, as well as the durations of processing and wait between process tasks. The use of value stream maps (VSMs) is an effective manner in engaging frontline healthcare workers, hospital administrators, and support staff to collaborate on addressing waste in healthcare processes.

This chapter serves as an introduction to constructing and utilizing VSMs in Lean Healthcare initiatives. In the spirit of Jimmerson (2010), this chapter approaches Lean Healthcare in a way that is accessible and inclusive to all healthcare workers, whether a physician, nurse, support worker, or managers. As a case example, VSMs depicting current- and future states of a medical coding and billing (MCB) workflow will be proposed. MCB refers to the process associated with recording and submission of data associated with patient encounters for the purpose of remuneration. The chapter is structured as follows. First, Lean Healthcare and its associated wastes will be characterized. Next, VSMs will be described, including the symbols for their diagrams, their development processes within Lean Healthcare initiatives, and their use within an overarching Lean Healthcare initiative. Finally, MCB processes and their associated wastes will be described, and subsequently used as an example of representing healthcare processes in VSMs.

25.2 Lean Healthcare

Lean originates from the ideas of Taichi Ohno (1988) during his development of the production system at Toyota. The premise of the Lean system is that all wastes (or *muda*) must be eliminated. Waste has been defined for healthcare as "anything not necessary to produce the product or service" (Ransom et al. 2005). The key to eliminating this waste is to identify it, throughout all stages in all processes involved in production. Key in identifying waste is its conceptualization. Originally within Lean, waste can occur in seven ways: unneeded confusion, excessive motion, waiting, overprocessing (or requiring more effort than needed to process one item), excess inventory, defects, and overproduction (or producing more of a product than needed).

A version of these seven original wastes has been adapted for Lean Healthcare (Jimmerson 2010). The first waste is *confusion*. Confusion can be caused by situations such as unclear instructions, not knowing where equipment is located, or not knowing where to send paperwork, resulting in repeated work or medical errors.

Table 25.1 Sources of waste in Lean Healthcare (Jimmerson 2010)

Waste	Occurs when
Confusion	Uncertainty exists in workflow
Motion/conveyance	Unnecessary movement (body/place to place) occurs
Waiting	Process idle, waiting for another event or more processing
Overprocessing	Unnecessary amount of work is performed for a task
Inventory	Inventory stock numbers are disconnected from actual demand
Defects	Medical errors, sometimes requiring more work
Overproduction	Tasks are performed more times than necessary

The second waste is *motion/conveyance*. Motion refers to the motion required to complete a task, and conveyance refers to moving patients and materials from place to place. Both result in time and energy wasted during a process. The third waste is *waiting*. When waiting for a procedure or an event to occur, patients can get anxious and idle staff costs money. The fourth waste is *overprocessing*. This manifests as performing more tasks than necessary to produce the same amount of work. The fifth waste is *inventory*. This can consist of any stored supplies in amounts that are more than necessary, for example, obsolete inventory, any waste pertaining to inaccurate demand forecasting, and any labor associated with maintaining waste inventory. The sixth waste is *defects*. Medical procedures performed to correct medical errors can be classified as waste due to defects. The seventh waste is *overproduction*. Overproduction occurs when more work than necessary is being performed. Table 25.1 summarizes these wastes.

25.3 Value Stream Maps

Simply put, a VSM is a diagram that represents a process, and value stream mapping entails the activities associated with creating these diagrams (Jimmerson, 2010). Specifically, VSMs are concerned with determining at what steps value is added to the person making the request. In the current state VSM, non-value adding steps will be mapped, in order that they are identified, communicated, and scrutinized by mapping process participants. In the future state VSM, a new ideal process is created by the mapping process participants. This new map depicts a waste-free process with activities that only contribute value to the person making the request.

Designed to be expressed on one sheet of paper, in portrait orientation, a VSM is characterized by three components. Each of these components is meant to be depicted on the upper, middle, and lower third of the paper. The upper third is for depicting the request for services and how the request is made. The middle third is for depicting the fulfillment of the request, and all of the tasks and inventories

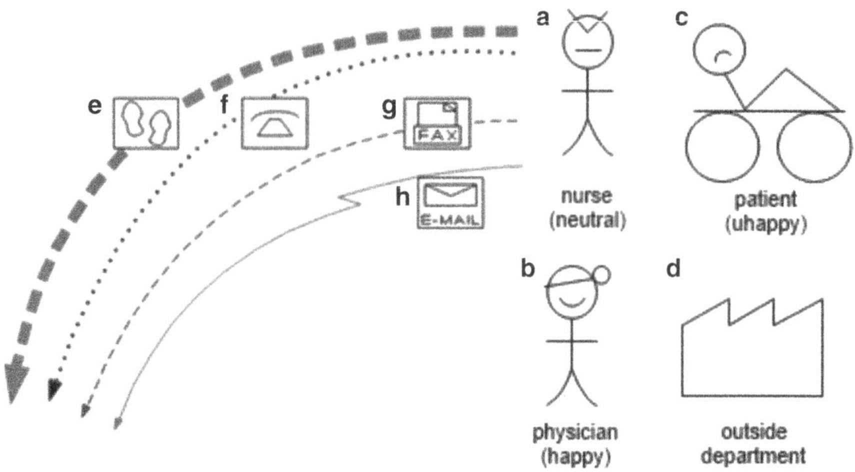

Fig. 25.1 People (**a**–**d**) and request (**e**–**h**) symbols, which can be used to depict a service request. These typically appear on the *top* third of the VSM. Symbols created in eVSM (eVSM.com)

involved in fulfilling that request. The lower third is used for showing the data related to fulfilling that request, including the time that it takes to perform each task or idle time waiting in queues, or similar data. Each of the sections contains various symbol depicting aspects of the processes. These symbols can come from a standard set, or can be created as needed and described on the document itself. These sections and the symbols contained within them will be explained in more detail below. eVSM (www.evsm.com), a software application for modelling VSMs, was used to create the models.

25.3.1 Top Section

The top section contains two types of information pertaining to the information about the request for the service. This section is meant to describe all actions, events, and details that take place before the process is actually triggered. This can include gathering information, waiting for other processes to finish, or waiting for some sort of notification. Figure 25.1 includes some symbols typically used on the top section of a VSM.

25.3.1.1 People

The various people that are included in forming the request are depicted on the top section. The requester of the process is typically included in the top right corner,

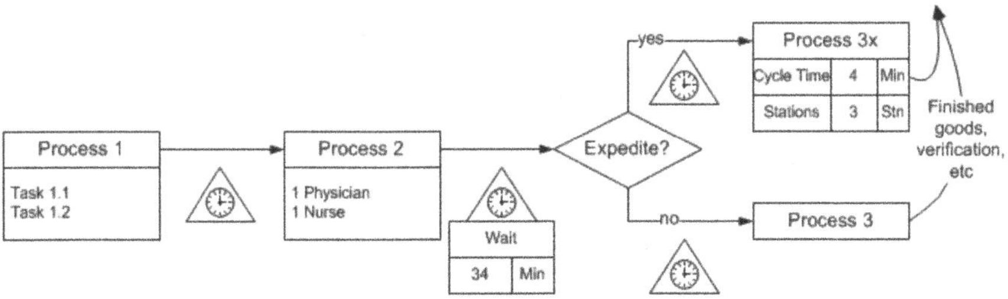

Fig. 25.2 Symbols for processes, flows, decisions, waiting, and their associated data, which can be used to depict a process workflow. These typically appear on the *middle* third of the VSM. Symbols created in eVSM (eVSM.com)

although it can contain interactions with others before the work has actually commenced. Various people, such as nurses (a), physicians (b), and patients (c), are represented by stick figures. The symbols can also be used to express the satisfaction of the person in the process. They can be happy, neutral, or unhappy (as depicted). Other departments (d) or organizations can also be depicted.

25.3.1.2 Requests

The requests that the people make for the service are also included on the top section. The people included on the map need to establish contact with the department that runs the process to make the request. This request can be communicated in several ways. The pattern of the lines themselves indicates the nature of the different ways the request can be made. This can indicate that the request is a (e) push, (f) expedited, (g) Kanban, or (h) made by electronic means. The medium in which the request is made is also depicted. This can include (e) foot travel, (f) telephone, (g) fax, or (h) email.

25.3.2 Middle Section

The middle section contains information about the processes that constitute the work performed. Included in this is any wait times between processes. The left side of the diagram shows where the request is received and the work starts. As the work progresses, it moves towards the right, where the work is eventually finished and the request is fulfilled. Additionally, arrows at this side can represent any action that happens after the process is finished, such as delivery of finished goods or a notification to the requestor. Figure 25.2 depicts how the work processes are modelled in this section.

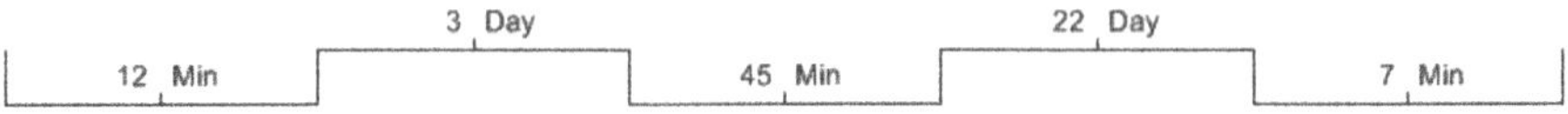

Fig. 25.3 Symbols depicting process and wait time duration in VSM. These typically appear on the *bottom* third of the VSM. Symbols created in eVSM (eVSM.com)

25.3.3 Processes

The process symbol can represent something where work that adds value to the work unit is completed (represented by boxes). Although a process is likely to be represented by only a box with a name in the beginning of the map's development (as in Process 3), versions throughout the development may include extended details about the process. These details may include information associated with cycle time, number of stations or other relevant information (as in Process 3x), the various tasks that are involved in completing that process (as in Process 1), or the number of people involved in the process (as in Process 2).

25.3.3.1 Flows and Waiting

The arrows represent the sequence of value- and non-value-added activities, as the work flows from start to completion. The flow may be dependent on decisions made at certain points of the flow. This is represented by the diamond, while each possible decision can be represented by labels on or near each of the flows. At the end, an arrow can represent what happens to the work, including where it is delivered, or if anybody is notified that the work is completed, for example. The triangles represent times between processes, when no value is being added to the work unit. These can represent a queue, FIFO, inventory, or other goods at rest. The triangles used to represent work-at-rest in this particular diagram contain a clock, which means that there is a wait time between each process. When data pertaining to the wait is collected, it can be entered in a table underneath the wait symbol.

25.3.4 Lower Section

On the lower section of the diagram is where information regarding the timeline of the process is contained as demonstrated in Fig. 25.3. The steps in the process and any waiting times between tasks in the process are represented in the middle section of the VSM. The times associated with each step in the process are depicted on the timeline, contained in the lower section of the VSM, underneath these steps. The timeline is shaped in a way so that it contains peaks and valleys. The valleys contain the times it takes to complete each of the steps in the process, and the peaks contain

Fig. 25.4 Additional descriptive symbols used in VSM. These can appear anywhere on the diagram, as needed. Symbols created in eVSM (eVSM.com)

the duration of wait times between processes. If the numbers contained here cannot be acquired from existing sources, some basic data collection (timesheets, for example) can be used to create an average for each of the stages.

Time can also be depicted in the boxes. When time is depicted in this way, it can show the highs and lows, conveying the variation in each individual process.

25.3.5 *Assorted*

There are a number of symbols that can appear in any section of the diagram, to indicate information other than the details concerning the request, work performed, or duration of each process. Sometimes the creator of the diagram will want to describe something about the context of the process, or give description in a way that doesn't neatly fall into the category of request, process, or duration. Figure 25.4 presents some examples of commonly used symbols to allow the people involved in constructing these diagrams to convey this information. A Kaizen, or problem (a), symbol can be placed anywhere on the diagram where a problem is identified and opportunity exists for collaboration amongst team members to solve. This symbol, depicted as a sort of explosion, is useful for drawing attention to actual problems on current state VSMs. A cloud, or solution (b), symbol can be placed anywhere where a solution has been implemented, likely on a future state or a new current state VSM. Whenever any extra detail in an area is important, a callout (c) can be used to display this information, using its arrow to indicate the exact area that the detail pertains to.

25.4 How to Create Value Stream Maps

Generally speaking, VSMs are used to articulate, communicate, and conceptualize processes, for the overall goal of improving the process (George 2003; Jimmerson 2010). With that in mind, VSMs are used as a tool in an overarching methodology

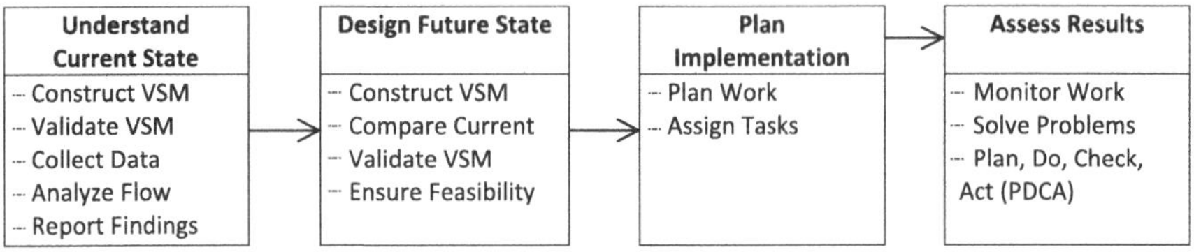

Fig. 25.5 Lean Healthcare process improvement methodology using VSMs. Adapted from Jimmerson (2010)

of Lean Healthcare process improvement. The process, depicted in Fig. 25.5, is adapted from Jimmerson (2010) and described below.

25.4.1 Understand Current State

The first step in improving the process is to understand the current state of the process. An initial version of the current state VSM is drawn. This version is validated by showing it to other people who work the process. This is a good way to get buy-in from the people that are being consulted.

Even when the diagram is first constructed, sources of waste can be identified. It may however be necessary to gather data to add more credibility to the diagram. At times, gathering the type of data you need can be a challenge, as it may require extra resources, such as a dedicated staff member or extra labor, during an already demanding process. A simple data gathering technique would have people fill out times that a certain process is completed on a spreadsheet or a sheet of paper, although this method requires the disruption of a person's process. If this data already existed in a database, this would be the easiest to acquire, although it is likely that the exact data that suits the problem does not exist. It has been recommended that small amounts of data are sufficient, as low as eight or ten cases (Jimmerson 2010), yet more would be valuable as well.

In analyzing the flow, there are several things that you want to look for. These would include repeated processes, similar processes, areas of confusion, redundant processes, and non-value adding processes. If you have gathered data, you will be interested in processes that have a large variance. That is, the time it takes to complete a process varies to a large degree. This can be assessed by calculating the standard deviation, or merely by calculating the difference between the highest and lowest times. Processes that have a large variance warrant further investigation. Also of interest here are cases that have resulted in defects. Particularities or common elements of these cases may indicate root problems.

25.4.2 Design Future State

The next step is to conceptualize the future state VSM that is desired by the change. This future state should be built to bring the processes closer to an ideal state, but not so close that the actual changes made are infeasible or likely to fail. This map also needs to be drawn and validated in consultation with the people who are involved in the process. This is a good way to ensure that the process is feasible. As well, consultation is a commonly used strategy to secure buy-in from the people that will have to experience the change, reducing the likeliness that they will resist any changes and derail improvement efforts.

When creating the future state of a process, it is important to keep in mind the *ideal state* of healthcare, in order that healthcare processes can produce the best possible result. Five qualities of an ideal process in healthcare have been proposed by Jimmerson (2010), based on previous work by Tucker and Spear (2006). First, healthcare should be delivered in a manner that is *defect-free*, so that exactly what is needed is delivered, without a single problem. Second, healthcare should be delivered *without waste*, or *muda*, so that there are no activities within a process that do not contribute to the value eventually received by the requestor. Third, *individual attention* to patients must be achieved in processes that support flexibility, yet considering the importance for standardizing processes. Fourth, healthcare services should be available *as they are demanded*. Fifth, any problems experienced in the system must be *immediately responded to*, with the purpose of not repeating that problem in the future.

25.4.3 Plan Implementation

At this point the current state of the process is thoroughly understood, and the vision is created for an improved future process. The next step is to determine how to implement the new process. The way in which Lean process improvements are implemented depends on a variety of factors; therefore, there is no one right way to do this. Factors such as the people involved, the likeliness that they will resist change (Jick and Peiperl 2003), or any patient safety concerns are just a few of the issues that can come into play when implementing process improvements. As a result, there are a variety of tools that can be used to implement Lean process improvements. Jimmerson (2010) uses a simple table outlining (1) exactly what changes need to be made, (2) person responsible for this change, (3) estimated completion time of the improvement, and (4) the expected outcome for each of the process. Each change should be a portion of work that is attainable and clearly specified. Indeed, the changes to be made and the related details should be validated by the people who are impacted by them. Progress on each item should be evaluated periodically, and if need be, reassessed.

25.4.4 *Assess Results*

During implementation, problems and barriers are likely to surface, hindering the ability to implement lasting changes. Addressing problems in this phase amounts to tactically addressing issues to reach an overall strategic future state. Various tools exist for problem solving including fishbone diagrams (Ishikawa 1990) and Five Whys (Ohno 1988). Another technique that is used in assessing the results of changes is called the Plan–Do–Check–Act (PDCA). This technique involves iterating between planning to understand the root cause of a problem, putting in a plan in place to address the problem, measuring the impact that the plan had in addressing the problem, and then establishing new rules for the process (Deming 1986).

Integral to implementing PDCA is the A3 technique, named after the A3 standard size paper (Sobek and Smalley 2008) that the corresponding report is drawn on. The report typically contains (a) information about the specific problem being addressed, (b) current condition and problem statement, (c) goal statement, (d) root-cause analysis, (e) countermeasures taken against the problem, (f) effect of the countermeasures, and (g) any follow-up action taken. This report can be used to communicate the current status of an ongoing project, as well as be used to propose new projects.

25.5 Value Stream Mapping Case Example in Medical Coding and Billing

In this section, current and future VSMs will be proposed for the processes rounding MCB in Ontario, Canada. MCB refers to the accurate and timely recording and submission of data associated with patient encounters for the purpose of remuneration. As a result of the complexities inherent in the MCB processes, it has been estimated that up to 15 % of a physician's gross annual income may be lost as a result of such billing process deficiencies (Blanchfield et al. 2010). This high degree of lost income makes the MCB processes a candidate for a Lean Healthcare initiative. The current state VSM will depict the MCB process with all of its wastes, and the future state VSM will depict the MCB processes with all the wastes identified in the first diagram eliminated.

The MCB process is triggered after a chargeable patient encounter. A chargeable patient encounter could occur when the physician performs a diagnostic procedure on the patient, or when the physician performs a service on the patient. After the procedure is performed, the doctor must send information associated with the procedure to the payer, whether it is a government ministry, health insurance provider, or other. The MCB process consists of three tasks. First, as each of the procedures that are remunerable by the payer has a code associated with it, the physician selects the correct code that corresponds to diagnostics or service procedure performed

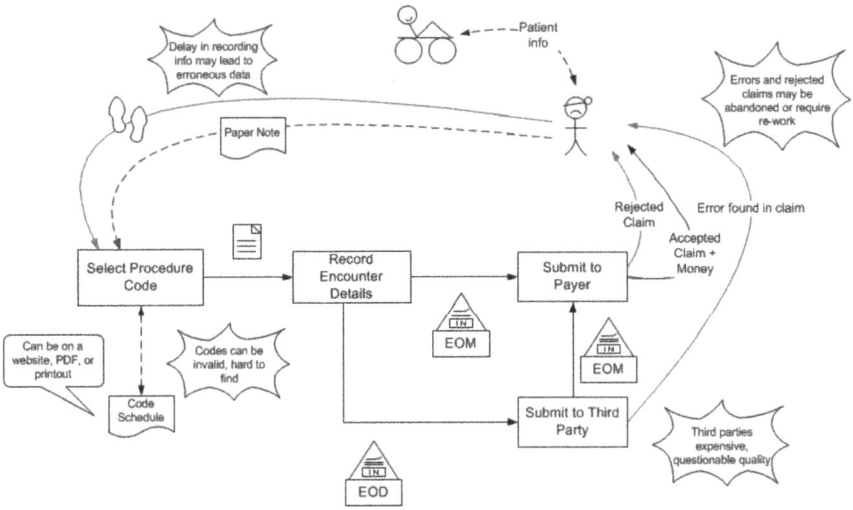

Fig. 25.6 Proposed current state VSM for an illustrative medical coding and billing process. Diagram created in eVSM (eVSM.com)

during the patient encounter. Second, the physician records data associated with a patient encounter, such as the services performed, identity and demographics of the patient, and so on. This information is then either sent directly to the payer or a batch of information is sent periodically, for the purpose of reimbursement.

The processes associated with MCB can be quite complicated, which leads to more resources dedicated to their management (Blanchfield et al. 2010). First, physicians must capture the patient encounter with specific demographic and health information (including patient name and other identifying information) and select appropriate diagnostic and service code from the schedule. Significant complexity can exist in selecting the correct service or diagnostic code given the incredible number of potentially applicable codes dictated by the service type, location of the patient encounter, on-call and after-hours assessment, as well as many additional variables. Second, the codes in the schedule are revised on a regular basis, reflecting revisions to funded services. The consequence of charge entries that contain errors is the rejection of the charge by the payer, and payment for these services to the physician is withheld. Therefore, it is in the best interest to ensure the submission of accurate and error-free charge entries.

The VSM depicting a typical yet generalized current state of this process is depicted in Fig. 25.6. The request begins after a patient encounter, when the physician must gather information, pertaining to the patient, the service and diagnostics performed, and other details about the encounter. In an outpatient situation, the on-call physicians may have to perform these services away from their office, compelling them to either memorize the data or write details on a paper note, so it can be properly recorded later. When the data is to be recorded, the correct service and diagnostic codes applicable to the patient encounter must be guaranteed. This may require looking up the codes on the Ontario Ministry of Health (the healthcare service payer in Ontario) website, on a saved file, or on a print-out of this document. After the correct codes are found, the physician will record the rest of the data associated with the encounter. This is commonly recorded on a paper log sheet or a computer record. The physician then has the option of sending daily records to a third party billing agent or monthly records directly to the payer. If the doctor chooses to use a billing agent, the billing agent eventually sends the monthly report to the payer, after performing a level of error checking on the batch of data. Successful submissions are responded with reimbursement. Errors detected by third party billing agents or rejected submissions to the payer require rework.

Before gathering data, some problem areas can be seen, as denoted by the Kaizen symbols. First, any delay in recording the data can lead to erroneous entries in the main patient encounter records. Such a situation can be conceived as waiting, as in waiting to enter the data into the main record. Notes can get lost, details can be forgotten, or the physician can be distracted between the time of the patient encounter and the recording of the data. In an outpatient situation, having to move to the physician's office to record the data on the main record may also represent unnecessary conveyance. Second, the codes can be hard to find in a printed out document, or a file document saved on a computer. An extra step is required if a website needs to be accessed to reach this information. Or else, a chance in service and diagnostic coding can occur, rendering useless the codes currently memorized by the physician. This can be classified under confusion, if the physician is unsure of the accuracy of the code, or has to search for the correct code using an inefficient method. Third, the use of a third party billing agent may be considered overprocessing, or performing an unnecessary amount of work for a task, if a less wasteful error checking mechanism can be found. Fourth, defects can be defined as rejected or erroneous submissions.

Figure 25.7 depicts a future state VSM of the MCB process, with previously identified sources of waste reduced or eliminated. An integral implementation to the future state of the MCB process is the use of a mobile phone application developed for recording patient information at the point of care, as well as accessing an up to date database of service and diagnostic codes. Recording the data at the point of care eliminates the wait to input data into the main list. Features on the application can include a level of error checking at the point of data entry, resulting in reduced erroneous claims sent to the payer and less resources spent checking data in the form of third party agents.

25.6 Discussion and Conclusion

The value stream mapping technique, as applicable to Lean Healthcare and as described in this chapter, is useful for detailing the different types of waste that can be eliminated in the current state of healthcare processes, while proposing

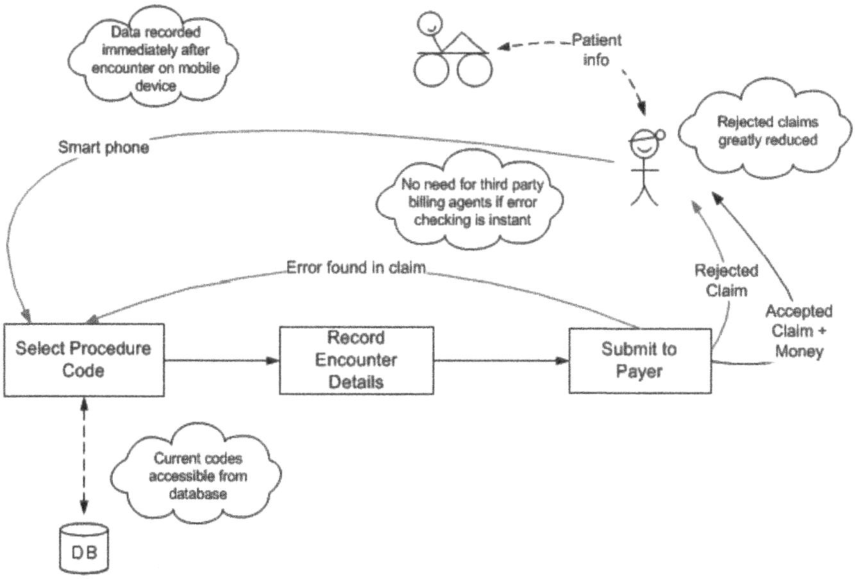

Fig. 25.7 Proposed future state VSM for an illustrative medical coding and billing process. Diagram created in eVSM (eVSM.com)

redesigned processes for a future state. Such process workflow redesign will bring an organization closer to a theoretically ideal state. The creation and use of VSMs occur in an approach with four phases. First, the current state VSM is used to identify sources of waste inherent in current processes. Second, a future state VSM is created, depicting a process with waste eliminated, yet realistic to achieve. Third, work is assigned to implement the applicable changes, and finally progress towards these goals is periodically monitored.

The case described here was a generic case involving MCB, or the processes associated with recording details about a patient encounter for the eventual purpose of receiving remuneration from a healthcare system payer. In this case, a current state map was used to describe the typical sources of waste that occur in these processes, and a future state map proposed how a technology can reduce waste in these processes.

As Lean becomes more popular in healthcare, several issues may affect its successful adoption in the healthcare environment. As managers, these issues are worth considering while crafting a Lean deployment strategy, in healthcare organizations in particular, in order to avoid failure of deployment or any other negative consequences. As the success of Lean does rely on the competency of frontline workers, barriers may impact the ability for meaningful participation in quality improvement, such as low skill and experience in process modelling in this population (de Koning et al. 2006). As well, members of the organization may simply be skeptical that the participation and effort required by Lean will result to any lasting changes or significant improvement in performance (Joosten et al. 2009). There are many more issues like these, too numerous to mention here. In planning deployment of Lean in the healthcare organization, the managers must do so strategically, considering the critical factors associated with their respective organizations, while providing the support required for such a change (Zidel 2006).

25.7 Questions

1. What are the seven Lean wastes as applied to healthcare? Propose some real world examples of Lean waste in healthcare from your experiences as a healthcare worker or a patient.
2. One issue that has been identified with deploying Lean in a healthcare context is frontline worker buy-in. Other than the ones mentioned in this chapter, what would you propose are barriers for frontline healthcare workers to meaningfully participate in these initiatives? How would you address these barriers?
3. VSMs are considered by some to be accessible means in articulating healthcare processes to a variety of healthcare workers. Having seen examples of VSMs and their development process, do you agree with this statement? Why or why not?
4. Although sources of waste in healthcare processes can be detected simply by drawing a current state VSM, is it acceptable to implement a proposed solution without first collecting data to describe aspects of the current state? Why or why not?

References

Agarwal, A., Xenodemetropoulos, T., Abdelrahman, Y., Dohan, M., McKibbon, A., & Tan, J. (2012). ChargeMed: Development of a Mobile Application for Medical Billing and Coding in the Ontario Healthcare Environment. HICSS 2012. Proceedings of the [45th] Annual Hawaii International Conference on System Sciences (CD-ROM), Maui, Hawaii.

Blanchfield, B., Heffernan, J., Osgood, B., Sheehan, R., & Meyer, G. (2010). Saving billions of dollars—and physicians' time—by streamlining billing practices. *Health Affairs, 29*, 1–7.

de Koning, H., Verver, J. P. S., van den Heuvel, J., Bisgaard, S., & Does, R. J. M. M. (2006). Lean six sigma in healthcare. *Journal for Healthcare Quality, 28*(2), 4–11.

Deming, W. (1986). *Out of the crisis*. Cambridge, MA: MIT Press.

George, M. L. (2003). *Lean six sigma for service: How to use lean speed and six sigma quality to improve services and transactions*. New York: McGraw-Hill.

Ishikawa, K. (1990). *Introduction to quality control*. Tokyo: 3A Corporation.

Jick, T., & Peiperl, M. (2003). *Managing change: Cases and concepts* (p. 515). Boston, MA: McGraw-Hill/Irwin.

Jimmerson, C. (2010). *Value stream mapping for healthcare made easy*. New York: Productivity Press.

Joosten, T., Bongers, I., & Janssen, R. (2009). Application of lean thinking to health care: Issues and observations. *International Journal for Quality in Health Care, 21*(5), 341–347.

Ohno, T. (1988). *Toyota production system: Beyond large-scale production*. New York: Productivity Press.

Ransom, S., Joshi, M., & Nash, D. (2005). *The healthcare quality book: Vision, strategy and tools*. Chicago, IL: Health Administration Press.

Sobek, D. K., II, & Smalley, A. (2008). *Understanding A3 thinking: A critical component of Toyota's PDCA management system* (p. 184). New York, NY: Productivity Press.

Tucker, A. L., & Spear, S. J. (2006). Operational failures and interruptions in hospital nursing. *Health Services Research, 41*(3 Pt 1), 643–662. doi:10.1111/j.1475-6773.2006.00502.x.

Zidel, T. (2006). *A lean guide to transforming healthcare: How to implement lean principles in hospitals, medical offices, clinics, and other healthcare organizations*. Milwaukee, WI: ASQ Quality Press.

Chapter 26
Using Value Stream Mapping to Improve Processes in a Urology Department

Chris M. Gonzalez, Kwok Hung Lau, and Nilmini Wickramasinghe

Abstract In order to realise the healthcare delivery goals of access, quality and value, it is necessary to examine existing processes to identify opportunities to redesign them and incorporate ICT (information communication technologies) to enable effective and efficient processes that do facilitate the delivery of superior healthcare. Value stream mapping technique can be used in identifying wastes in the process for elimination so as to improve overall efficiency and throughput. The following discusses this in the context of a urology clinic at a large hospital in the MidWest, USA.

Keywords Value stream mapping • Waste elimination • Process re-engineering • ICT • Workflow • Urology

26.1 Introduction

In most outpatient settings waiting, delays and cancellations are sadly too common. One might be tempted to think that this is why a patient is called a patient. Both patients and providers are significantly affected by the waste of time due to waiting,

C.M. Gonzalez
NorthWestern Memorial Hospital, Galter 20-150, 675 N. St. Clair, Chicago, IL 60611, USA
e-mail: CGonzalez@nmff.org

K.H. Lau
School of Business IT and Logistics, RMIT University, GPO Box 2476, Melbourne, VIC 3001, Australia
e-mail: E02653@ems.rmit.edu.au

N. Wickramasinghe (✉)
Epworth HealthCare & Department of BITL & HIRi, RMIT University, GPO Box 2476 Melbourne, VIC 3001, Australia
e-mail: nilmini.work@gmail.com

N. Wickramasinghe et al. (eds.), *Lean Thinking for Healthcare*, Healthcare Delivery in the Information Age, DOI 10.1007/978-1-4614-8036-5_26,

delays and cancellations. Moreover, the quality and cost of healthcare delivery are also negatively impacted (Kywi 2007; Ganiban 2004; Inchingolo 2007; Schnellen 2008; Smith 2007; Wickramasinghe et al. 2007a, b).

Quality is defined in three ways. The first is result quality. This is the most important, because it is responsible for patient satisfaction, which is essential for the success of healthcare institutions. The second is structural quality, which includes the conditions, required to succeed, i.e. number of employees and their skills, the infrastructure, the equipment, the organisation structure and the collaboration within a team. This kind of quality is the simplest to measure. The third and easiest to impact is process quality. It includes the workflow and the information flow. If all of these three quality pillars are high, the overall quality will be also at a high level. However, if there are big differences between these, then patients and providers alike will feel this imbalance and total quality will be negatively impacted.

The impression of lack of quality mostly lies in process quality problems. But it is easy to solve these problems, because there are no big capital investments to be made. Improving the workflow lies in reducing process variation that impact flows (Institute for Healthcare Improvement 2003). While some variability is normal, other variation is not and should be eliminated. Waits, delays, bottlenecks and backlogs are not the result of lack of commitment on the part of staff. The answer to improving workflow lies in redesigning the overall, system-wide work processes that create the flow problems. Optimal care can only be delivered when the right patient is in the right place with the right provider and the right information at the right time.

To illustrate this and thereby show how it is possible to enhance quality and value in an outpatient setting, the following discusses a three-phase case study performed at a urology setting in a large MidWest hospital in the USA. Phase 1 occurred in 2006–2007, phase 2 2007–2008 and phase 3 commenced in Oct 2008.

26.2 Background to Urology Clinic: Initial Position

In 2006, the outpatient urology department of a large MidWest hospital was convinced that quality and hence value was being compromised since its patients did not consistently move smoothly through the system. Specifically, patients on one hand and providers on the other hand were wasting too much time with waiting. This was taken as a clear sign that processes need to be improved. However moving from needing to improve processes and what to do to improve these processes was critical.

The outpatient urology department has very few emergency patients. Most of the patients that come to the urology clinic make an appointment before they come. Hence the clinic should not have to struggle with flow variation—the ebb and flow of patients arriving throughout the day—as is typical in emergency departments. So it should be possible for the urology department to control patient flow with effective scheduling. The urology clinic however does have to manage clinical variability—different patients' conditions they have to medicate and treat. In addition, they have to handle professional variability, i.e. the fact that their providers have different techniques regarding how they medicate the patients and how they organise their workflow.

Hence, some of the variability cannot be eliminated or reduced, rather it must be managed, because it is not possible to eliminate the different types of problems from which patients suffer. However, other types of variability are often caused by individual preferences and these should be reduced if not eliminated.

26.3 Preparations

There are many factors that can have an effect on the process of healthcare delivery: technical, organisational, structural, economic, human, etc. The best way to find out the reasons that cause the existing process problems was to analyse the complete urology department. In order to do this, an ethnographic research methodology was adopted and the activities of the urology clinic were critically observed and evaluated. It also was necessary to see the urology clinic from different points of view. Therefore physicians, medical assistants, medical technicians, receptionists and patients have been interviewed. For these interviews protocols and questionnaires were prepared.

26.4 Observation and Interview Results

26.4.1 Kind of Patients

In the urology department three kinds of patients appear. One is the new patient, who visits the urology clinic for the first time. It is possible that he/she has been to the hospital before, but he/she has never visited in the urology department before. Another kind is the returning patient who visits the urology department on a previous occasion. It is possible that the reason of his/her visit is only a checkup or that he/she wants to talk to the doctor about the last medical problem or it can also be possible that he/she has a new medical problem. The third kind of patient is the patient who comes for a procedure, like a biopsy, for example. This is the only reason for his/her visit.

26.4.2 Workflow

It was not easy to clearly identify the workflow in the urology department. The first reason was that the workflow differs, depending on the kind of patients. The second reason was that there is no standard workflow, because the work is done in different ways, depending on the medical assistant and the doctor in the treatment care team. Figure 26.1 shows the approximated workflow with a new patient.

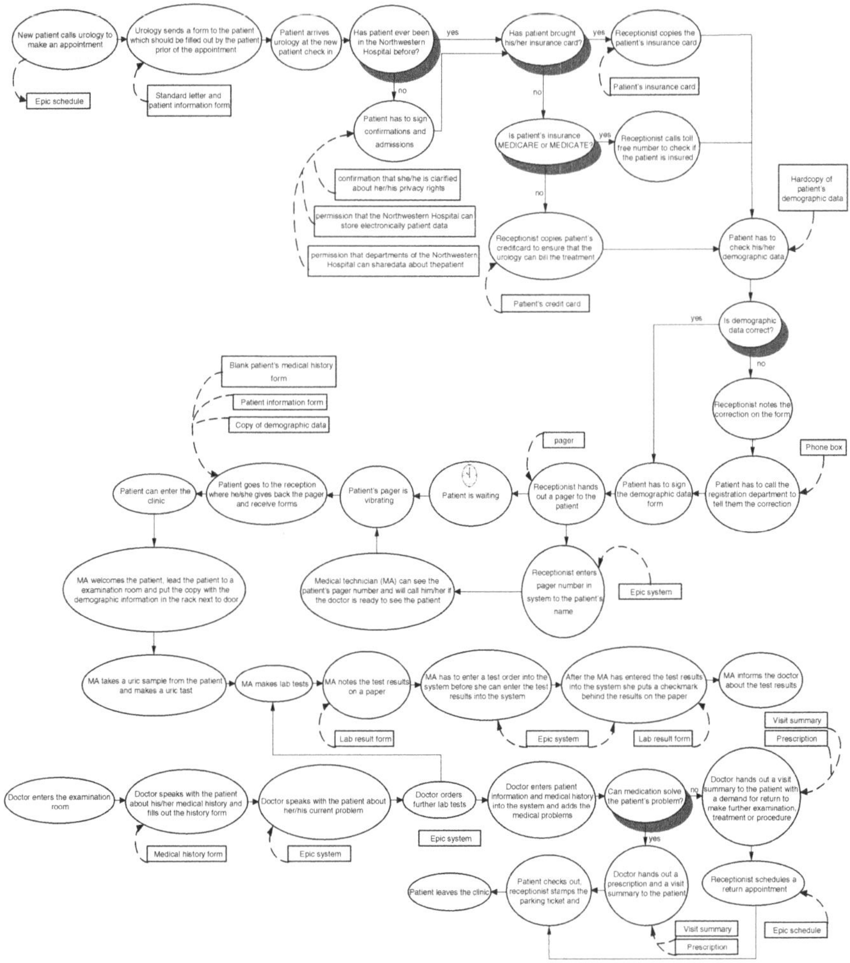

Fig. 26.1 Workflow in the urology department

After a patient has called the urology clinic to make his/her first appointment, the urology department sends out a patient information form per mail that the patient needs to fill out (medical/social/family history, review of systems). Prior to his/her appointment he/she should also call the registration department to give them his/her demographic data (address, insurance information, information about employer, in some cases information about the legal guardian).

When the patient arrives at the urology department, he/she needs to check in at the new-patient front desk. The receptionist hands out printed demographic data to the patient that he/she can check if the data is correct. If the data is incorrect, the patient must use a special phone in the waiting room to call the registration department to correct the data. The receptionist will mark the errors on the printed form and the patient has to sign the form with the demographic data. If the patient has never been at the hospital, he/she needs to sign these additional forms at the check in: confirmation that he/she is clarified about his/her privacy rights, permission that the hospital can store patient data on the electronic medical record and permission that departments of the hospital can share data about the patient. Furthermore the receptionist copies the patient's insurance card. If the patient has forgotten his/her card and the insurance is MEDICARE or MEDICAID, the receptionist can call a toll free number to check, if the patient is really insured. If the patient is insured at another insurance company, the receptionist will copy the patient's credit card to make sure that the urology can bill the patient for the treatment.

The receptionist hands out a pager to the patient and he/she will enter the pager number into the system. When the doctor is ready to see the patient, then the medical assistant (MA) will call the patient's pager. The patient comes back to the front desk. The receptionist hands out a copy of the demographic data, the patient information form and a blank patient medical history form to the patient that he/she can bring to the doctor. Then the patient can enter the clinic.

The MA welcomes the patient and leads him/her to one of the three examination rooms. She takes the paper with the demographic information about the patient and puts it in the special rack besides the door. Then she takes a urine sample from the patient.

The MA makes some tests with the urine. She writes the results from the tests on a paper form. Before she can enter the results into the system, she has to enter a lab test order into the system. Then she can add the results to the order in the system; after that she makes a checkmark behind the results on the paper form and informs the doctor about the results.

Next, the doctor enters the examination room. The patient hands over the information and medical history form to the doctor. Then the doctor will have a longer conversation with the patient about his/her medical history and about his/her current problem. Depending on the patient's problem, the doctor orders further lab tests. He leaves the examination room in the meantime to enter the data about the patient into the system. Depending on the tests results he will decide if he can immediately treat the patient or if he/she has to come for a second visit. Then he will hand out the patient a visit summary and in some cases a prescription or a demand for a return visit.

The patient leaves the clinic through the check-out. There the patient hands out the summary and his/her demographic data to the receptionist. The receptionist checks the summary; if another visit is required, he/she will schedule a new appointment. The demographic data are needed for the billing. Then the receptionist stamps the parking ticket and the patient can go.

26.5 Findings

The first problem is incomplete patient history forms. When patients make a first appointment, the urology clinic usually sends a form to the patients or asks them to download the form at the urology website. The patient should bring the completed form along with him/her at the time of appointment. The majority of patients don't bring the form duly completed. So they have to fill out the form in the waiting room while the doctor is waiting.

Another problem is the inflexible scheduling. The EMR only allows 15 min slots in scheduling. So the urology clinic usually allocates 15 min appointments for returning patients and 30 min appointments for new patients. Sometimes it is unnecessary to give a 15 min appointment to a returning patient, because the doctor knows that he only has to talk with the patient for 5 min, for example. The rest of the time the doctor is waiting for the next patient.

The next problem is poor communication between the staff members creates waste of time. The doctor is done and ready for the next patient. The clock says that it is 10 min before the next appointment. The EMR shows him that the next patient has already arrived at the urology clinic, but the doctor doesn't know if the patient is ready for the examination or if the patient is filling out forms. So the doctor is waiting for the receptionist to forward the patient or for the medical assistant calling in the patient. Possibly the patient is also waiting for the doctor meanwhile.

Duplicate lab orders confuse the lab staff and mean needlessly waste of time for the doctor. After the examination, the doctor tells the lab staff, if he needs some blood or urine analysis. Then he enters the lab order into the system. The lab staff subsequently sees the electronic order on his/her screen.

There is no clear communication between the urology department and other departments throughout the hospital. This means for the patient that he/she has to return many times which is not helpful to increase the patient's contentment. When the doctor needs an X-ray image or a CT analysis, for example, the patient has to make a new appointment with radiology. For this appointment the patient has to come a second time to the hospital. To speak with the doctor in urology and to continue the examination, the patient has to come a third time to the hospital.

The doctor often doesn't really know the reason for the patient's visit till he can speak personally with the patient. This often leads to unexpected extensions of the patient's visit. The doctor expects that the visit of a returning patient will take not so much time, for example, because he expects that he only has to do a regular checkup. But some returning patients have new problems, about which they want to talk to the doctor. So the doctor has to spend more time with those patients than he expected.

Yet another waste of time problem is caused by the system, because there is no account for each staff member and the urology team doesn't correctly use the shared mode functionality from the system. Here is an example: When the MA wants to enter results into the system, it can happen that he/she has to wait while the doctor is using the system at the same time or if the doctor has forgotten to close the workspace.

The system's features are inadequately being used; it turned out to be another problem. While the system could take on many jobs, the crew is struggling with these jobs. Here is an example: If a patient is too late and the receptionist has waited more than 20 min, she will cancel the appointment in the system. Instead the receptionist needs to check the clock the whole time; the system could automatically cancel the appointment 20 min after the scheduled time, if the patient hasn't arrived at the urology department yet.

The inexplicit division of labour also leads to a not satisfying patient support service and to additional work for the health care team. In one case a patient has arrived at the reception and he was a new patient. He needed to fill out some forms. He told the receptionist that he has arthritis and that he can't write. The receptionist told the patient that he shall take the blank form to the doctor, so that the doctor can fill out the form with the patient together. This is not the doctor's job and extends the time he has to spend with the patient.

Additional work for the doctor is also caused by inexplicit distribution of jobs. A new patient needs to fill out several forms. The receptionist gives these filled out forms to the patient so that he/she can give them to the doctor. Later the doctor has to enter all the information from the forms into the system.

26.6 Value Stream Mapping

The above investigation and analysis clearly indicate that the current efficiency of the system is relatively low due to a number of problems. In addition to the issues of incomplete patient forms, inflexible scheduling, poor communication between the staff members and departments, lack of transparency and inexplicit division of labour, there is the problem of waste in terms of unnecessary manual checks and data entry, duplicated activities, excessive waiting time and underutilisation of resources. Most of these non-value-adding (NVA) wastes can significantly be reduced upon proper planning and design of the whole healthcare delivery process. They can also be minimised through the use of information technology to enhance visibility and enable automation. To identify the sources of waste and the locations of bottlenecks so as to help redesign the whole process, the use of the value stream mapping (VSM) technique is proposed.

VSM is a lean manufacturing technique originated from "just-in-time manufacturing" or "Toyota production system" introduced by the Japanese automobile manufacturing company Toyota (Browning and Heath 2009; Cox and Chicksand 2005). It is commonly used to analyse and design the flow of materials and information required to bring a product or service to a consumer effectively and efficiently while maintaining quality. Nowadays, lean manufacturing or production usually refers to a collection of principles governing waste elimination and value creation (see, e.g. Womack and Jones 2003) that have been applied in different industries, organisations and countries (Calloway 2004; Holweg 2007).

The essence of VSM is to map the current state of a production or delivery process to a value stream. First of all, a product, product family or service has to be identified. Then, the main objective of the mapping is to identify all the value-adding (VA) and NVA activities involved in the process. Efficiency of the process cycle can then be calculated based on the total lead time and the total processing time. The more NVA activities involved in the process, the lower the efficiency will be. These NVA activities will need to be removed or reduced so as to increase the total value of the stream. This may involve redesigning the whole process, adoption of a pull instead of a push strategy during production or service delivery, the use of information technology for visibility and automation, etc. Next, a revised value stream map for the new or future state of the process can be created upon re-engineering the process to eliminate the identified waste in the flow. Again, efficiency of the new process cycle can be calculated using the new total lead time and processing time to determine the extent of improvement. This will help justify the process re-engineering or redesign if the value of the stream has been significantly increased as a result. Finally, a plan to work toward the future state condition can be developed to guide the migration and to allocate resources. VSM has now been adopted in many other disciplines apart from manufacturing and can be applied to nearly any value chain (Manrodt et al. 2008; Shan et al. 2008).

In the healthcare industry, VSM has been widely used to help improve efficiency and service quality. For example, Kaale et al. (2005) used VSM to develop a time VSM tool for emergency department triage at the York Hospital Emergency Department. The objective is (1) to identify activities that "add value" to the patient encounter versus those that are "wasteful" (non-value added), (2) to delineate bottlenecks to flow, and (3) to establish a baseline framework for improvement by creating a "map" of the existing triage process. Their analysis revealed that most activities in the triage process did not add value to the patient's encounter and should be removed. Teichgräber and de Bucourt (2012) applied VSM techniques to eliminate non-value-added waste for the procurement of endovascular stents. They found that only 2 out of 13 processes for the procurement of stents were value-adding. Out of the 11 NVA activities, 5 are totally unnecessary and could be eliminated. Decision point analysis also revealed that using a pull instead of a push system to trigger the movement of a unit after removal can help improve inventory control and reduce unnecessary stock.

Using VSM, the current and the future state value streams of the urology department under investigation are shown in Figs. 26.2 and 26.3, respectively. It can be seen from Fig. 26.2 that the current process involves a lot of manual operation in information processing and archiving which are time-consuming and NVA. This is because, to the patient, the value of the service delivery process lies only in receiving the diagnosis from the doctor. Time spent in all other activities is NVA although some of them, such as checking in or taking and testing a urine sample, are necessary but non-value-adding (NVA). Time spent in waiting for checking of insurance, demographic information, diagnosis, etc. is totally unnecessary if automation and a pull approach are adopted in the process. As the actual processing times in the various activities involved in the process vary from patient to patient, the time values shown in the current state map are just averages and approximate figures. Nonetheless, they reflect to a reasonably accurate degree the overall cycle time of

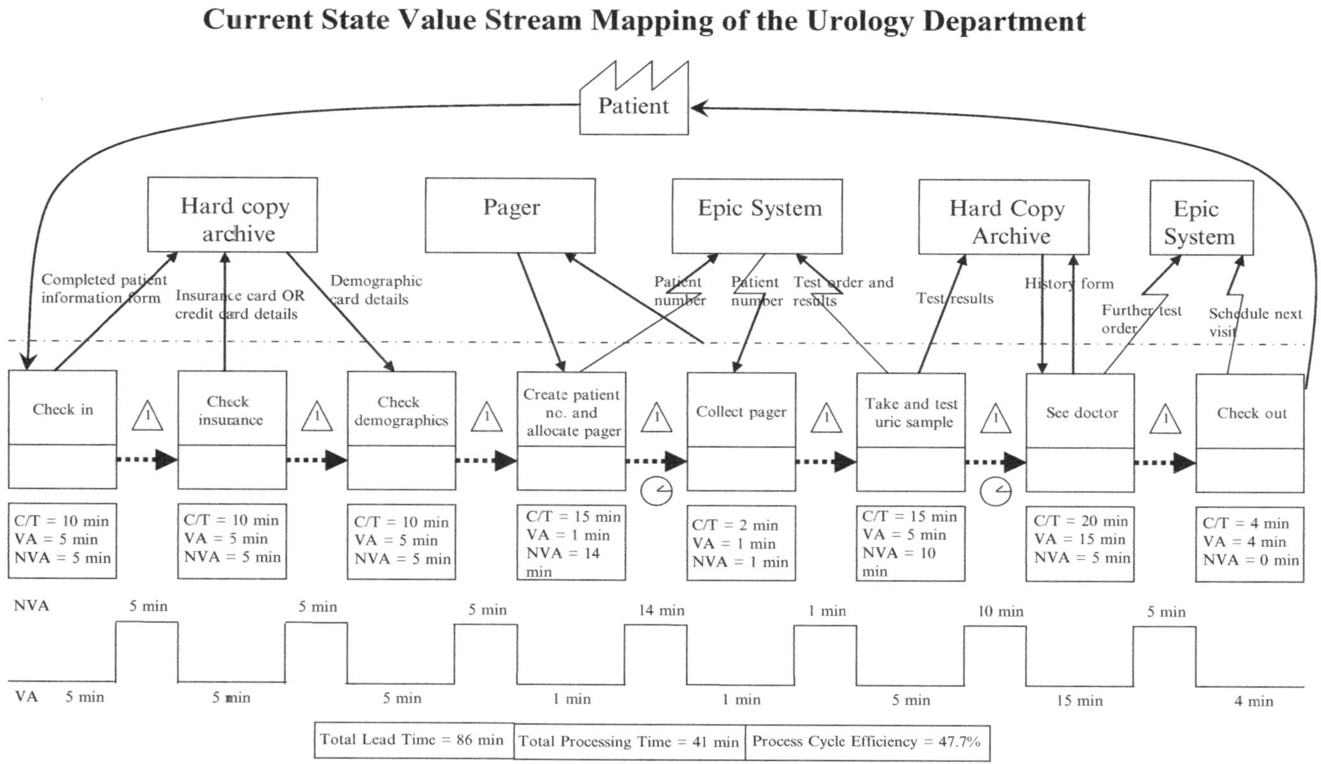

Fig. 26.2 Current state value stream map of the process

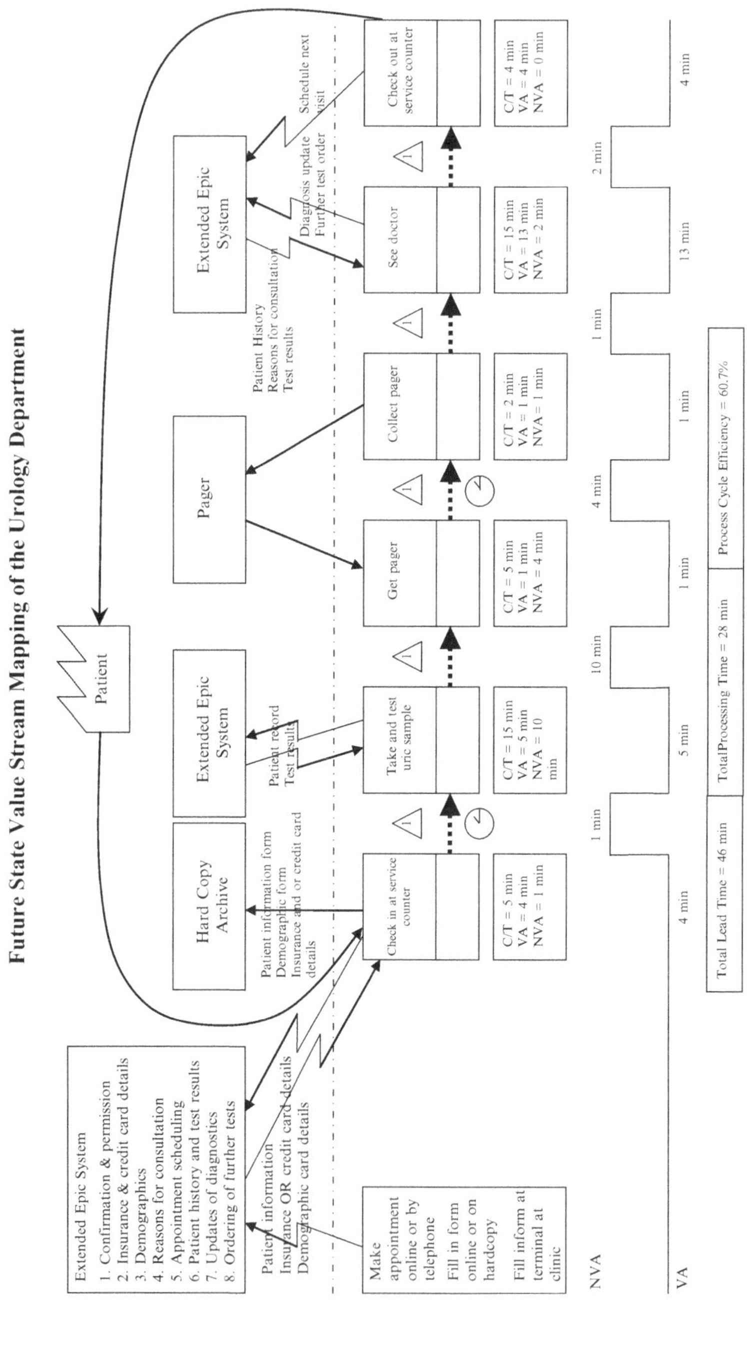

Fig. 26.3 Future state value stream map of the process

the current situation. Using these figures, the total lead time and the total processing time of the current state add up to 86 and 41 min, respectively, thereby giving a process cycle efficiency of 47.7 %.

To reduce the time-consuming and unnecessary manual document checking activities so as to reduce the non-value-added waiting time of patients, information technology in terms of an extended EMR can be used. The extended EMR can automate the patient check in process online or through an operator-assisted process prior to the appointment. This will significantly expedite the check-in process at the urology department and reduce the total lead time, thereby increasing throughput of the system. Also, to increase perceived value of the service, NVA activities, such as taking and testing a urine sample, can be done before the beginning of the wait for diagnosis. To further reduce cycle time, the extended EMR can be used to facilitate record retrieval, updating and archiving. The Web-enabled system ensures a high level of interoperability by allowing parallel multiple accesses to a patient record at the same time. This also helps remove bottlenecks that occurred in the current linear sequence of operation. As shown in Fig. 26.3, the redesigned process is more streamlined with fewer stages involved despite the fact that relatively little change is needed to resource requirement apart from the extended EMR system. Although many of the procedures may have to be reengineered so as to make use of the extended EMR system as a major interface for data entry and retrieval, the flow is basically identical to that of the current state, thereby minimising the inconvenience caused to the patients as well as the ambulatory staff. As a result of the process rationalisation, the new total lead time and the new processing time are estimated to be 46 and 28 min. They represent a 47 and 32 % reduction, respectively, which is quite a significant saving. The new process cycle efficiency is estimated to be 60.7 % representing a 13 % increase when compared with that of the current situation. This figure can further be improved upon continued process redesign to reduce non-value-added time in the process.

26.7 Conclusions from Phase 1

26.7.1 Suggestions for Improvement

To eliminate the bottleneck of completing and signing forms, the patients with internet access could be asked to make the appointment online. Then they could be more easily fill out the forms, making the first appointment a smoother entry into the system. The urology department also could put up a kiosk in the waiting room, where the patients can fill out online forms. The urology department could post the forms that have to be signed in the internet, so that the patients can download them and print them out. The patients also should be able to download the brochures (e.g. "Your Privacy Rights") that they can read before they sign confirmations and permissions.

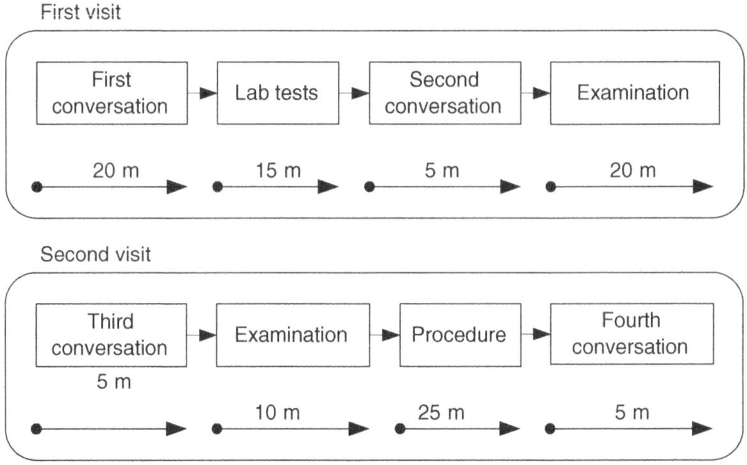

Fig. 26.4 Exemplary and simplified standard of a medical condition's treatment

Another issue are the forms themselves. The urology department should redesign them, because some questions are not clear. They can ask the receptionist, he/she will know which questions are confusing for the patients, because the most of the time patients ask him/her if they don't know how to fill out the forms. The letter the urology department sends to the new patients is confusing. The letter says that the patient should be at the reception 15 min prior to his/her appointment. But on the letter is a red sticker that says the patients should be at the department 10 min prior the scheduled appointment. If someone receives a letter overcrowded with information and with a red sticker, what will this person prefer to read? What will this person think is more important—letter or red sticker? And if this person decides to read both, what will he/she keep in mind?

If a patient calls to make an appointment for a return visit, the receptionist could ask the patient, why he/she wants to see the doctor—Still the same problem? Another problem? Only checkup? Or if the patient is transferred by a general practitioner, they could ask him/her about the patient's problem. If the urology department can establish the online scheduling, they could force the patients to specify the reason of their visit. The urology department has to find out why the patient wants to see the doctor before he/she comes to clinic; this will be helpful to improve the time management.

Next, the urology department has to eliminate the inflexible scheduling. The EMR should allow arbitrary time slots. If the department could find a way to find out the visit reasons of the return patients, then they can introduce an intelligent scheduling. Therefore they have to establish standards depending on the patient's medical condition so that they can classify the time needed for different treatments (see Fig. 26.4).

It is very important that the urology department improves the usage of the EMR features. At the moment they only use the system to enter and store data. But the system can assume many other jobs with which the staff is struggling with at the moment. To quote an example: If a patient is too late and the receptionist has waited more than 20 min, she will cancel the appointment in the system. Instead of this, the EMR could automatically cancel the appointment 20 min after the scheduled time, if the patient hasn't arrived.

The system also could be used to improve the communication between the reception and the clinic. The system should show the receptionist when there is an examination room empty or when the doctor is ready to see the next patient that he/she can forward the patient to the clinic. Otherwise the system should not only show that a patient has arrived, it also should show the clinic staff that the patient is ready to enter the clinic. The communication between the clinic staff could be improved by the system, too. If they only use the system to exchange lab orders and results, they can save time while cutting down duplicate work.

Therefore it is important that every team member has his/her own account. Then it would be possible to introduce a better user interface which is personalised and serves every team member the needed information. The lab staff only needs a list of lab orders and a user interface where he/she can enter the results, for example.

To improve their healthcare delivery, the urology department should check if they can use the EMR or another technology to improve the communication and collaboration with other departments in the hospital so that they can finish the patient's treatment in a faster and more efficient way.

It is also important that the urology department establishes a concrete division of labour which can only be diverged for a good reason. Therefore they need concrete work descriptions that specify which person is responsible for which task. With a business process model, they could describe all steps of each jobs and who is responsible for it. If everybody knows what is his/her responsibility, the work will be done more efficiently with less confusion. First it seems that building up business processes and job descriptions is hard work but the advantages which the department will retrieve are rewarding. It will be helpful to find out who is overloaded and who is unchallenged, so that labour can be newly distributed. The bottom line is it will be helpful to improve the contentment of the staff, to advance the healthcare delivery and to raise the satisfaction of the hospital's customers, which in turn extends the good reputation of the hospital. And this means more patients will opt for the hospital when it comes to their medical condition which again means more income (see Fig. 26.5).

26.7.2 List of Recommendations

- Improve the process of completing and signing patient to eliminate this bottleneck.
- Eliminate inflexible scheduling and improve an intelligent scheduling to improve the time management.

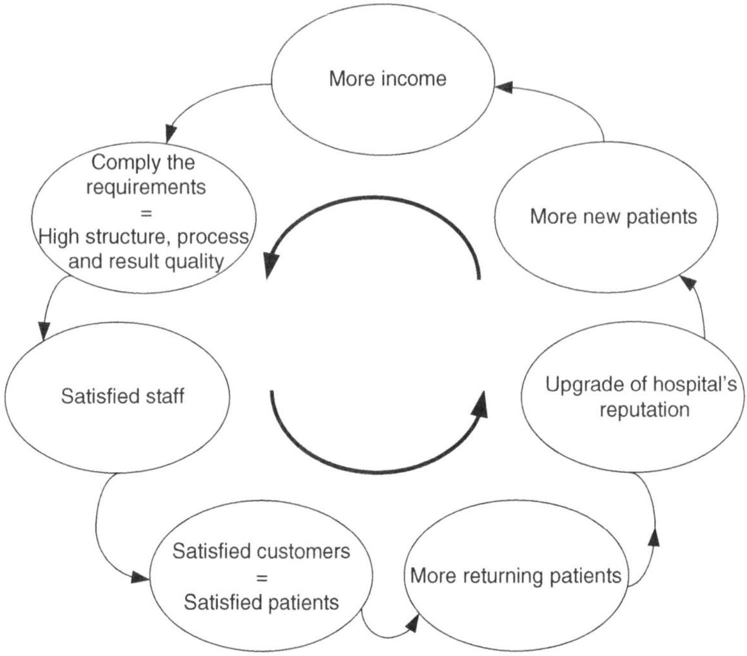

Fig. 26.5 Success circle

- Improve communication between reception and clinic to make the workflow smoother.
- Eliminate needless work by adapting the workflow to the EMR in order to eliminate wasting of time.
- Improve communication between the urology department and other departments to make healthcare delivery more efficient.
- Find a way to specify the reason of the patient's visit before they arrive at the urology department to improve the time management.
- Try to use all features which the EMR has to offer to ease the daily routine.
- Establish job descriptions and business processes to improve the quality of healthcare delivery.
- Create medical treatment standards to lower the variability.

26.7.3 Summary

The urology department can reduce the waste of time; they can improve their workflow and can raise the contentment of the providers and the patients. The bottom line is that they can advance the quality of healthcare delivery. The above-listed issues can be a beginning and if the urology department tries to realise them, they will get rewarded. It is not a difficult challenge and it doesn't need a big investment. What is needed is a team—staff members who are freed of their duties for a while or an extern project team—which will reorganise the process of healthcare delivery in the urology department while they put the above-listed issues into practice. However it is important to note that such changes should be effected first before any further technology solutions and e-health initiatives are introduced in order to realise the healthcare value proposition. This chapter has thus served to illustrate the benefits of applying the concept of VSM to healthcare in an attempt to identify areas that can be improved and thereby realise superior healthcare operations in practice.

Acknowledgements The author wishes to acknowledge Katharina Gaensler of the University of Cooperative Education Heidenheim, Germany for her invaluable assistance on this project.

References

Browning, T. R., & Heath, R. D. (2009). Reconceptualizing the effects of lean on production costs with evidence from the F-22 program. *Journal of Operations Management, 27*(1), 23–44.
Calloway, W. (2004). Lean thinking. In M. M. Srinivasan (Ed.), *Streamlined: 14 principles for building and managing the lean supply chain*. Phoenix: Thomson Business and Professional Publishing.
Cox, A., & Chicksand, D. (2005). The limits of lean management thinking: Multiple retailers and food and farming supply chains. *European Management Journal, 23*(6), 648–662.
Ganiban, J. (2004, April) Protecting your PACS purchase. *Radiology Today*. Retrieved from http://www.radiologytoday.net/archive/rt_042604p8.shtml
Holweg, M. (2007). The genealogy of lean production. *Journal of Operations Management, 25*(2), 420–437.
Inchingolo, P. (2007). Picture archiving and communications systems in today's healthcare. *WMA J.*
Institute for Healthcare Improvement. (2003). Optimizing patient flow—Moving patients smoothly through acute care settings innovation series. http://www.ihi.org. Accessed January 2011.
Kaale, R. L., Vega, D. D., Messner, K., Eitel, D. R., Johnson, D. E., McKniff, S., et al. (2005). Time value stream mapping as a tool to measure patient flow through emergency department triage. *Annals of Emergency Medicine, 46*(3), 23.
Kywi, A. (2007). PACS is a crowd-pleaser in healthcare. *Health Management Technology*. Retrieved from http://www.healthmgttech.com/archieves/0305/0305pacs_crowdpleaser.htm
Manrodt, K., Thompson, R., & Vitasek, K. (2008). The lean journey. *Logistics Management, 47*(4), 35–38.
Schnellen, M. (2008). Developing a model to analyze the physic and information processes of an emergency department. In N. Wickramasinghe & E. Geisler (Eds.), *Encyclopaedia of healthcare information*. Hershey: IGI.
Shan, R., Chandrasekaran, A., & Linderman, K. (2008). In pursuit of implementation patterns: The context of lean and six sigma. *International Journal of Production Research, 46*(23), 6679–6699.
Smith, E. (2007). *Optimizing patient care and radiologist workflow through integrated patient-related data and image management*. Misys Healthcare Systems. http://www.besmith.com. Accessed January 2011.
Teichgräber, U. K., & de Bucourt, M. (2012). Applying value stream mapping techniques to eliminate non-value-added waste for the procurement of endovascular stents. *European Journal of Radiology, 81*(1), e47–e52.

Wickramasinghe, N., Tumu, S., Bali, R. K., & Tatnall, A. (2007a). Using Actor Network Theory (ANT) as an analytic tool in order to effect superior PACS implementation. *International Journal of Networking and Virtual Organisations, 4*(3), 257–279.

Wickramasinghe, N., Bali, R., & Geisler, E. (2007b). The major barriers and facilitators for the adoption and implementation of knowledge management in healthcare operations. *International Journal of Electronic Healthcare, 3*(3), 367–381.

Womack, J. P., & Jones, D. T. (2003). *Lean Thinking*. New York: Simon and Schuster.

Chapter 27
A Technology-Mediated Solution to Reduce Healthcare Disparities

Nilmini Wickramasinghe, Ray Arias, and Chris Gonzalez

Abstract As healthcare costs in the USA continue to rise exponentially, it becomes a strategic imperative for healthcare organizations to examine all areas of their healthcare delivery and identify those which are currently inefficient and ineffective and then work to design and develop solutions that provide superior healthcare and that support a healthcare value proposition of excellence in access quality and value. Moreover, given the current emphasis on identifying meaningful use of technology in healthcare in the USA, it becomes prudent to develop appropriate technology solutions that not only comply with this requirement but also facilitate superior healthcare delivery to ensue. One area within healthcare delivery that this is particularly relevant and germane is when we look at healthcare disparities that currently exist. One key area within healthcare disparities relates to access to language services in healthcare or more specifically supporting limited English-proficient patients (LEP patients). This chapter discusses how the development of a real time online technology-mediated solution to support LEP patients can address key effectiveness and efficiency issues and provide superior healthcare and thereby serve to reduce a key healthcare disparity.

Keywords Limited English-proficient (LEP) patients • Healthcare delivery • Meaningful use of technology • Healthcare disparities • Title VI

N. Wickramasinghe (✉)
Epworth HealthCare & Department of BITL & HIRi, RMIT University,
GPO Box 2476, Melbourne, VIC 3001, Australia
e-mail: nilmini.wickramasinghe@rmit.edu.au

R. Arias
Arias Information Solutions LLC, Chicago, IL, USA

C. Gonzalez
Northwestern Memorial Hospital, Galter 20-150, 675 N. St. Clair, Chicago, IL 60611, USA
e-mail: CGonzalez@nmff.org

N. Wickramasinghe et al. (eds.), *Lean Thinking for Healthcare*, Healthcare Delivery in the Information Age, DOI 10.1007/978-1-4614-8036-5_27,

27.1 Introduction

For many decades the USA has been noted as being a melting pot of cultures and people from different ethnic backgrounds. This has indeed brought a richness and depth to the USA and has served to play a key role in shaping this country's history and future. One of the challenges of such a multicultural society is that all people have access to all things despite varying English language proficiency. One area where English language proficiency should not impinge on access to and quality of service is with healthcare. Improving access to language services in healthcare has been an ongoing issue that continues to be at the forefront of various healthcare agendas (Amazon 2011; Armbrust et al. 2010). Today, when healthcare delivery in the USA is at a major crossroad (Au et al. 2009), it becomes imperative to address this issue. Moreover, given that this is the age of technology, it makes sense to look for a technology-enabled solution that might address this problem.

27.2 Background

Currently over 23 million Americans have limited English proficiency, which in turn has a negative impact on their ability to receive appropriate healthcare delivery (Youdelman, 2008; Flores et al. 2008). Language barriers in the healthcare setting can lead to problems such as delay or denial of services, issues with medication management, and underutilization of preventative services (Green et al. 2005; Jacobs et al. 2004; Gandhi et al. 2000). In addition, difficulty in communication also may limit clinicians' ability to understand patient symptoms and effectively provide treatment (Karliner et al. 2004; Barrett et al. 2008). Moreover, existing research suggests the quality of communication between patients and providers is strongly associated with providers' ability to deliver better and safer care for LEP patients (Ponce et al. 2006a, b; Institute of Medicine 2003; Interpreter Services Work Group Report to Minnesota Legislature 2008). Language services, such as translation and interpretation, can facilitate this communication and thus improve healthcare quality, the patient experience, adherence to recommended care, and ultimately health outcomes (Flores 2005; Jacobs et al. 2004; Karliner et al. 2004; Kallick 2007; National Committee for Quality Assurance 2008).

Although Title VI of the Civil Rights Act 1964 always has required that entities receiving federal funds provide language services to those with LEP, the law has not often been enforced in healthcare settings (Jacobs et al. 2004; Chen et al. 2007; DrTango Inc. 2011). However, awareness of the need to provide language services in healthcare has increased in recent years (Perkins and Youdelman 2008).

27.3 Problem Statement

Today there are over 60 million Americans who speak languages other than English and that number is expected to grow over the next decade. Findings from several recent studies conducted and funded by the United States Department of Health and Human Services reveal that language barriers are a real source of additional cost to the already overworked American Healthcare System. Estimates rise to $20 billion per year for this additional cost.

27.4 Model

Succinctly stated then the key issues of this problem are as follows (Fig. 27.1):

- High cost and quality impact of language barriers on US healthcare system (medical errors).
- 60 million LEP healthcare interactions each year.
- $100B + direct and indirect costs/year.
- Only 20 % of LEP patients received proper healthcare coordination.
- Federal government is also at significant litigation risk due to non-service to the LEP population.

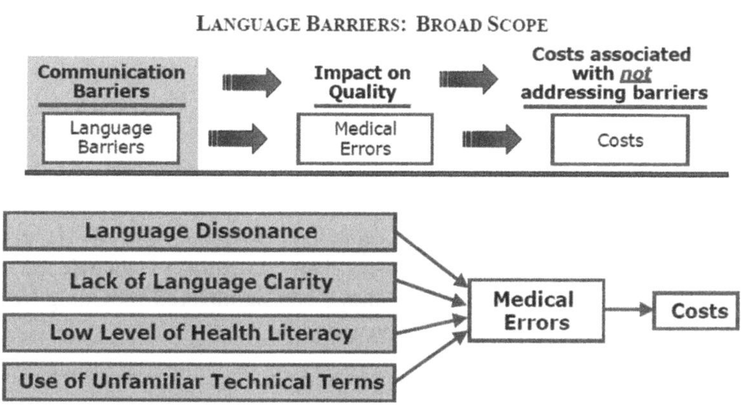

Fig. 27.1 Problem in a nutshell. Reproduced with the permission of Arias IS LLC

27.5 Technology Solution

Cloud computing is a new computing technology that offers dynamically scalable reconfigurable resources and services to clients on demand via the Internet (Gilbert 2010; Julisch and Hall 2010). It is currently noted as being one of the most significant information technology (IT) advances in recent years that is expected to transform the IT industry in many ways by facilitating the creation of business value and innovation (Armbrust et al. 2010; Julisch and Hall 2010; Troshani et al. 2011).

With cloud computing, adopters can access resources (e.g., their documents and data) and capabilities (e.g., specific functionality such as word processing, email, software development environments) ubiquitously from any device anywhere anytime, while being able to rent computing power and storage from providers on demand (Troshani et al. 2011). It is anticipated that this will in turn result in fundamental impacts on both lifestyles and organizational cost structures (Etro 2010). Moreover, cloud computing is expected to provide significant efficiency improvements; promote growth, competition, and business creation; and enhance overall national macroeconomic performance (Dutta and Mia 2011; Etro 2010).

As it is relatively new, the definition of cloud computing is still expected to evolve overtime; currently, most scholars subscribe to the definition that cloud computing is an arrangement that enables the convenient provisioning of configurable software capabilities and underlying hardware resources across numerous host computers that are connected via a network (Mell and Grance 2010; Svantesson and Clarke 2010). There are five essential features that characterize cloud computing (Mell and Grance 2010; Troshani et al. 2011):

- On-demand self-service whereby consumers can obtain computing capabilities or resources (e.g., network storage or server time) without necessarily requiring service provider interaction.
- Broad network access whereby computing capabilities or resources can be accessed ubiquitously using any device (e.g., mobile phones, laptops).
- Resource pooling whereby location-independent computing resources and capabilities are assigned dynamically to consumers according to demand.
- Rapid elasticity whereby computing capabilities and resources are rapidly scalable and can be purchased by consumers at any time in any quantity.
- Measured service whereby resource usage can be metered providing transparency to both service providers and consumers.

In addition, cloud computing capabilities and resources include various applications and services, storage, processing power, memory, network bandwidth, and virtual machines which are classified into three broad categories (Julisch and Hall 2010; Mell and Grance 2010; Troshani et al. 2011):

- Software as a service (SaaS) which includes software applications controlled by providers that consumers can access and run through thin client interfaces (e.g., web browsers). Examples include web-based mail services such as Gmail.

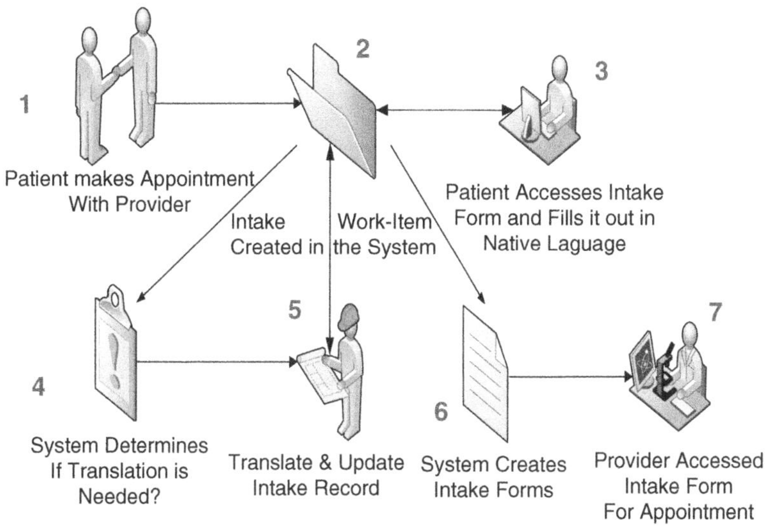

Fig. 27.2 Conceptual model. Reproduced with the permission of Arias IS LLC

- Platform as a service (PaaS) which includes provider-controlled platforms comprising development tools and run time environments which cloud consumers can use to develop their own software applications. Examples of PaaS include Google Apps and Microsoft Azure.
- Infrastructure as a service (IaaS) which includes provider-controlled fundamental computing resources such as virtual machines, storage, and networks where consumers can run arbitrary applications including operating systems. Examples include Amazon's Elastic Compute Cloud (Amazon EC2).

Given the possibilities afforded to us by recent technology most especially the advent of cloud computing and WEB 2.0, it now becomes possible to design and develop a technology-based solution to facilitate the intake and registration process of LEP patients and thus try to address this issue. The following presents a possible intake assist solution designed and developed to address this. Figure 27.2 provides the conceptual model from which the solution is then derived.

Based on this conceptual model, 13 critical stages have been identified to describe the patient encounter as depicted in Fig. 27.3. All these 13 steps of care must be addressed in the technology solution and/or suite of solutions.

From the 13 steps of the healthcare encounter, the next three key technology functions were identified including intake assist, outtake assist, and analytics assist (Fig. 27.4), and hence a solution suite has been conceptualized to address the problem. Figure 27.5 illustrates key steps of the first functional area intake assist.

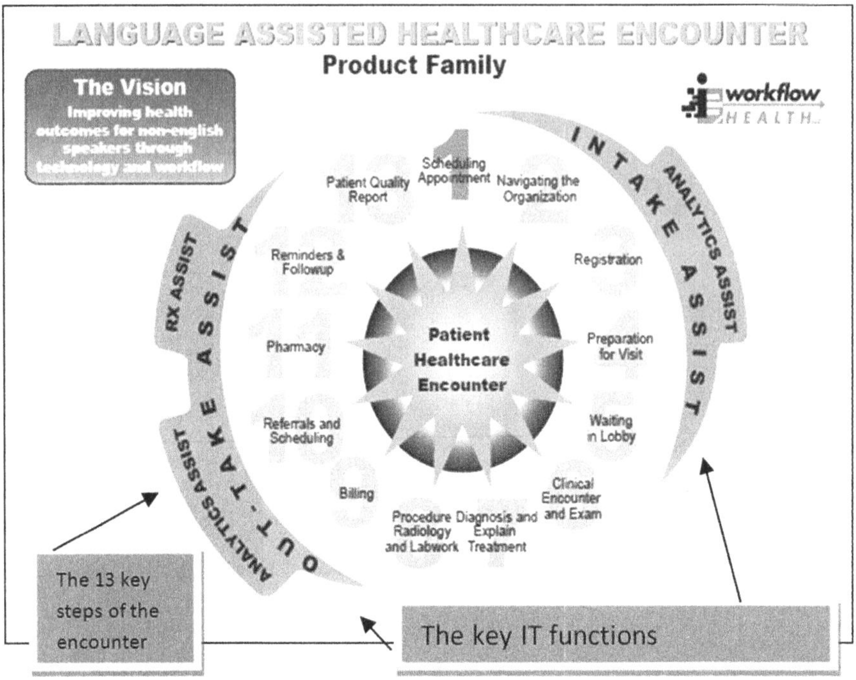

Fig. 27.3 The 13 steps of the healthcare encounter. Reproduced with the permission of Arias IS LLC

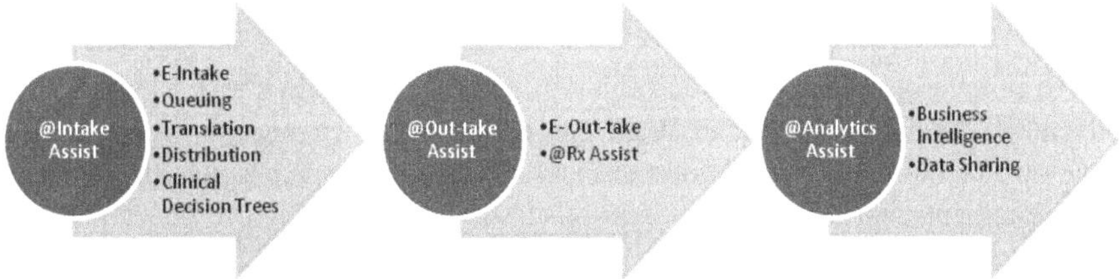

Fig. 27.4 Key technology function areas. Reproduced with the permission of Arias IS LLC

27.6 The Solution

The language-assisted intake and workflow solution designed is presented in Fig. 27.5 and has many advantages over the present strategies employed by healthcare organizations in dealing with LEP patients. In particular, it serves to reduce

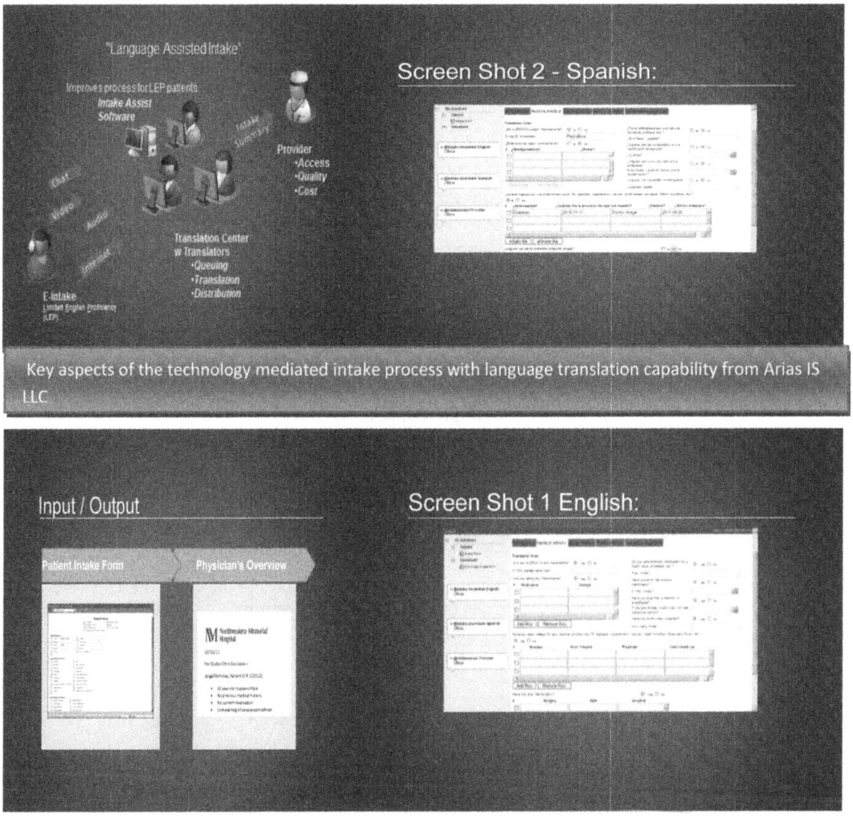

Fig. 27.5 The technology solution for intake with language assistance. Reproduced with the permission of Arias IS LLC

language barriers that in turn lead to a delayed or missed diagnosis and/or increased or needless hospital admissions as well as have a positive impact on access of care for patients. In addition, the cost benefits include reduction of the costs associated with EHRs (electronic health records) and significant savings with regard to non-compensated translator costs. Finally, the solution ensures healthcare facilities comply with government mandates and Title VI and is indeed as an example of meaningful use of technology.

The key benefits of this proposed solution are many and far reaching and include several aspects as noted below and summarized in Table 27.1 while Table 27.2 provides a comparison of the before and after scenarios:

- Provider administrators can test the impact of offering a (software as a service) cloud-based patient intake process for serving LEP and non-LEP patients vs. traditional paper methods.

Table 27.1 Key benefits

Who	How	What	When
Patient calls for appointment	Call in	Call in and scheduling process remains the same	At patient's request
Clinic admin	Clinic facility	Uses current scheduling system to identify appointment, also logged into intake assist system for associate registration number and offers appointment to patient • Mails or emails traditional intake form • Invites LEP or English-speaking patients to appoint 30 min early to complete intake form locally	At patient's call in
Patient	Remote or in clinic	Completes intake form via paper or in advance of visits (30 min early to complete form online)	At patient's convenience
Translator	Remote	Completes form where translation is required	In advance of physician appointment
Clinic admin	Clinic facility	Places completed intake form in physician queue	After form is completed
Physician	Clinic facility	Conduct diagnosis	Schedule appoint-ment time
Physician	Completes survey	Assessment of experience with form	After visit
Patient	Completes survey	Assessment of experience with form	After visit

- Improve administration process by integrating e-based enrollment option into clinic workflow.
- Reduce cost of dealing with paper forms.
- Make it easier to serve LEP patients.
- Can assess the usability of electronic form for other purposes.
- Providers (physician can test the value of using language-specific digital medical history forms).
- Clear concise information on medical/social/family history forms.
- Translated "reason for visit" information from which to begin diagnosis.
- LEP patients have the opportunity to complete intake in their own language (beginning with Spanish).
- Improve the comfort/quality of responding to intake in native language.
- Provide more detail from which the provider/physician can begin clinical diagnosis.

Table 27.2 Before vs. after

Actor	Before	Using intake assist
Spanish-speaking patients	• Handed an English language intake form and were asked to fill it out to the best of their ability	• Asked to participate in beta study, if agreeable directed to intake kiosk
	• Often had a family member fill out the form, forms were often difficult to read and were incomplete	• Offered Spanish language form which was translated into English per study description by medically competent interpreter
	• If no family member was present, a Spanish-speaking staff administrator was taken off their job and asked to serve as interpreter and fill out the form with patient and increased the cost of serving an LEP patient	• In some cases family member filled out form and in other cases interpreter filled out form
	• Completed forms were often difficult to read and of marginal value to physician provider	• No problems observed in using kiosk
	• Cultural behaviors limited the ability to gather information, Older Hispanics, men and women are very reluctant to volunteer information	• Form presentation was clear and understandable by patient
	• Completed form given to administration desk	• Completed form given to administration desk
	• Completed form was placed in patient intake folder and was available to physician, was not available for other purposes	• Completed form in electronic format was available for other purposes
English-speaking patients	• Given paper form	• Given option of using electronic intake kiosk with drop-down menus and input boxes
	• Filled out form to the best of ability	• Faster intake form completion
	• Very often completed forms were not easy to read and of minimal value to physician	• Intake form presentation was clear and understandable by patient
	• Completed form was placed in patient intake folder and available to physician, was not available for other purposes	• Completed form was placed in patient intake folder and available to physician and available for other purposes

(continued)

Table 27.2 (continued)

Actor	Before	Using intake assist
Physician	• Used a paper handwritten intake form from which to begin patient encounter • Often difficult to read • Information was missing or out of place	• Physician presented an electronic-typed form • More complete format • Detailed medical history • Detailed family history • Physicians had capability to request form modification for additional questions or format
Administration	• Begins with request for appoint and scheduling of appointment • Request for completion of paper forms prior to actual appoint, on appointment date	• Appointment setting is conducted using traditional method, but patient is sent email with site information for online completion of form in native language • Front desk administration offered patient option to fill out form in office in native language • Administration was able to produce multiple copies of forms for other uses such as intakes for ambulatory surgery

Table 27.3 Barriers and facilitators

Barriers	Facilitators
Deployment of physical kiosk could be an overarching barrier to beginning the trial when Internet connectivity is required	Ubiquitous wireless technology in the Feinberg setting allowed the placement of kiosk in available waiting area
Workload as an inhibitor of administrator training	Dedicated staff came in 30 min early for training purposes
Unavailability of patient schedules in advance appointments	Front desk staff provided patient appointment schedules well in advance for purpose of establishing translation load requirements
Availability of translation support	Third-party resources eliminated the need to use Spanish-speaking staff to translate intake forms
Disruption of normal activities	Preplanning of sequence of workflow mitigated disruptions of workflow
Availability of kiosk technology to meet patient demand	Preplanning and utilization of appropriate queuing models

Like all IT projects there are naturally impediments to success or barriers and facilitators (Wickramasinghe et al. 2012). It is important to capture these and then address them so that the full potential of the solution can be realized (Wickramasinghe et al. 2012). Table 27.3 captures the major barriers and facilitators.

27.7 Discussion

The solution proposed in the proceeding serves to address a key challenge faced by healthcare facilities due to LEP patients. Specifically it aims to leverage the advantages afforded to us by WEB 2.0 and current technology developments and intelligent applications as well as incorporate leading management principles in order to streamline the intake and registration process so that effective and efficient delivery of care can ensue to all patients. This in turn serves to support a healthcare value proposition of cost-effective, superior-quality, and hassle-free healthcare encounters.

The US healthcare provider setting is working to deliver the best possible patient care. At the same time, it must also meet cost of service objectives and provide physicians the best possible tools to meet patient's expectations of best practice. Technology in its many forms and applications can be employed and adapted to accomplish these goals.

A critical aspect in healthcare delivery is communication and coordination. Technology that facilitates communication and coordination between the patient and the provider (physician and administration) will thus have an important role. All healthcare interactions begin and end with communication between the provider and patient. This is a determining factor in successful health outcomes. With greater clarity and availability of patient information, there is a greater probability of meeting patient need and managing the cost of delivering service. For example, it is well documented that language barriers (communication barriers) between patients and providers are a leading cause of healthcare disparities. Communication barriers are not limited to the interactions between the patient and physician but also include the patient's interactions with the physician supporting healthcare infrastructure (administration).

Communication barriers impact:

- Patient–physician communication:
  - Inability of physicians to understand a patient's need and thus increase the potential for medical errors and the associated higher cost of service.
  - Poor communications between the physician and patient extend the healthcare encounter and create delays in physician access.
- Patient–administration communication:
  - The ability for the patient to follow procedural or pharmacy instructions which leads to patients incorrectly following instructions with detrimental consequences that serve to impact negatively on quality of healthcare outcomes and have the potential for significant cost of care implications
  - The ability for patients to provide or understand billing or insurance information which leads to confusion, patient dissatisfaction, and unnecessary time spent on nonproductive activities
  - The ability to follow up with the next steps in a treatment protocol which leads to potentially compromised outcomes and higher cost of service

The proposed intake assist solution is an effort to understand the impact of using a technology solution, i.e., an electronic intake format for gathering patient information from both English-speaking and non-English-speaking (LEP) patients to address these communication barriers and thereby support the delivery of a healthcare value proposition of superior access, quality, and value. Clearly the impacts for process improvement and increasing service quality are considerable and far reaching. However the technology solution must be fully developed first. Some key findings from a small pilot study run at Northwestern Memorial's urology clinic to show proof of construct demonstrated the benefit and viability of such a solution. Table 27.4 highlights the key points.

27.8 Conclusions

To underscore the importance of the online intake assist solution, Table 27.5 serves to compare and contrast with and without the technology scenarios. This table clearly presents a compelling case for the proposed technology solution. The next

Table 27.4 Key findings

Actor	Event	Outcome
English-speaking patient	*Intake*—English-speaking patients were offered option of traditional paper intake form or completing the electronic form at kiosk with touch screen and drop-down menu capabilities	• Technology is not a barrier 80 % of the patients offered the electronic option chose to use it. Several patients commented that the electronic version was much faster to use and more consistent with a modern healthcare setting. Others inquired if the electronic form was transferable to other departments. Yet others commented "no one uses paper anymore" • High patient satisfaction with intake process For those patients that chose the electronic version, patient satisfaction ranged on the scale of 4 or 5 with 5 being the highest on a 1–5 scale • Potential age barriers The Department of Urology serves an aged skewed population. As a general rule the younger the patient the more likely they were to opt for the electronic format
Spanish-speaking patient	*Intake*—Spanish-speaking patients were offered the options of the traditional paper intake form in English or completing the electronic form at kiosk with touch screen and drop-down menu capabilities in Spanish. Consequently, each Spanish-speaking patient opted for the electronic version of the form offered in their native language	• Forms translated into native language In each case at the electronic kiosk, translator services were incorporated to facilitate the completion of the intake form. Spanish-speaking patients were afforded the opportunity to complete the intake in their language while the administration and physician were provided an English-translated version of the intake form • High patient satisfaction with intake process In each case customer satisfaction was rated a 5 on a 1–5 scale. Multiple copies of the completed intake form given to each patient for potential use in other departments

(continued)

Table 27.4 (continued)

Actor	Event	Outcome
Physician and patient	English- and Spanish-speaking patients were queued to meet with the physician in a business as usual manner	• Physician satisfaction with electronic form Physicians who had access to the electronic forms regardless of language spoken by the patient rated the clarity of the information on the electronic form higher than the handwritten form. Also, physicians stated that the quantity of the information was greater and offered a clearer picture of the patient medical, family, and social status. Physician satisfaction with the electronic form over the handwritten form was ranked higher because the electronic form was easier and faster to read. See Appendix for sample of handwritten and electronic form
Administration and patient	Once the intake forms were competed (English and Spanish), they were handed to the front desk for administration, placed in the patient intake folder, and placed in queue for the physician. The form is reviewed by the physician. It is generally not used beyond physician review for other purposes	• Form redundancy After the physician encounter, patients were often asked to complete other forms very similar in content to the original intake form. Form redundancy is a major detractor to patient satisfaction and high-cost component to administrative efficiency. No other forms have a language assistance component. The impact of this is obvious, i.e., when a dietary requirement is needed before a test can be conducted and this requirement is not met due to language barrier, the procedure is rescheduled wasting valuable resources on time, equipment, and skilled staff

Table 27.5 With/without intake assist

	With intake technology	Without intake technology
Patient	• E-form for English and Spanish speaker—faster easier input and greater patient satisfaction	• Handwritten intake form
	• Language support—patient satisfaction and greater accuracy of information input	• Limited opportunity for information input
	• Greater input control—greater quality and quantity of information input	• Language dissonance
	• More information	• Lack of information control
Physician	• Greater quality and clarity of patient intake information at the beginning of encounter	• Unclear handwritten intake forms
	• Customized intake opportunity based on physician requirement (adaptive technology)	• Longer patient interview
	• Faster understanding of patient need	• Limits physician access
Administration	• Greater provider access	• Hand-carried paper information
	• E-forms that can be reused for other needs	• No electronic flexibility
	• Direct entry into EMR	
	• Consistent method for dealing with non-English speakers	

steps include designing and developing the outtake assist functions and analytics assist functions. Furthermore, if the solution is truly to realize its full potential, it must embrace the key principles of lean thinking and six sigma.

References

Amazon. (2011). *Announcing Amazon simpleDB in the EU region*. Retrieved from http://aws.amazon.com/about-aws/whats-new/2009/09/22/announcing-amazon-simpledb-in-the-eu-region/

Armbrust, M., Fox, A., Griffith, R., Joseph, A. D., Katz, R., Konwinski, A., et al. (2010). A view of cloud computing. *Communications of the ACM, 53*(4), 50–58.

Au, M., Taylor, E., & Gold, M. (2009). *Improving access to language services in health care*. Princeton, NJ: Policy Brief Mathematica Policy Research Inc.

Barrett, S., Dyer, C., & Westpheling, K. (2008). *Language access: Understanding the barriers and challenges in primary care settings*. McLean, VA: The Association of Clinicians for the Underserved.

Chen, A., Youdelman, M., & Brooks, J. (2007). The legal framework for language access in healthcare settings: Title VI and beyond. *Journal of General Internal Medicine, 22*, 362–367.

DrTango Inc. (2011). *A comparison of DMHC and CDI SB853 requirements*. Retrieved January 2001, from http://www.sb853.com/pdf/regulations-Table.pdf

Dutta, S., & Mia, I. (2011). *The global information technology report 2010–2011*. Geneva: World Economic Forum and INSEAD.

Etro, F. (2010). The economic consequences of the diffusion of cloud computing. In S. Dutta & I. Mia (Eds.), *The global information technology report 2009-2010*. Geneva: World Economic Forum and INSEAD.

Flores, G. (2005). The impact of medical interpreter services on the quality of health care: A systematic review. *Medical Care Research and Review, 62*(3), 255–299.

Flores, G., Torres, S., Holmes, L., Salas-Lopezs, D., Youdelman, M., & Tomany-Kprman, S. (2008). Access to hospital interpreter services for limited English proficient patients in New Jersey: A statewide evaluation. *Journal of Healthcare for the Poor and the Underserved, 19*(2), 391–415.

Gandhi, T., Burstin, H., Cook, E., Puopolo, A., Haas, J., Brennan, T., et al. (2000). Drug complications in outpatients. *Journal of General Internal Medicine, 20*, 149–154.

Gilbert, F. (2010). Cloud service contracts may be fluffy: Selected legal issues to consider before taking off. *Journal of Internet Law, 14*(6), 17–30.

Green, A., Ngo-Metzger, Q., Legedza, A., Massagli, M., Philips, R., & Iezzoni, L. (2005). Interpreter services language concordance and health care quality. *Journal of General Internal Medicine, 20*, 1050–1056.

Institute of Medicine. (2003). *Unequal treatment: Confronting racial and ethnic disparities in health care*. Washington, DC: The National Academic Press.

Interpreter Services Work Group Report to Minnesota Legislature. (2008). *Interpret services for patients in medical and dental settings*. Retrieved January 2010, from http://www.health.state.mn.us/dics/pqc/hci/ISWGreport08.pdf

Jacobs, E., Shepard, D., Suaya, J., & Stone, E. (2004). Overcoming language barriers in health care. *American Journal of Public Health, 94*(5), 866–869.

Julisch, K., & Hall, M. (2010). Security and control in the cloud. *Information Security Journal: A Global Perspective, 19*(6), 299–309.

Kallick, D. (2007). *Working for a better Life*. New York: Fiscal Policy Institute.

Karliner, L., Perez-Stable, E., & Gildengorin, V. (2004). The language divide. *Journal of General Internal Medicine, 19*, 175–183.

Mell, P., & Grance, T. (2010). The NIST definition of cloud computing. *Communications of the ACM, 53*(6), 50.

National Committee for Quality Assurance. (2008). *Standards aimed at improving health care for diverse groups, released for Public comment Dec 1*. Retrieved January 2010, from http://www.ncqa.org/tabid/916Default.aspx

Perkins, J., & Youdelman, M. (2008). *Summary of state law requirements addressing language needs in health care*. Washington, DC: National Health Law Program.

Ponce, N. A., Hays, R. D., & Cunningham, W. E. (2006a). Linguistic disparities in health care access and health status among older adults. *Journal of General Internal Medicine, 21*(7), 786–791.

Ponce, N. A., Ku, L., Cunningham, W. E., & Brown, E. R. (2006b). Language barriers to health care access among Medicare beneficiaries. *Inquiry, 43*(1), 66–76.

Svantesson, D., & Clarke, R. (2010). Privacy and consumer risks in cloud computing. *Computer Law & Security Review, 26*(4), 391–397.

Troshani, I., Rampersad, G., & Wickramasinghe, N. (2011) On cloud nine? An integrative risk management framework for cloud computing. In Bled eConference, June 12–15, 2011.

Wickramasinghe, N., Bali, R., Kirn, S., & Sumoi, R. (2012). *Critical issues for the development of sustainable e-health solutions*. New York: Springer.

Youdelman, M. K. (2008). The medical tongue: U.S. laws and policies on language access. *Health Affairs, 27*(2), 424–433.

Part V
Case Studies

1.1 Introduction

In order to make processes more effective and efficient it is necessary first to identify, analyze and redesign (unfreeze—redesign—freeze) the already existing processes. This approach was probably first brought to general attention of scholars and practitioners by the work of Deming and his colleagues (Deming 1982; Juran 1988; Sanders et al. 1999; Hall and Johnson 2009; Jacka and Keller 2011). However, the father of process modeling and designing processes for effective and efficient management dates back to Taylor (Gilbreth and Gilbreth 1924; Taylor 1911).

Business process mapping then refers to activities involved in defining exactly what a business entity does, who is responsible, to what standard a process should be completed and how the success of a business process can be determined (Wikipedia 2012). The main purpose behind business process mapping is to assist organizations in becoming more efficient. Thus, a clear and detailed business process map or illustration allows outside firms to come in and look at whether or not improvements can be made to the current process. While to date process mapping of healthcare processes is not as prevalent as other areas of business process mapping the following four chapters illustrate its use and benefits in case studies that focus on process mapping of emergency departments of four respective hospitals in the Stuttgart area in Germany. The four chapters are summaries from respective student projects supervised by Professors Kirn and Wickramasinghe. They are intended to illustrate the benefits of using process mapping techniques and tools in real life scenarios but are not intended to suggest effective or ineffective management in terms of healthcare practice.

All four case studies have a common approach. At first students collected data in the particular emergency departments in order to build a very detailed business process model using event driven process chains. Afterwards they analysed the processes and identify inefficiencies (especially unnecessary waiting times). Subsequently students made recommendations for possible improvements and critically assessed them by indicating the barriers and facilitators.

Besides, two of the groups integrated their idea for improvement into the process model and tried to show a reduction of throughput times by using the simulation tool MedModel®.

The four groups focused on different problems in the emergency department:

1. The group considering Marienhospital Stuttgart focused on the implementation of a Triage system
2. The group considering Klinikum Esslingen focused on the implementation of Kiosk Check-In
3. The group considering Katharinenhospital Stuttgart focused on the improvement of the bed management process
4. The group considering Robert-Bosch-Krankenhaus Stuttgart focused on the improvement of different parts of the process, e.g. transportation process

We believe the following four case studies which by no means cover all the possibilities of using simulation to facilitate business process mapping and redesign help to demonstrate the benefits of such exercises and their applicability to healthcare contexts.

References

Deming, W. E. (1982). *Out of the crisis*. Cambridge: Cambridge University Press.
Gilbreth, F., & Gilbreth, L. (1924). *The quest of the one best way*. West Lafayette, IN: Purdue University, Frank and Lillian Gilbreth Papers, Society of Industrial Engineers, The University of California.
Hall, J. M., & Johnson, M. E. (2009). When should process be art, not science? *Harvard Business Review, 87*, 58–65.
Jacka, M., & Keller, P. (2011). *Business process mapping*. New York: Wiley.
Juran, J. M. (1988). *Juran on planning for quality*. New York, NY: Free Press.
Sanders, D., Ross, B., & Coleman, J. (1999). The process map. *Quality Engineering, 11*(4), 555–561.
Taylor, F. W. (1911). *The principles of scientific management*. New York, NY: Harper and Bros.
Wikipedia. (2012). Retrieved July 29, 2012, from http://en.wikipedia.org/wiki/Business_process_mapping

Chapter 28
Process Models, Its Inefficiencies and Recommendations of the Emergency Department of the Marienhospital

Lara Henzler, Daniel Mengele, Tahnee Platz, Kristina Riemann, and Janine Steffen

Abstract Waiting times play an important role in emergency departments. Even though all emergency departments serve the same purpose, none are exactly the same as every single one is unique in its setup and requirements. This was the biggest challenge facing us when we were compiling a general valid theory to optimize waiting times.

In this study, we observed the emergency department of the Marienhospital, and it was our aim to point out processes that are inefficient and point out potential to reduce sources of errors. We already studied literature, observed the workflow, analysed the data and illustrated the current process. In this chapter, we will describe and model the target process and discuss the results.

Keywords Emergency department • Simulation • Triage • EPC

28.1 Case Study

28.1.1 General Survey

This case study is about the process and its existing (or non-existent) inefficiencies in the emergency department of the Marienhospital, a catholic hospital situated in the south part of Stuttgart, Germany. The emergency department of the Marienhospital is interdisciplinary and deals with approximately 40–60 patients per day. A layout of the emergency department can be seen in Fig. 28.1 with its waiting room, the

---

The material in this case study was prepared originally for Project Seminar SS 2012 at the University of Hohenheim, Germany, under the supervision of Profs Kirn and Wickramasinghe.

L. Henzler (✉) • D. Mengele • T. Platz • K. Riemann • J. Steffen
University of Hohenheim, Stuttgart, Germany
e-mail: daniel-mengele@web.de

N. Wickramasinghe et al. (eds.), *Lean Thinking for Healthcare*, Healthcare Delivery in the Information Age, DOI 10.1007/978-1-4614-8036-5_28,

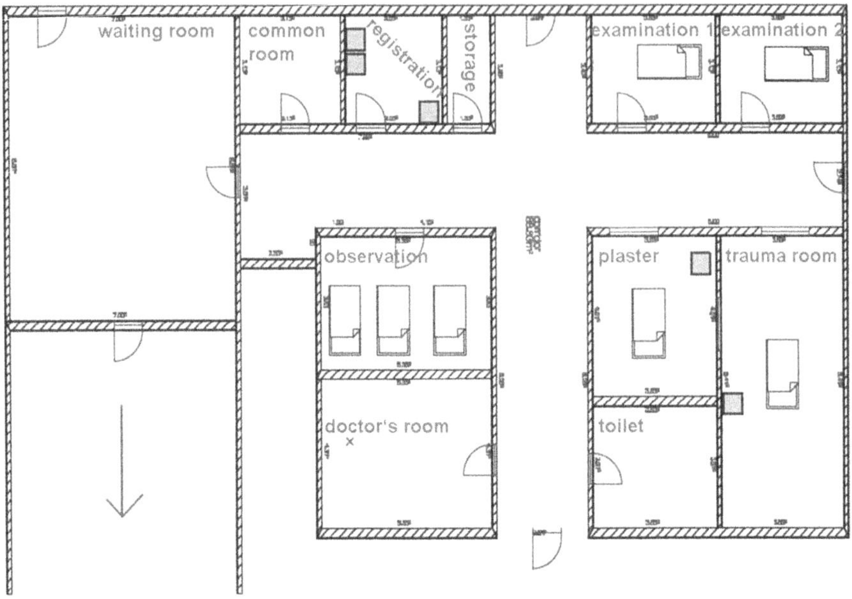

Fig. 28.1 Layout Marienhospital

registration, two examination rooms, a trauma room, a plaster and observation room with three beds, and each has a monitor and two common rooms. The Marienhospital works with an ERP system called ORBIS, a hospital information system from Agfa Healthcare GmbH in Germany.

What is truly special about the Marienhospital is that they rent out premises to the Notfallpraxis. Not only that, they (the Notfallpraxis) also use the Marienhospital's technical equipment. It is a pool of general practitioners who have no functional collaboration with Marienhospital. The Notfallpraxis is on duty during times when a general practitioner is not—which means nights Mondays to Thursdays from 7 p.m. to 7 a.m., Fridays from 2 p.m. to 7 a.m. and on weekends and on bank holidays 24 h/day. The patients are often confused and cannot distinguish the difference between the emergency department and the Notfallpraxis. This misunderstanding is strengthened by the fact that both organizations use the same entrance. Thus, the patients do not see any differences between them and think they belong together. During our observations, it often happened that the patients came to the registration of the emergency department and asked for further information. This information cannot be given by the emergency staff due to the fact that they work with a different ERP system and due to legal reasons that we do not wish to elaborate on here. What makes the situation even more difficult is that from 1 a.m., the admission for the Notfallpraxis is made by Marienhospital. In the mornings, the emergency department collects the admission data and hands it out to a staff from the Notfallpraxis. Furthermore, people who arrive at night as walk-in patients are urged to be treated by the Notfallpraxis, as well.

28.1.2 Proceeding

In the context of a research project of the information system chair of the University of Hohenheim, we analysed the process of the emergency department of the Marienhospital. After gaining an overview of the literature concerning emergency departments, Event-driven Process Chains and the optimal process of an emergency department itself, we were sent to the emergency department to get an overview and primarily to monitor waiting and examination times. For this reason, we were given a document with all required times, for instance, time of arrival, time of first contact with nurse, time of first contact with doctor, time of blood sample taking and so on. After spending approximately 150 h in emergency department and collecting time data from 97 patients, we aggregated those times and calculated the averages. Furthermore, we mapped a current process flow map and used the times we had established in it.

We gave thought and discussed the current flow map and tried to show inefficiencies. Some of these are presented in Chap. 28.1.4 as a suggested process map.

This suggested process map we tried to simulate, the methodology and its results can be seen in Chaps. 3 and 4.

28.1.3 Current Process Flow Map

First of all, the current process flow map of the Marienhospital will be described in the following. The current process flow of the emergency department in the Marienhospital is split up into nine subprocesses. At first, the patient arrives in emergency department either by ambulance or by 'walk-in' and is admitted by an employee or a member of nursing staff. After waiting time, the patient has to undergo some nursing staff actions before blood taking is done. Parallel to nursing staff actions and blood taking, there is the first contact with doctor as well as X-ray or CT examination. After this the patient has second contact with doctor. Finally, the patient has either no admission to ward or has an admission to ward, and there is a bed management needed.

At the beginning of the current process flow, an injured or sick patient arrives in the emergency department. Relating to the arriving, there are two possibilities: via ambulance vehicle or via 'walk-in'. The data collection in Marienhospital shows that 46.58 % of 146 observed patients arrived via ambulance vehicle and 53.42 % arrived via 'walk-in'.

If patients arrive via ambulance vehicle, they were handed over to doctor on duty by paramedics. After handover, the patient is admitted administrative in ORBIS system (software of the emergency department) and the admission log by an employee or member of nursing staff. For this admission, the employee or member of nursing staff needs patients' insurance card, transportations documents, former examination results (if available) and additional assurance form if the patient is not already registered in the system.

The subprocess for patients who arrive in IER via 'walk-in' is quite similar to the subprocess for patients via ambulance vehicle except for one difference: If a patient walks into the emergency department, there is at first the question, if the patient is in the right place or if he has to go to the 'Notfallpraxis'. Patients who walk in during opening hours of the 'Notfallpraxis' must leave the emergency department and go to the 'Notfallpraxis'. If the patient is right in emergency department, he is admitted administrative in ORBIS system and the admission log by an employee or member of nursing staff. Similar to the first subprocess, the registration needs patients' insurance card, transportations documents, former examination results (if available) and additional assurance form if the patient is not already registered in the system. From the data collection in Marienhospital, results show an average length of time of 5 min for administrative admission.

Relating to the administrative admission, there is the first identified process inefficiency. On the admission log, which is a standard draft for each patient, is a field for the triage of an arriving patient, but this field or rather the triage system itself is not in use. The nursing staff evaluates the arriving patients by experience which could be problematical, because urgent patients could be misjudged by members of nursing staff who are too inexperienced.

If the arriving patient is admitted, the current process flow continues with the third subprocess: waiting time. The patient has to wait in the waiting room until an examination room, a member of nursing staff and/or a doctor are available. On average, the patient has to wait 1 min until he/she has the first contact with nursing staff and 3 min until the first contact with a doctor. Parallel to the waiting time, the patient is allocated to internal medicine, neurology, or accident surgery by a member of nursing staff. After allocation, the patient's admission log is put into the correct doctor's shelf compartment.

After classification and waiting time, the patient is called up for bringing to one of the fifth examination rooms in the emergency department (observation room, trauma room, plaster room, U1 and U2).

The decision concerning the transfer to examination room is done by a member of nursing staff and depends on seriousness and type of illness/injury and availability of the examination room. In doing so the relocation to the observation room is intended for patients with life-threatening condition, in which the evaluation of the patient is made by intuition. Patients in the observation room are connected to monitor which observes the patient's condition and gives the alarm if the condition is too critical. The allocation to all other rooms is indeed spontaneously (depending on availability) done by members of nursing staff and either documented or systematic, which is another process inefficiency.

After transferring the patient to one of the examination rooms, a member of nursing staff checks vital signs and ECG of the patient and the results are registered in the patient record. The data collection in Marienhospital shows that the first contact with nursing staff takes 9 min on average, the second contact takes 6 min on average and the third contact takes 7 min on average. In total the average length of time is about 8 min per patient.

If vital signs and ECG of the patient are checked, the member of nursing staff has to decide about the blood taking, whereupon two possibilities exist: blood withdrawal is needed and blood withdrawal is not needed. If the blood withdrawal is needed, because of medical reasons, for further examinations (like X-ray or CT) or on doctors' order, a caregiver or the doctor himself takes the blood from the patient. In doing so the blood withdrawal is done to 88 % by caregiver, and the average length of time is about 5 min. When the blood withdrawal is finally done, the blood is taken away to the laboratory by emergency department staff.

If there is no need for blood withdrawal because of medical reasons (e.g. patient is too weak) or the blood taking is declined by the patient (e.g. because other hospitals or the paramedic have done that before), the patient goes to the next subprocess in the current process flow.

After the blood taking follows in the further current process flow normally the first contact between the patient and a doctor. During this first contact, the doctor examines the patient and collects the first findings about patient's illness/injury. This first verdict is registered in ORBIS and the patient label, but some doctors record their findings first manually until they enter them into the system. Based on the data collection, the first contact with a doctor takes 9 min on average. Furthermore, when the doctor has the first findings about patient's illness/injury, he/she decides if a CT or an X-ray is required to verify the diagnosis.

At first the explanation of the current process flow regarding a required CT: If the decision is made that a CT is required, the patient has to be registered for a CT in ORBIS by the doctor. After registration, the patient has to wait for his/her examination. Normally the patient has to wait in the examination room or in the waiting area, but sometimes there are also patients who wait on the corridor until their examination is ready. Another identified process inefficiency is the fact that in some cases the doctor or a member of nursing staff has to ask actively by phone if the examination for the patient is ready. If the examination is ready, the patient exits the IER with the aid of a caregiver or a member of nursing staff and goes to the CT where he/she is examined. After the CT examination, which takes 26 min on average, the patient comes back to the IER for further examination. However, it is also possible that sometimes patients will be transferred directly to ward after CT examination.

In addition to the decision about a required CT, the doctor also has to decide if there is an X-ray required to verify the diagnosis. If there is a need for an X-ray, the current process flow is very similar to the CT process. At first the patient has to be registered for X-ray examination in ORBIS by the doctor. Afterwards the patient has to wait (in examination room, in waiting area, or sometimes on corridor) until the examination is ready. When the examination is ready, the patient exits the IER with the aid of a caregiver or a member of nursing staff and goes to X-ray which takes 23 min on average. After the examination, the patient comes back to the IER or in some cases goes straight to ward.

If the CT and/or X-ray examination is done and in case that there is no need for a CT or an X-ray examination, the patient goes directly to the next subprocess: the second contact with a doctor. In this subprocess, the doctor starts further examinations based on the results of blood taking, ECG, vital signs, CT and X-ray.

Furthermore, the doctor has also the possibility to use additional examinations like sonography for verifying the diagnosis. This further examination by the doctor takes totalling (1./2./3. medical examination) 10 min on average, but there are also huge differences between working day and weekend (e.g. 2. medical examination: on working day: 13 min; on weekend: 8 min).

If the patient's ailment is diagnosed and in treatment, the doctor enters the diagnosis into the system (ORBIS) and the admission log so that the system is updated.

Moreover, the laboratory results for patient's blood are given by the employee of the lab. These results are registered in ORBIS and are only available through actively accessing the patient's health record in the system. The need of an active accessing by a member of nursing staff or a doctor is also an identified process inefficiency, which should be optimized through electronic tools. Another problem is the average length of time about 2 h and 27 min until the laboratory values are available and the huge difference between working day and weekend. On working day, the average length of time until laboratory values are available is about 3 h and 27 min, while the average length of time on weekend in contrast is about 1 h and 49 min.

In the further current process flow, the doctor has to come to a decision regarding the patient's admission to ward. This decision is made on the basis of illness heaviness, condition of the patient and which further examinations are planned (e.g. coloscopy). Based on the data collection, 49.32 % of the 149 observed patients had an admission to ward, whereas 50.68 % of the patients get discharged by doctor.

In case of patient's admission to ward, the doctor has to locate available beds in ORBIS and by telephone. However, the location of available beds is an identified process inefficiency mainly on working days, because many doctors are searching simultaneously for available beds and the actual amount is not registered contemporary. So the doctor has to use the telephone in addition to ORBIS for calling different wards (on average 1.25 telephone calls per patient), which takes the time they should normally use for treating patients. If the doctor has finally an available bed located, he contacts the ward for the reservation and the confirmation of the bed. After the confirmation through ward, a member of nursing staff requires the transport of the patient, who is finally collected by nursing staff from ward and leaves the emergency department. The average length of time between request the transport and patient's collection is about 9 min, but there are also huge differences between working day and weekend (average length of time on working day: 7 min; average length of time on weekend: 16 min). This difference is founded on the fact that on working days an additional caregiver service (called Johanniter) supports the nursery staff from ward, so the patient's transport to ward can be done faster.

If the doctor indeed decides to discharge the patient, he/she has to prepare the patient's report with the aid of ORBIS and Microsoft Office draft. However, there could be long waiting times during peak times until the patient's report is prepared. After the preparation, the patient's record is given to the patient by doctor or sometimes by a member of nursing staff and the patient leaves the emergency department finally. Based on the data collection results for the total length of stay in emergency department, an average length of time is about 2 h and 7 min.

28.1.4 Identified Process Inefficiencies

As already shown in the description of the current process flow, there are some identified process inefficiencies in the emergency department of Marienhospital.

The first identified inefficiency is the patient's allocation to an examination room. Normally the patient should be allocated depending on type and heaviness of his/her illness/injury and depending on the planned examinations by doctor. However, in the current process flow, the allocation of the patients is done spontaneously (depending on availability of the rooms) and on request by members of nursing staff. An exceptional case is indeed life-threatened patients, who are always allocated to observation room or trauma room.

One possible solution for the inefficiency depending the allocation of patients could be a software, which is integrated into the current IT system and operable from nurse station. Within the software, the allocation of examinations rooms could be easily switched from available to unavailable (and the other way round) by the members of nursing staff. An expanded version of this solution could be the possibility to change the room's status immediately in every examination room with the aid of a button/touch panel. This button/touch panel changes the room's status within the system and shows the current availability on a screen in the nurse station.

Another identified inefficiency refers to the laboratory results of patient's blood. These results are registered in ORBIS and are only available for the doctor or the member of nursing staff through actively accessing the patient's health record in the system. One possible solution for this process inefficiency could be an integrated software, which opens automatically a pop-up message if the results of a patient's blood are available. Since there are different types of blood results, another idea would be giving each type a little icon in the patient's file of the system. So in the overview of all current patients, it can be seen which results have already been taken and which are still to be taken; these could be shown greyed out.

This solution enables a significant reduction of waiting time until blood results are available could possible reduced considerable and the further examination process could go on faster.

The third identified process inefficiency refers to the subprocess bed management. If the doctor has decided that the patient has to go to ward, he/she has to locate available beds in ORBIS. The problem in this connection is the fact that mainly on working days many doctors are searching simultaneously for available beds and the actual amount is not registered contemporary in the system. So the doctor has to use the telephone in addition to ORBIS for calling different wards and locating an available bed, which takes the time they should normally use for treating patients. A possible solution for this inefficiency is the implementation of a software, which shows the actual amount of available beds within different wards. Simultaneously the system should allow the doctor to reserve an available bed on ward without calling them additionally by telephone. So the time which is previously needed for locating an available bed by telephone could be reduced and used for the treatment of patients.

Another part of the process that does not run smoothly is the application for CT. After the decision that a CT scan is necessary, the physicians apply the patients for the examination. For this procedure, they use ORBIS. After that the patient is told to walk over or—if he/she is not able to walk—to wait in the waiting room until someone picks him/her up. In some cases, we observed that the nurses had to call the CT ward to ask why the patient is not back yet, or why nobody picked him/her up. In most of the cases, they get the response that the capacities of the CT scan are running at rates and that they have to wait a bit longer. To avoid such waiting times and additional phone calls, we suggest that ORBIS should show the physicians and nursing staff how many patients are already applied to CT or other examinations like X-ray, so that they are able to appraise how long it will take to get CT scans. This enables them to plan further examinations better and more efficient. For example, if the physician knows that already eight other patients are waiting for CT and he/she knows that his/her patient not only needs CT but a sonography as well, he/she could first do the sonography and then send the patient to the CT examination. This way, the results of the sonography will be available sooner, the patient has reduced waiting times, and the staff would not have to make additional calls.

The last identified inefficiency refers to the missing triage system in the emergency department of Marienhospital. Even if there is a field for the triage of arriving patients on the admission log, this field or rather the triage system itself is not in use. The nursing staff evaluates the arriving patients by experience which could be problematical, because urgent patients could be misjudged by members of nursing staff who are too inexperienced. In order to evaluate arriving patients correctly and give the members of nursing staff the necessary safeness in doing so, the following triage process should be implemented into the current process flow between arriving/admission of the patient and the patient's transfer to an examination room (Fig. 28.2).

28.2 Simulation

28.2.1 Method Simulation and Software

Robinson defines simulation as an 'imitation of a system'. This implicates that a simulation is used to simplify a real situation, either computer based or physical. For instance, it is not just a software which can simulate. From a certain point of vew Las Vegas can be called a simulation, since you can find the Eiffel Tower, the New York skyline and so on . Of course, this is a very static example, with no consideration of time. This consideration is one of the major aims in simulation—next to the reduced costs and the quick ability to change parameters, which are not possible in real life.

Simulation with software can be defined as an 'imitation on a computer of a system as it progresses through time'. To sum up, it can be said that simulation is a good ability to model variability, to simulate restrictive assumptions and to cause a high degree of transparency (Robinson 2004, p. 2ff).

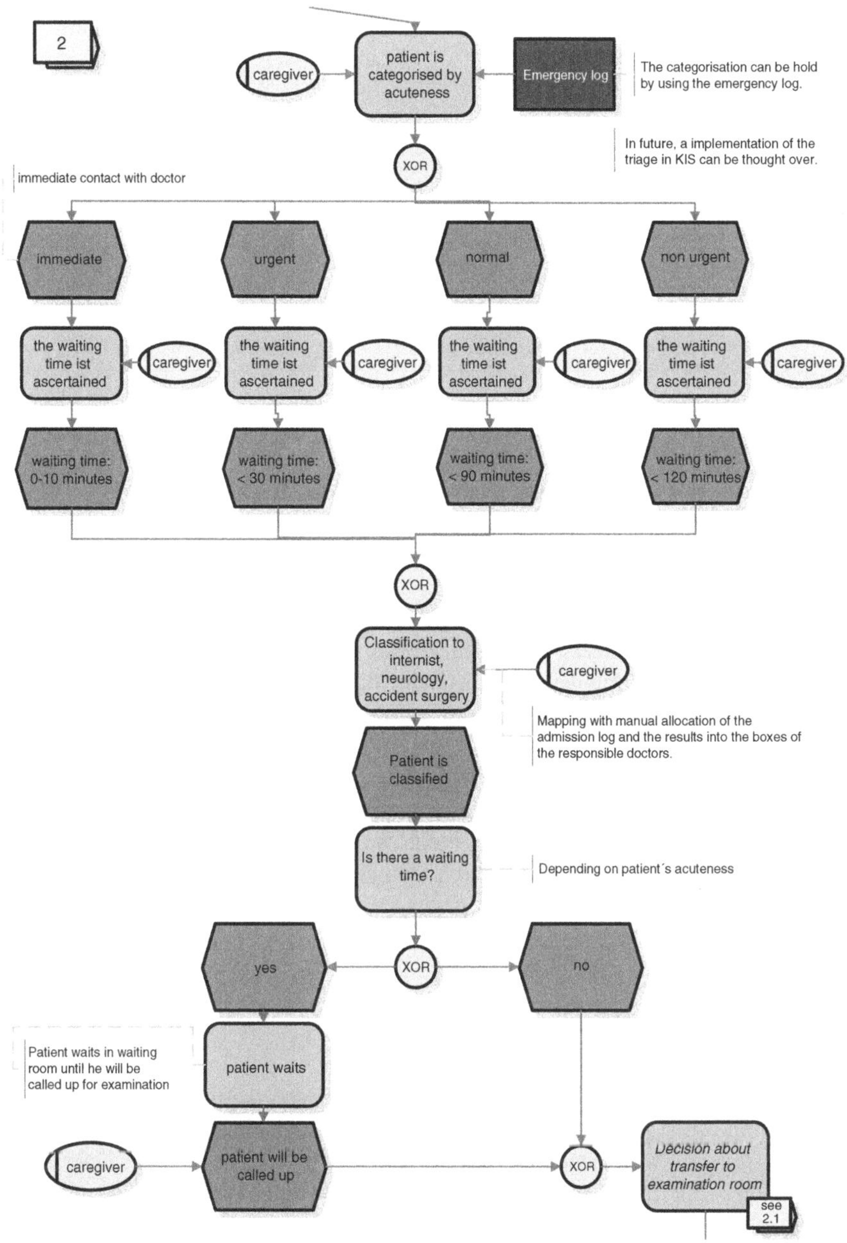

Fig. 28.2 Suggested process flow

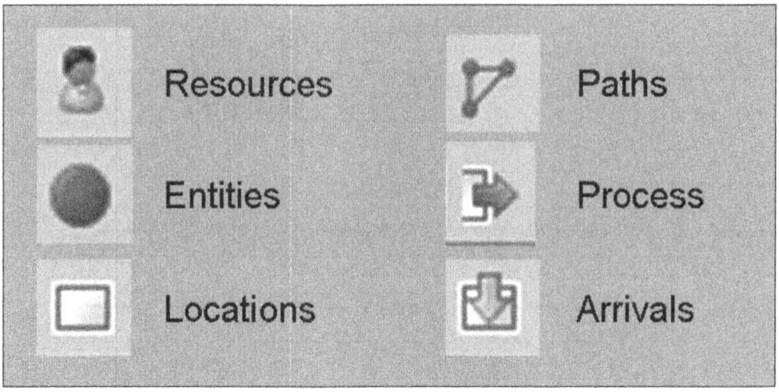

Fig. 28.3 Items of the MedModel

These assets we tried to simulate in the MedModel software. MedModel is a Windows-based simulation tool which specialized in healthcare systems. It is a product of the ProModel Corporation, 'a leading business process optimization and decision support company' (ProModel 2012).

With this model, a process can be mapped, simulated and analysed. Furthermore, it should help engineers and managers in decisions about innovations. Universitätsklinik Tübingen, Universitätsklinik Hamburg, Universitätsklinik Leipzig and Klinikum Esslingen are just some of the hospitals using this simulation tool (ProAspect 2012).

Figure 28.3 shows the items that are mostly used in the model. By using entities (e.g. patients) and resources (doctors or nurses) with optional capacities, routing paths with probabilities and locations (e.g. waiting room), the simulation can be accomplished. The arrivals are needed to define the patients' frequency. In the following subchapter, it will be described how we used those items.

28.2.2 Building the Actual Simulation

First of all, we tried to build a realistic situation. For this reason, the responsible of the Marienhospital provided us a layout of the Marienhospital. This helped us mapping the situation: with locations we could animate the Marienhospital's emergency department, which contains the waiting room, administration, two examination rooms, plaster room, trauma room, observation room, entrance, CT and X-ray. Every location was given a capacity as its realistic situation, so the observation room is equipped with three capacities due to its three beds, the entrance got an infinite capacity and the waiting room a capacity of 20 seats.

Figure 28.4 shows the pasted layout with its locations.

Second, the entities and the resources had to be defined. As there is no current documented triage system, there was no need to define different types of entities.

Fig. 28.4 Locations

Thus, we defined in the current process only one type of entity, in other words, one type of patient. As resources, we categorized a receptionist, who is responsible for the administration, three doctors and three nurses. The mentioned path in Fig. 28.3 describes the aisleways for movement. We have defined the movement of the doctors and nurses by moving back to the doctors' room and the nurses' station, respectively.

The processes are defined as followed:

- From entrance to administration with the collected 5-min administration
- From administration to waiting room with the collected average time of 1 min
- From the waiting room to the diverse examination rooms with the collected times of first doctor's and nurses contact (9 min each)
- From the diverse examination rooms back to the waiting room with the collected times of second contact (doctors: 13 min, nurses: 6 min)
- From the diverse examination rooms to the CT with the probability of 33 % with a defined average time of 23 min
- From the diverse examination rooms to X-ray with the probability of 33 % with a defined average time of 26 min
- All back to waiting room
- Defined exit

As an arrival, it was defined that a patient arrives every 9.6 min.

The challenge was to abstract the main processes and to fill in the data from the data collection mentioned in Chap. 1. In consideration of the complexity of the tool and in the context of a term paper, not all processes have been simulated. For instance, we desisted a second examination in the rooms and the doctors' other duties and responsibilities, which has nothing to do with the emergency department or the patient itself.

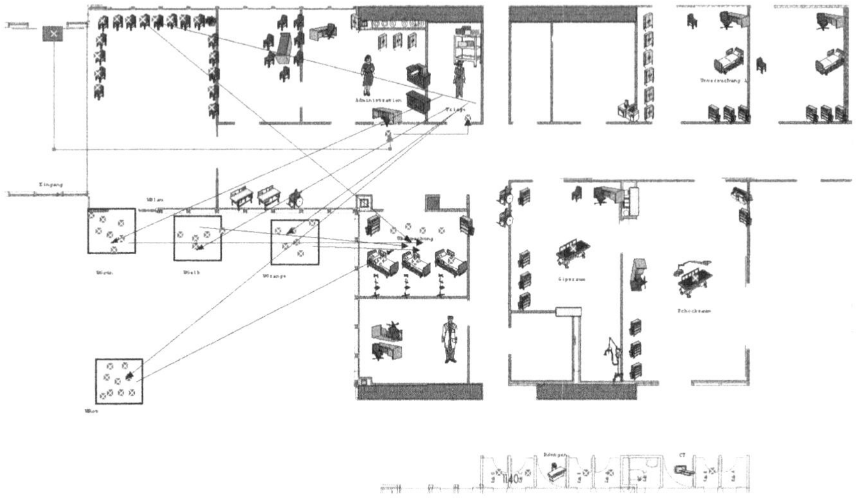

Fig. 28.5 Simulation of triage

28.2.3 Building the Recommended Simulation

First of all, it was very difficult to simulate our raised and above-mentioned recommendations. We came to the conclusion that only one recommendation can be built: the triage. The aim of this simulation is to ascertain whether the risk of a slowdown of the implementation of a separate triage system is given. For this reason, we build the model as followed:

- Patient arrives.
- From entrance to administration (all times were adapted from current process).
- From administration to triage: Patient will be classified in five different types—red for very urgent, orange for urgent, yellow for semi-urgent, green for normal and blue for not urgent cases.
- From triage to waiting room (as mentioned: same times as in current process).
- From waiting room to examination room (for simplification reasons, we raised the capacity of the room to seven beds, which reflect the real bed capacity of all rooms).
- From examination room to exit (since we only want to compare the recommended triage, we did not consider the following processes).

As seen in Fig. 28.5, we separated the waiting room in five different fictive ones, which helps us in programming the priorities: We defined that the 'red patient' comes first, the 'orange patient' has to wait till the 'red waiting room' is empty, the 'yellow patient' has to wait till the 'red and the orange waiting room' is empty and so on. As we know in the previous chapter, usually the rule that the yellow patient has to wait for the maximum of 30 min—this challenge is due to the complexity of the tool unfortunately not mapped.

28.3 Discussion

28.3.1 Barriers and Facilitators of Simulated Recommendations

The activities in an emergency department are to be subject to a strict legal framework. If there are more patient in the emergency depatmend than capacities allow to be treatet, still all of them have the right to medical treatment. Due to limited resources, such as personnel, medical equipment or patient beds, it is not possible to treat all patients at the same time, especially during peak times. Somebody needs to decide which patient enjoys the higher treatment obligation (Mackway-Jones et al. 2011).

Patients with life-threatening diseases have to be cured immediately. Accordingly, it often occurs that patients with less life-threatening diseases or injuries have to wait much longer than patients in life-threatening critical condition. As a result, it is a problem to figure out who comes first, when there are many patients with life-threatening diseases, but less treatment opportunities. Every case manager decides similar, but marginally different, because of his/her subjective opinion and experiences (Anon n.d.).

Intuitive assessment can lead to a misinterpretation of the patient's condition, especially when nurses have to deal with stress, hectic or even panic (Decker 1996, S. 111). There are many reasons why each nurse decides differently in respect of the assessment results.

Instead of individual assessments, nurse's decisions are influenced by prejudices, earlier actions and stereotypical thinking. Or in the heat of the moment, for example, when nurses feel personally affected, it might come to fast and not well-considered decisions. Furthermore, given the excitement of the incidents, nurses might forget to ask detailed questions or document the information for the physicians (Decker 1996, S. 112).

Another negative aspect of an intuitive assessment is that the decisions are neither documented nor communicated to the patient; thus the patient cannot retrace the rank order. There was no document that guarantees legal security and recorded the patient's condition when a person came to the emergency department. These issues require a system everybody can understand and is able to apply in the appropriate situation (Anon n.d.).

Due to less documentation possibilities on the registration form, significant information which might be helpful for the physician diagnose get lost (Ersteineschätzung in der Notaufnahme). At this point the triage model forces the nurses to answer all questions in the form, even if the information seems to be unnecessary to them. The triage system solves these problems due to a predefined question form which leads step by step to a descriptive assessment in a form of a decision tree (Cruz-Cunha et al. 2011).

Furthermore, the triage will be documented, thus the patient can retrace the rank order (Anon n.d.) and the resulting documentation ensures safety to the personnel. It is much easier for the nurses and physicians to justify their actions, and they cannot be blamed personally if patients may suffer harm from long waiting time (Mackway-Jones et al. 2011). Moreover, triage would satisfy legal requirement in respect of §135 a SGB V which says the hospitals are bound by law to implement measures to improve healthcare quality within the hospital and its surrounding (§135 a SGB V).

When the decision of a triage model is made, it is realistic that the processing of implementations will take from 6 to 12 months. In advance nurses, physician and all persons who take up an interface position should be trained. This is very important in case of the cooperation between the emergency department in the hospital and the ambulance service or other hospitals. Different triage models could have different standards and could be misinterpreted by nurses and physicians. Therefore, it is indispensable to be informed how other triage model work and which one is used by the cooperating partners (S. 92 Ersteinschätzung in der Notaufnahme).

As you can see the positive aspects predominate, and in our opinion there would be no barriers why the Marienhospital should not implement a triage model. Analysing the financial point, the Marienhospital has to spend a specific amount on personnel trainings. Therefore, external coaches can be hired. One seminar provider is the company 'ZeQ' in Mannheim, which is a specialist in the healthcare sector. It is a consulting company and offers seminars for implementing a triage model in hospitals for the management. The costs for a seminar would be 1,300 EUR[1] for up to 20 persons. Furthermore, the Institut für Notfallmedizin (IfN) der Asklepios Kliniken Hamburg GmbH offer in-house trainings where nurses, physicians and other employee get information about different triage models, triage procedures and further helpful information. The costs vary in respect of the duration, complexity and participants. For a 2-day seminar with up to 22 participants, the cost will approximately be 275 EUR per person (Institut für Notfallmedizin, Asklepios Kliniken).

28.3.2 Suggested Solutions

Month ago the Marienhospital already designed a triage model as you can see in Fig. 28.6. The triage system consists of four levels. To categorize the patient to one of these levels, it is important to use specialized charts for every illness or injury. These charts help to categorize the patients in the groups: very urgent (red), urgent (yellow), normal (green) and not urgent (blue).

Each category contains questions. For example, they are asking if the patient can breathe and whether the patient is shocked. If one of these questions would be answered with yes, the patient is in group number one, which means immediate treatment (LBK Hamburg kein Datum). If he/she is not part of the first group, he/she has to wait inside the waiting room. This assessment should take a maximum of 1 min (Süß 2009).

But the triage system is not in use because of missing personnel coaching. We highly recommend to organize a seminar where an external company trains the

[1] This is an information from Mr. Bärauch representing ZeQ, Mannheim.

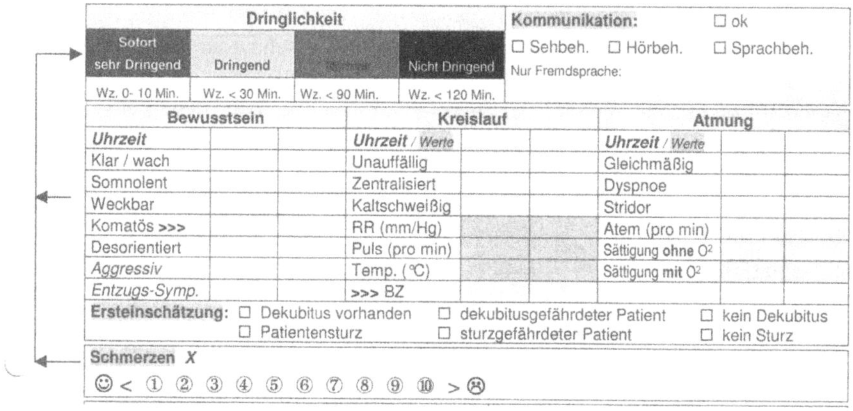

Dringlichkeit				Kommunikation:
Sofort sehr Dringend	Dringend		Nicht Dringend	☐ ok ☐ Sehbeh. ☐ Hörbeh. ☐ Sprachbeh. Nur Fremdsprache:
Wz. 0- 10 Min.	Wz. < 30 Min.	Wz. < 90 Min.	Wz. < 120 Min.	

Bewusstsein			Kreislauf			Atmung		
Uhrzeit			*Uhrzeit* / Werte			*Uhrzeit* / Werte		
Klar / wach			Unauffällig			Gleichmäßig		
Somnolent			Zentralisiert			Dyspnoe		
Weckbar			Kaltschweißig			Stridor		
Komatös >>>			RR (mm/Hg)			Atem (pro min)		
Desorientiert			Puls (pro min)			Sättigung **ohne** O2		
Aggressiv			Temp. (°C)			Sättigung **mit** O2		
Entzugs-Symp.			>>> BZ					

Ersteinschätzung: ☐ Dekubitus vorhanden ☐ dekubitusgefährdeter Patient ☐ kein Dekubitus
☐ Patientensturz ☐ sturzgefährdeter Patient ☐ kein Sturz

Schmerzen *X*

☺ < ① ② ③ ④ ⑤ ⑥ ⑦ ⑧ ⑨ ⑩ > ☹

Fig. 28.6 Triage field

nurses, physicians and employees from the hospitals ED management. When we were talking to physicians and nurses from the Marienhospital, we got confirmation that the implementation would make the triage process easier, and the most important argument is that the personnel would feel safer, but bureaucracy and financial barriers slow down the implementation.

28.4 Conclusion

When we first came to the emergency department, we recognized that the classification of patients regarding their degree of priority was not as we imagined.

At the beginning of this project, we read about Manchester Triage and other systems, which make it possible to identify the patients who have to be treated immediately or the ones who can wait, because their injuries or illnesses are not life threatening.

Systems like the Manchester Triage are common in today's emergency departments and offer numerous advantages to them, especially to reduce mistakes right at the start.

Since the emergency department of Marienhospital does not use such a classification system, but is about to implement one, we decided to model this process to demonstrate difficulties with the identification of the patient's degree of priority and then generate specific solutions for these problems.

The simulation gives the impression that the emergency department runs smoothly. During their stay at the emergency department, the patients are treated in 90 % of the time. The nurses and physicians also do not work at full capacities at any time. Unfortunately, these results do not reflect reality. Neither a physician nor the nursing staff will follow the same route at any time or takes over a single job in a given time. There are several reasons why these predefined routes are interrupted or changed: 1. Patients won't always remain in the waiting or examination rooms, as recommended by medical staff, since they want information, e.g. about the expected waiting time or about further treatment. This behaviour can interfere in the workflow of the medical staff. 2. Physicians order special treatment for patients to decide about further treatment or they have to consult with their associates and nurses have to carry patient to other wards personally. The simulation model does not describe such incidents, and as a consequent it is not comparable to reality.

One explanation that physicians are not at full capacity is that in reality they have more responsibilities, than in the model. They need to treat patients at their ward or at the Notfallpraxis, or sign up patients for X-ray or different extra examinations, or search for an empty bed, so that the patient can go to ward. Same applies to the nurses, who have to face the same problems. The simulation does not show how many times patients talk to the nurses because they are tired of waiting for treatment or lab results, or that they have to bring every single blood withdraws to the lab.

After modelling the process with implemented triage system, we recognized that the patients have to face longer waiting times until first contact with the nursing staff. One positive point is that patients with higher degree of priority are actually treated first and do not have to face long waiting times, which is the primary goal of the triage.

For a better and more realistic process, image and optimization solutions are further extensive data collection at the emergency department just as increasing degree of complexity in modelling necessary, which was not possible for us with the given resources and lack of knowledge over the capabilities of the MedModel system.

In conclusion that thanks to advertent observation, through the analysis of the collected data in combination with evaluating literature at beginning of the project, we learned a lot about processes in emergency departments, especially the Marienhospital and could thus use these knowledge to generate solutions for reorganizing the process which will improve the whole process.

References

Anon. (n.d.) *LBK Hamburg Ersteinschätzung nach dem Manchester-Triage-System*. Retreived April 3, 2012, from http://www.bag-zna.de/pdf/symposium/mts.pdf

Cruz-Cunha, M. M., Varajao, J., Powell, P., & Martinho, R. (2011). *ENTERprise information systems. Communications in computer and information science* (Bd Nr. 221, p. 228). Berlin: Springer.

Decker, F. (1996). *Führen im Rettungsdienst, 2. Aufl* (pp. 111–112). Berlin: Springer.

Mackway-Jones, K., Marsden, J., Windle, J., Published by Krey, J. (2011). 3. edition. (pp. 294–295). Bern: Verlag Hans Huber.

ProAspect. (2012). *MedModel*. Retrieved July 14, 2012, from http://www.proaspect.de/produkte/medmodel/default.html

ProModel. (2012). *About us*. Retrieved July 12, 2012,from http://www.promodel.com/aboutus/

Robinson, S. (2004). *Simulation: The practice of model development and Use*. Chichester: Wiley.

Süß, J. (2009). *Implementierung einer interdisziplinären Notfallaufnahme*. Norderstedt: GRIN.

Chapter 29
Simulation Study: Clinical Center Esslingen—Process Analysis in the Emergency Department

Corinna Klink, Daniel Denkert, Mario Vargheamidis, Nils Kern, and Tobias Lörch

Abstract The following simulation study deals with the process inefficiencies identified in the emergency department of the clinical center Esslingen, the possible solutions to solve the existing problems and their simulation with the simulation tool MedModel. By using this tool it is to show if and how the recommendations might change process efficiency.

The first part of this simulation study outlines the current process flows in the emergency department, followed by a short introduction to the MedModel software. In the second part the process of creating the simulation will be described as well as its results and the conclusions that can be drawn from them.

Keywords Waiting queue • Kiosk check-in • Simulation • Administration • Emergency department

29.1 Case Study

29.1.1 Current Process Flow Maps

In this chapter, the current situation in the emergency department (ED in the following) of the clinical center Esslingen is going to be displayed. Therefore the processes will be verbally described and sections of our process flow maps will be described in detail, whereas the complete model can be found in the Appendix.

The material in this case study was prepared originally for Project Seminar SS 2012 at the University of Hohenhiem, Germany under the supervision of Profs Kirn and Wickramasinghe.

C. Klink (✉) • D. Denkert • M. Vargheamidis • N. Kern • T. Lörch
University of Hohenheim, Stuttgart, Germany
e-mail: Corinna.Klink@web.de

N. Wickramasinghe et al. (eds.), *Lean Thinking for Healthcare*, Healthcare Delivery in the Information Age, DOI 10.1007/978-1-4614-8036-5_29,

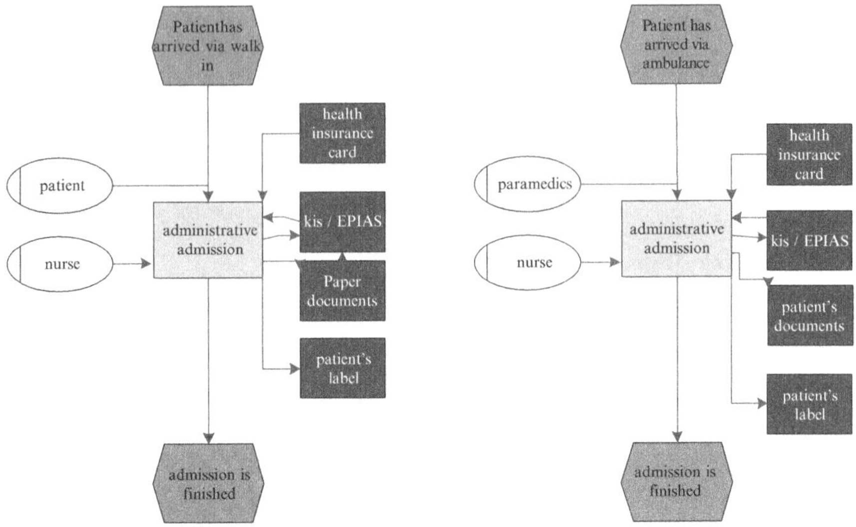

Fig. 29.1 Differences in admission, depending on way of arrival

People can arrive in the ED either as walk-in patients or via ambulance. In case of an arrival via ambulance, the ED-team gets informed via radio transceiver, so they can prepare the necessary rooms or equipment. If the patient is in a very critical condition, he will be brought into the resuscitation room. Otherwise a common surgery room is sufficient.

Depending on how the patient arrived, the admission will be carried out differently. In case of a walk-in arrival, the patient has to go into the reception room himself. Ambulance patients are registered by paramedics. The administrative personnel won't get to see the patient in this case and has to rely on information given to them by the ambulance men. Figure 29.1 shows the differences in admission of walk-in and ambulance patients.

After the admission is finished, the triage needs to be executed. This is important to categorize patients and their urgency to be treated. The triage is carried out by a nurse, who is also located in the reception room. Again, walk-in patients are triaged in a different way than patients arriving via ambulance. Walk-in patients get questioned by the triage nurse, whereas the triage of the ambulance patient is done with the help of the paramedics. The triage nurse can't have a personal look at the injured person, because she would have to leave the registration room to go see the patient personally who is located either in a treatment room or in a niche. After the triage categorizing, the triage status of the patient is set and entered into the triage system, named *epias*. The status can be either blue, green, yellow, orange, red, or immediate, depending on symptoms and pain intensity. The status also determines the default waiting time, which actually differs often (especially in status blue and green) from the actual waiting time, due to current workload in the ED.

Walk-in patients are sent into the waiting area after being registered and triaged, or directly sent into a treatment room, if injury is severe and a room is ready.

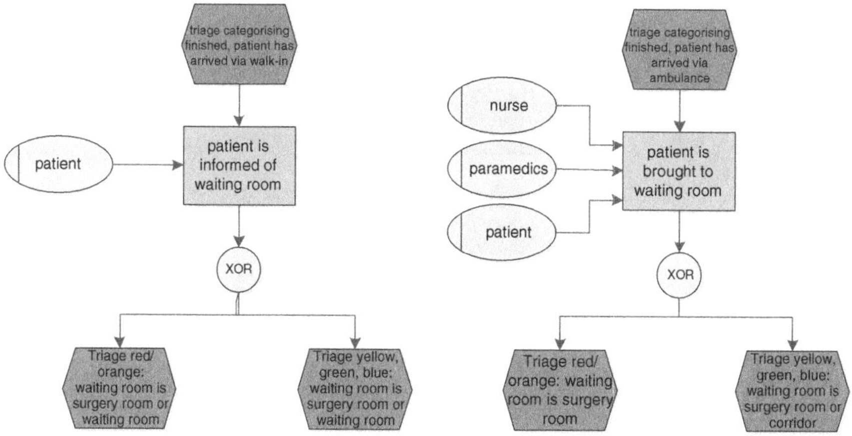

Fig. 29.2 Waiting areas, dependant on way of arrival

Patients who arrived via ambulance get carried into a treatment room directly by the paramedics. In case no room is empty, they will be brought into a transportation niche for waiting (Fig. 29.2).

The location of the patient is always entered into the system, so the staff is able to locate them at any time. At the beginning the patient is either in the waiting room, a treatment room, or in a niche in the corridor. After starting his personal clinical pathway, he might change locations quite often. That's why employees have to spend time entering changes in the system. For example, when a patient is send to X-ray, a care staff member needs to change his location in the system from "treatment room" to "X-ray." If someone forgets to enter the change, other staff members being on the lookout for a certain patient will have a hard time finding him. Therefore it is very important to keep the data in the system updated all the time.

If a patient is located in the waiting room at the beginning, he gets called up via speakers or is being fetched by an employee personally. In the optimum, a patient gets called in before his ascertained waiting time runs out. As already mentioned, this is not always the case, since especially triage statuses blue and green are forced to wait longer if more severe cases arrive in the meantime.

When a patient is located in a treatment room, the first attendance starts. During the first attendance by care units, nurses check the patient's injury and start treating if necessary (e.g., disinfecting wounds or stop bleedings). Afterwards a doctor tends to the patient. He examines the patient and treats him if necessary (e.g., saturation). If further examination is necessary the patient is send to X-ray, CT, or echography by the doctor. The diagnosis center is located on another floor than the ED; therefore the patient has to leave the ED temporarily. Since further diagnoses are often necessary (in 101 out of 150 cases, according to our observations; see Fig. 29.3) staff members sometimes have a hard time keeping track of a patient, because they would have to always observe the elevator to make sure to not miss someone going to or

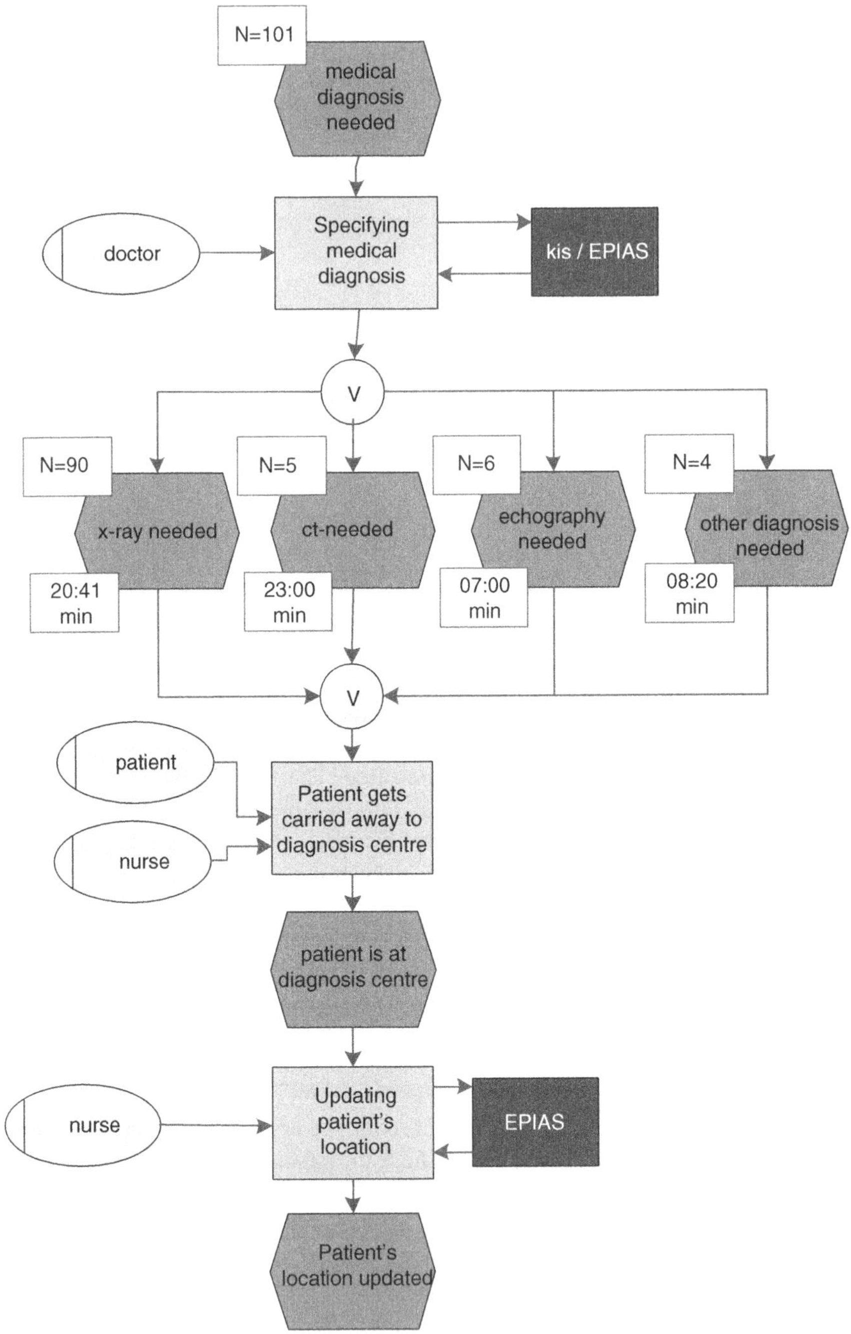

Fig. 29.3 Changing of location and updating of data

returning from X-ray, CT, or echography. One has to also keep in mind, that in some cases, a patient needs more than one of those examinations or even has to do one of them more than one time.

After additional examinations, a patient either goes into the waiting room again or he can get right back into a treatment room. This depends on workload. Again, his change of location has to be registered in the system. Afterwards the second attendance takes place either through a care unit or a doctor or both. If further treatment is necessary, it is carried out in the treatment room (e.g., applying a bandage) or in a specially designed and equipped room (e.g., for saturation or applying a cast).

Sometimes the consultation of doctors of another specific field is necessary. The consultation can happen via communicative devices (e.g., telephone) or personally, if the other physician is also located in the clinical center Esslingen.

If a patient needs to be taken in as an inpatient, certain preparations need to be done (see Fig. 29.4). The hospital ward has to be called to get information about bed occupancy. If there's no bed available, another ward has to be contacted or maybe even another hospital. Depending on the patient's condition and the location of the destined ward he can either walk to the specific ward himself or get transported there. Also patients who don't need to be taken in as an inpatient might get transported back home. That's mostly the case when they already arrived via ambulance or if they are not able to walk.

The visit in the ED ends when a patient leaves it by himself, by going to a ward or by being transported home.

29.1.2 Identified Process Inefficiencies

29.1.2.1 Problem 1: Manual Updating of Patient's Location

Entering the data and clinical pathway of all patients manually makes demands on care staff time. Information like treatment, room assignment, staff assignment, start and end time of X-ray, CT, and sonography has to be registered. Therefore staff members need to spend a lot of time being on the lookout for patients returning from medical examination, taking place elsewhere, and entering time, and whereabouts.

29.1.2.2 Problem 2: Mixed Waiting Rooms and No Further Information

There is a mixed waiting room for patients needing surgical or internistic treatment. Staff members have a hard time keeping an overview and because of possibly long waiting times the risk of infection increases. Also patients are not familiar with the split-up between these two areas, so they are not able to understand different waiting times (e.g., if a person with laceration is called up after someone who has "only" abdominal pain) and maybe get annoyed. Staff members need to calm patients that don't feel taken seriously and deal with a lot of questions concerning the remaining waiting time.

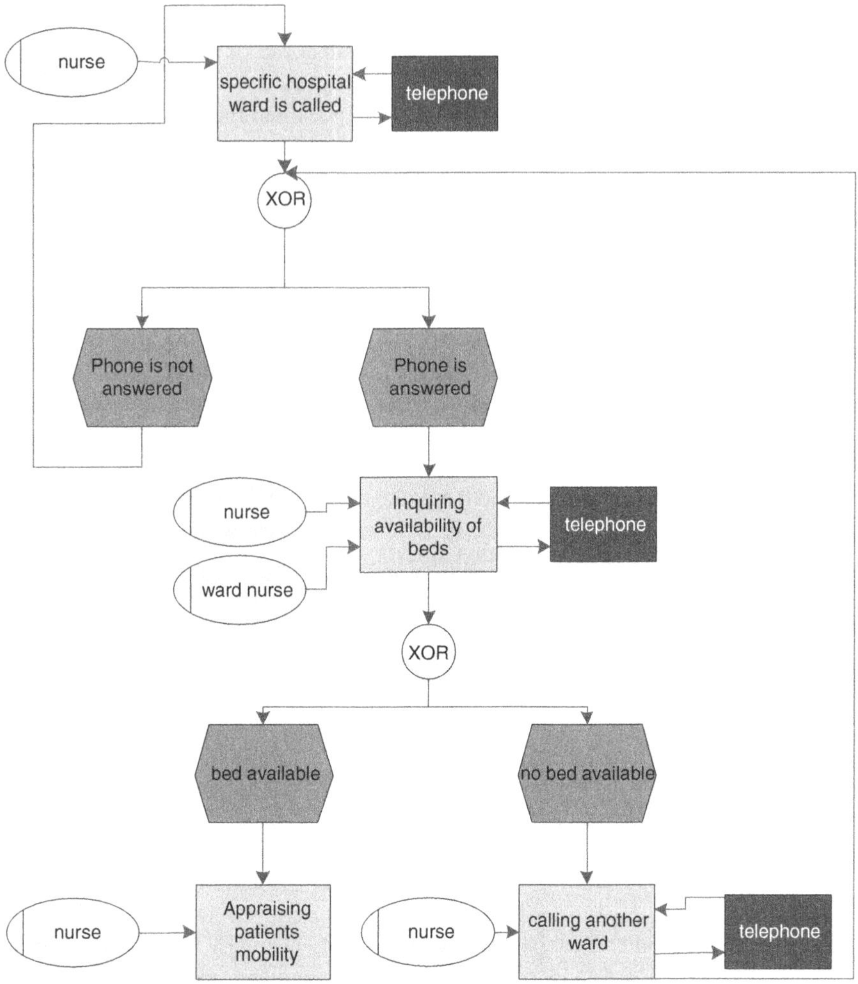

Fig. 29.4 Patients needs residential treatment

Also, patients are not informed of the triage-concept and they don't know about the capacity within the ED. If there is an emergency and all the doctors are needed, the waiting time for other patients increases naturally. If they're not informed, they won't be able to fully understand and keep asking for estimated waiting time, even if the personnel is not able to give information.

29.1.2.3 Problem 3: Admission Step-by-Step

Because of discretion, patients are only allowed to enter the reception/triage room one after another. For that reason long waiting queues arise. They not only result in frustration, but are also quite critical, since the urgency (before triage) is not assessable yet. At the moment, registration and triage takes place simultaneously. Therefore patients are interrogated by two persons at a time, they need to switch from answering administrative questions (e.g., professional association) and medical questions (e.g., if the wound is bleeding strong).

29.1.2.4 Problem 4: Admission as Inpatient

If the doctors decide that an ambulatory treatment isn't sufficient, the patient needs to be taken in as an inpatient. After checking with the bed-assignment-management, the doctors or care staff inform the administration staff of the transfer. They need to enter this information into the MIS, including information about what ward the patient is going to. This process of passing on information takes time and often happens in an asynchronous manner. That way it might happen that a patient has long gone to a hospital ward before the transfer is registered in the system. This leads to data that isn't current and reliable. For the administration and triage personnel it is an additional task that has to be carried out besides registration processes and triage.

29.1.3 Recommendations and Suggested Process Flow Maps

29.1.3.1 Recommendation 1: Using RFID Technology

Implementation of a system, which is able to automatically locate a patient. Patients could be equipped with wristbands that work with RFID technology. Checkpoints for scanning the RFID-chips within the wristbands could be set up in the doorframes of the various treatment rooms. Passing patients would be registered automatically, so the identification of a patient, as well as his passing through a certain checkpoint (e.g., walking into the elevator that leads him to X-raying) allow conclusions of his localization. No staff member is needed, since the computer-system is updated self-acting.

Staff members might be equipped with RFID as well. Logging into the system manually for registering start and end time of attendance wouldn't be necessary that way. The MIS would be able to automatically document in which room a patient is located and which doctor is responsible for his treatment.

This way staff members would be able to perform their actual tasks and the data would be consistently and current.

Alternatively, more employees could be hired that are responsible for entering data into the MIS. A medical education wouldn't be necessary, since only administrative tasks need to be carried out (Fig. 29.5).

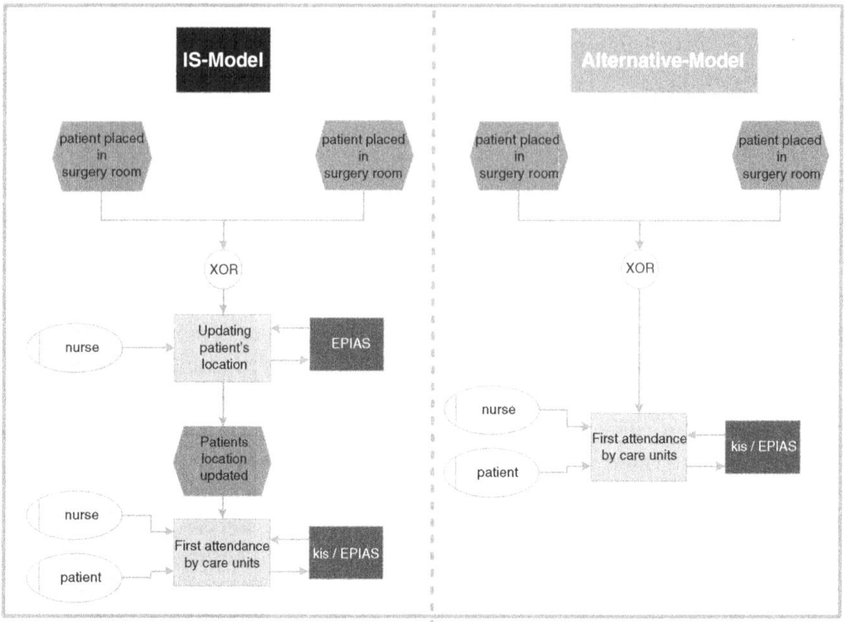

Fig. 29.5 Alternative model—RFID technology instead of manual updating

29.1.3.2 Recommendation 2: Split up Waiting Areas

Split up the waiting area of surgical or internistic cases. This way the staff could have an easier overview of number of patients and the patients might be more patient, if there are only 5 other people waiting than 15. Plus, the risk of infection would be decreased. A computer monitor might be installed in the waiting room, showing the current number of patients (divided into surgical and internistic patients), emergencies, number of patients in treatment (so the waiting persons don't get the impression that nothing's moving or feel like the doctors are having a coffee break) and maybe the triage-levels (patients knowing their own triage-level and especially the level of others might also have negative effects, such as not feeling taken seriously and lack of understanding) (Fig. 29.6).

29.1.3.3 Recommendation 3: Using Kiosk Check-in-Systems

A possible solution could be the use of a Kiosk check-in-system. Those can already be found at airports or libraries, they work against queues by transferring standardized information between customers and companies. The registration process in the ED, at least part of it, consists of repetitive data and information, such as name, date of birth, family doctor, telephone number, health insurance company, etc. Installing only a few input terminals might increase efficiency and decrease waiting time.

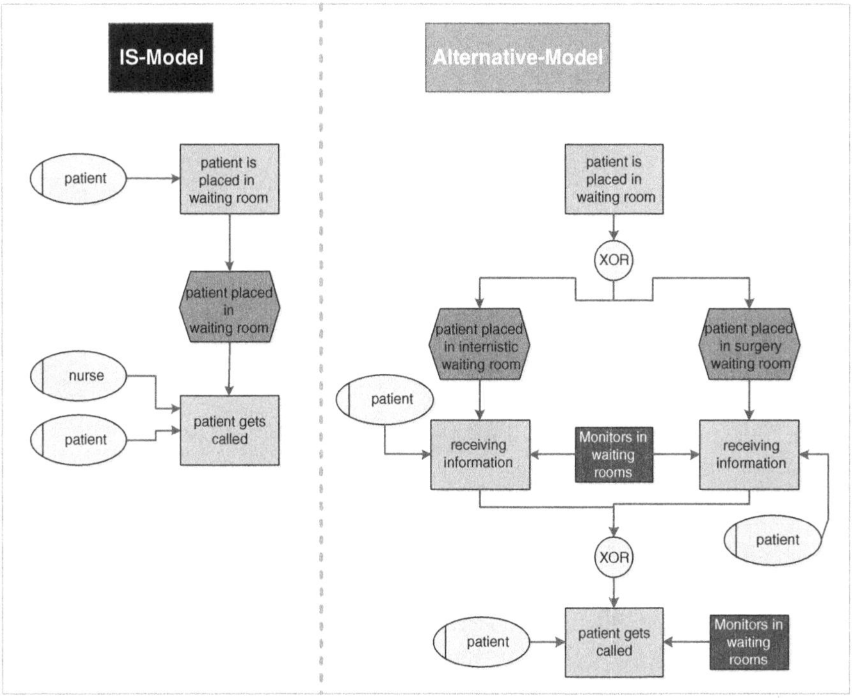

Fig. 29.6 Alternative model—split up waiting areas

Of course there are always cases, that don't follow a standardized procedure, but a majority of administrative work could be carried out by the patients themselves. If further inquiry is necessary, most of the relevant data is already included in the system and the staff only has to enter little information manually. This way, employees responsible for registration tasks would be disburdened and in the best-case only the triage process would need a person-to-person interaction. Patients won't get frustrated, if they can help speeding up the registration process and there would be no interference between triage and administrative personnel (Fig. 29.7).

29.1.3.4 Recommendation 4: Eliminating Unnecessary Process Steps

The unnecessary process step of passing on information between medical and administrative staff members could be eliminated. After booking a bed and eventually ordering transportation, the doctors or care employees could enter this information into the MIS themselves. This way the data would be more current and localization of patients would be simplified. Also the administrative and triage employees could concentrate on more urgent tasks such as registration and triage (Fig. 29.8).

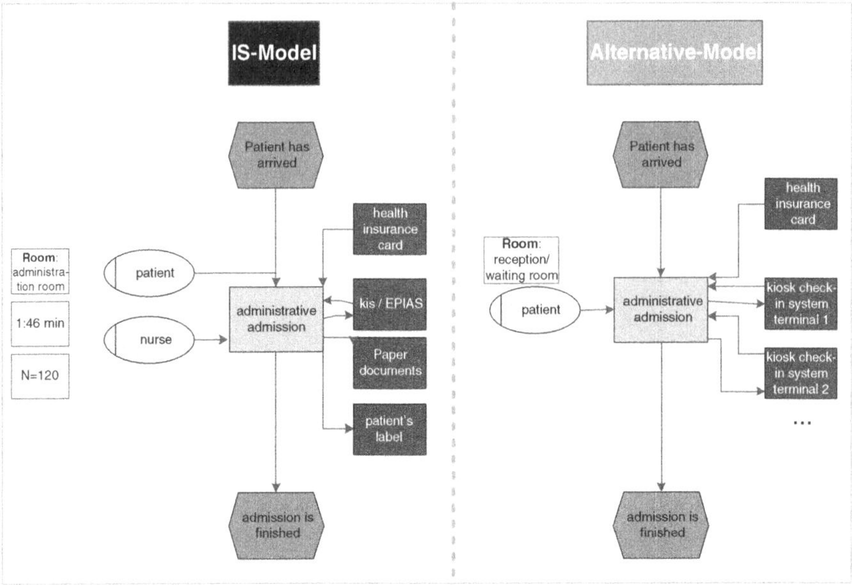

Fig. 29.7 Alternative model—using Kiosk check-in-systems

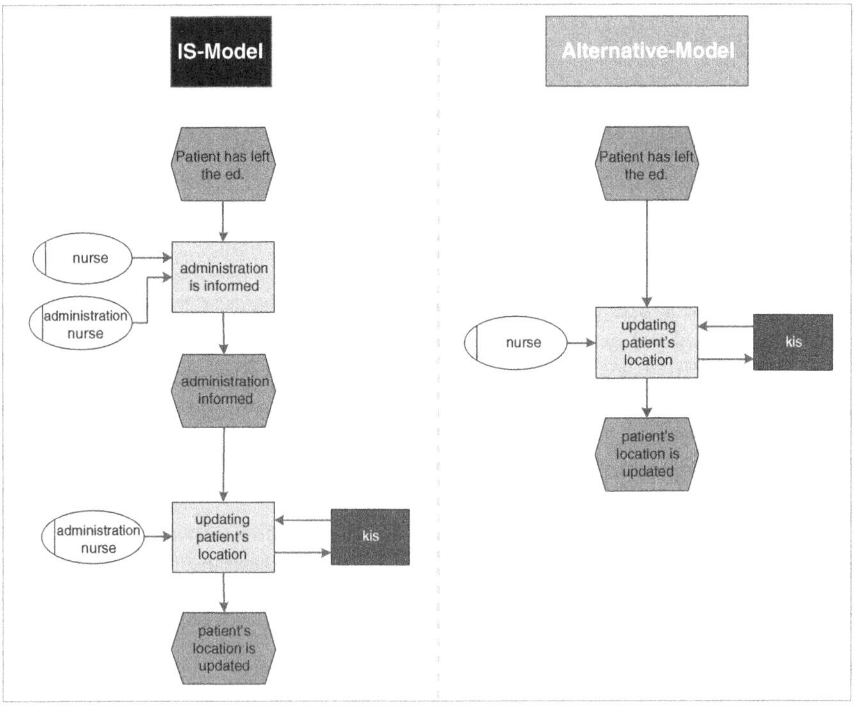

Fig. 29.8 Alternative model—unnecessary step eliminated

29.2 The Simulation

29.2.1 Method Simulation and Software

Understanding the various business processes proceeding in an enterprise today seems to be much challenging due to their complexity and wide range—a phenomenon the ED of a hospital is no exception either. The various participants (doctors, nurses, paramedics,...) need to collaborate under specific time pressure in mutual dependence. Every step needs to be exactly matched to his forerunner and all of them have to follow a fixed sequence.

In order to perceive a workflow this manifold, it is helpful to create a model with graphical presentation to easily understand the various steps that need to be done. As already shown, visualizing business processes can be done with a modeling language such as Event-driven process chains (EPCs). With this EPC, one can easily analyze the progress of the process.

While EPCs only offer a static view, a simulation tool can be used in order to cover the dynamic point of view; this is indeed necessary to analyze the impact of potential changes to the model parameters. As already mentioned, several problems were identified during the process analysis in the clinical center Esslingen and based on these observations, several possible solutions were discussed and verbalized. In order to verify and evaluate these possible solutions, the simulation tool "Medmodel" can be used. This software is a subdivision of "ProModel" and includes a hospital-specific simulation environment.

29.2.1.1 Locations, Entities, Processes, and Resources

The basic logic of MedModel contains a division of locations, entities, processes, and resources. Locations are used to collect the entities on a specific position and to send them to the following one. To have an exact model, one can import a plant layout; the locations then can be visualized with several icons for ideal recognition. Entities represent the items of the simulation; in the hospital-specific context, the patients form the entities. In this area, arrivals need to be defined, so the simulation can run properly. Processes are mandatory to execute the simulation due to the fact that they contain all routes the patients follow. With additional "operations," patients can exactly be matched and differed; for example, not every patient has to have X-ray, so the patients need to be defined via manifold operations (see Sect. 29.2.2 for further informations). All processes are visualized with the help of an arrow, so one can easily comprehend the routes a patient passes by. Finally, resources need to be specified; resources form a sort of entity that are required to accomplish the process. In this case, the resources are doctors, nurses, and the administrative staff. These resources receive a particular USE-time they need to complete their tasks and for blocking them.

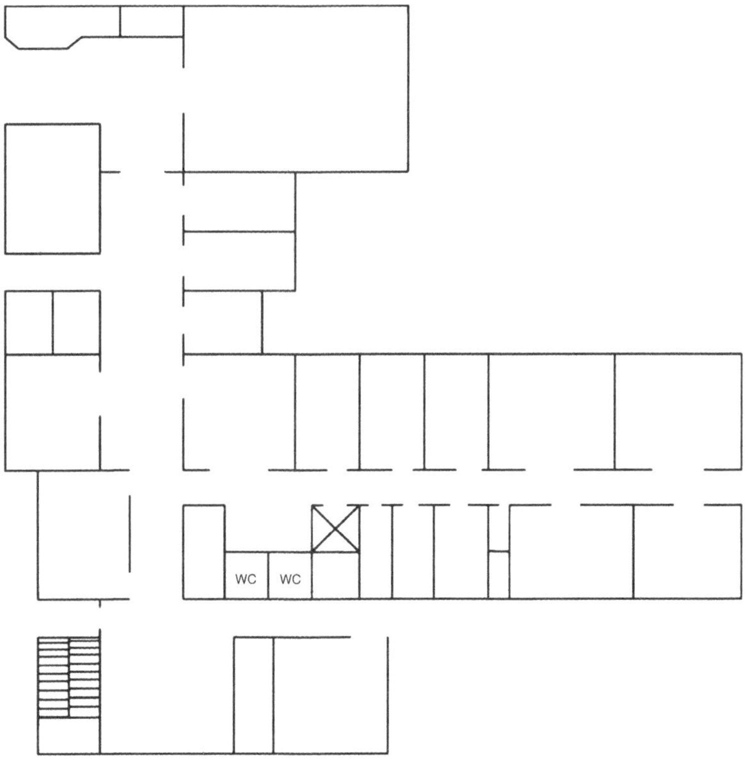

Fig. 29.9 Floor plan of ED Esslingen

When locations, entities, processes, and resources are well defined, one can run the simulation. After having finished, the integrated Output-Viewer collects all relevant statistics. Having saved these, one can rebuild the model (e.g., according to the suggested solutions) and then run the simulation again—the new statistics than can be compared to the previous ones. With this output, possible modifications then can be evaluated.

29.2.2 Building the Simulation

First of all, with the creation of a model with MedModel the selection and the creation of a background takes place. For this, a construction plan of the emergency department was requested. Since the construction plan contained a lot of information (superficial contents and numbers of every single room as well as the dimly representation of the furniture), the plan had been retraced with the Adobe Illustrator true to the scale. Afterwards, the new traced plan was defined as background (Fig. 29.9).

In order to create the model close to reality, the locations had been generated based on the construction plan. Following Locations reappear in the simulation model (the simulation contains German notations, so they are also used in the following to ensure comparability):

- WalkIN Eingang (Walk-in entrance)
- Anmeldung (Registration)
- Triage
- Wartezimmer (Waiting room)
- Behandlung 1 (Treatment room 1)
- Behandlung 2 (Treatment room 2)
- Behandlung 3 (Treatment room 3)
- Behandlung 4 (Treatment room 4)
- Wundversorgung (Wound treatment room)
- Gipsraum (Room for casts)
- X-ray
- Wartezimmer 2 (Waiting room 2)
- Ausgang (Exit)

Other Locations were added additionally in order to devise the model graphically. However, these Locations were not respected in the processing and therefore are not listed. All Locations were completed with symbols which the software provides and they were configurated visually appropriate. In addition, Entity Spots were added to every Location and their capacity was defined. An Entity Spot serves to a visual representation of entities which "wander" through the system.

29.2.2.1 Routing

After the determination of the locations, the routing system was defined. In order to represent the process cycle of the Walk-In patients, the already built EPK model was used. It became clear that there have to exist different types of patients for whom there has to be made in each case an independent process. Based on these reflections, the routing system was determined. A Walk-In patient appears at the entrance in order to go to the registration and to the triage. After a patient has received a status of the triage (was not simulated), he or she goes to the waiting room. There, the patients disperse in the treatment rooms 1–4 in order to go afterwards to the exit, the wound treatment, or to the X-ray. Already here it was pointed out that there have to exist many types of patients. If a patient goes to the wound treatment, for example his wound is sutured and he is able to leave the room to go to the exit. If it is necessary to X-ray a patient, he has to go to the X-ray and afterwards to *Wartezimmer 2*. *Wartezimmer 2* is only a fictitious waiting room and was created for reasons of modeling in order to be able to assign the already X-rayed patients a higher priority; otherwise the software cannot distinguish the X-rayed patients from the patients who are for the first time in the waiting room. The patients are distributed to

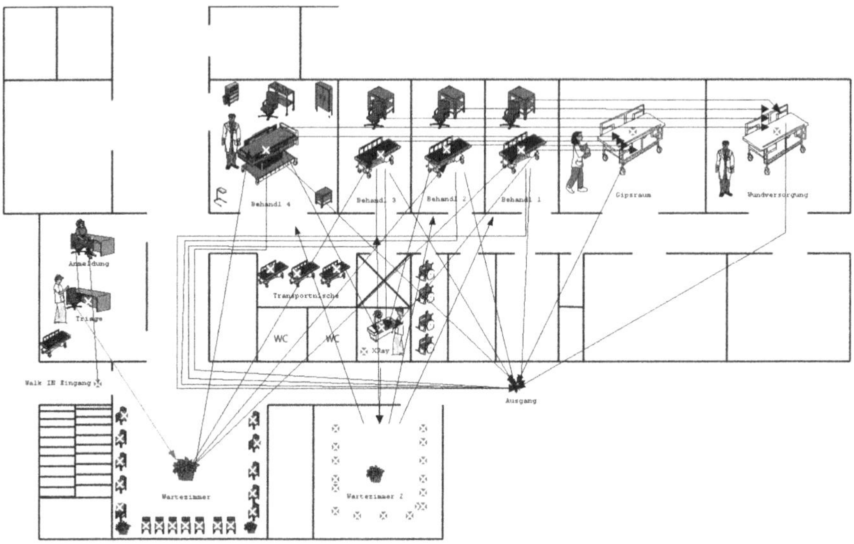

Fig. 29.10 Routing

treatment rooms 1–4, beginning is the waiting room 2. In the treatment rooms, there follows another distinction of the patients, for example those who get a salve bandage and who go afterwards to the exit and patients which have a fracture and where it is necessary to apply a gypsum. These patients go to the room for making gypsums where they are treated and then they leave the emergency department (Fig. 29.10).

29.2.2.2 Entities and Processing

In order to distinguish the types of patients named above, it is necessary to determine an own entity-type for every distinction. With this processing model a distinction is made between the following entities:

- WI
- WI EXIT
- WI Wundversorgung (WI wound treatment)
- WI Röntgen (WI X-ray)
- WI Geröntgt Gips (WI X-rayed cast)
- WI Geröntgt Exit (WI X-rayed exit)

Different avatars were assigned to the entities in order to make a graphical representation during the simulations processing. The acronym *WI* stands for Walk-In. At the beginning, a *WI*-patient enters the emergency department and passes through the registration as well as the triage and then goes to the waiting room. Afterwards, he goes to the treatment rooms 1–4 and is distinguished in the entity-type *WI EXIT*, *WI Wundversorgung*, and *WI Röntgen*.

By means of a distribution function, which is defined in the User Distributions, 30 % of the *WI* patients become *WI EXIT* patients, 10 % are assigned to wound treatment (*WI Wundversorgung*), and 60 % are converted to *WI Röntgen* patients.

The distribution values for the most part are based on the collected data for the hospital Esslingen. A *WI Exit* patient is treated by the doctor and leaves afterwards the emergency department, whereas a *WI Wundversorgung* patient is taken to the wound treatment room in order to leave the emergency department afterwards. *WI Röntgen* patients go after the first contact with the doctor in the treatment room to *X-ray* and then go to the fictitious *Wartezimmer 2*. There they get (as mentioned above) a higher priority and afterwards they go to the treatment rooms 1–4.

After a second contact with the doctor they are again distinguished in the entities *WI Geröntgt Gips* and *WI Geröntgt Exit*. Here, 15 % of the *WI Röntgen* patients become *WI Geröntgt Gips* patients who go after the diagnosis in the treatment room to the room for making gypsums, where they get a cast. Subsequently they can leave the ED.

Eighty-five percent become *WI Geröntgt Exit* patients who immediately leave the emergency department after the treatment. The distinction of the entity-types happens in the Processing of the respective Locations by the means of a RENAME command.

29.2.2.3 Resources

Resources represent the employees of Esslingen's ED and can stand for doctors, nurses, or care staff members. In the is-model, the following Resources have been defined:

- Arzt (Doctors) (2×)
- Anmeldung Schwester (Administration-nurse)
- Triage Schwester (Triage-nurse)
- XRay Schwester (X-ray-nurse) (2×)
- Gips Schwester (Cast-nurse)

The number of Resources doesn't represent the actual number of employees. In reality, the ED of the clinical center Esslingen is managed in shifts, so a discrepancy of manpower, subject to time of day, isn't unusual. For reasons of simplification, this fact has not been included in the model. Instead a fixed number of employees working throughout the whole day was modeled. The resources *Anmeldung Schwester, Triage Schwester, XRay Schwester, and Gips Schwester* are bound permanently to Locations and interact with entities. The Resource *Doctor* is not bound to a Location, but switches between treatment rooms 1–4 and the wound treatment room. To interact with an entity, a USE command has to be defined for the relevant

Resource in the Processing settings. The following USE-times were taken from the data records of the study:

- Anmeldung Schwester → 1:46 min
- Triage Schwester → 1:00 min
- XRay Schwester → 17:41 min
- Gips Schwester → 20:31 min
- Doctor's contact after X-ray before exit (X-ray findings with no further treatment necessary) → 9:14 min

The following times have been estimated. Because of the new breakdown in different entity-types, data is not existent.

- Doctor's contact before exit (time for examination without further treatment) → 18 min
- Doctor's contact before wound treatment (time for examination before wound treatment) → 2 min
- Doctor's contact before X-raying (time for examination before X-raying) → 5 min
- Doctor's contact wound treatment → 16 min
- Doctor's contact before applying of cast (X-ray findings with following applying of cast) → 4 min

Alternative Model

In the alternative model the approach of implementing a Kiosk Check-In system is displayed. Therefore the whole process of registration (Walk-In, registration, and triage) had to be considered. To make the implementation of a Kiosk Check-In terminal more clearly, a second is-model—based on the first is-model—has been created. An additional Location was added between the Walk-In entrance and the registration room. This Location was called *Warten Anmeldung* and represents a graphical waiting line in front of the registration room. Additionally the capacity of the waiting room was set to "infinite" to avoid a backlog of patients. This way the process of registration can be analyzed separately. The frequency of arriving patients was modified as well. Now every 1.5 min. a patient enters the ED. This modification is necessary to show the effect of the Kiosk Check-In system on the registration process compared to a registration without Kiosk Check-In.

As an addition to the second is-model a Kiosk Check-In terminal has been added to the alternative model in form of a Location. The terminal allows the autonomous registration of patients within 45 s. The duration of 45 s was estimated and implemented in the Processing settings of the location with the help of a WAIT command. The Location *Warten Anmeldung* still exists, but the patients now disperse between the common registration and the Kiosk Check-In terminal. This happens by using probabilities, which need to be defined in the Routing settings of the Location *Warten Anmeldung* (menu item "Rule"). The values of the distribution are estimated (70 % of the patients use the Kiosk Check-In terminal, 30 % use the common registration). The nurse responsible for registration needs 1:46 min. and patients arrive every

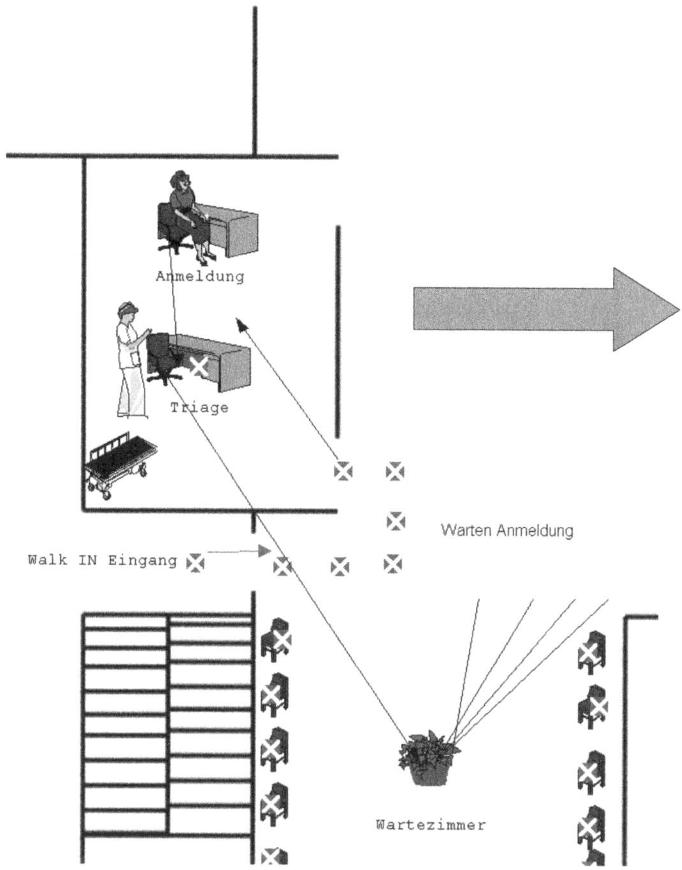

Fig. 29.11 Is-model without Kiosk check-in

1.5 min (identical to the is-model). To ensure a direct comparison to the second is-model, the capacity of the waiting room is also set to "infinite" (Figs. 29.11 and 29.12).

29.2.2.4 Problems Occurring During the Building of the Simulation

While trying to create a working simulation a lot of problems were identifies and solved. The following chapter will give a summary of the most serious ones.

At the beginning a simulation with Walk-In patients and patients arriving via ambulance was planned. Because of the complexity of the simulation tool MedModel the Routing for these types of patients could be generated, but not the Processing. To create the Processing, a lot more time for building the simulation and becoming acquainted with the software would have been necessary. Additionally the required

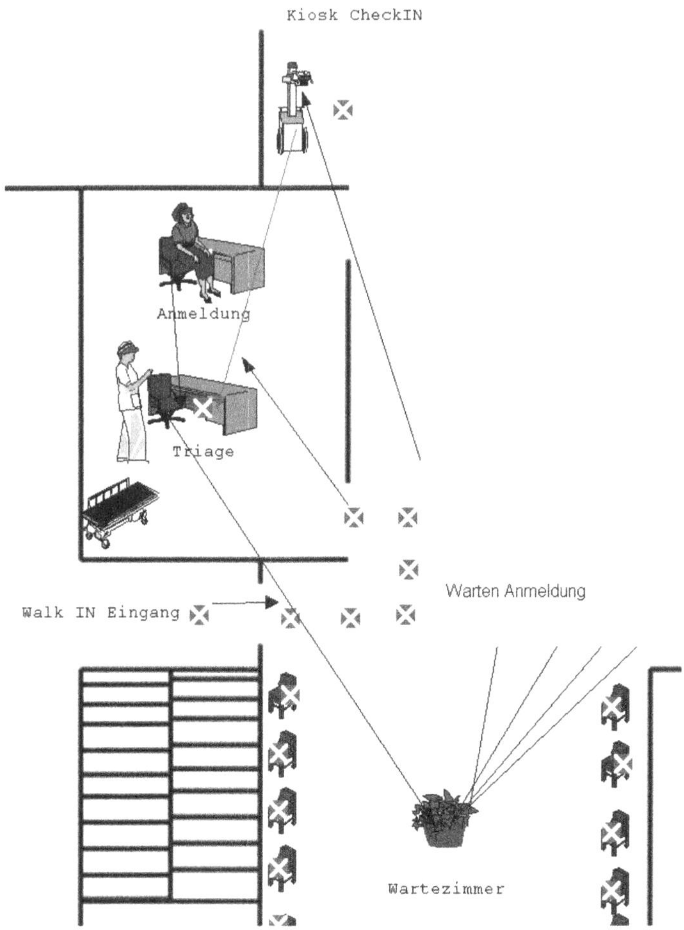

Fig. 29.12 Alternative model with Kiosk check-in

knowledge of commands wasn't existent to create such a complex system. That's also why the is-model was shortened and simplified by including only two doctors and care units that are bound to their Location, not considering working in shifts. Plus, the patients arriving via ambulance and the different triage states weren't regarded.

In a first try of modeling, the Processing of the entities was afflicted with problems, so the first try was dismissed. Since the Routing features different ways to the exit, various types of patients are needed. At the beginning we attempted to distinguish patient types by using distributions and spread them to the correspondent locations. The distribution function was defined in the "User Distribution" and added to the Operation of the relevant Location. In each Location, where a distinction of patient types takes place, an "if… then" relation was defined for every potential patient type in the operation setting. The following problem occurred: The types of

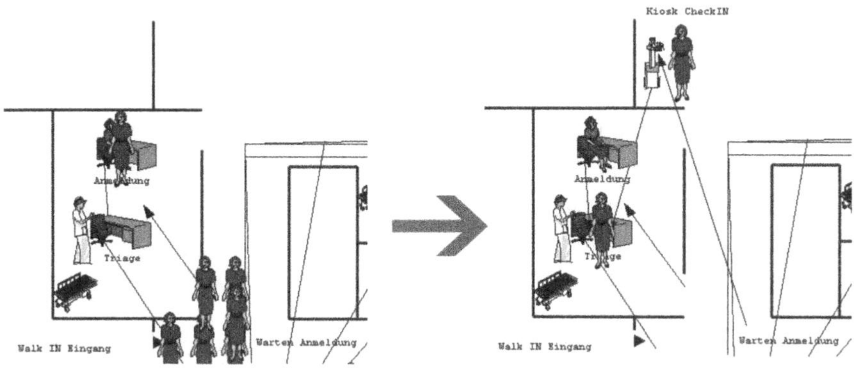

Fig. 29.13 With the help of the Kiosk check-in system, the queues could be resolved

patients had to be distinguished several times and furthermore they needed to appear more than one time in the same Location. That's also the reason why patients didn't visit certain treatment rooms and therefore the resource *Arzt* couldn't "use" them. Based on that, we tried to send entities and resources to the respective Locations with the help of the SEND command. That attempt also failed. The solution was to generate different entities, transform them into the desired entity via the RENAME command and distribute them to the Locations.

29.3 Discussion

29.3.1 Results from the Simulation

In the following section, the results of the simulation are to be presented. While collecting the process times in the clinical center Esslingen, at certain times we noticed an appearance of queues in front of the administration corner. To solve this problem, as shown before, we recommended the implementation of a Kiosk check-in system. In the simulated IS-version based on the documented times, the problem of waiting queues was nonexistent—due to the fact, that waiting queues only arise during peak hours, what, unfortunately, could not be defined within the simulation. Hence, a modification of arrival frequency was necessary to generate them. With a frequency of 1.3 (what means that every 1.5 min a new patient is arriving), the waiting queues became observable. With the help of the Kiosk check-in system, the queues could be resolved (Figs. 29.13 and 29.14).

On the left side, one can see the situation before the adoption of a Kiosk check-in system. The location "Warten_Anmeldung" is fully occupied; in contrast, with the Kiosk check-in system (as pictured on the right side), one can see a discharge of this location.

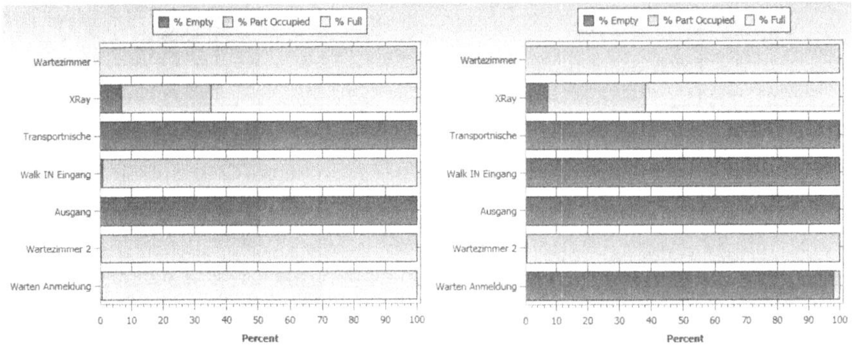

Fig. 29.14 Statistics with frequency of 1.3

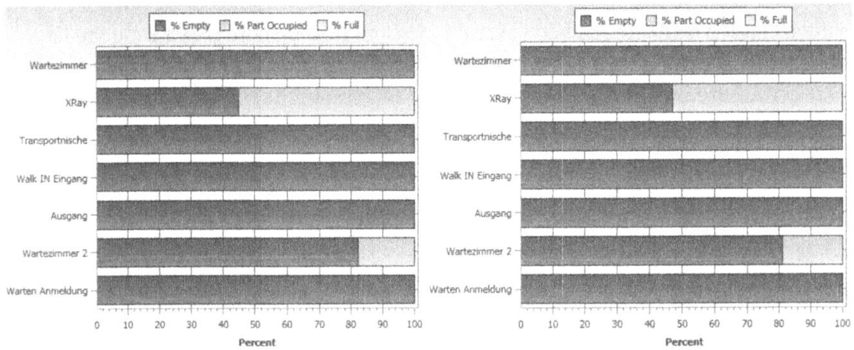

Fig. 29.15 Statistics with a frequency of 20

In addition, the total number of patients passing through the ED could be increased from 6,905 patients to 7,754.

As said, a frequency of 1.3 was required to generate and visualize the waiting queues; based on this frequency, the Kiosk check-in system would be able to reduce the waiting time. To have a realistic view, a frequency of 20 was adopted (Fig. 29.15).

On the left side, one again can see the situation before the adoption of the system, whereas the right side visualizes the adopted system version. With this frequency of 20 (that is approximately realistic for the ED Esslingen) one can see an empty "Warten_Anmeldung" location due to the fact that the administration (without the Kiosk check-in system) only needs about 1:46 min to apply the patients files.

Therefore, a Kiosk check-in system indeed would be able to resolve the problem of waiting queues; however, these queues only arise during peak hours. So all things considered, the system would not really be necessary because of an in this regard insufficient amount of patients passing through the ED for the variations to become noticeable.

29.3.2 Barriers and Facilitators of Simulated Recommendations

As already mentioned, the Kiosk check-in system in general offers several advantages that also could be applied to hospitals in order to achieve a faster handling.

The essential benefit is to have a faster and more efficient administration. On the one hand, patients themselves are able to complete their registration; on the other hand, more administration corners are available, so there is the advantage of reducing the waiting times that go along with the administration process, especially during peak hours. With the help of these additional spots, the administration nurse can be disencumbered and the process itself can be shortened. With these reduced waiting times and the lack of a waiting queue to queue up, the patients first impression when arriving might be even affirmative.

In addition, a multiple language support can be adopted with the Kiosk check-in system. When the communication between the administration nurse and the patient is difficult due to language barriers, the system can help to simplify the administration process with the help of a support of different languages.

The Kiosk check-in system undoubtfully offers various benefits. However, potential negative aspects ought to be considered too. When adopting a Kiosk check-in system, one needs to ensure the acceptance: some patient groups, e.g., the elderly population, might not be able to run the administration process properly. For these patients, additional personnel assisting them would be indispensable, leading to higher amount of personnel expenses. Furthermore, the patients can be unable to run the system by virtue of their injuries: a patient walking in with a broken arm might not have the ability to handle a touchscreen. Without entourage, another assistant might be required to offer a helping hand or the patient would be forced to anyway utilize the face-to-face administration corner.

Besides, the cost-benefit-ratio should be kept in view. With an amount of several thousands of Euros, the acquisition costs of the system are quite demanding. The additional benefits, in contrast, are not that outstanding—at least for the ED of the clinical center Esslingen.

29.4 Conclusion

Generally, the simulation tool MedModel is suited to show the process of implementing a Kiosk Check-In system. It offers graphic elements for visualization and tables to display statistic results of the simulated problem. To create a functional model, several estimations and assumptions need to be made, because of missing data and the short time for training. Some suggestions, such as installing a monitor in the waiting room, which should increase the patient's satisfaction, could not be modeled since happiness is not measurable. Probably it is possible to simulate every process with measurable data by using MedModel. However the realization of the identified problems is way too time consuming, because of complex structures within the processes, as well as in the software.

The concept of Kiosk Check-In was the best solution to simulate, due to the fact that it was one of the major problems we identified and its realization was possible without including too many complex elements, commands, and relations.

Despite major problems in handling the tool, we were able to create a simulation that can picture our idea of possible solutions. The simulation may provide knowledge about the most important issues. But to actually illustrate a realistic process, with all its relevant elements, functions, and relations, a long time is needed to get to know the software, practice the simulation, and identify possible sources of errors.

In conclusion, you can say that regarding a low frequency of arriving patients, as it is the case in the clinical center Esslingen, a solution as the Kiosk Check-In system isn't cost-efficient. Since this concept can prove its efficiency only in peak times of patient arrivals.

Although several problems could be identified, none of them were really severe, since they only occurred under certain premises (e.g., peak times). Therefore it is quite probable that some of the recommendations might not be economic in a long-term view, because the costs and efforts would exceed the benefits.

Chapter 30
Emergency Department Katharinenhospital Stuttgart

Melanie Bathelt, Sabrina Hamm, Ayse Cakmak, Stefanie Guder, and Steffen Ebach

Abstract The Interdisciplinary Emergency Department of the Katharinenhospital, as well as other hospitals, needs to constantly increase its quality, keep the costs to a minimum, and improve its processes. To support this, students of the University of Hohenheim did an observation of the existing processes. This case study shows the results of this observation, which include a description and process models about the existing process. The process consists of part processes like administration, triage, nurse and doctor contacts, treatment, and bed management. There will also be a discussion of recommendations on how the process could be improved further.

Keywords ED • Triage • Bed management • New processes

30.1 Introduction

The case study is about the analysis of processes in the Emergency Department (ED) of the Katharinenhospital which is a part of the Klinikum Stuttgart.

The authors of this case study, students of the University of Hohenheim, were in the ED for several days to observe and document the work flow and to ascertain statistic data.

The material in this case study was prepared originally for Project Seminar SS 2012 at the University of Hohenheim, Germany, under the supervision of Profs. Kirn and Wickramasinghe.

M. Bathelt (✉) • S. Hamm • A. Cakmak • S. Guder • S. Ebach
University of Hohenheim, Stuttgart, Germany
e-mail: M_Bathelt@uni-hohenheim.de

N. Wickramasinghe et al. (eds.), *Lean Thinking for Healthcare*, Healthcare Delivery in the Information Age, DOI 10.1007/978-1-4614-8036-5_30,

Main objective of this study was to identify problems in the process and to work out proposals for solution. An EPC model was created and is the chief subject of the present case study.

The existing processes in the Emergency Department of the Katharinenhospital will be analyzed and discussed in the following chapters. The main focus is about the improvement of the triage process and the execution of the bed management. The problems will be worked out and proposals for solution will be suggested. The particular proposals for solutions will be observed from a critical point of view and proved about their practicability.

The whole case study is based on some key elements of economic theory. Process management is not attributed to a specific group of persons within the hospital, but a challenge of the entire ED and as a result every employee is involved. Value can only be created if all persons of the ED are highly integrated in the execution of the processes. When improvements are implemented in the ED, this should be done within a change management. This secures an optimal implementation.

30.2 Background

The healthcare system in Germany is one of the best among the world (Gries, Zink, Bernhard, Messelken, & Schlechtriemen, 2006, p. 1). Since 1883, Germany has a mandatory health insurance system. There are two possibilities to be insured, either governmental or private. In 1997, the Federal Republic of Germany (FRG) counted 80,024 million inhabitants in Germany. On the one hand 88 % of the German population had a governmental health insurance and on the other hand 8.91 % of the German population was private-insured. Only 0.18 % of the total population was uninsured. This approximates 150,000 people. Therefore, everyone can come easily to an Emergency Department to get an emergency medical care (Platz, Bey, & Walter, 2003, p. 2).

The hospitals in Germany have two different Emergency Departments. They have established either an interdisciplinary emergency medicine (Interdisziplinäre Notaufnahme, INA) or a Centralized Emergency Department (Zentrale Notaufnahme, ZNA).

Interdisciplinary Emergency Departments are separate and independent departments in the hospital with their own direction. Every day, they offer a 24 h service (Walter & Fleischmann, 2007, p.659). Every person can come to the Interdisciplinary Emergency Department, regardless of what symptoms he has and which medical care he needs, because the physicians in the Interdisciplinary Emergency Departments are all-rounders. This presupposes specialized physicians from different departments who work together in a team in the Interdisciplinary Emergency Department. All of them have an operating experience and a large knowledge in emergency medical care. Every physician can treat every patient, so each patient has a physician and a nurse who are responsible for him. This form of an ED brings many advantages. There is no need for a lot of specialized physicians anymore, because the doctors of Interdisciplinary Emergency Departments are generalists who treat each patient. This helps to reduce costs for specialized physicians. Moreover the responsibilities of doctors and nurses are clearly defined and there is a constant high quality in human health. Interdisciplinary Emergency Departments reduce also the waiting times for patients. There is no need to wait for a certain doctor and it is a faster handling of the patients (Hogan & Fleischmann, 2008, pp. 30–31). Interdisciplinary Emergency Departments are therefore very attractive for patients and accident ambulances. Each year, the number of patients in Interdisciplinary Emergency Departments is increasing about 10–20 % (Walter & Fleischmann, 2007, p. 658).

However, this large knowledge and skills in emergency medical care of physicians from Interdisciplinary Emergency Departments are not profound and adequate. It is not a replacement for a family doctor or specialist. It is quite the opposite. The physicians in Interdisciplinary Emergency Departments make the emergency medical care, for example, stabilizing, diagnosing, treating, and scheduling. Further treatment will be made by a family doctor or a specialist (Walter & Fleischmann, 2007, p. 658).

In Germany, more and more Centralized Emergency Departments are established since the last decade. The reasons for establishing a Centralized Emergency Department are the economic pressure and changing medical and political environment (Bey, Hahn, & Moecke, 2008, pp. 275–276).

The Centralized Emergency Department is a structural association of several disciplines in an emergency room. There is an autonomous medical management, which reports directly to the medical director and can design by itself about its structures and processes (Zehnder, 2007, p. 51).

Aims and advantages of the Centralized Emergency Departments are to bring different services for patients together, which means a higher quality in medical care, satisfaction of patients, cost reduction, and the optimum utilization of resources that are in the room (Bey et al., 2008, p. 275).

But for all those positive aspects, there are also disadvantages in this option of establishing an Emergency Department. The physicians in Centralized Emergency Departments are not specifically trained for emergency care. They work without a supervision that could improve, help, and give feedback to their work (Bey et al., 2008, p. 275).

No matter which possibility of Emergency Departments' organization is taken, fact is that the number of patients in Emergency Departments is increasing from year to year as well as the costs. The establishment of the best alternative for each hospital is of a great importance. For each patient the number of emergency help is 112 and is significantly important.

30.2.1 Literature Review

During the last 20 years Emergency Department (ED) overcrowding and waiting times have become a major topic in the emergency medicine. Since the mid 1980s a significant increase in overcrowding in EDs has been reported in the literature worldwide. According to the German Hospital Federation for Emergencies, the number of patients in the EDs in Germany increases dramatically. Due to the EHEC-suspicions 21 million patients got a medical treatment in an ED in 2010—a rise of more than 18 % (L.N. Schaffrath, 2011, Digital Medien GmbH). Cultural, social, economic, and demographic changes are mentioned as reasons. Furthermore there is a consistent argumentation that ED overcrowding leads to several negative effects like risking patient safety and lower patient satisfaction. Logically a lot of research to identify and eliminate the causes has been done during the last years. With this contribution we want to illustrate the current state of the ED overcrowding research in the Katharinenhospital.

30.3 Case Study

30.3.1 Background

For our seminar in information systems we students are sent in groups to the ED to see and model the processes which are running in the ED during the patient's habitation. Observation was conducted over a duration of 8 days. During this time, medical and nursing personnel were monitored. The Emergency Department of the Katharinenhospital is an interdisciplinary ED. It was found in December 2010.

Goals of the new founded ED are to be upfront with every patient suffer twenty-four-seven and an equal high standard medical and human treatment quality.

The ED has 22 divan beds, 10 in cabins with curtains and 12 in separated rooms. Some rooms even have an own toilet. The ED commands over the hospital's SAP system and its own created emergency software called ECare as well. ECare is a system with pictures and attends process of the ED. With the help of ECare all patient movements or treatments are documented. Every physician or caregiver has access to the system from the computer stations, which are in the middle of the ED, shown in Fig. 30.1.

The Emergency Department has one entrance where all patients come in and after treatment is finished get out. They want to avoid that patients leave the ED without being seen or patients get lost because of confusion.

For this complex system, the ED needs a good managed team for a smooth process. There exists only one team well functioning separation. The doctors have an explicit competence and responsibility for the patients during their place of residence. Between 7 a.m. and 11 p.m. the ED guarantees that there is an internal and surgeon specialist present.

These are managed by a team, consisting of a physician responsible for medical matters, i.e. Prof. Dr. Schilling, who is assisted by two executive medical assistants, i.e. Mrs. M. Sauter for nusing matters and her representative Fig. 30.2. Besides the direction team there exists an ED council, which includes two members of the doctors team and two members of the caregivers team. The council gives advice to the direction team.

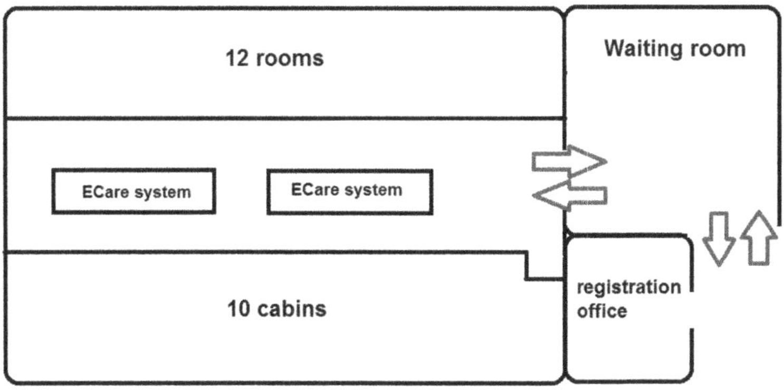

Fig. 30.1 Map of the ED

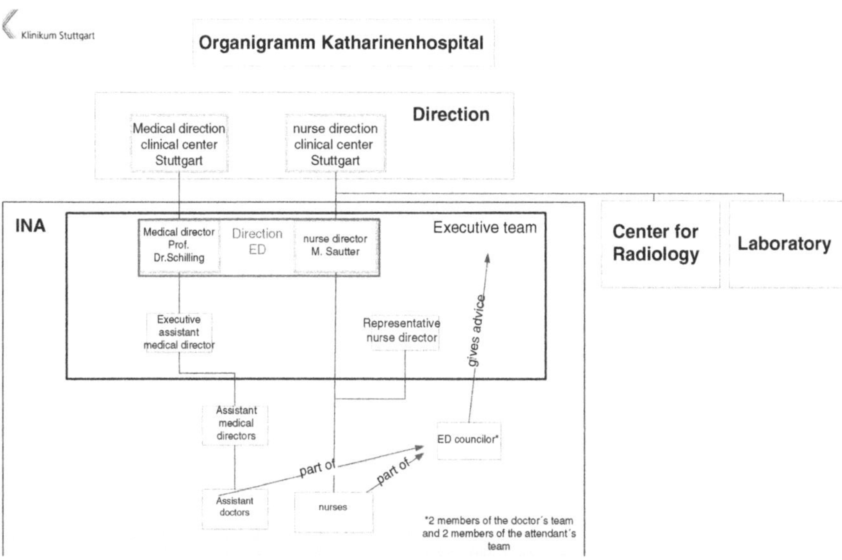

Fig. 30.2 Organigram of the Katharinenhospital

30.3.2 Methodology

To get information about how long each task in the ED takes and to measure how long waiting times are, we went to the Katharinenhospital. There, we watched the process of a patient entering the ED until leaving again and wrote down times on when certain tasks were happening. There was no exclusion of certain patients; we wrote down everybody who entered the ED, no matter what the disease was. After we had gotten an idea of the process, we created an EPC model. It shows the details of the whole process, which will be discussed in Chap. 30.3.3. The EPC model is attached at the end of this chapter.

Table 30.1 Table of the calculated times

Time calculated	Start	End
Administration time	Start of administration	End of administration
Time for triage	Start of triage	End of triage
Waiting time for triage options 1 and 2	Start of administration	Start of triage
Waiting time for triage option 3	Start of administration	Start of triage
Time of first nurse contact	Start of first nurse contact	End of first nurse contact
Time of first doctor contact	Start of first doctor contact	End of first doctor contact
Time for taking a blood sample	Start of taking a blood sample	End of taking a blood sample
Time for the X-ray	Patient leaves the ED for the X-ray	Patient comes back from the X-ray
Waiting time for an X-ray	End of first doctor contact	Patient leaves the ED for the X-ray
Time for a CT	Patient leaves the ED for a CT	Patient comes back from the CT
Waiting time for a CT	End of first doctor contact	Patient leaves the ED for a CT
Time of sonography	Start of sonography	End of sonography
Time of other examinations	Start of other examination	End of other examination
Time of consil	Start of consil	End of consil
Time for treatment	Start of treatment	End of treatment
Time for searching a bed with case manager	Start of searching a bed	End of searching a bed
Time for searching a bed without case manager	Start of searching a bed	End of searching a bed
Time until decision for sending patient to a station	Start of first doctor contact	Decision about sending the patient to a station
Waiting time for a transport	Time of ordering a transport	Pick-up time of the patient by a transporter
Time of the patient in the ED	Patient enters the ED	Patient leaves the ED
Waiting time for a bed	Decision that the patient goes to a station	Patient gets picked up and taken to the station

For the times we stopped, we used a documentation table that was given us by the University and the hospital. The table asked for times for certain tasks in the ED that were important to write down for later calculations. With those times, we were able to calculate the length of the different tasks as well as waiting times that occurred for patients. Table 30.1 shows which times had been taken and how they were used for calculation.

30.3.3 Results

In this chapter, the process of a patient entering the ED until leaving again is being described. Our group modeled this process in an EPC process model, which can be

Table 30.2 Calculated times

Time calculated	Average time	Minimum	Maximum	Median	Number (n)
Administration time	0:01	0:00	0:16	0:01	128
Time for triage	0:01	0:00	0:07	0:01	127
Waiting time for triage options 1 and 2	0:08	0:00	0:25	0:07	85
Waiting time for triage option 3	0:03	0:00	0:08	0:02	34
Time of first nurse contact	0:06	0:00	0:55	0:04	128
Time of first doctor contact	0:07	0:00	0:39	0:06	128
Time for taking a blood sample	0:03	0:01	0:09	0:03	40
Time for the X-ray	0:20	0:05	0:46	0:18	27
Waiting time for an X-ray	0:28	0:01	2:33	0:14	22
Time for a CT	0:26	0:13	0:56	0:21	10
Waiting time for a CT	1:16	0:47	1:29	1:23	7
Time of sonography	0:08	0:04	0:17	0:08	7
Time of other examinations	0:09	0:02	0:40	0:05	16
Time of consil	0:15	0:06	0:29	0:13	8
Time for treatment	0:40	0:01	3:07	0:21	46
Time for searching a bed with case manager	0:26	0:00	1:00	0:07	5
Time for searching a bed without case manager	0:03	0:01	0:14	0:02	9
Time until decision for sending patient to a station	1:40	0:12	4:16	1:19	15
Waiting time for a transport	0:30	0:04	2:06	0:15	9
Time of the patient in the ED	1:54	0:11	22:42	1:23	106
Waiting time for a bed	1:47	0:36	3:00	1:47	11

found in the attachment. An overview of our calculated times is shown in Table 30.2. We calculated the average time and a median for every task or waiting time. Table 30.2 also shows a maximum, minimum, and the number of cases (n) that we used for the calculation, for every task. All the times are shown in hours.

There will be further calculations for the triage process, that are shown later in Chap. 30.3.3.4.

We divided the whole process in smaller process parts, so it would be easier to understand. In the following, the process will be described very detailed and calculated times were added to the specific tasks.

30.3.3.1 Patients' Arrival

When patients feel sick, they want to get easy and fast treatments. For this, many patients go to the emergency Department. There are two options how they can get to the ED; either they walk-in, mostly with relatives or friends, or they are accompanied by the ambulance. In the case that the patient is being picked up by an ambulance, he gets first-aid by an ambulance doctor before arrival.

30.3.3.2 Walk-In

If the patient walks in, he will be registered by the administrative nurse. She is sitting at the information desk and asks the patient about his symptoms and his insurance information. With the insurance card, where all data about the patient is secured, the registration time is very fast. If the patient has forgotten his insurance card, the nurse will have to type in all information about the patient manually. After this process the patient is registered in the ED's ECare system. The patient's information is automatically transferred to the hospital's SAP system, which is used inside the ED. After the patient is registered, the nurse prints out forms with information about the patient and gives it to the responsible nurse or the triage nurse. Sometimes, the patient is already being triaged at the registration desk. In this case, he gets a triage color. If the triage will be done later, his color is grey. At the end of this process, the patient will be forwarded to the ED or the waiting room. This depends on how busy the ED is at the time.

30.3.3.3 By the Ambulance

If the patient is accompanied by the ambulance, he will be pushed into the ED in a wheelchair or on a barrow by the aid men. Severely hurt patients are taken straight to the shock room. In this case, the administrative nurse takes care of informing everybody in the hospital who is needed to treat the patient in the shock room. Two nurses and at least one doctor from the ED will be sent to the shock room as well. If the patient is not severely hurt and can be treated in the ED, the registration is the same as already described in the "walk-in" process. In some cases, the patient is being registered right at the beginning; if a treatment is necessary first, the registration will be done during the process. The ambulance doctor gives information about the patient's condition to the nurses and doctors in the ED right after their arrival.

30.3.3.4 Triage

The triage is a process in which the waiting time for each patient is ascertained. There exist three manners of execution of the triage process in the Katharinenhospital.

The first option is that the patient gets his triage in a normal treatment room from a nurse. In option 2 the patient gets his triage in the triage room from the triage nurse. Both options take place either right after the administration or after waiting in the waiting room, depending on how busy the ED is and on how severe the patient's condition is. In option 3 the patient gets his triage during the administration. In the following, options 1 and 2 will be described. Option 3 will not be described more precisely because it takes place during the administration process and is done without examination.

First Option

The nurse decides on which time she is going to execute the triage. There are no specific determinants when the triage process is supposed to start. After the decision that the triage should be done, the nurse calls for the patient. In this instance, there are three possibilities:

- The patient is not available. His family members might be able to let the nurse know where the patient is to find. Or the nurse will come back later, when the patient is ready to enter the ED.
- The patient is not findable in spite of repeated calls. He might have left the ED because of long waiting times and will come back later. In our observation, there was one case, when a patient went shopping because he didn't want to wait in the ED.
- The patient is available and can be picked up by the nurse. She takes him into the treatment area of the ED. Family members have to wait outside until they are asked to enter as well.

After being picked up and taken into the treatment area, the patient is taken to a room. This can be a cabin with a curtain or a room cabin with a curtain, a room, or the surgery room (e.g., for sewing or a cast). The nurse decides for the room depending on the sickness of the patient. The nurse also brings the paperwork that was printed out at the administration to the room and places it into the box at the room entrance. After the patient has been taken into the room the triage is executed.

The nurse checks out the symptoms that are necessary for the triage, according to the Emergency Severity Index (ESI) (www.esitriage.org). Sometimes, also the vital parameters are measured right away (e.g., blood pressure). The categories red, orange, yellow, green, and blue are categorized through specific symptoms.

- Immediate (red) means that an immediate life-saving intervention is required. The patient is acrotic. The defined waiting time for this category must be 0 min.
- The emergent category (orange) means that there is a high risk situation. The patient is confused, lethargic, and disoriented. He has severe pain and the vital parameters are in a danger zone. Such a patient doesn't have to wait longer than 10 min.
- The urgent category (yellow) is described by no danger zone vitals and many different resources are needed. The defined waiting time is at the maximum 30 min.
- Semi-urgent (green) means that there is one different resource needed and the waiting time has to be below 90 min.
- Nonurgent (blue) means that no different resources are needed. In this case the waiting time must not exceed 120 min (Table 30.3; Fig. 30.3).

In the Katharinenhospital in average, none of the ESI-defined waiting times were exceeded. But in the categories emergent (orange) and urgent (yellow) concerning the maximum value of the waiting time, there are some exceedances. The maximum waiting time according to ESI of category emergent is 10 min; the maximum value

Table 30.3 Waiting times for the different categories of ESI

	Immediate	Emergent	Urgent	Semi-urgent	Nonurgent
Waiting time till first care contact	$n=1$	$n=11$	$n=39$	$n=46$	$n=8$
	Ø=1 min	Ø=4,55 min	Ø=7,69 min	Ø=10,57 min	Ø=8,75 min
	min=max=1 min	min=1 min	min=1 min	min=0 min	min=2 min
		max=15 min	max=63 min	max=85 min	max=31 min
	$m=1$ min	$m=3$ min	$m=5$ min	$m=7$ min	$m=6$ min
		$w=14$ min	$w=62$ min	$w=85$ min	$w=29$ min
Waiting time till first physician contact	$n=1$	$n=11$	$n=39$	$n=46$	$n=8$
	Ø=1 min	Ø=13,09 min	Ø=19,97 min	Ø=20,09 min	Ø=27,13 min
	min=max=1 min	min=3 min	min=2 min	min=2 min	min=2 min
		max=28 min	max=63 min	max=77 min	max=106 min
	$m=1$ min	$m=10$ min	$m=19$ min	$m=19$ min	$m=10$ min
		$w=25$ min	$w=61$ min	$w=75$ min	$w=104$ min

n=sample size, min after equal sign=minutes, min before equal sign=minimum, Ø=average, m=median, w=wingspread

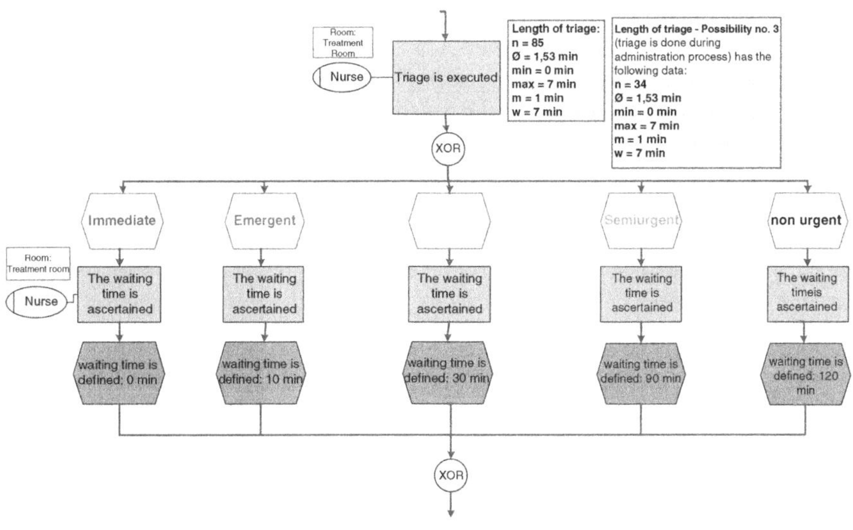

Fig. 30.3 Subprocess of the triage

in the data ascertainment was 15 min till first care contact and 28 min till first physician contact. The maximum waiting time was exceeded in one case by a sample size of 11 patients.

The maximum waiting time according to ESI of category urgent is 30 min; the maximum value was 63 min till first care contact and 63 min till first physician contact. The maximum waiting time was exceeded in two cases by sample size of 39 patients. This means that there are only two outliers which could be attributed to a specific situation.

The minimum waiting time till first care contact of category semi-urgent (green) was 0 min. Consequently this minimum waiting time was lower than in categories red and orange which is unexpected. This can be attributed to the small sample size of 1 patient in category immediate (red) and 11 patients in category emergent (orange).

The median of the waiting time in category emergent (orange) was 3 min till first care contact and 10 min till first physician contact. This shows that over 50 % of the patients were treated by a nurse after a waiting time under 3 min and by a physician after a waiting time below 10 min. This is the case in all categories: the median always lies under the average waiting time and under the predefined waiting time. Also, the median of the waiting time till the first physician contact always was higher than the median of the waiting time till first nurse contact. This is comprehensible because the normal work flow in the ED of Katharinenhospital determines that the first treatment is done by the nurse (with exceptions by patients of category immediate). The physician needs for his work some pre-information about the medical conditions of the patient. For example, the vital parameters have to be measured before the first physician contact takes places.

Within the data ascertainment the triage options 1 and 2 weren't distinguished. Accordingly it was not documented whether the triage took place in the triage room or in a normal treatment room. Following, the described waiting times and the statistic data refer to both options.

The wingspread of waiting time till first care contact was 29 min and till first physician contact was 104 min. This is reasonable because of the different predefined waiting times for each category of ESI. Within the particular categories the wingspreads were also high: For example, the wingspread of the waiting time of category urgent is 62 min until first care contact and 61 min until first physician contact. It has to be clarified from a medical point of view if these are systematical bias.

The average waiting time from the start of the administration—which is in Katharinenhospital equatable to the arrival of the patient—till the triage was executed was 8.2 min at a sample size of 85 patients. The maximum value of the waiting time till triage execution was 25 min. This would be an exceedance of the defined waiting time for categories immediate and emergent according to ESI. The median of the waiting time till triage execution was 7 min. This shows that 50 % of the 85 patients got their triage after a waiting time which lies under 7 min.

The length of the execution of the triage is in average 1.53 min at a sample size of 85 patients. The medium is 1 min, so 50 % of the patients were triaged in a timeframe up to 1 min. But the maximum length of the triage execution is 7 min. This shows that there were some outliers.

After finishing the execution of the triage, the nurse leaves the room. The patient has to wait until the doctor will have time to enter the room. The results of the triage have to be documented. For this, the nurse enters the triage color and the results of the triage in the system, ECare. When the nurse is done, the color and the corresponding waiting time appear on the screens that are arranged in the whole ED.

Second Option

The second option is similar to option 1 but there are some differences that will be discussed in the following.

The description of option 2 starts at the known process point when the patient is being picked up by the triage nurse and is taken to the triage room. The triage room is room number 1—the first room on the left side in the ED. The triage nurse checks out the symptoms which are necessary for the triage according to the ESI in the triage room. The waiting times were already described in triage option 1. After finishing the execution of the triage, the triage nurse and the patient are leaving the triage room. The nurse has a first concrete idea of what the patient's problem is. Depending on the sickness, the patient is taken to a cabin with a curtain, a room cabin with a curtain, a room, or a surgery room (e.g., for sewing or a cast). If there is no unoccupied treatment room, the patient is sent back to the waiting room. He has to wait in the waiting room until a nurse calls for the patient and brings him to a treatment room. The results of the triage have to be documented in ECare by the triage nurse as well.

Third Option

As mentioned above, option 3 includes the triage in the administrative process without further examination.

Concerning the waiting time for a patient to get his triage there was a sample size of 34 patients. The average waiting time until the triage execution was 2.53 min. The median of the waiting time till triage execution was 2 min. Consequently the median of the waiting time till triage execution was lower in option 3 than in options 1 and 2 which are described above. This is reasonable because in option 3 the triage was executed during the administration process.

The length of the execution of the triage is in average 1.53 min at a sample size of 34 patients which is the same average duration compared to options 1 and 2. The median is also 1 min and the maximum length of the triage execution is 7 min. This shows that from the viewpoint of the triage length there are no significant differences between option 3 and options 1 and 2. This is unexpected: In option 3 the triage is executed during the administration without a medical examination and is not briefer than the triage duration of the real triage in options 1 and 2.

30.3.3.5 First Contact with the Nurse

After the triage, the patient gets into the treatment room. The nurse enters the room to measure the vital parameters, like blood pressure or pulse, and asks about the patient's condition. In average the time of the nurse examining the patient is about 6 min. After the nurse finished measuring, she enters the results in the ECare system. The doctor now has basic information about the patient visible on the screen before he enters the room.

Sometimes the first contact with the nurse is at the same time as the triage. If the patient came in the ambulance the first contact with the doctor and with the nurse were mostly at the same time.

30.3.3.6 First Contact with the Doctor

The patient's information about the triage and the vital parameters are visible on the screen for the doctor. Depending on how many patients he has to take care of and on the triage color, he decides which patient he will contact next. The doctor enters the room and tries to figure out how he can help the patient by asking him questions about his symptoms and his condition. With finishing the first contact, the doctor orders further tests or examinations to get more information about the patient. This process takes about 7 min in average.

30.3.3.7 Sonography

The doctor decides to do a sonography examination for the patient. He will get the sonography machine into the treatment room to do the examinations. For this process we observed seven patients with the average time of 8 min. After the examination is finished, the results can be seen in the system.

30.3.3.8 X-Ray

The doctor gave the order for an X-ray. Depending on the patient's condition either he will be asked to walk to the X-ray room or the nurse will order a transporter for him. Either way, the patient has to wait in the ED until the doctor gets the allowance for his patient to go upstairs to get his X-ray. Waiting times are varying, depending on how busy the radiology is. A problem in this process was for patients to find their way to the X-ray room right away. After the X-ray is taken the patient will come back into his room in the ED and the results are visible in the system. Within 27 patients we have an average time of 20 min for the patient leaving the ED until he comes back.

30.3.3.9 Computer Tomography

The order for a computer tomography (CT) is given by the doctor as well. The CT room is outside of the Emergency Department. This is why patients have to leave the ED for this examination either by walking themselves or by being taken by a transporter ordered from the nurse. Waiting times for the CT are varying as well. The patient has to wait in the ED until the doctor gives him the allowance to leave for his examination. The observed average time for 10 patients to leave the ED until they enter their room again was about 26 min. When the CT is done the doctor can look at the results in the system.

30.3.3.10 Blood Test

If the doctor needs to get a blood test, he will give the order to a nurse to take a blood sample from the patient. The nurse takes about 3 min average to get a blood sample (40 patients observed). After the blood sample is taken, the nurse will stick a tag with the patient's identification marking on the sample and brings it to a container in the ED. The administrative nurse calls the laboratory to pick the sample up and do the test. When the lab figured out the results they will enter them into the system, so that they will also be visible in the ED.

30.3.3.11 Other Examinations

If the doctor needs other examinations as the ones named above, like for example, a electrocardiogram, he will order them as well. Depending on the examination it will be done by the doctor himself or by the nurse. Other examinations take for 19 patients about 9 min. At the end of the examinations the results will be put into the system as well.

The doctor can order several tests at the same time and they will be done one after the other like described above. Sometimes the doctor might not order another test or examination until after he has had the chance to evaluate the results from examinations ordered earlier. This might happen if the gotten results won't give him enough information for the needed treatment.

30.3.3.12 Arrangements

After looking at the test results the doctor needs to find a diagnosis for his patient and decides what the next steps will be. This can be a treatment if it can be done in the ED, a council if the doctor needs the opinion of a specialist, or the patient might have to be transferred to a station or to another hospital.

30.3.3.13 Council

The council will always be done, if the emergency doctor needs more specific information about the patient's disease. A council can be done for every kind of disease. To do a council, the emergency doctor will call the specific council doctor by phone. If the council doctor is available, he will come as soon as possible to the ED. There, he can look at all treatments the ED doctor has done already and do his council.

After the council doctor has examined the patient, he will talk to the ED doctor about his opinion and they will try to find a solution for what will happen next to the patient and how further treatment looks like. When the council doctor is finished, he will leave the ED and the ED doctor takes over again and takes care of further treatment or arrangements. The time of when the council doctor enters the ED until the finishing of the council is in average 15 min for 8 patients.

30.3.3.14 Treatment

When the ED doctor knows what kind of disease the patient has, he can decide about the treatment himself. The treatment will be done by the doctor and the nurse is assisting him. The time when the treatment begins until the treatment is over took in average 40 min for 46 patients. After the treatment, the doctor has to write the doctors letter. The average time of waiting for the doctors letter was 33 min for 45 patients. But there are also a few people that had to wait longer than 2 h and one person had to even wait for more than 3 h.

After receiving the doctors letter, all patients can go home or to another station or hospital. The time between entering the ED and leaving the ED with the doctors letter was in average 1:54 h for 106 patients.

30.3.3.15 Different Hospital

Because the process has a lot to do with other hospitals we do not focus on it. We wanted to concentrate on internal processes. That's the reason why we do not have any data about this process. The ED decides that the patient has to go to another hospital. The reasons could be that the Katharinenhospital won't treat the patient, because a different hospital is more specialized in the specific disease, or there is no free bed for the patient. The nurse will call other hospitals to find a place for the patient.

There are two possibilities. It could be that they do not have a bed for the patient. In this case, the nurse has to call another hospital. If they have a free bed the nurse books it. Her next step is to call and book a mobile intensive care unit (MICU) to transport the patient to the other hospital. The MICU will come and pick the patient up when he is ready to leave the ED.

30.3.3.16 Bed Management

For 15 patients the doctor made a decision if the patient has to go to a station or not. It was done in average 1:40 h after the first contact between the doctor and the patient. That could be if the patient has to be watched or further treated and for this has to stay in the hospital. If the patient has to be sent to a station, the doctor of the ED has to search for a bed. The time of finding a bed inside the hospital needs in average 26 min if the case manager is inside the hospital. Five people had to go to a station when the case manager was inside the hospital. It took just about 3 min if the case manager wasn't available. Nine patients had to go to a station when the case manager was not available.

If the ED doctor finds a bed he has to inform the station doctor about the patient. He will do this by calling at the station and talking to the responsible doctor. When the station doctor is informed, the nurse of the ED can order the transportation to pick up the patient and take him to the station. The transporter takes the patient either in a bed or in a wheelchair out of the ED. In average the time between ordering the transportation and the beginning of the transportation is 30 min. It was done for nine patients. Most of the cases needed less than 30 min. Only in a few cases the time was much longer than 30 min.

30.3.3.17 Searching a Bed

If the doctor begins to search a bed, he has at first to think about what time and weekday it is. If it is between Monday and Friday from 8 a.m. until 4 or 6 p.m. the case manager of the station will be inside the hospital and the doctor can phone him. Outside this timeframe, the case manager won't be there and the doctor has to directly call the station. The processes of calling the station or the case manager are similar. Because of this, we will only show the process for calling the case manager. To make sure where the differences are, we will show the differences in times between the two cases.

The first step will be that the doctor calls the case manger via phone. There is not any personal contact between the doctor and the case manager. Now there are two possibilities.

- The ED doctor does not get through to the case manger. In this case, the doctor needs to try to call him again later. In our statistics, the ED doctor phoned the case manager 12 times and only once he couldn't reach him. The ED doctor phoned the station 10 times and every time somebody was available.
- The second possibility is that the doctor gets through to the case manager. In 12 times the doctor phoned the case manager and out of that he reached him 11 times. When the doctor called the station, his call got answered every time. When the doctor gets through, he has to ask for a bed.

The case could occur that there is no free bed for the patient. In our observation, a doctor asked the case manager 11 times for a free bed and in 5 times he couldn't get one. Ten times the doctor asked the station for a free bed; only one time there was no bed available. So in 45 % of asking the case manager for a free bed there was one available. In 80 % of asking the station a bed was free for the patient. If there is a free bed available, the doctor will book it and the search for a bed is over.

30.3.4 Recommendation

In the existing process of the ED of the Katharinenhospital, we observed several flaws in the process. In this chapter we would like to make some recommendations on how those flaws can be improved. The two main parts of the process that we would like to discuss are the triage process and the process of searching for a bed on a station in the Katharinenhospital. In the end of this chapter, there are more critical points we would like to recommend, that aren't concerning a whole process part.

30.3.4.1 Triage

As described in previous chapters, patients have to wait when the ED is very busy and when the patient's medical problem is not severe. But often patients have to wait although the ED is not very busy. Unnecessary waiting times should be avoided by having the administrative nurse observing the waiting times of patients sitting in the waiting room. The specifications of ESI for waiting times should be observed strictly.

In the existing triage process, the nurse decides at which time she is going to execute the triage. There are no specific determinants that determine the starting point of the triage process. It seemed that every nurse decides on her own when the patient is going to be triaged. This is shown by the unspecific triage, done by the nurse during administration. We recommend that the triage should be done directly after administration.

When the nurse comes and takes the patient into the ED, the family members have to wait outside until they are asked to enter as well. The family members often do not understand why they have to stay in the waiting room. They want to back up their family member. Even though it is comprehensible that the doctor wants to look after the patient without family members at first, there could be an advantage from a medical point of view if the family members accompany their relatives: In many cases they know about the medicaments and the disease of the patient. A proposal for solution is that one family member is allowed to accompany the patient. If this is not possible, the nurse should explain the reason why the family members have to stay in the waiting room. This way, there would be a better understanding of the relatives and the patients for the rules in the ED.

Another problem refers to the point of time in which the triage is executed. The accomplishment of the triage takes place after the patient has already waited in the waiting room. Consequently, the waiting times were ascertained although the patient has already waited. In options 1 and 2, the average waiting time from the start of the administration—which is in the Katharinenhospital equatable to the arrival of the patient—until the triage was executed 8.2 min at a sample size of 85 patients. The maximum value of the waiting time until triage execution was 25 min. This would be an exceedance of the defined waiting time for the categories immediate and emergent according to ESI. The median of waiting time until triage execution was 7 min. This shows that 50 % of the 85 patients got their triage after a waiting time below 7 min. In option 3, there was a sample size of 34 patients. The average waiting time until the triage execution was 2.53 min. The median of the waiting time until triage execution was 2 min. Consequently the median of the waiting time until triage execution was lower in option 3 than in options 1 and 2. This is reasonable because in option 3 the triage was executed during the administration process.

According to the ESI rules, triage should be done before the patient is sent to the waiting room. This was not always the case in the Katharinenhospital. Our recommendation would be to follow those rules and while or right after the administration. Many patients tell their medical problems and symptoms already during the administration process, so the triage nurse could already listen and decide if a more specific triage is necessary or if the patient can go straight to the waiting room.

Another idea for the Katharinenhospital would be that the triage room would be placed within the waiting area instead of the main area of the ED. This way, patients could be triaged right after the administration, before being asked to take a seat in the waiting room or to enter the ED where they would get a room or a cabin to wait to see the doctor. This process would contribute to a better structure of the first steps that a patient has to go through after entering the ED. The triage would have a fix time of when it would be done and the local structure would support this process.

We observed that when the first contact with the nurse or triage nurse is over, she does inform the patient about further steps. But what they didn't tell the patient was the approximate waiting time until the first doctor contact starts. In our opinion it would be again helpful for both sides if the nurse could give the patient an approximate waiting time for a better appreciation of the system. This way, patients get not as impatient as quickly if waiting time is longer when the ED is busy.

For a better understanding of our recommendations for this process, we modeled a target process as an EPC model. It shows how the process could look like when critical process points are optimized and is illustrated in Fig. 30.4. In our target process the triage takes place directly after the administration process. This way, the triage is actually done before the patient is sent to the waiting room. Furthermore, a triage room exists and it is in use, not only as an option but also as the regular room in which the triage is executed. During the whole time, one triage nurse, that is especially trained in the execution of the triage according to ESI, is responsible for all the triage executions.

The triage nurse decides if it is necessary to take the patient to the triage room or if it is enough to just look at him and listen to his symptoms asked at the administration, to do the triage without an explicit analysis. Already, this decision constitutes a pre-triage, because the triage nurse bases her decision on her experience. If triage in the triage room is necessary, the triage nurse asks the patient to follow her into the triage room. The triage room is placed in the waiting room area or right at the entrance of the main ED area. This way, the patient doesn't have to cross the whole ED to get to the triage room.

When the triage is executed the triage nurse checks out the symptoms of the patient, which are needed for the triage according to the ESI. Afterwards she categorizes the patient in one of the categories immediate (red), emergent (orange), urgent (yellow), semi-urgent (green), and nonurgent (blue). The vital parameters (e.g., blood pressure) can also be measured. Waiting times for each color are ascertained. This is why the triage should be done before the patient has to wait in the waiting room.

After the nurse has finished the triage, she made a decision on how long the patients waiting time will be by choosing a color. Our recommendation would be that she lets the patient know about how long his waiting time will be. The probability that dissatisfaction occurs will decline that way.

Then, the triage nurse accompanies or sends the patient back to the waiting area or takes him straight to a room or cabin. The results of the triage are documented in ECare. That means that the color and the corresponding waiting time appear on the screens which are arranged in the whole ED. The physicians and the other nurses can see the specific symptomatic situation and the waiting times on the screens.

30.3.4.2 New Process Bed Management 1

A recommendation on how to improve the process of bed management would be that the case manager is 24 h a day available and also on weekends. Our idea would be a department of case managers that can work together on the bed management in

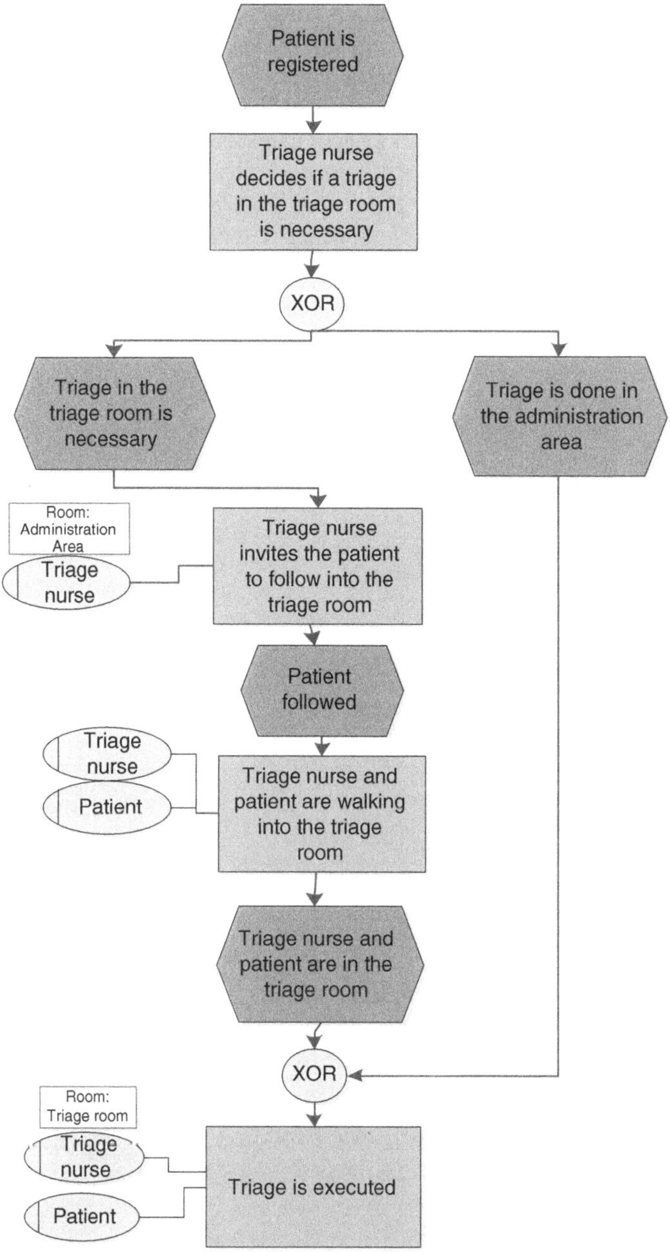

Fig. 30.4 Subprocess of the optimized triage process

total. This way, the process would also be easier if a doctor ordered and booked a bed and later changes his mind about which station the patient needs to go to. In the old case, he would have needed to cancel the bed with the case manager, he booked the bed with at first, and then find the case manager from the new station to book another bed. If the case managers aren't responsible for just one specific station, the doctor would only need to let them know the change and the case manager can find to book a new bed. This saves the doctor time.

We would also recommend that instead of having every doctor to call a case manger, there would be a computer system that sends the bed request to the case manger. A possibility could be that the doctor writes the first three preferences of stations the patient can go to, into the system. The case manager team gets a message and can start to search for a station with a free bed. When a bed is found, they type it into the system and the doctor gets a message to confirm the bed. If changes need to be made for a different bed, the process will be done again.

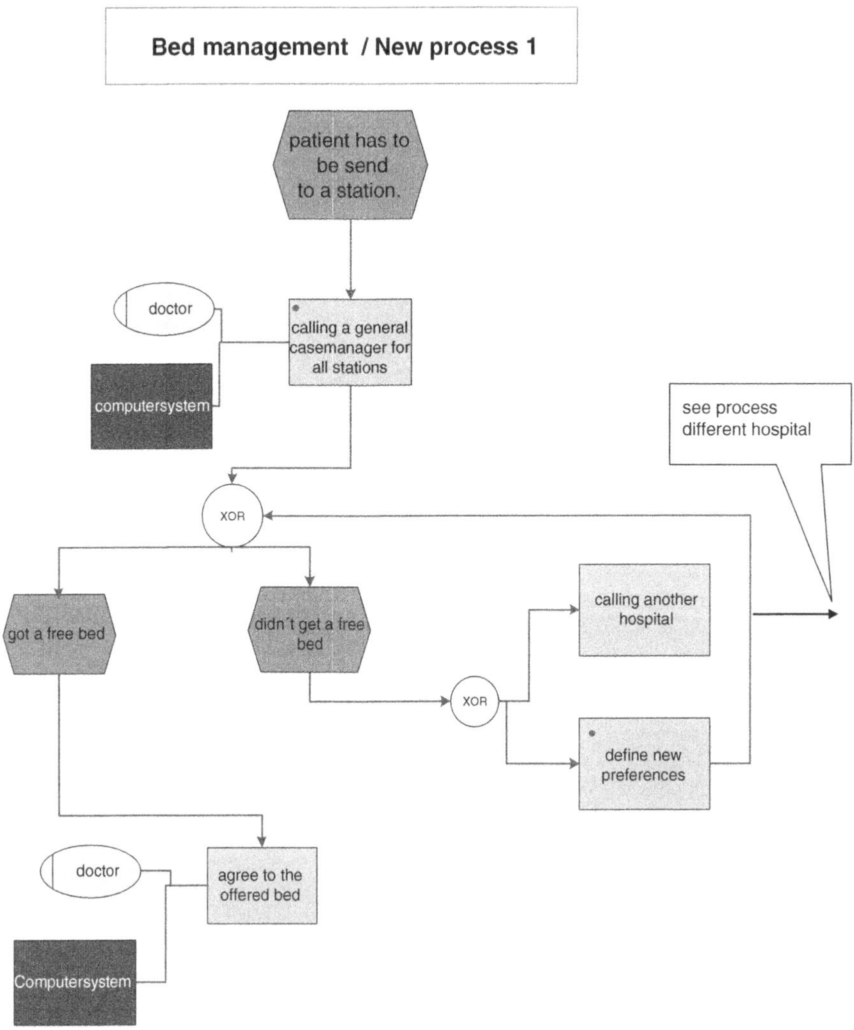

Fig. 30.5 Bed management new process 1; see process *different hospital*

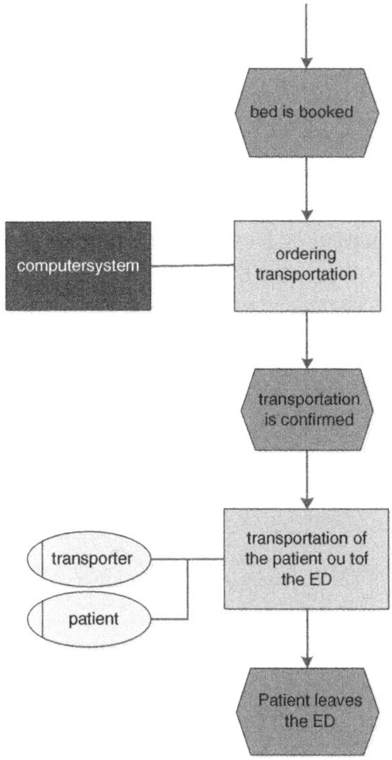

Fig. 30.5 (continued)

There could be the possibility that there is no free bed inside the preferences of the doctor. In this case the case manager needs to ask the doctor if the patient could also go to a different station or if the patient should rather be sent to a different hospital. The case manager sends the doctor the options he has and the doctor needs to agree on which bed he would like for his patient.

Another feature of the computer system should be that with the final confirmation of the bed, the computer system will automatically call the transportation team for transportation to the specific station. If the transportation team gets more transportation offers at the same time, they should do them in order of the triage color. The transportation team will pick up the patient. At this point the patient leaves the ED (Fig. 30.5).

30.3.4.3 New Process Bed Management 2

This option for the process of bed management will not change the original process as much as the first option. The only difference is that there will be a special nurse or administration nurse who will be responsible for all bed management processes inside the ED. This way, the doctors don't have to spend extra time with trying to reach the case manager. Instead, they can concentrate on the treatment of their patients (Fig. 30.6).

30.3.4.4 Other Improvements

During our time at the Emergency Department, we've noticed some other problems in and around the process that can't be modeled in an EPC. Those problems could improve the physicians' and nurses' work flow if they will be improved.

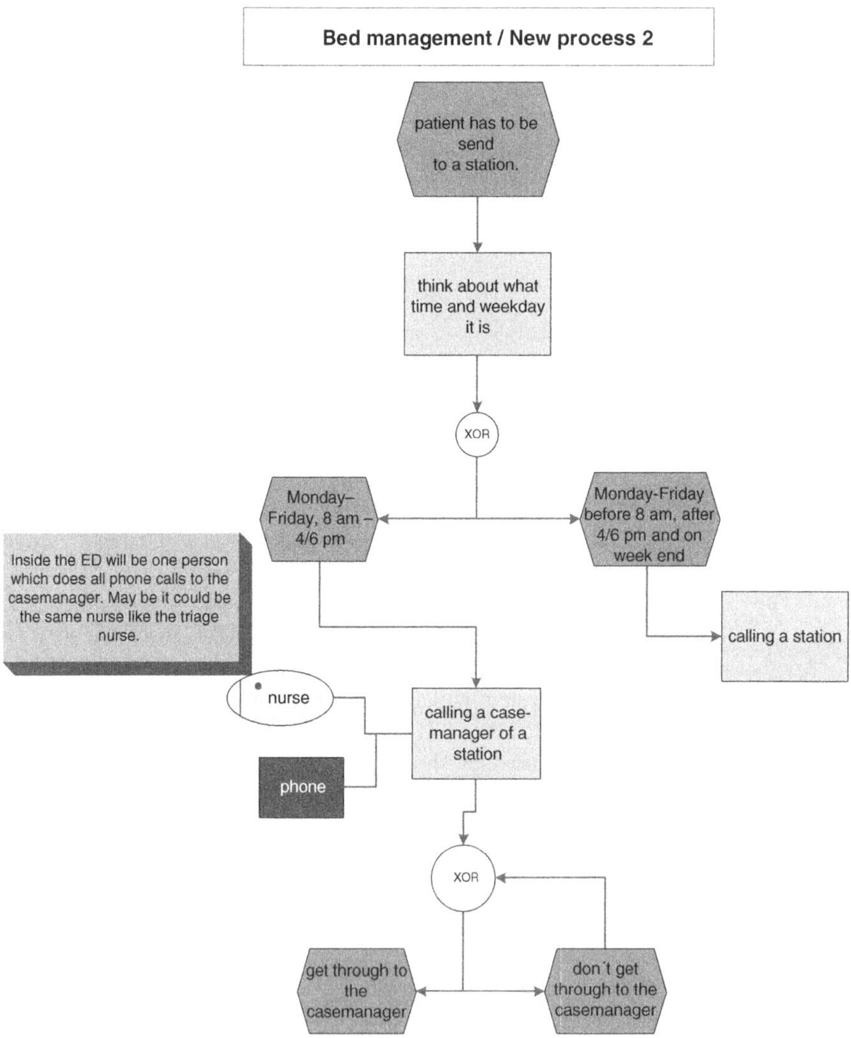

Fig. 30.6 Bed management new process 2

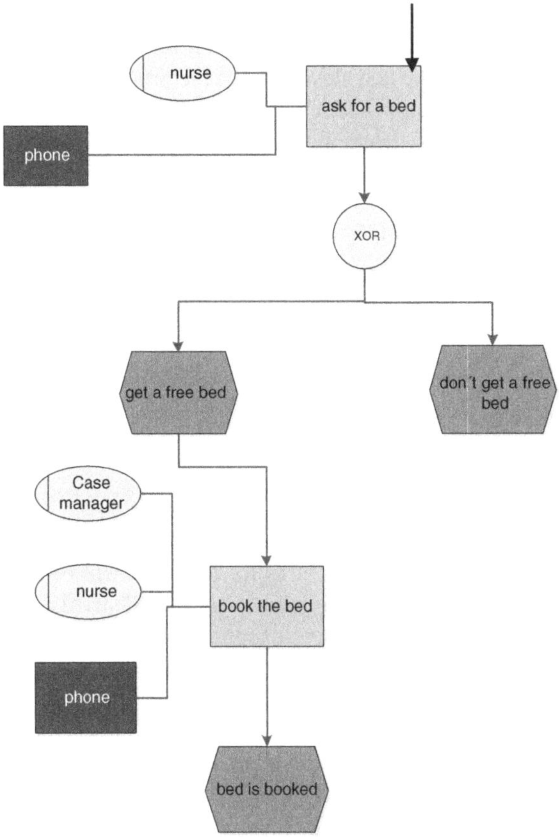

Fig. 30.6 (continued)

First, we've noticed that the ED registration desk is often used as the hospital's information desk. All day long, there were people coming to the registration and asking for directions or help. Our proposal is to make a clear patient guidance system with signs at the entrance or a simple info point at the entrance.

For better transparency we would recommend to put a monitor into the waiting room, so that patients can see their waiting time until they'll get in the ED for treatment. The screen could also show what reasons make the waiting time longer, e.g., if there is an emergency. This will help to get a better understanding from the patients for waiting times.

While watching the doctors and nurses in a busy time, we observed that doctors wanted to make a sonography on two different patients at the same time. The problem was that there exists only one sonography machine in the ED and there didn't seem to be a certain place for it. So doctors had to search the ED for the machine, because it was left in empty rooms. Our suggestion would be that the ED gets at least one other sonography machine and that the team finds one place where it will always be taken back to after usage.

Further, we also suggest that ED gets its own transporter twenty-four-seven, because there were times when patients had to wait very long to get a transportation, which increased waiting time and slowed down the process.

Also, we felt a better atmosphere if male and female nurses work together, instead of only female nurses. We would suggest a quotation of male and female nurses in one shift.

Last, we saw that some doctors take a long time to type the doctors letter, which increases the waiting time for the patient until he can leave the ED. Our suggestion would be that doctors and maybe also nurses get the offer for a ten-finger seminar. Another improvement for this problem could be to get a recording software.

30.4 Discussion

30.4.1 Triage

At first, we want to clarify our main aims for improvement of the triage process. The triage process has to fulfill all requirements of the ESI strictly and has to be time-saving. A smooth work flow and the avoidance of redundancy have to be achieved. Of course, such advances are not for free. The Katharinenhospital has to invest in such improvements. Therefore an accurate cost–benefit analysis has to be done to defend and justify the investments.

To avoid waiting times when the ED is not very busy the administration nurse has to observe the waiting times of the patients sitting in the waiting room. This is not related to specific costs; but it needs more attention of the administration nurse, which might keep her from other tasks. The administration nurse should get a good understanding of the importance of these waiting times, so she accepts the extra work and no barriers occur that endanger the improvements for the process.

That one family member might be allowed to accompany the patient could improve the triage process and the further treatment of the patient because the family members could be helpful with information for the doctor or by being psychological support for the patient. This would facilitate the physician's work. At the same time it also has to be considered that family members may disturb the treatment. It has to be pondered from a medical point of view if the additional information and the company of the family members overcompensate the disturbing factor. It would depend on the condition of the patients; for example, for elderly patients or diffused patients it would probably be useful. When it is decided that no family member is allowed to accompany the patient, the family members should be informed about the reasons. This is not a cost-factor and improves the satisfaction of the involved people. It is important to recognize that hospitals are in a competitive situation and content patients will come back if it would be necessary in the future.

Informing the patient about the approximate waiting time is another improvement which has to be analyzed critically. The communication of the information itself does not create huge costs. It can be done when the triage nurse already informs the patient about further steps. But creating this information is much more difficult. The triage nurse has to estimate the approximate waiting times, which is dependent on the actual situation in the ED. But with practical knowledge this is realizable. The costs of a computer-calculated waiting time have to be considered closer. Therefore all advantages have to be expressed in terms of money to compare the costs and the created benefits. An important fact is that repeated demands of uninformed patients disturb the process and are additional work for the nurses. A further improvement could be the illustration of the waiting times on a screen in the waiting room. This could lead to problems with privacy rights of the patients if their names would be shown on the screens. Another idea would be to give every patient a number that is shown on the screen and identifies the patients.

To execute the triage directly after the administration would be our main improvement. Only this way, the specifications of ESI would be observed and not circumvented. Waiting times mustn't be ascertained after the patient has already waited. Circumventing the ESI may lead to juridical problems which can entail inestimable high costs. But there are human barriers because the nurses are used to perform the process of the administration and the process of the triage in their practiced manner. They have to be informed about the requirements of the ESI and the importance of the new sequence. Therefore an information course would be suitable. The improvements have to take place within a systematic change management to handle the barriers and to overcome occurring problems that endanger the implementing of the improvements.

The placement of the triage room in the waiting area is probably expensive because of the current architecture of the ED. The waiting area of the ED would have to be rebuilt. The current triage room is placed in the first room of the main area of the ED so the patients at least do not have to cross the whole ED. Therefore, the costs of a new triage room placed in the waiting area would probably not be compensated.

As mentioned above, there exist three options of executing the triage in the Katharinenhospital. This isn't a standardized process yet. In Australia, for example, the whole way of the patient through the hospital is standardized. There exists a so-called patient flow model. A standardized patient flow model secures that every patient is guided through the ED in a determined way. Removing the different manners and instead establishing one way of execution the triage would approach to such standardization.

30.4.2 Bed Management 1

In our first bed management solution there are a lot of factors which will be new. These are:

- Case manager is 24 h every day available
- Case manager department
- New computer system
- Transporter team is connected to the computer system

The first point, that the case manager is 24 h available every day, would be very good for the ED. They wouldn't have to call the station directly and don't have to think about which time and weekday it is. It would also be better for stations because they can use their resources for the patients instead of answering phone calls and trying to organize their beds. A problem could be that the hospital needs a bigger team of case manager. This would be expensive and the hospital has to think if the effort would be worth the benefit.

This problem could maybe be solved by the case manager department. The case managers inside the stations wouldn't be needed anymore and instead can build a team of case managers in a special department. The team could work together and help each other if there are some problems. The working structure could be changed. The team, for example, could be split up and work in little groups in shifts 24 h the whole week.

A problem could be how the case manager department gets the information about the free bed situation in different stations. It would not be much of an improvement if the department phones the stations directly. The case manager should have a computer system that shows him how many beds are free for new patients and which are reserved already. This system could work similar to the ECare system. There, the doctors of the ED can see which patient is in which room. The system could have data about every station that is also connected to every station. There, the nurses or doctors organize their beds and the case manager team has access to the plan as well; at least to see which beds are free, because they wouldn't need any other data about the patients.

Workload for the staff of the stations would increase to put the data about the bed situation inside the computer system. An idea would be that the system, that is used so far for bed organization, will be connected to the system for the case manager and exports data about the bed situation. If the system can't be changed this way, another idea is to reduce the effect of increasing workload by using special RFID-Chips. The station team could lay RFID-Chip inside the rooms where patients occupy a bed and the case manager department could see where the RFID-Chips are.

The case manager team needs a department room. The hospital has to figure out if they have a free room or department that they could give to the case manger team. Maybe, the space of other departments could be reduced or the hospital needs to build a new one. This would result in high costs though and it would be better to find a place for the case manager team that already exists in the hospital. If the computer system is good enough, the case managers might be able to stay, where they are right now and communicate over the computer with each other. The hospital could think about investing in groupware systems to support the communication and the group work.

The third point of improvement is the special computer system. It has to be developed from a specialized company, so that all important parts of the hospital can be involved. This will be very expensive. But the hospital has to balance those costs against the phoning costs of the hospital and the time that is used for those. They are calls from the ED doctor to the station or case manager as well as the calls from the ED nurse to the transportation team that wouldn't be necessary anymore.

This would save the doctors and nurses a lot of time that could be used for the patients and their diseases or other important tasks in the ED. This way, the quality will also increase.

The fourth and last changing factor will be that the transporter team will also be integrated into the computer system. At the moment, the transporter team is only reachable via phone. This will be changed by the new computer system. The transporter team would get the information for the next transport by the computer system, which saves time on both sides. To save even more time, the transporter should get the next order of transportation directly after finishing the first order. So it would be good if there is a transmission of sending the information about the next transportation from the computer system straight to the transporters. This could be done with a mobile phone. All transporters would see on their phone at all times which patient has to be sent from which station to which other station. The computer system would take care of the ordering of the patients that have to be transported after the triage system. If one transporter finished his last order he will click on the first transportation order on the phone and will fulfill it. On all other mobile phones this transportation order would disappear. If a doctor needs a transportation very fast, he can click a certain button to speed up the process. With clicking the button the transporter team will get the information that this order has to be done before the others. If the doctor uses this fast transportation he has to explain in a few words why he is using it. The case manager team has to control this in spot tests. This way no doctor can use it without a need.

All in all, the whole changing process would be very expensive. The costs developed by the computer system, trainings how to use the system, and new rooms for the new department will add up. But there are also a lot of factors why the changing process should be done. The quality of treatment can increase, the doctors can use the free time more for the treatment of the patients, this can fasten the process, and the communication will be better between the stations. To do all these changes at the same time would be very difficult. The hospital needs a long-term concept on how to do those changes and in which order they should be done. It will be very important to give the employees the feeling that the changing process will help them to do their work in a better way instead of making them feel like they're part of an economical process that has to be improved.

30.4.3 Bed Management 2

The second process on how to do the bed management in a better way will be much easier, but the changes are not as advanced as in the first process. The second idea was that the ED has its own case manager who will take care of the whole bed searching processes inside the ED.

This would make it easier for the doctors to tell the case manager which patient needs a bed on which station. There would be a direct conversation instead of communicating through technical systems. The doctors can give the searching process to the case manager and can concentrate on their work. This way, resources are used in a better way. A problem of this solution is that the ED needs a person who is the case manager. They might need to employ a new person for this assignment. This will be expensive. Another possibility would be that one of the employees will do the case manager work additionally. But the nurses and doctors have already a lot to do so it would be very difficult to find somebody who can do it. Maybe one of the case managers from the other stations could take over the task as well, but this might result in a change of the whole case manager system. They wouldn't be responsible for one station anymore, but for several at the time.

We think that the working process and the working time can be reduced with the changing of a few things. These things will be explained in chapter "Discussion Other Improvements". With this changing the time of one person inside the ED can be reduced and this person can do the case manager work.

30.4.4 Other Improvements

We mentioned to put a sign or a small info point at the entrance for a better overview for the patients because every day patients interrupt the work of the nurses at the registration desk for asking where other stations are or for the way to some treatment rooms. We asked Prof. Dr. Schilling about how often the interruption takes place and he answered that there are interruptions up to 50 times a day.

So a simple sign or an info point with a person, whose function is to give further information to the patients at the entrance, would be helpful. The problem with the info point can be more costs for more staff. But at the same time, the staff from the ED would have fewer interruptions and could better focus on their own tasks.

There would also be a problem with time because the hospital does three shifts. For a twenty-four-seven assistance at the info point you would need more than one person at the info point. It would be good to figure out when the most people show up at the ED to ask for information and to figure out at which times a person at the info point would be useful. At night times, for example, it will probably not be as important to have somebody at the info desk the whole time.

Further, we noticed that a monitor with waiting times of the patient doesn't exist in the waiting room. A Monitor would give transparency to the patient on how long he has to wait. Also relatives can get information about the treatment time and further information. Barriers would be IT-problems, because of the privacy of patient's information. If a patient got there first and has to wait longer, there should be an illustration on why this is for better understanding.

Another suggestion was a second sonography machine because of the high frequent use of the machine. In addition all the machines should stay in one central room where everybody gets easy access. The new machine will cost money but the hospital can treat more patients at the same time. This way, the whole process can be faster and more patients can be treated overall.

Waiting times for transportation to treatment rooms or to other stations were partially very long. This is lost time that patients are laying in treatment rooms in the ED because other patients could be treated instead. The ED already has its own transporter but only from 10 a.m. until 6 p.m. on weekdays. It would be much more efficient if the ED would get its own transporter twenty-four-seven. It would have to be discussed if this is rentable, but we think you could treat much more patients if the transportation time would be reduced; especially on the weekend when transportation time is very high and the number of patients increases.

Some of us noticed a fierce atmosphere if male or female nurses worked separately. Our suggestion was a quotation of male and female nurses during their shifts. It is complex to enforce this because many nurses switch shifts so they can be with others they like to work with. To get this quotation accepted, comprehension from the staff is needed, as well as an improvement of working atmosphere in general.

As our last point we suggested that the doctors should get a ten-finger seminar for better writing, because some of the doctors type kind of slow. For doctors it might be hard to relearn their way of typing, but others might be thankful to get the chance to improve it. So another suggestion was to get a recording software where the doctors can speak their diagnostics and the system will write them automatically. They have to change or type in only a few things which would save time but cost money. The hospital has to discuss how effective such a software would be and how many it would cost to buy such a software.

All in all, the improvements discussed in this chapter are not as huge, time-consuming, and expensive and some of them should be easy to realize. It is up to the Katharinenhospital what they would like to change and if our solutions are considered as a possibility.

30.5 Conclusion

This was an interesting case study and we got to know a field that we didn't know much about before this seminar. What we learned out of this case study is that people don't like to be controlled. If you are going to observe them, they should be informed of the process and what it is for, so there is a better understanding and comprehension. We also learned that doctors really don't have an easy job to take care of their patients as good as they can but at the same time have to stay economically and try to keep the costs and the recourse use low.

The Interdisciplinary Emergency Department in the Katharinenhospital is already pretty advanced and has a good structure in its process. This structure is very helpful for patients as well as for the staff to have an organized process that they can all follow and that makes them feel more comfortable. But as always, there are still improvements that can be made.

We think that there are some improvements in our suggestions that are realizable pretty easily and others will be a lot harder because of economical reasons.

Most changes will result in high costs and they will only be realized if the hospital sees a big enough advantage in them. The Katharinenhospital is responsible for the next step now. We would recommend that there will definitely be an improvement in the bed management process, but also in the timing of the triage, so that the rules of the ESI are followed better.

The hospital needs to decide which of our recommendations are economically realizable with the recourses they have. Maybe, if not all of our recommendations are possible, there is a chance to realize parts of them, so that the Interdisciplinary Emergency Department will improve further and the care of their patients increases.

30.6 Attachment

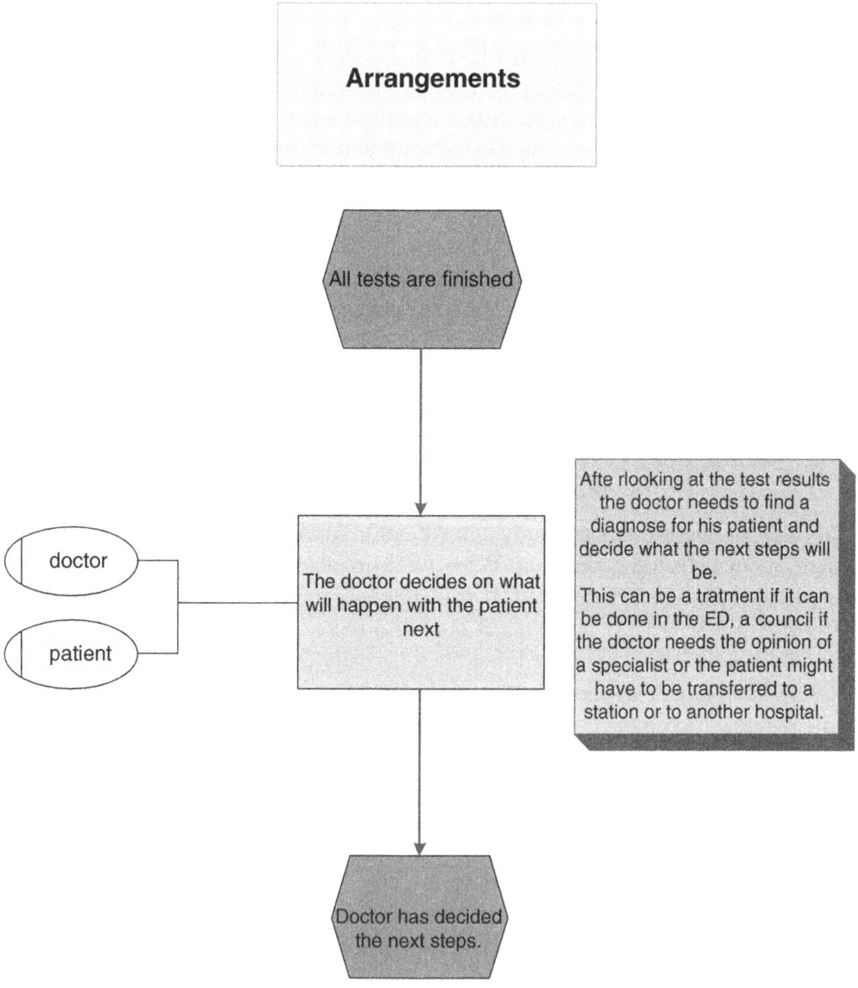

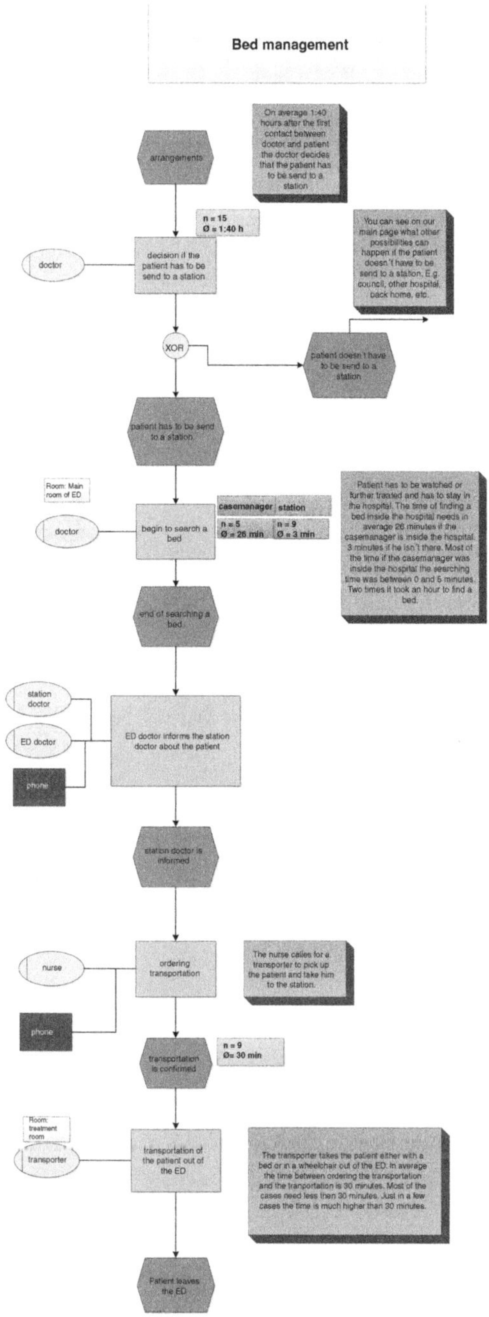
Bed management
On average 1:40 hours after the first contact between doctor and patient the doctor decides that the patient has to be send to a station
arrangements
n = 15
Ø = 1:40 h
doctor
decision if the patient has to be send to a station
You can see on our main page what other possibilities can happen if the patient doesn't have to be send to a station. E.g. council, other hospital, back home, etc.
XOR
patient doesn't have to be send to a station
patient has to be send to a station.
Room: Main room of ED
doctor
begin to search a bed
casemanager
station
n = 5
Ø = 26 min
n = 9
Ø = 3 min
Patient has to be watched or further treated and has to stay in the hospital. The time of finding a bed inside the hospital needs in average 26 minutes if the casemanager is inside the hospital. 3 minutes if he isn't there. Most of the time if the casemanager was inside the hospital the searching time was between 0 and 5 minutes. Two times it took an hour to find a bed.
end of searching a bed
station doctor
ED doctor
phone
ED doctor informs the station doctor about the patient
station doctor is informed
nurse
ordering transportation
The nurse calles for a transporter to pick up the patient and take him to the station.
phone
transportation is confirmed
n = 9
Ø= 30 min
Room: treatment room
transporter
transportation of the patient out of the ED
The transporter takes the patient either with a bed or in a wheelchair out of the ED. In average the time between ordering the transportation and the tranportation is 30 minutes. Most of the cases need less then 30 minutes. Just in a few cases the time is much higher than 30 minutes.
Patient leaves the ED

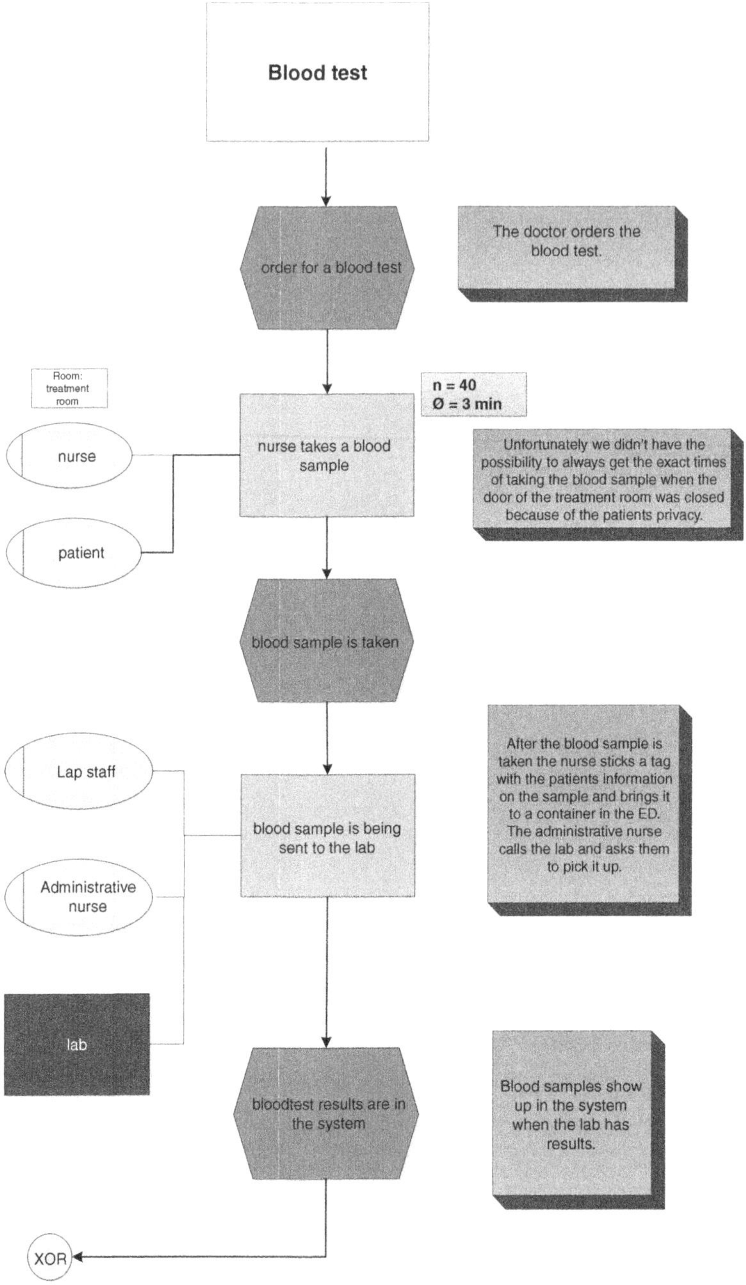
Blood test
order for a blood test
The doctor orders the blood test.
Room: treatment room
nurse
patient
nurse takes a blood sample
n = 40
Ø = 3 min
Unfortunately we didn't have the possibility to always get the exact times of taking the blood sample when the door of the treatment room was closed because of the patients privacy.
blood sample is taken
Lap staff
Administrative nurse
lab
blood sample is being sent to the lab
After the blood sample is taken the nurse sticks a tag with the patients information on the sample and brings it to a container in the ED. The administrative nurse calls the lab and asks them to pick it up.
bloodtest results are in the system
Blood samples show up in the system when the lab has results.
XOR

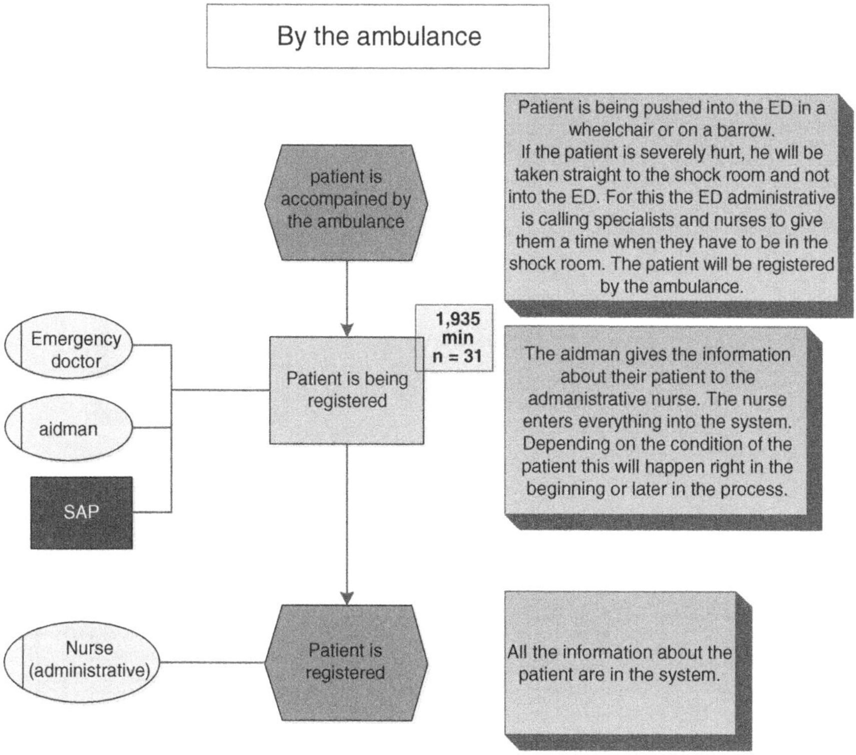
By the ambulance
patient is accompanied by the ambulance
Patient is being pushed into the ED in a wheelchair or on a barrow.
If the patient is severely hurt, he will be taken straight to the shock room and not into the ED. For this the ED administrative is calling specialists and nurses to give them a time when they have to be in the shock room. The patient will be registered by the ambulance.
Emergency doctor
aidman
SAP
Patient is being registered
1,935 min
n = 31
The aidman gives the information about their patient to the admanistrative nurse. The nurse enters everything into the system. Depending on the condition of the patient this will happen right in the beginning or later in the process.
Nurse (administrative)
Patient is registered
All the information about the patient are in the system.

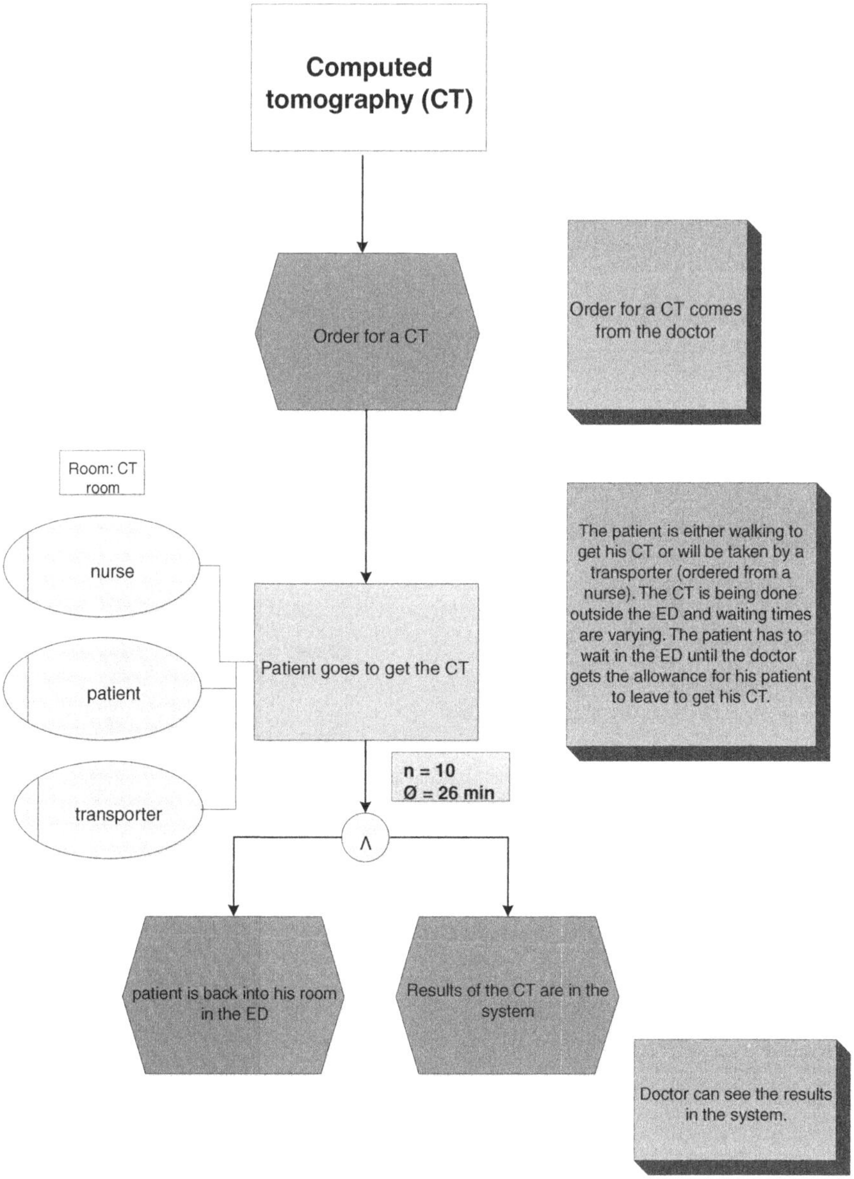
Computed tomography (CT)
Order for a CT
Order for a CT comes from the doctor
Room: CT room
nurse
patient
transporter
Patient goes to get the CT
The patient is either walking to get his CT or will be taken by a transporter (ordered from a nurse). The CT is being done outside the ED and waiting times are varying. The patient has to wait in the ED until the doctor gets the allowance for his patient to leave to get his CT.
n = 10
Ø = 26 min
∧
patient is back into his room in the ED
Results of the CT are in the system
Doctor can see the results in the system.

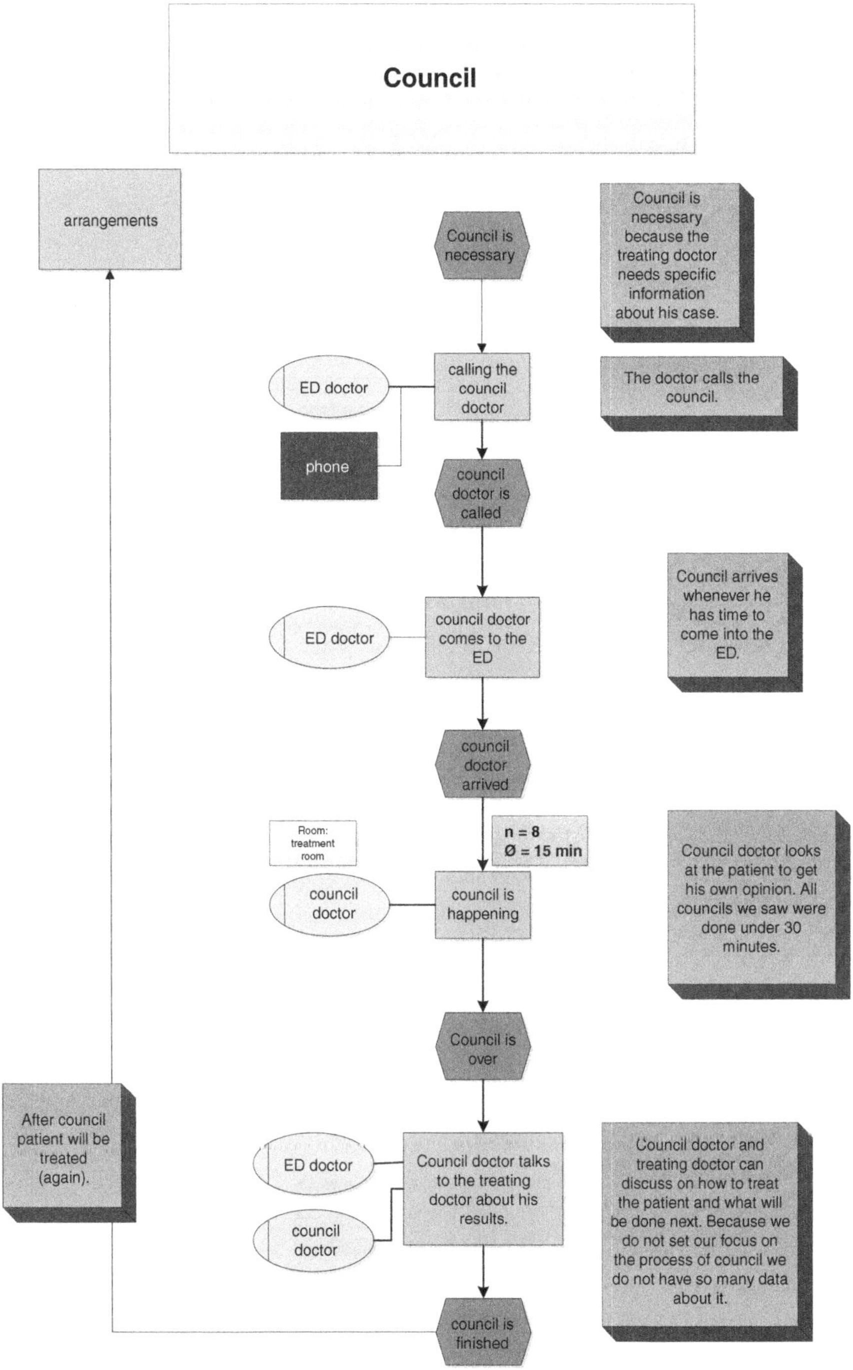
Council
arrangements
Council is necessary
Council is necessary because the treating doctor needs specific information about his case.
ED doctor
calling the council doctor
phone
The doctor calls the council.
council doctor is called
ED doctor
council doctor comes to the ED
Council arrives whenever he has time to come into the ED.
council doctor arrived
Room: treatment room
n = 8
Ø = 15 min
council doctor
council is happening
Council doctor looks at the patient to get his own opinion. All councils we saw were done under 30 minutes.
Council is over
After council patient will be treated (again).
ED doctor
council doctor
Council doctor talks to the treating doctor about his results.
Council doctor and treating doctor can discuss on how to treat the patient and what will be done next. Because we do not set our focus on the process of council we do not have so many data about it.
council is finished

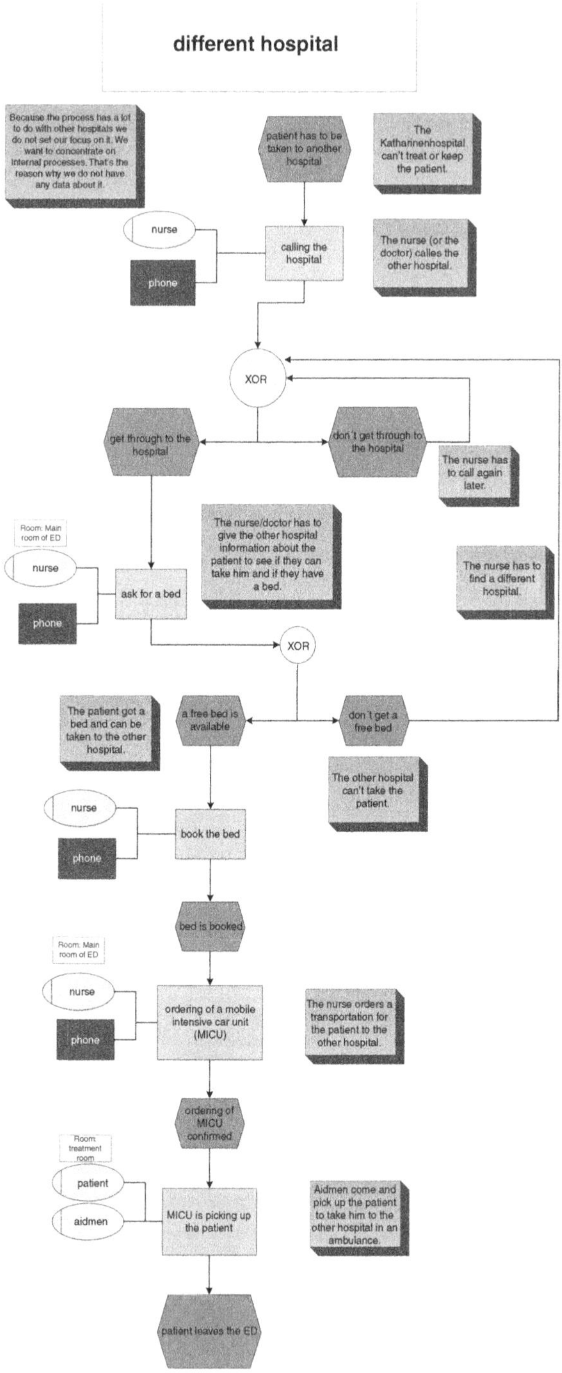
different hospital
Because the process has a lot to do with other hospitals we do not set our focus on it. We want to concentrate on internal processes. That's the reason why we do not have any data about it.
patient has to be taken to another hospital
The Katharinenhospital can't treat or keep the patient.
nurse
phone
calling the hospital
The nurse (or the doctor) calles the other hospital.
XOR
get through to the hospital
don't get through to the hospital
The nurse has to call again later.
Room: Main room of ED
nurse
phone
ask for a bed
The nurse/doctor has to give the other hospital information about the patient to see if they can take him and if they have a bed.
The nurse has to find a different hospital.
XOR
The patient got a bed and can be taken to the other hospital.
a free bed is available
don't get a free bed
The other hospital can't take the patient.
nurse
phone
book the bed
bed is booked
Room: Main room of ED
nurse
phone
ordering of a mobile intensive car unit (MICU)
The nurse orders a transportation for the patient to the other hospital.
ordering of MICU confirmed
Room: treatment room
patient
aidmen
MICU is picking up the patient
Aidmen come and pick up the patient to take him to the other hospital in an ambulance.
patient leaves the ED

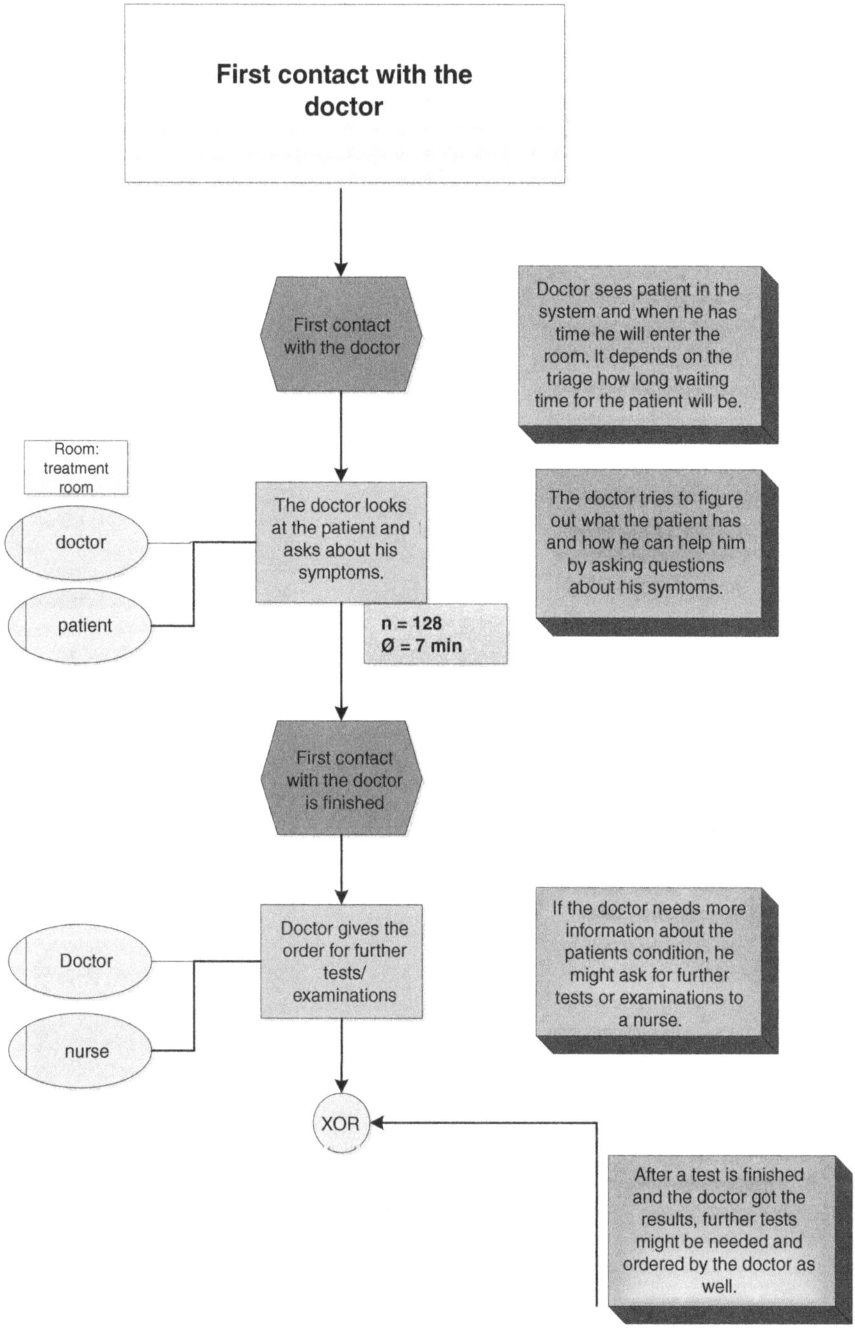
First contact with the doctor
First contact with the doctor
Doctor sees patient in the system and when he has time he will enter the room. It depends on the triage how long waiting time for the patient will be.
Room: treatment room
doctor
patient
The doctor looks at the patient and asks about his symptoms.
n = 128
Ø = 7 min
The doctor tries to figure out what the patient has and how he can help him by asking questions about his symtoms.
First contact with the doctor is finished
Doctor
nurse
Doctor gives the order for further tests/ examinations
If the doctor needs more information about the patients condition, he might ask for further tests or examinations to a nurse.
XOR
After a test is finished and the doctor got the results, further tests might be needed and ordered by the doctor as well.

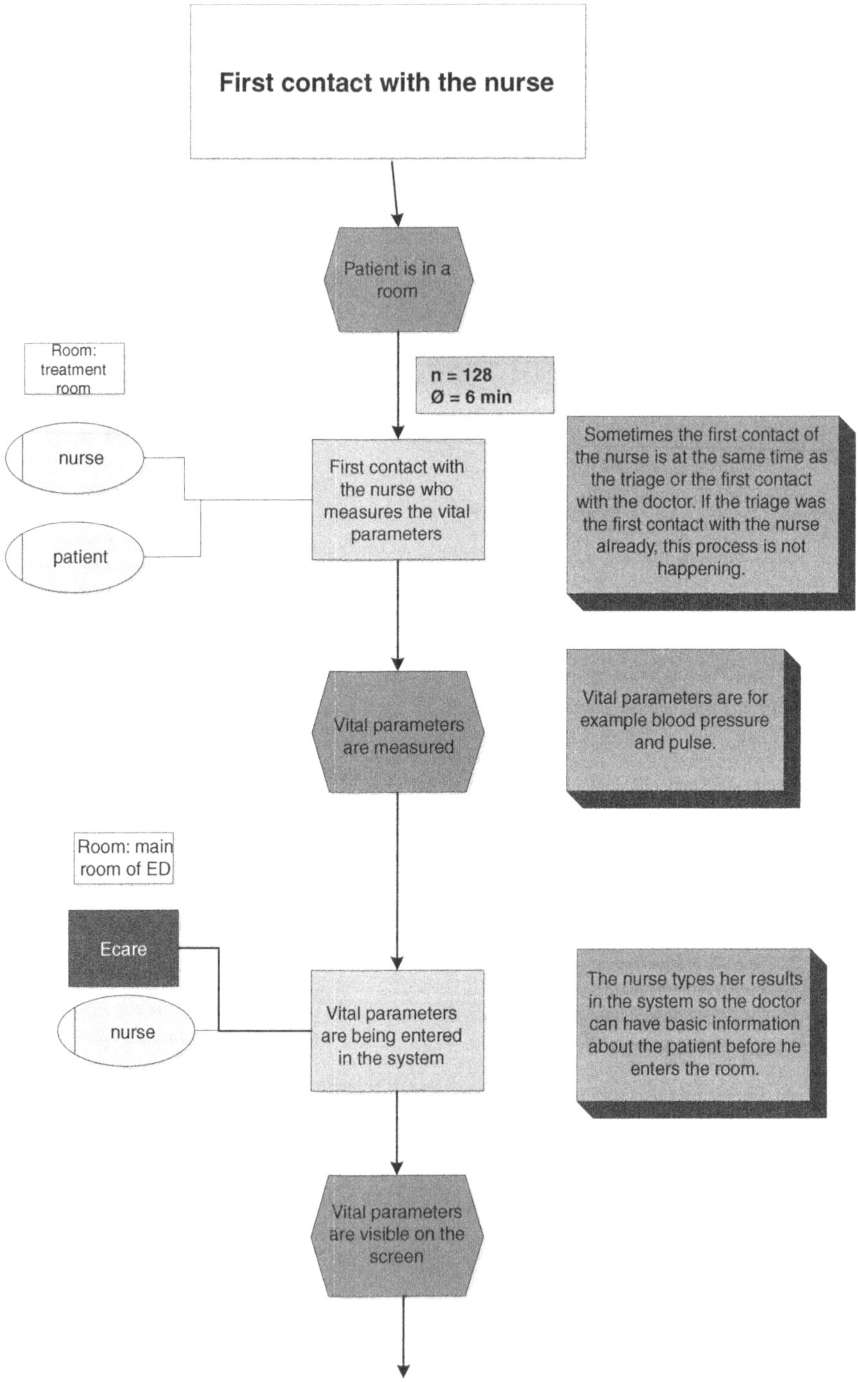
First contact with the nurse
Patient is in a room
Room: treatment room
n = 128
Ø = 6 min
nurse
patient
First contact with the nurse who measures the vital parameters
Sometimes the first contact of the nurse is at the same time as the triage or the first contact with the doctor. If the triage was the first contact with the nurse already, this process is not happening.
Vital parameters are measured
Vital parameters are for example blood pressure and pulse.
Room: main room of ED
Ecare
nurse
Vital parameters are being entered in the system
The nurse types her results in the system so the doctor can have basic information about the patient before he enters the room.
Vital parameters are visible on the screen

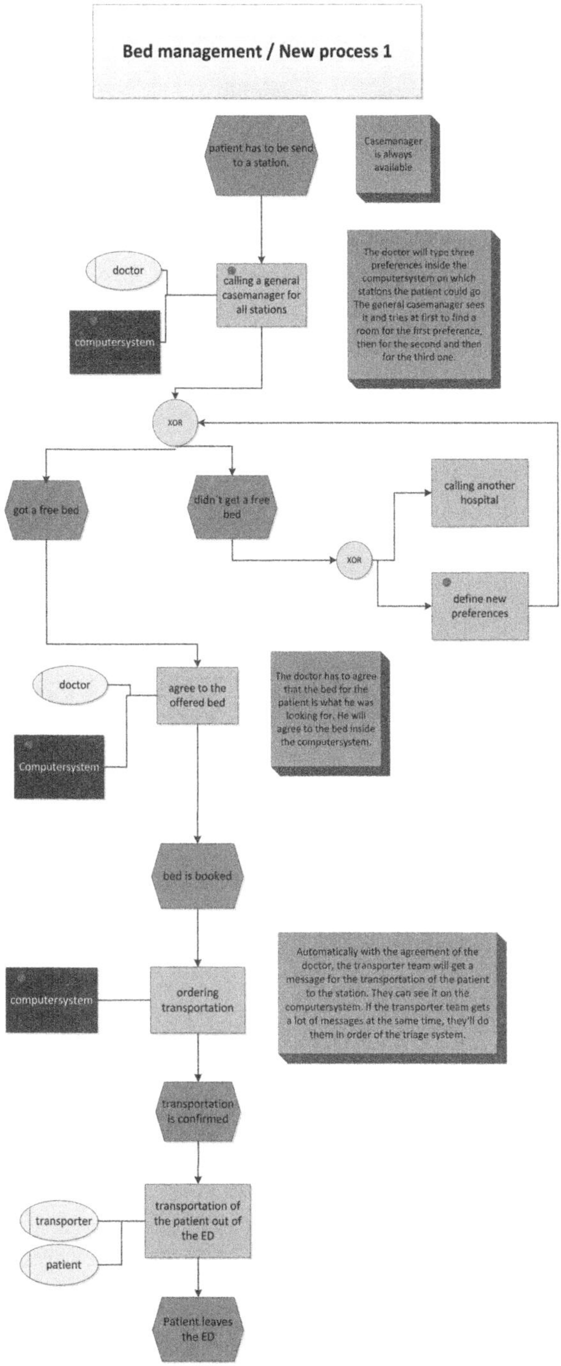
Bed management / New process 1
patient has to be send to a station.
Casemanager is always available
doctor
computersystem
calling a general casemanager for all stations
The doctor will type three preferences inside the computersystem on which stations the patient could go The general casemanager sees it and tries at first to find a room for the first preference, then for the second and then for the third one.
XOR
got a free bed
didn't get a free bed
XOR
calling another hospital
define new preferences
doctor
Computersystem
agree to the offered bed
The doctor has to agree that the bed for the patient is what he was looking for. He will agree to the bed inside the computersystem.
bed is booked
computersystem
ordering transportation
Automatically with the agreement of the doctor, the transporter team will get a message for the transportation of the patient to the station. They can see it on the computersystem. If the transporter team gets a lot of messages at the same time, they'll do them in order of the triage system.
transportation is confirmed
transporter
patient
transportation of the patient out of the ED
Patient leaves the ED

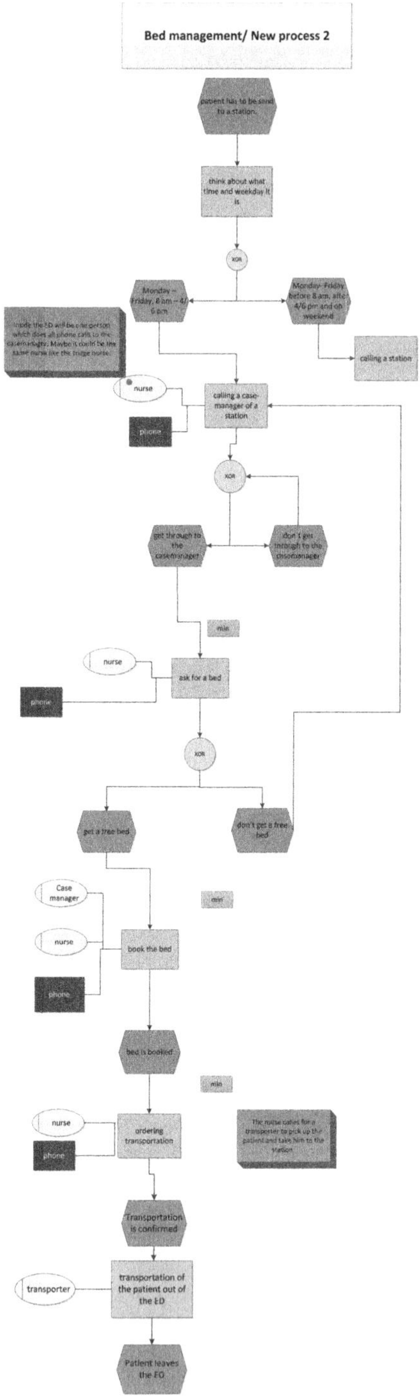
Bed management/ New process 2
patient has to be send to a station.
think about what time and weekday it is
XOR
Monday – Friday, 8 am – 4/6 pm
Monday- Friday before 8 am, after 4/6 pm and on weekend
calling a station
Inside the ED will be one person which does all phone calls to the casemanager. Maybe it could be the same nurse like the triage nurse.
nurse
phone
calling a case-manager of a station
XOR
get through to the casemanager
don't get through to the casemanager
min
nurse
phone
ask for a bed
XOR
get a free bed
don't get a free bed
Case manager
nurse
phone
min
book the bed
bed is booked
min
nurse
phone
ordering transportation
The nurse calles for a transporter to pick up the patient and take him to the station
Transportation is confirmed
transporter
transportation of the patient out of the ED
Patient leaves the ED

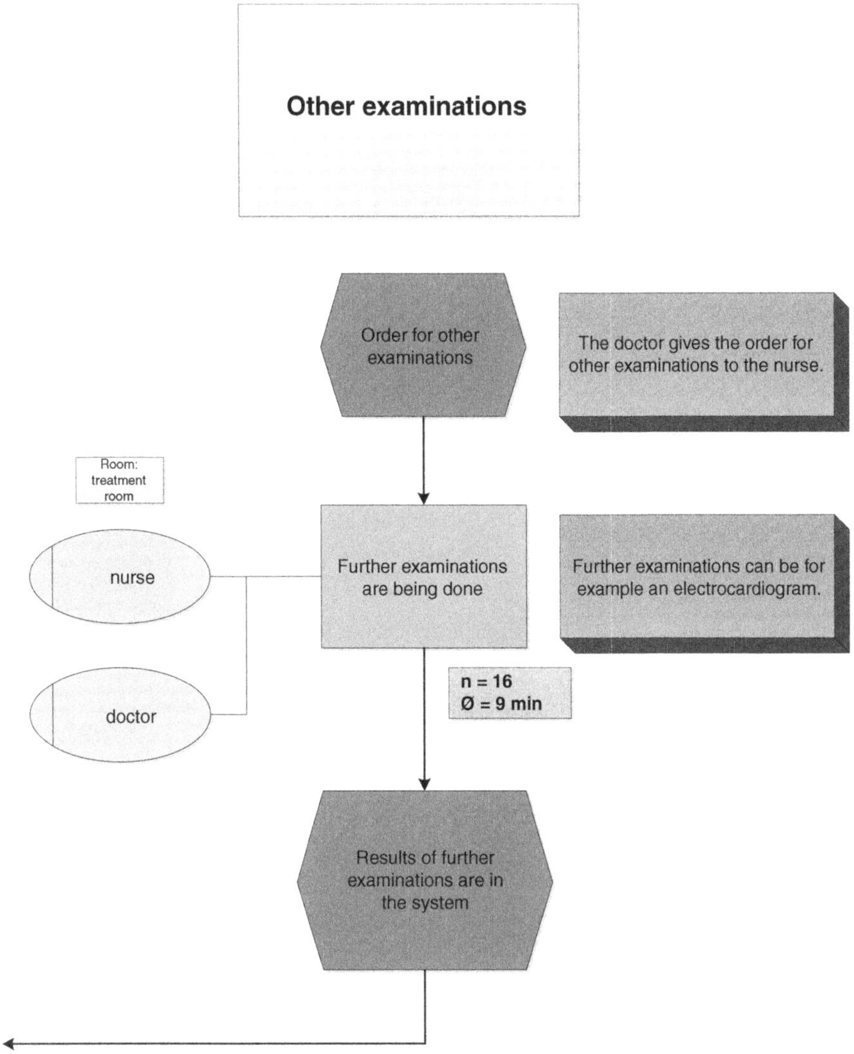
Other examinations
Order for other examinations
The doctor gives the order for other examinations to the nurse.
Room: treatment room
nurse
Further examinations are being done
Further examinations can be for example an electrocardiogram.
doctor
n = 16
Ø = 9 min
Results of further examinations are in the system

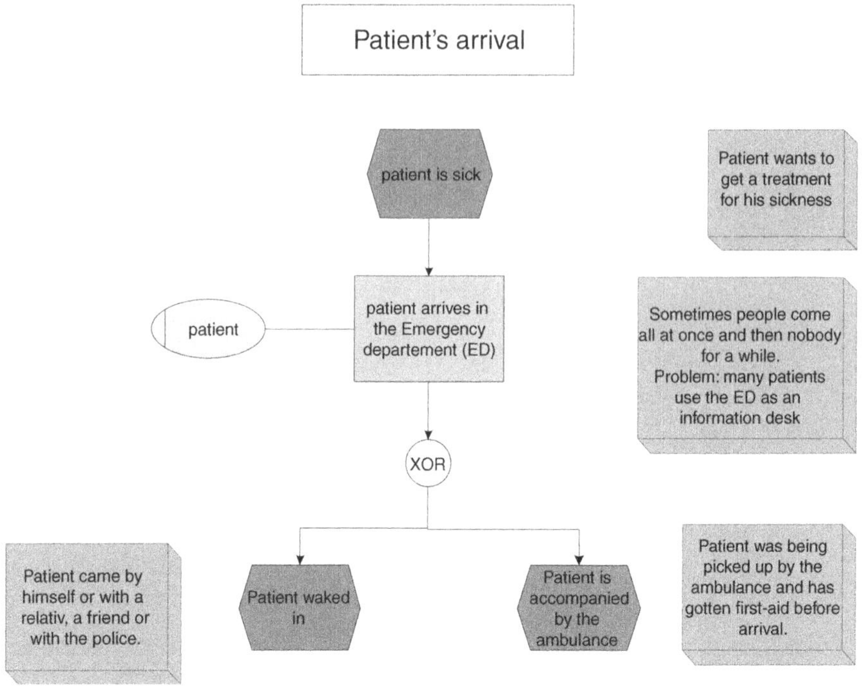
Patient's arrival
patient is sick
Patient wants to get a treatment for his sickness
patient
patient arrives in the Emergency departement (ED)
Sometimes people come all at once and then nobody for a while.
Problem: many patients use the ED as an information desk
XOR
Patient came by himself or with a relativ, a friend or with the police.
Patient waked in
Patient is accompanied by the ambulance
Patient was being picked up by the ambulance and has gotten first-aid before arrival.

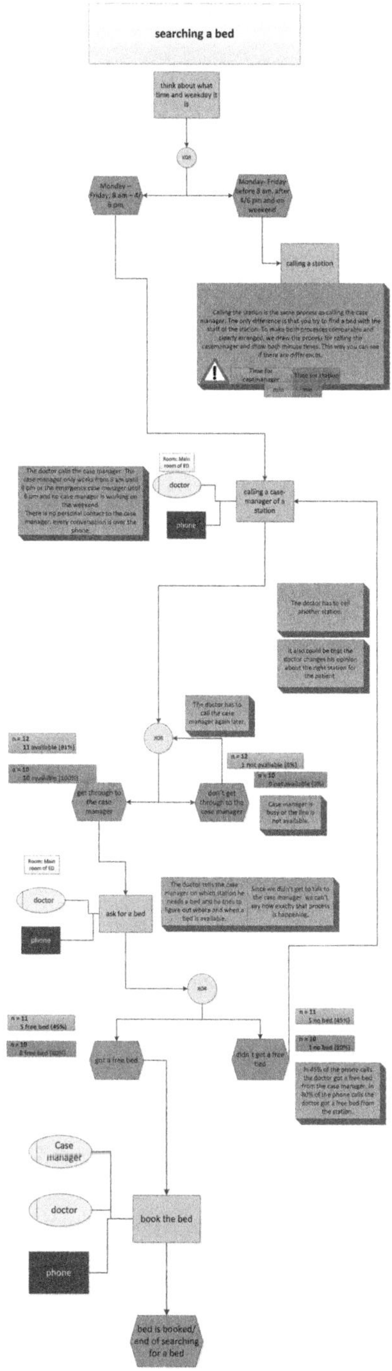

searching a bed
think about what time and weekday it is
XOR
calling a station
calling a case-manager of a station
doctor
phone
XOR
get through to the case manager
don't get through to the case manager
ask for a bed
doctor
phone
XOR
got a free bed
didn't got a free bed
Case manager
doctor
phone
book the bed
bed is booked/ end of searching for a bed

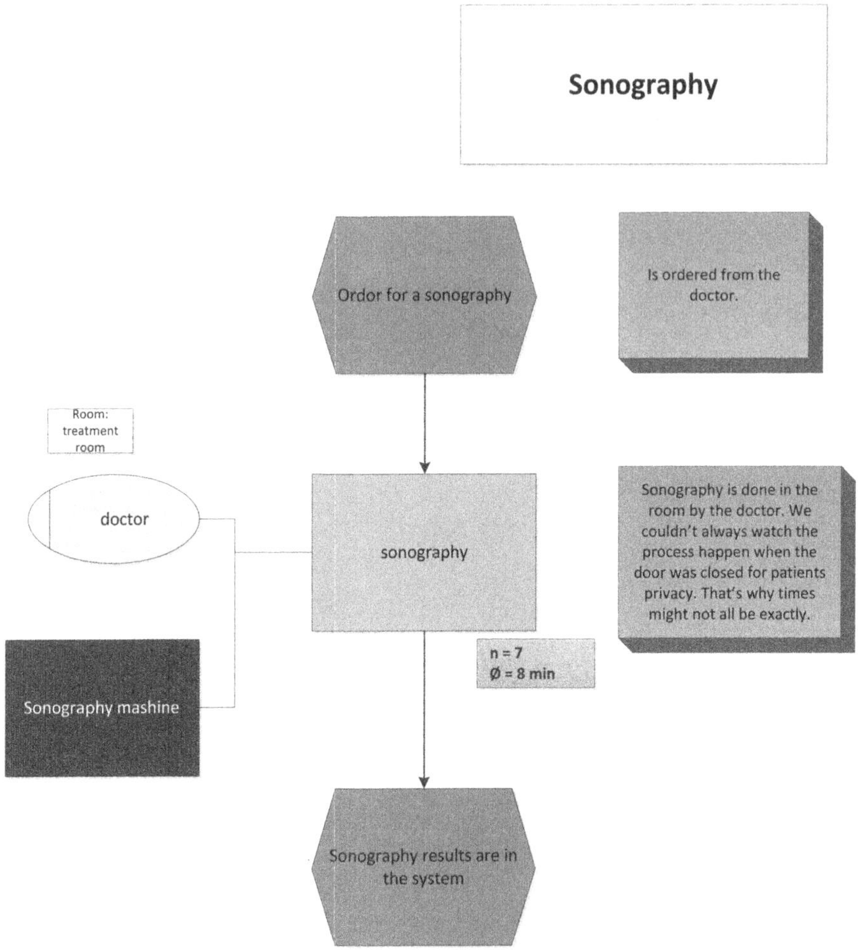
Sonography
Ordor for a sonography
Is ordered from the doctor.
Room: treatment room
doctor
sonography
Sonography is done in the room by the doctor. We couldn't always watch the process happen when the door was closed for patients privacy. That's why times might not all be exactly.
Sonography mashine
n = 7
Ø = 8 min
Sonography results are in the system

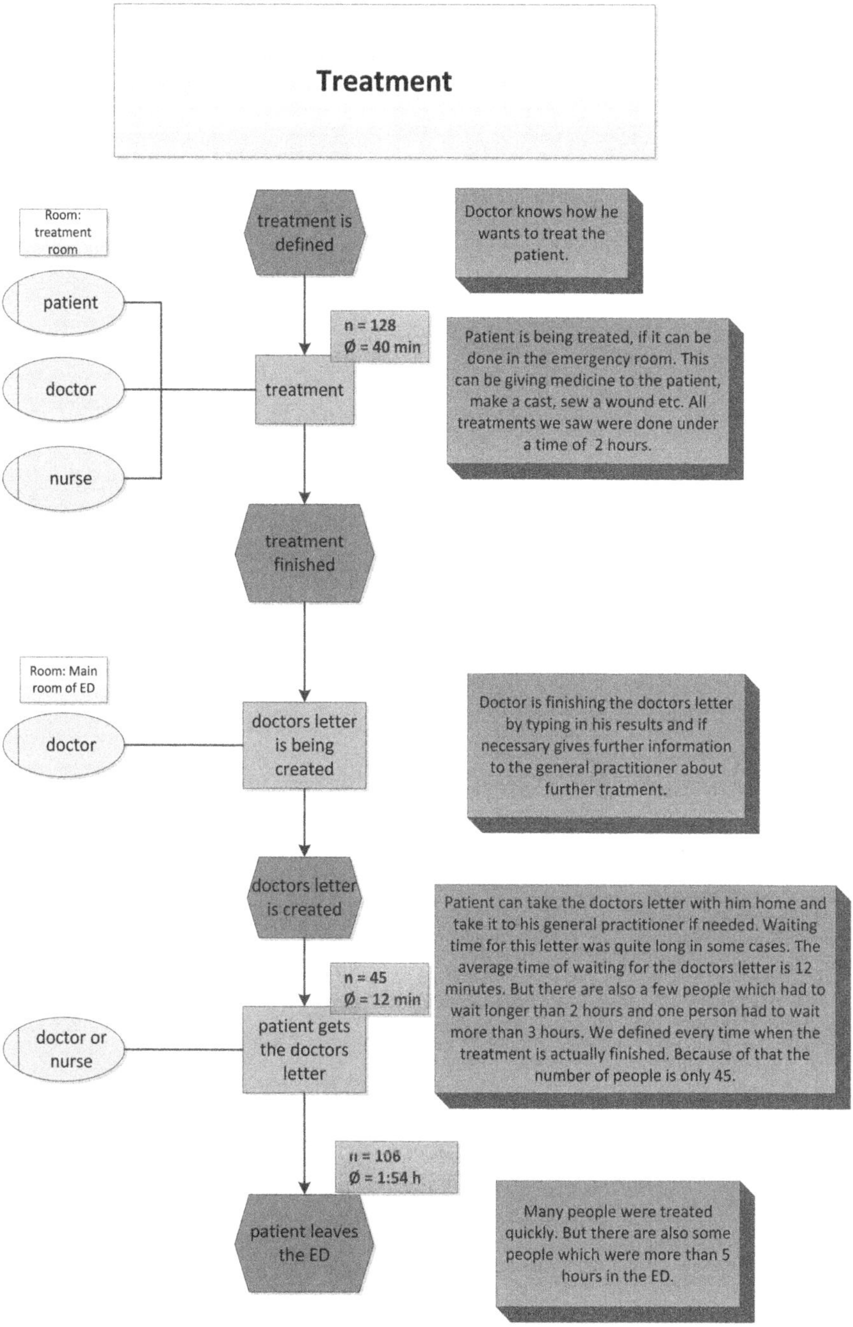
Treatment
Room: treatment room
treatment is defined
Doctor knows how he wants to treat the patient.
patient
doctor
nurse
n = 128
Ø = 40 min
treatment
Patient is being treated, if it can be done in the emergency room. This can be giving medicine to the patient, make a cast, sew a wound etc. All treatments we saw were done under a time of 2 hours.
treatment finished
Room: Main room of ED
doctor
doctors letter is being created
Doctor is finishing the doctors letter by typing in his results and if necessary gives further information to the general practitioner about further tratment.
doctors letter is created
Patient can take the doctors letter with him home and take it to his general practitioner if needed. Waiting time for this letter was quite long in some cases. The average time of waiting for the doctors letter is 12 minutes. But there are also a few people which had to wait longer than 2 hours and one person had to wait more than 3 hours. We defined every time when the treatment is actually finished. Because of that the number of people is only 45.
n = 45
Ø = 12 min
doctor or nurse
patient gets the doctors letter
n = 106
Ø = 1:54 h
patient leaves the ED
Many people were treated quickly. But there are also some people which were more than 5 hours in the ED.

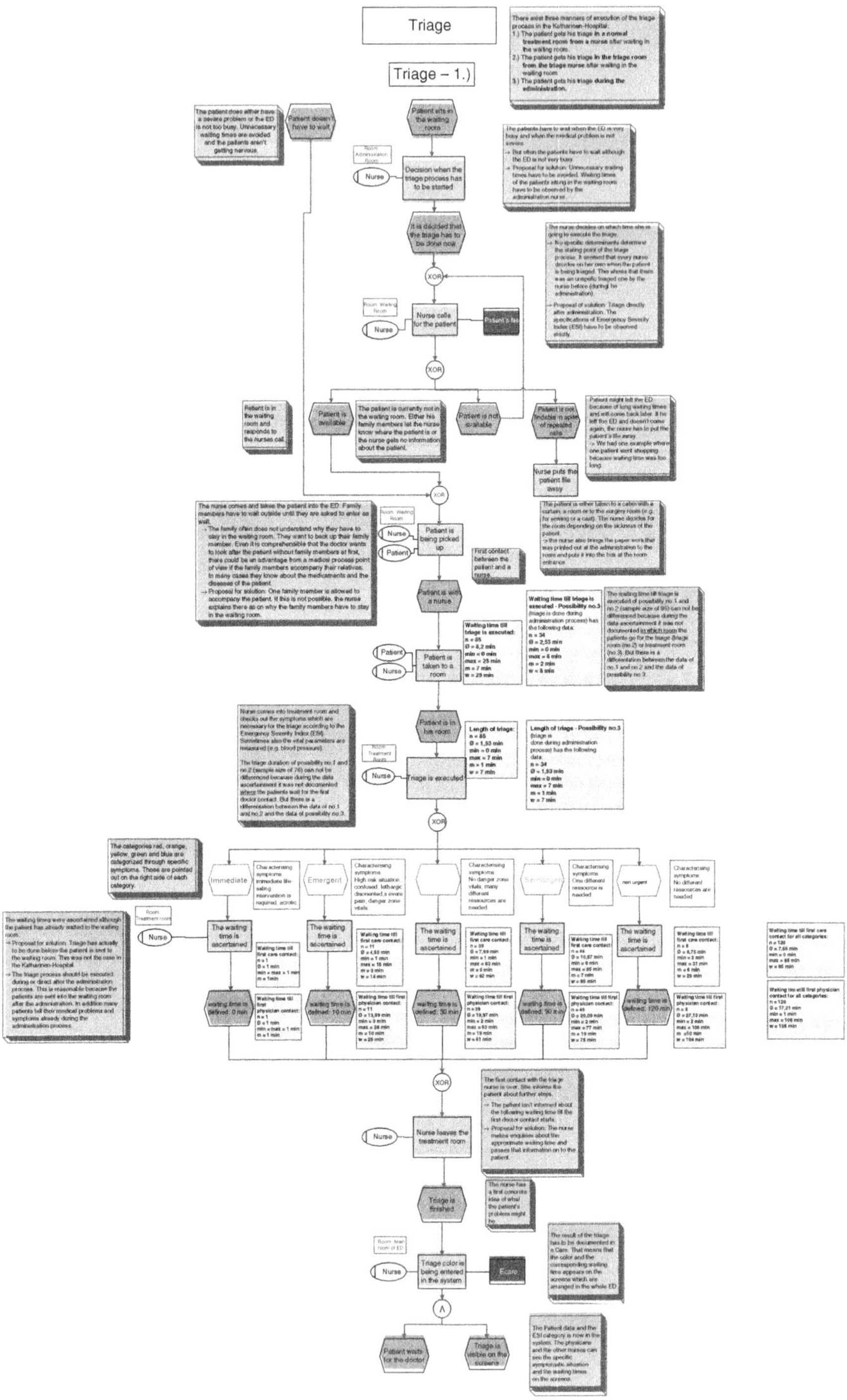
Triage
Triage – 1.)
Patient sits in the waiting room
Patient doesn't have to wait
Decision when the triage process has to be started
Nurse
It is decided that the triage has to be done now
XOR
Nurse calls for the patient
Patient's file
Patient is available
Patient is not available
Patient is not findable in spite of repeated calls
Nurse puts the patient file away
Patient is being picked up
Patient
Patient is with a nurse
Patient is taken to a room
Patient is in his room
Triage is executed
Immediate
Emergent
Semiurgent
non urgent
The waiting time is ascertained
waiting time is defined: 0 min
waiting time is defined: 10 min
waiting time is defined: 30 min
waiting time is defined: 90 min
waiting time is defined: 120 min
Nurse leaves the treatment room
Triage is finished
Triage color is being entered in the system
Ecare
Patient waits for the doctor
Triage is visible on the screens

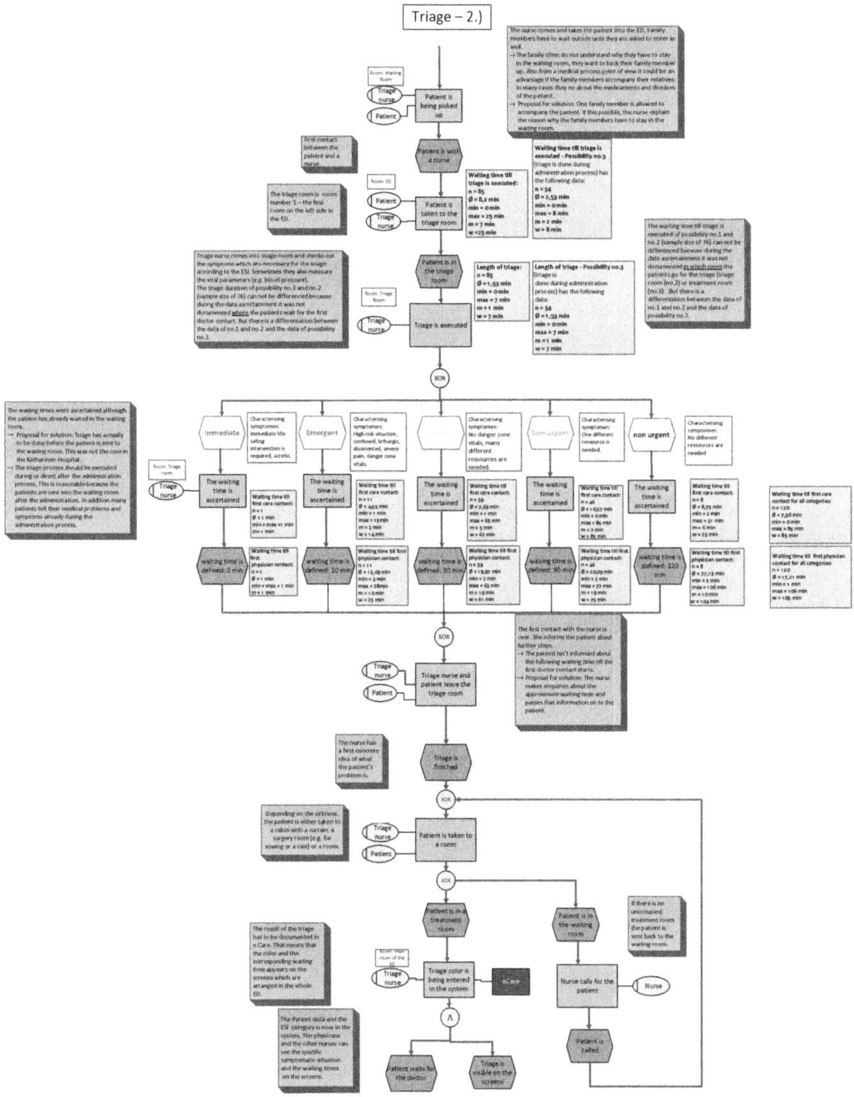
Triage – 2.)
The nurse comes and takes the patient into the ED. Family members have to wait outside until they are asked to enter as well.
→ The family often do not understand why they have to stay in the waiting room, they want to back their family member up. Also from a medical process point of view it could be an advantage if the family members accompany their relatives: In many cases they no about the medicaments and diseases of the patient.
→ Proposal for solution: One family member is allowed to accompany the patient. If this possible, the nurse explain the reason why the family members have to stay in the waiting room.
Room: Waiting Room
Triage nurse
Patient
Patient is being picked up
First contact between the patient and a nurse.
Patient is with a nurse
Waiting time till triage is executed - Possibility no.3 (triage is done during administration process) has the following data:
n = 34
Ø = 2,53 min
min = 0 min
max = 8 min
m = 2 min
w = 8 min
Room: ED
The triage room is room number 1 – the first room on the left side in the ED.
Patient
Triage nurse
Patient is taken to the triage room
Waiting time till triage is executed:
n = 85
Ø = 8,2 min
min = 0 min
max = 25 min
m = 7 min
w = 25 min
The waiting time till triage is executed of possibility no.1 and no.2 (sample size of 76) can not be differenced because during the data ascertainment it was not documented in which room the patients go for the triage (triage room (no.2) or treatment room (no.3)). But there is a differentation between the data of no.1 and no.2 and the data of possibility no.3.
Triage nurse comes into triage room and checks out the symptoms which are necessary for the triage according to the ESI. Sometimes they also measure the vital parameters (e.g. blood pressure).
The triage duration of possibility no.1 and no.2 (sample size of 76) can not be differenced because during the data ascertainment it was not documented where the patients wait for the first doctor contact. But there is a differentation between the data of no.1 and no.2 and the data of possibility no.3.
Patient is in the triage room
Room: Triage Room
Triage nurse
Triage is executed
Length of triage:
n = 85
Ø = 1,53 min
min = 0 min
max = 7 min
m = 1 min
w = 7 min
Length of triage - Possibility no.3 (triage is done during administration process) has the following data:
n = 34
Ø = 1,53 min
min = 0 min
max = 7 min
m = 1 min
w = 7 min
XOR
The waiting times were ascertained although the patient has already waited in the waiting room.
→ Proposal for solution: Triage has actually to be done before the patient is sent to the waiting room. This was not the case in the Katharinen-Hospital.
→ The triage process should be executed during or direct after the administration process. This is reasonable because the patients are sent into the waiting room after the administration. In addition many patients tell their medical problems and symptoms already during the administration process.
Immediate
Characterising symptomes: immediate life-safing intervention is required, acrotic.
Emergent
Characterising symptomes: High risk situation, confused, lethargic, disoriented, severe pain, danger zone vitals.
Characterising symptomes: No danger zone vitals, many different ressources are needed.
Semiurgent
Characterising symptomes: One different resource is needed.
non urgent
Characterising symptomes: No different ressources are needed
Room: Triage room
Triage nurse
The waiting time is ascertained
waiting time is defined: 0 min
waiting time is defined: 10 min
waiting time is defined: 30 min
waiting time is defined: 90 min
waiting time is defined: 120 min
XOR
The first contact with the nurse is over. She informs the patient about further steps.
→ The patient isn't informed about the following waiting time till the first doctor contact starts.
→ Proposal for solution: The nurse makes enquiries about the approximate waiting time and passes that information on to the patient.
Triage nurse
Patient
Triage nurse and patient leave the triage room
The nurse has a first concrete idea of what the patient's problem is.
Triage is finished
XOR
Depending on the sickness, the patient is either taken to a cabin with a curtain, a surgery room (e.g. for sewing or a cast) or a room.
Triage nurse
Patient
Patient is taken to a room
XOR
Patient is in a treatment room
Patient is in the waiting room
If there is no unoccupied treatment room the patient is sent back to the waiting room.
The result of the triage has to be documented in e.Care. That means that the color and the corresponding waiting time appears on the screens which are arranged in the whole ED.
Triage nurse
Triage color is being entered in the system
eCare
Nurse calls for the patient
Nurse
Λ
The Patient data and the ESI category is now in the system. The physicans and the other nurses can see the specific symptomatic situation and the waiting times on the screens.
Patient waits for the doctor
Triage is visible on the screens
Patient is called

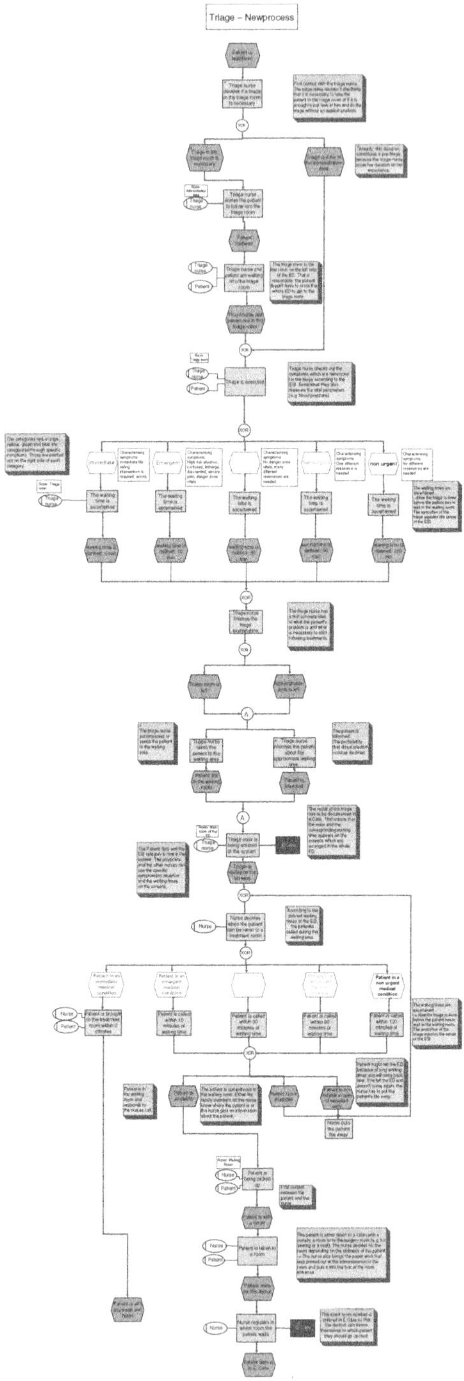
Triage – Newprocess
non urgent

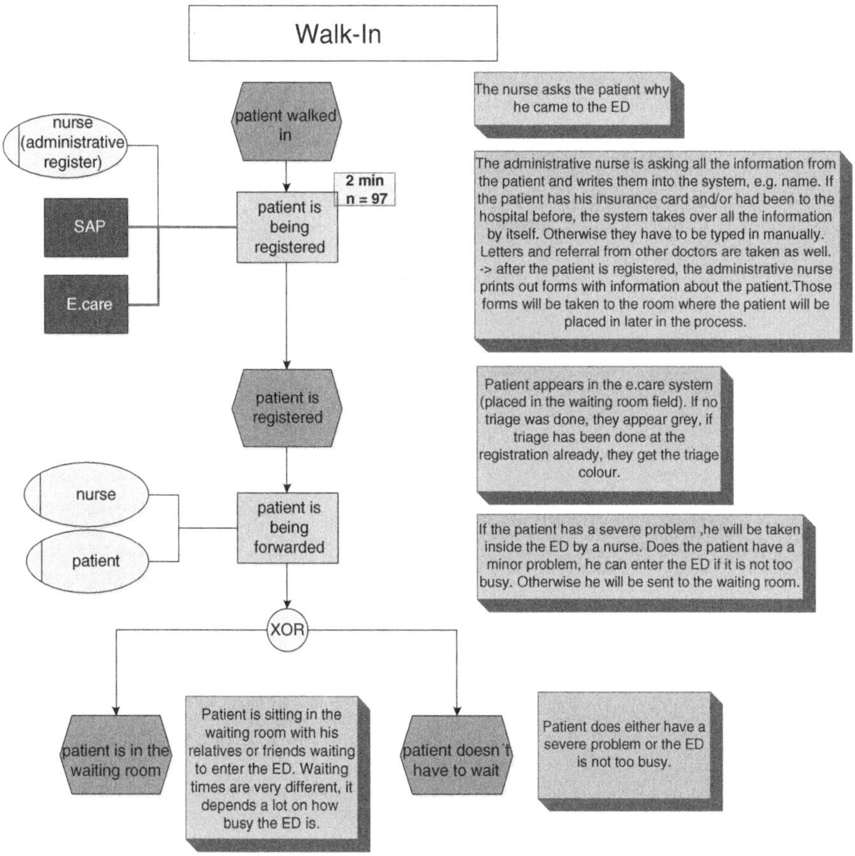
Walk-In
patient walked in
The nurse asks the patient why he came to the ED
nurse (administrative register)
SAP
E.care
patient is being registered
2 min
n = 97
The administrative nurse is asking all the information from the patient and writes them into the system, e.g. name. If the patient has his insurance card and/or had been to the hospital before, the system takes over all the information by itself. Otherwise they have to be typed in manually. Letters and referral from other doctors are taken as well. -> after the patient is registered, the administrative nurse prints out forms with information about the patient.Those forms will be taken to the room where the patient will be placed in later in the process.
patient is registered
Patient appears in the e.care system (placed in the waiting room field). If no triage was done, they appear grey, if triage has been done at the registration already, they get the triage colour.
nurse
patient
patient is being forwarded
If the patient has a severe problem ,he will be taken inside the ED by a nurse. Does the patient have a minor problem, he can enter the ED if it is not too busy. Otherwise he will be sent to the waiting room.
XOR
patient is in the waiting room
Patient is sitting in the waiting room with his relatives or friends waiting to enter the ED. Waiting times are very different, it depends a lot on how busy the ED is.
patient doesn´t have to wait
Patient does either have a severe problem or the ED is not too busy.

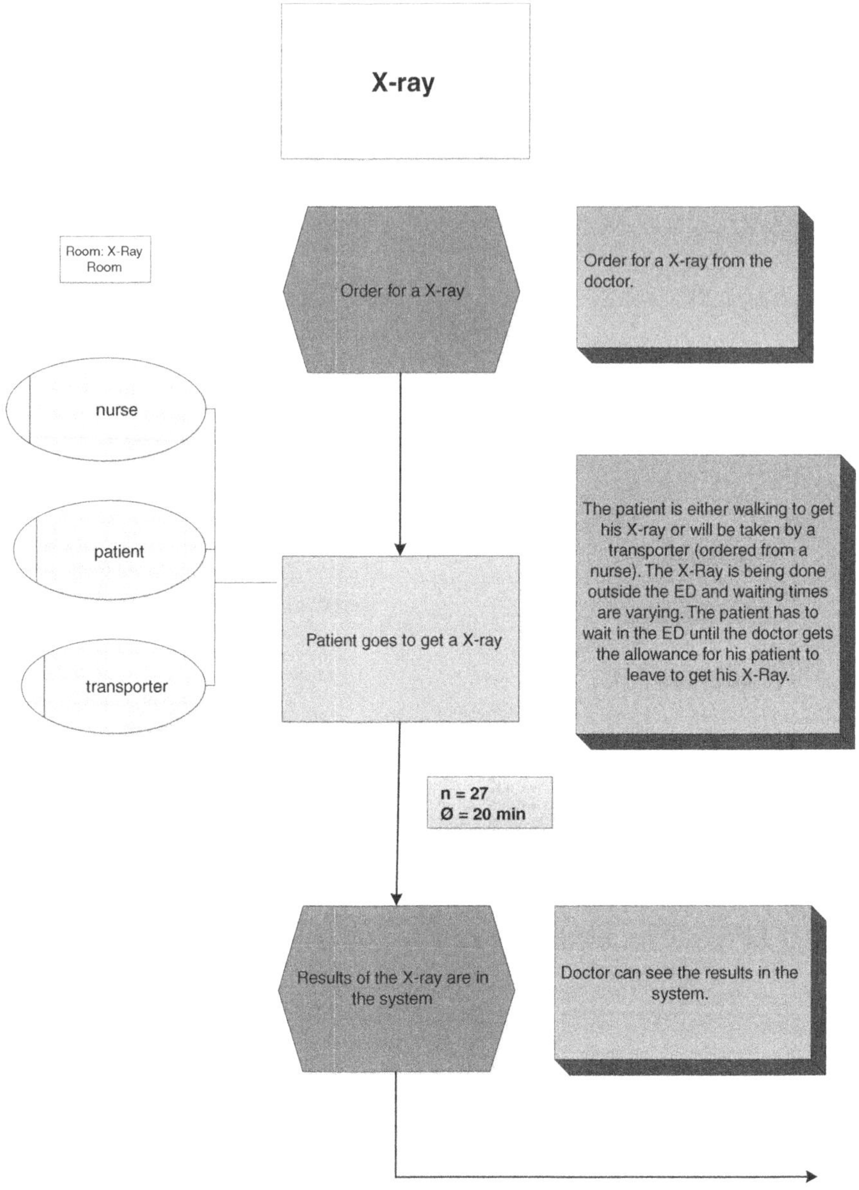
X-ray
Room: X-Ray Room
Order for a X-ray
Order for a X-ray from the doctor.
nurse
patient
transporter
Patient goes to get a X-ray
The patient is either walking to get his X-ray or will be taken by a transporter (ordered from a nurse). The X-Ray is being done outside the ED and waiting times are varying. The patient has to wait in the ED until the doctor gets the allowance for his patient to leave to get his X-Ray.
n = 27
Ø = 20 min
Results of the X-ray are in the system
Doctor can see the results in the system.

References

Bey, T. A., Hahn, S. A., & Moecke, H. (2008). The current state of hospital-based emergency medicine in Germany. *International Journal of Emergency Medicine, 1*(4), 273–277. doi:10.1007/s12245-008-0076-5.

Gries, A., Zink, W., Bernhard, M., Messelken, M., & Schlechtriemen, T. (2006). Realistic assessment of the physician-staffed emergency services in Germany. *Der Anaesthesist, 55*(10), 1080–1086. doi:10.1007/s00101-006-1051-2.

Hogan, B., & Fleischmann, T. (2008). Kompetent und unabhängig. Interdisziplinäre Notaufnahme-Konzeption und personelle Besetzung. *Krankenhaus Umschau, 77*(2), 30–32.

Platz, E., Bey, T., & Walter, F. G. (2003). International report: Current state and development of health insurance and emergency medicine in Germany. The influence of health insurance laws on the practice of emergency medicine in a European country. *The Journal of Emergency Medicine, 25*(2), 203–210. http://www.sciencedirect.com/science/article/pii/S0736467903001732.

Walter, B., & Fleischmann, T. (2007). Interdisziplinäre Notaufnahme. *Das Krankenhaus, 7*, 657–660.

Zehnder, A. (2007). Strategischer Erfolgsfaktor. *kma - Das Gesundheitswirtschaftsmagazin, 37*(1), 50–52.

Chapter 31
Business Process Modeling and Measuring Waiting Times in a German ED: An Approach for Identifying Improvements

Mirjam Bathelt, Emanuel Grabler, Jan Lipka, and Tobias Reutemann

Abstract This case study is about the modeling of the business processes in the interdisciplinary ED of the Robert-Bosch-Hospital in Stuttgart, Germany. An EPC process model for the complete stay of a patient was created. Time intervals for different subprocesses were measured to support the model and to identify waiting times. The case study works out that the modeling of current business processes is a good basis for finding improvements.

Waiting times and weaknesses were identified in the improvable implementation of the MTS, the bed management, and the insufficient integration of the IT systems.

Keywords Business process modeling • Waiting times • EPC • Process analysis ED

31.1 Introduction

The examination object of the present case study is the emergency department (ED) of the Robert-Bosch-Hospital. This hospital is part of the Klinikum Stuttgart. The head of the ED-center in Robert-Bosch-Hospital and chief physician of the department for general internal medicine and nephrology is Prof. Dr. med. Mark Dominik Alscher. Assistant medical director of the ED-center and of the division for general internal medicine and nephrology is Dr. med. Christoph Wasser. He was the person in charge and the reference person for the group of students who visited the ED during the execution of the case study. During these weeks of execution there was a

The material in this case study was prepared originally for Project Seminar SS 2012 at the University of Hohenhiem, Germany under the supervision of Profs Kirn and Wickramasinghe.

M. Bathelt (✉) • E. Grabler • J. Lipka • T. Reutemann
University of Hohenheim, Stuttgart, Germany
e-mail: M.Bathelt@uni-hohenheim.de

N. Wickramasinghe et al. (eds.), *Lean Thinking for Healthcare*, Healthcare Delivery in the Information Age, DOI 10.1007/978-1-4614-8036-5_31,

close cooperation between the students and the Robert-Bosch-Hospital. The group of students was in the ED for several days over a period of a few weeks. They observed the processes and documented their observance. With the help of this data they were able to analyze the processes in the ED of Robert-Bosch-Hospital.

The goals of the case study were the creation of a complete EPC process model for the ED at the Robert-Bosch-Hospital and also the statistical survey for some key factors (e.g., patient cycle time) to support the validity of the model. Constructing thereon the analysis of the current process and reflections about reengineering were two major aims. Furthermore the analysis of the IT architecture to support the processes at best was another goal of the case study.

The main attention is on some key economic principles which are highly important for the specific situation in an ED. They build the economic base of the case study. E-health itself aims to increase efficiency in healthcare, thereby decreasing costs. So inefficient parts of processes in the ED which for example can be ascribed to redundancy decline the value and have to be improved. Moreover the whole process has to fulfill the requirement of sustainability.

In the following, the subsistent workflows of the Robert-Bosch-Hospital will be demonstrated, discussed, and analyzed. At this, only the internistic surgical cases will be regarded—the accident surgical cases are not a component of the analysis. After pointing out critical positions and problems of the partial processes, proposals for solution will be recommended. These suggestions will be regarded from a critical point of view and will be analyzed about their workability. The main improvements refer to a better communication, an improved technological support, and new rooms. The communication between hospital and patients as well as the hospital staff among themselves has to be redefined.

31.2 Background

All over the world healthcare is a huge cost driver. Over the years you can recognize that health expenditures are constantly increasing. German health costs amount a bit more than 10 % of the gross domestic product. Australia's health insurance costs contain a higher amount of private expenditure on health. In Germany healthcare is provided by a two tier healthcare system. From 82.14 million inhabitants of Germany 70.23 million enrollees use public health insurance and 8.62 million enrollees use private health insurance taking a substitutive function. You can only choose between a public and a private health insurance. There is no possibility to upgrade your public health insurance with the private health insurance in some cases. Australia's two tier healthcare system is different. In comparison to Germany there is no private health insurance, but it is provided a private hospital insurance presenting a complementary function to the public health insurance. You can add it additionally to your public health insurance. Germany has got 48,030 pharmacists working in 21,602 pharmacies; in Australia there are 16,300 pharmacists and 4,992 pharmacies. Furthermore in Germany, there are 2,087 hospitals and 319,697 doctors; in Australia there are 1,315 hospitals and 59,500 medical practitioners. In Australia 4,107 inhabitants are concentrated on one pharmacy. In Germany there are 3,803. In Australia the amount is a little bit higher because most of the people are living in big cities and therefore less pharmacies are necessary to support the inhabitants of Australia, but in Australia are relatively more pharmacists working than in Germany (Wickramasinghe 2012).

Concerning emergency departments in Germany, there are two different types of them: The interdisciplinary type and the subject-specific type. Regarding the interdisciplinary emergency department all kinds of branches of study are represented. In comparison to the interdisciplinary one, the subject-specific either only receives trauma surgical patients or nonsurgical ones.

To improve the German healthcare system and to inform the doctor better about the patient, especially in emergencies the new electronic health card is introduced step-by-step since October 2011. In 2013 every patient will have the new one. Results of other doctors can be stored on the e-health card. It isn't necessary to send the results to the family doctor via mail. The patient brings the e-health card with him and checks in, the results will be automatically transferred. This implicates that the doctor doesn't have to type in the results because it's already done by the IT system and therefore reduces consumption of time. Because of the use of the patient's picture misusage can be eliminated and costs decreased.

In case of a change of the address it can easily be edited on the card and will automatically be updated in every IT system the card gets connected, e.g., at the dentist's, at the hospital's, at the family doctor's (Bundesministerium für Gesundheit 2012).

31.2.1 Literature Review

One of the major topics when it comes to Emergency Departments is the influence of process speed on treatment delays and resulting patient overcrowding. Literature considering patient overcrowding and decreasing patient satisfaction is nowadays published in nearly every modern country of the world as it is a global phenomenon. A detailed overview about patient crowding development and resulting problems offers the article "Optimizing Emergency Department Front-End Operations" written by Wiler et al. (2010). The study shows that patient visits in US Emergency Departments increased about 20 % only in the last 2 years and connects this result with the necessity of optimizing processes inside the Emergency Department to keep patient and also staff satisfaction stable and ensure the quality of treatment in US hospitals. The main part of this work shows several approaches to achieve that goal. While some of them are already implemented in several hospitals some of them also rely on a reconstruction of processes or technologies involving other healthcare system organizations. Regarding this Case Study German authors also already addressed publications to the field of emergency department process improvement concerning the challenges of modern ED's over the last years. A mentionable text was published by Fleischmann (2007) called "Rettungsdienst und Notaufnahme." Fleischmann takes a look at several problems in the ED, regarding staff issues or unclear responsibilities. An interesting fact for the German healthcare system is that Fleischmann connects those issues with the shift to interdisciplinary emergency departments, which occurred over the last years in Germany.

31.3 Case Study

31.3.1 Background

The goal of this case study was to have a cross-disciplinary view and apply business information modeling techniques in healthcare and ED department environment. After a literature review to get a basic understanding of an ED the students visited the ED and created the process models.

31.3.2 Methodology

The ED was visited 4 times at the weekend as well as 4 times during the week. Each time we stayed from 10 a.m. to 10 a.m. so that all peak times were covered on the one hand, but on the other hand this time interval also enabled the chance for cases of nonpeak times to become a sample of the case study.

Whenever a patient entered the ED during this time interval the time of arrival was noted and the steps until his actual departure were tracked. During the stay we also measured different waiting times and the length of the treatments the patient received.

An overall number of 114 data samples were collected. After this data was analyzed by using STATA 11 software and we calculated for each time interval the average value, the median, variance and standard derivation, and minimum and maximum values. Because of the small number of cases in some time intervals the statistic might not be so meaningful in these cases. The analyzed data helped to identify critical points in the processes and supported and validated our process model.

The actual EPC process model is based on our experience and observations in the ED and supported by the collected data. The stay of a patient was divided into different subprocesses and these subprocesses were modeled in detail. The software used for creating the EPC models was Microsoft Visio (The complete process models are included in the Appendix.) (Table 31.1).

Table 31.1 Measured time intervals in minutes

Measured timeframe	Number of observations	Average	Minimum	Maximum	Standard deviation	Variance	Median
Total time in ED	100	179.48	2	457	94.34	8.900,55	173.0
Administration	109	4.34	1	63	8.32	69.28	3.0
Triage	106	3.87	1	26	4.43	19.47	3.0
Time until							
First nursing contact (walk-in)	76	2.64	0	60	7.16	51.22	1.0
First nursing contact (all triage-levels)	101	20.80	0	143	25.04	627.02	12.0
First nursing contact (triage: blue)	4	31.50	4	59	31.75	1.008,33	31.5
First nursing contact (triage: green)	44	25.66	0	143	27.22	740.83	18.5
First nursing contact (triage: yellow)	44	18.39	0	131	23.35	545.08	11.5
First nursing contact (triage: orange)	7	4.71	0	10	4.31	18.57	4.0
First nursing contact (triage: red)	2	2.00	2	2	0.00	0.00	2.0
First physician contact (all triage-levels)	99	55.55	0	237	48.86	2.387,52	46.0
First physician contact (triage: blue)	4	41.50	24	59	20.21	408.33	43.5
First physician contact (triage: green)	43	75.23	0	237	57.71	3.330,71	74.0
First physician contact (triage: yellow)	39	51.00	0	135	34.31	1.177,32	46.0
First physician contact (triage: orange)	7	14.43	5	27	7.96	63.29	13.0
First physician contact (triage: red)	3	0.33	0	1	0.58	0.33	0.0
Length							
First nursing contact	94	11.18	1	55	8.88	78.77	10.0
First physician contact	95	7.95	1	34	4.97	24.73	7.0
Blood draw	34	3.82	1	8	1.71	2.94	3.5
X-ray	48	33.31	2	132	29.95	896.77	25.0
CT	16	19.25	1	65	15.21	231.40	14.5
Sono	6	20.50	7	34	10.67	113.90	18.0

(continued)

Table 31.1 (continued)

Measured timeframe	Number of observations	Average	Minimum	Maximum	Standard deviation	Variance	Median
Other testings	7	17.43	1	65	22.69	515.29	10.0
Further treatment	16	11.81	1	35	8.80	77.50	10.0
Council	14	9.14	1	32	9.71	94.29	5.0
Second nursing contact	14	9.29	1	24	7.45	55.45	9.5
Second physician contact	20	7.30	2	19	4.34	18.85	7.0
Laboratory	12	50.33	14	104	23.31	543.33	51.5
Bed search	13	1.54	1	3	0.78	0.60	1.0
Between bedding decision and transport to ward	21	95.19	5	267	86.68	7.514,26	65.0

31.3.3 Results

31.3.3.1 Walk-in

Walking In into an Emergency department is one of two ways a patient could arrive. Usually the patient walks directly to the administration desk and waits until the staff there is able to start the administration and register him at the ED. There are two reasons why the patient might have to wait in front of the administration desk before his administration and triage can get started.

One reason is a waiting queue in front of the administration desk. Since the arrival of new patients is more or less random distributed there are not much ways to affect the development of a waiting queue. Actually we experienced a waiting queue only a few times. However in combination with the second factor for waiting time in front of the administration desk this might increase into a major problem.

The second case in which a patient has to wait until the administration and the triage can begin appears when the administration desk is not occupied the moment the patient arrives. Often only one person is in charge of the administration desk. This person does both: the administration and the triage. So the working area has to be left quite often for some reasons. For example every time the administration process is completed the patient file has to be transferred manually into the treatment room by walking into it. We will discuss this issue in Sects. 13.3.3.3 and 13.3.3.4. So the administration desk is often empty for many minutes.

The measured average waiting time for the first contact with the ED hospital was 2.6 min and the median waiting time was 1 min. This comes from some experienced extreme values (>15 min) which is pushing the average time a little bit up.

There seems to be not much time and in general many patients do not have to wait at this point. But if one has bad luck and arrives at a time the administration desk is not occupied and maybe in combination with a waiting queue, the waiting time can be very long. Since at this point the patient is not triaged and registered there is no chance that he could receive a preferred treatment and some urgent cases might be undetected. In fact this is a blind spot. Even the patient is physically at the ET, no one has noticed and categorized his issues yet.

31.3.3.2 Ambulance Arrival

By ambulance is the second possibility a patient could get into the treatment area. After the ambulance has arrived at the parking lot the patient is brought directly into the treatment area. There are different ways of the ED personal as to how to handle the arrival. In urgent emergency cases the patient is receiving immediately medical treatment from the physicians. In this case the patient was often preregistered before his arrival to give the ED staff the possibility to prepare. In other not so urgent cases the patient is taken over to a nurse or is "parked" at the corridor because there are no free rooms or resources available.

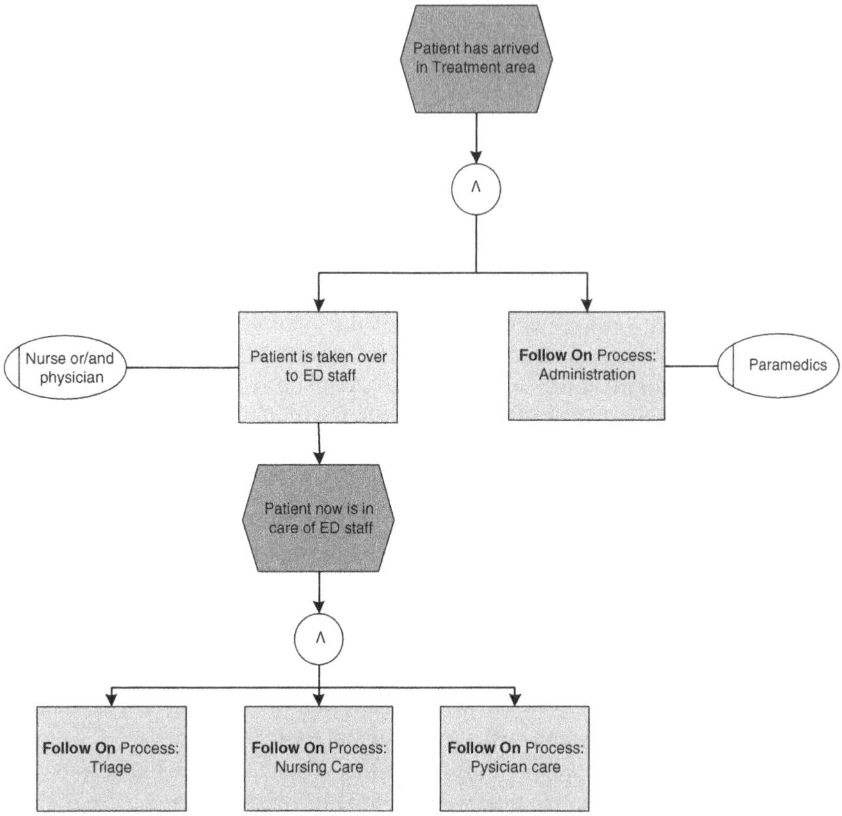

Fig. 31.1 Extract from EPC process after the patient has arrived in the treatment area

In all cases after the patient is taken over to the ED staff a paramedic walks out of the treatment area in order to register the patient. Sometimes this leads to confusion because the paramedic does not know where to go and that the Administration is taken place outside the treatment area.

In general we noticed that processes and procedures are not standardized and that there are no best practices as to how to handle the arrival of a new patient. But the waiting times that occur here are minor and not so critical to the patient safety (Fig. 31.1).

31.3.3.3 Administration

Whether a patient has walked in or arrived by ambulance in both cases he must get registered at the ED and some administrative work hast to be done.

In the walk-in case the patient himself provides the necessary information at the administration desk. If there is an ambulance arrival a paramedic walks with the necessary patients documents (insurance card etc.) from the treatment area to the administration desk where the administration is completed. The staff there receives the insurance card and creates a patient file.

The process described above is the basic administration process. When the patient is a walk-in patient this cannot clearly be separated from the triage process. The triage nurse or the person who is in charge of the administration and the triage often does this thing parallel. For example while questions about the patient disease are asked the triage nurse also fills in administrative data into the pc. For this reasons it was difficult to measure a clearly separated time interval for administration and triage. So the statistics for these processes should be treated with caution.

Theory administration process and triage process should be clearly separated and done by different persons: the administration staff and the triage nurse. But during our visits the administration desk was often only occupied with a normal administration staff member, only a few times there was an additional triage nurse.

This shortage on personal leads to overlapping and unknown responsibilities and makes standardization more difficult, because in which way the Triage and administration is performed depends on which person is in charge (Fig. 31.2).

We noted that the personnel at the administration desk is often overburdened and suffers from the overlapping and not clearly defined processes.

31.3.3.4 Triage

In Robert-Bosch-Hospital the Triage is executed according to the Manchester Triage System (MTS). During the triage process the waiting time subject on different symptoms is ascertained.

In Robert-Bosch-Hospital two possibilities of the triage process exist: In possibility 1 the *triage nurse* executes the triage process in the little triage area. A member of the administration staff has done the administration before. In possibility 2 the *administration staff* does the triage *during the administration process*. No triage nurse is present. The main differences between possibility 1 and 2 refer to the person who executes the triage and the place where the Triage is executed.

In the following, possibility 1 will be described more precisely. Subsequently possibility 2 will be considered.

In possibility 1 the administration is concluded by the administration staff. The administration staff introduces the triage nurse and the now introduced triage nurse takes the patient into the little triage area. The little triage area is not a specific room. It is located in the administration area next to the administration desk. As soon as the triage nurse and patient are in the little triage area the execution of the triage can start. The patient is categorized by the MTS by acuteness. During the data ascertainment 106 patients were classed by MTS. By this sample size the average execution time of the triage was 3.9 min. The appropriate median of 3 min shows that more than half of the patients were treated by nurse or physician after a waiting time

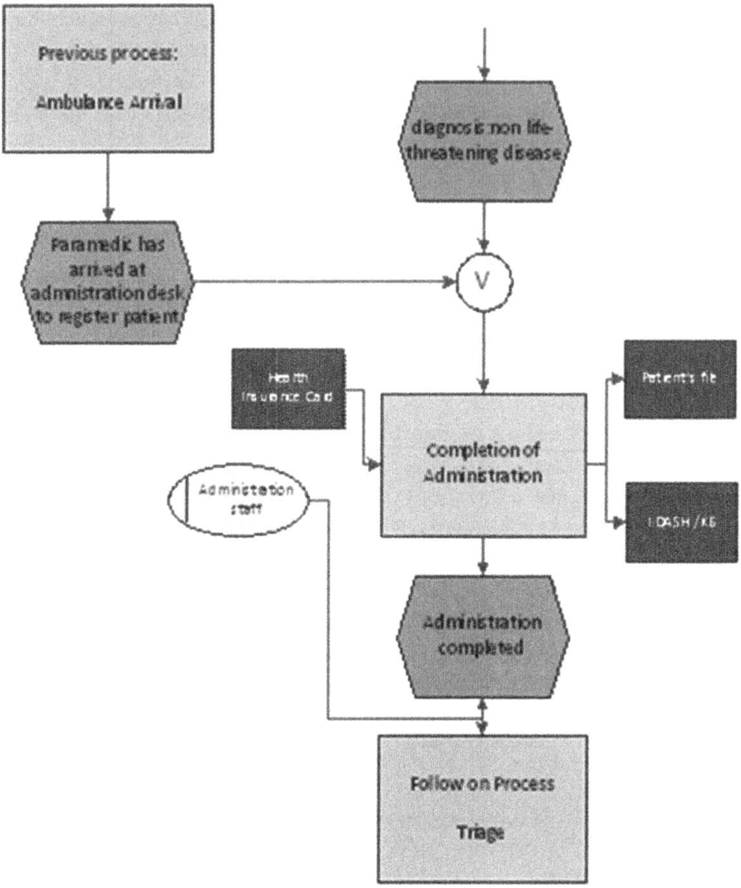

Fig. 31.2 Extract from EPC process for the administration

under the average waiting time. The corresponding standard derivation of 4.41 min shows that there are some outliers which pushed the average value.

The nurse checks out the physical condition of the patient. Therefore she checks up specific symptoms. There are five different categories (immediate, emergent, urgent, semiurgent, nonurgent) in the MTS which are categorized through these particular symptoms. The symptom evaluation is transformed in waiting times on the bases of the triage key.

The symptoms of *category immediate* (*red*) are insufficient breathing and shock. There mustn't exist any waiting time for such a categorized patient.

Category emergent (*orange*) means that the patient has severe pain and abnormal pulse. The defined waiting time is at the maximum 10 min.

The symptoms of *category urgent* (*yellow*) are moderate pain and lasting sickness. Such a patient doesn't have to wait longer than 30 min according to MTS.

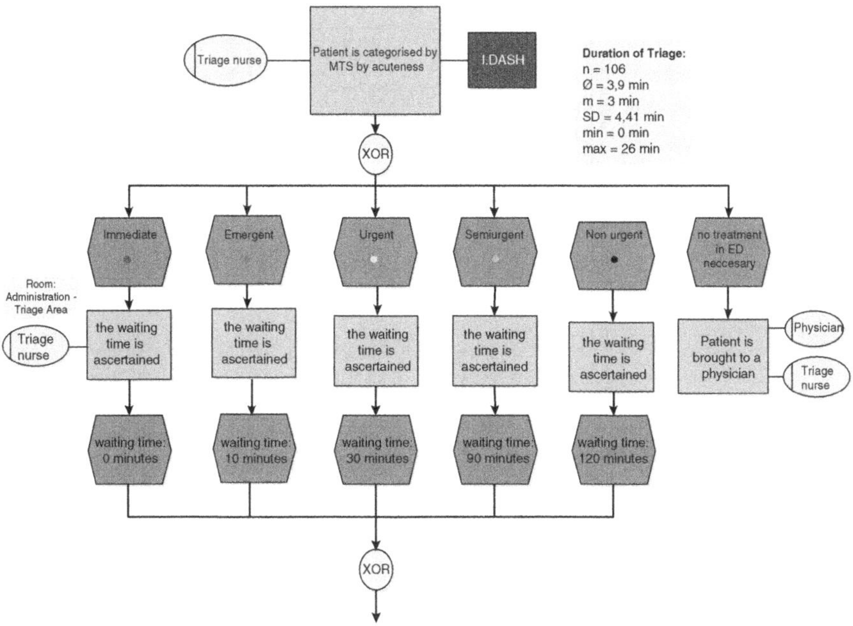

Fig. 31.3 Extract from the existing triage process in RBK

The semiurgent category (*green*) is described by sickness and a younger problem. In this case the waiting time has to be under 90 min.

In other respects the triage nurse chooses *category nonurgent* (*blue*). In this case the waiting time mustn't transcend 120 min (Fig. 31.3, Table 31.2).

In Robert-Bosch-Hospital the waiting times predefined by MTS were not transcended in average. But individual waiting times transcended the defined waiting time.

The median is under the average waiting time in each category. That means that more than half of the patients of each category were treated by nurse or physician after a waiting time under the average waiting time. This shows that some outliers pushed the average value.

In category urgent (yellow) the maximum value is 131 min till first nurse contact, while the maximum value till first physician contact is 135 min. The acceptable waiting time according to MTS is only 30 min. This shows that in individual cases the defined waiting time is highly exceeded.

In category semiurgent (green) the maximum value is 143 min till first nurse contact and 237 min until first physician contact. The acceptable waiting time according to MTS is only 90 min. In some cases the defined waiting time is highly exceeded.

Category nonurgent (blue) has no exceedances. The maximum value till first nurse contact is 59 min and until first physician contact also is 59 min. Both lie

Table 31.2 Waiting times

	Immediate	Emergent	Urgent	Semiurgent	Nonurgent
Waiting time until first nurse contact	*n* = 2	*n* = 7	*n* = 44	*n* = 44	*n* = 4
	Ø = 2 min	Ø = 4.7 min	Ø = 18.4 min	Ø = 25.7 min	Ø = 31.5 min
	m = 2 min	*m* = 4 min	*m* = 11.5 min	*m* = 18.5 min	*m* = 31.5 min
	SD = 0 min	*SD* = 4.3 min	*SD* = 23.3 min	*SD* = 27.2 min	*SD* = 31.8 min
	min = 2 min	min = 0 min	min = 0 min	min = 0 min	min = 4 min
	max = 2 min	max = 10 min	max = 131 min	max = 143 min	max = 59 min
Waiting time until first physician contact	*n* = 3	*n* = 7	*n* = 39	*n* = 43	*n* = 4
	Ø = 0.3 min	Ø = 14.4 min	Ø = 51 min	Ø = 75.2 min	Ø = 41.5 min
	m = 0 min	*m* = 13 min	*m* = 46 min	*m* = 74 min	*m* = 41.5 min
	SD = 0.6 min	*SD* = 8 min	*SD* = 34.3 min	*SD* = 57.7 min	*SD* = 20.2 min
	min = 0 min	min = 5 min	min = 0 min	min = 0 min	min = 24 min
	max = 1 min	max = 27 min	max = 135 min	max = 237 min	max = 59 min

n = sample size, Ø = average, *m* = median, *SD* = standard degression, min without a number before = minimum, max = maximum, min with number before = minutes under the prescribed waiting time of 120 min. In comparison with category semiurgent and urgent the maximum waiting is lower. This is attributed to the extremely low sample size of category nonurgent of only four patients.

The median of the waiting time for all categories until first physician contact is distinct higher than the median of the waiting time until first care contact. This is reasonable and is referable to the fundamental structure of the processes in the ED, because the patient is first treated by the nurse. She does the preliminary examination (e.g., taking of a blood sample) so that the physician has more information about the patient (e.g., blood panel). The standard derivation of the waiting time until first physician contact in category emergent, urgent, and semiurgent is distinctly higher than the standard derivation of the waiting time until first nurse contact. This shows that the spread around the arithmetic average is more bold.

A couple of times a green categorized patient is preferred to a yellow categorized one because he is acquainted to the hospital staff.

Sometimes no treatment in ED is necessary. In this case the patient is brought to a physician for a short check to confirm the triage nurses assessment that no treatment in ED is needed. After finishing the execution of the triage the results, that means the specific color and the corresponding waiting time, are documented in I.Dash. Now the patient data and the MRT category is in I.Dash and all nurses and physicians can see the specific waiting situation on the screens. The triage itself is finished. Afterwards it has to be clarified if an internistic or accident surgical case is existent to be able to bring the patients in the right waiting room. The waiting room for the internistic patients differs from the waiting room of the accident surgical patient: The accident surgical waiting room is directly in front of the administration desk whereas the internistic waiting room is not located in the administration area. Therefore the triage nurse records and categorizes the specific symptoms. In I.Dash it can be seen if the patients has an internistic or accident surgical problem. Afterwards the triage nurse brings or sends the patient in the right waiting room. If an internistic case exists she sends the patient into the internistic waiting room. Otherwise if an accident surgical case is existent the patient is sent into the accident surgical waiting room. If the patient walks on his own there is a problem: the internistic waiting room is difficult to find. The patient is not informed about his waiting time automatically before sending him to the waiting room. If the patient asks about his waiting time, the answer is inaccurate and not bindingly. The patient is now seated. Because of no given information and waiting time the patient gets nervous. He walks to the administration desks and asks about his waiting time or asks ED staff who walks through the waiting room. The answer is uncertain and not bindingly. Dissatisfaction might occur. After seating the patient in the waiting room the triage nurse brings the patient's file in the treatment workplace. While the administration nurse walks to the treatment workplace, the administration desk is not occupied.

Subsequently the nurse calls for the patient. There are two possibilities: the patient is still in the waiting room or he is not available. If the patient is not present in the waiting area, he will be called again.

If the patient is unfindable he will be called again later. If he has left the ED the patient's file will be put away. When the patient responds to the nurse's call he is brought into the treatment room. This is documented in I.Dash. Now the patient waits in the treatment area. ED staff can see via I.Dash in which room the patient currently waits. If the patient is able to sit and the ED is overcrowded, the patient will be brought out of the treatment room and will be seated in the waiting room again.

The data does not distinguish between the two possibilities of the triage process. The main difference between possibility 1 and possibility 2 is the executing nurse: in possibility 1 the triage nurse executes the triage whereas in possibility 2 the administration nurse does the triage. During the data ascertainment this possibilities weren't distinguished. Consequently it was not documented in the data ascertainment which nurse executed the triage.

In the following, *possibility 2* is considered. There are some differences to possibility 1 which will be discussed and which will be in the focus of the following analysis. The main process is comparable to the process of possibility 1. The starting point of the triage process is *during the administration*. The triage is executed by the administration staff.

The administration nurse asks the patient for the symptoms. The patient describes his symptoms and the medical problem that brought him to visit the ED. It is only a verbal description—the administration staff does not have the time to do a real triage execution. On this basis the patient is categorized by MTS by acuteness. The specifics of the triage (e.g., symptoms, maximal waiting times) are equally to those in possibility 1. As mentioned the data does not distinguish between the two possibilities of the triage process. So the statistical analyses between the two possibilites do not differ. Afterwards the administration nurse documents the results of the triage in I.Dash and the triage is finished. She also clarifies whether an internistic or accident surgical case is existent and brings or sends the patient to the right waiting room. Subsequently the triage nurse brings the patient's file to the treatment workplace.

While the administration nurse walks to the treatment workplace, the administration desk is not occupied. The rest of the process doesn't differ from the process of possibility 1.

31.3.3.5 Nursing Care

Before the patient gets in touch with the nurse for the first time he has to wait. His waiting time depends on the Manchester Triage level he was categorized. At the Robert-Bosch-Hospital the waiting time for the first contact with the nurse was about 31.5 min when he was triaged blue, with green he had to wait 25.66 min on average, with yellow 18.36 min, with orange 4.71 min, and with red 2 min. Approximately the waiting time for all patients averages 20.80 min. Because of restricted resources patients with less life-threatening diseases have to wait longer to get the treatment they need of course. Sometimes patients will be triaged in the treatment room for the first time when there is no triage nurse available or the desk clerk is unsure about the Manchester Triage level. In the beginning of the nurse's treatment the nurse measures the patient's blood pressure in the treatment room. It occurred that a patient was determined for the surgical department, but instead was transported to the nonsurgical department. The nurse didn't know that the patient was sent to the wrong department and the transport had to be made retrogressive. After the blood pressure measure is done it will be documented in Gap.It! and I.Dash. Secondly, the nurse compiles the blood withdrawal injections in the hallway. Therefore she has to leave the treatment room and it generates consumption of time because of the long distance. Because of different blood counts different injections for the blood withdrawal process have to be used. So the nurse has to open every single injection manually. This fact increases consumption of time. ID codes for blood withdrawal are printed by the desk clerk, not at the nurse's work place. That consumes the desk clerks time because of the transport. The desk isn't occupied by the desk clerk during the transport. As a result, patients arriving in the emergency department have to wait until the desk clerk has completed the transport. Blood withdrawal needs most of the time and freezes following processes, e.g., doctor's first contact because of analyzing the blood first before being able to think about a diagnosis. The nurse takes the blood and it lasts 3.82 min on average. After the blood is taken by the nurse in the treatment room, it will be recorded in Gap.It! and I.Dash and will be sent to the laboratory afterwards in the hallway of the emergency department. The nurse has to put a long distance back. Hence manifests in occurring unnecessary time consumption. Blood results are on Sundays much more faster than on other weekdays. On Sundays less patients arrive in the emergency department, so less blood withdrawals have to be analyzed. There could be a personal overutilization on other days in the laboratory. Human resources could be tried to get shifted to the laboratory when they're derated, but there could be some education measures necessary to transform human resources to laborants. Now the nurse does an ECG in the treatment and writes the results down in Gap.It! and I.Dash. A woman with cystitis was given an infusion and seated in the waiting room, triage level could be set down from yellow to green. Patients being able to sit due to a lack of space will be seated in the waiting room. Additionally, nurses have to absolve further services like bringing the patient to the toilet, cleaning, giving infusions and painkillers, doing urine tests, transporting the patient to the wards or to the X-ray/CT waiting room. This needs a lot of time. Human resources and rooms are difficult to organize because of peak hours and emerging overutilization.

31.3.3.6 Physician Care

After analyzing the blood by the laboratory worker in the laboratory, the blood results will be sent to the doctor electronically via Gap.It! and will be looked up by the doctor at the doctor's work place. On average the blood results take 50.33 min time to get analyzed. This might be a consequence because of less human resources in the laboratory in matters of the amount of patients especially at high peaks and the purpose of machines and analyzing techniques. Then the doctor visits the patient for the first time in the treatment room and simultaneously thinks about a diagnosis. After the diagnosis is settled and registered in Gap.It! the doctor instructs himself or the nurse for further treatment in the treatment room or their work place. Either the doctor instructs the nurse to do a CT, X-ray, or other nursing treatments or he does a sonography or other physician treatment. If the patient gets a treatment for a CT or X-ray, the emergency department nurse will bring the patient to the CT/X-ray waiting area or the patient will be transported by a CT/X-ray nurse. If it's the patient's turn, he will be called and investigated in the CT room or X-ray room. Therefore by then examination result will be looked up in Gap it! to set up the CT and X-ray at its best. Now the CT or X-ray is completed. The duration of an X-ray lasts for 33.31 min on average, the one for a CT lasts for 19.25 min on average. X-rays could probably last longer because there is perhaps less staff employed than in the CT area. Sometimes it occurs, that patients return to the emergency department on their own before being X-rayed, because they didn't want to wait for so long. Afterwards the patient will be brought back either from a CT or X-ray nurse or from an emergency department nurse. In case of the need of a sonography, the doctors do a sonography in the treatment room and it takes 20.5 min on average. After completing the sono the doctor fills in the results in I.Dash and Gap it! Other physicians or nursing care may be applying pain killers, sewing wounds, and doing a urine test. The doctor or nurse looks the already done measures and already settled diagnosis up in Gap it! and writes down the new done measures in I.Dash and Gap it! Writing down the physician and nursing treatment measures is necessary for letting oneself and other nurses now that the measure is already done and reduces doubles. The duration for further treatment is about 17.42 min on average. After carrying out those treatment options it occurs the question of additional treatment. By using Gap.It! the doctor can decide whether an additional treatment is necessary. For example the patient has a complex fracture of the leg, the doctor first instructs the nurse to do an X-ray, but the results are indefinite. So he comes to the conclusion that a CT should be additionally done or the illness of the patient changes by occurring new symptoms like a stomache. Then an accessory sonography would make sense. When the additional treatment is finished the council will be started by a second doctor. After finishing the council the data will be documented in Gap.It! and I.Dash. Because of finishing the patient's treatment it occurs the question whether there is a change of department or a need of stationary treatment required. If stationary treatment is necessary, a treatment contract will be entered, if not, the patient will be discharged. In case of a department change from nonsurgical to surgical or the other way around the whole process starts at the beginning of the nursing care.

31.3.3.7 Bed Management

With the decision to move a patient to ward, the posttreatment processes between the emergency department and the ward staff begin. During the time of observation about 40 % of all patients, treated in the ED, were sent to ward afterwards.

The first step before transferring the patient finally to ward is to search an available bed. An important fact regarding the bed Management is that compared to other countries like Australia the whole responsibility for searching a bed lies with the physicians themselves instead of with the nursing staff. The observation showed that there is no usage of a best practice solution noticeable. Sometimes the wards inform the ED's physicians prematurely about available beds or physicians already know about available beds on the ward where they have their regular shift on. Also during shift change physicians instruct their followers with information about available beds they got during their shift. To finally allocate a bed to an ED patient, the physicians have to call the wards to make sure the beds are indeed free as expected. If the responsible physician has no information about available wards, he has to call all suitable wards on after another until a free bed was found. According to emergency department's internistic senior physician Wasser, M.D. the RBK is using a Bed Management System to always show the ED physicians available beds on the different wards and support them to find a bed faster. But also he mentioned that the benefit of this system is limited, as the ward staff has to keep their bed occupancy up to date manually. Because of that the ED's physicians cannot rely on the system, as it often contains wrong information about the bed availability, and physicians have to call the wards anyway to get safe information and to finally allocate a patient to a ward. Besides all the wards for the different specialities the RBK has a ward, called 3D, especially for patients coming from the emergency department. On daily shift the ED physicians try to send most patients to the different special wards, as on night shift they need free beds on 3D, because 3D is the only ward that has two nurses even at nightshift what makes it easier to get patients transported there then to other wards. Normally the search for an open bed begins with the decision that a patient needs further treatment on ward. This doesn't necessarily mean that the patient will be transported in the next few minutes as beds gets searched often before the patient is finally stabilized to get transported to ward or the transport process itself is delayed for several reasons. The I.Dash program includes a function where the ED can mark the patient as "treatment completed" but as this function has to be filled in automatically the System is often not kept up to date and made often difficult to understand when a patient-treatment was actually finished during the time of observation.

31.3.3.8 Transport Process

The bead search merges in most cases into the transport process without any delays. When the ED physician has finally found an available bed at ward he still has to solve the important question of how the patient is going to be transported to his reserved spot. In the Robert-Bosch-Hospital exist two major possibilities of patient transportation. The first one is the standard transport by ward nurses. Ordinarily it is done by nurses from the ward the patient is transported to. This case is also the critical one which contains the biggest problems for the Emergency Department. The main reason therefore is that the transport in this case gets often delayed as the ward nurses are too busy to react on the transport requests by the

Emergency Department. Patient transport from the Emergency Department is not a highly prioritized task for ward nurses in the Robert-Bosch-Hospital. According to Wasser M.D. the reason for this is mostly financial. As an example he mentioned that a delayed preparation for a surgery and the resulting underutilization of an operating room costs the hospital far more than they would earn from faster patient transport and a faster patient cycle times in the Emergency Department. Although this seems reasonable the Emergency Department's intern bed management gets more complicated because of it. Obviously the time between the decision of accommodation and the actual transport is rising enormously because of that. For example the largest value during the observation was 267 min. But besides the delay of the transport itself the problem is that the Emergency Department often does not even get clear information about when the patient will finally be transported as for the ward nurses it is hard to estimate the amount of time they will need to finish their higher prioritized tasks. Not only the Emergency Department can get problems in their bed allocation but also the patient satisfaction suffers from bad information about their transport. During the observation it happened several times that stabilized patients sat in the floor with the information that they will be transported in the next minutes but in the end waited there for sometimes more than an hour.

To solve that transport problem the Robert-Bosch-Hospital created a second transport solution by establishing a hospital intern transport service. The transport service just came up a few weeks before the observation took place. Its purpose is to relieve the ward staff from the duty of transporting patients from the emergency department to ward. The transport service consists of nonmedical employees like for example young people who are doing a voluntary social service for a year. Until now the reactions on the transport service are very positive as Emergency Department staff said that the transport service most of the time reacts a lot faster on requests and transport delays are reduced in those cases since the service was established. However the transport service cannot replace the transport by ward staff, as it is not available on a 24/7 basis. Also as mentioned before the employees are not medically trained, because of that the transport service can only be used for unproblematic patients without any serious dangers while being transported. For example a patient with cancer who came to the emergency department with a feeling of faintness could not be transported to ward for hours as he had to wait for the ward nurses to arrive although the transport service was available at this day. The reason was the preexisting illness that could cause several problems during the transport, so that already legal issues made in impossible to get the patient transported by nonmedical staff. Still till now the transport service seems to be a positive step to improve the internal patient transport.

When the transport staff finally arrives at ward he gets instructed by the Emergency Department nurses about any important issues regarding the patient. This process is normally pretty fast as ward and Emergency Department staff are good coordinated and exchange their information fast and accurately.

31.3.4 Recommendations

31.3.4.1 Administration

The administration desk often is not occupied when a patient arrives at the ED. Until the first contact with the ED staff has taken place the patient is in a blind spot. He is not triaged yet and nobody knows if there might be an emergency. Overlapping and no clearly defined processes are leading to overburdened personnel.

- Installation of a bell in front of the administration desk. This would be an easy and simple way to reduce waiting times. A time interval (for example 30 s) must be defined after which the nurse should arrive at the desk. This would also allow the nurses and the administration staff to leave the desk if it is necessary and there are no currently no patients.
- The main reason why a triage nurse or the administration staff might leave the administration desk is to transport the patient file into the treatment area. This often takes several minutes. By publishing the patient file and data electronically to the doctors in the treatment area the administration desk there would be no reason any more for an employee to leave the desk that often. The employee also gets unburdened. Prerequisite for this solution would be an enhancement and an integration of the IT systems in the ED. Furthermore it is unknown if the doctors and nurses would accept this new way, because many of them would like to speak with the person who has first received the patient.
- Another possibility to unburden the employees at the administration desk would be to move the administration of ambulance patients into the treatment area. Here a basic administration could be done by a paramedic or nurse at a computer terminal. The paramedic also would not have to leave the treatment area anymore to register a patient. If some things are missing the administration could be completed later by an employee at the desk who has electronically access to the data. Again an integration of the IT systems would be a prerequisite.

31.3.4.2 Triage

During the data ascertainment in the ED of Robert-Bosch-Hospital several problems surfaced. The data evaluation revealed weak spots and gave first hints for proposals of solution. In an accurate analysis these proposals were worked out.

The responsibilities between the triage nurse and administration staff are not clearly defined.

- Sometimes the administration staff does the triage during the administration process. Sometimes the triage nurse does the triage and the administration also. The proposal for solution is that the responsibilities between the triage nurse and administration staff have to be clearly defined. The triage has to be done by a special qualified triage nurse and not during the administration without an examination. In Australian EDs, this is already usual.

Another problem is that the little triage area is not a specific room.

- It is located in the administration area next to the administration desk. The patients who are sitting in the accident surgery waiting room can see the triage examination. A special triage room is necessary. This improvement would protect patient's privacy.

As shown in the data analysis of the maxima, the defined waiting times are exceeded in some cases.

- Every exceedance circumvents the MTS. According to the defined waiting times of the MTS all patient should be called during this waiting time. This is important to ensure the health of every single patient.

As mentioned in the description of the current triage process, a couple of times a green categorized patient is preferred to a yellow categorized one because he is acquainted to the hospital staff.

- Personal issues have to come second and must not influence the waiting time. The MTS should not be circumvented.

After the execution of the triage, the triage nurse brings the patient in or sends the patient to the right waiting room.

If the patient is sent and walks on his own there is the mentioned problem: the internistic waiting room is difficult to find.

- The proposal for solution is the installation of red quadrats on the floor. As a consequence the patient is able to find the waiting room on his own.

Another problem might occur. The patient is not informed about his waiting time automatically.

- Because of not given information and waiting time the patient might get nervous. He walks to the administration desks and asks about his waiting time or asks ED staff who walks through the waiting room. The answer is uncertain and not bindingly. Dissatisfaction might occur. The patient himself only sees the other patients in the waiting room. He does not know how many other patients are located in the treatment area. The suggested improvement relates to more communication between the triage nurse and the patient. The patient has to be informed about his approximately waiting time to avoid dissatisfaction and intranquility in the waiting area. The patient should be informed about the triage system also. It has to be communicated that the process differs from ones in medical practices.

Another problem occurs owing to the transmission of the patient's file. While the administration nurse itself walks to the treatment workplace, the administration desk is not occupied.

- Only by possibility 1 there is a little and discontented practiced solution: If a triage nurse is present and doesn't do a triage at this moment, she can undertake the administration. This has to be improved. The administration desk has to be occupied: for example the patient's file is transferred electronically to the treatment workplace or another person is accountable for the transmission of the patient's file.

Another issue occurs after the patient was already in the treatment room. If the patient is able to sit and the ED is overcrowded, the patient will be brought out of the treatment room and will be seated in the waiting room again.

- The patients often do not understand why they have to sit—in part with infusion—in the waiting area again. Consequently it should be avoided that patients are sent back to the waiting room.

The To-Be-Process includes all proposal for solutions and guaranteed a smoothly process operation. The To-Be-Process builds on possibility 2 where triage nurse executes the triage process in the little triage room. A member of the administration staff has done the administration before. It is highly important that the triage is done by a special qualified triage nurse and not during the administration without an examination. Furthermore the triage nurse is in operating distance to the administration staff. To accelerate the process the triage nurse listens to the administration process because many patients already describe their medical problem during the administration process. Moreover the responsibilities between the triage nurse and administration staff are clearly defined. The triage nurse is the case manager and has all information about the actual patient. The triage nurse takes the patient into the triage room which is a specific room located next to the administration. The other patients in the accident surgery waiting room cannot see the triage examination. Patient's privacy is protected. Now the triage is executed: the patient is categorized by MTS by acuteness. Subsequently the results of the triage, that means the specific color and the corresponding waiting time, have to be documented in I.Dash. The patient data and the MRT category is now in I.Dash. All nurses and physicians can see the specific waiting situation on the screens. The categorization according to MTS is bindingly. The color of the triage category is permanent on the screens instead of appearing and disappearing. Afterwards it has to be clarified if an internistic or accident surgical case is existent to be able to bring the patients in the right waiting room. Now the triage nurse is able to calculate the approximate waiting time for the patient and the patient gets informed about his waiting time automatically. The possibility, that the patient becomes nervous, declines. Unnecessary requests for his waiting time at the administration desk are mostly avoided. The patient knows that many patients are already in the treatment area. The triage nurse communicates that the process differs from ones in medical practices. Subsequently she brings or sends the patient to the right waiting room. If the patient walks on his own he can follow the red quadrats on the floor. The patient is now able to find the waiting room on his own. Now the patient's file is transferred in the treatment workplace. The administration desk is always taken. One possibility is that the patient's file is transferred electronically to the treatment workplace. Another possibility is that one person is accountable for the transmission of the patient's file. Subsequently the nurse calls for the patient. There are two possibilities: the patient is still in the waiting room or he is not available. If the patient is not present in the waiting area, he will be called again. When the patient responds to the nurse's call he is brought into the treatment room. This is documented in I.Dash. Now the patient waits in the treatment area. ED staff can see via I.Dash in which room the patient currently waits.

31.3.4.3 Nurse and Physician Care

ID codes are printed by the desk clerk. Everytime he transports the ID codes the desk isn't occupied and patients arriving in the emergency department have to wait.

- The ID codes for blood should be first printed at the nurse's work place and it should be used everywhere (in Gap.It!, I.Dash, SAP, at blood withdrawals, and at urine tests) the same ID code for one patient, e.g., the ID from the health insurance card. So the desk at the reception would be always occupied, codes only have to be printed, when they're necessary, it can be done by the nurse, the ID codes are consistent and therefore results in a time-reducing process.

Taking and analyzing blood and other examples is very long lasting, equally X-raying and doing a CT.

- Because of the freezing character of blood withdrawals for follow-on processes, blood should be always taken in the ambulance. The blood withdrawal injections can be handed to the nurse during the check-in of the patient.
- Generally, taking blood should be the first step the nurse does during her first visit. This increases velocity of follow-on processes and should be standardized.

Improvements could be done in the laboratory because the whole physician process bases on the laboratory's results. On Sundays the laboratory results are as faster as usual ever because of the underutilization in the emergency department. By establishing a human resources management system free human resources can be shifted to the laboratory. New employments would be very cost intensive. This would accelerate the blood analysis process and the doctor can set up a diagnosis faster.

- By already compiled blood withdrawal boxes with the most needed blood counts, the nurse only has to open the box, not every single injection. This might decrease consumption of time.
- After the blood is taken the nurse does not have to walk through the whole hallway, a blood transport station should be installed in the nurse's work place. It decreases consumption of time and distance the nurses can concentrate even more on the patient.
- Employing experienced doctors would decrease costs. So smear tests would only be used when they are really necessary. Inexperienced doctors sometimes ordered an unnecessary smear test even though the patient hadn't got any symptoms and wasn't in a home for the aged.
- After the diagnosis the treatment is initiated. More persons should be responsible for the X-ray on the weekend. Often it occurs that people without being X-rayed

return to the emergency department. More people in the X-ray can be realized by the human resources management system with constant costs instead of increasing ones.

Human resources are hard to manage due to unexpected high peaks.

- Establishing a human resources management system would improve the capacity utilization of human resources. As already mentioned, the laboratory works very well at the weekend, defiles in the laboratory can be balanced during the week and there could be a chance for blood results to be as fast as on Sundays. Maybe nurses from the emergency department could be shifted to the laboratory when there is no high peak in the emergency department. Emergency department nurses could even be transformed to transport nurses. As a result the whole treatment process could be provided faster and the nurses get more experience in different areas and because of the diversified activities it won't get boring. Concerning the possibility of a human resources management system, it could be realized in the whole new integrated IT system. Nurses get a notification at the PC when they are needed e.g., in the laboratory and can change their tasks when there is an underutilization in the emergency department. Ulterior it can be tried to employ people from the federal volunteer service or honorary persons supporting the emergency department in the bed transport or creating internships for chemistry students to help in the laboratory.
- Advanced training in the resuscitation room should be very quick and informing and settled at a time where there is no expected peak in the emergency department to ensure the best possible supply for the patient.

Migrants and foreigners often can't communicate in an adequate way with the nurses and doctors in German. It is hard for the nurses and doctors to understand the patients properly.

- On account of a high amount and wide range of migrates and foreigners language skills of nurses and doctors have to be boosted for better communication and understanding. Nurses should be able to speak most used and necessary sentences in German, English, and Turkish. As a result, it decreases consumption of time, distance between patients, doctors, and nurses. Even more distinct diagnoses because of better understanding can be settled.

General recommendations:

- Already done and very beneficial for the emergency department is to place patients in the waiting room when they are able to sit for providing more space in the emergency department.
- All IT systems should be synced automatically for supporting the nurse's and doctor's work process and enabling them to concentrate even more on the patient.
- A death room should be installed, so no other beds, even whole rooms will be blocked.
- When a patient is shifted from a department to another, the process shouldn't begin with measuring the blood pressure, because it's already done.

31.3.4.4 Bed Management

The physician has the whole responsibility in the bed searching process. During the time he is searching for a bed he cannot treat other patients.

- The role of the Emergency Department nurses needs to be strengthened, so that they can assume the responsibility for the bed searching process and unburden the physicians.

The wards still need to be called each of them individually to get reliable information about available beds, although a bed management system was already implemented, because the information shown in the system are often not up to date and the function is limited on showing available beds.

- The less costly solution would be to keep the current bed management system but to ensure that the responsible ward staff keeps it always up to date so that the Emergency Department always sees available instantly when they take a look at the system and can call the wards for a bed allocation more target-oriented and efficient.
- Another solution that is linked with higher costs is to extend the bed management system with several features. A possibility to keep the system up to date might be the integration of the bed management with the system used at the ward for patient management comparable with the integration of I.Dash in the Emergency Department, so that when a patient file gets closed and a patient leaves ward the bed management system gets automatically updated and the bed gets marked as available in the system.
- To solve the problem that the bed search and allocation is still done via phone and the responsible person at the Emergency Department relies on the availability of the ward staff in the moment they call so that they can get a response and do not have to call over and over again. The bed management system could be extended so that via the system the Emergency Department staff can send a request to all wards that are suitable for the patient who needs to be transported. The ward nurse gets a message on a beeper or a similar device with the incoming bed request and reminded in a regular interval until they answer the request. The Emergency Department staff on the other hand receives a message as soon as they get a positive response from a ward. This way the active bed search would be abbreviated, as after sending a request the ward staff could continue with their regular duties.
- As also visible in the process models, a more complex and beneficial bed management system would avoid media disruptions during the bed search process.

31.3.4.5 Transport Process

Bed planning in the Emergency Departments gets even more difficult as they do not get specific information about when the ward nurses will arrive to transport patients from the Emergency Department.

- There has to be a deadline until the ward has to complete the patient transport, as there has to be an opportunity for the Emergency Department to estimate their bed allocation.
- Although it is reasonable that there are issues that are more relevant for the ward staff then the patient transport, it is important that patient gets transported in an acceptable amount of time, as already existing Emergency Department overcrowding gets even more problematic when patient discharge gets stuck often.
- A possible solution might be to integrate a regular point of time in the daily ward schedule, when the ward nurses have to fulfill open transport requests. This way the ward staff could plan their transports better without skipping or delaying their other responsibilities.

The transport service is limited on medical unproblematic cases and is only available on a few days during the week, although the response on it was highly positive.

- The transport service could at least occasionally be supported by medical staff when the occupancy rate on wards or other medical units is not as high as on usual shifts.
- A research should be done to show if overall the hospital benefits from offering the transport service also on a financial basis. If the profit is high enough the hospital should think about extending the transport service to make it available for more cases. This extension could either be to employ medical staff especially in the transport service, so that it could also be used to transport more critical patients or just an increase of semiprofessional staff so that the transport service gets available more often or in the best case over the whole week.

31.4 Discussion

All suggested solutions aim at a fluent, time-saving, and redundancy avoiding process in the ED. But there are some barriers which prevent the implementation of every single suggested solution from an economic point of view. The costs of the whole healthcare system in Germany are enormous. The designing of the processes in the ED of Robert-Bosch-Hospital has to be cost-saving to avoid an improvement of the process but a degradation of the cost situation.

Defining the responsibilities between the triage nurse and administration staff is not related to big costs. It leads to more specialization and consequently to more effectiveness. But there has to be a facilitator so that the administration nurse (who does not execute the triage anymore) does not feel overlooked. It has to be communicated that the triage nurse now released the administration nurse. Otherwise there is a human barrier which complicates the implementation and the success of the improvement.

Building up a specific triage room is related to costs of planning and building up this room. These costs are not to be underestimated. So a barrier of this improvement is the economic cost situation. The economic advantages of the new triage room have to be confronted with these costs. Therefore all advantages (the privacy of the patients, the better way of the triage execution etc.) have to be transformed in terms of money.

As shown in the data analysis of the maxima, the defined waiting times are exceeded in some cases. Of course the requested aim is to eliminate every single exceedance. But this is not a realistic aim: there are always outliers according to special situations and it is plain and simple not possible. It is important to reduce these outliers so that there do not exist systematic errors which occur regular anymore. For example exceeded waiting times because of wrong categorized patients have to be eliminated.

The installation of red quadrats on the floor helps patients to find the internistic waiting room on their own more easily. There are no significant barriers: neither special technology nor much money is needed. The advantage of a more fluent process without interruptions and demands should not be underestimated.

Informing the patient about his approximately waiting time is not as easy and low-priced as it seems. If the information is based on the specific waiting situation on the specific day in the ED, you need some calculations—maybe even a calculation system. A critical cost-benefit analysis should be done. Giving information about the triage system and communicating the process differences to medical practices is much cheaper and increases the understanding of the patient. There are different ways: verbal explanations or illustrations. Illustrations have the advantage that they do not cost time during the process in the ED.

By publishing the patient file and data electronically to the treatment area the administration would be occupied. There is an economic barrier: the electronic data exchange has to be extended to enable this data transmission. But in order to reach a huge process improvement these costs would be amortized very quickly. There could be a human barrier, too. Maybe the physicians favor the transmitted papers. Therefore an explanation of all advantages of the new solution and the preferability of the electronic data exchange has to be done within a systematic change management. A person who is accountable for the transmission of the patient's file is more expensive and should not be considered closer.

An important factor which determines the success of every suggested solution—independent of the specific solution and its barriers—is the way how the improvement of the triage process is implemented in the ED. The implementation should be done within a change management which is a systematic approach.

Concerning the view from the economic angle, the possibility of employing more staff to improve the whole process isn't enforceable because of the cost barrier, but it can be tempted to fetch free human resources from other departments to the emergency department, to the laboratory, to the bed transport service, to the X-ray, or the other way around via the human resources management system. Additionally, a good way of keeping the costs low would be providing internships for chemistry students in the laboratory performing easy tasks or employing voluntary people to help the nurses transporting the patients to the intended ward.

Measures should always be considered, if the planned ones make sense and decrease costs or consumption of time sustainably. It can be questioned if the process gets perceptible faster by using already compiled blood withdrawal boxes and due to the incremental demand of space, but it should be tried.

A new blood transport would cause enormous costs, but the nurses in the nonsurgical emergency department can try to adjust with the trauma surgical nurses to help each other with the transport. Nurses from the nonsurgical emergency department can hand it over to the nurses in the trauma surgical department when while spying them on the hallway in the emergency department.

As mentioned in the text, there is nothing to be said against to change the steps of the nursing care. Defrosting of the follow-on processes would push the blood withdrawal as first step of the nursing care.

Equally the blood taking process in the ambulance should be standardized, but issues could be occurring due to judicial conflicts. Prophylactically, possible occurring judicial subjects should be discussed before implementing the new process.

In times of a constant increase of IT used in the emergency department, it has to be questioned whether it can be too much. For example WLAN-devices to localize the patient are very useful because of making the positioning in I.Dash independent. Nurses wouldn't have to do it manually, but the WLAN-devices could get lost easily in a short period of time due to desist to allude the patient to return it or by other means.

The most improving measures can be tried to be implemented in the IT system. Therefore most of the time can be reduced. Nurses, desk clerks, and doctors have to type in everything twice.

31.5 Conclusion

To be still extant in the increasing competition within the healthcare system, it might be very useful for an ED to have its processes analyzed from outside observers. This cross-disciplinary approach could lead to new innovative ideas and help to avoid organizational blindness. Here the EPC model is a good basis for all participants to communicate with each other. So our study showed that the execution of the daily work in the ED can be improved to secure an optimal sequence of the different operations.

Although this study tried to have a very general view of the processes in an ED during the study some interesting questions came up which are out of scope. These fields might be a good starting point further to research based on this study:

- *Simulation, validation, and comparison*: A further step would be the simulation of the to-be processes. An interesting approach would also be the comparison with other process models created in Germany and the world. In general the EPC provides an easy way of modeling and simulation so this could be a good basis for an worldwide comparison and discussion

- *IT integration*: Many IT solutions in the hospitals in Germany suffer from insufficient integrated IT systems. Creating a new system architecture for hospitals is on the one hand a research field that offers a great potential. On the other hand, during the special restrictions in the healthcare industry also very challenging.
- *Change management in an ED*: While the new processes and solutions are designed this step could be easily forgotten although it is the most important. ED is strictly hierarchy organized. And like in many other organizations there might be a general suspection about changes. But if the personnel stand not behind even the best solution will fail. So another important research field would be how to adopt the typical change management techniques in an ED environment.

References

Anon. (2012). *Bundesministerium für Gesundheit: Elektronische Gesundheitskarte*. Zugriff am 10.07.2012. http://www.bmg.bund.de/krankenversicherung/elektronische-gesundheitskarte.html

Fleischmann, T. (2007). Rettungsdienst und Notaufnahmen: Die Schnittstellen-problematik unter der Lupe. *Rettungsdienst, 30*, Heft 8, S. 814–817.

Wickramasinghe, N. (2012). Presentation: healthcare Australia—Germany.

Wiler, J., Gentle, C., Halfpenny, J., Heins, A., Mehrota, A., Mikhail, G., et al. (2010). Optimizing emergency department front-end operations. *Annals of Emergency Medicine, 55*(2), 142–160.e1.

Erratum to

Using Technology Solutions to Streamline Healthcare Processes for Nursing: The Case of an Intelligent Operational Planning Support Tool (IOPST) Solution

Nilmini Wickramasinghe, Bridie Kent, Fatemeh Hoda Moghimi, Malte Stien, Lemai Nguyen, Bernice Redley, Nyree Taylor, and Mari Botti

N. Wickramasinghe et al. (eds.), *Lean Thinking for Healthcare*, Healthcare Delivery in the Information Age, DOI 10.1007/978-1-4614-8036-5_23,

DOI 10.1007/978-1-4614-8036-5_32

The publisher regrets that in the print and online versions of this book the affiliation of Dr. Lemai Nguyen on the chapter 23 is incorrect. The correct affiliation appears below.

Here is the correct affiliation:

Dr. Lemai Nguyen
Deakin University School of Information and Business Analytics
70 Elgar Road, Burwood, Victoria 31253125
Burwood, Victoria, Australia
email: lemai.nguyen@deakin.edu.au

The online version of the original chapter can be found at
http://dx.doi.org/10.1007/978-1-4614-8036-5_23

Epilogue

Globally healthcare delivery is turning to ICT (Information Communication Technologies) as a silver bullet to remedy its current woes of escalating costs, increasing ageing population, increase in the prevalence of chronic of chronic disease and pressures on providers to deliver quality, patient-centred healthcare. However, to date many are becoming disenchanted with ICT because too often it is failing to deliver the promised nirvana. We believe that one key reason is connected to the fact that simultaneous to the application of ICT it is necessary to also incorporate key management principles and techniques; one such management perspective being lean thinking.

With this in mind, we set about to compile the preceding content to share with our readers the benefits of incorporating lean thinking and related or complementary perspectives can afford to healthcare delivery. Clearly, in one volume it is not possible to delineate all possibilities but we believe we have provided sufficient depth and breadth, covering macro- and micro-perspectives as well as providing case studies that demonstrate how to move forward with key lean thinking initiatives. We trust you have found this illuminating, useful and instructive and we wish you all the best as you move forward to do your part to develop superior patient-centred healthcare solutions.

Nilmini Wickramasinghe, Nov 2012

N. Wickramasinghe et al. (eds.), *Lean Thinking for Healthcare*, Healthcare Delivery in the Information Age, DOI 10.1007/978-1-4614-8036-5,

Index

N. Wickramasinghe et al. (eds.), *Lean Thinking for Healthcare*, Healthcare Delivery in the Information Age, DOI 10.1007/978-1-4614-8036-5,

I

M

N

O

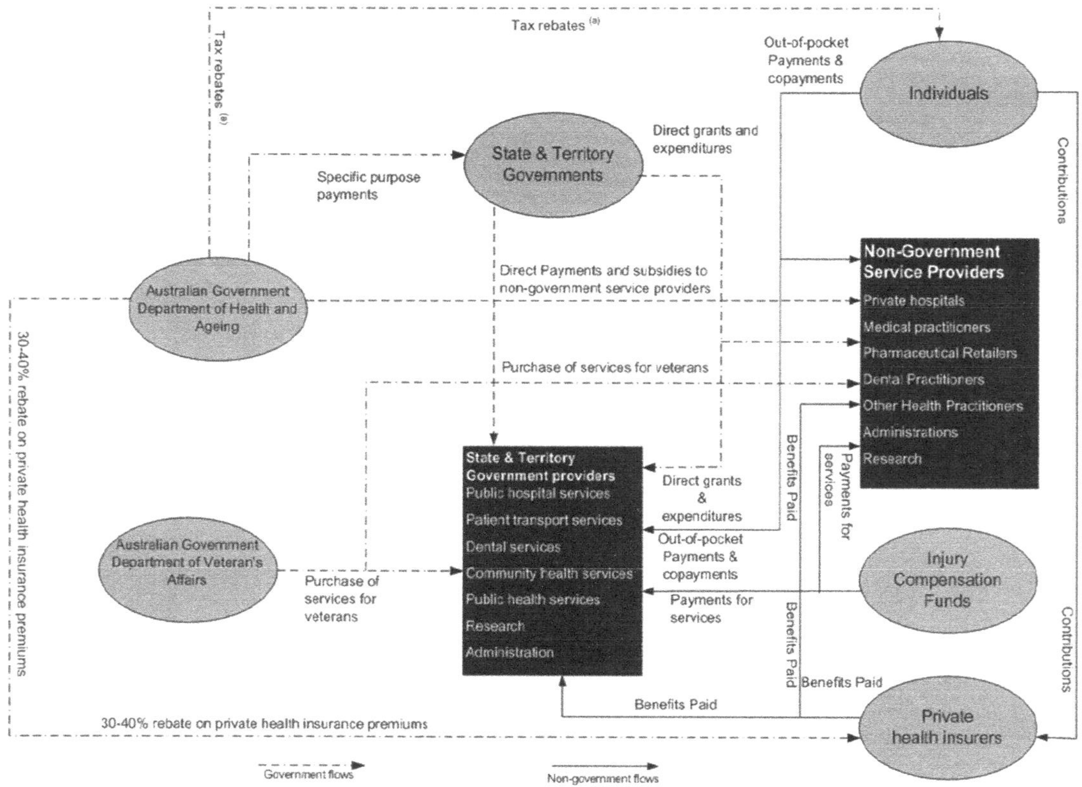

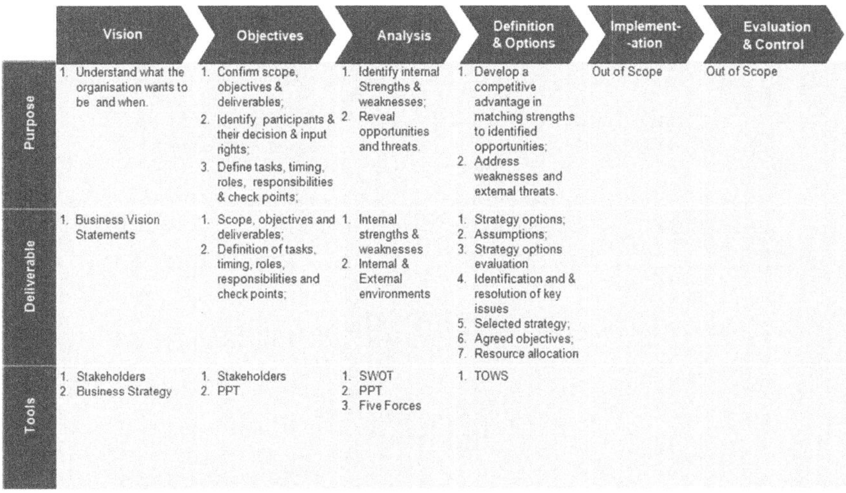

Table 30.3 Waiting times for the different categories of ESI

	Immediate	Emergent	Urgent	Semi-urgent	Nonurgent
Waiting time till first care contact	$n=1$	$n=11$	$n=39$	$n=46$	$n=8$
	$\varnothing=1$ min	$\varnothing=4{,}55$ min	$\varnothing=7{,}69$ min	$\varnothing=10{,}57$ min	$\varnothing=8{,}75$ min
	min = max = 1 min	min = 1 min	min = 1 min	min = 0 min	min = 2 min
		max = 15 min	max = 63 min	max = 85 min	max = 31 min
	$m=1$ min	$m=3$ min	$m=5$ min	$m=7$ min	$m=6$ min
		$w=14$ min	$w=62$ min	$w=85$ min	$w=29$ min
Waiting time till first physician contact	$n=1$	$n=11$	$n=39$	$n=46$	$n=8$
	$\varnothing=1$ min	$\varnothing=13{,}09$ min	$\varnothing=19{,}97$ min	$\varnothing=20{,}09$ min	$\varnothing=27{,}13$ min
	min = max = 1 min	min = 3 min	min = 2 min	min = 2 min	min = 2 min
		max = 28 min	max = 63 min	max = 77 min	max = 106 min
	$m=1$ min	$m=10$ min	$m=19$ min	$m=19$ min	$m=10$ min
		$w=25$ min	$w=61$ min	$w=75$ min	$w=104$ min

n = sample size, min after equal sign = minutes, min before equal sign = minimum, $\varnothing$ = average, m = median, w = wingspread

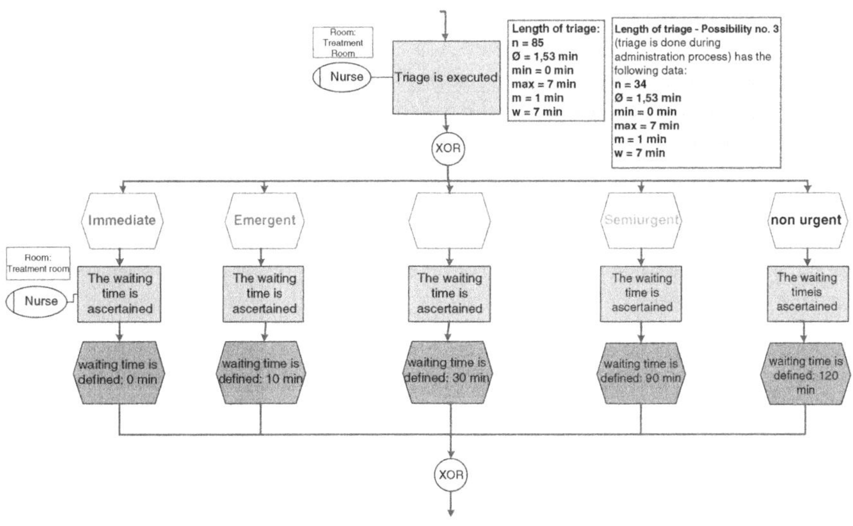

Fig. 30.3 Subprocess of the triage

in the data ascertainment was 15 min till first care contact and 28 min till first physician contact. The maximum waiting time was exceeded in one case by a sample size of 11 patients.

The maximum waiting time according to ESI of category urgent is 30 min; the maximum value was 63 min till first care contact and 63 min till first physician contact. The maximum waiting time was exceeded in two cases by sample size of 39 patients. This means that there are only two outliers which could be attributed to a specific situation.

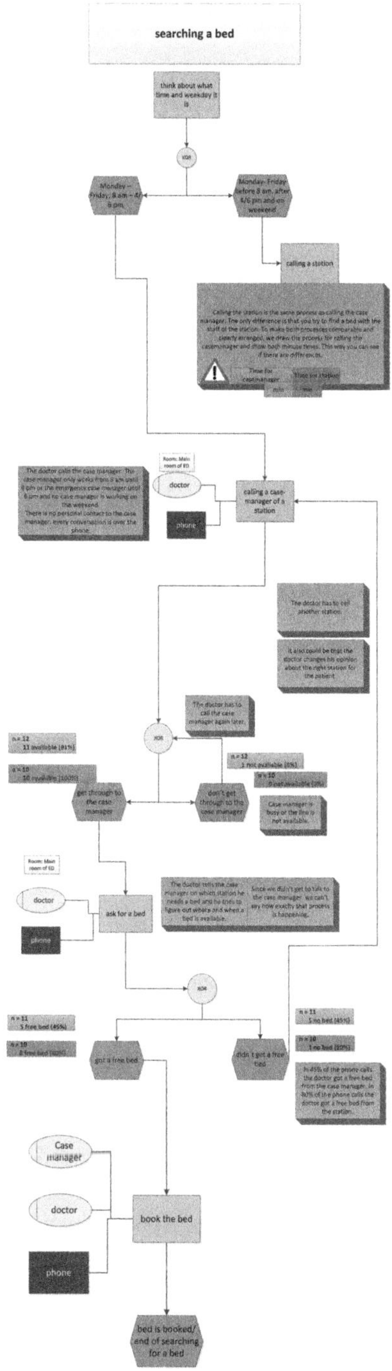
searching a bed
think about what time and weekday it is
XOR
Monday – Friday, 8 am – 4/6 pm
Monday- Friday before 8 am, after 4/6 pm and on weekend
calling a station
Time for casemanager
Room: Main room of ED
doctor
phone
calling a case-manager of a station
The doctor has to call another station.
It also could be that the doctor changes his opinion about the right station for the patient.
The doctor has to call the case manager again later.
XOR
n = 12
11 available (91%)
n = 10
get through to the case manager
don't get through to the case manager
n = 12
1 not available (8%)
Case manager is busy or the line is not available.
Room: Main room of ED
doctor
phone
ask for a bed
The doctor tells the case manager on which station he needs a bed and he tries to figure out where and when a bed is available.
Since we didn't get to talk to the case manager, we can't say how exactly that process is happening.
XOR
n = 11
5 free bed (45%)
got a free bed
didn't get a free bed
n = 11
5 no bed (45%)
In 45% of the phone calls the doctor got a free bed from the case manager. In 80% of the phone calls the doctor got a free bed from the station.
Case manager
doctor
phone
book the bed
bed is booked/ end of searching for a bed

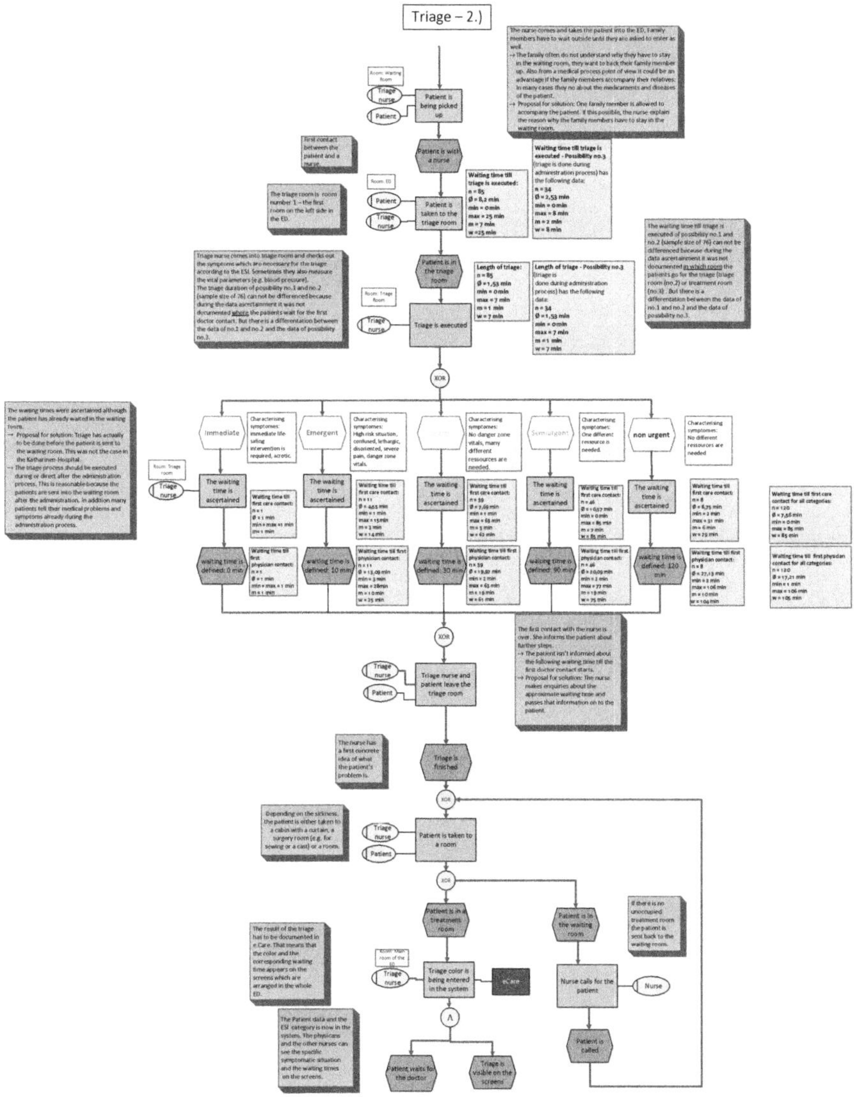
Triage – 2.)
The nurse comes and takes the patient into the ED. Family members have to wait outside until they are asked to enter as well.
→ The family often do not understand why they have to stay in the waiting room, they want to back their family member up. Also from a medical process point of view it could be an advantage if the family members accompany their relatives: In many cases they no about the medicaments and diseases of the patient.
→ Proposal for solution: One family member is allowed to accompany the patient. If this possible, the nurse explain the reason why the family members have to stay in the waiting room.
Room: Waiting Room
Triage nurse
Patient
Patient is being picked up
First contact between the patient and a nurse.
Patient is with a nurse
Room: ED
The triage room is room number 1 – the first room on the left side in the ED.
Patient is taken to the triage room
Waiting time till triage is executed: n = 85 Ø = 8,2 min min = 0 min max = 25 min m = 7 min w = 25 min
Waiting time till triage is executed - Possibility no.3 (triage is done during administration process) has the following data: n = 34 Ø = 2,53 min min = 0 min max = 8 min m = 2 min w = 8 min
The waiting time till triage is executed of possibility no.1 and no.2 (sample size of 76) can not be differenced because during the data ascertainment it was not documented in which room the patients go for the triage (triage room (no.2) or treatment room (no.3). But there is a differentation between the data of no.1 and no.2 and the data of possibility no.3.
Triage nurse comes into triage room and checks out the symptoms which are necessary for the triage according to the ESI. Sometimes they also measure the vital parameters (e.g. blood pressure). The triage duration of possibility no.1 and no.2 (sample size of 76) can not be differenced because during the data ascertainment it was not documented where the patients wait for the first doctor contact. But there is a differentation between the data of no.1 and no.2 and the data of possibility no.3.
Patient is in the triage room
Room: Triage Room
Triage is executed
Length of triage: n = 85 Ø = 1,53 min min = 0 min max = 7 min m = 1 min w = 7 min
Length of triage - Possibility no.3 (triage is done during administration process) has the following data: n = 34 Ø = 1,53 min min = 0 min max = 7 min m = 1 min w = 7 min
XOR
The waiting times were ascertained although the patient has already waited in the waiting room.
→ Proposal for solution: Triage has actually to be done before the patient is sent to the waiting room. This was not the case in the Katharinen-Hospital.
→ The triage process should be executed during or direct after the administration process. This is reasonable because the patients are sent into the waiting room after the administration. In addition many patients tell their medical problems and symptoms already during the administration process.
Room: Triage room
Immediate
Characterising symptomes: immediate life-safing intervention is required, acrotic.
Emergent
Characterising symptomes: High risk situation, confused, lethargic, disoriented, severe pain, danger zone vitals.
Characterising symptomes: No danger zone vitals, many different ressources are needed.
Semiurgent
Characterising symptomes: One different resource is needed.
non urgent
Characterising symptomes: No different ressources are needed
The waiting time is ascertained
waiting time is defined: 0 min
waiting time is defined: 10 min
waiting time is defined: 30 min
waiting time is defined: 90 min
waiting time is defined: 120 min
Waiting time till first care contact for all categories: n = 120 Ø = 7,56 min min = 0 min max = 85 min w = 85 min
Waiting time till first physician contact for all categories: n = 120 Ø = 17,21 min min = 1 min max = 106 min w = 105 min
XOR
The first contact with the nurse is over. She informs the patient about further steps.
→ The patient isn't informed about the following waiting time till the first doctor contact starts.
→ Proposal for solution: The nurse makes enquiries about the approximate waiting time and passes that information on to the patient.
Triage nurse and patient leave the triage room
The nurse has a first concrete idea of what the patient's problem is.
Triage is finished
Depending on the sickness, the patient is either taken to a cabin with a curtain, a surgery room (e.g. for sewing or a cast) or a room.
Patient is taken to a room
Patient is in a treatment room
Patient is in the waiting room
If there is no unoccupied treatment room the patient is sent back to the waiting room.
The result of the triage has to be documented in e.Care. That means that the color and the corresponding waiting time appears on the screens which are arranged in the whole ED.
Triage color is being entered in the system
eCare
Nurse calls for the patient
Nurse
The Patient data and the ESI category is now in the system. The physicans and the other nurses can see the specific symptomatic situation and the waiting times on the screens.
Patient is called
Patient waits for the doctor
Triage is visible on the screens

Erratum to

Using Technology Solutions to Streamline Healthcare Processes for Nursing: The Case of an Intelligent Operational Planning Support Tool (IOPST) Solution

Nilmini Wickramasinghe, Bridie Kent, Fatemeh Hoda Moghimi, Malte Stien, Lemai Nguyen, Bernice Redley, Nyree Taylor, and Mari Botti

N. Wickramasinghe et al. (eds.), *Lean Thinking for Healthcare*, Healthcare Delivery in the Information Age, DOI 10.1007/978-1-4614-8036-5_23,

DOI 10.1007/978-1-4614-8036-5_32

The publisher regrets that in the print and online versions of this book the affiliation of Dr. Lemai Nguyen on the chapter 23 is incorrect. The correct affiliation appears below.

Here is the correct affiliation:

Dr. Lemai Nguyen
Deakin University School of Information and Business Analytics
70 Elgar Road, Burwood, Victoria 31253125
Burwood, Victoria, Australia
email: lemai.nguyen@deakin.edu.au

The online version of the original chapter can be found at http://dx.doi.org/10.1007/978-1-4614-8036-5_23

N. Wickramasinghe et al. (eds.), *Lean Thinking for Healthcare*, Healthcare Delivery in the Information Age, DOI 10.1007/978-1-4614-8036-5_32,

V

W

Z

Lightning Source UK Ltd.
Milton Keynes UK
UKOW06n0948030616

275524UK00015B/277/P

9 781461 480358